D0286138

THE FUTURES OF AMERICAN STUDIES

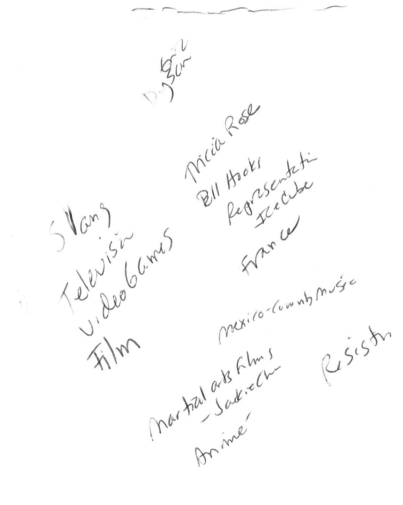

NEW AMERICANISTS ✧ *A Series Edited by Donald E. Pease*

THE

FUTURES OF

AMERICAN STUDIES

Edited by Donald E. Pease and Robyn Wiegman

Duke University Press   Durham & London

2002

© 2002 Duke University Press   All rights reserved   Printed in the United States of America on acid-free paper ∞   Designed by C. H. Westmoreland   Typeset by Keystone Typesetting, Inc.   Library of Congress Cataloging-in-Publication Data appear on the last   printed page of this book.

Contents

C O U N T E R H E G E M O N I C

A F T E R W O R D

Acknowledgments

While this book was long in the making, it did not suffer from the absence of a dedicated and timely editorial assistant, Kyle Julien, who paid attention to every detail at every turn and managed to manage with wit and clarity a large group of contributors and, most importantly, demanding co-editors. Our thanks to him for his endurance.

We have also benefited from the advice and encouragement of the editorial team at Duke University Press: Reynolds Smith and Sharon Parks Torian, both of whom worked diligently to keep us on task and to see the project through from its first glimmer at the 1997 Dartmouth Institute on American Studies.

We wish to thank Dean Edward Berger and Dean Jamshed Bharucha for the support they have provided from the office of the Dean of the Faculty at Dartmouth, Michael Mastanduno for the unfailing generosity of the Dickey Center for International Development, Dean Barry Scherr for funding from the Dartmouth Humanities faculty, and in particular Dean Sandra Gregg without whose dedication and friendship the Dartmouth Institute in American Studies would never have gotten off the ground.

And finally, our thanks to the anonymous reviewers of the manuscript for the press, the contributors, and the many participants at the Dartmouth Institute who have helped make that venue a challenging intellectual event for thinking about the pasts as well as the futures of the field.

The following were previously published: Lindon Barrett, "Identities and Identity Studies: Reading Toni Cade Bambara's 'The Hammer Man,'" *Cultural Critique* 39 (Spring 1998): 5–29; Winfried Fluck, "The Humanities in the Age of Expressive Individualism and Cultural Radicalism," *Cultural Critique* 40 (Fall 1998): 49–71; Amy Kaplan, "Manifest Domesticity," *American Literature* 70, no. 3 (1998): 581–606; Paul Lauter, "American Studies, American Politics, and the Reinvention of Class," in *From Walden Pond to Jurassic Park: Activism, Culture, and American Studies* (Durham: Duke University Press, 2001), 34–63; Gunter H. Lenz, "Toward a Dialogics of International American Culture Studies: Transnationality, Border Discourses, and Public Culture(s)," *Amerikastudien / American Studies* 44, no. 1 (1999): 5–23; George Lipsitz, " 'Sent for You Yesterday, Here You Come Today': American Studies Scholarship and the New Social Movements," *Cultural Critique* 40 (Fall

1998): 203–25; Lisa Lowe, "The International within the National: American Studies and Asian American Critique," *Cultural Critique* 40 (Fall 1998): 29–47; Walter Benn Michaels, "Autobiographies of the Ex-White Men," *Transition* 7, no. 1 (1998); 122–143; Donald Pease, "C.L.R. James, *Moby-Dick* and the Emergence of Transnational American Studies," *Arizona Quarterly* 56, no. 3 (2000): 93–123; Janice Radway, "What's in a Name? Presidential Address to the American Studies Association, 20 November 1998," *American Quarterly* 51, no. 1 (1999): 1–32; John Carlos Rowe, "Post-Nationalism, Globalism, and the New American Studies," *Cultural Critique* 40 (Fall 1998): 11–28; Robyn Wiegman, "Whiteness Studies and the Paradox of Particularity," *boundary 2* 26, no. 3 (Fall 1999): 115–150.

THE FUTURES OF AMERICAN STUDIES

Futures

Donald E. Pease and Robyn Wiegman

The future . . . breaks absolutely with constituted normality and can only be pro-
claimed, presented, as a sort of monstrosity.—Jacques Derrida, *Of Grammatology*

That is why I am unable to choose a single symbolic act to represent this most
recent stage of the movement; our direction is so clearly paradoxical that no one
can say just where we are now, let alone prophesy where we may be headed.
—Gene Wise, "Paradigm Dramas in American Studies"

We have organized the various contributions to *The Futures of American Studies* within the context of an essay Gene Wise published over two decades ago.
Perhaps the most frequently cited text on the history of the field, " 'Paradigm Dramas' in American Studies: A Cultural and Institutional History of
the Movement" (1979) attempts to assess the impact of social movements on
the disciplinary and interdisciplinary formations of American studies and,
in this, it serves as a crucial document for any project concerned with the
temporalities of this twentieth-century interdisciplinary field.[1] Jay Mechling
amply demonstrates the pertinence of the essay to conceptualizations of the
future of American studies in his 1999 reevaluation of Wise in *Locating American Studies: The Evolution of a Discipline*. For Mechling, " 'Paradigm Dramas' "
was an exercise in minor prophecy that opened the field to its "utopian" possibilities. He selected the following list of predictions from the essay as veri-
fications of Wise's prescience: a pluralistic rather than a holistic approach
to American culture, the rediscovery of the particular, the repudiation of
American exceptionalism, and the rise of comparativist and cross-cultural
approaches to American studies.[2] While the twenty-five years that have in-
tervened make the present appear consistent with Wise's description of
emergent futures, we are less invested in writing continuity with his essay—
and thereby founding this *Futures* as the fulfillment of that past—than in
examining the various strategies of temporal management through which
" 'Paradigm Dramas' " sought to negotiate the future.

Overall, Wise intended the phrase *paradigm dramas* to accomplish a range
of disparate and overlapping functions: it would represent the field of Ameri-

can studies as involved in an ongoing conflict over its organizing schemas; it would continue what he called the reflexive turn that American studies had recently taken in the 1970s; and it would thereby provide guidance for the future course of the (inter)discipline. "When handling ideas in a cultural context," Wise explained, Americanist scholars "have employed a 'climate of opinion' mode of explanation" (295). Insofar as this mode of understanding installed a relationship between the general culture and its particular components (ideas, individuals, or institutions), wherein the "particulars simply re-act" to the general, climate-of-opinion history proved "too rigidly hierarchical" to do justice to the "experience of our own fragmented culture" (296). To replace this metaphor drawn from the weather, Wise turned to keywords from the theatrical world. "Paradigm dramas" viewed "historical ideas not as 'enveloped' by their surrounding climates, but rather as a sequence of dramatic acts—acts which play on wider cultural scenes, or historical stages" (296). In this way, Wise put into service terms that advanced the dynamic aspects of the emergent field while recasting the entire history of American studies as the outcome of the monumental actions performed by exemplary figures such as Vernon Parrington, the founder of the American studies movement, and Perry Miller, the founder of the academic field. The collaboration between the movement Parrington represented and the academic discourse Miller fashioned to represent the movement's imperatives shaped the institutional boundaries, objects of study, and methods of analysis of the field of American studies. As the effects of "offering a way to create order and direction from masses of disparate materials on the whole history of American experience" (298), the founders' respective "paradigm dramas" lay claim to the power to conjoin the disparate purposes of the American studies movement with the scholarly imperatives of an academic field.

" 'Paradigm Dramas' " must thus be understood not simply as a history of the field, but as a founding gesture. Like most founding gestures, this one gave monumental status to an origin retrospectively invoked, thereby giving the past authority over the contours of the present in a management strategy that seemed aimed to contextualize, if not override, the present threat of rupture and incoherence. In so doing, Wise sought to repair the conceptual ground of a field whose fissuring into multiple programs and subfields at once reflected and gave expression to the aspirations of social movements that had exceeded the "founding" field's epistemological grasp. The canonical objects of analysis, protocols of reading them, and the interpretive narratives that had secured Wise's field identity were brought into the ambit of the crisis he diagnosed. In the wake of this encounter, Wise strained to invent a paradig-matic drama that would enable him to feel at home in any of the possible trajectories of the emergent field. That this effort would fail is certain from the outset, as the project of identifying with the field's formative past at the very moment of its passing writes the present as subordinate, because always in reference, to the temporal priority of the origin. The reproductive me-chanics of the past thus function to ward off through incorporation into temporal order the threat of present and future dissolution. This does not mean that Wise could accurately be labeled a conservative, though it is to say that in generating a coherent past for the field, he made history the founda-tion for managing the temporal uncertainty that diversification brought to both the nation and the field.

From our perspective, then, Wise's prescience was tempered by his in-ability to locate a coherent identification with any of the alternative fu-tures made possible by social movements, and hence the utopian possibilities Mechling notes were not simply undercut, but in some sense foreclosed precisely at the moment when Wise seemed to open the future to a range of possibilities (what Wise called the "diversification" of the field [319]). But countering Wise's project at this late date is not finally the point. We are more interested in examining the implications of the unacknowledged drama we have begun to chart than in arguing with any of the essay's substantive claims. This drama involved Wise's anxieties over the recognition that the field would not reproduce any of the paradigms that he characterized as representative of the American studies movement. The temporal crisis of his essay (and the problematic of time that his paradigmatic desire most power-fully demonstrates) provides a space for thinking about the anxiety over futurity that *America* as a nationalist icon and *American studies* as a field forma-tion both evince. Wise's paradoxical desire to escape the crisis that he believed pervaded the field of American studies and at the same time to reshape the field within the essay's paradigmatic scenarios turned " 'Paradigm Dramas' " into what Michel Foucault has called a heterotopia. Foucault proposed that a heterotopia be understood as different from—and to constitute an alternative to—utopia in that it occupied a special type of space, one to make new and different sense of all other spaces.[3] It is Wise's heterotopic desire to avert the cognitive impasses that the new interdisciplinary formations had precipitated within the field of American studies which brings certain passages in the essay into intimate proximity with what might be called the temporally uncanny dimensions of his heterotopia. These untimely passages, as we will call them, do not belong to the historical moment of the essay's composition, but produce instead the conditions of possibility for reconsidering the temporal problematic of futurity both for and within American studies as a field. It is in this sense that we understand the present volume as part of an unfinished encounter with the emergence of futurity that Wise's essay provoked.[4] Our title thematizes this concern by organizing a range of critical meditations as orientations toward the futures of American studies, thereby exploiting what, following Foucault, we might call the heterochronic potentials of " 'Paradigm Dramas.' "

It is Wise's correlation of the field's paradigmatic social drama with a form of history making as futurity that discloses our somewhat perverse rationale for linking essays in this volume on the futures of American studies to " 'Paradigm Dramas.' " Insofar as the essays collected here are constituted out of knowledges that were unincorporable to Wise, each essay inhabits a possible future that Wise's claim for the priority of a monumental past functioned to foreclose. Moreover, while our essays differ among themselves in their assumptions about the present status of American studies and in their speculations about the future, individually and collectively they call into question Wise's attempt to represent the field's history (and thereby to manage its futures) in terms of the dramatic unfolding of field-integrating paradigms. The contributors to this volume do not assume that the field of American studies is reducible to the dimensions of a single overarching paradigm, nor do they think that the genealogy of the field can be adequately described as a struggle to predominate among conflicting paradigms. These essays thus wager the futures of Wise's present as the productive present of a field whose organization of objects of study, critical histories, and methodologies have not been brought into coherent order with either the recent past of social movement or the field's retrospectively constituted origins.

In setting *The Futures of American Studies* in the context of Wise's account of the field's disposition in 1979, then, we hope to produce the present dispositions of American studies out of the futures that Wise had foreclosed in the past. Insofar as the essays here deliver the future mutations of American studies from a past mode of representation in which it was incubating, they transform the defensive strategies expressive of Wise's future fears into the portals through which alternative futures will have entered American studies.[5] To explicate the inextricable connections that we adduce between the futures of American studies and Wise's strategies of temporal foreclosure, we want to provide a deeper consideration of his strategies before discussing the essays in this volume. The introduction is divided into sections devoted to considerations of Wise's strategies of temporal management, of the untimely moments in Wise's essay in which futurity emerged at the paradoxical sites of its foreclosure, and of the present futures of American studies as a field.

Paradigm Trauma

" 'Paradigm Dramas' " is overtly cast by Wise as a critical journey "back over the history of American studies during the course of the twentieth century" in order to consider the two questions that he locates as definitive of the field: " '*What imperatives are there in the larger American culture and social structure, and in the culture and social structure of academe, which have made possible the quest for an integrating "American Studies"?*' and '*How have these imperatives changed over time?*' " (294–95). As this opening suggests, Wise is not primarily concerned with challenging the ideal of an "integrating" American studies but with the ways in which social and academic pressures have affected the field's self-defining quest. His notion of "representative acts" and "paradigm dramas" are the means through which he will chart changing imperatives in order to "crystallize possibilities for integrated American Studies in each stage of the movement's history" (295).

Wise's staging of the history of the field begins prior to its academic institutionalization, which underlies in part the force of the word *movement* that defines it implicitly as a knowledge project more expansive than the academic field. Its representative act is characterized as a "revolt against formalism" and is embodied in the lifework of Vernon Louis Parrington, whose 1927 *Main Currents in American Thought* inaugurated the intellectual history paradigm that would define, through a series of elaborations, American studies until the mid-1960s (298). For Wise, Parrington is the intellectual founder of American studies because of the way he forged "an immensely usable past . . . usable not just in the obvious sense of making the past relevant to urgencies of the present . . . [but] also in offering a way to create order and direction from masses of disparate materials on the whole history of American experience. In this sense, he demonstrated in his scholarship how an integrating 'American Studies' might be done" (298). Parrington as a representative figure is critical, Wise writes, to "this pre-institutional stage of American Studies because he did it almost all *alone*" (300). By this, Wise is referring to the fact that Parrington never earned more than a B.A. and was turned away from Harvard for doctoral work in his mid-thirties because of his age. His monumental study, *Main Currents*, was a decade in the making and made it to print through happenstance, not the securities of scholarship supported by academic institutions. As "a passionate mind encountering a dynamic world, sans the mediating forms of convention," Parrington is cast as an outsider whose dramatic quest to articulate "what American experience is like" made possible the emergent consensus among scholars in the 1940s, 1950s, and 1960s concerning the field (298, 300).

Wise's second representative act, which brings with it new contexts and imperatives for an integrating American studies, is embodied in the figure of Perry Miller, cast as the founder of American studies as an academic enterprise. For Wise, Miller's now famous "jungle epiphany" in *Errand into the Wilderness* (1956) evinced "the urge to impose form upon experience, to seize upon the American past and insist that it answer questions he is driven to ask of it" (302). As with Parrington, the quality of mind at work at integrating American experience was not conventional: "It is the human drive . . . to explain things, to make one's own experience, and the world around that experience, comprehensible" (303). But unlike Parrington, Miller experienced institutional prestige, claiming a "coveted professorship at Harvard" where the first Ph.D. in the history of American civilization was awarded in 1940 (to Henry Nash Smith) by the program Miller helped to found (303). By 1947, Wise tells us, "more than 60 institutions were offering undergraduate majors in the field," and American studies as a whole was organized intellectually by a "substantive consensus on the nature of American experience, and a methodological consensus on ways to study that experience" (306). The key aspects of this consensus paradigm, what Wise named the "intellectual history synthesis," included the following assumptions: 1) that there is an "American mind"; 2) that what distinguishes this mind is its "location in the 'New' World"; 3) that while the mind can be found in "anyone American," its greatest expression is in "the country's leading thinkers— Williams, Edwards, Franklin, Cooper, Emerson, Thoreau, Hawthorne, Melville, Whitman, Twain, Dewey, Niebuhr, et al"; 4) that the mind's enduring form is expressed in a set of recurrent themes: "Puritanism, Individualism, Progress, Pragmatism, Transcendentalism, Liberalism"; and 5) that while the study of the popular is important, "America is revealed most profoundly in its 'high' culture" (306–7). Wise is careful to assert that this consensus was not programmatic, in the sense that scholars were not forced to conform to its accepted meanings—"total conformity is not required for a communal paradigm to function" (307).

With the intellectual history synthesis thus operating as a paradigm that expresses both free intellectual inquiry and the spirit of the American mind encountering and shaping all things "new," Wise turns to the third stage of the movement's history, the consolidation of consensus into the myth-symbol school, "the decade and a half following 1950" that "look like the 'Golden Years' of the movement" (308). Wise tempers the simplicity of this retrospective coherency by pointing out the corporate nature of American studies in this postwar era, marking it as the turning point for a fully insular academicization of the movement's project. His representative act is a seminar taught by Robert Spiller and Thomas Cochran at the University of Pennsylvania which focused on twentieth-century American cultural values. American Civilization 900 was supported by a five-year $150,000 Carnegie Corporation grant and was ultimately a kind of failure, with "too much organized activity and too much diffused prestige ever to focus down on its basic task—bringing together perspectives from history, literature, and social science to explain values in twentieth-century America" (309). As American studies expanded with corporate backing, the national movement did so as well, with the founding in 1949 of *American Quarterly*, and two years later the American Studies Association as a national professional body.

For Wise, it is the institutional structure of increased corporatism that tempers his affection for this stage of the field's history, not a skepticism concerning the content of the enterprise still defined as the extrapolation of the intellectual history synthesis put into play by Parrington. By defining the underbelly of the "Golden Years" in this way—as the structural transformation of scholarship—Wise turns to the fourth stage of his history, which has all the hallmarks of a "depressing story" (317):

> By the middle of the 1960s . . . the intellectual history synthesis which had served American Studies so well for so long was shattered; and academies across the country were threatened by forces which charged them with being bastions of reaction, not a haven for free, inquiring minds. Similarly, many saw American Studies not as a vanguard movement on the frontiers of scholarship—the movement's prior image of itself—but as an overly timid and elitist white Protestant male enterprise which tended to reinforce the dominant culture rather than critically analyzing it. (312–13)

In this, the "'coming apart' stage of American Studies," the representative act is Culture Therapy 202, a course taught by Robert Merideth at Miami University (312–13). Cast against Parrington's and Miller's "dramatic personal gestures" to explicate American culture and Spiller's and Cochran's corporate institutionalism, which nonetheless hoped to "articulate that culture, not basically to criticize it," Merideth symbolized the introduction of a negative critical project, one that positioned the American studies scholar antagonistically in relation to the field's self-defining object of study (312). With critique now a centerpiece of American studies, Wise simultaneously describes and laments the consequences of cultural trauma when "emotional searing events like assassinations and riots" and "gigantic institutions . . . wreak havoc on people's lives" (314). It "was hard to assume without question," he writes, "that America is an integrated whole; division and conflict, not consensus, seemed to characterize the culture. . . . Hence we have seen, since the mid-sixties, a proliferation of subcultural studies focusing on one or another aspect of American life" (314). Viewed from this perspective, "American Studies has been in decline ever since" (314).

Wise does not end his history here, however, but seeks to define the characteristics of the present and its paradoxical possibilities for the field's future. To a certain extent, the last part of his essay works to resist the "depressing story" he has told about the undoing of the American studies movement by forms of social revolt that radically challenged what we tend to call today (though Wise did not) the nationalist project of the field's golden years: "[A] case can be made that measuring the movement through indices of growth and energy and activity, American Studies has never been stronger and healthier" (317). By growth, Wise means the proliferation of American studies programs; by energy and activity, he is referring to the vitality of the American Studies Association, which in 1967 began to hold national (as opposed to regional) conferences. Nonetheless, Wise offers no representative act to define the present; the "coming apart" stage of the 1960s is followed instead by a "direction [that] is so clearly paradoxical that no one can say just where we are now" (317). With this, Wise sounds his sour notes once again before a final attempt to move forward:

> American Studies today lacks a single synthesis with the influence, say, of the old symbol-myth-image explanation. It also lacks any clear consensus on a "usable" American past. Hence intellectually the last decade has brought disintegration in the movement. But if in one sense dis-integration means decline, in another sense it may mean simply diversification. . . . We are less inclined now to take readings from a single vantage point on *The* American experience; instead, we look upon American from a variety of different, often competing, perspectives. (319)

The present is thus for Wise without a coherent order—it fails to embody the very historical paradigm of singular figures and representative acts that he used to define the field's past. Positioned now as a witness to the disintegration of the paradigm he has called into being, he turns in the essay's final section toward what we call the emergent aspects of the field that have come to render the work of the first three stages marginal in their contemporary currency.

This new trajectory is broadly signified by the term *American culture studies*, which, like the more coherent stages Wise defines, features a fraternity of scholars who comprise its ranks and define its intellectual and institutional predilections. Wise credits the emergence of new understandings of culture with an institutional relocation of the field's training and scholarship from Harvard to Penn. Bruce Kuklick's 1972 critique in *American Quarterly*, "Myth and Symbol in American Studies," ushers in an "essentially negative" project: "He dis-assembled humanistic symbol-myth-image assumptions, but he advanced no alternative assumptions—humanistic or otherwise—to take their place" (320). Kuklick's work was built on by his colleague Gordon Kelly, who returned to arguments about method in American studies in order to develop more social scientifically oriented protocols for study in the field. This shifted the humanistic focus on literature and its specific articulation of high culture to new methodological grounds, decentering the author, the canon, and ideals of homogeneity in favor of explorations of the social as a structure dependent on context, the popular, and the everyday. The " 'new ethnography' of the seventies" thus featured "every person [as] a culture bearer" and drew attention to the ways in which American experience was itself constituted out of a range of cultural activities and materials (323, 324).

In addition to the "concern for anthropological definitions of culture [and an] emphasis on social structures," Wise also defined a " 'reflexive' temper" as a central characteristic of emergent American studies work (331–32). This reflexiveness is best characterized in the intellectual and institutional labor of Jay Mechling, who studied at Penn and would become a leader in the American studies program at the University of California, Davis. Along with Robert Merideth and David Wilson, Mechling helped to design a new kind of curricular structure for the field; their published statement, "American Culture Studies: The Discipline and the Curriculum," won the *American Quarterly* award for the journal's best essay in 1973. The Davis group, as Wise calls them, was critical of the institutional position occupied by most American studies projects (then totally reliant on the disciplines, most often literature or history, for faculty and curricular support) and sought instead to become their own permanent programmatic or departmental site. In addition to his role in redefining the institutional aspiration of the field, Mechling also chaired the standing committee of the ASA responsible for the annual bibliographic issues of *American Quarterly*. "More than any other single forum, the bibliographical issues have stimulated critical self-consciousness in the movement," Wise writes before listing the many new topics that the forums handled, including "film studies, American Indian studies, above-ground archaeology, folklore, women's studies, autobiography, still photography, structuralism, drama, Afro-American Studies" (329). In a crucial way, Mechling stands as a key figure in Wise's delineation of the fruitful possibilities of a new American studies; while not a representative figure, Mechling can nonetheless stoke Wise's desire to guarantee the field's proliferation—its extension into futurity—through institutional autonomy and academic legitimacy, even if the content of the emergent field cannot yet be organized into a stage making intellectual synthesis.

This does not mean, of course, that Wise has given up on synthesis altogether. The implicit shift in his investments from a lineage of great thinkers to an autonomous American studies as an interdisciplinary endeavor revives some of the history that his essay so anxiously brought into being in order not to lose. It does this by offering him a way to reclaim the centrality of the critical mind and the possibility of interdisciplinarity as a form of integration. American culture studies requires, he writes, a "different quality of mind, a connecting mind which can probe beyond the immediacy of the situation to search for everything which rays out beyond it. Such a connecting imagination is precisely what integrating culture studies, at their best, are structured to encourage" (336). Thus returning on new ground to some of the very self-defining features of American studies from which he began, Wise can reaffirm his production of history as central to futurity by writing the implications of the social movements as reclamations of the past: "Finally, the quest for subcultural 'roots' of the last few years has resensitized Americans to the inescapable power of the past—has emphasized that a people which presumes to outrun its history never does so in fact. . . . Several in the movement seem more inclined now to take sounding on their own past as a means of identifying what American Studies is, and envisioning where it may be heading" (336). In this, his essay's final move, Wise refuses to encounter the futures brought into being that would challenge his identifications with the field's past by bringing the past—as a coherent form and referent—to mark the meaning of both the present and the future. Time as an unruly force that can circumvent both movement and futurity is thus managed—and in more ways, as we will show, than one.

Time Control

There is no future and we are in it.—unknown author, Graffiti

In its affective dimension, " 'Paradigm Dramas' " possessed affinities with more recent expressions of what the Australian critic Meaghan Morris has provocatively called future fear—"the fear that most speculation about the future to which I could ever have access is 'academic' in the sense that society as I know it will likely collapse, or be transformed unimaginably, within my lifetime."[6] Morris is concerned that the time scholars take to reflect about the future will always lag behind the speed of its eventuation and lack the cognitive wherewithal to accommodate the gigantic dimensions that the future has recently been made to assume—the millennium, the new world order, the epoch of globalization. Wise's anxieties differ from Morris's, however, in that they are not merely speculative but give reference to an academic field that had already been "transformed unimaginably" within his lifetime. Wise had encountered futurity as what was nonsynchronous with the time kept by the field and nonsymbolizable in its terms. An absent cause that could only be experienced in its devastating effects, futurity named, for Wise, what hurt.

Hence, his account of the field's past grandeur constituted an effort to mitigate his anxieties over the loss of temporal control and a defensive reaction against uncertainty. In the guise of providing an accurate description of the field's genealogy, the essay afforded him the occasion to struggle for symbolic control over the temporality that would usher in future organizations of the field. Take, for instance, the following passage:

> With the demise of the Parrington paradigm, the movement has lacked a larger cultural synthesis, an image of a "usable" American past to lend it purpose and direction. Where the old synthesis got intellectual mileage from setting America off against Europe—New World against Old—*now we tend to see* both America and Europe on one side of a cultural and economic chasm, with the poorer, often newer, nations of the world on the other. Seen from this vantage point, America does not look as new and innocent, as idealistic, as pragmatic as it once did. Thus American Studies is deprived of its previous fascination with watching a freshly-born culture as, Adam-like, it goes about creating and naming and using new things in the world. (314–15; emphasis added)

Throughout this passage, Wise experiences the future in its effects on the field it has superseded, which means that he views the emergent in terms of its catastrophic challenge to the paradigm it is displacing. Vernon Parrington's model of the usable past has toppled over like a fallen idol. The American Adam, along with the immense signifying machine through which the myth-symbol school made sense of the changes in his new world, have also undergone semiotic depletion within the landscape that they had formerly brought into symbolic order. In witnessing the destruction of the mythological figure out of whose symbols and images his field identity had been formed, Wise encounters the future's dismantling of his integrative powers: "Seen from this vantage point, America does not look as new and innocent, as idealistic, as pragmatic as it once did" (315).

In negotiating his way through the field's potential decline, Wise does not so much come to identify with the emergent as constrain it from within the foundational assumptions of the paradigm it has displaced. For instance, in describing the past perfect of America's innocence and newness, Wise personifies the organizing logic of the vanishing perspective and casts its affect as quintessential loss: "American Studies is deprived of its previous fascination with watching a freshly-born culture" (315). The emergent critique cannot alter the status of the new as foundational for American studies as a field; it can only deprive the field of that enabling perspective. Even the phrase "now we tend to see," which ostensibly describes his adoption of the emergent visual standpoint toward American things, restricts that position to an unwanted tendency. Wise's rhetorical strategy throughout the passage works to represent what "we" now see from the standpoint of what "we" now lack, which orders the relationship between the emergent and the residual antagonistically, as a contest between temporally contentious visual positions. The perspective from which Wise visualizes American studies as in decline cannot coincide with the viewpoint from which "now we tend to see both America and Europe" (314). The latter viewpoint cannot inhabit the same visual field that permitted the former view (that American studies has been in decline) without one or the other undergoing a corrective revision. The field can only be represented as in decline if "we" regarded American studies' previous vision as progressive. In sighting the emergent from the perspective it would displace, Wise paradoxically deploys the field perspective to which he can never return at the very instant of its critical demise. In this way, he retains the authority of the displaced paradigm in his anxious confrontation with a future that threatens not simply to eradicate it, but to lose all purpose and direction for American studies in the process.

Having thus described the transmutation of the field into an afterimage of its previous identity, Wise provides an account of the effects of this loss on the field's positioning among the disciplines: "Pursuing further this declension theme, we can say that, unquestionably, American Studies is no longer working on the frontiers of scholarship. During the fifties and early sixties, symbol–myth–image scholarship came uniquely out of an American Studies perspective, and it influenced scholars in traditional disciplines too, particularly in intellectual history and in literary history. Very little of that is happening with American Studies now" (315). Here, Americanist knowledge is precisely what the emergent field can no longer know. The time of American studies—the historical time in which it flourished and its immanent structure of the repetition of the same—has been displaced. It has not been fulfilled or renovated; it has been displaced by a form of temporality that will not take place (i.e., become new) in its terms. The trauma that the loss of a paradigm for the present engenders is thus informed by two kinds of temporal splittings: between the past and the present as a continuous relation to the future; and between the present and the future as a coherent template for identity production. In his inability to found a paradigmatic identity for the future orientations of the field, Wise remains a spectral alterity within the emergent field of American studies.

While our analysis of Wise's rhetorical emplottment of a field-forming perspective provides the means for discerning his anxiety over futurity, it is just as important to read " 'Paradigm Dramas' " as deeply anxious about the status of the past. Indeed, the essay struggled to conserve the past against the very charges that the emergent "subcultural" formations brought to bear on it.[7] For Wise, such charges—of elitism, masculinism, corporatism, and racism—were nearly unutterable as issues generated by the intellectual history synthesis that his essay made foundational for the field. Instead, he shifts to the register of academic institutionalization, defining the corporatization of American studies in the 1950s as the political beginning of the field's radical end. The following passage is especially illuminating as an example of Wise's strategy of casting the underside of the golden years in institutional terms and thereby preserving the intellectual project of the field from a sustaining critique by the emergent knowledges of the sixties:

> Perhaps because people in American Studies often fancy themselves "American Adams" (and now "Eves") . . . Americanists still tended to see themselves in the image of a Parrington—that is, lone intellectual adventurers fired by a personal vision of the culture, and driven to put scholarly form on that vision. This vision is not wholly false. *Virgin Land* and *The American Adam* and *The Jacksonian Persuasion* and *The Machine in the Garden* are all passionately personal books; they are not intended as simply objective "contributions" to corporate

knowledge. Yet the social and economic structure of American scholarship had been fundamentally transformed since the days of Parrington, and those who still envisioned themselves isolated "American Adams" by the 1950s and 60s were largely deceived. (310)

The temporal displacements that Wise here effects are striking: he locates the status of Parrington as a model available to that ever belated woman, "Eve," who can constitute a part of the American collective "now" through an identification with those "lone intellectual adventurers," even as that vision of American culture studies has been undermined by changes in the structure of American scholarship in those decades in which the very social consciousness of Eve was on the cusp of its collective articulation. In this way, Wise manages the past perfect of Parrington, whose exemplary vision and individualism—his quintessential American Adamness—needs to be preserved against (because it can already stand as the model for) the incursion of other historical demands, other forms of critical collective recognition.

The incorporation of Eve at the moment of delineating the rotten underside of the golden years functions symptomatically in a history designed to delineate the "vision" and "passionately personal" from the "corporate." Hence, the field's origins are preserved as definitively separate from the appropriations of the nationalist apparatus of the Cold War university, which is to say that, for Wise, there is nothing critically amiss about the intellectual history synthesis, with its masculine adventurers, that would inspire its appropriation by state and corporate forces in the period after World War II. Most tellingly, this shift from intellectual formation to institutional context enables him to suggest, however implicitly, that the anti-institutional forces of social movement that emerged in the 1960s were resuscitations of Parrington's individualist and alienated anti-institutional position that founded American studies as an intellectual movement. While Wise cannot define the subcultural formations of American studies in any way that can incorporate within them his identifications with the field, he nonetheless manages to narrate the field's origins in such a way that they appear internally resistant to "subcultural" knowledge as intellectual critique. When Wise looked to the Davis group and to the possibility of an institutionally autonomous academic project for American studies, severed from its reliance on the disciplines and capable of sustaining its object of study on its own, so to speak, his failure to render social movements as knowledge was complete.

Masquerading as an objective description of the field, then, Wise's " 'Paradigm Dramas'" constituted an encompassing project of boundary management that assumed the form of attempting to establish control over the future of the field. Its putative capacity to synchronize the field's entire history within an encompassing drama was a compensatory mechanism designed to make up for the loss of the field's integrative powers. In representing the changes in the field's history in terms of paradigm dramas, Wise regulated the temporal dynamics of both social and disciplinary change.

The Shock of Futurity

The futurity Wise seeks to control entails a revision of the field and of the nation that would undermine, in its seeming negativity, the critical assumptions on which Wise's own generational identifications were borne. In place of the nostalgic representation of the field's past as dedicated to independent thought and a synthesizing methodological modality, the new social movements introduce, as we delineate in this section, a counter-history that cannot be emplotted as the next stage of a progressive narrative of American studies as a radical individual or intellectual movement.[8] To the extent that Wise tries at his essay's end to find a potential heir (Jay Mechling) who can connect some of the impulses of the founding stages to the sixties and thus provide a positive and continuous future, he reproduces the forms of canonical history making that the academic institutionalization of social movements would so fervently contest. From this perspective, Mechling's 1999 return to Wise's "'Paradigm Dramas'" in a collection on the "evolution" of American studies as a discipline confirms the one version of the future that Wise's essay found possible—a version that would substitute the now lost synthesis of American experience with an institutionalized project whose disciplinary history would keep the lost synthesis alive as origin, as the founding principle. History in this sense rescues the past from the present, while the institutionalization of American studies as a discipline provides the mechanism for ensuring that Wise's version of the past would have a permanent futurity. Wise's "'Paradigm Dramas'" must thus be understood as history making in the most profound sense, and in this it has deep ties to the field formation that Wise inherited and that the sixties seemed by 1975 to have radically redressed.

The American studies in which Wise received his training named the academic site where the disciplines of literature, history, politics, sociology, and government were assigned the task of both studying and understanding the United States' geopolitical boundaries. Often referred to today as "exceptionalist" in its conceptual orientation, the field operated by spatializing assumptions drawn from the realm of international politics in which the United States was represented as a circumscribed territory. At the same time, it temporalized these assumptions within the narrative of the nation's history as autonomous and liberatory. American literature and American history tended to homogenize the popular memory that they also produced, and literature and history departments supplied the institutional sites wherein the field of American studies collaborated with the press, the university system, the publishing industry, and other aspects of the cultural apparatus that managed the semantic field and policed the significance of such value-laden terms as *the nation* and *the people*. The myth-symbol school of American studies was central to this formation, generating an imaginary homogeneity out of discrepant life worlds. In proposing that every moment of historical time constituted the occasion for the potential repetition of the sacred time of the nation's founding, the national mythos supplied the means of producing what Benedict Anderson has called the empty homogeneous time of the imagined national community.[9] The national mythology's endless repetition of the moment of the nation's founding produced the basic unit of "progress," which the processes of "Americanization" at home and abroad were implicitly made to "universalize."

At once a mode of inquiry, an object of knowledge, and an ideological rationale, the transdisciplinary reach of the myth-symbol school traversed academic disciplines and claimed the power to integrate their incompatible knowledges within a single interdisciplinary agenda. This interdisciplinary formation was constructed in reaction against what its practitioners described as the fragmentation of knowledge accompanying specialized academic disciplines. Thus the logic of the nation as a knowable whole was grafted onto the concept of interdisciplinarity as it was made to serve a unifying function. Through an interdisciplinary approach, Americanists used the myth-symbol school to rework daily life into images encouraging belief in the isomorphism of the sovereign people, U.S. territory, and national culture. The knowledges produced thus served the ever increasing needs of a centralized state apparatus.

By the late 1960s, the aspiration for radical social transformation produced within the new social movements led to the repudiation of the American studies movement precisely for its complicit identification with the exceptionalist state apparatus that the field purported to interpret. The radical democratic discourses developed within the feminist, civil rights, and gay and lesbian movements of the 1960s dramatically reshaped the nation's social and political landscape. Arguing that their task was to break the constraints of an enveloping imperial culture, architects of the sixties counterculture moved away from the privileged standpoints provided by myth-symbol and other unifying paradigms to reveal the field's internal critical limits. These movements thereby involved American studies in a project of reformulation, one that resulted in a reconfiguration of its intellectual position within the academy. It is that reconfiguration that generates for Wise a crisis over futurity as the older exemplary acts and unifying paradigms are hobbled in the face of certain disintegrating social impulses.

As is now well known, the academic response to these movements resulted in the formation of interdisciplinary fields, disciplinary subfields, and academic programs that refused either to accede to American studies' dominant assumptions or to be reduced to its categories. These academic fields emerged at the intersections of a range of critiques: of feminism by women of color, of heterosexist liberal pluralism by gay and lesbian activists, and of U.S. imperialism by both antiwar and third-world activisms. Challenging education as a specific form of citizen construction and normative cultural reproduction, proponents of these movements formed programs in the 1970s to register their critique, resulting in the (uneven) proliferation of African American studies, Latino/a studies, Asian American studies, Native American studies, gay and lesbian studies, and women's studies. Each of these fields challenged the hegemonic understanding of objects of study, identities, and scholarship that had predominated, bringing pressure to bear on the belief that American studies comprised a unitary field of knowledge. They demanded that American studies be construed as a critical and self-reflexive rather than as a normative category. As a consequence of these challenges, professors of American studies could no longer un-self-consciously claim to do justice to their subject without critically evaluating the field's role in the reproduction of social and economic inequalities. Members of American studies and participants in these movements thus engaged in a relationship of negative reciprocity: scholars in emergent identity-based (inter)disciplines defined themselves and their projects against those of establishment American studies and vice versa. As a consequence, American studies became the Other against which cutting-edge scholarship was to be defined, and national identity movements and anti-imperial discourses became the Other the field excluded to effect coherence. As we have discussed, Wise tellingly described this moment as the "coming apart" stage of the American studies movement.

If we understand the drama of Wise's essay as a struggle to regulate the field's conceptual order, we might read its symbolic action as an attempt to persuade members of the emergent subdisciplinary and interdisciplinary discourses to reorganize themselves in the normative image of members of a paradigm community—or risk the abandonment of a coherent future. After all, Wise's history of the field, parsed into four paradigmatic moments, is itself a form of pedagogical instruction about the relation between the modalities of movement and academic institutionalization. Parrington's act of founding American studies as a social movement was followed by Miller's institutionalization of the American studies movement as the myth–symbol paradigm. Against this celebratory interaction came the third and fourth stages: the American Studies Association's consolidation of the field into a professional enterprise, and the crisis precipitated by the social reaction directed against that enterprise. In staging the institutional history of the field in this way, Wise represented the challenges that new social movements posed to the future organization of the field as a recapitulation of the paradigmatic relationship between the social movement Parrington organized and the myth-symbol paradigm with which Miller transformed it into an academic field. According to the temporal logic underwriting this dramatic turn of events, Miller's paradigm retroactively transformed the social imperatives of Parrington's movement into the objects of study and methods of analysis of the field of American studies. The symbolic action of the essay thus works to position the criticism which activist scholars directed against the field of American studies as a repetition of the field's foundational antagonisms. The field crisis in Wise's present was thus transformed into an event that had already taken place at the time of the field's institutionalization, and hence the historical transformation then taking place was symbolically suspended so that the shock of different futures could be contained in the repetition of the field's founding.

Untimely Passages

Insofar as Wise's essay constituted an effort to recover the use value of the past, it might be understood as having performed the work of producing a temporal common sense for the field of American studies. The temporal dynamic of its hegemonizing discourse reaffirmed progressive models from the past as the precondition for the reproduction of the present in the future. Wise recognized the challenges that heterogeneous movements posed to the ideology of U.S. progress underwriting the temporal logic of the field. That is why the temporality out of which Wise reorganized the field's history denied these socially transformative projects any standing within the field's history. Despite his having refused them the right to become present within the terms of his drama, however, Wise nevertheless felt the temporal pressure they exerted. Indeed, Wise's very efforts to assimilate their field-transformative modes of eventuation within the temporal contours of his consensual dramas led to his encounters with temporalities that the field could not synchronize. It is toward these nonsynchronous temporalities that we now turn.

In the following passage, for instance, the futurity that " 'Paradigm Dramas' " refused to represent (as in, 'to make present in the present') happened—as the social movements produce a generalized force of eventfulness that traversed the entire field: "Hence we have seen, since the mid-sixties, a proliferation of subcultural studies focusing on one or another aspect of American life. But we have very little of wide influence in the movement attempting like the old symbol-myth-image works, to integrate the whole culture. Intellectually American Studies has never recovered from the earthquake-like jolts of the sixties, and the consciousness those events forced upon the culture" (314). This passage constitutes a struggle over the control of the productive and reproductive functions of American studies and, by implication, over the legitimate definition of U.S. society. As a strategy of time control, Wise might be understood here to mobilize a hegemonic understanding of the disputed terrain of American studies by making the differences represented by social movements into subcultural "aspect[s] of American life" and thereby incorporating subcultural studies within the relations of domination and subordination that had previously organized the field. This reading would be predicated on the fact that the passage leaves unaddressed the material conditions of inequality which the relations of subcultural to cultural inevitably reproduce. Hence, the shared assumptions that produced the continuity of the field now effectively silence (indeed continue to silence) critical interrogation of the social structure's asymmetries of power and their resulting economic and social inequalities. The silence can be identified as a set of values that, on the one hand, deny social divisions and, on the other, identify them as being natural and inevitable. Thus positioned within the institutional boundaries of American studies as "subcultural studies," these alternative disciplinary formations were made to share the values, attitudes, and norms of the dominant—if not directly then at least in their categorical subordination to an aspect of American life.

As an instance of untimely passages, however, the passage opens up radically different temporalities. For when he depicts the crisis that subcultural studies effected within the field in terms of "earthquake-like jolts," thereby returning to the metaphor of weather that he previously rejected, Wise finds in the forces of nature a language for describing what remains nameless from within the paradigmatic dramas used to cast the intellectual history and shape of the field. Unpredictable, without origin, but temporally disruptive, the subcultural traverses the field and shakes its foundation. Such seismic changes mutate into multiple interruptions of the temporality through which the field had formerly measured its progress. These subcultural formations do not "progress," however, they proliferate and, in this, their disruptive temporalities are productive of altogether different futures at the sites of their emergence. Unable to take place within the temporal register through which Wise regulated the field, futurity becomes associated, in affect if not always in Wise's narration, with the past's self shattering. But this is not the whole of it. For as that which could not become present within the field's available representations, the forces that these field movements put into play carried with them temporalities that were nonsynchronous with the field's contemporaneity. Because they multiplied into subcultures rather than reproducing themselves within the dominant paradigm, their disruptive temporalities literally interfered with the continuation of the field. The utopian possibility that Mechling notes takes place here, where the subcultures' powers of proliferation exceeded Wise's ambit of control, proliferating beyond the limits of his strategy of temporal management.

At another important moment in his essay, the chronology authorizing Wise's drama shows signs of alternative knowledge by exceeding the limits of the territorial imaginary that underwrote the myth-symbol school of American studies's golden years. As Wise described it, the golden age fulfilled the intellectual imperatives of the field's origins and lasted from its academic founding until the mid-sixties. During these years, American studies worked at "the frontiers of academic scholarship" by encroaching on the boundaries of other academic disciplines and reshaping their projects into the inclusive metaphors of the myth-symbol school (315). It was able to accomplish this work because of a limitation inherent to academic disciplines. Traditional academic disciplines establish a set of rules out of which they produce a regulated order of knowledge and authorize specific practices through which that order can be regulated, even as they may lack the overarching rationale that American studies eagerly supplied. But in the following passage, the field is described as having come unmoored from the bounded territorial imaginary on whose frontiers it formerly accomplished its encroachments and to have lost the rationale through which it assimilated other disciplines to the national telos. Such unmooring precipitates an untimely convergence between academic field and social movement:

> In scholarship, we have become something of a "parasite" field—living off the creations of others. . . . We do this in two different ways. In some cases, we draw from new work in the traditional disciplines—from the discipline of history, for example, we draw from family studies, demography, community studies, and, more generally, from social history; from literature, we draw from autobiography and structuralism; from anthropology, we draw also from structuralism, cognitive anthropology, techniques of field work, and remnants of culture-personality analysis. In other cases, American Studies has drawn from, or rather given a home to, studies which have their real base of vitality in the culture at large. This is particularly true of women's studies, perhaps the most vital and interesting new field in the movement today. But it is also true with black studies, Hispanic studies, American Indian studies, ecology studies, and so on. (315)

While our earlier discussion of "'Paradigm Dramas'" emphasizes Wise's anxiety over the loss of control of the field's past and future dispensations, this passage is remarkable in its confrontation with the residual (the past) and the emergent. Here, Wise represents the transformation of both a self-enclosed field of American studies into a hybridized borderland and the centered field identity into a parasitic border dweller who is not the source of integrative activities but is itself the outcome of a series of negotiations.

As a border dweller in between social movements and the disciplinary formations it formerly made out of them, Wise's American studies comes to inhabit two different temporalities—it has regressed to its past condition of a social movement dependent on the hospitality of established disciplines for the institutionalization of its knowledge, and it is also a contemporary academic field which can either draw from the vitality of the new social movements or give a home to them. It is the mutual interference between its status as a field and a movement that has transformed the American studies over which Wise aspired to exercise temporal control into a hybridized zone where the emergent inhabits the residual. Here, already existing disciplines intersect with social formations whose demands are not compatible with the disciplines' cognitive categories and are unanswerable in their terms. In this untimely scene, the multiple cognitive and sociopolitical negotiations that take place at this busy intersection cannot be subordinated to the operations of a paradigm. The failure to manage the time of emergency that " 'Paradigm Dramas' " charts thus serves as a critical instance of the unfinished encounter with the future that essays in this volume will retrospectively address.

Radical Imaginaries:
How Futurity Will Have Entered the Field

In the previous section, we focused on two untimely passages in Wise's essay where futurity erupted within the field, inhabited his field identity, and generated the mutual interference between field formation and social movement. Such irresolveable tensions between social movements and the already instituted field can be conceptualized as a relationship of disruption between the field-imaginary and what Cornelius Castoriadis calls "the radical imaginary." For Castoriadis, the radical imaginary activates the knowledge of the historicity that the field-imaginary has disavowed.[10] In this, the radical imaginary exploits the paradoxical sites in which the field-imaginary encounters the lack of closure in its system of signification, opening spaces for the emergence of futures that do not reproduce the field's contours and that cannot be reduced to its categories. Future-oriented and linked to the emergence of unanticipated transformations and unpredicted rearrangements of the institutional order, the radical imaginary announces the possibility of a break from previous historical determinations. For our purposes, it is imperative to think the radical imaginary outside the already constituted categories within the institutional boundaries of the field-imaginary and to link this outside with the disruptive temporalities of the social movements traversing the field.

While Wise experienced the radical imaginary's effects on the field as an occasion to counter futurity's disruptions through temporal management strategies, we have organized this volume as a return to " 'Paradigm Dramas' " in order to install different relationships to the emergent futures he seemed unable not to fear. Rather than authorizing his strategies of denial, the essays collected here relocate his foundational gestures in the hybridized zone in between emergent and residual whereby futurity enters the field.[11] These Americanist scholars exploit the radical imaginary and construct multiple pasts and imagine disparate futures out of the nonsynchronous historical materials embedded within American studies as a heterotopia. " 'Paradigm

Dramas'" might be described, then, as a site wherein American studies undergoes change through the taking place within the present dimension of the futures the social movements that Wise had denied epistemological emergence. But as readers will see, the predicted correlation between the academic field and the movements that it only partially accommodates differs across the essays in significant ways. Through various conceptualizations of the dynamic interactions between American studies as a social formation and as an interdisciplinary formation, the essays collected here engender different morphologies for the futures of American studies. In an effort to differentiate their modes of temporalization, we have designated the rubrics *comparativist* and *differentialist* to describe the futures that have emerged out of the challenges which disparate social movements posed to the discourses organizing the academic fields. And we have proposed *counterhegemonic* and *posthegemonic* to specify the different temporalizations that academic knowledges assume when they empower the work of social movements. While most of the essays comprising these intertextual relays do not specifically engage Gene Wise's essay, individually and collectively they materialize the futures he foreclosed. That is to say, they inhabit the problematic of present futures and past presents that animated Wise's essay in its unfinished encounter with the future that American studies now occupies.

Open Futures: Posthegemonic American Studies

Playing off this line of intertextual commentary, the opening essay of *The Futures of American Studies*, Janice Radway's "What's in a Name?" returns to Wise's discussion of Parrington as a pretext for convoking the multiple past histories sedimented in the pluralization of the term *studies* so as to retrieve congeries of groups comprising the American studies movements. As the 1998 presidential address to the American Studies Association, Radway's essay challenges the naturalization of such categories as the nation-state and questions the reification of the American studies movements as a single unitary culture. By convoking the convention around the question of the name its members wished to be called, Radway operationalized Castoriadis's notion of the radical imaginary. The question "What's in a Name?" introduced a temporal disruption between the already instituted association and one of the instituting acts that the already instituted order could not accommodate to its existing categories. For if the name of "American" could not secure for the association a place in the future to which its members would want to answer, perhaps a crisis in the name could. *America, Americanness,* and *Americanization*: all of these terms have their own intelligibility. By raising the question of the name, Radway challenged practitioners in the field to account for how the unintelligible and unrepresentable can be brought to bear on the field.

Radway's practices of citation and redescription of Wise's essay released a range of possible futures that " 'Paradigm Dramas' " had foreclosed. She quoted Wise's assertion that the first substantive consensus on what he called the American experience was dominated by the conviction that "There is an American Mind . . . and that mind is more or less homogeneous. Though it may prove to be complex and constructed of many different layers, it is in fact a single entity" (Wise 306). Whereas Wise had written " 'Paradigm Dramas' " to buttress the members of the American Studies Association against the threats posed to the nationalist hegemony, Radway asked the members to reconsider whether it was the "American Mind" that brought them into affiliation with one another. Her address dissociated the ASA from the field-imaginary that had fostered destructive hegemonic masculinity and white supremacist attitudes so as to reinstitute the American Studies Association outside a nationalist denominative. Radway's broad survey of the changes which had transpired within American studies underscored the importance of the contributions of women's studies, black studies, queer studies, international American studies, ethnic studies, Asian American studies, and post-colonial and poststructuralist theory to American studies.

The interrogative power of "What's in a Name" drew on the declining power of the nation-state to subordinate the emergent disciplines of the sixties and seventies to the mandates of the national narrative. Radway laid claim to the radical democratic idea mobilized by such challenges to national-ism and structured in an understanding of what she calls the "intricate inter-dependency" of questions of race, gender, identity, and sexualities outside the framework supplied by the nationalizing narrative. In "The International within the National: American Studies and Asian American Critique," Lisa Lowe argues that any effort to come to terms with the futures of American studies involves a reckoning with the imperialist history that has led some members of the association to be ashamed of the name. Lowe evokes the future out of the formerly disavowed knowledges of the U.S. colonial and imperialist histories to which racialized subjects bear singular witness. As an example of such a reckoning, she explains how the construction of the "Asian American" resulted from the convergence of U.S. nationalism with policies of racial exclusion, gender subordination, and labor stratification. At the heart of Lowe's argument is an examination of the complicity of such political and legal institutions with this history—and with the structures of academic knowledge formations that continue to bifurcate the realms of the economic, political, and cultural. Lowe discovers that existing immigration laws do not merely reflect existing social relations, but that they reproduce the relations of social and economic production, and that these relations are further inscribed in the way the university organizes the relationship between identity studies and traditional disciplines.

Lowe finds the feminized masculinity of the "Asian American male" evidence of the gendering and the racialization of immigrant labor that must be recalled if the future is not to reproduce indecent relations of production from the past. José Muñoz's "The Future in the Present: Sexual Avant-Gardes and the Performance of Utopia" alludes to a related temporal dialectics elaborated on in C. L. R. James's work *The Future in the Present*. But instead of struggling to eliminate a historical practice, Muñoz draws on the utopian potentials of the future as a context in which to investigate the singular temporalities of what he calls the sexual avant-garde. In *The Future in the Present*, James observed that present instantiations of actually existing socialist reality had affirmed their future actuality. Muñoz finds a comparable dialectical utopianism in the live sex acts performed in the New York City gay clubs which Mayor Giuliani was, at the time of the essay's composition, in the process of closing down. But Muñoz is unlike James in that he worries over the ways in which their future orientation might remove the presentness of these live sex acts from history. He therefore proposes that these performances not be relegated to a single temporality, but that they be understood to take place simultaneously in the present and in the future.

Amy Kaplan's contribution to this volume is also interested in the ways in which the forging of discrepant temporalities can perform the work of social transformation, but unlike Lowe and Muñoz, who devote their attention to the utopian dimensions of social change, Kaplan demonstrates the ways in which the state harnesses uneven temporalities to the work of empire building. In "Manifest Domesticity," Kaplan discerns an equivalence between the social logic of domesticity and the political logic of empire. In particular, Kaplan demonstrates how the discourse that produced this equivalence engendered a series of analogies out of it which correlated the work of clearing the domestic landscape of indigenous tribes with quotidian labors ordinarily associated with cleaning house. Kaplan describes how the ideology of domesticity permitted Americans to understand internal colonialism as a form of housekeeping so that they might thereafter construe imperial adventure abroad as a public duty. In pointing out the role gender played in enforcing the geographical distinction between the domestic and the foreign, Kaplan also unearths a historical discourse which associated the native peoples who were resettled by U.S. domestic enterprises with a recalcitrant and archaic temporality to represent the projects of internal colonialism as historically progressive. Her work thus produces its own utopian desire at the site of a critical refusal to maintain the gendered divisions of labor and spatial organizations of the domestic that would constrain the field-imaginary wholly within the nation's time.

In "C. L. R. James, *Moby-Dick*, and the Emergence of Transnational American Studies," Donald E. Pease reexamines James's reading of *Moby-Dick* from the perspective of the subordinated populations who were the victims of the state's temporal as well as its economic and geographical colonization. James composed his rereading of *Moby-Dick* while awaiting deportation on Ellis Island in 1953. He articulated the figures of the "mariners, renegades, and castaways" that he recalled from within Melville's narrative with the un-Americans who, like him, had passed through Ellis Island. But after constructing this correlation, James does not clamor after Americanization. He instead finds in *Moby-Dick* the prediction of a future that constitutes an alternative to the present. By replacing the need for national belonging with the openness to unassimilated otherness represented by the "mariners, renegades, and castaways," James constructed an open-ended circuit of transnational and international relations as a strategic substitution for nationalism. The emergence in James's work of acts of narration with the demonstrated competence to effect transnational and international relations that were then excluded from the official national narrative turn this work from the historical past toward the postnational future that has emerged within our historical present. Its recollection, Pease concludes, constitutes one of the possible futures of a transnational America(s) studies.

Present Futures: Comparativist American Studies

The contributions by Radway, Lowe, Muñoz, Kaplan, and Pease are posthegemonic in that they presuppose the end of U.S. hegemony but that they do not propose counterhegemonies. In designating them as posthegemonic, we intend to indicate the basis for their affiliation with the projects in this volume that do articulate counterhegemonies. Posthegemonic and counterhegemonic American studies emerge out of the reinstituting powers that social movements produce as they traverse and intersect with disciplinary formations. Comparativist and differentialist American studies are concerned with the articulation of the knowledges circulating through these movements to already instituted disciplinary and interdisciplinary formations. John Carlos Rowe's essay in this volume, "Postnationalism, Globalism, and the New American Studies," performs this work of translation in that it proposes to survey the knowledges produced out of these transnational movements in the context of the different formations of American studies they would empower.

Rowe proposes courses in comparative American studies as alternatives to the interdisciplinary models of American studies that move from the U.S. center. Comparative American studies calls for a rethinking of cultures and identity formations in the face of the nation-state's failure to function as guarantor. It would compare the diverse modernisms of the Americas as well as their disparate constructions of race, gender, and ethnicity. Rowe correlates comparative American studies and the future of American studies with the prediction that it will become all the more significant with the decentralization of the academy. He represents comparative American studies in hemispheric and transnational terms as a field that is interdisciplinary in method and that would offer multicultural perspectives on the peoples and cultures of the Americas. Comparative American studies draw from anticolonialist and anti-imperialist political movements an understanding of the ways in which different relations with U.S. and European colonialism gave rise to countries with different social structures and places in the global economy. It would focus as a consequence on the diverse modernisms of the Americas and different constructions of race, gender, and ethnicity. The global analytic of the new American studies would no longer move from the U.S. center. Programs in American studies would be reshaped anew in different institutional sites out of their specific negotiations with globalization.

In "*Salesman* in Moscow," Dana Heller deploys this alternative model to the work of showing how U.S. culture is generated by another culture and in a context that cannot be recuperated in Americanist terms. Rather than looking for similarities to her situation within the United States, Heller uses her experience as a teacher of *Death of a Salesman* as an occasion to take stock of the changes of the United States' place in the world and of her place as an

Americanist scholar. The relation to the field-imaginary that Heller takes up in this essay might be understood as a counter to the one that Wise wrote " 'Paradigm Dramas' " to consolidate in that she does not fear the loss of her field, but turns her essay into the occasion to enter the zone in between her field identity and its disidentification (and in between the field's present and future) that Wise had foreclosed. As she taught this national masterwork to students at Moscow State University, their dialogues produced a zone of cultural interaction in which the play underwent dramatic changes in condition, what Heller calls the Russianization of *Death of a Salesman*, which entailed removing it from the properties of autonomy, artifact, Americanness, and canonicity. Like Willy Loman, the play itself became commodified as a negotiable form of cultural capital. By allowing the radical imaginary to operate in this context, Heller welcomes the opportunity to reimagine herself as the Russians saw her, even as this change of outlook requires her to decenter her Americanist identity so as to understand it from another critical perspective.

Winfried Fluck's "The Humanities in the Age of Expressive Individualism and Cultural Radicalism" constitutes a comparable effort at decentering a dominant U.S. perspective. His analysis of the New American studies is grounded in the differences between the scholarship in American studies that grows out of the European American Studies Association and what Fluck describes as the new Americanists' expressive individualism. Instead of honoring the claim that this scholarship is the necessary outgrowth of the bankruptcy of the European Enlightenment's foundational narratives of human emancipation, Fluck proposes that expressive individualism is premised on the European Enlightenment's privileged addressee—the liberal individual. But in turning the market rather than culture into the arena in which their work is produced and in whose terms it is to be valued, expressive individualists have also turned the overvaluation of differences into the primary form of value. If individual differences constitute the only way to create and exchange value, then the proliferation of increasingly eccentric interpretations comprises expressive individualists' mode of scholarly production. As a consequence of expressive individualists' displacement of culture with the market, the pursuit of truth has been displaced by the proliferation of different meanings.

For this situation to change in the future, Fluck concludes his exercise in comparativist scholarly traditions, U.S. Americanists must critically reevaluate the conditions of their scholarly production. In "Autobiographies of the

Ex-White Men: Why Race Is Not a Social Construction," Walter Benn Michaels has examined the mode of scholarly production with a comparably intense form of critical scrutiny. But in place of proposing that the market be supplanted by the cultural sphere as the proper site of scholarly inquiry, Michaels investigates the mistakes in logic that have overseen the transformation of the demands of social movements in the multiculture into academic disciplines. Michaels opens this provocative analysis with an examination of the contradictory social logics informing the recommendation of the editor of the journal *Race Traitor* that whiteness be abolished. While Fluck might have found the recommendation (as well as Michaels's reading of it) symptoms of the worst excesses of the ideology of expressive individualism, Michaels deploys the social logic of race to interrogate its correlation with the discipline called whiteness studies. Whereas the discipline called for whites to disidentify with the white supremacist positioning of an unmarked subject position, Michaels proposes that this call in fact continues the genocidal logic that made the abolition of blackness and Indianness a potential historical reality. Michaels produces a distinction between race as an ontological and race as a performative category to argue that those proponents of whiteness (and ethnic and identitarian) studies who claim that race is a social construction have confused actions and choices with identities.

In "Color Blindness and Acting Out," Carl Gutiérrez-Jones conducts a careful examination of the cultural implications of Michaels's decision to analyze the knowledges produced within ethnic studies and identity programs from the standpoint of their contradictions in logic. Rather than considering Michaels's project an example of an academic maverick who is intent on establishing a unique position in the profession, as Fluck might have, Gutiérrez-Jones finds Michaels's resistance to the antiracist demands of scholars in identity studies symptomatic of a collective reaction formation. Gutiérrez-Jones has thereby resituated Michaels's project within the context of the white male backlash against the renewed attention to multiculturalist questions in general and to race in particular. He thereafter proposes that the substitutions that Michaels has produced, which would replace terms such as *race*, *culture*, *identity*, and Holocaust with the logical contradictions out of which they are composed, betoken a series of "stranded judgments." According to Gutiérrez-Jones, Michaels's strictly logical accounting of the issues of race and ethnicity conceal the white male's feeling of racial injury.

Futures Imperfect: Differentialist American Studies

When Gutiérrez-Jones characterizes Michaels's response as representative of white liberals' rage at the inroads of identity politics into the U.S. academy, he writes from the perspective of a scholar working in ethnic studies. Gutiérrez-Jones's commitments to comparativist programs in U.S. American studies predispose him to defend whiteness studies as comparable to ethnic studies in its political commitments. But in "Whiteness Studies and the Paradox of Particularity," Robyn Wiegman finds whiteness studies an expression of the white supremacy that it pretends to disavow. Wiegman's analysis agrees with Gutiérrez-Jones that white liberals are presently overtaken by a collective trauma over the loss of their privilege. But she finds the field itself to be organized out of strategies of disavowal that bear greater similarity to Gene Wise's fortress American studies than to contemporary ethnic studies programs. Like Wise's " 'Paradigm Dramas,' " the proponents of whiteness studies construct a field out of a traumatized sense of the loss of a former identity.

Throughout her essay, Wiegman examines the ways in which transforming white identities into objects of study does not disinvest but reinvests those identities with white supremacist academic power. By examining the emerging disciplinary apparatus of whiteness studies, Wiegman explores the ways in which this new field brings into crisis the relationship between disciplinary commitments to objects and the social and historical contexts through which objects are empowered as sites of knowledge in the first place. By examining the disciplinary apparatus of whiteness studies at the historical moment of its emergence, Wiegman discloses the difference between its claim to solidarity with the particularist identities of minoritarian movements and the universalist privilege concealed within this claim to be a marked, hence particularized, identity. Insisting on the differences between the empowering knowledges formed within social movements and their transformation into disciplinary objects, Wiegman establishes the distinction between comparativists and differentialists. Whereas comparativists exploit the similarities between social and academic formations, differentialists position their projects at the site of this intersection in order to scrutinize the distinctions.

In "Identities and Identity Studies: Reading Toni Cade Bambara's 'The Hammer Man,' " Lindon Barrett turns this intersection into the analytic practice that he calls, following Kimberlé Crenshaw, "intersectionality." Unlike the modes of interpretation that would construe race, gender, and sexuality as more or less stable analytic categories, intersectionality commits Barrett to undertake the critiques and transformation of these social categories. Barrett examines how the categories of identity—ethnicity/race, class, sexuality, gender—which are made into salient stable categories by the cultural codes of the dominant culture, intersect, transfigure, and remain co-implicated in one another. Ethnicity and race are socially reproductive categories, for example, and they propagate a heteronormative vision of racial identities that forecloses recognition of their gender insubordination. In order to get at the difference between how these categories work intersectionally and how they are put to use in academic disciplines, Barrett asks how American studies can "engage the mutually constitutive categories of ethnicity/race, gender, and sexuality without replicating the cultural inequities which they seek to expose"? When American studies produces knowledges that ignore intersectionality, Barrett concludes, it reiterates rather than contests given ideological systems.

Instead of comparing more or less stable social categories, Wiegman and Barrett have examined how these categories are produced at and as the site of the intersection where disciplines and movements become one another's futures. But they have conducted their analyses of this site within U.S. territorial borders. The transnational and international aspects of differentialist American studies are made vivid in "Hemispheric Vertigo: Cuba, Quebec, and Other Provisional Reconfigurations of 'Our' New America(s)." Here, Ricardo Ortíz builds on José David Saldívar's reading of José Martí's *Our America* to reconceptualize transnationality along intersectional lines. More specifically, he uses the configuration of an unprecedented North Americas system along an Ottawa-Miami-Havana axis as the conceptual matrix through which to interpret a cross-national and multicultural performance. Ortíz discusses Gloria Estefan's decision to perform her 1997 Montreal concert in Cuban Spanish rather than English in terms of the contradictory alliances that decision organized. For Ortíz, transnationality names a property that belongs to a social movement. It is produced by a form of social motion that also produces the people who can be understood to belong to this movement and complicates their understanding of historical rootedness. Ortíz demonstrates how American borders fail to resist traffics in cultural and other forms of capital which in their increasingly vertiginous circulations further the disintegration of the cultural and national spaces these borders had traditionally defined.

Ortíz discerns in transnationality the resource for opening the intranational perspective of American studies to pan-hemispheric considerations. But in "Marriage as Treason: Polygamy, Nation, and the Novel," Nancy Bentley is concerned with the ways in which U.S. nationalism was itself produced out of the citizenry's differentiation from an alien nation construed as internal to national borders: the phantom presence of Mormonism as an internal yet foreign religious nation against which and in terms of which nineteenth-century U.S. culture was formed. Bentley analyzes the interdependence of "consent" and the "sovereignty" status of the citizen through their collective cultural differentiation from Mormonism. Specifically, she explores how nineteenth-century antipolygamy novels produced a symbolic space wherein the sovereign citizen and the sovereign state co-constituted themselves. Bentley's account of how these novels materialize the social force exerted by the notion of consent is compelling. She proposes that a woman's consent was construed in these narratives as at once a literary sentiment and an active social force deployed by judges in articulating their legal reasons for opposing polygamy. She concludes that these fictive works significantly transformed the legal and civil status of women.

Bentley's interpretation of the role played by popular novels in constructing a hegemonic understanding of a woman's powers is informed by the difference that feminist theory makes to the official understanding of U.S. legal history. Whereas Bentley constructs a bridge conjoining novelistic representations of consent with the procedural logic underwriting juridical decisions, Gillian Brown has produced a thematic bridge linking the recovered memory of child abuse with the liberal democratic discourse out of which the United States had emerged. Throughout "Litigious Therapeutics: Recovering the Rights of Children," Brown cites Thomas Paine's and John Locke's conceptualizations of the injured child as the imaginary basis for political and civil entitlements. She thereby demonstrates an inextricable relationship between discourses that might have otherwise been construed as utterly incompatible. The vulnerability to harm that the child is helpless to overcome conjures a picture to which Thomas Paine alluded when he represented the American colonists as children who suffered at the hands of George III. According to Brown, it was Thomas Paine's picturing of them as wounded children which aroused the colonists' commitment to the future. In their struggle to obtain independence from their abusive parent, the colonists had conveyed to their posterity the redress that liberal individualism affords.

Brown's picturing of its institutions within the context of the recovered memory syndrome radically undermines the liberal tradition's self-portrait. In "American Studies in the 'Age of the World Picture': Thinking the Question of Language," William V. Spanos associates Americanists' world picture with U.S. imperial ventures worldwide. But unlike Brown, Spanos is not interested in supplying the U.S. picture with a critical genealogy. He has instead undertaken a mode of analysis that would release a difference internal to the U.S. picture of itself that cannot become representable within any of the official portraits. To make vivid the difference between this spectral figure and official representations of the nation, Spanos stages its emergence from within the frame of Francis Fukuyama's "end of history" narrative. Fukuyama claimed that U.S. history ended with the collapse of its Russian enemy and with the global triumph of neoliberalism. Spanos adds the memory of the Vietnam War to the end of U.S. history. This extraneous image of the exercise of genocidal violence against a recalcitrant Other reveals the specter within U.S. history. It is this internally disavowed figure, Spanos observes, that produces the national desire to reduce all of the globe into the U.S. imperial imaginary.

Futures Past: Counterhegemonic American Studies

Wiegman, Barrett, Ortíz, Bentley, Brown, and Spanos have all called attention to the distinction between the aspirations for change informing the movements which intersect the field and the different objects and projects to which these energies are put in the academy. But from the time that he published the bibliographical essay, "The Special American Conditions: Marxism and American Studies" in 1986, Michael Denning has been engaged in reshaping the disciplinary formations developed in the field of American studies into an instrument for social transformation. In that essay, Denning explicitly mentioned Wise's interpretation of the significant relationship between the needs of the Cold War and the myth-symbol school of reading.[12] But instead of accepting Wise's description of the field-integrating function of the school, Denning analyzed the way in which Matthiessen in particular had deployed myth-symbol approaches as substitutes for Marxist analyses of culture. In reading back into their texts the Marxism it had been designed to censor, Denning retrieved a dimension of American studies as a field and as a configuration of movements that Wise could neither suppress nor acknowledge. In his efforts to recover the past for which Wise's mode of telling the official stories had served as a substitute, Denning returned to the moments that Wise ascribed to the founding of American studies as a movement and specifically to the figure Wise described as most responsible for demonstrating in his scholarship how an integrating American studies might be done: namely, Vernon Parrington.

According to Wise, Parrington did not merely supply the movement with a usable past, he also endowed the whole of the American experience with a purpose (298, 314). In transforming Parrington's literary career into a synecdoche for the "whole of the American experience," Wise suppressed the conflicting accounts of U.S. history that emerged out of completely different strains within the American studies movement. Denning's *The Cultural Front* demonstrates how the very intellectuals from the 1930s and the 1940s who had been powerfully influenced by certain aspects of Parrington's work had also collaborated in antiracist projects that forged counterhegemonic linkages between American studies as an academic field and as a participant in an international social movement. According to Denning, this group proved Gramsci's claim that "a new social group that enters history with a hegemonic attitude, with a self-confidence which it initially did not have, cannot but stir up from deep within it personalities who would not previously have found sufficient strength to express themselves fully in a particular direction."[13]

Disrespectful of Wise's efforts to integrate American studies into a homogeneous movement, the counterhegemonic essays gathered in this collection, like Denning's book, have reconnected the pasts buried under hegemonic representations with the possible futures for which they substituted. In place of an alternative hegemony, these essays reimagine the field as an international space that engenders multiple collective identifications and organizational loyalties. Individually and collectively, they convoke networks of association and of intersections that create and reflect social spaces mediating with distant and dissimilar ones.

"Work and Culture in American Studies" continues the argument of *The Cultural Front* and enables Denning to elaborate on the claim that race and ethnicity had become the means through which the working classes experienced their lives and mapped their communities with a much needed theoretical rationale. This essay is part of Denning's larger project to bring the vital political and social traditions that the Cold War had suppressed back into connection with contemporary social and political conditions. Here, Denning constructs a genealogical account of the emergence of culture as the encompassing category for the field of American studies which established the centrality of the cultural front to the construction of American studies as a social formation. Denning is interested in particular in retrieving from that historical moment a labor theory of culture that would undermine the privileging of mental over manual labor. He argues that the conceptual processes which are invoked to distinguish cultural artifacts from the material outcomes of labor do not in fact sustain the distinction that they are intended to enforce. Insofar as both forms of cultural work arise out of the execution of preconceived designs, they are inextricably linked forms of cultural production.

In " 'Sent for You Yesterday, Here You Come Today': American Studies Scholarship and the New Social Movements," George Lipsitz turns to Denning's *The Cultural Front* to elaborate on the significance of this alternative past for the future of American studies. Lipsitz explains how the intellectual work and artistic productions of the cultural front were unlike Parrington's in that their projects were not confined to academic inquiry but emerged directly from their social activism. Their work disclosed "the relationship between politics and culture, between ethnic identity and class consciousness, between the myth of American exceptionalism and the always international identities of the U.S. nation-state and between cultural theory and cultural practice." When Lipsitz associates his project with the historical formation that Denning has retrieved, he intends to demonstrate how the knowledges produced within that historical movement can address questions posed by the global economy.

Whereas Lipsitz and Denning return to the historical era in which popular front politics functioned as the rallying point for a variety of counterhegemonic formations, Günter Lenz's "Toward a Dialogics of International American Culture Studies: Transnationality, Border Discourses, and Public Culture(s)" demonstrates the impact of a wide range of discursive formations—British cultural studies, the discourse of the borderlands, and the critique of U.S. imperialism—on the field of American studies. The counterhegemonic aspect of Lenz's account inheres in his description of American culture as itself the product of a range of complex processes. "American culture is not the homogenized powerful, imperializing or globalizing Other," Lenz remarks, "but it is in itself multiplicitous, inherently differentiated and conflicted, and always changing in active response to alternative multicultural and intercultural discourses and experiences." It is as a consequence of these internal divisions that programs in American studies assume different shapes in relation to their institutional locations and out of their specific negotiations with the impact of globalization.

Like Lenz, Paul Lauter is committed to breaking away from centrist mod-

els of Americanism to consider the economic processes, institutional projects, and political effects of American studies as a field. One of Gene Wise's
contemporaries, Lauter has repeatedly turned his positioning as a scholar in
American studies into the occasion of adopting his field identity to address
changing political circumstances rather than to construct the defense against
change. Lauter's initial understanding of American studies was grounded in
his own struggles with the imperatives of the Cold War state. But as a student
at NYU in the 1950s, he also learned from other interdisciplinary programs
like ethnic studies and women's studies about how to establish linkages between academic disciplines and social movements, as well as how to align
knowledges, practices, and laws in ways that could effect social change. In
"American Studies, American Politics, and the Reinvention of Class," Lauter
deploys his lived history of what Denning has called cultural front politics to
demonstrate their pertinence to contemporary questions.

If Denning returns to Wise's account of Parrington's integration of the
American studies movement in order to recover a political history of the
movement that Wise had suppressed, Lauter exemplifies how that restored
history could be placed in the service of forging a counterhegemonic role for
the new American studies. In "The End of Academia: The Future of American Studies," Eric Cheyfitz builds on this conversation by arguing that non-
comparable logics organize academic rationales and political formations. He
thus insists that a distinction be preserved between the academic politics that
in some universities have resulted in a multicultural curriculum and concrete
forms of social action. In insisting on such distinctions, Cheyfitz does not
refuse solidarity with the counterhegemonic projects of Denning, Lipsitz,
and Lauter, but he does insist that the failure to recognize the differences
between these realms can lead to the most fraudulent kinds of academic
posturing as a masquerade for political work.

In "Nation dot com: American Studies and the Production of the Corporatist Citizen," Russ Castronovo analyzes American studies in the context of
what Bill Readings has described as the global university. He examines the
ways in which American studies unintentionally offers the university a corporatist model that would profit from the scholarship of even the most critical
Americanists. The globalization of the American economy and culture, Castronovo observes, might have turned even the most transnational and interdisciplinary initiatives of the field into a continuation of corporate capitalism
by other means. But if American studies has become the institutional space in
which to continue corporate capitalism, it has also provided the opportunity
to reflect critically on its assumptions and resist its hegemony.

In sorting the essays for this volume under one or another of these rubrics—comparativist, differentialist, counterhegemonic, and posthegemonic—we are interested primarily in considering the ways in which each of these field-movement projects animates a different temporalization of the future and in how these temporalities converge, overlap, and deconstruct each other. While the comparativist model suggests that a significant transformation of the field has already been accomplished, the differentialists' interrogations of the categories through which the comparativists have represented their model reject the idea that this model constitutes a movement forward. Moreover, if the counterhegemonists return to subaltern political pasts to materialize alternative futures, the posthegemonists might be understood to disclose the ways in which those alternative futures install hegemonies of a different order.

In staging the emergence of these disparate futures of American studies at the fault lines and within the untimely moments of Gene Wise's " 'Paradigm Dramas,' " we have attempted to unreify the temporal dimensions within which the field has produced its past imaginaries and to wrest adumbrations of the *inter*national, the *trans*national, and the *post*national out of the Cold War consensus. In supporting this project, the essays collected in this volume undertake the analyses, contestations, and reversals of American studies' temporal norms. In releasing the futures that quite literally haunted Wise's history-making text, these mobile temporal formations also refuse the self-satisfactions of presentism and encourage the reconceptualization of the field of American studies as itself a heterotopia. The relationships obtaining among the essays gathered might thus be described as elaborating a heterotopology, a relational field comprised of different and intrinsically fluid social formations that engenders multiple collective (dis)identifications and organizational (dis)loyalties. Produced by discourses and social processes that do not conform to distinct identity categories, these essays effect field identities that are open-ended rather than self-enclosed processes. Since these field identities name the vehicles through which these discourses reproduce themselves, no hard and fast distinction separates what is produced and what regulates the production. Field identity appears instead as the result of a series of never completed partial identifications.

If, by way of these operations, the temporalities of the futures of American studies can be imagined as partaking of the heteronomy animating the radical imaginary, they might consequently be described as a heterochronic. The futures of American studies, that is to say, might be conceptualized not as what comes after the most recent organization of the field but after the manner in which they struck Gene Wise a quarter-century ago—as what is other than presentable in the field of American studies.

Afterward: Futures Now?

Throughout this volume we have operated on the assumption that thinking about the futures would release the field's most creative aspects. And we have promoted this understanding by staging this release within the context of Gene Wise's aversions to futurity. But we cannot conclude this volume without considering an alternative conceptualization. In "ConsterNation," Dana Nelson provocatively argues that any gesture of "future thinking" emanates from a desire for a realm that is free from political struggle and thus constitutes blockage in the organization of what she calls radical democracy. And she further views the deterritorialization of the nation into postnational, international, and transnational formations as the projection of an antidemocratic formation. She asks whether the dilemma posed between the political value of multicultural agendas and the ideological and bureaucratic forces mounted against them constitutes a false choice. And she wonders whether that false choice constitutes the rationale for the desire for the escape to futurity. If "ConsterNation" names the feeling of helplessness and confusion as we look again to America's alternative multicultural or patriotic future, Nelson wants to rethink politicalness as disagreement.

Dana Nelson wants this future now—so do we.

Notes

1   Gene Wise, " 'Paradigm Dramas' in American Studies: A Cultural and Institutional History of the Movement," *American Quarterly* 31, no. 3 (1979): 293–337. Subsequent references are cited parenthetically in the text. The piece was republished in *Locating American Studies: The Evolution of a Discipline*, ed. Lucy Maddox (Baltimore: Johns Hopkins University Press, 1999), 166–210.
2   Jay Mechling, "Commentary," in *Locating American Studies*, ed. Maddox, 211–14.
3   Michel Foucault, "Of Other Spaces," *Diacritics* 16, no. 1 (1986): 22–27. Wise's essay was radically heterotopic in that it contained within its spaces the historically incompatible temporalities of American studies as an academic field and as a congeries of heterogeneous social movements. Wise's efforts to avert the epistemological crises which resulted from the coexistence of these discrepant temporalities led him to construe " 'Paradigm Dramas' " as a space in which

to make new and different sense of all other spaces within the field of American studies.

4 Nearly all of the essays included here began as plenary talks at the Dartmouth College Institute of American Studies in the four years leading to and including the quintessential mark of futurity, the year 2000. We want to thank Sandra Gregg for her ongoing wisdom and organizational skills in providing leadership for the institute's direction and the many scholars who have participated over the years in deliberating on the issues raised here.

5 The proposition that essays in this volume transpose Wise's anxieties over futurity into resources of hope might improperly suggest that our emergent futures gratify a hope that Wise had articulated. Through his repeated acts of foreclosure, Wise acknowledged that the field's possible futures had already inhabited its spaces—but as that which he felt compelled to disavow. The futures that emerged could not be assimilated to already constituted categories or included within existing arrangements. Neither could they ratify an ideology of progress. Insofar as futurity happened through the catastrophic destruction of the field machinery through which Wise had accomplished these disavowals, he would have experienced these resources of hope—and indeed the actualization of the field in such terms—as the fulfillment of his worst fears.

6 Meaghan Morris, "Future Fear," in *Mapping the Futures: Local Cultures, Global Change*, ed. Jon Bird et al. (New York: Routledge, 1993), 38.

7 "Paradigm dramas" as the vehicle for Wise's historical narrative of the field also functioned to keep in play a critical genealogy that the emergent discourses of the sixties were definitively challenging. As we have discussed, the myth-symbol synthesis of American literature and American history concentrated its core beliefs within key foundational texts—*Errand into the Wilderness, American Renaissance, Virgin Land, American Adam, The Machine in the Garden*—which oversaw the translation of American studies as a movement into the methodological assumptions, objects of inquiry, and modes of analysis through which the founders had instituted American studies as an academic field. To render this past usable in the face of the sixties crisis, Wise used *paradigm dramas* to articulate the myth-symbol paradigm with the anthropologist Victor Turner's account of the social dramas through which cultures reflected on and thereafter transformed themselves. Turner had modeled his explanation of "social dramas" after Northrop Frye's description of literary mythology as educating the social imagination. Frye proposed that the literary understanding of drama might be extrapolated into an analytic category capable of representing as well as effecting social change. In placing Turner's model into the service of defining the conflicts over the future of American studies, Wise reaffirmed the explanatory power of the myth-symbol paradigm to which Turner's model was indebted—at the very moment that the paradigm had lost its epistemological authority throughout the academy. See Victor Turner, "Social Dramas and the Stories about Them," in *On Narrative*, ed. W. J. T. Mitchell (Chicago: University of Chicago Press, 1981), 152.

8   The following critical reappraisal of the American studies movement advanced by the scholar-activist Christopher Lasch is representative of the radical knowledge produced within the new social movements: "The infatuation with consensus; the vogue of a disembodied 'history of ideas' divorced from considerations of class or other determinants of social organization; the obsession with 'American Studies' which perpetuates a nationalist myth of American uniqueness—these things reflect the degree to which historians have become apologists, in effect, for American national power in the holy war against communism." Lasch, "The Cultural Cold War: A Short History of the Congress for Cultural Freedom," in *Towards a New Past: Dissenting Essays in American History*, ed. Barton J. Bernstein (New York: Pantheon, 1968), 323.

9   Benedict Anderson, *Imagined Communities: Reflections on the Origin and Spread of Nationalism*, rev. ed. (London: Verso, 1991).

10 Castoriadis writes: "This element . . . which gives . . . a specific orientation to every institutional system, which overdetermines the choice and the connections of the symbolic networks . . . the basis for articulating what does matter and what does not . . . is nothing other than the imaginary of the society and of the period considered." Cornelius Castoriadis, *The Imaginary Institution of Society* (Cambridge, Mass.: MIT Press, 1987), 145.

11 Two important essays, not reprinted in this volume, produce the radical imaginary from Wise's history-making essay. Amy Kaplan's " 'Left Alone with America': The Absence of Empire in the Study of American Culture" rereads the moment in Wise's essay in which he describes Perry Miller's "jungle epiphany" as a casebook example of paradigm formation. For Wise, Miller's scholarly project carried "the urge to impose form upon experience, to seize upon the American past and insist that it answer questions he is driven to ask of it" (302). He thus concludes that Miller's project did not arise from "the conventional desire simply to make a 'contribution to scholarly knowledge,' " but was instead animated by his need to break through the academic conventions that he regarded as impediments to the gratification of his "primordial drive" (302). When Amy Kaplan returns to this scene foundational to the institution of American studies, she proposes a different understanding of Miller's epiphany. Whereas Wise described American studies as a field whose representative action entailed the containment of the culture's diversity within a paradigm that symbolized it, Kaplan's redescription of this scene generates a supplemental scenario within what Wise described as the founding moment of American studies. Kaplan found what Toni Morrison has described as the "Africanist presence" in Miller's "epiphany," and she reads this as the disavowed context for the institution of the field of American studies. In place of locating, as did Wise, Miller's remarkable synthesizing powers, Kaplan diagnoses Miller's staging of his academic vocation against the backdrop of his imperial adventure in the Congo as symptomatic of the involvement of his "primordial drive" with the history of U.S. imperialism. According to Kaplan, the transactions conducted in this occluded scene entailed struggles over racial

equality and colonialism as the unacknowledged knowledges which the field's epistemological categories had reproduced yet disavowed. When Miller invested himself with the authority to describe European settlers' imperial adventures in the North American wilderness while in the Congo, he tacitly represented, as Kaplan observes, the Congo and the New England wilderness as equivalent spaces within the imperial world system. Although Miller characterized his vocation to recount the Puritans' "errand into the wilderness" as an ambition comparable to Gibbons's *Decline and Fall*, Kaplan finds a more appropriate cultural antecedent in Conrad's *Heart of Darkness*.

Because the supplementary events Kaplan discerns within Miller's scene could not be assimilated into Wise's paradigm drama, this extraneous scenario effected a disruption of the drama through which Wise had recovered the coherence of the field. In redescribing the founding moment of American studies as an academic field, Kaplan reveals the conceptual limits of Wise's American paradigms by supplanting them with the discourse of the "borderlands," the name Kaplan uses for the paradoxical site of contacts, collisions, and encounters that produce new hybrid cultures. "The site of the borderlands," Kaplan explains, comprises "multidimensional and transterritorial" spaces that "not only lie at the geographical and political margins of national identity but as often traverse the center of the metropolis." Borderland intellectuals would sacrifice certainties for the contradictions and ambiguities that inform present and future field identities. Their borderlands discourse would link "the study of ethnicity and immigration inextricably to the study of international relations and empire." Amy Kaplan, " 'Left Alone with America': The Absence of Empire in the Study of American Culture," in *Cultures of United States Imperialism*, ed. Kaplan and Donald E. Pease (Durham, N.C.: Duke University Press, 1993), 16–17.

At the same time, Kaplan's formulation of the discourse of the borderlands draws on José David Saldívar's description of this paradoxical space in *The Dialectics of Our America: Genealogy, Cultural Critique, and Literary History* (Durham, N.C.: Duke University Press, 1991), esp. 49–84. Here, Saldívar represented the borderlands as the discursive terrain in which U.S. representations of American things engage in dialogic transactions with other cultures' descriptions of American things. Saldívar produced a dialogue with Kaplan in his 1998 essay "Remapping American Cultural Studies," where he returned to her revisionist description of Perry Miller's jungle epiphany to insist on indissoluble differences between the assimilationist practices of U.S. imperial culture and unassimilable ethnic minorities. According to Saldívar, the discourse of U.S. imperialism has depended on a conceptual apparatus that the field of American studies has reproduced. The apparatus was comprised of a relay of mutually constitutive terms, recognizable signs, metaphors, and master narratives. This apparatus preexisted cultural contact and permitted its projection onto other cultures. In tracing the coordinates of a different mapping of the field of American studies, Saldívar deployed a reading of Captain John Gregory Bourke's imperial adventure along what he called the "American Congo" in support of the claim that America was itself a cartographical artifact produced within the discourse of U.S. imperialism. In elaborating the significance of borderlands to his remapping of the field, Saldívar characterized the cultures emerging at these margins as negotiating non-nationalistic claims to representation and identity. See the chapter "Remapping American Cultural Studies," in Saldívar's *Border Matters: Remapping American Cultural Studies* (Berkeley: University of California Press, 1997), 159–83, esp. 161–64.

As a result of the usages to which Americanists like Kaplan and Saldívar have put them, Wise's transitional scenarios have not remained anchored to the past. Obeying the logic of what Freud has analyzed as a primal scene, Wise's dramas have translocated into sites for the construction of alternative futures that he could not have imagined in the past. " 'Paradigm Dramas' " might be described, then, as a site wherein American studies undergoes change through the taking place within the present dimension of the futures the social movements that Wise had denied presentification. But the predicted correlation between the academic field and the movements that it only partially accommodates differs in significant ways.

12 Michael Denning, " 'The Special American Conditions': Marxism and American Studies," *American Quarterly* 38, no. 3 (1986): 357.

13 Michael Denning, *The Cultural Front: The Laboring of American Culture in the Twentieth Century* (London: Verso, 1996), 145.

POSTHEGEMONIC

✧

What's in a Name?

Jan Radway

I

In the spring of 1960, less than ten years after the founding of the American Studies Association, its first president, Carl Bode, of the University of Maryland, sat down to recall the moment of the association's founding. Assuming that the members of the American Studies Association might be interested in the story of how he started the organization, Bode intended his tale to provide guidance for the future. He hoped his narrative would point to both the strengths and the weaknesses of the American studies movement and of the American Studies Association itself. Although this short piece was not Bode's presidential address—at the time, such addresses were not required of ASA presidents—it was, nonetheless, one of the first instances of the now familiar American studies genre, the genre conceived in response to the question, "does American Studies have a distinctive method?" Like so many others who have since followed his lead, Professor Bode sought to define American studies, to specify its peculiar method, and to lay out an argument for why American studies might, in his words, "lead a counterreformation in college curriculums."[1]

I want to recall Carl Bode's essay for a particular reason. Indeed, I want to acknowledge it respectfully as a precedent precisely because it does not focus only on the scholarly and intellectual field of American studies. It also looks at the American Studies Association itself and deliberately asks about the role it should play in a larger social and political context. I, too, want to think about the American Studies Association as an organization fostering specific forms of knowledge production at this particular historical moment because I want to ask what the association should do now to build on the rich body of work that has developed in the last twenty years or so, work that has made the annual ASA conference both possible and tremendously exciting.

That work—pursued by feminists, by those working on the question of race, by ethnic studies scholars, by people working on gay, lesbian, and queer histories, by those preoccupied with the lives of the laboring classes and with the achievements of the indigenous populations of this continent—that work has challenged some of the early assumptions that grounded the field of

American studies. It has challenged what Donald Pease called "the disciplinary unconscious and field imaginary" of American studies, the presumption that American culture is exceptional in some way and that it is dominated by consensus.[2] As nearly all recent presidents of the American Studies Association have pointed out in their presidential addresses, this new work has insisted on the importance of difference and division within American history, on the significance of "dissensus," in Sacvan Bercovitch's suggestive phrase.[3]

But note the difficulties in expressing the point here, the problem of how to think difference and the idea of a specifically *American* studies together. My own sentence put it this way—"the importance of difference and division *within* American history." It is not easy to deal with either the most generative or the most limiting effects of difference if you already assume the unity and coherence of a distinctly American history. Is difference merely to be posed as a qualifier of some prior whole? Does the perpetuation of the particular name, American, in the title of the field and in the name of the association continue surreptitiously to support the notion that such a whole exists even in the face of powerful work that tends to question its presumed coherence? Does the field need to be reconfigured conceptually in response? Should the association consider renaming itself in order to prevent this imaginary unity from asserting itself in the end, again and again, as a form of containment?

These are the questions I want to pose by drawing attention to Carl Bode's very brief anecdote about the naming of the association. I want to ask "what's in a name?" and "what do names do?" I want to take up the challenges issued by Mary Helen Washington in last year's presidential address, "Disturbing the Peace: What Happens to American Studies If You Put African American Studies at the Center?"[4] In particular, I want to take to heart the caveat Washington provided in her recommendation of John Sayles's film, *Lone Star*, as a prophetic allegory about how to change the field of American studies. In recommending *Lone Star*'s particular depiction of what she called "cultural menudo," Mary Helen Washington observed that, in Sayles's film, "the resolution of disputes is not as important as the freer play of long-silenced voices." She continued: "In *Lone Star*, cultural traditions and styles more often collide rather than intersect and interweave; and what I love about Sayles's depiction of this process is that he doesn't allow differences of language, politics, historical vision, etc. to dissolve in a soothing movement toward consensus; he presents the multicultural moment as one of tension, struggle, discomfort and disagreement" (16). The question I aim to pose is what the association can do at this particular moment, on the brink of a new century, and at the edge of the so-called American continent, to ensure that its very name does not enforce the achievement of premature closure through an implicit, tacit search for the distinctively American common ground.[5] With this aim in mind, I want to note here that, in response to Mary Helen Washington's caveat, I have deliberately sought to avoid using the pronoun "we" through-out this essay as a way of refusing the presumptive and coercive enclosure it usually enacts when used in institutional situations of this kind. I have resisted the comforting assumption that there is an unproblematic "we" as a way of recognizing that the many who associate their work with American studies often have distinctly different interests, agendas, and concerns.

Carl Bode's mention of the naming of the American Studies Association is very brief. He first notes that a small group of literary scholars, historians, and nonacademics met on March 22, 1951, in response to his efforts to organize a society that "would help to define American civilization" (347). He hoped that its stress on synthesis would counter the increasing emphasis on "specialism." In this account, Professor Bode further reports that "business went briskly," and then he observes, "We argued about naming the society— American Civilization Society vs. American Studies Association—but few other things caused any debate." His reference to an argument about the worth of highlighting "civilization" rather than "studies" is tantalizing here. One wonders what the arguments were. I have not been able to recover the details of the discussion, but it does seem plausible given what I know about the debates of the time that disagreement might have centered on the validity of highlighting the unity of American society, on the question of whether that society actually had developed anything so coherent as a civilization, on whether it might be better to feature the looser, more contingent idea of multiple "studies" in the organization's title rather than assuming from the outset that those studies would amount to the history of an organic whole.[6]

It is interesting to juxtapose the final choice of "studies" with what appar-ently didn't cause any debate at this first organizational meeting, that is, the question of whether or not to use the word *American*. If, as his omission of any reference to this point suggests, Bode and his colleagues did not debate the use of the term *American*, their application of it to quite diverse studies of the history and culture of the United States might be seen as a function of the precise historical context within which they worked. As many have observed, the American Studies Association was a product of a Cold War context that produced a desire to delineate what was exceptional about U.S. culture at a time when public debate was structured by the perceived opposition between the aggressive empire of the Soviet Union and the supposedly disinterested, democratic republic of the United States. It was this interest in American exceptionalism, really, that led to the desire for an interdisciplinary method that would be equal to the notion of American culture conceived as a unified whole, a whole that manifested itself as a distinctive set of properties and themes in all things American, whether individuals, institutions, or cultural products.

From the beginning, then, there has been a highly productive tension in both the field and the association, a tension exemplified by conflicting impulses embedded in the name. On the one hand, there is a strong tradition in American studies of asserting the exceptionalism of American society and of delimiting the extent of that exceptionalism geographically. Gene Wise summarized what he called this first "substantive consensus on the nature of the American experience" in his important article, " 'Paradigm Dramas'." It was dominated, he suggested, by the assumption that "There is an 'American Mind.' That mind is more or less homogenous. Though it may prove to be complex and constructed of many different layers, it is in fact a single entity." He continued, "What distinguishes the American Mind [in this view] is its location in the 'New' world." Wise suggested further that the consensus assumed that the American mind could theoretically be found in any American, but it presumed further that it "comes to most coherent expression in the country's leading thinkers—Williams, Edwards, Franklin, Cooper, Emerson, Thoreau, Hawthorne, Melville, Whitman, Twain, Dewey, Niebuhr, et al." The "al," of course, was still white, straight, middle-class, and male.[7]

On the other hand, there has been an alternative tradition to this late 1940s and 1950s consensus, a tradition that Linda Kerber, Allen Davis, Martha Banta, Alice Kessler-Harris, Elaine Tyler May, and Patricia Nelson Limerick explored in their presidential addresses, a tradition that Michael Denning has recently shown was present in the earliest stirrings of what would become the American studies movement.[8] In his important book, *The Cultural Front,* Denning has performed the immense service of telling another origin story about the development of the American studies field, a story that places the origins of the field not in the Cold War decades but much earlier, in the decades of the thirties and the forties. As George Lipsitz has pointed out, Denning recovers the diverse radical roots of the first practitioners of American studies and shows how those practitioners sought to understand the United States precisely so as to critique its racism, classism, sexism, and xenophobia.[9] Denning demonstrates persuasively that cultural critique was not a new impulse in American studies when it began to dominate the field in the 1970s and 1980s. Rather, he suggests, some students of American history have always attempted to counter the notion of American exceptionalism both by pursuing the question of the place of the United States in an international context and by suggesting that the apparent democratic consensus in fact excluded many from participating in defining it or from enjoying its supposed benefits.[10] This tradition has focused on what I like to call, after Stuart Hall, "the popular," that is, the everyday lives, political activities, and cultural productions of the subordinated populations of the United States.[11] It has tended to focus on practices and structures of feeling that bind people to communities that are larger or smaller than the American nation, communities that have sometimes been international in scope, sometimes more locally based, and sometimes bound more to political goals than to space or territory.[12] This work has been enabled and encouraged, I want to suggest, by the founders' judicious decision to highlight the possibility of multiple, different studies of things diversely American.

Despite the richness of this alternative American studies tradition, it was not until very recently that it managed to bring to awareness another piece of the disciplinary unconscious embedded in the choice of the word *American* to describe the association and the field it was meant to foster. Indeed, it has been less frequently remarked on in the accounts of the Cold War origins of American studies that, in addition to underwriting the notion of American exceptionalism, the early consensus in the field tended to elide the idea of the American with the culture of the United States.[13] In so doing, it unconsciously erased the fact that other nations, groups, and territories had already staked their own quite distinctive claim to the concept and name American. Indeed there would be no mention in the *American Quarterly* for decades of the earlier, alternative account of the concept of American culture articulated by José Martí in his important essay, "Nuestra America," published almost simultaneously in January 1891 in Mexico City and in New York.[14] The pronominal "nuestra," the "our" in Martí's title, referred not to the American culture of those born within the borders of the United States, but to a different America, the America of those who claimed South and Central America, the America of the Caribbean basin, as their home. As Martí makes clear, that America included both Haiti and Cuba, the sites of important revolutionary movements opposing European and United States imperialism.

In settling on the term *American* to delimit their area of study, then, the founders of this association, no doubt without intending to, compounded earlier imperial gestures. In naming the society in this way, they repeated a particular nation-state's claim to the powerful historical concept of America. Thus they repeated the usurpation by the United States of the right to employ a word that had originally been mobilized by Europeans to name geographically dispersed lands that they themselves had imperially expropriated for their own use from indigenous peoples who named the locales they occupied in their own, diverse and distinct languages. The apparent lack of self-consciousness about this gesture was almost certainly a function of the raw economic and political power wielded by the United States, which enabled it to obliterate by inattention other nations' or groups' claims to the term.

The elision of American culture with the United States and the consequent backgrounding of U.S. imperialism that it produced has now been placed on the agenda of the ASA by scholars and intellectuals building explicitly on the alternative traditions of American studies as well as on earlier critiques of imperialism produced by people like Martí, José Rizal, W. E. B. Du Bois, C. L. R. James, Franz Fanon, and others. They have taken to heart the fluidity embedded in that word *studies* that was highlighted in the field's title and then read that fluidity back into the once reified concept of an organic America assumed to be congruent with the borders of the United States. This new work made a particularly prominent intervention in the field of American studies with the appearance of the volume *Cultures of United States Imperialism*, edited by Amy Kaplan and Donald Pease. That volume provided the inspiration for the 1998 ASA conference in Seattle and suggested its theme, "American Studies and the Question of Empire."[15]

I want to call attention to this rich body of work that has developed at the intersection between American studies' alternative traditions and certain strains in critical race theory, Black Atlantic studies, women's studies, postcolonial theory, subaltern studies, and transnational feminist and queer studies, to name only a few of the influences here. I would then like to explain why I think this turn to the question of American imperialism, both domestically and internationally realized, is not only important but potentially transformative of the field of American studies itself.

I want to suggest, in fact, that this new work fundamentally challenges certain deeply embedded assumptions about the concepts of identity and culture that, despite an increasingly prominent critique of them, still tend to enclose and contain the effects of difference within American studies often through the structuring principles of syllabi, anthologies, and even conference programs and panels.[16] I hope to suggest finally that the complex, increasingly elaborated and refined discussion of the social, political, cultural, and intellectual consequences of both internal and external forms of U.S. imperialism has begun to demand new ways of thinking the relationship between geography, culture, and identity. I believe that this work of reconceptualization should now be placed at the heart of the field's agenda and that the association should itself seek ways to foster it through every means possible. The ultimate question is whether this can be adequately done in the current historical context, dominated as it is by a rapidly advancing global neocolonialism that specifically benefits the United States, by an association whose very name still so powerfully evokes the ghostly presence of a fantasmatic, intensely longed-for, unitary American culture.[17]

II

Space will not permit a full scale intellectual history of American studies' radical traditions nor even of the field's now extensive engagement with the question of difference. I only want to note here that some of the earliest scholarship on questions of gender, race, ethnicity, and class, and to a certain extent on sexuality, did find a hospitable space within American studies, a place where the challenges this work posed to familiar canons and dominant traditions could be formally delivered. Indeed many scholars working on these questions presented their work at American studies conferences. They were able to do so because committed individuals connected with the association have always worked diligently to open the conference proceedings, the organization itself, and the pages of the journal to new modes of thought.

Although the resulting work has varied widely and was differently inflected in order to advance diverse agendas, it seems clear to me that its collective force challenged the earlier consensus view, the notion that the American democratic idea uniformly included within its purview all those who inhabited the United States. By noting the ways in which certain populations were not only excluded from the so-called American experiment but also included within other communities defined not by national belonging but by gender, race, class, or ethnic affiliation, this scholarship early on centered on questions of subjectivity—in the parlance of the time, on questions of identity.

The term *identity politics* of course has a complex history, and it has been used both approvingly to delineate various forms of political opposition to an unexamined nationalism and disparagingly as an epithet aimed at questioning the value of so-called minority identifications.[18] Within American studies, it seems to me, the causes of identity politics have generally been taken very seriously. Scholars within the field have conscientiously attempted to respond to demands that they examine something more than the activities of educated, middle-class, straight, white men. Important work has been done as a result. In the past, however, these forms of non-national identification sometimes were essentialized and rendered as secondary qualifications to others deemed overarching or primary. What this often amounted to was an additive intellectual politics, a politics of inclusion, a move that left intact the assumed privilege of territorial paradigms and the priority of the nationalist community. So-called minority identities and projects were construed as having come not from the core or center but from the periphery. Since difference thus conceived was assumed to be divisive, a constant reiteration of the need to seek common ground developed in response. American studies was concomitantly envisioned as a more capacious umbrella containing more multitudes than it had been able to encompass before. I take this idea of America as "a stable container of social antagonisms" to be the subject of Nikhil Pal Singh's bracing critique, just published in *American Quarterly*, of both past and recent defenses of American liberalism which have sought to justify the idea of common ground against the supposedly divisive claims of multicultural difference.[19]

The liberal solution to the question of difference has increasingly been made untenable, however, by new work on race especially, but also by work on sexuality, ethnicity, gender, and class. Much of this work has made a critical theoretical break with earlier formulations of identity. Sometimes (but not always) informed by poststructuralist understandings of the ways in which subjectivities are constructed, this work has detached the question of difference from various bodily, cultural, and geographic essentialisms, and it has begun to explore the complex, intersecting ways in which people are embedded within multiple, conflicted discourses, practices, and institutions. Within American studies, this break appeared particularly acute when work on difference explicitly began to engage the question of how American nationalism was actively constructed at specific moments, at specific sites, and through specific practices.

I am thinking here of work like that done by Amy Kaplan, Lauren Berlant, Lisa Lowe, George Sanchez, Hazel Carby, Wahneema Lubiano, Vicki Ruiz, Eric Sundquist, David Roediger, Carolyn Porter, José Saldívar, Eric Cheyfitz, George Lipsitz, Robyn Weigman, Lisa Duggan, Betsy Erkkila, Gary Okihiro, Robin Kelley, Nancy Hewitt, Dana Nelson, Chandra Mohanty, George Chauncey, and so many others. Although this work is not uniform and is, in fact, animated by quite different theoretical commitments—indeed some of it is not explicitly poststructuralist—I do think it collectively poses the question of how American national identity has been produced precisely in opposition to, and therefore in relationship with, that which it excludes or subordinates. This work has begun to show that American nationalism is neither autonomously defined—which is to say, exceptional—nor is it internally homogenous. Rather, it is relationally defined and historically and situationally variable because it is dependent on and therefore intertwined with those affiliations, identities, and communities it must actively subordinate in order to press the privileged claims of the nation on individuals and groups.[20]

I believe that this work calls for a new way of formulating the objects of American studies.[21] Instead of a form of attention that tends to isolate and reify those things that are the focal point of concern—whether a culture, an event, a political subject, or an institution—this new work demands an attention to relationships of connection and dependence, relationships I like to characterize generally as *intricate interdependencies*. I use that term somewhat loosely here to describe a range of radically intertwined relationships that have been brought to the fore in recent attempts to rethink nationalism, race, culture, ethnicity, identity, sex, and gender. Let me point to two sites where the effort to explore the consequences of imperial power relations has foregrounded the need for relational thinking and highlighted the importance of intertwined, material, and conceptual dependencies. This work bears portentous implications for the way American studies might be practiced in the future.

There is a large body of work on the social and cultural formation of the subject, which attempts to dislodge the question of identity from its attachment to some form of biology. Indeed, this desire sits at the heart of a good deal of feminist work on gender, queer work on sex, and antiracist work on the category of "race." In the interests of space, I have decided only to say a few things about the work on race here as a way of drawing attention to the larger effort to displace essentially defined bodies for complex social subjects produced at the intersection of a number of discourses, practices, and institutions.[22] Some of the key features of this work can be found in an essay by Wahneema Lubiano entitled "Like Being Mugged by a Metaphor," as well as by the volume she recently edited, *The House That Race Built*.[23]

Neither Lubiano's essay nor the larger volume itself is designed simply to

question race as a function of biology nor to argue merely that "race" is a
socially constructed category. Rather, they aim to argue more radically that
the state and the political economy of the United States are themselves entirely dependent on the internal, imperial racialization of the population.
What this means is that the American national subject is produced as white
and that the process of production takes place in an overdetermined fashion
through the knotted, inextricably intertwined relationship between practices
of symbolic representation and specific economic, educational, and political
policies that simultaneously name and subordinate black populations. As
Lubiano puts it, "the constructions of our various beings as a group are both
material and cultural. The material and the cultural are neither completely
separate nor do they operate autonomously. The idea 'Black people' is a
social reality. Black people are a dominated group politically and economically, even if every member is not always dominated under all circumstances"
(73). The United States is thus utterly dependent on its obsession with blackness. In fact, that obsession is constitutive of the state and the way it functions
on behalf of some. The United States are intricately intertwined as a national
and state entity with those it must dominate in order to establish, in however
illusory a fashion, the conceptual stability of, and material security for, a
particular ruling group. George Lipsitz has documented in excruciating detail how this is actually managed in his recent book, *The Possessive Investment
in Whiteness*.[24]

American national identity is thus constructed in and through relations of
difference. As a conceptual entity, it is intricately intertwined with certain
alterities that diacritically define it as something supposedly normative, normal, and central. As a material and social entity, it is brought into being
through relations of dominance and oppression, through processes of super-
and subordination. To take the measure of this national entity, it is necessary,
then, to focus on these constitutive relationships, these intricate interdependencies, which ironically are figured as deep fissures and fractures in the
national body. America is not an organically unified, homogeneous thing.
Nor should it be isolated for simple veneration, as an object in a museum.
This, it seems to me, is Lubiano's important point when she says that the
myth of America must be de-aestheticized.

I should point out here that, in this article, Lubiano also raises troubling
questions about the political work of intellectuals and university-based scholars. She suggests, in fact, that a conceptual instrument like multiculturalism,
which she ultimately supports, might function as just another technology for

racializing the world if it is used by intellectuals to construct and study black-ness without also tracing out how that blackness is wholly functional for the state. This may also be true of the notion of the American in American studies. If intellectual practice in the field does not examine the ways in which the construction of a national subject works to the economic and political advantage of some and precisely against the interests of others, then American studies runs the risk of functioning as just another technology of nationalism, a way of ritually repeating the claims of nationalism by assuming it as an autonomous given, inevitably worthy of scholarly study.[25]

There is another large body of work on the social and cultural formation of the subject, which extends the critique of an aestheticized America by pursuing another set of intricate interdependencies. This work attempts to dislodge the question of identity from its attachment to essentialized notions of culture and geography. Much of this work has been done as part of the examination of the effects of U.S. imperialism around the globe. I would like to acknowledge the important contributions of Chicana/Chicano studies and point as well to the contributions of recent work on the effects of the U.S. presence in the Pacific Rim, especially in Hawai'i, Guam, and the Philippines. The nature of these contributions is laid out with exceptional clarity in two essays in the Kaplan-Pease volume, José Saldívar's "Américo Paredes and Decolonization," and Vicente Diaz's "Pious Sites: Chamorro Culture between Spanish Catholicism and American Liberal Individualism."[26] Both of these essays strain after a new understanding of the concept of culture by seeking to de-reify it. That is, they abandon the conceptualization of culture as an organic, homogeneous thing bound to a fixed territory and attempt to reconceptualize it as the result of complex social processes deeply bound up with the exercise of power at specific, concrete sites.

José Saldívar aims to criticize what he calls the "spatial materialism and the politics of cultural identity" (294) that have grounded traditional American studies. He does so by analyzing the influential and generative work of Américo Paredes, whom he characterizes as a "border intellectual." Noting that the Texas-based Paredes refused to be identified as a Mexican immigrant to the United States, Saldívar suggests that Paredes's "antidisciplinary border project" (293) grew out of his desire to acknowledge the fact of U.S. military aggression against the land of his ancestors. In Saldívar's view, Paredes sought to trace out the ways in which the imposition of an Anglocentric economic and cultural hegemony on the land appropriated from Mexico failed to produce the desired Americanization of the people living there. In his important book on the *corrido*, "*With His Pistol in His Hand*," and in his novel, *George Washington Gómez: A Mexicotexan Novel*, Paredes documented the complex ways in which border dwellers produced their own distinctive world and a point of view that acknowledged that they were neither simply Mexican nor American, nor even some third, homogenous cultural identity.[27] Rather they were deeply and continuously affected by the clash of cultures at a site characterized by a "serious contest of codes and representations" (295). The point of view that this social situation generated, and which Saldívar characterizes as "in betweenness" (308), was not equivalent to the simple physical oscillation between two homogeneous and autonomous cultures. Rather, it generated an ambivalent subject, a subject produced not by the simple contiguity of cultures, but by mutual contestation of social histories and habits—by the interleaving and interweaving of cultural practices—a situation achieved through the complex processes of migration, appropriation, domination, and subordination, and by the sense of loss, active remembrance, adaptation, and borrowing that they produced.[28]

Culture, in this view, is not something one "has" as the consequence of being situated at a particular geographic location. Rather it is a meaning effect produced by hierarchical relationships established between different spaces and the communities that give them significance. Culture becomes remarkable because a sense of alterity is produced through the social confrontations and interdependencies that result from these interconnections.[29] Hence, for Paredes, as Saldívar suggests, "the consensus rhetoric of American Studies with its emphasis upon the motto, '*e pluribus unum*' had to be negated and supplemented with a more sophisticated sense of 'culture' as a site of social struggle" (295). This is as true for culture within the boundaries of the United States as it is for culture in the borderlands and beyond. The very notion of the American is intricately entwined with those "others" produced internally as different and externally as alien through practices of imperial domination and incorporation.

Like Saldívar and Paredes, Vicente Diaz also seeks to "trouble . . . national and cultural boundaries" (313) by examining the complexities of Chamorro cultural history in Guam. He does so by tracing the successive ways in which local histories and practices in the Marianas were deeply affected by the social transactions promoted by the global economic and political policies of imperial states. Thus he traces the ways in which Chamorro traditions and self-understandings have been transformed by their encounters with Spanish Catholic and U.S. state imperialism. He does this by disentangling the histories embedded in the architectural mélange of the capital city, Agana, and by exploring what he calls the "troubled entanglements among indigenous and exogenous ideas and practices" (313) in two nearly contemporaneous events in 1990, the suicide of former governor Ricardo Bordallo and the passage of an antiabortion law by the Guam legislature. What Diaz is able to show is how both places and events in Guam are deeply affected by cultural histories that are neither finished nor past but actively engaged and demonstrably effective in the present through the persistence of memories, dreams, desires, and even spirits.

Through a careful analysis of the intertwined practices and rhetorics comprising the suicide and the passage of the abortion law, Diaz demonstrates that, in both events, indigenous Chamorro, Spanish Catholic, and American liberal beliefs and practices contest each other in ways that act to blur the distinctions between them. Diaz suggests that Chamorro culture has not simply been superseded by Spanish Catholic culture, nor has the latter been displaced by American liberalism. Rather, the practices and representations of which all three are constituted intersect, interweave, *and* are transformed as a result. He suggests that because of this, it is essential to see "how Chamorro cultural continuity makes a home within intrusive foreign systems . . . that sought to reconsolidate themselves in imperial and evangelical imperatives among people . . . who also sought to reconsolidate their own notions of self and society" (334). Chamorro, Spanish, and American cultures are thus intricately intertwined and dependent on each other for their mutual self-definition through confrontation and exchange.

Much of the work on borderland culture and on the cultural complexities of the Pacific Rim challenges the idea that culture can be adequately conceived as a unitary, uniform thing, as the simple function of a fixed, isolated, and easily mapped territory. Similarly, Saldívar and Diaz suggest that cultural identity can no longer be conceptualized as a naturalized essence or property thoroughly saturating individuals because of their socialization within a particular locale. Instead, identity must be conceptualized as a specific, always changing relationship to multiple, shifting, imagined communities, communities that, despite the fact that they are always imagined, are situated in specific places at particular moments and amidst particular geographies.

This work does not, therefore, diminish the importance of place or geography in the effort to understand societies and culture. Rather, it demands a reconceptualization of both as socially produced through relations of dependence and mutual implication, through relationships established socially and hierarchically between the near and far, the local and the distant. It suggests that, far from being conceived on the model of a container—that is, as a particular kind of hollowed-out object with evident edges or skin enclosing certain organically uniform contents—territories and geographies need to be reconceived as spatially situated and intricately intertwined networks of social relationships that tie specific locales to particular histories. The feminist geographer Doreen Massey conceptualizes this interweaving of locale and history as a particular "space," that is, as "the sphere of the meeting-up (or not) of multiple trajectories, the sphere where they coexist, affect each other, maybe come into conflict. It is the sphere both of their independence (*co-existence*) and of their interrelation." Subjects and objects, she adds, "are constructed through the space of those interrelations."[30]

It seems to me that new work on cultural borderlands and hybridities challenges the claims to intellectual validity of fields that unwittingly continue to perpetuate a set of assumptions criticized recently by Akhil Gupta and James Ferguson, assumptions that bounded territories are naturally disconnected, that cultures are isomorphically tied to those spaces, and that identities follow necessarily and unitarily from them. This work suggests instead that territories and geographies need to be understood as always hierarchically interconnected, which is tantamount to saying, in the words of Gupta and Ferguson, that, "spaces are always related to each other through the social relations that control them."[31] Culture needs to be reconceived as a site of perpetual social struggle, as the location where particular forms of power produce opposition and contestation in the very act of trying to control it. Culture is not a matter of coherence and consensus. Rather, it is the always shifting terrain on which multiple social groups form, actively solicit the identification of some, hinder that of others, and ignore the counterclaims made by still others. Identity is never unitarily achieved as a result, not even by the claims of nationalism. As David Lloyd points out, "it is a paradox of nationalism that though it may often summon into being a 'people' that is to form and subtend the nation-state, it is always confronted with that people as a potentially disruptive *excess* over the nation and its state. . . . If nationalism calls forth a people for the nation-state, its mode of subjectification still cannot exhaust the identifications available to the individuals thus summoned" (189). From this perspective, ethnic, queer, feminist, or working-class identities cannot be conceived as separate essences sheltered within a more capacious, ontologically prior American identity. Rather, they must be seen as cross-cutting, insurgent, oftentimes oppositional identifications.[32] Sometimes those identifications are with subnational communities; at other times, they are with trans- or international communities. In either case, they pose a profound challenge to the integrity of the very idea of an American whose identity is fully accounted for by residence in the territory of the United States.

III

What does all this mean for American studies at this particular historical moment? If the notion of a bounded national territory and a concomitant national identity deriving isomorphically from it are called into question, why perpetuate a specifically American studies? Has enough work been done at this point to complicate and fracture the very idea of an American nation, culture, and subject, such that its continued presence in the name of the field and in that of the association no longer functions as a form of premature closure or as an imperial gesture erasing the claims of others to use of the name? In order to promote work that would further reconceptualize the American as always relationally defined and therefore as intricately dependent on "others" that are used both materially and conceptually to mark its boundaries, would it make sense to think about renaming the association as an institution devoted to a different form of knowledge production, to alternative epistemologies, to the investigation of a different object?

A name change can seem a superficial gesture, or the disrespectful, willful dismissal of a significant past, or it can function as the signifier of something more positive. It is not clear to me whether changing the name of this association would amount to one or another of these possibilities. Would finding another name for the ASA do little to alter the parameters of the field and the forms of knowledge production generated within it? Would it amount only to a dangerous and ill-timed denial of the achievements of a field that many believe has done more to foster diversity in personnel and intellectual point of view than have numerous other scholarly disciplines? Or would a name change renew the field by pushing scholars to reconceptualize its proper object of study by asking questions about culture for which they do not already have the answers?[33] I am uncertain about how to respond to these questions, in part because every name change I can think of produces as many objections to it as it does potentially positive effects. Although I think that, in the end, the name *American studies* will have to be retained, I believe it is worthwhile to open up a speculative discussion of the name for several key reasons.

The activity of exploring potential new names is generative because names are never simply descriptives. They also function as directives and sometimes as promises; as such, they have to be enacted and embodied in constitutive practices; their promise demands to be realized. Thinking of possible ways to rename the field and the association can help to identify new practices that might be taken up by participants as a way to institute the relational perspectives I have been recommending here. The act of trying out new names, it seems to me, can therefore work to suggest how a different relation to the name *American studies* might be taken up or realized by those who are seeking to redefine it.[34] If the study of human social interaction is not to be spatialized and essentialized in isomorphic ways at this historical moment, if the boundaries of the American are not to be naturalized or taken for granted or mapped onto the United States alone, how should the parameters of the field be delineated, how should objects of study be constituted?

Let me sketch out three possibilities for renaming the association and the field and the advantages and problems they might pose. I can't in good faith argue for any one of these against the others, but I have found that the effort to think them through is fruitful precisely because it helps to clarify what might be desirable in the future. At the same time, because each name change generates certain dissatisfactions and hints at the potential objections that might be made by others, this thought experiment demonstrates both how difficult it is to shed some of the field's most basic presuppositions and how hard it will be to negotiate within a world that is increasingly wary of the multifarious forms of power exerted by the United States and by dominant modes of thought. Ultimately, I think, the process of examining the imperatives contained within different names can at least suggest concrete actions which the association might take now to help ensure that the field's proper objects of study can be further transformed.

One possibility would be to name the field and the association with greater modesty. The field could be called United States studies and the association could be renamed the Association for the Study of the United States with the proviso that analysis of the United States would have to foreground its relationships to the rest of the world as well as to non-national communities. Such a move would have the advantage of refusing to repeat the imperial gesture whereby competing claims to the name *American* were erased. In keeping with this greater awareness of international power relations, the association could additionally be reconfigured as the *International* Association for the Study of the United States, following the lead taken by the International Forum for U.S. Studies organized at the University of Iowa. This would acknowledge the fact that analysis of the United States and its history, people, and cultures is not carried out solely within the borders of this country. Indeed those positioned beyond its borders and hence at a remove from ordinary and taken-for-granted ways of seeing and doing things can frequently denaturalize the familiar with greater effectiveness and thereby see culture and convention where others see only the world.

It should be noted, however, that, as Jane Desmond and Virginia Dominguez have effectively cautioned in their article, "Resituating American Studies in a Critical Internationalism," the act of renaming the association an international one would enjoin on all those associated with it certain responsibilities.[35] It would be necessary to ensure that international scholars and scholarship occupied something more than a token position within it. At the association's conference, in the pages of its journal, and in the notes of scholars who associate themselves with the field, the work produced by scholars living and teaching outside the United States ought to figure crucially in arguments about the nature of this country's history and cultures.

The present association has made important strides in this direction, but it could do more to institutionalize an international, comparative agenda. A growing number of individual scholars from outside the United States (especially from the European Association of American Studies) have been welcomed at recent ASA conferences. The association has also institutionalized ties with the Japanese Association for American Studies and sponsored joint conferences with the Canadian Association for American Studies. But the work of international scholars is still often cordoned off in special international panels rather than integrated within panels that feature United States–based scholars. And the ASA as an organization has yet to explore the possibility of formalizing connections with other worldwide associations for the study of the culture of the Americas, including the Latin American Studies Association. By placing the United States (conceived always in a global context) at the heart of the field's work while formally acknowledging that that work is carried out internationally, this new name might be successful at challenging the chauvinism Américo Paredes and others found embedded in the name of *American studies*, the sense that only U.S. citizens understand the United States.

The problem with this name change, of course, is that it would not necessarily address the questions I have raised about the reification of cultures. Even more to the point, by associating the field with the political rather than the conceptual borders of the nation-state, such a name might actually promote even less questioning about the nature of the U.S. nation and nationalism as the implicit objects of study of the members of the association. Even more worrisomely, such a name might lead to a greater isolationism in the intellectual construction of the United States, a sense that its embeddedness in changing international contexts is not essential to its definition. This would perpetuate and perhaps worsen the tendency to believe that something essential and fundamentally different happens when individuals and families migrate to the United States, that those people become entirely other cultural subjects than they were before.

A second possibility, then, might be the Inter-American Studies Association. After all, in her presidential address some five years ago, Cathy Davidson suggested that "postcolonialism is the theory; inter-American studies is the practice."[36] José Saldívar himself has also recently repeated this call for inter-American studies in *Border Matters*, and Eric Cheyfitz argued for something similar when he proposed "Americas Cultural Studies."[37] Betsy Erkkila has argued for another related formulation in her article, "Ethnicity, Literary Theory, and the Grounds of Resistance."[38] The name inter-American studies would have the advantage of comparatively connecting the study of U.S. history and cultures to those of North, Central, and South America and to the countries and cultures of the Caribbean as well. By focusing on transnational American social and cultural relations, inter-American studies could foster the investigation of regional cultural flows, of peoples, ideas, institutions, movements, and products.

At the same time, such a name would implicitly place the entire American field in relation to the imperial Europe that first began to define it. The refocused field could comparatively explore the complex economic, political, social, and cultural relations that produced the various American societies that have emerged in the so-called new world. A field organized on such principles could conceivably challenge the naturalization of nations as discrete units of analysis, and it might even question the theoretical reification of culture on the model of a distinct and unitary thing. By recognizing that the American idea has been pursued somewhat differently in different contexts, such a field might be able to foster an understanding of culture as a complex site of economic, social, and representational contestation and exchange, transactions produced by contiguities and circulation through relationally defined borders.[39]

In attempting to foster inter-American studies, a redirected association would need to institutionalize connections with the Latin American Studies Association, with the Canadian Association for American Studies, the European Association of American Studies, the Canadian Studies Association, the National Association for Ethnic Studies, the National Association of African-American Studies, the National Association of Hispanic and Latino Studies, and any number of others. It would be extremely important, however, that possibilities be explored with sensitivity and with attention to the fact that such a gesture could easily be seen as another imperial act of containment, erasure, or even co-optation. Clearly, an Inter-American Studies Association should not be conceptualized as a means for preempting the work of organizations developed previously according to other rubrics. It must not be conceived as an umbrella organization uniting and overseeing the work of more specific, local, American studies organizations. Inter-American studies would need to be conceptualized and organized as a comparative site, a place where scholars with many different focal points of interest in the diverse Americas come together to explore the connections and divergences in their scholarship. An association renamed in this way would need to seek out other organizations and explore with them what sort of an alliance might be useful to all concerned.

Still, there are drawbacks to this new name as well. Although inter-American studies could well foster attention to regional cultural flows and thus to the hybridity of cultural identities, one has to ask why the American continents and the Caribbean should be singled out as a coherent region? Why contain the flows in this particular geographic way? What is the justification for isolating this region as somehow different from all others? Wouldn't the relationship of the United States to the countries of the Pacific Rim be just as important for the definition of American citizenship, say, or for understanding labor and legal history in the United States?[40] What about the virtually unstoppable export of U.S. cultural products around the globe at the end of the twentieth century? Doesn't that phenomenon potentially enlarge the purview of inter-American studies even further? Would one want to investigate Singapore, for instance, or some of the major cities in India, where U.S. mass culture has had an enormous impact, as zones where the American interacts with other cultural processes? This could seem an even more troublesome imperialist gesture than the one the proposed name change is attempting to undo if it did not focus carefully on the reciprocal nature of the exchanges involved.

Should space and geography, then, be thrown out entirely as an organizing rubric for the investigation of human culture? What about a third possibility, something like the Society for Intercultural Studies? Such a move offers distinct possibilities, but it comes with major drawbacks as well. To begin with, if the field were organized in this way, it might better foster the study of non-national and transnational forms of identity construction. By training its gaze on complex processes of cultural flows, on the hybridities they produce, and even on the reactionary formations that develop in their wake, this reconceived field might do a better job of attending to the many ways in which the logic of nationalism is and has always been contested. A society that was not hemmed in by the need to peg cultural analysis of community and identity formation to geography might better be able to attend to the full variety of cultural negotiations, negotiations that do not recognize national borders but flow across them to solicit the identifications of attentive and like-minded individuals.

In particular, such a field might more effectively focus on the study of identities and communities based on interests, actions, and politics rather than on simple location or position. Additionally, by focusing on exchanges, crossings, and mutual influences, by placing the idea of the transaction rather than that of the boundary or limit at its conceptual heart, such a field might more successfully develop a pedagogy predicated on relations, not on mutually exclusive divisions. It might then develop as a technology for fostering interdependence rather than autonomy, responsible mutuality rather than satisfied self-regard. The field might provide something other than a civic-minded pedagogy for the national subject. It might imagine a pedagogy designed to foster what David Noble has called "unpredictable creativity." It might seek to foster fluidity and flexibility in a mobile, always changing subject who lives both here and there, in the present and in the past, for the future and for others.[41]

Institutionally, a society renamed in this mode might then sensibly pursue the cause of multilingualism. In fact, I think this is a good idea even if the American Studies Association is never renamed. It would make a good deal of difference, I think, if this association, in whatever incarnation, came out in favor of at least a bilingual, if not a multilingual student body.[42] Jane Desmond and Virginia Dominguez have already made this recommendation, and I think the association's council could recommend this policy to departments and programs in American studies. I believe that American studies programs should require extensive knowledge of a language other than English and that the question of what life is like when it is lived between and among different languages should be structurally embedded at the heart of the curriculum. I believe that American studies programs should demand that their students develop the skills to read American studies work in languages other than English.

There are clear drawbacks, of course, to the name intercultural studies. No doubt one may wonder about the loss of specificity this might promote. Would such a name change make this field another form of what is now known as cultural studies? Would something important be lost in the process? What is the value of local specificity in an age of global capital? How important is it to remember that people live everyday lives embodied and locally situated? Similarly, how important is it to understand and preserve the ways in which knowledges are themselves particular and situated, that is, generated in, and relevant to, specific contexts and histories? Do those who focus their attention on the United States have a special responsibility at this historical moment to track the ways in which processes of global integration disproportionately work to benefit a relatively small number of U.S. citizens? Would lack of attention to the ways in which the effects of global processes are always felt locally simply aid and abet forces of global integration? Is this a moment of historical watershed in which it would be particularly dangerous to do away with the respect for local contexts? I believe that it is.

I come back, then, to American studies, the field, and to the American Studies Association as an organization with a particular name and a complex history, embedded in the contradictions of a particular historical conjuncture. What is to be done? Is it possible to honor the past and to build on the successes of the field and the association even while mounting a responsible but vigorous critique of past myopias and earlier paradigms? I believe that it is. I do not think this field or this association need to fear change. Together they have fostered it in the past and embraced its effects; they can do so again. Change, however, won't come on its own. Changes will have to be made deliberately and actively, with an eye to their potential consequences. Although the association probably does not need to be renamed in order to reconfigure for the future, I do believe it should at least seek ways to institutionalize new forms of bifocal vision, a capacity to attend simultaneously to the local and the global as they are intricately intertwined. Such a project will entail the fostering of a relational and comparative perspective. It will also require that the association actively pursue the intellectual and political consequences of difference by establishing connections with other organizations, whether they be subnational in focus, differently national, transnational, or regional. It will entail a recognition of the theoretical centrality of working-class and ethnic studies, women's studies, queer studies, and Native American studies to a reconceived American studies project. At the same time, it will require conversations with others who have very different points of view, a fact that will require even greater disciplinary and political openness. I believe the association must promote multilingualism within American studies programs and departments and within its conference proceedings. Finally, as a way of foregrounding the complexity of the social relations that produce the cultural flows, transactions, and exchanges that are now to be highlighted, the association must seek ways to foreground the intricate calibrations between the structural and the cultural. This will require more extensive attention to social theory and to the new work being done in the social sciences. Attention to the complexity of cultural construction will require renewed and refined thinking about the intricacies of social behavior and social action. This is a complex agenda, I know, but it seems to me that this field and the ASA, which have both changed dramatically since their inception, can embrace further change and actively seek to bring it about in order to face the challenges of the future.

Notes

I would like to thank my research assistant, Jessica Blaustein, for her terrific help with this essay. I would also like to thank my students for their rigorous questioning over the last several years and for the many times they have introduced me to new work. Finally, I would like to acknowledge the assistance I have received from many friends who read and critiqued an earlier version of this address. That group includes, in no particular order, Kathy Rudy, Cathy Davidson, Barry Shank, Shantanu Duttaahmed, Jane Desmond, Virginia Dominguez, Nancy Hewitt, Alberto Moreiras, José Saldívar, Sybille Fischer, Wahneema Lubiano, and Larry Grossberg. I would also like to thank the members of a seminar at the University of Kansas who also commented extensively on an earlier version of this essay and had an enormous impact on the final version.

1 Carl Bode, "The Start of the ASA," *American Quarterly* 31, no. 3 (1979): 347. Subsequent references are cited parenthetically in the text. The headnote to the essay clearly notes that it had been written in 1960. Although it is conventionally said that what distinguishes American studies as a field is its investment in interdisciplinarity, it seems to me that it has been equally characterized by its critical, theoretical, and methodological self-consciousness. That is to say, as a form of intellectual investigation and study that specifically challenged older,

more naturalized configurations of knowledge production in both the humanities and the social sciences, American studies has consistently had to think critically about the intentions and imperatives that pushed it to construct its object of knowledge differently. In fact, in 1958, only eight years after the founding of the association, *American Quarterly* began publishing an annotated list of "Writings on the Theory and Teaching of American Studies" as part of its annual bibliography issue. In that year, the list included forty entries alone under the heading of "The Philosophy of American Studies." Since the very beginning, then, the field has consistently asked itself a series of questions including: why study American culture? exactly what *is* American culture? and what are the best ways to go about examining American culture?

I see this essay as another instance in this now long-standing tradition and hope that it generates thoughtful conversation about how American studies might construct its proper object differently at a moment when complex global processes are augmenting the circulation of capital, commodities, and people and therefore challenging older ways of thinking about the autonomy of cultures, nations, and identities. My claim here is that this new context at least demands the rethinking of justifications for the study of American culture if not also the rethinking of the very idea of American culture itself.

2 Donald Pease, "New Americanists: Revisionist Interventions into the Canon," *boundary 2* 17 (1990): 1–37. For an example of work that fundamentally challenged older configurations of the American, see Nina Baym's important and now classic essay, "Melodramas of Beset Manhood: How Theories of American Fiction Exclude Women Authors," *American Quarterly* 33, no. 2 (1981): 123–39, where her questions about traditional ways of thinking about the nature of the American experiment are inspired by feminist frameworks. Baym specifically criticizes the theoretical presumptions and methodological habits by which the traditional canon of representative American literary texts had been constructed based on an unconsciously gendered way of thinking about American experience.

3 Sacvan Bercovitch, *The Rites of Assent: Transformations in the Symbolic Construction of America* (New York: Routledge, 1993).

4 Mary Helen Washington, "Disturbing the Peace: What Happens to American Studies If You Put African American Studies at the Center?" *American Quarterly* 50, no. 1 (1998): 1–23. Subsequent references are cited parenthetically in the text.

5 I want to make it clear here that I am only strategically questioning the search for common ground and not necessarily challenging its worth on an absolute, theoretical basis. Though I believe the move to invoke common ground at this precise historical moment is problematic precisely because questions about the nature and significance of difference are both volatile and consequential for the lives of many, and because any move to define the nature of the common very likely would be controlled by those already in power holding to a dominant set of assumptions, values, and beliefs, I do feel that the future of a diverse popu-

lation will depend on the capacity to articulate a conception of a shared public culture that will both depend on difference and protect and celebrate it as well. It seems to me that a new commons will very likely have to be established through the difficult process of coalition building rather than through the incorporative processes that tend to characterize efforts to define common ground in a society built fundamentally on the idea of property and private space.

6   See, for instance, Robert Spiller, "American Studies, Past, Present, and Future," in *Studies in American Culture: Dominant Ideas and Images*, ed. Joseph J. Kwiat (Minneapolis: University of Minnesota Press, 1960), 207–20; and Spiller, "Unity and Diversity in the Study of American Culture: The American Studies Perspective," *American Quarterly* 25, no. 5 (1973): 611–18, where he observes about the founding of the association: "We said by our actions if not by our words: There is now in existence a well-formed total and autonomous American culture and it is our business to find out just what it is, how it came into being, how it functions, and how it should be studied, researched and taught" (613). Although he acknowledges that there is diversity in American culture, he suggests that such diversity does not challenge the prior idea of the whole. Spiller writes, "Actually, there never was such a thing as an ethnically, geographically and temporally pure culture; nor was there ever a culture that was not made up of an infinite number of variations and subcultures; *but such qualifications of the concept of total culture do not invalidate it where the gestalt is clearly enough defined to overcome the problem of inner diversity and conflict*" (613; emphasis added). It should be clear from these comments that, in this particular conceptualization of American culture, difference is figured as troublesome to the idea of the whole, as something to be overcome and managed by a totalizing formulation, rather than as a feature that is integral to, and constitutive of, the notion of the entity itself.

7   Gene Wise, " 'Paradigm Dramas' in American Studies: A Cultural and Institutional History of the Movement," *American Quarterly* 31, no. 3 (1979): 306. It was this canon of quintessentially American authors, of course, that Nina Baym was questioning in "Melodramas of Beset Manhood," where she suggested that "This myth of artistic creation, assimilating the act of writing novels to the Adamic myth, imposes on artistic creation all the gender-based restrictions that we have already examined in that myth. The key to identifying an "Adamic writer" is the formal appearance, or, more precisely the *informal* appearance of his novel. The unconventionality is interpreted as a direct representation of the open-ended experience of exploring and taming the wilderness, as well as a rejection of "society" as it is incorporated in conventional literary forms. There is no place for a woman author in this scheme. Her roles in the drama of creation are those allotted to her in a male melodrama: either she is to be silent, like nature; or she is the creator of conventional works, the spokesperson of society" (138).

8   Linda K. Kerber, "Diversity and the Transformation of American Studies,"

American Quarterly 41, no. 3 (1989): 415–31; Allen F. Davis, "The Politics of American Studies," *American Quarterly* 42, no. 3 (1990): 353–74; Martha Banta, "Working the Levees: Building Them Up or Knocking Them Down?" *American Quarterly* 43, no. 3 (1991): 375–91; Alice Kessler-Harris, "Cultural Locations: Positioning American Studies in the Great Debate," *American Quarterly* 44, no. 3 (1992): 299–312; Paul Lauter, "Versions of Nashville, Visions of American Studies," *American Quarterly* 47, no. 2 (1995): 185–203; Elaine Tyler May, " 'The Radical Roots of American Studies,' " *American Quarterly* 48, no. 2 (1996): 179–200; Patricia Nelson Limerick, "Insiders and Outsiders: The Borders of the USA and the Limits of the ASA: Presidential Address to the America Studies Association 31 October 1996," *American Quarterly* 49, no. 3 (1997): 449–69; Michael Denning, *The Cultural Front: The Laboring of American Culture in the Twentieth Century* (London: Verso, 1996). See also Denning's first version of this argument in " 'The Special American Conditions': Marxism and American Studies," *American Quarterly* 38, no. 3 (1986): 356–80.

9 George Lipsitz, " 'Sent for You Yesterday, Here You Come Today': American Studies Scholarship and the New Social Movements," *Cultural Critique* 40 (1998): 203–25.

10 The masthead of the *American Quarterly* also makes it clear that, despite its tendency to focus on domestic events, institutions, and movements, an interest in the place and role of the United States in international contexts did exist within the association from the beginning. Indeed, in the Fall 1949 issue of the journal, the title page was headed by the following note: "The aim of *American Quarterly* is to aid in giving a sense of direction to studies in the culture of the United States, past and present. Editors, advisers, and contributors are therefore concerned not only with the areas of American life which they know best but with the relation of each of those areas to the entire American scene and to world society." This headnote has been used continuously throughout the history of the AQ. For the most part, however, and until recently, the material in the journal has tended to focus on domestic events and concerns of the United States and its citizens.

11 Stuart Hall, "Notes on Deconstructing the Popular," in *People's History and Socialist Theory*, ed. Raphael Samuel (London: Routledge and Kegan Paul, 1981), 226–39.

12 I am indebted here to the work of Akhil Gupta and, in particular, to his perspective on nationalism and transnationalism. See especially his essay, "The Song of the Nonaligned World: Transnational Identities and the Reinscription of Space in Late Capitalism," in *Culture, Power, Place: Explorations in Critical Anthropology*, ed. Gupta and James Ferguson (Durham, N.C.: Duke University Press, 1997), 179–202. I should also note that that entire volume (along with recent discussions in the field of anthropology) has been enormously influential in the formation of my own thinking about the issues under discussion in this essay.

13 Note the equation of the culture of the United States with the concept of

American culture in the *American Quarterly* masthead description mentioned in note 10 of this essay.

14 José Martí, "Our America," in *Our America: Writings on Latin America and the Struggle for Cuban Independence*, ed. Philip S. Foner, trans. Elinor Randall (New York: Monthly Review, 1977), 84–94.

15 Amy Kaplan and Donald E. Pease, eds., *Cultures of United States Imperialism* (Durham, N.C.: Duke University Press, 1993). I also want to acknowledge here how much my thinking in this essay has been influenced by the recent volume edited by Lisa Lowe and David Lloyd, *The Politics of Culture in the Shadow of Capital* (Durham, N.C.: Duke University Press, 1997). In addition, I have found very helpful an essay by Paul Giles, "Reconstructing American Studies: Transnational Paradoxes, Comparative Perspectives," *Journal of American Studies* 28 (1994): 335–58. There he writes, "A question arises whether American Studies might not have become a redundant tautology, the residue of an age of patriotic empire-building that bears little relevance to the increasingly transnational networks of the 1990s" (337). He continues, "for all the talk about post-national narratives and comparativist perspectives, it remains very difficult to dislodge many of the primary, foundational assumptions of American Studies, because such assumptions are often bound unconsciously to a residual cultural transcendentalism that fails to acknowledge the national specificity of its own discourse" (344).

16 On this point, see Carolyn Porter, "What We Know That We Don't Know: Remapping American Literary Studies," *American Literary History* 6 (1994): 467–526. There she argues that "the lip service paid to the severance of the U.S. from its claim of title to American—in the by now habitual disclaimers we offer in courses on 'American' literature, as well as in just such scare quotes used to signal our understanding that 'American' is a misnomer—are more than marks of bad faith. They also signal the failure of too many of us to 'rethink' what we thought we already know in the context of what we all know that we do not know—how to reconceptualize a field that is clearly no longer mappable by any of the traditional coordinates" (471).

17 As I write this, I am acutely aware that this work is not work I myself have done in my own scholarly investigations. Indeed, I want to make it clear here that, despite the feminist focus of *Reading the Romance* and an effort to think the notion of a fractured subjectivity and questions of difference in *A Feeling for Books*, I place my own work within the traditional, Americanist, highly spatialized paradigm of culture that I believe the new work on race, ethnicity, sexuality, and gender explicitly challenges. Although I was attempting to question certain fundamental assumptions about gender in the first book and about the categorization and functioning of print culture in the second, the framing of each study remains within certain dominant ideological assumptions of the time, assumptions that justify the treatment of American cultural genres in isolation. My thoughts in this essay are now prompted by an engagement with the work of others that challenges this fundamental presupposition.

That engagement has taken place in my classes and in conversation with my students. It is also the product of several formative experiences that occurred while working on other projects.

I am thinking particularly of conversations with Professor Nicolás Kannelos that took place during the first organizational conference about volume 4 in the American Antiquarian Society's *History of the Book in America* project. I am co-editing the fourth volume of this project with Carl Kaestle of Brown University. Our volume covers the years 1880 to 1945. We invited Kanellos to our first organizational conference for this volume along with a number of other well-respected scholars of American culture and book production. We were hoping to emphasize the increasing diversification of the population during our period and to focus on the impact this had on book production and consumption. More specifically, Professor Kaestle and I were hoping to include a specific essay on the Hispanic press in a section of the book devoted to the functions of print culture for diverse audiences and communities.

Although Kanellos applauded our intent, he also provided a powerful critique of our assumptions which, despite our interest in difference, had located the center of book production in "the trade," on the east coast of the United States, and conceptualized American print culture as primarily English-speaking. He pointed out that if the Hispanic press only appeared in a section on readers and uses of print, there would be no way to tell the story of the different history, chronology, and functions of print production within primarily Spanish-speaking communities in the United States from a time even before English colonization. He also noted that the story of Spanish-language print production in the United States would have to trace movements across the U.S.-Mexican border and throughout Central and South America and would need to think about economic, social, and cultural relationships to Spain and Mexico as well as to the United States. His larger point was that our outline presumed a narrative point of view located at some putative American center assumed to be within the continental United States and therefore conceptualized difference as something foreign emerging from the periphery and beyond the border, which could only thereby modify the main story but not contest and reconfigure its outlines or structure completely. He urged on us a more complicated narrative structure, one that would recognize that print culture in the United States has been simultaneously realized multiply and differently at different sites and that those different forms of print culture are the product of radically different histories and chronologies. To do justice to their stories, it would be essential not to make one a secondary subplot within the lineaments of another.

Kaestle and I did attempt to reorganize the planned structure of the volume in response to Kanellos's critique (including acknowledging in our volume title that our concern is principally with the print culture of the United States, not with that of all the Americas). Still, we fear that we have not managed this reconfiguration as fully as we should have. As Carolyn Porter has pointed out, it is extremely difficult to reconceptualize research subjects in a larger field that can no longer be responsibly mapped according to traditional coordinates or through the use of a familiar set of organizing metaphors—like that of center and periphery or theme and variation, both of which have been prominent in narratives about culture which attempt to acknowledge the presence of difference. My aim in this essay is to encourage a conversation that would seek to define what those new coordinates might be.

18 For an important review of, and commentary on this history, see Avery F. Gordon and Christopher Newfield, eds., *Mapping Multiculturalism* (Minneapolis: University of Minnesota Press, 1996).

19 Nikhil Pal Singh, "Culture/Wars: Recoding Empire in an Age of Democracy," *American Quarterly* 50, no. 3 (1998): 471–522.

20 This way of thinking is what I was referring to earlier in making a distinction between internal and external U.S. imperialism. It seems to me that American nationalism and American national identity have historically been constructed through a set of relationships of power that actively subordinate both internal, non-national communities and other nations to the privileged claims of the U.S. nation-state. For a discussion of the role of subordination and superordination within nationalism more generally, see David Lloyd, "Nationalisms against the State," in *The Politics of Culture*, ed. Lowe and Lloyd, 173–200. Subsequent references are cited parenthetically in the text. For a discussion of the way in which processes of identity formation are always relational and carried out for some purpose, see George Bisharat, "Exile to Compatriot: Transformations in the Social Identity of Palestinian Refugees in the West Bank," in *Culture, Power, Place*, ed. Gupta and Ferguson, 204–33. There he argues, "I would venture to say that statements about identity are virtually never idly made but are typically coded with implications for future action and sometimes with claims, being fielded with reference to some, not necessarily conscious, purpose. The negotiation of an identity is thus a step toward an end, not an end in itself: identity is always 'identity for' something" (205).

21 I am specifically not suggesting here that American studies must somehow be reduced to ethnic studies, or gender studies, or sexuality studies. Nor am I suggesting that the U.S. nation or American nationalism should no longer be at the heart of American studies. Rather, what I am suggesting is that the very notion of the U.S. nation and the very conception of American nationalism must now be understood as relational concepts, that is, as objects and/or figures constructed precisely in and through a set of hierarchical relationships with groups, communities, and nations defined somehow as other, alien, or outside. I am further suggesting that this way of thinking can and should be generalized, so that subjects like the one I recently examined, the Book-of-the-Month Club, might also be understood as constructed precisely in dynamic and working relationship to other formations that are actively being affected and controlled through that relationship. Had I understood the full implications of this way of thinking when I first conceptualized my research

project back in 1985, I might have looked more carefully at the way the club's creation of a middlebrow culture, with its pretensions to being national in scope, worked precisely to subordinate both certain ethnic cultures and the culture of the working classes in the United States. Although I discuss both these aspects of the club's history in *A Feeling for Books*, they are treated as secondary or as additional concerns in a larger narrative about middle-class desire, not as the defining and organizational architecture of the entire study itself. Had they been the latter, I might have constructed the study in a much more comparative fashion, examining not only what was happening to middlebrow culture through the club, but also what was happening to the cultures of the working classes in local or union newspapers, in community-based theaters, and in neighborhood venues.

22 It seems to me, however, that this section of the address could easily have been written by foregrounding the ways in which the queer work on sex and feminist work on gender have both called essentialized identities and cultures into question and fostered a practice of attending to mutually constitutive relationships.

23 Wahneema Lubiano, "Like Being Mugged by a Metaphor," in *Mapping Multiculturalism*, ed. Gordon and Newfield, 64–75; and Lubiano, ed., *The House That Race Built* (New York: Random House, 1997). Subsequent references are cited parenthetically in the text.

24 George Lipsitz, *The Possessive Investment in Whiteness: How White People Profit from Identity Politics* (Philadelphia: Temple University Press, 1998).

25 I am here adopting terminology used by Michel Foucault to describe the ways in which intellectual paradigms function because I think his use of the word *technology* helpfully welds material practices to conceptual articulation. Foucault generally uses the word to characterize ways of producing and organizing knowledge about the world as well as to describe particular ways of acting within the meaningful world thereby produced. He suggests that, in identifying or relying on certain features, events, and objects in a social world, human actors call those very features, events, and objects into being precisely as things worthy of remark and/or control. He notes in volume 1 of *The History of Sexuality*, for instance, that bourgeois society of the nineteenth century did not simply describe or repress a previously existing "sex." Rather, by putting "into operation an entire machinery for producing true discourses concerning it," bourgeois, psychologists, physicians, clergyman, and scholars called into being the very category of sexual behavior they simultaneously sought to organize and to manage. Michel Foucault, *The History of Sexuality*, vol. 1, trans. Robert Hurley (New York: Vintage, 1990), 68.

I believe Foucault's move is important for the way in which it recognizes that actions within a world are also always ways of conceptually ordering the world, and vice versa, that ways of knowing the world are also always ways of acting on it. In this particular context, *technology* is especially suggestive because it can be applied to the ways in which book clubs, legal decisions, world's fairs, entertainment spectacles, museum exhibits, and any number of other activities functioned as technologies of nationalism by conceptually and materially producing the American against that which was identifiably not American. At the same time, it can be applied to the very practices of problem definition, research design, and intellectual argumentation associated with American studies that have operated to carve out a bounded American world open to observation, investigation, and analysis. The importance of Foucault's terminology in this context, then, is that the word refigures practices of knowledge production as conceptual actions rather than as mere passive descriptions of already existing things.

The question is whether American studies as just such a technology of knowledge production has done enough to challenge its own once dominant conceptual frameworks for organizing the world so as to fundamentally alter the kind of action it exercises within it. American studies must ask whether, in spite of the powerful challenges posed by its alternate traditions, it continues to function in subtle, still unconscious ways as a technology of imperial political relations, as a practice helping to create an American nation poised both to contain and include those who would challenge it from within and to interact with and dominate those defined as different on the far side of the border.

26 José David Saldívar, "Américo Paredes and Decolonization," in *Cultures of United States Imperialism*, ed. Kaplan and Pease, 292–311, and Vicente M. Diaz, "Pious Sites: Chamorro Culture between Spanish Catholicism and American Liberal Individualism," in *Cultures of United States Imperialism*, ed. Kaplan and Pease, 312–39. Subsequent references are cited parenthetically in the text.

27 Américo Paredes, *"With His Pistol in His Hand": A Border Ballad and Its Hero* (Austin: University of Texas Press, 1958); Paredes, *George Washington Gómez: Mexicotexan Novel* (Houston: Arte Publico, 1990).

28 I should note here that it is this sense of the subject as conflicted, ambivalent, haunted by ghosts, and internally divided by history that *A Feeling for Books* attempts to enact by narrating my own complex relationship to, and investments in, both middlebrow culture and the culture of the academy. That project was enabled by my engagement with feminist explorations of the personal voice and also by the efforts made by African American, Chicana, and other women of color to challenge the very idea of a singular womanly identity. On this point, see Denise Riley, *"Am I That Name?": Feminism and the Category of "Women" in History* (Minneapolis: University of Minnesota Press, 1988).

29 For a particularly clear and cogent discussion of these issues, see James Clifford, *Routes: Travel and Translation in the Late Twentieth Century* (Cambridge, Mass.: Harvard University Press, 1997).

30 Doreen Massey, "Spaces of Politics" in *Human Geography Today*, ed. Doreen Massey, John Allen, and Philip Sarre (Cambridge: Polity Press, 1999), 283.

31 Akhil Gupta and James Ferguson, "Beyond 'Culture': Space, Identity, and the Politics of Difference," in *Culture, Power, Place*, ed. Gupta and Ferguson, 35.

32 On this, see Lowe and Lloyd, "Introduction," *The Politics of Culture*, ed. Lowe and Lloyd, 1–32; and Lisa Duggan, "Queering the State," *Social Text* 39 (1994): 1–14.

33 I want to acknowledge the influence of Dipesh Chakrabarty on this particular formulation. He gave an enormously moving account of the history of sub-altern studies at a conference in October 1998 at Duke University entitled "Cross-Genealogies and Subaltern Knowledges," in which he suggested that subaltern studies benefitted from the youth of its early practitioners because, as students, they operated under the assumption that they were asking many questions to which they did not have already formulated, preset answers.

34 Thanks to Alberto Moreiras for this suggestion about name changes and the possibility of taking up a different relationship to a familiar name.

35 Jane C. Desmond and Virginia R. Dominguez, "Resituating American Stud-ies in a Critical Internationalism," *American Quarterly* 48, no. 3 (1996): 475–90.

36 Cathy Davidson, "Loose Change," *American Quarterly* 46, no. 2 (1994): 130.

37 Eric Cheyfitz, "What Work Is There for Us to Do? American Literary Studies or Americas Cultural Studies," *American Literature* 67 (1995): 843–53.

38 Betsy Erkkila, "Ethnicity, Literary Theory, and the Grounds of Resistance," *American Quarterly* 47, no. 4 (1995): 563–94.

39 Thanks to Jane Desmond for stressing the importance of exchange in addition to contestation.

40 Thanks to Virginia Dominguez for stressing the importance of the Pacific Rim, the "fluid West" in her words, to the definition of American culture.

41 David W. Noble, *The End of American History: Democracy, Capitalism, and the Metaphor of Two Worlds in Anglo-American Historical Writing, 1880–1980* (Min-neapolis: University of Minnesota Press, 1985). For a discussion of the impor-tance of Noble's formulations, see George Lipsitz's discussion of his book in the essay, " 'Sent for You Yesterday, Here You Come Today,' " 20–26.

42 By taking this action, the association would be making the kind of change that would fundamentally alter some of its deepest, most unconscious assumptions (the notion, for instance, that American literature is literature written in En-glish), and it would therefore ensure that the field's supporting paradigms functioned as a very different technology of knowledge production. This could serve as an effective counter, then, to the recent passage of English only laws, which are clearly aimed at immigrants and function themselves as tech-nologies for the production of a certain kind of Anglicized American.

The International within the National

AMERICAN STUDIES AND ASIAN AMERICAN CRITIQUE

Lisa Lowe

All too often, the periodization of immigration to the United States schemat-ically presumes Anglo-European immigration as the nation's originary past) while racialized immigration is temporalized as if it is a recent event, follow-ing the Immigration and Nationality Act of 1965. In contradistinction, I want to observe that the longstanding phenomenon of racialized immigra-tion, brought into visibility through recent episodes of anti-immigrant nativ-ism most forcefully felt in California around Proposition 187 in 1994, and recast through California's attempts to ban affirmative action in 1996, is not merely contemporary. Rather, racialized immigration is indeed, along with American empire, part of a longer history of the development of modern American capitalism and racialized democracy, a longer, more notorious past in which a nation intersected over and over again with the international contexts of the Philippines, Puerto Rico, Mexico, Korea, or Vietnam. The material legacy of America's imperial past is borne out in the "return" of immigrants to the imperial center, and whereas the past is never available to us whole and transparent it may often be read in the narratives, cultural practices, and locations of various immigrant formations; these fragmentary, displaced memories of America's imperialism can be refigured as alternative modes in which immigrants are the survivors of empire, its witnesses, the inhabitants of its borders. Walter Benjamin wrote memorably in his "Theses on the Philosophy of History," that "nothing that has ever happened should be regarded as lost for history."[1] Following Benjamin, this essay suggests that if one seeks the futures of American studies, it may well involve, however delayed, partial, or allegorized, a tireless reckoning with America's past—its past as empire, its international past.

I suggest Asian American critique as one site that may call this reckoning into being. Asian American critique asks us to interrogate the national ontol-ogy through which the United States constructs its international "others," and through which the nation-state has either sought to transform those others into subjects of the national, or, conversely, to subordinate them as objects of that national ontology. In framing this critique, I address the phenomenon of Asian immigration to the United States, as a racial formation, as an economic sign, and as an epistemological object, and pose the question of that object's intelligibility as a pressing question for the American university. I begin by specifying the ways in which the "new" Asian immigration conjoins with the earlier history of Asian racialization and then ask why that racial formation continues to be relatively illegible within scholarly disciplines within the university—including American studies. Furthermore, in the discourses in which it is legible, why is the status of Asian racial formation one of analogue, duplicate, counterfeit, or aestheticized commodity? Why is it not treated as a historical phenomenon that requires a transformation of disciplinary formations? Let us stress that the force of Asian American studies is not the restoration of a cultural heritage to an identity formation, but rather that the history of Asian alterity to the modern nation-state highlights the convergence of nationalism with racial exclusion, gendered social stratification, and labor exploitation. If this is so, what do Asian Americans and the specificity of Asian American critique bring to the table of American studies? Finally, how do we make Asian American critique intelligible, how do we locate that intelligibility institutionally, and what forms of practice necessarily issue from its emergence into intelligibility?

As Racial Formation

From roughly 1850 to World War II, Asian immigration to the United States was the site for the eruptions and resolutions of the contradictions between needs of the national economy and the role of the political state, and, from World War II onward, the locus of contradictions between the nation-state and the global economy.[2] Economic development deals with its systemic crisis of declining profits by seeking out cheaper factors of production, especially labor. In the earlier period, the recruitment of Chinese, Japanese, Filipinos, and South Asians to the United States was motivated by this imperative. Industries utilized racialized divisions among laborers to maximize their profits, but they also needed the exclusion of immigrant groups to prevent a superabundance of inexpensive labor and the disenfranchisement of existing labor forces to prevent capital accumulation by those groups. Through immigration exclusion acts and laws against naturalization of Chinese in 1882, South Asians in 1917, Japanese and Koreans in 1924, and Filipinos in 1934, the state barred these immigrants from the political sphere as "nonwhites" and "aliens ineligible to citizenship," and accordingly distanced Asian Americans from the terrain of national culture. The contradiction between the economic need for inexpensive, tractable labor and the political need to constitute a homogeneous nation with a unified culture was resolved through the legislation of Asian immigrants that racialized these groups as nonwhites even as it consolidated immigrants of diverse European descent as "white." The history of the legislation of the Asian as alien and—after the repeal acts of 1943–52—the administration of the Asian American as citizen, is at once the genealogy of this attempt at national resolution and the genealogy of a distinct racial formation for Asian Americans, defined not in terms of biological racialism but in terms of institutionalized legal definitions of race based on national origin.

Legal theorist Neil Gotanda has argued that the sequence of laws that excluded immigrants from China, Japan, India, and the Philippines, combined with the series of repeal acts overturning these exclusions, constructed a common racial categorization for Asians that depended on consistently racializing each national origin group as "nonwhite."[3] Gotanda observes that in each of the separate statutes between the Magnuson (1943) and the McCarran-Walter Acts (1952), individual Asian national origin groups were allowed to become U.S. citizens as exceptions to the 1790 whites-only statute; he argues that the categorization of Asians as diverse, racialized ethnic groups, rather than as a single racialized category, supported and obscured the powerful naturalization and centrality of the white category. In other words, through the legal enfranchisement of specific Asian ethnic groups as exceptions to the whites-only classification, the status of Asians as nonwhite is legally restated and reestablished. The historical racialization of Asian-origin immigrants as nonwhite aliens is actually rearticulated in the very processes of legal enfranchisement and the ostensive lifting of legal discriminations in the 1950s.

When this legal history is seen in the context of political economic forces, we see that legal institutions have functioned as flexible apparatuses of racialization and gendering in response to the material conditions of different historical moments. Instead of understanding the law as merely a part of the superstructure that reflects social relations, I am suggesting that legal institutions reproduce the relations of production as racialized gendered relations and are therefore symptomatic and determining of the relations of production themselves. In other words, immigration law reproduces a racially segmented and stratified labor force for capital's needs, inasmuch as such legal disenfranchisements or restricted enfranchisements seek to resolve such inequalities by deferring them in the promise of equality on the political terrain of representation through citizenship. The legal genealogy of the Asian immigrant contributes to what Michael Omi and Howard Winant have called a "racial formation": the shifting construction of racial meanings formed in the dialectic between state categorization and social challenges to those categorizations, and the sociohistorical process by which racial meanings are created, lived, and transformed. They write: "The racial order is equilibrated by the state—encoded in law, organized through policy-making, and enforced by a repressive apparatus. But the equilibrium thus achieved is unstable, for the great variety of conflicting interests encapsulated in racial meanings and identities can be no more than pacified—at best—by the state."[4] Extending Omi and Winant's work, I suggest that racial formation is the dialectical struggle between, on the one hand, the racial state that serves the economy and facilitates its needs for exploitable labor by racializing through the law and repressive apparatuses, and, on the other, the social movements, collective projects, and cultural practices that continually redefine racial meanings in ways that seek to reorganize those racialized and gendered capitalist relations.

It should be equally clear that racialization along the legal axis of definitions of citizenship has also ascribed gender and sexuality to the Asian American subject. While race may be theorized as an abstraction, it is not lived, experienced, or determined abstractly; there is never a moment in which race exists as simply race. Up until 1870, American citizenship was granted exclusively to white male persons; in 1870, men of African descent could become naturalized, but the bar to citizenship remained for Asian men until the repeal acts of 1943–52. Whereas the "masculinity" of the citizen was first inseparable from his "whiteness," as the state extended citizenship to nonwhite male persons, it formally designated these subjects as "male" as well. The 1943 enfranchisement of the Chinese American into citizenship, for example, constituted the Chinese immigrant subject as male; in the 1946 modification of the Magnuson Act, the Chinese wives of U.S. citizens were exempted from the permitted annual quota; as the law changed to reclassify "Chinese immigrant" as eligible for naturalization and citizenship, female immigrants were not included in this reclassification but were in effect specified only in relation to the changed status of "the Chinese immigrant" who was legally presumed to be male. Thus the administration of citizenship for Asians was simultaneously a technology of racialization and gendering. John

Kuo Wei Tchen has demonstrated that, from the late nineteenth century until the 1940s, Chinese immigrant masculinity had been socially and institutionally marked as different from that of Anglo- and Euro-American "white" citizens owing to the forms of work and community that had been historically available to Chinese men as the result of the immigration laws restricting female immigration.[5] Sucheng Chan, Judy Yung, and Gary Okihiro have explored the ramifications of the Page Law of 1875 and a later ban on Chinese laborers' spouses that effectively halted the immigration of Chinese women and prevented the formation of families and generations among Chinese immigrants; in addition, female U.S. citizens who married "aliens" lost their own citizenship.[6] In conjunction with the relative absence of Chinese wives and family among immigrant bachelor communities, and because of the concentration of Chinese men in "feminized" forms of work—such as laundry, restaurants, and other service-sector jobs—Chinese male immigrants could be said to occupy a non-heterosexual, "feminized masculinity" in relation to white male citizens. The racialization of this feminized masculinity becomes the material trace of the history of this gendering and sexualization of immigrant labor. Historian Nayan Shah has analyzed the ways that public health policies constructed urban Chinese bachelor immigrants as "diseased." Shah's work suggests that urban planning and public health discourses were crucial in figuring Chinese bachelors as threats to American society and notions of white male citizenship increasingly signified through heterosexual marriage and a middle-class domesticity, both of which were legally and practically at odds with Chinese immigrant masculinity.[7]

As Economic Sign

Since World War II, the capital imperative has come into greater contradiction with the political imperative of the nation-state, with capitalism requiring an economic internationalism in order to increase labor and capital, and the state needing to be politically coherent and hegemonic in world affairs in order to determine the conditions of that internationalism. During the period of unprecedented aggregate growth of global capitalism in the 1950s to the 1960s, the Western domination of Asia that had been expressed through direct colonialism, as in the Philippines, was transformed into a U.S. development project by way of modernization. In the struggle for leadership in the postwar global order, the United States sought to achieve the military superiority, economic supremacy, and ideological predominance necessary to determine the terms of the postwar economic internationalism, and to establish secure access to raw materials and markets.[8] In this sense, the foreign policy that framed wars in Korea and Vietnam responded equally to the need to take economic supremacy and to contain the Soviet Union diplomatically. Although the U.S. wars in Korea and Vietnam reflected the general desire to incorporate the Asian economies into the industrial core, the twenty-year period in which the United States vied for power over the rimlands of Northeast Asia, Southeast Asia, and Taiwan also constituted a theater in which the United States performed its technological modernity and military force in relation to the Asiatic world, a process legitimated by the emergence of the Soviet Union's and China's global influences.[9] Yet the wars in Korea and Vietnam were as much a stage for the ideological lesson that the United States could and should determine how capital could move globally as they secured the material conditions for that movement.[10] The wars of the 1950s to 1970s laid the groundwork for the U.S. investment and material extraction in Asia that took place only later in the 1980s with global restructuring, and displaced Korean and Vietnamese populations, some of which have immigrated to the United States. By the 1990s, the United States had reached a period of "imperial overstretch" marked by the decline of its economic hegemony and the emergence of Japan and Germany as forceful players in the field of economics. The contradictions of U.S. capital investment and development in Asia further found expression in the rapid growth of the newly industrializing countries in Asia—Hong Kong, Singapore, South Korea, and Taiwan.

The emergence of successful capitalist states in Asia has necessitated global restructuring for U.S. capital, reinvigorating American anxiety about Asia, an anxiety that is clearly not new. Though predictions of Asian productivity supplanting European economic dominance have gripped European and American imaginations since the nineteenth century, since World War II, Asia has emerged as a particularly complicated double front of threat and encroachment: on the one hand, Asian states have become prominent as external rivals in overseas war and in the global economy; on the other hand, Asian immigrants are still a necessary racialized labor force within the domestic national economy. Indeed, it is precisely this doubleness and the unfixed liminality of the Asian immigrant—geographically, linguistically, and racially at odds with the context of the national—that has given rise to the necessity of endlessly fixing and repeating stereotypes such as the threatening "yellow peril," or alternatively, the domesticated "model minority." Yet the discursive fixing of the Asian is not exclusively a matter of stereotypical representation in the cultural sphere; as I have been arguing, it has historically been instantiated through the state's classification of racialized Asian immigrant identities. The state announces its need to fix and stabilize the identity of the immigrant through legal exclusions and inclusions, as well as through juridical classifications. Whereas earlier immigrants from Asia were classified as "aliens," contemporary Asian immigrants are reclassified as "legal" and "illegal," "citizen" and "non-citizen," and "U.S.-born" and "permanent resident"; these are the current modes through which the liberal state discriminates, surveys, and produces immigrant identities. The presence of Asia and Asian peoples that currently impinges on the national consciousness sustains the figuration of the Asian immigrant as a transgressive and corrupting foreignness and continues to make Asians an object of the law, the political sphere, as well as national culture.

Since the 1970s, as manufacturing moved internationally to make use of low-wage labor markets, the proportion of the U.S. workforce engaged in manufacturing has fallen as the proportion working in services has increased. The structural transformations of the economy have produced an increased demand for immigrants to fill minimum-wage, unskilled and part-time jobs, yet these same economic processes have initiated new waves of anti-immigrant nativism and renewed the state's rationalization for the legislation of immigration. Several strategies have been employed to meet the capital imperative: U.S. capital moved to Asian and Latin American sites of cheaper labor and production, and the 1965 Act "opened" immigration, renewing domestic labor supplies. Since 1965, the profile of Asian immigration consists of both low-wage service-sector workers as well as proletarianized white-collar professionals, the former a group that at once supplies laborers for services and manufacturing, and the latter that furnishes a technically trained labor force serving as one form of "variable capital" investment in the U.S. economy.[11] If the nineteenth-century racialized and gendered formation of Chinese male immigrants as laborers sublated the contradictions between economic imperatives and the state, then these contradictions reemerge in the demographic composition of the post-1965 Asian immigrant group, a group still racialized and exploited, yet they are complicated by class and gender stratification.

Since the 1980s, the increased proletarianization of Asian, Latina, and Caribbean immigrant women's labor in the United States is an index of new forms of contradiction and is commensurate with the gendered character of the international division of labor that makes use of neocolonized and racialized immigrant women as a "flexible" workforce in the global economy. The sweatshops of the garment industry located in San Francisco or Los Angeles, for example, employ immigrant women from Mexico, El Salvador, Guatemala, Hong Kong, South Korea, Thailand, and the Philippines, while in these same countries of origin, U.S. transnational corporations are also conducting garment assembly work, making immigrant women and women working in Asia and Latin America virtually part of the same workforce. Yet this dimension of the new Asian immigration is rendered invisible by the stereotypes of new Asians as exclusively technical professionals or successful independent merchants. Likewise, the current specter of ethnicized "Asian capital corrupting American democracy" is significant for the ways in which it disavows both historical and contemporary racialized labor exploitation. But as with all fetish constructions that simultaneously acknowledge as they substitute and disavow, the trope of Asian capital acknowledges yet displaces the particular history I have briefly outlined here: Asian participation in the nation has been historically confined to the economic sphere, first as labor, and currently as labor and capital; the confinement to the economic sphere has been predicated on exclusion from the political sphere of citizenship and democratic politics, as well as from the terrain of national culture.

The 1965 act opened immigration, but in the process it initiated not fewer but indeed more specifications and regulations for immigrants of Asian origins. Immigration, in this sense, continues to be an important historical and discursive site of Asian American formation, the locus through which the national and global economic, the cultural and legal spheres are modulated. Whether that determination is mediated through immigration exclusion or inclusion, the nation-state attempts to produce and regulate the Asian as a means of resolving economic exigencies. Hence, "new Asian immigration" must be understood within the history of U.S. immigration policies and the attempts to incorporate immigrants into the developing economy, on the one hand, and within the expansion of the U.S. economy through colonialism and global restructuring, on the other.

As Epistemological Object

I wish to turn finally to discuss Asian American critique with respect to the contemporary university, the Asian American as an epistemological object, and to conclude by suggesting some of the contradictions brought into relief by the current struggles to establish Asian American studies—from Columbia University to the University of Maryland to Northwestern University.

Woodrow Wilson, when he served as president of Princeton University, often spoke of his vision of the university as a social institution working "in the nation's service." In this statement, he was not simply voicing a naive nostrum of what U.S. historians label progressivism.[12] He was also acknowledging a historical characteristic of modern civil society—that the educational apparatus is an especially significant instrument of social reproduction and that the university has played an important role in the formation of students as citizens for the nation. The traditional function of disciplinary divisions in the university is to uphold the abstract divisions of modern civil society into separate spheres: the political, the economic, and the cultural. The formation and reproduction of the modern citizen-subject is naturalized through those divisions of social space and those of knowledge. The historical exclusion of Asian immigrants and Asian Americans from the political and cultural spheres continues, and is reproduced, in the relative invisibility of that history of racialization within the modern university.

American national culture takes up the role of resolving the history of inequalities left unresolved in the economic and political domains: where the state is unable to accommodate differences, it has fallen to the terrain of national culture to do so. The modern university has thus been given the role of forming citizens through the education of students in national culture. This education forms citizens for the political sphere by disavowing the racialization and gendering of noncitizen labor in the economic sphere and through the teaching of national culture in the cultural sphere. The formation of citizens as subjects of national culture and modern civil society has required a fluency in national narratives and in those disciplinary divisions that suppress the history of racialization and racialized exclusion from citizenship. Let us understand, then, that student activism for Asian American studies in our contemporary moment is not an "identity" movement in search of cultural "roots"; it is a voicing of racial consciousness that seeks to bring this history into the university, that seeks to refuse this disavowal.

Civil rights activism in the 1970s was aimed at forcing into visibility conditions of segregation beneath the promises of inclusion and equal representation; many of the programs and departments of ethnic studies on the west coast of the United States were established as part of these struggles. Yet despite the gains of some ethnic studies projects, the contradiction nonetheless remains that many universities still maintain the study of culture as the

discrete sphere of Western culture, while addressing the demand for democratization of the university through the expansion (often at the expense of
humanities or social science research) of vocationalist curricula that aim to
train competitive professional and technical classes through the development
of business, engineering, and other programs. The result is a continuing
contradiction in which culture remains canonical in the traditional Western
European sense, while the educational system, claiming a multicultural conscience, serves to socialize and incorporate an increasingly heterogeneous
student population into the market economy. In the analysis of critical pedagogy theorist Martin Carnoy, the contradiction that brings new social groups
into the educational system for vocationalization but that continues to universalize a closed, autonomous notion of culture precisely implies "an exploitable political space for those who are willing to engage in the struggle
for change."[13]

In contemporary universities, this contradiction is visibly animated with
the emergence of interdisciplinary fields, such as ethnic studies, women's
studies, Third World studies, and some forms of cultural studies. Interdisciplinary sites mediate contradiction—or in Carnoy's terms, "exploitable political space"—to the degree that they can provide the sites from which to
reevaluate disciplinary methods that assume cultural autonomy and the universality of the subject. Interdisciplinary study may disrupt the empiricist
paradigms of science and social science within which the disinterested scholar
anatomizes, surveys, and classifies the non-Western, racialized, or female
Other as objects of knowledge. Interdisciplinary studies may challenge the
developmentalist historicism that requires the assimilation of "primitive,"
nonmodern, and racialized knowledges to the terms of Western rationalism:
this is the case with Arturo Escobar's work on the discourse of development
and the making of the "Third World," or Partha Chatterjee's analysis of
history as the nationalist narrative of the development of modern civil society.[14] In interdisciplinary women's studies, for example, work by and about
women of color—the work by Kimberlé Crenshaw addressing the marginalization of the intersection of race and gender under the law, say, or Chandra
Talpade Mohanty investigating racialized women's labor in the global economy, or Rosa Linda Fregoso's analysis of racial and gendered representation in
film—exemplifies interdisciplinary critical methods that refuse univocality,
totalization, and scholarly indifference.[15] This work redefines the traditional
separations of the scholar-subject and the object of study; it persistently
argues for the inseparability of the nonequivalent determinations of race,

class, and gender. Likewise, ethnic studies scholars like Robin D. G. Kelley, George Lipsitz, or José David Saldívar have never reproduced the methods of historical, sociological, or literary study merely to celebrate "ethnic culture" as an object separated from the material conditions of production and reception.[16] They have analyzed, in a critical, dialectical manner, the relationship between cultural artifacts and the social groups by which they are produced and which they, in turn, have helped to produce.

At the same time, institutionalizing interdisciplinary studies—whether American studies, ethnic studies, or Asian American studies—still contains an inevitable paradox: on the one hand, institutionalization provides a material base within the university for a transformative critique of traditional disciplines and their traditional separations; yet, on the other hand, the institutionalization of any field or curricula which establishes orthodox objects and methods submits in part to the demands of the university and its educative function of socializing subjects into the state. While institutionalizing interdisciplinary study risks integrating it into a system threatening to appropriate what is most critical and oppositional about that study, the logic through which the university incorporates areas of interdisciplinarity simultaneously provides for the possibility of these sites remaining oppositional forums, productively antagonistic to notions of autonomous culture and disciplinary regulation and to the interpellation of students as univocal subjects. In terms of Asian American studies, the approach to questions of reading texts, constituting objects of study, and teaching students can determine the extent to which Asian American studies serves the traditional function of the university and the extent to which it provides for a continuing and persistent site from which to educate students to be actively critical of that traditional function.

The Asian American as an epistemological object challenges both traditional disciplines and established interdisciplinary forms of study. On the one hand, owing to the history just outlined, in which Asian immigrants are admitted into the nation along the economic axis but excluded along the lines of political citizenship and national culture, the specific history of Asian American racial formation "discoordinates" the supposed separations integral to the development of subjects of modern civil society. Asian American history narrates the breakdown of the explanatory power of the abstract divisions of society into the political, the economic, and the cultural.[17] Asian American studies engages with traditional disciplines of history, literature, the arts, and fields of social science, and in the process, it requires a revision of the presumed objects and methods of study in these fields.

On the other hand, Asian American studies also contributes to existing interdisciplinary fields such as American studies, cultural studies, and women's studies. With respect to American studies, the history of Asian American formation highlights the production of race in the contradiction between national economy and the political state, and in the contradiction between the U.S. nation-state and the global economy, and it rewrites the history of the United States as a complex racial history. Like other racialized minority groups from Africa, the Caribbean, and Latin America, Asian American formation foregrounds for American studies the links between racial whiteness, nationalism, masculinity, and citizenship. At the same time, a focus on Asian Americans disrupts the usual racial binary of black versus white and, importantly, illuminates how this binary serves the perpetuation of racialized hierarchy within the history of the United States.

The exteriority of Asian Americans to national culture not only offers American studies critical insights into the role of national culture in the forming of citizens, but it also initiates a truly necessary inquiry into the comparative history of racialization, for example, the interrelationship of African American and Asian American racial histories. In the 1880s, as Chinese immigrants became "laboring subjects" yet were barred from political and social inclusion, the Fourteenth Amendment of 1870 admitted African Americans into citizenship as "American national subjects," but local ordinances barred African Americans from working as laborers in the western United States. Helen Jun argues that, while U.S. history has been constituted through a narrative that privileges the black and white racial crucible, the institutions and discourses that represent Asian immigrants as immutably foreign to the nation have not only constructed white national identity but have also been constitutive of, differentially, the history of black racial formation.[18] Grace Hong argues that throughout the twentieth century, Japanese Americans and African Americans have not been linked through a logic of identity, but through a relation of differential access to property rights by the state. She argues that the dispossessions that are a part of the internment for Japanese Americans, on the one hand, and segregation for African Americans, on the other, are uneven, but linked, manifestations of the privileging of private property ownership that structures U.S. society.[19] Furthermore, the history of U.S. colonialism and war in the Philippines, Japan, South Korea, and Vietnam, and the racialized immigration from these sites obliges us to rethink the history of the United States as a history of empire. In discussing the relationship between U.S. empire and labor segmentation in the southwestern and western United States in the early twentieth century, Eleanor

Jaluague argues that we must understand the interrelation and dependency of U.S. colonialism in the Philippines and the importation of Filipino laborers in California in order to understand the consolidation of whiteness and American citizenship during the New Deal era.[20]

Asian American racial formation also brings a uniquely situated analysis of the intersections of race, gender, and sexuality to American studies. The history of Asian immigration exclusion and regulated settlement that rendered Asian men a "feminized masculinity" estranged from middle-class domesticity, also hyperfeminized Asian women and made them emblematic of feminized domestic space. As David Eng's work on Asian American sexuality and Gayatri Gopinath's discussions of queer South Asian diaspora have demonstrated, these racialized constructions of both Asian masculinity and Asian femininity have tended to elide non-heteronormative sexualities as threats to national integrity or to foreclose such sexualities by placing them outside the boundaries of the nation and the family.[21] Chandan Reddy has likewise argued that the marginalization of Asian immigrants from the historical emergence of middle-class domesticity in the United States makes Asian Americans a site from which to understand family and domesticity as racialized practices in the reproduction of the unevennesses of capitalist social relations.[22]

A Politics of Knowledge

As we have seen, immigration has historically been a locus of racialization and a primary site for the policing of political, cultural, and economic membership in the U.S nation-state. Yet in our current moment, in the wake of California's Proposition 187 and federal and state immigration reforms that seek to restrict the rights and benefits of legal resident immigrants, we are witnessing what Balibar and Wallerstein would call a "re-racialization" of immigrants that constitutes "the immigrant" as the most highly targeted object of a U.S. nationalist agenda.[23] The efforts to deny undocumented immigrants medical care and schooling, and to prohibit legal immigrants from participating in state and federal programs, are the newest forms of surveillance for immigrant communities, particularly immigrant women, while these measures secure the conditions to ghettoize, marginalize, and extract low-wage labor from those same communities. In discussing Asian immigrant formation, I have hoped to draw attention to how these historical conditions have produced the emergence of Asian Americans as an oppositional racial grouping, and perhaps more importantly, how they give rise to new subjects whose horizons of definition force us to remap the development of the liberal political subject in America. This remapping that accounts for the different formation of Asian Americans opens up different possibilities for the reorganization of the university, and for political practice and coalition. I have not intended to render exceptional the racialization of Asians within the United States, but rather to specify the history of Asian American racialization as a critique of national history, so that it might be related to other histories of racialization—those of African Americans, Chicanos/ Latinos, Native Americans, and "white" Americans—in order to open possibilities of cross-race and cross-national projects.

In conclusion, permit me to venture a tentative thesis about the politics of knowledge implied by the relation between new Asian immigration and the current struggles to establish Asian American studies in universities east of California. The 1965 Immigration and Nationality Act has dramatically changed the demographics of Asian Americans; allowing for 170,000 immigrants annually from the Eastern hemisphere, it has rendered the majority of the constituency Asian-born, rather than U.S.-born, and the new immigrants from South Vietnam, South Korea, Cambodia, Laos, the Philippines, India, and Pakistan have diversified the already existing Asian American group of Chinese, Japanese, and Filipino descent. The current struggles for sites in which to study the history of Asian Americans mediates a particular impasse created by, on the one hand, the significant and substantial presence of post-1965 college-age Asian Americans in U.S. colleges and universities, and, on the other hand, the relatively small number of Asian American intellectuals within the academy at the present moment. The former could be said to be an index, as I've been suggesting, of global restructuring and the aftermath of U.S. colonial or development projects in Asia, while the latter is the condition of the racialized exclusion and cultural disenfranchisement of pre–World War II Asian immigrants. The demand for Asian American studies to answer to the student population exacerbates this impasse and brings the twin repressions of U.S. history—the United States as a modern racial state, and the United States as a modern empire—to the surface. I began with the question of which political practices would issue from the intelligibility of the history of Asian American racial formation. There are many political projects for Asian Americans outside of the university—for civil rights, for immigrant rights, in labor organizing, against racist violence. And the presence of Asian immigrants in low-wage labor makes clear that though enrollments of Asian Americans in some universities are greater than that of other Americans of color, many working-class Asian immigrants do not have access to the American university. At this particular moment, bringing Asian American history into relief through the struggle for educational space in universities east of California may be itself one form of political critique. Student activism and the demand for Asian American studies asks that the "newness" of Asian immigration be de-reified, asks that the history of new racialization be connected with the older one, and more importantly, that it be connected with the history of struggles against that racialization. These students seek, as Walter Benjamin's historical materialist, to "brush history against the grain," to force the American past into visibility as American studies' future (257).

Notes

Thank you to Jack Tchen and Eric Tang at New York University, Kandice Chuh at the University of Maryland, and Dennis Chong at Northwestern University, for their invitations to present earlier versions of this essay at their universities, and to Donald E. Pease and Robyn Wiegman for the invitation to "The Futures of American Studies" at Dartmouth College.

1 Walter Benjamin, "Theses on the Philosophy of History," in *Illuminations*, ed. Hannah Arendt, trans. Harry Zohn (New York: Schocken, 1969), 254. Subsequent references are cited parenthetically in the text.

2 See Lisa Lowe, *Immigrant Acts: On Asian American Cultural Politics* (Durham, N.C.: Duke University Press, 1996).

3 Neil Gotanda, "Towards Repeal of Asian Exclusion: The Magnuson Act of 1943, the Act of July 2, 1946, the Presidential Proclamation of July 4, 1946, the Act of August 9, 1949, and the Act of August 1, 1950," in *Asian Americans in Congress: A Documentary History*, ed. Hyung Chan Kim (Westport, Conn.: Greenwood, 1995), 309–28.

4 Michael Omi and Howard Winant, *Racial Formation in the United States: From the 1960s to the 1990s* (New York: Routledge, 1994), 53–55.

5 John Kuo Wei Tchen, "Modernizing White Patriarchy: Re-Viewing D. W. Griffith's *Broken Blossoms*," in *Moving the Image: Independent Asian Pacific American Media Arts*, ed. Russell Leong (Los Angeles: UCLA Asian American Studies Center and Visual Communications, 1991), 133–43.

6 Sucheng Chan, *Asian Americans: An Interpretive History* (Boston: Twayne, 1991); Judy Yung, *Unbound Feet: A Social History of Chinese Women in San Francisco* (Berkeley: University of California Press, 1995); Gary Y. Okihiro,

Margins and Mainstreams: Asians in American History and Culture (Seattle: University of Washington Press, 1994).

7   Nayan Shah, *Contagious Divides: Epidemics and Race in San Francisco's Chinatown* (Berkeley: University of California Press, 2001).

8   See William Appleman Williams, *The Tragedy of American Diplomacy* (Cleveland, Ohio: World Publishing, 1959).

9   Thomas J. McCormick, *America's Half-Century: United States Foreign Policy in the Cold War and After*, 2d ed. (Baltimore: Johns Hopkins University Press, 1991).

10 Bruce Cumings, *The Origins of the Korean War* (Princeton, N.J.: Princeton University Press, 1981–1990); Marilyn Young, *The Vietnam Wars: 1945–1990* (New York: Harper, 1991).

11 See Paul Ong, Edna Bonacich, and Lucie Cheng, eds., *The New Asian Immigration in Los Angeles and Global Restructuring* (Philadelphia: Temple University Press, 1994).

12 I thank Michael Bernstein for this observation.

13 Martin Carnoy, "Education, State, and Culture in American Society," in *Critical Pedagogy, the State, and Cultural Struggle*, ed. Henry A. Giroux and Peter L. McLare (Albany: State University of New York Press, 1989), 6.

14 Arturo Escobar, *Encountering Development: The Making and Unmaking of the Third World* (Princeton, N.J.: Princeton University Press, 1995); Partha Chatterjee, *The Nation and Its Fragments: Colonial and Postcolonial Histories* (Princeton, N.J.: Princeton University Press, 1993).

15 Kimberlé Crenshaw, "Demarginalizing the Intersection of Race and Sex: A Black Feminist Critique of Antidiscrimination Doctrine, Feminist Theory, and Anti-racist Politics," *University of Chicago Legal Forum* (1989): 139–67; Chandra Talpade Mohanty, "Women Workers and Capitalist Scripts: Ideologies of Domination, Common Interests, and the Politics of Solidarity," in *Feminist Genealogies, Colonial Legacies, Democratic Futures*, ed. M. Jacqui Alexander and Mohanty (New York: Routledge, 1997), 3–29; Rosa Linda Fregoso, "Recycling Colonialist Fantasies on the Texas Borderlands," in *Home, Exile Homeland: Film, Media, and the Politics of Place*, Hamid Nacify (New York: Routledge, 1999), 169–92.

16 Robin D. G. Kelley, *Race Rebels: Culture, Politics, and the Black Working Class* (New York: Free Press, 1994); George Lipsitz, *Time Passages: Collective Memory and American Popular Culture* (Minneapolis: University of Minnesota Press, 1990); José David Saldívar, *Border Matters: Remapping American Cultural Studies* (Berkeley: University of California Press, 1997).

17 On the discoordination of civil society, see Lisa Lowe and David Lloyd, introduction to *The Politics of Culture in the Shadow of Capital* (Durham, N.C.: Duke University Press, 1997), 1–32.

18 Helen Heran Jun, "Race For Citizenship: African Americans and Asian Americans" (Ph.D. diss., University of California, San Diego, in progress).

19 Grace Kyungwon Hong, " 'Something Forgotten Which Should Have Been

Remembered': Private Property and Cross-Racial Solidarity in the Work of Hisaye Yamamoto," *American Literature* 71, no. 2 (1999): 291–310.

20 Eleanor M. Jaluague, "Race, Immigration, and Contradiction in Carlos Bulosan's *America Is in the Heart,*" *Hitting Critical Mass* (forthcoming).

21 See David L. Eng, "Out Here and Over There: Queerness and Diaspora in Asian American Studies," *Social Text* 52–53 (1997): 31–52; and Gayatri Gopinath, "Nostalgia, Desire, Diaspora: South Asian Sexualities in Motion," *positions: east asia cultures critique* 5, no. 2 (1997): 467–89.

22 See Chandan Reddy, "Home, Houses, Non-identity: Paris Is Burning," in *Burning Down the House: Recycling Domesticity*, ed. Rosemary Marangoly George (Boulder, Colo.: Westview, 1998), 355–79. See also Evelyn Nakano Glenn, "Racial Ethnic Women's Labor: The Intersection of Race, Gender, and Class Oppression," *Review of Radical Political Economics* 17, no. 3 (1983): 86–108.

23 Etienne Balibar and Immanuel Wallerstein, *Race, Nation, Class: Ambiguous Identities* (London: Verso, 1991), especially 17–28.

The Future in the Present

SEXUAL AVANT-GARDES AND THE PERFORMANCE OF UTOPIA

José Esteban Muñoz

Futurity can be a problem. Heterosexual culture depends on a notion of the future: as the song goes, "the children are our future." But that is not the case for different cultures of sexual dissidence. Rather than invest in a deferred future, the queer citizen-subject labors to live in a present that is calibrated, through the protocols of state power, to sacrifice our liveness for what Lauren Berlant has called the "dead citizenship" of heterosexuality.[1] This dead citizenship is formatted, in part, through the sacrifice of the present for a fantasmatic future. On dance floors, sites of public sex, various theatrical stages, music festivals, and in arenas both subterranean and aboveground, queers live, labor, and enact queer worlds in the present. But must the future and the present exist in this rigid binary? Can the future stop being a fantasy of heterosexual reproduction? In this essay I want to argue for the disruption of this binarized stalemate and the enactment of what I call, following C. L. R. James, a future in the present. To call for this notion of the future in the present is to summon a refunctioned notion of utopia in the service of subaltern politics. Certain performances of queer citizenship contain what I will call an anticipatory illumination of a queer world, a sign of an actually existing queer reality, a kernel of political possibility, within a stultifying heterosexual present. I will gesture to sites of embodied and performed queer politics and describe them as outposts of actually existing queer worlds. The sites I consider are sites of mass gatherings, performances that can be understood as defiantly public—glimpses into an ensemble of social actors performing a queer world.

The Past for the Future: Queer Happenings

I begin this study of the future in the present by a turning to the past. Samuel R. Delany's memoir *The Motion of Light in Water* periodizes the advent of postmodernity through the evidence provided by two modes of avant-garde performance. These performances do more than represent an epistemic shift;

they enable the memoirist to procure a new vista on the world. The writer describes images from his then present (now squarely the past), and these pictures purchase a vision of the future. I want to suggest that these performances Delany described announced and enacted a new formation within the social.

The first of these performances was held in a 2nd Avenue studio apartment in New York's East Village during the summer of 1960. Delany and a cousin had stumbled on a performance Allan Kaprow titled "Eighteen Happenings in Six Parts." It was the first time the word "happening" had been used in a performance context. Delany explained that "many times now Kaprow's piece (today we would call it performance art) has been cited by historians as the equally arbitrary transition between the modern and the postmodern in cultural developments. But I don't believe I've read a firsthand account of it by any of its original audience."[2] The memoirist has missed some of the most interesting accounts of this performance genre. There is in fact a fascinating literature chronicling and documenting this artistic movement.[3] Delany's account is nonetheless valuable. He remembers entering an apartment that was taken up by polyethylene walls on painted wood frames. These walls divided the performance space into six sections of about eight feet by eight feet. The sections were accessible from a door-wide space on the outside, but separated from one another by semitranslucent walls through which one could make out "the ghost" of what was happening in the adjoining section. There were half a dozen or so wooden folding chairs in each room. The remembered performance that Delany narrates consisted of a child's windup toy being set on the ground and let run and then wound up again and again over the twenty-minute running time of the performance. Through the plastic walls the sounds and sights of other happenings partially filtered into the writer's cubicle. He could make out the buttery glow of a candle in one room while in another he heard the sounds of a drum.

The writer's expectations were severely challenged by this performance. He had assumed that the work would be "rich, Dionysian and colorful." He expected the happenings themselves to be "far more complex, denser and probably verbally boundable." He expected happenings that would crowd in on one another and form an interconnected tapestry of occurrences and associations rich in meanings and meaning fragments, full of resonance and overlapping associations, "playful, sentimental and reassuring." Yet the work he encountered was "spare, difficult, minimal, constituted largely by absence, isolation, even distraction" (183). Delany expected the six parts to be chronologically ordered, like acts in a play, but they were instead spatially organized. Delany writes that "it was precisely in this subversion of expectations about the proper aesthetic employment of time, space, presence, absence, wholeness and fragmentation, as well as the general locality of 'what happens,' that made Kaprow's work signify: his happenings—clicking toys, burning candles, pounded drums, or whatever—were organized in that initial work very much like historical events" (179). Delany admits that his expectations were formed by a modernist desire to see "meaningful plenitude," yet his disappointment waned once he had found the time to contemplate Kaprow's project, work that he found to be "more interesting, strenuous and aesthetically energetic." Delany concludes his recollection by claiming that " 'Eighteen Happenings in Six Parts' " was about as characteristic a work as one might choose in which to experience the clash that begins our reading of the hugely arbitrary postmodern" (179).

This avant-garde performance is intimately linked to another mode of "happening" that occurs later in the memoir. Delany was alerted to this particular performance venue by a painter friend in the East Village. His friend Simon had told him about the trucks parked by the river at the end of Christopher Street as a place to go at night for instant sex. Once the author passed the truck's threshold, he discovered that, on a regular basis, between 35 and 150 men slipped through the trailers, some to watch, but most to participate in "numberless silent sexual acts." Delany describes these acts as rituals that reconstructed intimacy: "At those times, within those van-walled alleys, now between the trucks, now in the back of the open loaders, cock passed from mouth to mouth to hand to ass to mouth without ever breaking contact with other flesh for more than seconds; mouth, hand, ass passed over whatever you held out to them, *sans* interstice; when one cock left, finding a replacement—mouth, rectum, another cock—required moving the head, the hip, the hand no more than an inch, three inches" (202). This scene is described as "engrossing," "exhausting," "reassuring," and "very human." The writer explains how the men in this space took care of each other by not only offering flesh but performing a care for the self that encompassed a vast care for others—a delicate and loving "being for others" (183).

He follows this description pages later with another retelling of the public sex performances. On his first visit to the St. Mark's Baths, Delany encountered a well-lit mass of perverts. Lighting made a difference insofar as the piers operated under the cover of a protective darkness that also kept the massiveness of the crowd available. In this respect he compares the piers to Kaprow's

"Eighteen Happenings in Six Parts." In the more formally theatrical happening "no one ever got to see the whole" because institutions like subway johns,
the trucks parked on the Christopher Street pier, pornographic theaters, and
other institutions of public sex accommodated these performances by cutting
them up, by making sure that the whole was distorted. In the blue light of the
St. Mark's Baths something was confirmed deeply for the then twenty-year-
old budding science fiction writer: "What *this* experience said was that there
was a population—not of individual homosexuals, some of whom now and
then encountered, or that those encounters could be human and fulfilling in
their way—not of hundreds, not of thousands, but rather of millions of gay
men, and that history had, actively and already, created for us whole galleries
of institutions, good and bad, to accommodate our sex" (267). This section of
The Motion of Light in Water is critiqued by historian Joan W. Scott, who
oddly employs this memoir as an example of gay history's reliance on unreconstructed narratives of experience, fixed identity, and "the visual."[4] (Lisa
Duggan has already pointed out the inappropriateness of making such an
argument on gay and lesbian history based on a writer's nonfiction memoir.)[5]
In that article Scott attempts to partially recant her reading of Delany, yet she
ultimately fails to comprehend the author's project. The Kaprow piece taught
Delany a valuable lesson about the way in which public culture is cut up
through the institutions of the majoritarian public sphere. The happening
thematized vision to show the ways in which vision is constantly compromised. Most of the memoir narrates through a Kaprowian understanding of
the alienation and segmentation that characterize the real. His moment of
seeing the whole of public sex is a utopian break in the narrative—it is a
deviation from the text's dominant mode of narration. Public sex culture
revealed the existence of a queer world and Kaprow's happening explained
the ways in which such utopian visions were continuously distorted. Delany
explains that "the first apprehension of massed bodies" signals a direct sense of
political power. This apprehension debunks dominant ideology's characterization of antinormative subject-citizens as "isolated perverts" (Delany, 266).
Kaprow's performance and the piers were adjacent happenings that only
presented shades of the whole; the blue light of the bathhouse offered a
glimpse of utopia.

I turn to this memoir of the sixties at this particular moment because it echoes
the current attack on cultures of sexual dissidence that New York City is
currently weathering. The city's draconian mayor has instituted a policy that

has rezoned the vast majority of public sex out of the city. New laws have closed down most adult bookstores, bars, movie theaters, peep shows and performance spaces that feature sexually oriented performances—everything from female strippers at straight bars to go-go boys at queer clubs have been partially zoned out of existence. This crackdown on public sex is part of Giuliani's notorious "quality of life campaign." The venues Delany employed to see "the massed bodies" signaling political power become harder and harder to glimpse. In many ways the fragmentation that will characterize this New York City's culture of public sex will be far more alienating than that described in Delany's chronicle of pre-Stonewall New York. While normative middle-class subjects enjoy a porn-free Manhattan, citizen-subjects who participate in the service economy of the sex industry will experience a level of harassment that surpasses even that experienced by other wageworkers like street vendors and taxi drivers. The mayor has recently instituted policies that clamp down on these professions, industries that, like that of sex workers, are heavily populated by people of color.

Times Square has entered its last phase of what I only half-jokingly call "late Disneyfication." Many local adult businesses have been replaced with more corporate representation, like massive Disney stores and Starbuck's franchises. Queers and other minoritarian subjects will be pushed further into the private sphere. Delany, in a recent text, has theorized what he calls "contact relations," as opposed to networking. Delany's thesis is a lucid and powerful one: "Given the mode of capitalism under which we live, life is at its most rewarding, productive, and pleasant when the greatest number of people understand, appreciate, and seek out interclass contact and communication conducted in a mode of good will."[6] Delany's work here uses his experience as a participant in Times Square's alternative erotic economy of public sex as the primary example of contact relations. Through anonymous and nonanonymous encounters, the writer experienced interactions that constituted powerful cross-race and interclass contact. The zoning of commercial sex culture will effectively replace these relations with basic networking. A salient example of networking and the new Times Square would be the example of the suburban tourists who are shuttled into the city in large tour buses. On the bus they interact exclusively with other tourists who have decided to venture into the big city. These tourists might then take in a show—let's just say it's Disney's "The Lion King"—and perhaps go out for dinner. These tourists will then hop on the bus and be safely deposited in their suburban homes. The only contact they will have outside of their class strata will be with representatives of the service industry who will take their tickets or serve their meals. This is the new Times Square, Giuliani's New York.

It is especially disturbing yet politically sobering to realize that the mayor's initiatives are supported by many gay voters. Lisa Duggan has recently described this phenomenon as homonormativity.[7] Duggan's term is meant to outline the retreat into the private sphere that conservative homosexuals have participated in in an effort to assimilate and perhaps purchase a seat at the table that right-wing gay pundits like Bruce Bawer and Andrew Sullivan long for.[8] This point resonates with an earlier theorization of sexual assimilation. Theodor Adorno, in an essay recently translated as "Sexual Taboos and Law Today," debunks the mythology of what he called "sexual liberation." Adorno explains that sexual liberation is "mere illusion":

> This illusion arose together with the phenomenon sociology elsewhere describes with its favorite expression "integration": the same way in which bourgeois society overcame the proletarian threat by incorporating the proletariat. Rational society, which is founded upon the domination of inner and outer nature and disciplines the diffuse pleasure principle that is harmful to the work ethic and even the principle of domination itself, no longer needs the patriarchal commandment of abstinence, virginity, and chastity. On the contrary, sexuality, turned on and off, channeled and exploited in countless forms by the material and culture industry, cooperates with the process of manipulation insofar as it is absorbed, institutionalized and administered by society. As long as sexuality is bridled, it is tolerated.[9]

Giuliani's gay support has everything to do with the way in which assimilationist homosexuals are willing to "turn off and on" their sexuality. The contract that they have signed onto demands that sexuality only be turned on within the shelter of the private sphere, in a darkness that is far murkier than the shadows that enveloped the trucks on Christopher Street in a pre-Stonewall 1960. The assimilationist homosexuals who back Giuliani are a sexual proletariat that has been swept into the conservative populism so powerfully characterizing this millennial moment. The contract they have signed is one of fake futurity. Rather than investing in children, they invest in an assimilation that is forever over the rainbow.

During sex panics like the current one, it seems especially important to enact a criticism that accomplishes a few tasks. Like Kaprow's happenings and Delany's memoir did, we crucially need to map our repression, our fragmentation, and alienation—the ways in which the state does not permit us to say "the whole" of our masses. It is also important to practice a criticism that enables us to cut through the institutional and legislative barriers that outlaw contact relations and obscure glimpses of the whole. These glimpses and moments of contact have a decidedly utopian function permitting us to imagine and potentially make a queer world. Such a criticism would work by allowing us to see "the future in the present."

C. L. R. James entitled his first volume of collected writing *The Future in the Present*.[10] This title riffs on an aspect of Hegelian dialectics suggesting that the affirmation known as the future is contained within its negation, the present. In his co-authored *Facing Reality*, a document that has been described as a classic document of the American left, James argues that a socialist future could be glimpsed by observing worker interaction and sociality within the space of the industrialized factory. Furthermore, he explains that the shop floor was an actually exiting socialist reality in the present. His most striking proof for this thesis considers the case of an anonymous worker at an unnamed factory: "In one department of a certain plant in the U.S. there is a worker who is physically incapable of carrying out his duties. But he is a man with wife and children and his condition is due to the strain of previous work in the plant. The workers have organized their work so that for ten years he has had practically nothing to do."[11] James looks to this situation and others like it throughout the world as examples of an already existing socialist present outside of the bureaucracy which was the Eastern Bloc. James argues that "the fundamental task is to recognize the socialist society and record the facts of its existence"; thus the scenes he describes are to be read as "outposts of a new society" (*Facing*, 137).

This idea in James, this notion of the future in the present, is manifest through his post-Trotskyist workerism, which has been critiqued widely. Today it is easy to dismiss an intellectual romanticization of labor. Two of James's most famous collaborators denounced this notion as delusional and naive. Cornelius Castoriadis (who contributed to the same book under one of his pen names, Pierre Chaulieu) has countered James's claims by explaining that "it is not difficult to understand that if socialist society already existed people would have noticed it." Raya Dunayevskaya, who founded the Johnson-Forest Tendency in American Marxism with James, stated that "the man who can write '*It is agreed that the socialist society exists*' need never face reality."[12] These are harsh words from allies and friends. Yet, despite these damning critiques, I am still drawn to this idea in James and its emphasis on the factory worker, particularly its framing of the social performer as something more than a cog. I contend that James's dialectic utopianism is *not* useless insofar as it helps us imagine the future without abandoning the present. James's formulation works as a refunctioned utopianism that is predicated on a critique of the present. I want to suggest that the reading practice that James describes helps us read the worldmaking potentialities contained in the performances of minoritarian citizen-subjects who contest the majoritarian public sphere.[13]

I use the term *minoritarian* to index citizen-subjects who, due to antagonisms within the social, like race, class, and sex, are debased within the majoritarian public sphere. The remainder of this essay will consider performances that I will describe as sexual avant-gardist acts whose ideological projects are both antinormative and critical of the state. Minoritarian performance—performances both theatrical and quotidian—transports us across symbolic space, inserting us in a coterminous time where we witness new formations within the present and the future. The coterminous temporality of such performance exists within the future and the present, surpassing relegation to one temporality (the present) and insisting on the minoritarian subject's status as world historical entity. The stage and the street, like the shop floor, are venues for performances that allow the spectator access to minoritarian life worlds that exist, importantly and dialectically, within the future and the present. James's workerist theory allows us to think of the minoritarian performer as a worker and the performance of queer worldmaking as a mode of labor. These performances are thus outposts of an actually existing queer future existing in the present.

Magic Touches: Queers of Color and Alternative Economies

Research has taken me to Jackson Heights, Queens. There I have visited and patronized the Magic Touch, a bar whose name signals a mode of contact between sex workers and consumers that can potentially be described as interclass and inter-race contact. As the clock ticks and the world of New York's culture of public sex faces extinction, I have made a point of soaking up as much of it as possible. This bar certainly did not compare to the illicit orgy on the piers that Delany chronicled. Yet it was very different from similar venues in the city, like the Gaiety in Manhattan.

The Gaiety is the only surviving gay burlesque show in New York City. A few years ago it was a hub of hustling and public sex activity. Patrons would not only interact with the performers, who were always available for private shows, but were equally interested in those sitting next to them. All sorts of sex would happen in this venue and others like it, including the now defunct Eros Theater and the Showpalace. The Gaiety has managed to stay in business by adopting many of the state's policies before the state actually instituted them. Now patrons are not allowed anywhere near performers, performers are strictly forbidden from negotiating private shows, and security guards patrol the aisles and make sure that patrons do not touch each other. The performers are almost exclusively white. All the dancers are conventionally attractive and extremely well-muscled. Most are based in Canada and travel to the Gaiety once a month to hustle on the side and strip on stage. The body types hold a powerful spot in the erotic imagination of mainstream homosexuality. I have described this phenomenon elsewhere as the "dominant imprint" that organizes mainstream desire in U.S. gay culture.[14] The dominant imprint is a blueprint of gay male desire and desirability that is unmarked and thus universally white. Patrons, like desiring subjects in mainstream gay culture, can never touch these boys unless they negotiate a private show in the adjacent lounge area. A private show averages about two hundred dollars. (Internet sites that discuss hustling from a consumer's perspective complain of the dancers' limited sexual repertoire. Two hundred dollars can generally buy one a "posing show," where a flexing hustler offers mostly visual pleasure to the often frustrated sex consumer.)[15] The dancers' inaccessibility and desirability are a combination of contradictory attributes recognizable in the dominant imprint. Tall, blonde white boys with pulsating muscles who barely dance and are instead objects to be desired from afar and engaged only in private conform to a culture of sex work that can be characterized as primarily being about privatized networking relations.

There is no such policing at the Magic Touch. The show is run like a contest there; a raffle selects judges for a competition. Contestants are judged on a range of attributes, which include both dancing and physical appearance. While the Gaiety's performers are mostly white, the Magic Touch's are Latino and African American. Since the Magic Touch is one of a few neighborhood gay bars in Queens, some lesbians and straight women also show up. The bar's clientele stands in sharp contrast to the Gaiety's—the Gaiety is populated by predominantly white men and tourists from Europe and East Asia, while the racial diversity I have encountered at the Magic Touch surpasses any I have seen at other gay clubs. Filipino queens sit next to older white daddy types who are across the bar from beeper-wielding Latino hustlers who seem to know the group of black men clustered around the jukebox. Some folks are Manhattanites braving the outer boroughs, and others hail from even deeper in Queens. The performers come out in uniforms—military garb, loose fitting hip-hop fashions, snug fitting gay club wear, blue-collar flannel drag—and strip to a G-string. They are instantly disqualified if they show anything that might be tucked inside the G-string. Their dancing styles vary—some let their bodies do all the work, while other boys are quite acrobatic. Hip-hop dance moves dominate the performers' routines. The movement can often be described as a highly sexualized break dancing. As soon as the contest is over and the winner has been crowned, the boys mingle with the audience for an hour or so. Tips are stuffed in bikinis and boots, deals are brokered, conversations ensue.

The dancers at the Gaiety do not seem to take as much pleasure in the dancing. Instead, most strut around the stage. During any one show a dancer at the Gaiety will dance to two consecutive songs. The music is almost exclusively contemporary pop. During the first song the dancer will perform a striptease to his jock or underwear. He will then walk backstage, and there will be a minute or two where the audience anxiously awaits the dancer's next appearance. During this pause, the dancer is getting erect or, as it is known in the professional lexicon, "fluffed." The erect dancer is greeted by a round of applause when he reemerges from backstage. Sometimes the dancer will have tied a rubber band or a cock ring around the base of his penis to allow him to maintain his erection a little longer. But more often than not the erection has faded by the middle of this next number. If the Magic Touch displayed such nudity it would be closed down. In fact, its dancers must wear more than a G-string since the new zoning laws prohibit female go-go dancers and male dancers to wear anything as revealing as bikinis. A few topless dance bars throughout Manhattan have survived by scrawling an "S" in front of former printed signs that now read "Stopless Dancing." The "stopless" dancers pole dance while wearing T-shirts. Most of the male go-go dancers wear athletic shorts as they rehearse their moves on stage. While the strippers at the Magic Touch are unable to take it all off, the customer is able to achieve physical contact when he tips his dancer of choice. The Gaiety's antiseptic lounge has a rough equivalent in the Magic Touch's ironically titled V.I.P. lounge. The V.I.P. area is actually the bar's basement. It includes a pool table and several pieces of run-down wicker furniture and white plastic picnic chairs. The contact enacted between dancer/stripper and spectator/john here is much more tactile and intense than that which happens upstairs.

One of my friends, an anthropologist who works with gay Filipino men in New York City, refers to the Magic Touch as the "Tragic Touch." This is a nickname given to the bar by some Jackson Heights locals. The *tragic* in this rewriting of the establishment's name is meant to poke fun at the pathos of the hustler/john relationship—the manner in which older men pay younger hustlers. From the vantage point of youth, we can clearly see the pathos of this relationship. Yet I want to suggest that it is a pathos that undergirds the ageism and, for lack of a better word, lookism of all gay male erotic economies. From yet another perspective, we can see this as something else, another formation: this economy of hustler/john is an alternative economy where flesh, pleasure, and money meet under outlaw circumstances. This economy eschews the standardized routes in which heteronormative late capitalism mandates networking relations of sex for money. This economy represents a selling of sex for money that does not conform to the corporate American sex trade always on display for us via media advertising culture and older institutions like heterosexual marriage. The hustler/john relationship represents a threat to these other naturalized performances of sex for money, in part because it promotes contact between people of different class and racial backgrounds. At the Magic Touch we see men of all colors relating to each other, forming bonds, and we see this in mass. We glimpse a whole that is diverse and invigorating in its eclectic nature. Some men come for voyeuristic pleasure, some come to meet other men who are spectators, others have come to participate in the age-old economy of hustler and john—all are performing outlaw sexuality. The new zoning legislation will only allow such establishments to function in industrialized spaces far away from public transportation and other businesses. Men who brave these industrialized zones will encounter far greater risks of gay bashing and robbery.

Stickering the Future

The phrase "Whose quality of life?" caught my eye. Someone had printed this line on a sticker attached to a street sign near my home. The rest of the text read, "It's a beautiful day. . . . 'Crime is down.' Police brutality is up. . . . What are you doing outside?" The sticker was signed by a Mickey Mouse head with the letters "f.t.m." superimposed over it—text below the mouse insignia explained that the acronym stood for "fear the mayor." The main text is a take off of ABC's ad campaign encouraging viewers to sit at home and watch TV despite a sunny day outside. I later encountered another sticker—

this one showed an image of two white men in baseball caps with their arms around each other. The men represented the contemporary white gay male clone, the type that populates certain neighborhoods in major U.S. cities, like New York's Chelsea or Los Angeles's West Hollywood. These images did not represent the dominant imprint but did resemble a look organized and formatted by the desire that is the dominant imprint. The text read "Can we afford to be normal?" Below the photo I found what at first glance appeared to be corporate megachain store The Gap's logo. But instead it spelled out G-A-Y. A slogan flanked the faux corporate insignia, reading "Heteronormativity. Fall into the trap." I understood this sticker to be associated with the previous one when I located the same familiar mouse head in the corner. This time the acronym was different—it read "r.h.q.," which stood for "resist the heterosexualization of queerness." I began to inquire as to the authorship of these inspired little stickers and soon traced them to a group of young activists in New York City who have launched an impressive sticker/wheat pasting campaign against the mayor's new directives. The group worked with the activist collective Sex Panic for a time but became disillusioned with that group's inability to incorporate questions of gender, race, and age into its critique of state censorship and homophobia. The group refuses to name itself in an attempt to remain a working collective and sidestep the essentializing effects that occur when a group identity is adopted. At times they employ the acronym "f.a.g.," which stands for feminist action group. At other times they appropriate the name of the suburban high school group that all white middle-class officials support—s.a.d.d. (students against drunk driving)— and resignify that acronym to mean "sex activists against demonization." The only constant graphic they retain in their guerrilla posturing and stickering is the outline of a Mickey Mouse head, which is meant to represent New York's ominous big brother. In their activist statement—a zine titled *Swallow Your Pride*—the group explains that "we choose to do a stickering/wheatpasting campaign because there are a lot of special perks to this kind of media. First, it's really cheap. Second, it reaches a different audience than the other options that are vaguely accessible: Internet, gay weeklies, and sometimes bigger newspapers. It's really local. People see the stuff on the street and in the city. It is not limited to people who have computers or read the newspaper regularly—which means younger people and poorer people."[16] This group has attempted to not replicate the mistakes of other important activists groups like Sex Panic, Act-Up and Queer Nation. Its guerrilla campaign has attempted to imagine and enact a modality of queer publicity that is calibrated to be responsive to modalities of difference that include race, class, gender, and sexuality. The young activist insistence on an integrated and intersectional queer critique can be discerned if we consider a sticker that reads "I ❤ Nushawn Williams." Williams is a young HIV-positive African American man who has been arrested for engaging in unprotected sex. He became a contemporary Typhoid Mary as sensationalized media reporting constructed him as the ultimate AIDS predator. The group's intervention in this case was a difficult and risky move. It is indeed a complex move to identify with someone who, while not behaving in a conventionally sexually responsible fashion, was, nonetheless, not the racialized monster constructed by the media's reporting.

The stickers function as performing objects inasmuch as they solicit a response from spectators. Sometimes people attempt to rip the stickers down, at other times people write directly on the stickers. The stickers themselves then become forums for public debate, where people work through pressing social issues in a sphere away from the corrupt mediatized majoritarian public sphere. The performances that the stickers demand from viewers open the possibility of critical thinking and intervention; they encourage lucidity and political action. They are calls that demand, in the tradition of African American vernacular culture, a response. The response is sometimes an outpouring of state ideology, yet at other times the responses are glimpses of an actually existing queer present in the future.[17]

One sticker in particular offers an important critique of the present that signals the coming of a new moment of queer activism and publicity. Washington Square has been one of the mayor's pet projects for years now. He first increased police presence at the park to truly militaristic proportions. The entire space of the park is blanketed by at least a dozen or so police officers at any given moment. A large police trailer is parked next to the park, and it has become command central. I cannot count the times over the last two years in which I have stood witness to three or four police officers jumping on one homeless drug dealer. (When I write drug dealer here, I mean homeless men who hustle tiny "dime bags" of marijuana.) This policing has a new technological dimension insofar as the park is now completely covered by video cameras that record everything happening inside or near Washington Square's arches. A week or so after these cameras appeared, I noticed the mouse head again. This time the acronym read "w.b.w.," which stood for "we are being watched." Another sticker soon followed. It had a great deal more text: "Smile!: You are on closed Circuit Television. The NYPD recently installed surveillance cameras in Washington Square Park. In our public urban spaces we are watched and harassed by an increasingly brutal police force. The use of state-sanctioned violence against queers, youth, people of color and the homeless in an effort to 'clean-up' this city must stop. Giuliani's 'quality of life' campaign is driving us out of the places where we have always hung out." The sticker functions as a mode of political pedagogy that intends to publicize the state's machinations of power. While technologies of surveillance colonize symbolic space, the anonymous performance of stickering contests that reterritorialization and harkens to another moment, a time and place outside of the state's electronic eye. This working collective is watching the watcher and providing a much needed counterpublicity to the state's power. In this work we also glimpse an avant-gardist sexual performance—which is to say a performance that enacts a critique of sexual normativities allowing us to bear witness to a new formation, a future in the present.

Mourning through Militancy: Matthew Shepard and Others

The point of seeing the whole of our masses did not become salient for me until I witnessed this theoretical formulation on the streets of New York, in the form of an uprising that was put down with brutal force by the New York City Police Department. The policing of this uprising worked so the masses would be unable to see the whole. Matthew Shepard was savagely beaten, bound to a fence, and left to die on a Wyoming road in the fall of 1998. The national attention this murder received was a surprise for many activists. Queer activists in New York City are very aware of the fact that, while crime is supposedly down under the Giuliani regime, violence against gays and lesbians is on the increase. In 1998 hate crime violence had increased by 8 percent.[18] Walking through the East or West Village, Chelsea, Brooklyn, or neighborhoods in Queens, queers have become very accustomed to seeing posters with the pictures of some queer person, often a queer person of color, who has been murdered or "disappeared" in New York. We see similar posters warning us of other predators who pray on our community. It was Shepard's telegenic face that secured a lot of media attention. His "traditional" good looks echoed certain aspects of a dominant imprint, and this certainly helped him become a flag many could rally around. Many of the activists who showed up for the Matthew Shepard political funeral the next day understood that if Shepard had not been a pretty white boy, there would have been no such outcry. We nonetheless seized the moment, took the streets, not only for Shepard, but for the countless women and men of all colors who have survived and not survived queer violence on the streets of New York City and elsewhere.

The official advance estimate for this vigil was five hundred; other estimates suggest that five thousand people showed up. The New York City police department responded to the outpouring of activism by calling in the troops. Marchers during this rebellion attempted to take to the streets, but the police insisted that this massive group walk exclusively on the sidewalk. A rupture came and people took to the streets. Violence ensued, horses were brought out, billy clubs were brandished, activists were pushed and knocked down. The protest's marshals, its leadership, were the first people arrested. I saw friends taken away, loaded on MTA buses commandeered by the police. My friend David wasn't planning to be arrested, but he was nonetheless randomly picked out of the crowd and taken to central booking. Rebecca avoided arrest but had a close call after she was shoved by a cop, her vigil candle spilling wax on another officer who turned angrily to her—in fear she apologized profusely hoping not be taken in. Most people had not planned to be arrested; this was supposed to be a somber political vigil. No one anticipated the horses, the bombardment of cops, the mass arrests, the force used against them. Many people on fragile antiviral drugs missed dosages and risked building up immunity to these precious drugs. The peaceful vigil became something else. It became a moment when queer people, frustrated and sick of all the violence they had endured, saw our masses. The police responded by breaking up the group, factioning off segments of our groupings, obscuring our mass.

The state understands the need to keep us from knowing ourselves, knowing our masses. It is ready, at the drop of the proverbial dime, to transform public transportation into policing machines, to call out thousands of cops to match thousands of activists, to wield clubs and fists. The state, like Delany, understands the power of our masses, a power that can only be realized by surpassing the solitary pervert model and accessing group identity. This entails resisting the privatization of queer culture that the Sullivans, Rotellos, and Bawers of the world clamor for. The next day the *New York Post* headline read "Gay Riot." It was more nearly a queer riot, where queer energies manifested themselves and the state responded with calculated force and brutal protocols. The riot was sobering insofar as the mechanisms of policing were partially displayed, revealed for an evening, and it became very clear to everyone present how the idea of queers making contact in a mass uprising scared the state. The utopian promise of our public performance was responded to with shattering force. Even though this impromptu rebellion was overcome easily by the state, the activist anger, a productive, generative anger, let those assembled in rage glean a queer future within a repressive heteronormative present.

Making Utopia

Adorno provided a succinct rendering of utopia when he described it as existing in "the determined negation of that which merely is." This negation points "to what should be."[19] The work I have considered here looks to what is and fashions important critiques of the present by insisting on the present's dialectical relation to the future. Our criticism should, like the cases I have surveyed, be infused with a utopian function that is attuned to what Ernst Bloch has called the "anticipatory illumination" of art and culture.[20] It is my contention that such illumination will cut through fragmenting darkness and allow us to see the politically enabling whole. Such illumination will provide us with access to a world that should be, that could be, that will be.

Notes

In the summer of 1998 I taught a graduate seminar at New York University on the question of cultures of sexual dissidence. Lee Edelman visited that course as an invited guest and presented work in progress on the questions of queers and the problem of futurity. Much of the thinking that informs this writing owes a debt to Edelman and that presentation. Another intellectual debt is owed to my comrade Fred Moten, with whom I have shared an archive as well as many drinks and conversations.

1   Lauren Berlant, "Live Sex Acts (Parental Advisory: Explicit Material)," *Feminist Studies* 21, no. 2 (1995): 379–404.

2   Samuel R. Delany, *The Motion of Light in Water: Sex and Science Fiction Writing in the East Village, 1960–1965* (London: Paladin, 1988), 179. Subsequent references are cited parenthetically in the text.

3   See, for example, essays by Michael Kirby, Allan Kaprow, and Ricard Schechner in *Happenings and Other Acts*, ed. Mariellen R. Sandford (New York: Routledge, 1994).

4   Joan W. Scott, "The Evidence of Experience" in *The Lesbian and Gay Studies*

Reader, ed. Henry Abelove, Michèle Aina Barale, and David M. Halperin (New York: Routledge, 1993), 397–415.

5   Lisa Duggan, "The Discipline Problem: Queer Theory Meets Lesbian and Gay History," *GLQ: A Journal of Lesbian and Gay Studies* 2, no. 3 (1995): 179–91.

6   Samuel R. Delany, *Times Square Red, Times Square Blue* (New York: New York University Press, 1999), 111.

7   Lisa Duggan, *The Incredibly Shrinking Public Sphere* (Boston: Beacon Press, 2002).

8   Examples of this right-wing impulse in current gay culture would include Andrew Sullivan, *Virtually Normal: An Argument about Homosexuality* (New York: Vintage, 1996) and Bruce Bawer, *A Place at the Table: The Gay Individual in American Society* (New York: Touchstone, 1994). Along with Duggan's text, two other important responses to the new gay conservatism are Phillip Brian Harper, *Private Affairs: Critical Ventures in the Culture of Social Relations* (New York: New York University Press, 1999), and Michael Warner, *The Trouble with Normal: Sex, Politics, and the Ethics of Queer Life* (New York: Free Press, 1999).

9   Theodor W. Adorno, "Sexual Taboos and Law Today," in *Critical Models: Interventions and Catchwords*, trans. Henry W. Pickford (New York: Columbia University Press, 1998), 72.

10   C. L. R. James, *The Future in the Present: Selected Writings* (Westport, Conn.: Lawrence Hill, 1977).

11   C. L. R. James, Grace Lee, and Pierre Chaulieu, *Facing Reality* (Detroit: Bewick, 1974), 137. Subsequent references are cited parenthetically in the text.

12   Qtd. in Kent Worcester, *C. L. R. James: A Political Biography* (Albany: State University of New York Press, 1995), 141.

13   The above paragraph is adapted from the last chapter of my book *Disidentifications: Queers of Color and the Performance of Politics* (Minneapolis: University of Minnesota Press, 1999).

14   See my essay "Dead White: Notes on the Whiteness of the Queer Screen," *GLQ: A Journal of Lesbian and Gay Studies* 4, no. 1 (1998): 127–38.

15   See http://www.atkol.com for an example of such internet sex consumer posting.

16   *Swallow Your Pride: A Hands-on Tool for Do-It-Yourself Activism*, independently produced activist zine, no pagination. The zine includes a return address: Amanda La Vita, 184 East 2nd Street #5F, New York, NY 10009. The zine itself is partially written as a how-to manual that gives instruction to would-be activists on how to make their own stickers and develop their own guerrilla activist projects.

17   I am grateful to Arin Mason, who participated in these stickering campaigns and suggested the stickers' status as performative objects in an excellent seminar paper.

18 See the LAMBDA Gay and Lesbian Anti-Violence Project Web site at http://www.lambda.org/glnvah.htm, for these statistics and more recent ones on antigay violence.

19 See Ernst Bloch and Theodor W. Adorno, "Something's Missing: A Discussion between Ernst Bloch and Theodor Adorno on the Contradictions of Utopian Longing," in *The Utopian Function of Art and Literature: Selected Essays*, by Bloch, trans. Jack Zipes and Frank Mecklenburg (Cambridge, Mass.: MIT Press, 1988), 12.

20 Ernst Bloch, "Art and Utopia," in *The Utopian Function*, 141.

Manifest Domesticity

Amy Kaplan

The "cult of domesticity," the ideology of "separate spheres," and the "culture of sentiment" have together provided a productive paradigm for understanding the work of white women writers in creating a middle-class American culture in the nineteenth century. Most studies of this paradigm have revealed the permeability of the border that separates the spheres, demonstrating that the private feminized space of the home both infused and bolstered the public male arena of the market and that the sentimental values attached to maternal influence were used to sanction women's entry into the wider civic realm from which those same values theoretically excluded them. More recently, scholars have argued that the extension of female sympathy across social divides could violently reinforce the very racial and class hierarchies that sentimentality claims to dissolve.[1]

This deconstruction of separate spheres, however, leaves another structural opposition intact: the domestic in intimate opposition to the foreign. In this context *domestic* has a double meaning that not only links the familial household to the nation but also imagines both in opposition to everything outside the geographic and conceptual border of the home. The earliest meaning of *foreign*, according to the *OED*, refers to the physical space "out of doors" or to concerns "at a distance from home." Contemporary English speakers refer to national concerns as domestic in explicit or implicit contrast with the foreign. The notion of domestic policy makes sense only in opposition to foreign policy, and uncoupled from the foreign, national issues are never labeled domestic. The idea of foreign policy depends on the sense of the nation as a domestic space imbued with a sense of at-homeness, in contrast to an external world perceived as alien and threatening. Reciprocally, a sense of the foreign is necessary to erect the boundaries that enclose the nation as home.

Reconceptualizing domesticity in this way might shift the cognitive geography of nineteenth-century separate spheres. When we contrast the domestic sphere with the market or political realm, men and women inhabit a divided social terrain, but when we oppose the domestic to the foreign, men and women become national allies against the alien, and the determining division is not gender but racial demarcations of otherness. Thus another part of the cultural work of domesticity might be to unite men and women in a national domain and to generate notions of the foreign against which the nation can be imagined as home. The border between the domestic and the foreign, however, also deconstructs when we think of domesticity not as a static condition but as the process of domestication, which entails conquering and taming the wild, the natural, and the alien. Domestic in this sense is related to the imperial project of civilizing, and the conditions of domesticity often become markers that distinguish civilization from savagery. Through the process of domestication, the home contains within itself those wild or foreign elements that must be tamed; domesticity not only monitors the borders between the civilized and the savage, but regulates those traces within itself.[2]

If domesticity plays a key role in imagining the nation as home, then women, positioned at the center of the home, play a major role in defining the contours of the nation and its shifting borders with the foreign. Those feminist critics and historians whose work has been fundamental in charting the paradigm of separate spheres, however, have for the most part overlooked the relationship of domesticity to nationalism and imperialism. Their work is worth revisiting here because their own language, echoing their sources, inadvertently exposes these connections, which scholars have just recently begun to pursue. Jane Tompkins, for example, lauds Catharine Beecher's *Treatise on Domestic Economy* as "the prerequisite of world conquest" and claims of a later version that "the imperialistic drive behind the encyclopedism and determined practicality of this household manual . . . is a blueprint for colonizing the world in the name of the 'family state' under the leadership of Christian women" (143, 144).[3] As her title indicates, Mary Ryan's *Empire of the Mother: American Writing about Domesticity, 1830–1860* employs empire as a metaphor framing her analysis; yet she never links this pervasive imperial metaphor to the contemporary geopolitical movement of imperial expansion or to the discourse of Manifest Destiny. This blind spot, I believe, stems from the way that the ideology of separate spheres has shaped scholarship; until recently it has been assumed that nationalism and foreign policy lay outside the concern and participation of women. Isolating the empire of the mother from other imperial endeavors, however, runs two risks: first, it may reproduce in women's studies the insularity of an American studies that imagines the nation as a fixed, monolithic, and self-enclosed geographic and cultural whole; second, the legacy of separate spheres that sees women as morally superior to men can lead to the current moralistic strain in feminist criticism, which has shifted from celebrating the liberatory qualities of white women's writing to condemning their racism. In this essay I try instead to understand the vexed and contradictory relations between race and domesticity as an issue not solely of individual morality nor simply internal to the nation, but as historically structural to the institutional and discursive processes of national expansion and empire building.[4]

My essay poses the question of how the ideology of separate spheres in antebellum America contributed to creating an American empire by imagining the nation as a home at a time when its geopolitical borders were expanding rapidly through violent confrontations with Indians, Mexicans, and European empires. Scholars have overlooked the fact that the development of domestic discourse in America is contemporaneous with the discourse of Manifest Destiny. If we juxtapose the spatial representations of these discourses, they seem to embody the most extreme form of separate spheres: the home as a bounded and rigidly ordered interior space is opposed to the boundless and undifferentiated space of an infinitely expanding nation. Yet these spatial and gendered configurations are linked in complex ways that are dependent on racialized notions of the foreign. According to the ideology of separate spheres, domesticity can be viewed as an anchor, a feminine counterforce to the male activity of territorial conquest. I argue, to the contrary, that domesticity is more mobile and less stabilizing; it travels in contradictory circuits both to expand and contract the boundaries of home and nation and to produce shifting conceptions of the foreign. This form of traveling domesticity can be analyzed in the writings of Catharine Beecher and Sara Josepha Hale, whose work, despite their ideological differences as public figures, reveals how the internal logic of domesticity relies on, abets, and reproduces the contradictions of nationalist expansion in the 1840s and 1850s. An analysis of Beecher's *A Treatise on Domestic Economy* demonstrates that the language of empire both suffuses and destabilizes the rhetoric of separate spheres, while an analysis of Hale's work uncovers the shared racial underpinnings of domestic and imperialist discourse through which the separateness of gendered spheres reinforces the effort to separate the races by turning blacks into foreigners. Understanding the imperial reach of domestic discourse might remap the way we read women's novels of the 1850s by interpreting their narratives of domesticity and female subjectivity as inseparable from narratives of empire and nation building.

I

Domesticity dominated middle-class women's writing and culture from the 1830s through the 1850s, at a time when national boundaries were in violent flux; during this period the United States doubled its national domain, completed a campaign of Indian removal, fought its first prolonged foreign war, wrested the Spanish borderlands from Mexico, and annexed Texas, Oregon, and California. As Thomas Hietala has shown, this convulsive expansion was less a confident celebration of Manifest Destiny than a response to crises of confidence about national unity, the expansion of slavery, and the racial identity of citizenship—crises that territorial expansion exacerbated.[5] Furthermore, these movements evoked profound questions about the conceptual border between the domestic and the foreign. In the 1831 Supreme Court decision *Cherokee Nation v. the State of Georgia*, for example, Indians were declared members of "domestic dependent nations," neither foreign nationals nor United States citizens.[6] This designation makes the domestic an ambiguous third realm between the national and the foreign, as it places the foreign inside the geographic boundaries of the nation. The uneasy relation between the domestic and the foreign can also be seen in the debates over the annexation of new territory. In the middle of the Mexican War President Polk insisted that slavery was "purely a domestic question" and not a "foreign question" at all, but the expansion he advocated undermined that distinction and threatened domestic unity by raising the question of slavery's extension into previously foreign lands.[7] In debates about the annexation of Texas and later Mexico, both sides represented the new territories as women to be married to the United States; Sam Houston, for example, wrote of Texas presenting itself "to the United States as a bride adorned for her espousals"; and President Taylor accused annexationists after the Mexican War of trying to "drag California into the Union before her wedding garment has yet been cast about her person."[8] These visions of imperial expansion as marital union carried within them the specter of marriage as racial amalgamation. While popular fiction about the Mexican War portrayed brave American men rescuing and marrying Mexican women of Spanish descent, political debate over the annexation of Mexico hinged on what was agreed to be the impossibility of incorporating a foreign people marked by their racial intermixing into a domestic nation imagined as Anglo-Saxon.[9] One of the major contradictions of imperialist expansion was that, while it strove to nationalize and domesticate foreign territories and peoples, annexation threatened to incorporate nonwhite foreign subjects into the republic in a way perceived to undermine the nation as a domestic space.

My point here is not to survey foreign policy but to suggest how deeply the language of domesticity permeated the debates about national expansion. Rather than stabilizing the representation of the nation as home, this rhetoric heightened the fraught and contingent nature of the boundary between the domestic and the foreign, a boundary that breaks down around questions of the racial identity of the nation as home. If we begin to rethink woman's sphere in this context, we have to ask how the discourse of domesticity negotiates the borders of an increasingly expanding empire and divided nation. Domestic discourse both redresses and reenacts the contradictions of empire through its own double movement to expand female influence beyond the home and the nation while simultaneously contracting woman's sphere to police domestic boundaries against the threat of foreignness both within and without.

At this time of heightened national expansion, proponents of "woman's sphere" employed the language of empire to both the home and women's emotional lives. "Hers is the empire of the affections," wrote Sarah Josepha Hale, influential editor of *Godey's Lady's Book*, who opposed the women's rights movement as "the attempt to take woman away from her empire of the home."[10] To educational reformer Horace Mann, "the empire of the Home" was "the most important of all empires, the pivot of all empires and emperors" (Ryan, *Empire of the Mother*, 112). Writers who counseled women to renounce politics and economics, "to leave the rude commerce of camps and the soul hardening struggling of political power to the harsher spirit of men," urged them in highly political rhetoric to take up a more spiritual calling, "the domain of the moral affections and the empire of the heart."[11] Catharine Beecher gave this calling a nationalist cast in *A Treatise on Domestic Economy*, when, for example, she uses Queen Victoria as a foil to elevate the American "mother and housekeeper in a large family," who is "the sovereign of an empire demanding as varied cares, and involving more difficult duties, than are exacted of her, who wears the crown and professedly regulates the interests of the greatest nation on earth, [yet] finds abundant leisure for theaters, balls, horse races, and every gay leisure."[12] This imperial trope might be interpreted as a compensatory and defensive effort to glorify the shrunken realm of female agency, in a paradox of what Ryan calls "imperial isolation" whereby the mother gains her symbolic sovereignty at the cost of withdrawal from the outside world (*Empire of the Mother*, 97–114). For these writers, however, metaphor has a material efficacy in the world. The representation of the home as an empire exists in tension with the notion of women's sphere as a contracted space because it is in the nature of empires to extend their rule over new domains while fortifying their borders against external invasion and internal insurrection. If, on the one hand, domesticity draws strict boundaries between the home and the world of men, on the other, it becomes the engine of national expansion, the site from which the nation reaches beyond itself through the emanation of woman's moral influence.

The paradox of what might be called *imperial domesticity* is that, by withdrawing from direct agency in the male arena of commerce and politics, women's sphere can be represented by both women and men as a more potent agent for national expansion. The outward reach of domesticity in turn enables the interior functioning of the home. In her introduction to *A Treatise on Domestic Economy,* Beecher inextricably links women's work at home to the unfolding of America's global mission of "exhibiting to the world the beneficent influences of Christianity, when carried into every social, civil, and political institution" (12). Women's maternal responsibility for molding the character of men and children has global repercussions: "To American women, more than to any others on earth, is committed the exalted privilege of extending over the world those blessed influences, that are to renovate degraded man, and 'clothe all climes with beauty'" (14). Beecher ends her introduction with an extended architectural metaphor in which women's agency at home is predicated on the global expansion of the nation:

> The builders of a temple are of equal importance, whether they labor on the foundations, or toil upon the dome. Thus also with those labors that are to be made effectual in the regeneration of the Earth. The woman who is rearing a family of children; the woman who labors in the schoolroom, the woman who, in her retired chamber, earns with her needle, the mite to contribute for the intellectual and moral elevation of her country; even the humble domestic, whose example and influence may be molding and forming young minds, while her faithful services sustain a prosperous domestic state;—each and all may be cheered by the consciousness that they are agents in accomplishing the greatest work that ever was committed to human responsibility. It is the building of a glorious temple, whose base shall be coextensive with the bounds of the earth, whose summit shall pierce the skies, whose splendor shall beam on all lands, and those who hew the lowliest stone, as much as those

who carve the highest capital, will be equally honored when its top-stone shall be laid, with new rejoicing of the morning stars, and shoutings of the sons of God. (14)

One political effect of this metaphor is to unify women of different social classes in a shared project of construction while sustaining class hierarchy among women.[13] This image of social unity both depends on and underwrites a vision of national expansion, as women's varied labors come together to embrace the entire world. As the passage moves down the social scale, from mother to teacher to spinster, its geographic reach extends outward from home to schoolroom to country, until the "humble domestic" returns back to the "prosperous domestic state," in a phrase that casts the nation in familial terms. Women's work at home here performs two interdependent forms of national labor; it forges the bonds of internal unity while impelling the nation outward to encompass the globe. This outward expansion in turn enables the internal cohesiveness of woman's separate sphere by making women agents in erecting an infinitely expanding edifice.

Beecher thus introduces her detailed manual on the regulation of the home as a highly ordered space by fusing the boundedness of the home with the boundlessness of the nation. Her 1841 introduction bears remarkable resemblance to the rhetoric of Manifest Destiny, particularly to this passage by one of its foremost proponents, John L. O'Sullivan, in his "The Great Nation of Futurity" of 1839: "The far-reaching, the boundless future will be the era of American greatness. In its magnificent domain of space and time, the nation of many nations is destined to manifest to mankind the excellence of divine principles; to establish on earth the noblest temple ever dedicated to the worship of the most high—the Sacred and the True. Its floor shall be a hemisphere—its roof the firmament of the star-studded heavens, and its congregation an Union of many Republics, comprising hundreds of happy millions, calling, owning no man master, but governed by God's natural and moral law of equality."[14] While these passages exemplify the stereotype of separate spheres (one describes work in the home and the other the work of nation building), both use a common architectural metaphor from the Bible to build a temple coextensive with the globe. O'Sullivan's grammatical subject is the American nation, which is the implied medium in Beecher's text for channeling women's work at home to a Christianized world. The construction of an edifice ordinarily entails walling off the inside from the outside, but in both these cases there is a paradoxical effect whereby the distinction between inside and outside is obliterated by the expansion of the home/nation/temple to encompass the entire globe. The rhetoric of Manifest Destiny and domesticity share a vocabulary that turns imperial conquest into spiritual regeneration in order to efface internal conflict or external resistance in visions of geopolitical domination as global harmony.

Although imperial domesticity ultimately imagines a home coextensive with the entire world, it also continually projects a map of unregenerate outlying foreign terrain that both gives coherence to its boundaries and justifies its domesticating mission. When in 1869 Catharine Beecher revised her *Treatise* with her sister, Harriet Beecher Stowe, as *The American Woman's Home*, they downplayed the earlier role of domesticity in harmonizing class differences while enhancing domesticity's outward reach. The book ends by advocating the establishment of Christian neighborhoods settled primarily by women as a way of putting into practice domesticity's expansive potential to Christianize and Americanize immigrants both in Northeastern cities and "all over the West and South, while along the Pacific coast, China and Japan are sending their pagan millions to share our favored soil, climate, and government." No longer a leveling factor among classes within America, domesticity could be extended to those conceived of as foreign both within and beyond American national borders: "Ere long colonies from these prosperous and Christian communities would go forth to shine as 'lights of the world' in all the now darkened nations. Thus the Christian family and Christian neighborhood would become the grand ministry as they were designed to be, in training our whole race for heaven."[15] While Beecher and Stowe emphasize domesticity's service to "darkened nations," the existence of "pagans" as potential converts performs a reciprocal service in the extension of domesticity to American women outside the perimeters of marriage. Such Christian neighborhoods would allow unmarried women without children to leave their work in "factories, offices and shops," or their idleness in "refined leisure" to live domestic lives on their own, in some cases by adopting native children. Domesticity's imperial reach posits a way of extending woman's sphere to include not only the heathen but also the unmarried Euro-American woman who can be freed from biological reproduction to rule her own empire of the mother.

If writers about domesticity encouraged the extension of female influence outward to civilize the foreign, their writings also evoked anxiety about the opposing trajectory that brings foreignness into the home. Analyzing the widespread colonial trope that compares colonized people to children, Ann

Stoller and Karen Sánchez-Eppler have both shown how this metaphor can work not only to infantilize the colonized but also to portray white children as young savages in need of civilizing.[16] This metaphor at once extends domesticity outward to the tutelage of heathens while focusing it inward to regulate the threat of foreignness within the boundaries of the home. For Beecher, this internal savagery appears to threaten the physical health of the mother. Throughout the *Treatise*, the vision of the sovereign mother with imperial responsibilities is countered by the description of the ailing invalid mother. This contrast can be seen in the titles of the first two chapters, "Peculiar Responsibilities of American Women" and "Difficulties Peculiar to American Women." The latter focuses on the pervasive invalidism that makes American women physically and emotionally unequal to their global obligations. In contrast to the ebullient temple building of the first chapter, Beecher ends the second with a quotation from Tocqueville describing a fragile frontier home centered on a lethargic and vulnerable mother whose

> children cluster about her, full of health, turbulence and energy; they are true children of the wilderness; their mother watches them from time to time, with mingled melancholy and joy. To look at their strength, and her languor one might imagine that the life she had given them exhausted her own; and still she regrets not what they cost her. The house, inhabited by these emigrants, has no internal partition or loft. In the one chamber of which it consists, the whole family is gathered for the night. The dwelling itself is a little world; an ark of civilization amid an ocean of foliage. A hundred steps beyond it, the primeval forest spreads its shade and solitude resumes its sway. (24)

The mother's health appears drained not by the external hardships inflicted by the environment, but by her intimate tie to her own "children of the wilderness" who violate the border between home and primeval forest. This boundary is partially reinforced by the image of the home as an "ark of civilization" whose internal order should protect its inhabitants from the sea of chaos that surrounds them. Yet the undifferentiated inner space, which lacks "internal partition," replicates rather than defends against the boundlessness of the wilderness around it. The rest of the treatise, with its detailed attention to the systematic organization of the household, works to "partition" the home in a way that distinguishes it from an external wilderness.[17]

The infirmity of American mothers is a pervasive concern throughout the *Treatise*, yet its physical cause is difficult to locate in Beecher's text. Poor health afflicts middle-class women in Northeastern cities as it does women on the frontier, according to Beecher, and she sees both cases resulting from a geographic and social mobility in which "everything is moving and changing" (16). This movement affects women's health most directly, claims Beecher, by depriving them of reliable domestic servants. With "trained" servants constantly moving up and out, middle-class women must resort to hiring "ignorant" and "poverty-stricken foreigners," with whom they are said in *American Woman's Home* to have a "missionary" relationship (332). Though Beecher does not label these foreigners as the direct cause of illness, their presence disrupts the orderly "system and regularity" of housekeeping, leading American women to be "disheartened, discouraged, and ruined in health" (18). Throughout her *Treatise* Beecher turns the absence of good servants—at first a cause of infirmity—into a remedy; their lack gives middle-class women the opportunity to perform regular domestic labor that will revive their health. By implication, their self-regulated work at home would also keep "poverty-stricken foreigners" out of their homes. Curiously, then, the mother's ill health stems from the unruly subjects of her domestic empire—children and servants—who bring uncivilized wilderness and undomesticated foreignness into the home. The fear of disease and of invalidism that characterizes the American woman also serves as a metaphor for anxiety about foreignness within. The mother's domestic empire is at risk of contagion from the very subjects she must domesticate and civilize, her wilderness children and foreign servants, who ultimately infest both the home and the body of the mother.[18]

This reading of Beecher suggests new ways of understanding the intricate ways in which domestic discourse generates and relies on images of the foreign. On the one hand, domesticity's "habits of system and order" appear to anchor the home as a stable center against a fluctuating social world with expanding national borders; on the other, domesticity must be spatially and conceptually mobile to travel to the nation's far-flung frontiers. Beecher's use of Tocqueville's ark metaphor suggests the rootlessness and the self-enclosed mobility necessary for middle-class domesticity to redefine the meaning of habitation to make Euro-Americans feel at home in terrain in which they are initially the foreign ones. Domesticity inverts this relationship to create a home by rendering prior inhabitants alien and undomesticated and by implicitly nativizing newcomers. The empire of the mother thus shares the logic of the American empire; both follow a double compulsion to conquer and domesticate the foreign, thus incorporating and controlling a threatening foreignness within the borders of the home and the nation.

II

The imperial scope of domesticity was central to the work of Sarah Josepha Hale throughout her half-century editorship of the influential *Godey's Lady's Book*, as well as to her fiction and history writing. Hale has been viewed by some scholars as advocating a woman's sphere more thoroughly separate from male political concerns than Beecher did (Sklar 163; Douglas 51–54). This withdrawal seems confirmed by the refusal of *Godey's* even to mention the Civil War throughout its duration, much less take sides. Yet when Hale conflates the progress of women with the nation's Manifest Destiny in her history writing, other scholars have judged her as inconsistently moving out of woman's sphere into the male political realm.[19] Hale's conception of separate spheres, I will argue, is predicated on the imperial expansion of the nation. Although her writing as editor, essayist, and novelist focused on the interior spaces of the home, with ample advice on housekeeping, clothing, manners, and emotions, she gave equal and related attention to the expansion of female influence through her advocacy of female medical missionaries abroad and the colonization of Africa by former black slaves. Even though Hale seems to avoid the issue of slavery and race relations in her silence about the Civil War, in the 1850s her own conception of domesticity takes on a decidedly racial caste, exposing the intimate link between the separateness of gendered spheres and the effort to keep the races apart in separate national spheres.

In 1846, at the beginning of the Mexican War, Hale launched a campaign on the pages of *Godey's Lady's Book* to declare Thanksgiving Day a national holiday, a campaign she avidly pursued until Lincoln made the holiday official in 1863.[20] This effort typified the way in which Hale's map of woman's sphere overlaid national and domestic spaces; *Godey's* published detailed instructions and recipes for preparing the Thanksgiving feast, while it encouraged women readers to agitate for a nationwide holiday as a ritual of national expansion and unification. The power of Thanksgiving Day stemmed from its center in the domestic sphere; Hale imagined millions of families seated around the table at the same time, thereby unifying the vast and shifting space of the national domain through simultaneity in time. This domestic ritual, she wrote in 1852, would unite "our great nation, by its states and families from the St. John to the Rio Grande, from the Atlantic to the Pacific."[21] If the celebration of Thanksgiving unites individual families across regions and brings them together in an imagined collective space, Thanksgiving's continental scope endows each individual family gathering with national meaning. Furthermore, the Thanksgiving story commemorating the founding of New England—which in Hale's version makes no mention of Indians—could create a common history by nationalizing a regional myth of origins and imposing it on the territories most recently wrested away from Indians and Mexicans. Hale's campaign to transform Thanksgiving from a regional to a national holiday grew even fiercer at the advent of the Civil War. In 1859 she wrote, "If every state would join in Union Thanksgiving on the 24th of this month, would it not be a renewed pledge of love and loyalty to the Constitution of the United States?"[22] Thanksgiving Day, she hoped, could avert civil war. As a national holiday celebrated primarily in the home, Thanksgiving traverses broad geographic circuits to write a national history of origins, to colonize the Western territories, and to unite North and South.

The domestic ritual of Thanksgiving could expand and unify national borders only by also fortifying those borders against foreignness; for Hale, the nation's borders not only defined its geographical limits but also set apart nonwhites within the national domain. In Hale's fiction of the 1850s, Thanksgiving polices the domestic sphere by making black people, both free and enslaved, foreign to the domestic nation and denying them a home within America's expanding borders. In 1852 Hale reissued her novel, *Northwood*, which had launched her career in 1827, with a highly publicized chapter about a New Hampshire Thanksgiving dinner showcasing the values of the American republic to a skeptical British visitor. For the 1852 version Hale changed the subtitle from "A Tale of New England" to "Life North and South," to highlight new material she had added on slavery.[23] Pro-union yet against abolition, Hale advocated African colonization as the only means of preserving domestic unity by sending all blacks to settle in Africa and Christianize its inhabitants. Colonization in the 1850s had a two-pronged ideology, both to expel blacks to a separate national sphere and to expand U.S. power through the civilizing process; black Christian settlers become both outcasts from and agents for the American empire.[24]

Hale's 1852 *Northwood* ends with an appeal to use Thanksgiving Day as an occasion to collect money at all American churches "for the purpose of educating and colonizing free people of color and emancipated slaves" (408). This annual collection would contribute to "peaceful emancipation" as "every obstacle to the real freedom of America would be melted before the gushing streams of sympathy and charity" (408). While "sympathy," a sentiment associated with women's sphere, seems to extend to black slaves, the goal of sympathy in this passage is not to free them but to emancipate white America from their presence. Thanksgiving for Hale thus celebrates national cohesiveness around the domestic sphere by simultaneously rendering blacks within America foreign to the nation.

For Hale, colonization would not simply expel black people from American nationality, but it would also transform American slavery into a civilizing and domesticating mission. One of her Northern characters explains to the British visitor that "the destiny of America is to instruct the world, which we shall do, with the aid of our Anglo-Saxon brothers over the water. . . . Great Britain has enough to do at home and in the East Indies to last her another century. We have this country and Africa to settle and civilize" (167). When his listener is puzzled by the reference to Africa, he explains: "that is the greatest mission of our Republic, to train here the black man for his duties as a Christian, then free him and send him to Africa, there to plant Free States and organize Christian civilization" (168). The colonization of Africa becomes the goal of slavery by transforming it into the civilizing mission of global imperialism. Colonization thus not only banishes blacks from the domestic union, but, as the final sentence of *Northwood* proclaims, it proves that "the mission of American slavery is to Christianize Africa" (408).

In 1852 Hale published the novel *Liberia*, which begins where *Northwood* ends, with the settlement of Liberia by freed black slaves.[25] Seen by scholars as a retort to *Uncle Tom's Cabin*, it can also be read as the untold story of Stowe's novel, beginning where she ends, with its former black slaves immigrating to Africa.[26] Although the subtitle, "Mr. Peyton's Experiment," places colonization under the aegis of white males, the narrative turns colonization into a project emanating from woman's sphere in at least two directions. In its outward trajectory, the settlement of Liberia appears as an expansion of feminized domestic values. Yet domesticity is not only exported to civilize native Africans; the framing of the novel also makes African colonization necessary to the establishment of domesticity within America as exclusively white. While Hale writes that the purpose of the novel is to "show the advantages Liberia offers to the African," in so doing it construes all black people as foreign to American nationality by asserting that they must remain homeless within the United States. At the same time, Hale paints a picture of American imperialism as the embodiment of the feminine values of domesticity: "What other nation can point to a colony planted from such pure motives of charity; nurtured by the counsels and exertions of its most noble and self-denying statesmen and philanthropists; and sustained, from its feeble commencement up to a period of self-reliance and independence, from pure love of justice and humanity" (iv). In this passage, America is figured as a mother raising her baby, Africa, to maturity; the vocabulary of "purity," "charity," "self-denial," and "love" represents colonization as an expansion of the values of woman's separate sphere.

The narrative opens with a threat to American domesticity on two fronts. The last male of a distinguished Virginia family is on his deathbed, helpless to defend his plantation from a rumored slave insurrection; the women of the family, led by his wife Virginia, rally with the loyal slaves to defend their home from the insurrection that never occurs. Thus the novel opens with separate spheres gone awry, with the man of the family abed at home, while white women and black slaves play the roles of protectors and soldiers. While the ensuing plot to settle Liberia overtly rewards those slaves for their loyalty by giving them freedom and a homeland, it also serves to reinstate separate spheres and reestablish American domesticity as white.

When the narrative shifts to Africa, colonization has the effect not only of driving black slaves out of American nationhood but also of Americanizing that continent through domesticity. A key figure in the settlement is the slave Keziah, who has nursed the white plantation owners. She is the most responsive to Peyton's proposal for colonization because of her desire both to be free and to Christianize the natives. Her future husband, Polydore, more recently arrived from Africa and thus less "civilized," is afraid to return there because of his memory of native brutality and superstition. This couple represents two faces of enslaved Africans central to the white imagination of colonization: the degenerate heathen, represented by the man, and the redeemed Christian, represented by the woman. Keziah, however, can only become a fully domesticated woman at a geographic remove from American domesticity. When Keziah protects the plantation in Virginia, her maternal impulse is described as that of a wild animal—a "fierce lioness." Only in Africa can she become the domestic center of the new settlement, where she establishes a home that resembles Beecher's Christian neighborhood. Keziah builds a private home with fence and garden and civilizes her husband while expanding her domestic sphere to adopt native children and open a Christian school.

Keziah's domestication of herself and her surroundings in Africa can be seen as a part of the movement in the novel noted by Susan Ryan, in which the freed black characters are represented as recognizably American only at the safe distance of Africa ("Errand into Africa," 572). Once banished from the domestic sphere of American nationality, they can reproduce themselves for readers as American in a foreign terrain. The novel not only narrates the founding of Liberia as a story of colonization, but Hale's storytelling also colonizes Liberia as an imitation of America, replete with images of an open frontier, the *Mayflower*, and the planting of the American flag. A double narrative movement at once contracts American borders to exclude blacks from domestic space and simultaneously expands U.S. borders by recreating that domestic space in Africa. Thus the novel ends with a quotation that compares the Liberian settlers to the Pilgrims and represents them as part of a global expansion of the American nation:

> I do not doubt but that the whole continent of Africa will be regenerated, and I believe the Republic of Liberia will be the great instrument, in the hands of God, in working out this regeneration. The colony of Liberia has succeeded better than the colony of Plymouth did for the same period of time. And yet, in that little company which was wafted across the mighty ocean in the *May Flower*, we see the germs of this already colossal nation, whose feet are in the tropics, while her head reposes upon the snows of Canada. Her right hand she stretches over the Atlantic, feeding the millions of the Old World, and beckoning them to her shores, as a refuge from famine and oppression; and, at the same time, she stretches forth her left hand to the islands of the Pacific, and to the old empires of the East. (303)

In Hale's view both slavery and domesticity are necessary to the imperial mission; African slaves are brought to America to become Christianized and domesticated, but they cannot complete this potential transformation until they return to Africa.

Hale's writing makes race central to woman's sphere not only by excluding nonwhites from domestic nationalism, but also by seeing the capacity for domesticity as an innate defining characteristic of the Anglo-Saxon race. Reginald Horsman has shown how, by the 1840s, the meaning of Anglo-Saxonism had shifted from a historical understanding of the development of republican institutions to an essentialist definition of a single race that possesses an innate and unique capacity for self-government.[27] His analysis, however, limits this racial formation to the traditional male sphere of politics. Hale's *Woman's Record* (1853), a massive compendium of the history of women from Eve to the present, establishes woman's sphere as central to the racial discourse of Anglo-Saxonism; to her, the empire of the mother spawns the Anglo-Saxon nation and propels its natural inclination toward global power.[28] In her introduction to the fourth part of her volume on the present era, Hale represents America as manifesting the universal progress of women that culminates in the Anglo-Saxon race. To explain the Anglo-Saxon "mastery of the mind over Europe and Asia," she argues that

> if we trace out the causes of this superiority, they would center in the moral influence, which true religion confers on the female sex. . . . There is still a more wonderful example of this uplifting power of the educated female mind. It is only seventy-five years since the Anglo-Saxons in the New World became a nation, then numbering about three million souls. Now this people form the great American republic, with a population of twenty three millions; and the destiny of the world will soon be in their keeping! Religion is free; and the soul which woman always influences where God is worshipped in spirit and truth, is untrammeled by code, or creed, or caste. . . . The result before the world—a miracle of advancement, American mothers train their sons to be men. (564)

Hale here articulates the imperial logic of what has been called "republican motherhood," which ultimately posits the outward expansion of maternal influence beyond the home and the nation's borders.[29] The manifest destiny of the nation unfolds logically from the imperial reach of woman's influence emanating from her separate domestic sphere. Domesticity makes manifest the destiny of the Anglo-Saxon race, while Manifest Destiny becomes in turn the condition for Anglo-Saxon domesticity. For Hale domesticity has a dual effect on national expansion: it imagines the nation as a home delimited by race and propels the nation outward through the imperial reach of female influence.

Advocating domesticity's expansive mode, *Woman's Record* includes those nonwhite women who Hale understood as contributing to the spread of Christianity to colonized peoples. In the third volume, Hale designates as the most distinguished woman from 1500 to 1830 an American missionary to Burma, Ann Judson, a white American (152). The "Fourth Era" of *Woman's Record* focuses predominantly on American women as the apex of historical development. In contrast to the aristocratic accomplishment of English women, "in all that contributes to popular education and pure religious sentiment among the masses, the women of America are in advance of all others on the globe. To prove this we need only examine the list of American female missionaries, teachers, editors and authors of works instructive and educational, contained in this 'Record'" (564). While Anglo-Saxon men marched outward to conquer new lands, female influence had a complementary outward reach from within the domestic sphere.

For Hale, African colonization can be seen as part of the broader global expansion of woman's sphere. In 1853 Hale printed in *Godey's Lady's Book* "An Appeal to the American Christians on Behalf of the Ladies' Medical Missionary Society," in which she argued for the special need for women physicians abroad because they would have unique access to the bodies and souls of foreign women.[30] Her argument for the training of female medical missionaries both enlarges the field of white women's agency and feminizes the force of imperial power. She sees female medical missionaries as not only curing disease but also as raising the status of women abroad: "All heathen people have a high reverence for medical knowledge. Should they find Christian ladies accomplished in this science, would it not greatly raise the sex in the estimation of those nations, where one of the most serious impediments to moral improvement is the degradation and ignorance to which their females have been for centuries consigned?" (185). Though superior to heathen women in status, American women would accomplish their goal imagining gender as a common ground, which would give them special access to women abroad. As women they could be more effective imperialists, penetrating those interior colonial spaces, symbolized by the harem, that remain inaccessible to male missionaries:

> Vaccination is difficult of introduction among the people of the east, though suffering dreadfully from the ravages of small-pox. The American mission at Siam writes that thousands of children were, last year, swept away by this disease in the country around them. Female physicians could win their way among these poor children much easier than doctors of the other sex. Surely the ability of American women to learn and practice vaccination will not be questioned, when the more difficult art of inoculation was discovered by the women of Turkey, and introduced into Europe by an English woman! Inoculation is one of the greatest triumphs of remedial skill over a sure loathsome and deadly disease which the annals of Medical Art record. Its discovery belongs to women. I name it here to show that they are gifted with genius for the profession, and only need to be educated to excel in the preventive department.
>
> Let pious, intelligent women be fitly prepared, and what a mission-field for doing good would be opened! In India, China, Turkey, and all over the heathen world, they would, in their character of physicians, find access to the homes and harems where women dwell, and where the good seed sown

would bear an hundredfold, because it would take root in the bosom of the sufferer, and in the heart of childhood. (185)

In this passage the connections among women circulate in many directions, but Hale charts a kind of evolutionary narrative that places American women at the apex of development. Though inoculation was discovered by Turkish women, it can only return to Turkey to save Turkish children through the agency of English women transporting knowledge to Americans, who can then go to Turkey as missionaries and save women who could not save themselves or their children. While Hale is advocating that unmarried women be trained as missionaries, the needs of heathen women allow female missionaries to conquer their own domestic empire without reproducing biologically. Instead, American women are metaphorically cast as men in a crossracial union, as they sow seeds in the bosom of heathen women who will bear Christian children. Through the sentiment of female influence, women physicians will transform heathen harems into Christian homes.

My reading of Hale suggests that the concept of female influence so central to domestic discourse and at the heart of sentimental ethos is underwritten by and abets the imperial expansion of the nation. While the empire of the mother advocated retreat from the world–conquering enterprises of men, this renunciation promised a more thorough kind of world conquest. The empire of the mother shared with the American empire a logical structure and key contradiction: both sought to encompass the world outside their borders; yet this same outward movement contributed to and relied on the contraction of the domestic sphere to exclude persons conceived of as racially foreign within those expanding national boundaries.

III

Understanding the imperial reach of domesticity and its relation to the foreign should help remap the critical terrain on which women's domestic fiction has been constructed. We can chart the broader international and national contexts in which unfold narratives of female development that at first glance seem anchored in local domestic spaces. We can see how such narratives imagine domestic locations in complex negotiation with the foreign. To take a few well-known examples from the 1850s, Susan Warner's *The Wide, Wide World* sends its heroine to Scotland, while the world of Maria Cummins's *The Lamplighter* encompasses India, Cuba, the American West, and Brazil. In E. D. E. N. Southworth's *The Hidden Hand*, the resolution of multiple domestic plots in Virginia relies on the participation of the male characters in the Mexican War, while the geographic coordinates of *Uncle Tom's Cabin* extend not only to Africa at the end, but also to Haiti and Canada throughout.[31] Such a remapping would involve more than just seeing the external settings anew; it would turn inward to the privileged space of the domestic novel—the interiority of the female subject—to find traces of foreignness that must be domesticated or expunged. How does this struggle with foreignness within woman's sphere shape the interiority of female subjectivity, the empire of the affections and the heart? While critics such as Gillian Brown, Richard Brodhead, and Nancy Armstrong have taught us how domestic novels represent women as model bourgeois subjects, my remapping would explore how domestic novels produce the racialized national subjectivity of the white middle-class woman in contested international spaces.[32]

Many domestic novels open at physical thresholds, such as windows or doorways, that problematize the relation between interior and exterior; the home and the female self appear fragile and threatened from within and without by foreign forces. These novels then explore the breakdown of boundaries between internal and external spaces, between the domestic and the foreign, as they struggle to renegotiate and stabilize their boundaries. This negotiation often takes place not only within the home, but also within the heroine. The narrative of female self-discipline that is so central to the domestic novel might be viewed as a kind of civilizing process in which the woman plays the role of both civilizer and savage. Gerty in *The Lamplighter*, for example, like Capitola in *The Hidden Hand*, first appears as an uncivilized street urchin, a heathen unaware of Christianity, whose anger is viewed as a "dark infirmity" (63) and whose unruly nature is in need of domesticating. We later find out that she was born in Brazil to the daughter of a ship captain, who was killed by malaria, the "inhospitable southern disease, which takes the stranger for its victim" (321).[33] To become the sovereign mother of her own domestic empire, Gerty must become her own first colonial subject and purge herself of both her origin in a diseased, uncivilized terrain and of the female anger identified with that "dark" realm. This split between the colonizer and the colonized, seen here within one female character, appears in *Uncle Tom's Cabin* racially externalized onto Eva and Topsy.[34]

My point is that, where the domestic novel appears most turned inward to the private sphere of female interiority, we often find the subjectivity of the heroine scripted by narratives of nation and empire. Even at the heart of *The Wide, Wide World*, a novel understood to be thoroughly closeted in interior space, where the heroine disciplines herself through reading and prayer, her favorite book is the popular biography of George Washington, the father of the nation. Her own journey to live with Scottish relatives can be seen as a feminized reenactment of the American revolution against the British empire. Similarly, in *The Hidden Hand*, the most inner recess of woman's sphere is conjoined with the male sphere of imperial conquest. While the American men in the novel are invading Mexico, in Virginia, a bandit, significantly named "Black Donald," invades the heroine's chamber and threatens to rape her. To protect the sanctity of her home and her own chastity, Capitola performs a founding national narrative of conquest. She drops the rapist through a trap door in her bedroom into a deep pit dug by the original owner in order to trick the Indian inhabitants into selling their land. The domestic heroine thus reenacts the originating gesture of imperial appropriation to protect the borders of her domestic empire and the inviolability of the female self.

Feminist criticism of *Uncle Tom's Cabin* has firmly established that the empire of the mother in Stowe's novel extends beyond the home to the national arena of antislavery politics. This expansive movement of female influence has an international dimension that helps separate gendered spheres coalesce in the imperial expansion of the nation by redrawing domestic borders against the foreign. In light of my reading of Hale's *Liberia*, we might remap the critical terrain of Stowe's novel to ask how its delineation of domestic space, as both familial and national, relies on and propels the colonization of Africa by the novel's free black characters. Rather than just focusing on their expulsion at the end of the novel, we might locate, in Toni Morrison's terms, the "Africanist presence" throughout the text.[35] Africa appears as both an imperial outpost and a natural embodiment of woman's sphere, a kind of feminized utopia, that is strategically posed as an alternative to Haiti, which hovers as a menacing image of black revolutionary agency. The idea of African colonization does not simply emerge at the end as a racist failure of Stowe's political imagination; rather, colonization underwrites the racial politics of the domestic imagination. The "Africanist presence" throughout *Uncle Tom's Cabin* is intimately bound to the expansionist logic of domesticity itself. *Manifest Domesticity* turns an imperial nation into a home by producing and colonizing specters of the foreign that lurk inside and outside its ever shifting borders.

Notes

1   Influential studies of this paradigm by historians and literary critics include Barbara Welter, "The Cult of True Womanhood," *American Quarterly* 18, no. 1 (1966): 151–74; Kathryn Kish Sklar, *Catharine Beecher: A Study in American Domesticity* (New Haven, Conn.: Yale University Press, 1973); Nancy F. Cott, *The Bonds of Womanhood: "Woman's Sphere" in New England, 1780–1835* (New Haven, Conn.: Yale University Press, 1977); Ann Douglas, *The Feminization of American Culture* (New York: Knopf, 1977); Nina Baym, *Woman's Fiction: A Guide to Novels by and about Women in America, 1820–1870* (Ithaca, N.Y.: Cornell University Press, 1978); Mary P. Ryan, *Cradle of the Middle Class: The Family in Oneida County, New York, 1790–1865* (Cambridge: Cambridge University Press, 1981); and Ryan, *The Empire of the Mother: American Writing about Domesticity, 1830 to 1860* (New York: Haworth, 1982); Mary Kelley, *Private Woman, Public Stage: Literary Domesticity in Nineteenth-Century America* (New York: Oxford University Press, 1984); Jane Tompkins, *Sensational Designs: The Cultural Work of American Fiction, 1790–1860* (Oxford: Oxford University Press, 1985); Gillian Brown, *Domestic Individualism: Imagining Self in Nineteenth-Century America* (Berkeley: University of California Press, 1990); and the essays in *The Culture of Sentiment: Race, Gender, and Sentimentality in Nineteenth-Century America*, ed. Shirley Samuels (New York: Oxford University Press, 1992). See also the useful review essay by Linda K. Kerber, "Separate Spheres, Female Worlds, Woman's Place: The Rhetoric of Women's History," *Journal of American History* 75, no. 1 (1988): 9–39. Subsequent references are cited parenthetically in the text.

2   On the etymology of the word *domestic* and its relation to colonialism see Karen Tranberg Hansen, ed. *African Encounters with Domesticity* (New Brunswick, N.J.: Rutgers University Press, 1992), 2–23; Anne McClintock, *Imperial Leather: Race, Gender and Sexuality in the Colonial Conquest* (New York: Routledge, 1995), 31–36.

3   Despite Tompkins's well-known debate with Ann Douglas, both critics rely on imperial rhetoric; while Tompkins applauds the imperialist impulse of sentimentalism, Douglas derides sentimental writers for their voracious reach that extends as far as the "colonization of heaven" and the "domestication of death" (240–72).

4   Even recent revisionist studies that situate woman's sphere in relation to racial and class hierarchies often overlook the international context in which these divisions evolve. In the important essays in *Culture of Sentiment,* for example, many of the racialized configurations of domesticity under discussion rely on a foreign or imperial dimension that remains unanalyzed. To take a few examples, Laura Wexler's analysis of Hampton Institute makes no mention of its founding by influential missionaries to Hawaii ("Tender Violence: Literary

Eavesdropping, Domestic Fiction, and Educational Reform," 9–38); Karen Halttunen's analysis of a murder trial revolves around the unclear identity of a white woman's foreign Spanish or Cuban lover ("'Domestic Differences': Competing Narratives of Womanhood in the Murder Trial of Lucretia Chapman," 39–57); Lynn Wardley ties domesticity's obsession with detail to West African fetishism ("Relic, Fetish, Femmage: The Aesthetics of Sentiment in the Work of Stowe," 203–20). Several essays note the comparison of slavery to the oriental harem, including Carolyn Karcher on Lydia Maria Child's anti-slavery fiction ("Rape, Murder, and Revenge in Slavery's Pleasant Homes: Lydia Maria Child's Antislavery Fiction and the Limits of Genre," 58–72), and Joy Kasson's analysis of Hirams's *The Greek Slave* ("Narratives of the Female Body: *The Greek Slave*," 172–90). The only essay to treat the imperial dimensions of domesticity is Lora Romero's "Vanishing Americans: Gender, Empire, and New Historicism" (115–27).

5   Thomas R. Hietala, *Manifest Design: Anxious Aggrandizement in Late Jacksonian America* (Ithaca, N.Y.: Cornell University Press, 1985).

6   *Cherokee Nation v. the State of Georgia*, in *Major Problems in American Foreign Policy: Documents and Essays*, ed. Thomas G. Paterson, 2 vols. (Lexington, Mass.: Heath, 1989), 1:202.

7   Qtd. in Walter LaFeber, *The American Age: United States Foreign Policy at Home and Abroad since 1750* (New York: Norton, 1989), 112.

8   Qtd. in George B. Forgie, *Patricide in the House Divided: A Psychological Interpretation of Lincoln and His Age* (New York: Norton, 1979), 107–8.

9   On popular fiction of the Mexican War, see Robert W. Johannsen, *To the Halls of the Montezumas: The Mexican War in the American Imagination* (New York: Oxford, 1985), 175–204.

10 Sarah Josepha Hale, "Editor's Table," *Godey's Lady's Book*, January 1852, 88.

11 From "The Social Condition of Woman," *North American Review* 42 (1836): 513; qtd. in Annette Kolodny, *The Land before Her: Fantasy and Experience of the American Frontiers, 1630–1860* (Chapel Hill: University of North Carolina Press, 1984), 166.

12 Catharine Beecher, *A Treatise on Domestic Economy* (Boston: Marsh, Capen, Lyon and Webb, 1841), 144. Subsequent references are cited parenthetically in the text.

13 Kathryn Kish Sklar is one of the few scholars to consider Beecher's domestic ideology in terms of nation building. She analyzes the *Treatise* as appealing to gender as a common national denominator, and as using domesticity as a means to national unity to counterbalance mobility and conflicts based on class and region. She overlooks, however, that this vision of gender as a fulcrum for national unity is predicated on a vision of that nation's imperial role (151–67). Jenine Abboushi Dallal analyzes the imperial dimensions of Beecher's domestic ideology in contrast to the domestic rhetoric of Melville's imperial adventure narratives in "The Beauty of Imperialism: Emerson, Melville, Flaubert, and Al-Shidyac" (Ph.D. diss., Harvard University, 1996), 60–105.

14 John L. O'Sullivan, "The Great Nation of Futurity," in *Major Problems in American Foreign Policy*, ed. Paterson, 1:241.

15 Catharine Beecher and Harriet Beecher Stowe, *The American Woman's Home* (Hartford: J.B. Ford, 1869), 458–59.

16 Karen Sánchez-Eppler, "Raising Empires Like Children: Race, Nation, and Religious Education," *American Literary History* 8 (1996): 399–425; Ann Laura Stoller, *Race and the Education of Desire: Foucault's History of Sexuality and the Colonial Order of Things* (Durham, N.C.: Duke University Press, 1995), 137–64.

17 Although the cleanliness and orderliness of the home promises to make American women healthier, Beecher also blames the lack of outdoor exercise for American women's frailty, as though the problematic space outside the home, the foreign, can both cause and cure those "difficulties peculiar to American women."

18 This generalized anxiety about contamination of the domestic sphere by children may stem from the circulation of stories by missionaries who expressed fear of their children being raised by native servants or being too closely identified with native culture. These stories would have circulated both in popular mission tracts and in middle-class women's magazines, such as *Godey's* and *Mother's Magazine*. See, for example, Stoller, *Race and the Education of Desire*, and Patricia Grimshaw, *Paths of Duty: American Missionary Wives in Nineteenth-Century Hawaii* (Honolulu: University of Hawaii Press, 1989), 154–78. The licentiousness of men was also seen as a threat to women's health within the home. In a piece on "Life on the Rio Grande," for example, celebrating the opening of public schools in Galveston, Texas, Sarah Josepha Hale quotes a military officer who warns that "liberty is ever degenerating into license, and man is prone to abandon his sentiments and follow his passions. It is woman's high mission, her prerogative and duty, to counsel, to sustain—as to control him." On the borderlands, women have the role of civilizing savagery in their own homes, where men's passions appear as the foreign force to be colonized. See Hale, "Life on the Rio Grande," *Godey's*, April 1847, 177.

In general, domesticity is usually seen as an ideology that develops in middle-class urban centers (and, as Sklar shows, in contrast to European values) and then is exported outward to the frontier and empire, where it meets challenges and must adapt. It remains to be studied how domestic discourse might develop out of the confrontation with foreign cultures in what has been called the "contact zone" of frontier and empire.

19 Nina Baym, "Onward Christian Women: Sarah J. Hale's History of the World," *New England Quarterly* 63 (1990): 249–70.

20 Sarah J. Hale, "Editor's Table," *Godey's Lady's Book*, January 1847, 53.

21 Sarah J. Hale, *Godey's Lady's Book*, November 1852, 303.

22 Qtd. in Ruth E. Finley, *The Lady of Godey's: Sarah Josepha Hale* (Philadelphia: Lippincott, 1931), 199.

23 Sarah J. Hale, *Northwood; Or, Life North and South: Showing the True Character of Both* (New York: H. Long and Brother, 1852). See her 1852 preface, "A Word

with the Reader," on revisions of the 1827 edition. Subsequent references are cited parenthetically in the text.

24   On the white ideological framework of African colonization, see George M. Fredrickson, *The Black Image in the White Mind: The Debate on Afro-American Character and Destiny, 1817–1914* (New York: Harper and Row, 1971), 6–22, 110–17; Susan M. Ryan, "Errand into Africa: Colonization and Nation Building in Sarah J. Hale's *Liberia,*" *New England Quarterly* 68 (1995): 558–83. Subsequent references are cited parenthetically in the text.

25   Sarah J. Hale, *Liberia; Or Mr. Peyton's Experiments* (1853; Upper Saddle River, N.J.: Gregg, 1968).

26   On *Liberia* as a conservative rebuff to Stowe, see Thomas F. Gossett, *Uncle Tom's Cabin and American Culture* (Dallas: Southern Methodist University Press, 1985), 235–36.

27   Reginald Horsman, *Race and Manifest Destiny: The Origins of American Racial Anglo-Saxonism* (Cambridge, Mass.: Harvard University Press, 1981), 62–81.

28   Sarah J. Hale, *Woman's Record* (New York: Harper, 1853). Subsequent references are cited parenthetically in the text.

29   Linda K. Kerber, *Women of the Republic: Intellect and Ideology in Revolutionary America* (Chapel Hill: University of North Carolina Press, 1980).

30   Sarah J. Hale, "An Appeal to the American Christians on Behalf of the Ladies' Medical Missionary Society," *Godey's Lady's Book*, March 1852, 185–88. Subsequent references are cited parenthetically in the text.

31   Susan Warner, *The Wide, Wide World* (1850; New York: Feminist Press, 1987); Maria Susanna Cummins, *The Lamplighter* (1854; New Brunswick, N.J.: Rutgers University Press, 1988); E. D. E. N. Southworth, *The Hidden Hand; Or, Capitola the Madcap*, ed. Joanne Dobson (1859; New Brunswick, N.J.: Rutgers University Press, 1988); Harriet Beecher Stowe, *Uncle Tom's Cabin* (1852; New York: Viking Penguin, 1981). Subsequent references are cited parenthetically in the text.

32   Nancy Armstrong, *Desire and Domestic Fiction: A Political History of the Novel* (New York: Oxford University Press, 1987); Brown, *Domestic Individualism*; Richard Brodhead, "Sparing the Rod: Discipline and Fiction in Antebellum America," in *The New American Studies: Essays from Representations*, ed. Philip Fisher (Berkeley: University of California Press, 1991), 141–70.

33   On the male characters' involvement in imperial enterprises in India in *The Lamplighter*, see Susan Castellanos, "Masculine Sentimentalism and the Project of Nation-Building," paper presented at the Nineteenth-Century Women Writers in the Twenty-First Century conference, Trinity College, May–June 1996.

34   On this split see Elizabeth Young, "Topsy-Turvy: Civil War and *Uncle Tom's Cabin*," chapter 1 of *Disarming the Nation: Women's Writing and the American Civil War* (Chicago: University of Chicago Press, 1999), 24–68.

35   Toni Morrison, *Playing in the Dark: Whiteness and the Literary Imagination* (Cambridge, Mass.: Harvard University Press, 1992), 6.

C. L. R. James, *Moby-Dick*, and the Emergence

of Transnational American Studies

Donald E. Pease

I publish my protest with my book on Melville because, as I have shown, the
book as written is part of my experience. It is also a claim before the American
people, the best claim I can put forward, that my desire to become a citizen is not
a frivolous one. —C. L. R. James, *Manners, Renegades, and Castaways*

On June 10, 1952, men in black suits from the Immigration and Naturalization Services abruptly interrupted C. L. R. James's research for the book he
intended to write that summer on Herman Melville. They removed him to
Ellis Island, where he was detained, awaiting deportation hearings for the
next four months. As warrant for his internment, the state agents cited the
McCarran-Walter Act, which, despite the fact that it was passed two years
after James had completed the examinations qualifying him for citizenship,
would nevertheless ultimately become the juridical instrument invoked by
the state to justify James's detainment.[1]

At a time in which the United States was increasingly dependent on third-
world labor, the McCarran-Walter Act put into place regulations concerning
the legal and economic conditions for citizenship that ratified neocolonial
distinctions. The bill authorized INS officials to apply different combinations
of rules and norms for the purpose of sorting immigrants into economic and
political classifications. The taxonomy to which INS officials subordinated
their clientele invoked racialized categories designed to reflect extant U.S.
geopolitical alliances and to expand U.S. markets at home and abroad.

The phrases whereby the bill distinguished immigrants that the state could
exclude on political grounds from migrants whose labor it could exploit
included within the former category of immigrants "any alien who has engaged or has had purpose to engage in activities 'prejudicial to the public
interest' or 'subversive to the national security.' "[2] In addition to granting the
state the right to expel subversives, the bill also called for a careful screening of
persons seeking to reside in the United States and installed cultural literacy as
one of the criteria whereby the state might determine whether or not "they"
were adaptable to the American way of life.

Although the state had kept James under scrutiny from the time of his formal application to become a legal resident in 1938, its designation of him as a subversive brought about a drastic change in his juridical relationship to the category of U.S. citizenship. The temporal flexibility invested in the phrase "who has engaged or who has had the purpose to engage in activities" subversive to the national security granted the INS powers of retroactive jurisdiction over the entire period of James's U.S. residency.

United States citizenship was grounded in the legal fiction whereby an individual citizen was construed as both legislator, the "I" who was the sender of the law, and subject, the "you" who was its addressee. By way of its derecognition of James's personhood, the state denied him the first-person pronominal powers necessary to support and defend his civil and political liberties. After the state pronounced him a security threat, James's legal sub-jectivity underwent demotion to the status of "you." As its secondary ad-dressee, James was subject to the law's powers of enforcement, but he was no longer recognized as the subject of its norms.[3]

James's loss of the power to speak as "I" also deauthorized the testifying phrases through which he could convey his claims before a court and invali-dated his interlocutory privileges within the civil society.[4] The state's restric-tion of his pronominal identifications to the "you" who must obey the law had also disallowed James membership in the "we" of "we the people" whose sovereign will the state was understood to represent. "You" could never become "we" because "you" named the subversive whom the state had refused the rights of dialogue with or as an "I."[5]

Jean-François Lyotard has proposed the term *differend* to describe the kind of juridical dilemma in which James was thereby embroiled. Lyotard defines a differend as a "case of conflict between at least two parties, that cannot be equitably resolved for lack of a rule of judgement applicable to both parties."[6] Because the damage for which James sought legal remedy originated with the legislation whose rules the courts were required to render applicable to their decisions, the judgment James sought exceeded the appellate courts' juridical authority. James could not appeal the state's ruling without calling for the repeal of the McCarran bill. But James could neither organize nor participate in a movement calling for the repeal of the McCarran bill without providing the state with an example of the activity for which he was accused. Moreover, any U.S. citizen who came to James's defense was liable to prose-cution for collaborating with a subversive.

In an effort to supply a rule of judgment the courts lacked, James produced an interpretation of *Moby-Dick* underwritten by a juridical standard through which he intended to define the illegality of the McCarran legislation and to represent as well the wrong against him that the state had perpetrated on McCarran's authority. At the time James published *Mariners, Renegades, and Castaways: The Story of Herman Melville and the World We Live In*, Americanist critics had already placed *Moby-Dick* into service as a weapon in the Cold War. In their readings of it as a prototypical national narrative, these critics deployed the United States' opposition to the Soviet Union to justify neo-colonialist policies in James's native Trinidad and elsewhere in the hemisphere. The United States bore the responsibility, these interpreters argued, to colonize life worlds—at home and abroad—as an effort to oppose the Soviet Union's anticipated colonization of them.

In a reading of *Moby-Dick* he published four years earlier, the literary critic Richard Chase had provided James's usage of the novel with an academic warrant. Chase represented Melville's novel as the foundational fiction of the Cold War state. Chase fostered an allegorical understanding of *Moby-Dick* that posited Ahab's monomania as the signifier of the totalitarian Other in opposition to which Ishmael's Americanness was defined, elaborated on, and defended. While subsequent interpreters would introduce at times ingenious variations on this theme, the essentialized opposition between Ishmael and Ahab would dominate readings of the novel in the field of American literary studies for the next fifty years.[7]

James believed that Americanist interpretations of *Moby-Dick* like Chase's corroborated the emergency powers of the national security state whose hegemony the field of American literary studies had indirectly legitimated. Engaging himself in the construction of a counterhegemony, James confirmed the prevailing understanding of Ahab as a "totalitarian type" (16). But after arguing that the security state had put into place the totalitarian rule it purported to oppose, he also generalized this type to include Ishmael, whom he described as "an intellectual Ahab" (44), as well as the members of the McCarran committee and the administrators of the national security state. As justification for this extension of the applicability of the type, James cited the administrators' individual and collective failure to repeal the state's emergency powers as signs of their complicity with Ahab's totalitarian rule.

In his efforts to delegitimize the state's emergency powers, James discriminated the people that the McCarran legislation presumed to represent—whom he correlated with Ahab's officers—from those who—like Ahab's crew—were its potential victims. James associated the emergency powers of the state with Ahab's transgression of his duly constituted authority and offered the following contrary proposition as the theme the book allegorized: "How the society of free individualism would give birth to totalitarianism and be unable to defend itself against it" (60).[8]

Correlating his experience with the INS authorities on Ellis Island to his reading of an exemplary national classic, James devised a signifying practice that was in one of its aspects a hermeneutic exercise and in another a juridical appeal. In the process of working on the book while detained on Ellis Island, James fashioned these discrepant facets into a personal memoir allowing him to come to terms with the ordeal he underwent there.

Stuart Hall has remarked on the juridical dimension of James's Melville book by recasting it as an imaginary conversation with an INS officer: "As a part of his defense, he made a wonderfully Jamesian gesture," Hall explains. "He attempted to present *Mariners, Renegades, and Castaways* as testimony to the fact that he was a much better American than the immigration authorities. It was as though he were saying, 'You do not understand your greatest artist, Melville, and I do. How can you expel me for un-American activities when I am telling you that next to Shakespeare, here is the greatest use of the English language? It is because you do not understand what your own author is telling you that you can expel me. You should welcome me—not throw me out.' "[9]

Hall's account is valuable for its discrimination of the civil liberties to which the state had legally denied James access from the cultural and political practices through which James continued to perform his citizenship. Hall's representation of this exchange between James and an INS officer communicates James's belief that U.S. citizenship be understood as the effect of disparate activities within a contested terrain for which the people rather than the state should act as arbiter. Hall has also usefully discerned the compensatory powers of James's interpretation, its capacity to provide imaginary restoration of the civic prerogatives the state had nullified.

While Hall's imaginary scenario underscores James's continued practice of a cultural form of U.S. citizenship, however, it overlooks the political and juridical dimensions of James's quandary. Moreover, Hall's depiction of James's Melville book as the symbolic gesture demonstrating the superiority of James's cultural literacy has ignored the irrelevance of this script to the state's absolute control over the writer's social destiny. Had he conducted his reading of *Moby-Dick* simply as evidence of his fluency in the literary idiom reproductive of the state's cultural capital, James would have indirectly legitimated INS policies. James's decision to continue the project the state had interrupted cannot be ascertained apart from the work's relation to his untenable legal position.

The state's representation of James as a security threat placed him outside the state's protection. Because he lacked any other form of secure placement, James's writing became for him a resolutely physical exercise. It provided James with a way corporeally to inhabit and keep record of his material presence within a space the state had defined as a geography for the bodily excluded. As he resumed daily the practice of writing, the role of Melville interpreter resubjectivized a Jamesian body otherwise denied any position the state was obliged to recognize. As the means whereby he disputed the state's authority, James's interpretation of Melville also materialized a site quite literally external to the state's boundaries.

Unable to argue against the McCarran legislation in his own name, James advanced his interpretation on the authority of figures that he described as the disavowed "heroes" of Moby-Dick. "It is clear," James remarks in explaining what led to their disavowal, "that Melville intends to make the crew the real heroes of his book, but he is afraid of criticism" (20). James referred one source of Melville's fear to the negative response he anticipated to narrating the crew's revolt against the Pequod's captain. After "Ahab had stated that the purpose of the voyage was different from that for which they had signed," James stipulated the rationale for the heroic action that Melville was afraid to narrate: "The men were entitled to revolt and to take possession of the ship themselves" (14).

James's decision to write about Moby-Dick from the standpoint of the figures Melville had felt prohibited from depicting as its heroes required that he position himself in resistance to what had restricted Melville's freedom of expression. Assuming the stance of the bodily relay required for the transmission of the mariners', renegades', and castaways' discontinued narratives, James thereafter interpreted Moby-Dick as Melville's previously unnarratable intentionality.

In accomplishing the intention Melville could not, James devised a series of interlocking homologies that respectively correlated: the criticism Melville feared with the violence that the state had directed against James's person; Ahab's exceeding his duly constituted powers with the state's emergency powers; mariners, renegades, and castaways with the change in legal status that the national people might undergo should the state decide to deprive them of their rights; and the Pequod's crew with his fellow detainees on Ellis

Island. James thereafter triggered the undischarged social energy that lay dormant within this relay with the proposal that the mariners' belated right to legal remedy be construed as a kind of legal precedent for the repeal of the McCarran legislation.

Mariners put into place a multilayered strategy. It produced a frame of intelligibility that supplied James with the categories and themes required to challenge the findings of the McCarran legislation, with the pronominal rights of an interpreting "I," and with an interpretive object through which to express his grievances against the state. As the continuation of the activity James had undertaken at the time of the state's forcible resettlement, the book was construable as the proximate cause for the state's action as well as documentation of the violence the state had exerted against his person. James's interpretation of Melville brought this example of his activities before the court of public opinion and invited its readers to decide on the justice of the state's actions.

In an effort to respond to the layered dimensions of James's project, I shall divide the following remarks into sections devoted respectively to a consideration of his engagement with the Cold War state and of how James's means of engagement implicated the past and the future(s) of American studies.

Taking Exception to U.S. Exceptionalism

The tradition of the oppressed teaches us that "the state of emergency" in which we live is not the exception but the rule.—Walter Benjamin, "Theses on the Philosophy of History"

Before its passage into law, the McCarran-Walter Act required the public's consent to its construction of subversives as exceptions to the state's democratic norms. McCarran solicited the public's acquiescence with declarations like the following, in which he claimed that the threat immigrants posed to the sovereignty of the national borders had precipitated a state of emergency: "Our entire immigration system has been so weakened as to make it often impossible for our country to protect its security in this black era of fifth-column infiltration and cold warfare with the ruthless masters of the Kremlin. . . . The time has long since passed when we can afford to open our borders indiscriminately to give unstinting hospitality to any person whose purpose, whose ideological goal, is to overthrow our institutions and replace them with the evil oppression of totalitarianism."[10]

Because the McCarran-Walter Act's antidemocratic measures openly violated more or less agreed upon political norms, it exposed a political paradox that, while foundational to the liberal state, was exacerbated throughout the Cold War. Within a liberal democracy it is the citizens who are sovereign. They accord certain powers to the state in return for the protection, education, and administration of a territorially bound national community. Because the state derives its powers from the sovereign will of the citizens, the state's actions can be construed as legitimate only when endowed with the prior consent of the sovereign will of the people. Due to the incompatible registers—the state's and the people's—in which political sovereignty operates, however, no political action can ever fully conform to this condition.[11]

Never fully authorized at the moment of its enactment, a political action always lacks the legitimacy that can only be conferred retroactively with the invocation of standards, norms, and rationales "incompletely thematized and consented to at its inception." The sovereign will of the people is, on the one hand, presumed to have already been given expression and, on the other, construed to entail a consensual process that must continually be accomplished. The interval in between a political action and the sovereign consent required to legitimate it discloses an "element of arbitrariness that cannot be eliminated from political life" (Connolly, *Pluralization*, 139).

The arbitrariness refers to the temporal lag in between the enactment of a policy like the McCarran Act and the people's recognition of the act as representative of their will. Although McCarran represented the bill's measures as the reflection of the citizenry's already declared consensus, the people the McCarran bill presumed to represent did not yet exist. The effort to afford the bill the appearance of representing a national consensus led to its affiliation with the discourse of U.S. exceptionalism. In representing the McCarran-Walter Act as an execution of the popular will purportedly expressed in that discourse, the legislators proposed that the public be understood to have already granted their consent to that bill's mandates.

United States exceptionalism constituted a political doctrine as well as a regulatory ideal assigned the task of defining, supporting, and transmitting the U.S. national identity. Throughout the Cold War, the state invoked the doctrine of exceptionalism to validate its emergency power to produce exceptions to democratic norms. What the doctrine declared exceptional in the U.S. political economy referred to institutions—class antagonism, totalitarian rule, a colonial empire—whose putative absence from the U.S. political economy provided the state with warrant to except exponents of such institutions from the national community.[12]

Scholars in the disciplines of American literature and history presupposed exceptionality as the normative framework guiding their interpretation and transmission of the national culture. The field of American studies promoted U.S. exceptionalism as the basis for the institutionalization of the American Studies Association in 1950. "It was this interest in American Exceptionalism," Janice Radway has recently noted, "that led to the desire for an interdisciplinary method that would be equal to the notion of American culture conceived as a unified whole, a whole that manifested itself as a distinctive set of properties and themes in all things American, whether individuals, institutions or cultural products."[13]

In the writings of the so-called consensus historians—Arthur Schlesinger, Daniel Boorstin, and Louis Hartz—the state discovered the means whereby it could secure retroactive consent for its exceptions. In stipulating the absence from the American past of the class system or the precapitalist colonial formations, which they described as the preconditions for totalitarian communism, these architects of U.S. exceptionalism provided the state with a historical justification for the production of "un-Americans" and for the latter's removal from the U.S. political order. Observing that Tocqueville had found U.S. political society exceptional in lacking the feudal traditions that had precipitated the violent confrontations in France's moment of transition, Louis Hartz advanced the claim that the absence of class conflict from a liberal capitalist order had rendered impossible the emergence of socialism within U.S. territorial borders. "One of the central characteristics of a nonfeudal society is that it lacks a genuine revolutionary tradition," Hartz noted approvingly. "And this being the case, it lacks also a tradition of reaction: lacking Robespierre, it lacks Maistre, lacking Sydney, it lacks Charles II."[14]

Richard Chase indicated the contribution American literature offered the emergency state when, in the preface to his Melville book, he explicitly affiliated its "purpose" with the effort to disassociate the American studies movement from the political radicalism of its earliest practitioners. Whereas C. L. R. James numbered Frederick Douglass, Lydia Marie Childs, José Martí, Randolph Bourne, Richard Wright, and Granville Hicks among the precursors for his scholarly project, Chase described that entire lineage as representative of the "progressive liberalism" whose practices he would except from American literary history. Chase's "purpose" was

to contribute a book on Melville to a movement which may be described (once again) as a new liberalism—that newly invigorated secular thought at the dark center of the twentieth century which . . . now begins to ransom liberalism from the ruinous sell-outs, failures, and defeats of the thirties. The new liberalism must justify its claims over the old liberalism. It must present a vision of life capable, by a continuous act of imaginative criticism, of avoiding the old mistakes: the facile ideas of progress and "social realism," the disinclination to examine human motives, the indulgence of wish-fulfilling rhetoric, the belief that historical reality is merely a question of economic or ethical values, the idea that literature should participate directly in the economic liberation of the masses, the equivocal relationship to communist totalitarianism and power politics. (vii)

While the purpose Chase describes in this passage would suggest an academic struggle between more or less equivalently empowered academics, the phrasing with which he concludes the passage—"the equivocal relationship to communist totalitarianism and power politics"—echoes rhetoric that the McCarran legislation had instrumentalized to justify its deportation of scholars like C. L. R. James. The legal apparatus for surveillance the Cold War state had recently put into place deployed similar language when it purged the American studies movement of members in political solidarity with the "progressive tradition" that Chase had repudiated.

In providing the doctrine of U.S. exceptionalism with the coordinated rationalities of literary interpretation and consensus history, the field of American studies had indirectly legitimated the McCarran legislation. Both disciplines produced what might be called a facilitating retroactivity for the construction of exceptions to the Americanist creed of tolerance for dissent and democratic inclusiveness. In its characterization of C. L. R. James as a dangerous subversive, the INS depended on the discourse of exceptionalism as a tacit warrant.

The McCarran-Walter bill could be construed as legitimate only if it reflected the prior consent of the people's sovereign will. McCarran and Walter solicited that consent by fashioning the historical absences U.S. historians had added to the master narrative of U.S. exceptionalism into grounds for their exclusion of subversives and aliens. In supplying the illusion that the unique conditions of the national history had already mandated the McCarran Act's exceptions to democratic inclusiveness, the discourse of exceptionalism closed the temporal gap in between the people that the act presumed to represent and the people constituted out of this legislation.

Instead of authorizing the reading of *Moby-Dick* that had declared Ahab's totalitarianism an exception to forms of democratic governance, James proposed that the McCarran-Walter Act continued Ahab's form of governance. In his revisionist reading, James focused on three figures who did not survive the wreck of the Pequod. Specifically, James's reading singled out Queequeg, the South Sea Islander, Tashtego, the Gay Head Indian from Massachusetts, and the African Giant Daggoo.

In the following passage, James associates the three harpooners with his fellow detainees on Ellis Island:

> This is my final impression. The meanest mariners, renegades and castaways of Melville's day were objectively a new world. But they knew nothing. These know everything. The symbolic mariners and renegades of Melville's book were isolatoes federated by one keel, but only because they had been assembled by penetrating genius. These are federated by nothing. But they are looking for federation. I have heard a young Oriental say that he would fight on either side [in the Cold War]—it didn't matter to him. What he wanted was a good peace, no half peace. This peace, however, he added almost as an afterthought, should include complete independence for his own little country. (186)

This passage is remarkable for the example James has supplied of the difference between Melville's "symbolic mariners"—who knew nothing—and his fellow detainees' knowledge of everything. The anecdote James reports to exemplify such knowledge, however, removes any meaningful distinction between exactly what these political refugees know and how they put it to the work of negotiating with the Cold War state. Throughout the Cold War, Asian countries acquired significance through their alignment with one or the other of the global hegemons. Both occupying powers conflated Asian countries with the systems of representation through which they administered and controlled their territories.

But with the declaration "that he would fight on either side (of the cold war)," the "young Oriental" has refused the discursive rules requiring that he identify himself as either friend or foe. Rather than agreeing to be constituted out of these categories of identification, he has suspended the Cold War's rules of discursive recognition and disrupted the discourse's mandatory bipolar logic. Having rendered the codes that would impose it indefinite and insecure, he decodifies their imposed identity. Because he cannot be stably located for or against either of these positions, his ambivalence has opened up a space internal to his country but extrinsic to Cold War governmental rule. Having made these opposed ideological systems appear reversible rather than mutually exclusive, his renegade positioning has actively removed the divide between East and West, enabling him an unimpeded transition from one side to the other.

Moreover, in proclaiming his loyalty to a "good peace" rather than either antagonist, James's interlocutor might be described as having set himself against Cold War rule by way of his identification with a "higher" rule internal to its code. The oppositional logic of the Cold War presupposed the attainment of a complete peace as at once the grounds for conflict and the condition that should supplant the warfare. But while its protagonists would acknowledge peace as their common goal, the Cold War's bipolar logic rendered it impossible for an occupied country to obtain any outcome other than a "half peace." By aligning his country with the "good peace" that predated the Cold War, James's fellow ward of the Cold War state has appealed to an element within the code that the code itself has recognized as a higher rule and has empowered with the authority to supplant it.

James's description of his fellow castaway's knowledge also characterizes his own project's relation to the state. Having been classified by the state as an exception to democratic norms, James has discovered a way to turn the paradoxical space in which the exception is located to his rhetorical advantage. Giorgio Agamben has analyzed the space of the exception with great precision. An exception "cannot be included in the whole of which it is a member and cannot be a member of the whole in which it is already included."[15] Included within a liberal democracy, exceptions name what that democracy must exclude to achieve unity and coherence. Because they name the limit to democratic inclusiveness, exceptions also produce what might be described as the illusion of an enveloping border for the members of the national democracy who have not been excluded. As members that the nation must exclude in order for the state to achieve coherence and unity, exceptions also designate the figures that a state produces when it establishes a historically specific concretization of the universalizing process known as nation-formation.

Exceptions describe what results when a state asserts the distinction between the nation as a universal form and its historically specific particularization. As a limit internal to the nation, an exception specifies the difference between nationalism as a universal modern norm and a state's historically specific concretization of that norm. When understood to specify the limits to the universalization of the nation-form, exceptions invite comparison with contingencies. Understood as social categories impossible to universalize, the contingencies of race, class, gender, and ethnicity often provide the state with the raw material for its construction of exceptions.

But the space of the exception is not reducible to these signifiers of the internally excluded. It would also include the rules of law themselves, which by definition cannot be subject to the norms they would regulate, as well as the state of emergency. A liberal democracy is understood to enter a state of emergency when its members are subjected to the extreme conditions of a war or a natural catastrophe. During an emergency, the state's requirement to protect the nation takes precedence over its obligation to acquire the people's consent for its decisions.

By observing that after Ahab "stated that the purpose of the voyage was different from that for which they had signed, the men were entitled to revolt and to take possession of the ship themselves" (14), James has fashioned Ahab as the totalitarian exception to a state's emergency powers. He has also described the crew as the democratic exception to Ahab's totalitarian rule. As the internal limit to Ahab's totalitarian governance, the crew holds the place of the rule of law, and, like the "young Oriental," they are comparably empowered by this higher law to overthrow Ahab's totalitarian order.

Because they owed "no allegiance to anybody or anything except the work they have to do and the relations with one another upon which that work depends" (20), the mariners in *Moby-Dick* produced a discontinuity with the oppressive conditions that prevailed under Ahab. Thus reimagined, Melville's castaways enabled James to talk back to the power of the Cold War state through figures who were likewise extrinsic to its forms of governance.

Remarking on the parallel between Ahab's illegal change of the contract and the emergency powers claimed by the Cold War state, James replaced the Ishmael–Ahab opposition, which establishment Americanists had proposed as the narrative's thematic center, with the unacknowledged knowledge that the "meanest mariners, renegades and castaways" constituted exceptions to both forms of totalitarian rule. In drawing on this subaltern knowledge to focus his reading, James also disclosed the state's interest in its disqualification.

With the observation that, while they bore its traces, Queequeg, Tashtego, and Daggoo lacked explicit knowledge of their histories, James engendered a creative collaboration between the consciousness of the experiences he underwent on Ellis Island and the unnarrated memory of the harpooners' pasts. This collaboration produced within James the recollection of the histories of colonial exploitation, Indian removal, and the African slave trade that Melville's fear had disallowed the harpooners. In articulating his knowledge of state power by way of reactivating the memories of these vanished intermediaries, James constructed partial and strictly provisional identifications with the national community.

Refusing compliance with the state's production of exceptions, James characterized dereferentialization and derecognition as the processes through which the state produced the absences that grounded the doctrine of exceptionalism, and he thereafter restored to Melville's crew the knowledges of class hierarchies, resettled populations, and internal colonialism that the doctrine had disqualified. James proceeded to link these derecognized knowledges with the other versions of subaltern knowledge circulating through Ellis Island. Then James positioned this knowledge in the temporal interval in between the McCarran Act and the consent to it that U.S. exceptionalism was understood to have manufactured—after the fact.

Throughout his interpretation of Melville, James exploited the incompatibility between the national citizenry's democratic norms and the state's emergency powers. He did so in order to exacerbate the asymmetrical registers—the state's and the people's—in which national sovereignty operated and to render it impossible for the discourse of exceptionalism to close the gap between these two levels. In removing the mask of exceptionalism from the bill's enactments, James demonstrated how McCarran's declaration of a danger to their security had produced the image of a totalized national community that McCarran thereafter claimed to represent. The McCarran Act had in effect granted the state the power to practice violence against the people in the name of preserving the state. Offering his case as proof, James claimed that it was McCarran's emergency measures that posed the real danger to U.S. democracy.

James intended his reanimation of the democracy's grounding paradox to effect two related political outcomes: the description of the McCarran-Walter Act as law-breaking rather than norm-preserving and the emergence within the social order of the subjects out of whose absences that order had constructed its coherence. In thus reversing the optic of governance from the state to these people, James expounded the ethical proposition that freedom and justice should not be sacrificed in the name of security. This proposition effectively reshaped his intepretation of *Moby-Dick* into a quasi-imperative: "You will have properly understood *Moby-Dick* only if you repeal the McCarran legislation."

Caliban on Ellis Island

Like Caliban, [James] could use the language he had been taught to push into regions Prospero never knew.—Sylvia Wynter, "Beyond the Categories of the Master Conception"

James's interpretation of *Moby-Dick* designated the doctrine of exceptionalism and the field of American studies in which it was produced as interdependent justificatory discourses responsible for the legitimation and normalization of the state's emergency powers. His efforts to impede their work led him to reconceptualize Ellis Island as an enclave lying in between the nation and the state where the state exercised a totalizing power. In negotiating his right to citizenship from within this space, James elaborated similarities between the emergency state and the colonial state apparatus. James's interpretive work compressed the field of American studies to the dimensions of the colonial encounter that he staged on Ellis Island and exposed U.S. history and literature as interlocking systems of state formation.

American studies transmitted an understanding of national U.S. history and literature that was formative of the autonomous citizen-subject on one level of operation and of the formation of a collective national identity on another. Under this description of its disciplinary effects, the field of American studies produced citizens accountable to the state and capable of promoting its interests. The vast majority of scholars in the field of American studies may have understood their belief in U.S. exceptionalism to be far removed from the Immigration and Naturalization Service's deportation policies. Through the juxtaposition of his reading of *Moby-Dick* with his transactions with the INS's bureaucratic apparatus, however, James discerned concrete and specific linkages between the two orders. The INS officers may have applied the rules determining the conditions of national belonging, but the tributary discourses of U.S. history and literature supplied the standards, norms, and rationales naturalizing them.[16]

Having compressed U.S. citizenship to the dimensions of his encounter with the colonial state apparatus, James redescribed the exchange structuring the U.S. symbolic economy during the Cold War as entailing the substitution of the state's actual colonization of its citizenry's life worlds for the grand narrative of U.S. exceptionalism developed within the field of American studies. In revealing Ellis Island as the mediator between the nation and the

Cold War state, James referred to the totalizing operations there as inter-changeable with the totalitarianism and colonialism that the doctrine of U.S. exceptionalism officially opposed.

In pursuing the analogy between his negotiation with the INS and a colo-nial encounter, James also established similarities between the imperial state's neocolonialization of third-world countries and the administrative state's colonization of domestic life worlds. According to James, the Cold War state positioned the national people in a quasi-colonialist structure. It thereby effected a relation of false reciprocity between domestic policies and na-tional security interests that transferred the foreign policy of Americanization abroad into an instrument for securing domestic solidarity at home.

The contradictory relations that James thereby delineated between the state and the nation reconfigured Americanization as an event that sedi-mented political, social, and economic registers within a layered structure that could not be reduced to a symbolic resolution. Interpretively connecting the internal colonialism of the national security apparatus to the structure of colonial relations still in force in his native Trinidad, C. L. R. James's account of his experiences on Ellis Island strategically materialized the site of a post-nation from within an Americanist narrative that had previously been de-ployed to effect just such an imaginary resolution.[17]

James's postcolonial knowledge of state subjection forced into visibility the foundational violence out of whose disavowal establishment American studies had been constituted. Interpretations fostered within the field had sought to dissolve the contradictory relations between the nation and the state. The "end of ideology" thesis put in their place the image of an inte-grated national identity that would displace historical contingencies and sub-sume cultural and political differences. In transforming incompatible matters into an imaginary coherence, the national mythology had constructed a fetish of national identity. Deploying Melville to bring into sight the dis-junctures between the imaginary wholeness of the national community and the nation's foundational disavowals, James unstitched the imaginary thread suturing the national community to the national security state.

In articulating this "other" realm (where state power operated uncon-cealed) to the narrated life world of the national community, James repre-sented Ellis Island as a colonial enclave within U.S. democracy. Here the state discriminated citizens who belonged to the national community from the island's inhabitants whom he represented as wards of a colonial state. In a version of what might be called postcolonial colonialism, citizens were encouraged to disavow knowledge of the state's violation of their democratic norms and to construe the persons who bore that knowledge as exceptions, like James's fellow islanders.

Interpreting *Moby-Dick* by way of a conceptual apparatus that uncovered colonialism and cultural imperialism as unacknowledged elements within the nation's official literary tradition, James represented himself as non-Americanizable in the official terms of that tradition. Writing from the position of the exception in between the state and the normalizing procedures that would legitimate its powers, James, instead of becoming Americanized or subjectivized in those terms, directed two questions to the architects of the Cold War canon: 1) How does the literary tradition Americanize migrants, refugees, and other stateless persons? and 2) What knowledge is foreclosed in the process?

The imagined domestic community through which the state conducted its policy of Americanization at home and abroad depended on the romance genre for the emplotment of its fantasy. The fantasy involved controlling the globe's ideological map. It was underwritten by an interpretive method produced within the field of American literary studies known as the myth-symbol school. The method derived its authority from endowing its practitioners with the capacity to represent entire cultures as ritual reenactments of this national fantasy. It yoked an anthropological imaginary to ritualistic explications of others' cultural stories and facilitated exchanges between literary and geopolitical realms that effectively transformed the field of American studies into an agency of neocolonialism. Its practitioners designed a cultural typology with which to interpret and thereafter to subsume other literatures and geopolitical spaces into a universal Americanism.[18]

The myth-symbol school's method of reading enacted the quasi-colonialist project of absorbing the mores and customs of third-world nations into an allegory of nation-formation that represented them as in the process of developing into an American nation. The colonialist component of this project absorbed the rituals of the so-called developing nations into an allegory of nation-formation underwritten by the quest romance. It consigned indigenous forms to the status of outmoded rituals. The disavowal of colonialism globally and the foreclosure of the tragic nationally comprised interlinked practices of the national romance.

Instead of reproducing this nationalizing mythology, James established concrete linkages between neocolonialism as a U.S. foreign policy and the practices of internal colonization in evidence on Ellis Island. In thereby reversing the direction of the symbolic economy that the American literary establishment authorized, James brought the Americanist mythos to its limit. He wrote from within a Melvillean life world that the myth-symbol school had translated into the terms of the national mythology. Then he operationalized his interpretation of Melville as a lever that, in demonstrating how American myths colonized others' life worlds, turned the national mythology inside out.

Unlike establishment Americanists, James wrote his commentary from the standpoint of a figure excluded from U.S. political culture. While James was reading the violence inherent to the reason of state from the perspective of Melville's frame narrative, he was also delineating the complex affiliation between this rationality and the interpretive assumptions grounded in it. Insisting on the inherence of acts of state violence to the literary establishment's image of the fulfilled national destiny, James removed *Moby-Dick* from the precincts of modern nationalism and linked its themes and events with his efforts to recover from state violence.

As an artifact within the tradition of modernist symbolism, *Moby-Dick* effected a synecdochal continuity between the present and the image of universal totality it was made to prefigure. The postnational emerged, in James's reading of Melville's text, at and as the interval in between the reason of state and the national mythology on which establishment American literature was grounded. Writing from outside that culture with an insider's knowledge of its workings, James's commentary uncovered in Melville's texts the political unconscious of official literary history: the codes and assumptions informing the structures of exclusion whereby the reason of state had secured its identification with the national mythology. Understood as a structure of containment, the pivot of the national metanarrative turned on the mythology of U.S. exceptionalism.

In James's account of their relationship, the nation's myth of itself ratified the social dynamic intrinsic to domestic Americanization. He invoked his own experiences on Ellis Island to criticize that dynamic as involving the exception of contingencies—ethnicity, race, gender, sexuality, race, and locale—which were represented as otherwise than Americanizable. On Ellis Island James rendered visible the act whereby the state made one people out of many. In doing so, he materialized the nation's internal limit. C. L. R. James, in occupying this always already traversed border in between being and becoming American, revealed how far apart the state's violent practices were from the desires of individuals who wanted to organize their societies differently. The antiexceptionalist strategies James subsequently devised here required that he confront U.S. citizens with the hard facts concerning their disavowed histories.

Promoting such knowledge demanded that James upset the relay of cultural relations supporting its denial. Two nodal points in this network of relations linked the ethnographic imaginary authorizing Melville's descriptions of Tashtego, Queequeg, and Daggoo to the criteria informing the deliberations of bureaucrats within the Immigration and Naturalization Service. An explanation of the strategies James deployed to disjoin these relays requires an understanding of the circular causality conjoining them. When resituated within the semiotic field brought into coherence by the INS, the taxonomies of cultural types that the public had learned from interpretations of Melville's narrative were made to signify a ranked hierarchical order.

The INS in turn conscripted the visual perceptions underwriting U.S. citizens' reading practices to reproduce and thereby authorize its categorizations. In visualizing "foreigners" according to INS categories, U.S. citizens linked them to formulations that also evaluated them. Members of other cultures thereafter became servants of INS categories that they could not escape and that seemingly legislated their existence. When they recognized immigrants as functions of distinguishable traits, U.S. citizens practiced what might be called visual imperialism. Visually sorting immigrants according to the INS's taxonomy involved citizens in the imperial practices whereby the U.S. colonized other life worlds.

But if cultural imperialism constituted a kind of optical unconscious for its citizens' visualization of cultural otherness, the assimilationist model through which they comprehended these processes rendered them unable to become conscious of this fact. Assimilation was the form U.S. exceptionalism assumed when it "naturalized" its citizens' cultural stereotyping. Assimilation actively disavowed the cultural imperialism immigration policies and visualization practices reproduced.

Immigrant narratives representing the United States as a haven from colonial and political oppression closed this circle by authorizing the mythology of U.S. exceptionalism. Each such story eclipsed the history of U.S. colonial relations. The myth of the United States as a promised land lacking the history of imperial domination and class oppression which haunted European memory effaced the middle passage narrative of slaves brought to the United States against their will, the stories of migrant laborers the state had newly colonized, and the accounts of migrants who felt their conditions had worsened.

James thoroughly understood how the negative reference to the state's production of exceptions to the official belief in U.S. exceptionalism regulated the citizenry's optical unconscious. He dedicated himself to showing U.S. citizens the knowledge that the discourse of exceptionalism could not include without breaking down. But before he could dismantle exceptionalism's hegemony, James was obliged to disrupt the structures supporting the disavowal through which it ruled. James contested these structures most vigorously at Ellis Island, the site of entry into and deportation from the United States.

James's redescription of Ellis Island did not altogether replace but complicated competing descriptions of it as a safe haven for political and colonial escapees. In writing there, James represented the emergency state's construction of exceptions to the credo of democratic inclusiveness as productive of a nodal point at which social relations within the domestic life world intersected with global capitalism and the international division of labor. And he transformed this intersection into the site whereon he imagined an alternative future.

A Postnational Fable of Transnational America(s) Studies

To establish his own identity, Caliban, after three centuries, must himself pioneer into regions Caesar never knew.—C. L. R. James, *Beyond a Boundary*

Thus far I have proposed the future field of American studies as the horizon onto which C. L. R. James projected his interpretation of *Moby-Dick*. Because imagining the future involves trading in counterfactuals, the remainder of this essay should be understood as the outline of a postnational fable, an allegory of the narrative strategies already described as well as the evocation, at the site of this fable, of a transnational America(s) studies.

On fashioning his brief against the Cold War state as a narrative of the stateless persons who had not survived the wreck of the Pequod, James also constructed an uncanny relationship to the time he served on Ellis Island. After linking the chronologically distinct moments of the Pequod's past with his involuntary incarceration, James imagined himself as if recalled into the past by figures whose present memory depended on the knowledges that James's reading of *Moby-Dick* constructed out of their traces. These Melvillean figures resembled James in lacking the condition of belonging to any nation. In establishing imaginary relations with them, James produced an extraterritorial site that was extrinsic to any of the themes through which the state assimilated persons to the national geography and that did not participate in the progressive temporality ascribed responsibility for the development of U.S. history and literature.

In his reading of *Moby-Dick*, James produced a fictive retroactivity whereby he represented the experiences he underwent on Ellis Island as having realized in historical time one of the national futures Melville had imagined a century earlier. Instead of ratifying the continuist and homogeneous time reproduced within U.S. literature and history, James redescribed his lived historicity as composed out of interruptive temporalities. Ransacking Melville's narrative for the figures through which he might communicate syncopated times required the representation of the experiences he underwent on Ellis Island as involving a disjoined temporality. *Mariners, Renegades and Castaways: The Story of Herman Melville and the World We Live In* associated James's contemporaneity with what might have become of Melville's past imaginings.

James transformed this temporality into a writing practice that conjoined slightly different orientations toward U.S. citizenship: at once not quite a citizen but also not yet not one, James characteristically split the difference between these dis-positions into the desire for forms of citizenship that, while incompatible with INS categories, were consistent with the relationships pertaining among the mariners, renegades, and castaways.

Participants in a transnational social movement, mariners, renegades, and castaways did not belong to a national community. The irreducible differences and inequivalent cultural features characterizing them refused to conform to a state's monocultural taxonomy and could not be integrated within a nationalizing telos. Not yet not a U.S. citizen, James produces through their motion the capacity to disidentify with the categories through which he would also practice U.S. citizenship.

Forever in between arrival and departure, the elements comprising the composite figure mariners, renegades, and castaways perform a process of endless surrogation. Each term names the movement of a "we" that is responsible for its constitution and that traces the presence within it of an alterity irreducible to an "I". In and out of the terminological places through which "we" pass, the figure produces multiple spatial and temporal effects. Each figure would appear to fill the absence in the space evacuated by the preceding figure and to empty that space in turn. Their goings and comings sound forth disparate absences and distant places that emerge from a past territorialized as the "third world" in James's bipolar world order.

The temporality that James's writing might be understood to enact in the relationship he adduces between their past and his present is neither the past definite that historians deploy to keep track of completed past actions nor the present perfect—the what has been of who I now am—of the literary memoirist. It is more properly understood as the future anterior tense. The future anterior links a past event with a possible future on which the past event depends for its significance. The split temporality intrinsic to the future anterior describes an already existing state of affairs at the same time that it stages the temporal practice through which that state of affairs will have been produced.

The future anterior tense provided James with a mode of conjectural reading with which to challenge McCarran's usage. As we have seen, the McCarran bill proposed to have represented a public will that it produced retroactively. The action James has employed the future anterior to produce "will have repealed" McCarran legislation—retroactively. In *Mariners* James correlates a past event—the collective revolt that did not take place in the past—as dependent on a future event—the repeal of the McCarran bill—by which the crew's revolt will have accomplished it. When he links the revolt that had not taken place on the Pequod with the possible future repeal of the McCarran legislation, the future repeal returns to the past to transform this virtual revolt into what will have been its legal precedent.[19]

As James traversed the temporal border separating Melville's symbolic mariners from his fellow wards of the Cold War state, he represented the state's linkage of its emergency measures with the doctrine of U.S. exceptionalism as part of the knowledge borne by the Ellis Island's castaways. James's subsequent efforts to supplant the emergency state's monopoly over the representation of contemporary historical events led him to connect the unstoried cultural anteriority of the mariners, renegades, and castaways with a future that could not have eventuated during the Cold War. James suggested that this other future also be understood as an alternative to the social and political conditions of the 1950s.

On November 28, 1952, now to permit this fable to catch up with James's allegorization, the Trinidadian critic and writer C. L. R. James completed his book on Herman Melville, *Mariners, Renegades, and Castaways: The Story of Herman Melville and the World We Live In*, that he had begun while detained and awaiting deportation on Ellis Island. In the following passage James attests to the site from which he wrote as a significant aspect of its exposition:

"Here was I just about to write suddenly projected onto an island isolated from the rest of society where American administrators and officials and American security officers controlled the destinies of perhaps a thousand men, sailors, 'isolatoes,' renegades and castaways from all parts of the world. It seems now as if destiny had taken a hand to give me a unique opportunity to test my ideas of this great American writer" (132–33).

Throughout this passage, James has traded on heterogeneous understandings sedimented within the word *destiny*. The range of meanings the term conjures up would include the state's imperial progress; the belief in "manifest destiny" through which it was rationalized; the violence with which state officials uprooted and then projected James onto Ellis Island; James's vulnerable political future; the chance configuration of events organizing the conditions of the book's composition, distribution, and transmission; the imagination informing James's critique of state policy; Melville's discontinued narrative intention; the process through which James assumed, continued, reperformed, and transmitted Melville's interrupted intention. All of the different values associated with *destiny* converged in James's decision to write his book. That event has condensed this entire chain of connotations into an opportunity that feels predestined.

Having been resettled on Ellis Island as a displaced person lacking national citizenship and awaiting deportation, James articulated his experience of these serial displacements into the transtemporal relay structuring the affiliation between himself, Melville's mariners, and his fellow Ellis Islanders. Imagining himself as if projected into a future by Melvillean figures likewise lacking placement, James has transformed the involuntary condition of forcible displacement into the precondition for the dynamic motion destining him there.

Recasting his confinement within Ellis Island as if continuous with the political space Melville had imagined in 1850, yet nonsynchronous with its temporality, then, James understood his stay on Ellis Island as an additional episode within Melville's masterwork. He thereupon experienced an oscillation between Melville's imaginary Pequod and his own political exile. According to the uncanny temporality underwriting James's commentary on *Moby-Dick*, Melville did not represent the contemporary political conditions of the Pequod's crew but those which will have prevailed on Ellis Island in 1952. The Pequod represented what Ellis Island will have been, and Ellis Island constituted a memory of the Pequod coming from James's political present.

At the time of James's detainment, Ellis Island was itself a highly contradictory space. It was a site where political refugees, migrant populations, nomads, expellees, and the dispossessed intersected with the international trade and immigration policies the state constructed to regulate their movements. Traversed by movements of people and information delocalized and transnational, Ellis Island resembled a federation of diasporas. The island's culture included contributions from national exiles as well as from colonials and postcolonials. It juxtaposed folkloric with transnational and cosmopolitan forms of expression.

The INS had resettled James on the island so as to segregate him along with other political deviants from the nation's civic and public spaces. But writing about *Moby-Dick* while incarcerated on the island enabled James to conduct an imaginary exchange of his immobilized condition of forced settlement for travel on a migratory vessel. This change of its geography transformed the island ghetto into a site of local resistance wherein he criticized the government's assimilationist policies and disclosed the impossibility of internalizing others within a homogeneous national space.

In place of submitting to the Ellis Island authorities, James positioned himself as if occupying the space splitting the narrative Melville intended from the security apparatus designed to censor it. Elucidating the difference between Melville's message and the fact that it could not be recognized as American, opened up the paradoxical space of the postnational through which James transmitted the future of American studies. In writing about *Moby-Dick*, the alternative Americas James discovered at work within Melville's work split at the seam where it would have otherwise been joined to the state. The administrative border of Ellis Island revealed the contour dividing the official national narrative from his renarration.

The disciplines within the field of American studies intersected with the United States as a geopolitical area whose boundaries field specialists were assigned at once to naturalize and police. Previous interpreters of *Moby-Dick* had accommodated its themes to the discourse of U.S. exceptionalism, through which they had demarcated and policed the national border. Rather than corroborating the exceptionalist imperatives organizing the field of American studies, James questioned the dominant discourses and assumptions within the field. He cast U.S. exceptionalism as a national fantasy installed within the field of American studies as an impediment to the emergence of this irrecuperably transnational movement. He brought the discrepant places and temporalities assembled on Ellis Island into critical relation with a field whose spatial boundaries were reflective of the binarized relations pertaining between the U.S. and its others.

The coalition gathered under the banner "mariners, renegades, and castaways" interrelated multiple international as well as transnational locales. Its members associated the movement's democratizing force with their shared condition of postnational migrancy. In place of corroborating the field's imperial imperatives, James's interpretation of *Moby-Dick* from the mariners' perspective minoritized the classic. Quite literally dialogic, his interpretation produced knowledges about *Moby-Dick* that turned it into a means of exchange and cultural transaction that could not be confined by a national telos.

Mariners transported James beyond the U.S. borders. In it James explored configurations of race and nationality in a transnational frame, and he conceptualized the United States as a geosocial space on the move across and between nations. After James extracted from *Moby-Dick* these extraterritorial properties, he rendered it impossible to determine to whose national culture it now belonged. The practices of aesthetic self-enactment which he generated out of it produced a fluctuating identity that avoided the state's categorical obsessions and challenged its belief that cultural identity is based on a national patrimony. In linking his experiences there with the floating culture on board the Pequod, James transformed Ellis Island into a mobile landscape whose geographically indeterminate space transgressed the national boundaries.

James thereby accomplished a transference of spatial and temporal properties which empowered him to redescribe the field of American studies as, like Ellis Island, a site where becoming American had become indistinguishable from becoming mariners, renegades, castaways. In effect, James reorganized the field as a space that Michel Foucault has called a "heterotopia." Written in a place that, while internal to the U.S., was external to the norms regulating other cultural spaces, *Mariners* permitted the analysis, contestation, and reversal of those norms. Heterotopia is the name of a space inhabited and defined by those who are passing through. It is comprised of transnational flows of people and information. James reimagined the field as a postnational space that engendered multiple collective identifications and organizational loyalties. It convoked networks of association and of intersections that produce juxtapositions confusing the same with the different, the near with the far, and that create and reflect social spaces mediating with distant and dissimilar ones.

In 1953, James activated Melville's future memory to continue this interruptive process. He subsequently articulated the figures he recalled from within Melville's narrative with the "un-Americans" who, like him, had passed through Ellis Island. Having replaced the need for national belonging with an openness to unassimilated otherness, James constructed an open-ended circuit of transnational and international relations. The emergence in James's work of acts of postnational narration with the demonstrated competence to effect transnational and international relations then excluded from the official national narrative turn this work from the historical past toward a postnational future that has emerged within our historical present. Its recollection constitutes one of the possible futures of transnational America(s) studies.

Notes

1   According to the itinerary James provided in *Mariners*, his examination was concluded on August 16, 1950, under the Act of 1918. The Internal Security Act was passed on September 23, 1950, and the Attorney General's decision was handed down on October 31, 1950. "But my appeal was rejected under the McCarran Act. I had therefore been denied due process of law; the McCarran Act had been applied . . . in the decision but could not have figured in the hearings." C. L. R. James, *Mariners, Renegades, and Castaways: The Story of Herman Melville and the World We Live In* (New York: n.p., 1953), 196. Subsequent references are cited parenthetically in the text.

2   Qtd. in Lisa Lowe, *Immigrant Acts: On Asian American Cultural Politics* (Durham, N.C.: Duke University Press, 1996), 9. David Campbell has observed the several ways in which the Cold War foreign policy resulted in the production of the national identity through the containment of threats to it. Foreign policy was understood as the "disciplining of ambiguity and the contingency of global politics by dividing it into an inside and an outside, self and other, via the inscription of the boundaries of the state." National identity was structured in the power to exert visual control over the political imaginaries of other cultures. "Danger was being totalized in the external realm in conjunction with an increased individualization in the internal field, the results being the performative reconstitution of the borders of the state's identity. In this sense the cold war needs to be understood as a disciplinary strategy that was global in scope but national in design." David Campbell, "Political Prosaics, Transversal Politics, and the Anarchical World," in *Challenging Boundaries: Global Flows, Territorial Identities*, ed. Michael J. Shapiro and Hayward R. Alker (Minneapolis: University of Minnesota Press, 1996), 64, 53.

3   See Costas Douzinas and Ronnie Warrington, " 'A Well-Founded Fear of

Justice': Law and Ethics in Postmodernity," in *Legal Studies as Cultural Studies: A Reader in (Post)Modern Critical Theory*, ed. Jerry Leonard (Albany: State University of New York Press, 1995), 197–229. According to Douzinas and Warrington, "Normatives can be seen as prescriptives or commands put into inverted commas that give them authority. The prescriptive says that 'x should carry out y.' Its normative reformulation adds 'it is a norm (or z decrees) that "x should carry out y." ' In a democratic polity political and legal legitimacy are allegedly linked with the fact that the addressor of the norm (the legislator) and the addressee of the command (the legal subject) are one and the same. The essence of freedom is that the subjects who make the law are also law's subjected" (210).

4 Jean-Francois Lyotard has observed that a just society is one that recognizes and allows all participants to have a voice, to narrate from their own perspective. It is desirable "to extend interlocution to any human individual whatsoever, regardless of national or natural idiom." Jean-Francois Lyotard, "The Other's Rights," in *On Human Rights: The Oxford Amnesty Lectures*, ed. Stephen Chute and Susan Hurley (New York: Basic Books, 1993), 139.

5 James described the limitations the state had imposed on his "I" in his representation of the following exchange when he requested that the District Director of the INS of the Port of New York send him to a hospital for the treatment of an ulcer. "Mr. Shaughnessy's reply was that if I did not like it there I was not going to be detained against my will. I could always leave and go to Trinidad where I was born and drink my papaya juice" (166).

6 Jean-Francois Lyotard, *The Differend: Phrases in Dispute* (Manchester: Manchester University Press, 1983), xi.

7 At a time in which the legal apparatus for surveillance had been put into place to purge universities of politically heterodox activities, Richard Chase's *Herman Melville* continued the state's policing measures by other means. He described the book's purpose as an effort "to ransom liberalism from the ruinous sell-outs, failures, and defeats of the thirties. . . . It must present a vision of life capable of avoiding the old mistakes: the facile ideas of progress and 'social realism' . . . the idea that literature should participate directly in the economic liberation of the masses, the equivocal relationship to communist totalitarianism and power politics." Richard Volney Chase, *Herman Melville: A Critical Study* (New York: Macmillan, 1949), vii. In "*Moby-Dick* and the Cold War," I discussed the Cold War mentality underwriting Melville criticism in some detail. *Moby-Dick* had entered the national canon as a sacralization of the nation's struggle with global totalitarianism. The canonical reading had discerned in Ishmael's survival the signs of a decisive victory in the imaginary war. This reading might be understood as a belated effort to discharge myself of an indebtedness I had not known that I had incurred in writing that essay. In "*Moby-Dick* and the Cold War," I situated Herman Melville's novel within the cultural politics of the Cold War. Not quite two years ago, the editors of a volume entitled *C. L. R. James: His Intellectual Legacies* sent me a reviewer's

copy of the book along with a note recommending that I read Cedric Robinson's essay "C. L. R. James and the World-System." In it Robinson analyzed my interpretation of *Moby-Dick* within the context of James's 1952 reading while incarcerated on Ellis Island. After observing that my refusal to find in Ishmael's narration a will that was any less totalizing than Ahab's constituted "an important addendum to James's indictment of Ishmael," professor Robinson complained that I had not taken my argument far enough. Cedric Robinson, "C. L. R. James and the World-System," in *C. L. R. James: His Intellectual Legacies*, ed. Selwyn R. Cudjoe and William E. Cain (Amherst: University of Massachusetts Press, 1995), 254. Had I adopted James's interpretive stance, it would have taken me beyond the boundaries of U.S. national culture and into the multicentered analysis of transnational cultural relations. See Pease, "*Moby-Dick* and the Cold War," in *The American Renaissance Reconsidered*, ed. Walter Benn Michaels and Pease (Baltimore: Johns Hopkins University Press, 1985), 113–54.

8 James will draw incomplete parallels between the McCarran Act and Nazi totalitarianism throughout *Mariners*. In the following passage, James at first explicitly correlates the emergency measures of the McCarran Committee with related forms of totalitarian rule, but at the paragraph's conclusion he restricts the latter attribution to his experiences in Nazi Germany: "The McCarran Act is an attempt to change the laws to correspond to the administrative policy. It may. But if and when the complete success has been achieved, there will also have been achieved the complete demoralization of the staff of the Department of Justice and large sections of the American people. It is a comparatively simple thing to mobilize majorities in Congress to pass laws, and for judges and administrators to set out to apply them. But you cannot reverse the whole historical past and the traditions of a people by packaged legislation and loud propaganda. Certain policies demand total destruction of a legal system, its replacement by a new one, totalitarian indoctrination of the population in the new doctrine, and storm-troopers or G. P. U. men to enforce them. Try to carry them out by grafting them onto a traditionally democratic system and the result is complete chaos. I saw precisely that happen step by step to a whole nation between 1934 and 1939" (173–74).

9 Stuart Hall, "C. L. R. James: A Portrait," in *C. L. R. James's Caribbean*, ed. Paget Henry and Paul Buhle (Durham, N.C.: Duke University Press, 1992), 12.

10 *Congressional Record*, 81st Cong., 1st sess., 1949, 95, pt. 4: 4993.

11 See William E. Connolly, *The Ethos of Pluralization* (Minneapolis: University of Minnesota Press, 1995), 39. Subsequent references are cited parenthetically in the text. Connolly draws on Paul Ricoeur's elegant formulation of this paradox: "It is of the nature of political consent, which gives rise to the unity of the human community organized and oriented by the state, to be able to be recovered only in an act which has not taken place, in a contract which has not been contracted, in an implicit and tacit pact which appears as such only in

political awareness, in retrospection and reflection." Paul Ricoeur, "The Political Paradox," in *Legitimacy and the State*, ed. William Connolly (New York:
New York University Press, 1984), 254.

12 Among important recent discussions of U.S. exceptionalism, see Michael
Kammen, "The Problem of American Exceptionalism: A Reconsideration,"
American Quarterly 45, no. 1 (1993):1–43; and Joyce Appleby, "Recovering
America's Historical Diversity: Beyond Exceptionalism," *Journal of American
History* 79, no. 2 (1992): 419–31.

13 Janice Radway, "What's in a Name? Presidential Address to the American
Studies Association, 20 November, 1998," *American Quarterly* 51, no. 1 (1999),
4, reprinted in this volume.

14 Louis Hartz, *The Liberal Tradition in America: An Interpretation of American
Political Thought since the Revolution* (New York: Harcourt, Brace, 1955), 5.

15 Giorgio Agamben, *Homo Sacer: Sovereign Power and Bare Life*, trans. Daniel
Heller-Roazen (Stanford, Calif.: Stanford University Press, 1998), 24. The
exception the state produces to engender the limits to the rule of democratic
governance might also be understood to embody the rule that has produced
the exception. As the limit internal to the national order but external to its
conditions of belonging, the exception can consent to this nonposition, or the
exception can do what the "young Oriental" did and turn the limit into legal
grounds for supplanting the entire order.

16 Michel Foucault has discussed the intimate relationship between the law and
the disciplines' naturalization of it: "From the nineteenth century to our own
day, [modern society] has been characterized on the one hand, by a legislation,
a discourse, an organization based on public right, whose principle of articulation is the social body and the delegative status of each citizen; and, on the
other hand, by a closely linked grid of disciplinary coercions whose purpose is
in fact to assure the coherence of this same social body. . . . Hence these two
limits, a right of sovereignty and a mechanism of discipline which define, I
believe, the arena in which power is exercised. But these two limits are so
heterogeneous that they cannot possibly be reduced to each other. The powers of modern society are exercised through, on the basis of, and by virtue of,
this very heterogeneity between a public right of sovereignty and a poly-
morphous disciplinary mechanism. . . . The disciplines may well be the car-
riers of a discourse that speaks of a rule, but this is not the juridical rule
deriving from sovereignty, but a natural rule, a norm. The code they come to
define is not that of law but that of normalisation." Michel Foucault, "Two
Lectures," in *Power/Knowledge: Selected Interviews and Other Writings, 1972–
1977*, ed. and trans. Colin Gordon (New York: Pantheon, 1980), 106.

17 James provided this postnational site with the following description: "The
whole of the world is represented on Ellis Island. Many sailors, but not only
sailors; Germans, Italians, Latvians, Swedes, Filipinos, Malays, Chinese, Hin-
dus, Pakistanis, West Indians, Englishmen, Australians, Danes, Yugoslavs,
Greeks, Canadians, representatives of every Latin American country" (183).

18 Apropos of Melville's ethnographic imaginary, Richard Chase quotes Melville's description of Queequeg as "George Washington cannibalistically developed." "Queequeg would do well enough in a side show, a hideous savage, the son of a cannibal king: 'Such a face! It was of a dark, purplish, yellow color, here and there struck over with large blackish-looking squares.' And he worshiped a 'curious little deformed image with a hunch on its back, and exactly the color of a three days' old Congo baby.' . . . The other harpooners are also creatures of folklore: of prodigious strength, they are imposing in their natural dignity and devoted to the spirit of the hunt" (82).

19 Jacques Derrida explains the significance of this retroactive temporality within the context of the *Declaration of Independence.* "We the people," as Jacques Derrida has explained their emplacement within the paradoxical logic of a representative democracy, "do not exist as an entity; it does *not* exist, *before* this declaration, not as *such.* If it gives birth to itself, as free and independent subject as possible signer, this can only hold in the act of the signature. The signature invents the signer. The signer can only authorize him- or herself, to sign once he or she has come to the end . . . if one can say this, of his or her signature, in a sort of fabulous retroactivity." "Declarations of Independence," trans. Tom Keenan and Tom Pepper, *New Political Science* 15 (1976): 10.

COMPARATIVIST

✧

Postnationalism, Globalism, and

the New American Studies

John Carlos Rowe

Curricula and scholarship in American studies have changed significantly over the past decade, reflecting the important influences of women's studies, ethnic studies, and postmodern and postcolonial theories. Earlier approaches, such as the Puritan-origins and myth-symbol schools, attempted to elaborate those features of American identity and social organization that are unique national characteristics. Often implicit in this nationalist approach to the study of U.S. culture was the assumption that the United States constituted a model for democratic nationality that might be imitated or otherwise adapted by other nations in varying stages of their "development."

The criticism of such American exceptionalism has focused on both its contributions to U.S. cultural imperialism and its exclusions of the many different cultures historically crucial to U.S. social, political, and economic development. In response to concepts of American identity shaped by Western patriarchy and Eurocentric models for social organization, more recent critical approaches have focused on the many cultures that have been marginalized by traditional American studies or subordinated to an overarching nationalist mythology. In articulating the various cultures and social identities in the United States, scholars have often focused on the cultural, political, and economic boundaries dividing these cultures both from the dominant social order and from each other.

Such "border studies" of the intersections and interactions of the different cultures of the United States must also include a reconsideration of national cultural boundaries. If a single nationalist mythology of the United States no longer prevails, then our understanding of just what constitutes the cultural border of the United States is no longer clear. Immigration has always shaped the United States in ways that demonstrate the shifting nature of such cultural boundaries. More traditional American studies relied on the model of a single dominant culture assimilating immigrant cultures in a gradual, evolutionary manner. In contrast, more recent approaches have stressed the cultural hybridities that have occurred historically among the many different cultures constituting the United States. Attention to these hybridities requires scholars to look at the multiple cultural influences involved in important social formations; such cultural complexity is often invisible when historical changes are viewed primarily in terms of the assimilation of "minor" cultures to a "dominant" social system.

The borders both of division and contact are also linguistic, and we should not equate and thereby confuse linguistic, cultural, ethnic, and national categories, even though there are many ways in which they may overlap and complement each other. In his recent "For a Multilingual Turn in American Studies" and his long-term project to republish non-English language works of U.S. literature, Werner Sollors has argued persuasively for the study of U.S. culture as a polylingual as well as multicultural discipline.[1] Despite the long history of an ideology of a monolingual United States—revived quite hysterically in recent years by E. D. Hirsch Jr. and Arthur Schlesinger Jr., among others[2]—the United States continues to be a multilingual society with large segments of its population working and living successfully in multilingual contexts. Statistical studies do not support the fear prevalent among conservatives and many liberals that recent immigrants fail to learn English or that polylingual communities, such as major metropolitan areas, are linguistically, culturally, and nationally fragmented. Recent studies, in fact, have shown that immigrant populations in the United States in the last half of the twentieth century have learned English—even as they have often preserved their native languages—more rapidly and universally than immigrants at any other time in U.S. history.[3] Far more likely to divide recent immigrants from U.S. "national culture," as it is sometimes called, are social disparities in educational and economic opportunities. Class hierarchies, in other words, are far more divisive of peoples in the United States in the late twentieth century than language or culture. Of course, class as a category is often bound up in social practice with historically established hierarchies of race, ethnicity, gender, sexuality, and religion. As Sollors and many of the respondents to his essay in the recent "American Crossroads" postings argued, the new American studies must address the multilingual reality of the United States in the curricular and scholarly reforms now under way in the field.[4]

By the same token, the dominance of the United States according to the nationalist paradigm has often led to the neglect of other nations in the Western hemisphere, each of which has its own complex multicultural and multilingual history, as well as its own interactions with the other nationalities of the region. The new American studies tries to work genuinely as a comparatist discipline that will respect the many different social systems and cultural affiliations of the Americas. Rather than treating such cultural differences as discrete entities, however, this new comparative approach stresses the ways different cultures are transformed by their contact and interaction with each other. If we are to preserve the name *American studies*, then we must take into account at the very least the different nationalities, cultures, and languages of the Western hemisphere, including Canada. If we find this field too large and challenging, then we should consider area studies models that would redefine the American studies taught at most U.S. colleges and universities today as "U.S. studies" or "North American studies." Such comparatist work thus focuses with special interest on just the points of historical, geographical, and linguistic contact where two or more communities must negotiate their respective identities. This new interest in border studies should include investigations of how the many different Americas and Canada have historically influenced and interpreted each other. With very different histories of responding to ethnic and racial minorities, as well as of constructing gendered and sexual hierarchies, these different Americas also help foreground the multilingual and multicultural realities of social life and economic opportunity in any of the Americas.

Such fundamental reconsiderations of what constitutes American studies as a field (or fields) of study should be accompanied by theoretical investigations of our methodologies for conducting research and interpreting data. The history of the impact of various critical theories and methodologies on American studies is complex and often contradictory; it is a subject especially in need of scholarly attention at this crucial moment in the reconceptualization of the field. As an interdisciplinary field, American studies declared its theoretical purposes from its earliest years in the 1930s, and yet American studies has often been particularly intransigent with respect to new theoretical models, ranging from modernist theories—like phenomenology, the Frankfurt School, structuralism, poststructuralism and deconstruction—to more contemporary approaches—like critical race theory, feminism, queer theory, and postcolonial theory.

A certain antitheoretical bias lingers in American studies, sometimes disguised by appeals to "native" methodologies or vaguely defined traditions of "American pragmatism."[5] At other times, an antitheoretical air surrounds those who insist that American studies has anticipated (and often does better) the knowledge production claimed by new methods. Such has often been the case with defenders of the myth-symbol school and specialists in popular culture, especially in their responses to ideological criticism, New Historicism, and cultural studies. Without even attempting to adjudicate these conflicting claims to priority for the centrality of culture as the key element constituting the object of study from the founders of American studies to recent theorists and practitioners of cultural studies, I would simply point out that the very claim for priority by some scholars in American studies ought to make new critical theories and cultural studies particularly appealing to them, rather than antagonists competing for scholarly attention and institutional space.[6]

Indeed, many of the most compelling postnationalist challenges to the study of the Americas as primarily (if not exclusively) coherent nation-states are the consequences of the impact of cultural studies on American studies and related area, ethnic, women's, and gender studies. Developing in part out of earlier "critical studies of colonial discourse" and "colonial studies," as well as the *Ideologie-Kritik* of the Frankfurt School, the materialist criticism and attention to popular and mass media of the Birmingham School, and important traditions of Latin American, African, South Asian, and East Asian anti-colonialist writings and political activism, cultural studies often investigates the relationship between the rise of the Western nation-state and the development of European imperial systems of economic, political, linguistic, and cultural domination.[7] Thus the relevance of a postnationalist perspective for the new American studies is evident in the new work being done on U.S. national ideology and its concomitant imperialist ambitions in North America, Latin America, and outside the Western hemisphere. The contemporary scholarly efforts to link the earlier "internal colonization" thesis of crucial American studies' scholars—like Robert Berkhofer, Richard Drinnon, Reginald Horsman, Annette Kolodny, Richard Slotkin, Ronald Takaki, and Jane Tompkins—with the argument that the United States has traditionally defined itself as a global power have obvious connections with the intellectual and political purposes of cultural studies' general interest in the origins, legitimation, and perpetuation of Euroamerican imperial and neoimperial forms of global domination.[8]

In its claims to encompass the many cultures and political organizations in the Western hemisphere, the new American studies threatens its own kind of cultural imperialism, a tendency often overlooked even by the most ideologically attentive scholars. We are now familiar with the ways American studies of the post–World War II era "often was enlisted in the service of quasi-official governmental policies and institutions" and how its "success" as a field of study could sometimes be tied to the exportation of "American" cultural ideals based on extraordinarily limited models of American identity and experience (Marx 54). There are commonly overlooked practical factors driving the popularity of American studies outside the United States, such as "the growing number of American-educated Ph.D.s teaching in other countries, the lure of relatively high-paying research grants and temporary teaching positions in the U. S., and the prestige of publishing in the U.S."[9] In short, the border dividing native and foreign versions of American studies is increasingly difficult to draw. We distinguish the new American studies from older versions not only for being more inclusive and diverse, but also for its vigilance with respect to its possible uses in the cultural imperialist agendas central to U.S. foreign policies from the Marshall Plan in postwar Europe to the multinational alliance we assembled to fight (and legitimate) the Gulf War. Yet just what separates cultural understanding from cultural imperialism is increasingly difficult to articulate in an age of technologically accelerated human and cultural mobility.

Often what U.S. specialists in American studies overlook is our tendency to universalize our own interests and to appeal, however unconsciously, to our own nativist expertise as implicated in a larger agenda of cultural imperialism that both includes and exceeds specific articulations of foreign policies. In another recent discussion by the "American Crossroads Project" electronic discussion group, Jim Zwick expressed his surprise at the equivocal response from non-U.S. scholars to his idea for a centennial conference on the Spanish-American and Philippine-American wars. Unaware that some non-U.S. scholars considered such a project as yet another effort by U.S. specialists to control the intellectual reception of these colonial wars, to disregard once again work already done by scholars in the Philippines, Spain, Cuba, and Latin America, and to publicize the latest U.S. theoretical approach (cultural studies, critical study of colonial discourse, etc.) as the most appropriate for specialists in other political and intellectual communities, Zwick found himself criticized for an intellectual "provincialism" he thought he was working to overcome.[10] Many recent scholars—like Paul Lauter, Emory Elliott, and Alice Kessler-Harris—have worked to expand the participation of non-U.S. American studies specialists in the American Studies Association and to increase the exchange of scholarly work at conferences (and now by way of the Internet) for the benefit of both U.S. and non-U.S. scholars and in recognition of the very different purposes, interests, and institutional configurations American studies may have around the globe.[11]

New institutes and forums for international scholars in American studies are doing important work at many different U.S. colleges and universities; such work is more important than ever, now that the United States Information Agency is being significantly downsized and valuable programs it sponsored lost to fiscal "exigencies."[12] As we contribute to this important work, however, we should remember the dialectical and dialogical purposes of such intellectual exchanges. An older international American studies in the 1950s and 1960s often drew on the cosmopolitanism of Euroamerican modernism, but its implicit cultural mission was to "enlighten" the foreign cultures from which it drew many of its most avant-garde materials and ideas. The new American studies requires a new internationalism that will take seriously the different social, political, and educational purposes American studies serves in its different situations around the globe. Local political, cultural, and intellectual issues are often interestingly woven into the curricula and pedagogy of American studies in non-U.S. cultures in ways U.S. scholars unfamiliar with those cultures (and their languages and histories) do not understand. Such hybridizations of local and international knowledges range from explicit efforts to circumvent repressive regimes and local censorship to subtler modes of responding to U.S. cultural imperialism by transforming the ineluctable importation of U.S. cultural goods. In short, U.S. and other Western hemispheric scholars have as much to learn from our international colleagues as they from us.

A common purpose linking these different versions of American studies should be the critical study of the circulation of America as a commodity of the new cultural imperialism and the ways in which local knowledges and arts have responded to such cultural importations—the study of what some have termed "coca-colonization."[13] What some cultural critics have termed the capacity of local cultures to "write back" against cultural and even political and economic domination should be considered part of American studies, even as we recognize the practical impossibility of expanding our scope to include all aspects of global experience simply because of the global pretensions of first-world nations like the United States. Nevertheless, the study of U.S. imperialist policies toward Native Americans should not be conducted without consideration of how native peoples responded to the specific historical circumstances investigated, just as the Philippine-American War should not be studied exclusively from the perspective of the United States or the response to the Vietnam War studied solely through U.S. texts. The Native American, Philippine, and Vietnamese perspectives must be represented in such studies (whether published research or classroom instruction), once again in keeping with the comparatist aims of the new American studies.

These are only some of the ways in which the new American studies should begin to reconstitute its fields of study, especially as the United States (along with other first-world nations) claims an ever greater responsibility for global economics, politics, language, and identity. I have written elsewhere about how we might adapt Mary Louise Pratt's theoretical model of the "contact zone" for articulating a comparative American studies that would include as one of its areas of specialization "comparative U.S. cultures."[14] Like the geopolitical, linguistic, cultural, ethnic, and economic borders I discussed above as crucial to the reformulation of American studies, the contact zone is a semiotic site where exchanges may occur from both (or more) sides, even when the configurations of power are inequitable (as they usually are). Intellectuals who work closely with peoples and issues relevant to the actual borders where immigration is controlled, economic destinies decided, and individual lives immediately and irrevocably affected often warn us not to generalize too casually or abstractly with regard to these "border regions."[15] We should heed their warnings and learn from their experiences, but we should also recognize that however real the border between the United States and Mexico or separating Southeast Asian or Haitian boat people from safety in the United States, they are also discursively constructed borders made all too often to have terrible physical consequences for those forbidden to cross them. In other words, we can begin to reconfigure such borders by establishing intellectual and cultural contact zones, where a certain dialectics or dialogics of cultural exchange is understood to be a crucial aspect of how the field of American studies is constituted and how the related territories of the Americas and the United States ought to be understood. In this respect, teaching and scholarship become direct, albeit never exclusive, means of effecting necessary social changes.

How is it possible for us to accomplish work so vast in scope and involving so many different specializations? One of the most common reactions to the progressive aims of the new American studies is to reassert the study of a "common" and "national" culture for reasons both ideal and practical. We must have a "common culture," Hirsch and others tell us, to avoid the intellectual anarchy into which we are already drifting. We must have a unified American studies discipline, department, program, and professional organization—which usually means one devoted to some version of nationalist study or American exceptionalism—because we haven't the resources, the time, or the expertise to do more, Sean Wilentz and others warn us as ethnic, women's, gender and sexuality, and cultural studies proliferate as new programs on college campuses around the world.[16] What, then, are the practical implications of the preceding description of what seems intellectually crucial for the new American studies to pursue if it is to avoid the mistakes of the past and draw on the best of its traditions?

Part of the problem facing those committed to this new vision of American studies is related to the increasingly antiquated model of the university, its disciplinary division of knowledges, and its model of instruction as the transmission of knowledge as information from an authority to receptive students. The conflict of the modern, Enlightenment model for the university and its liberal educational ideals with new conceptions of education, the character of knowledge, and the circulation of such knowledge is by no means unique to American studies.[17] We may simply face it more directly and immediately because we are in the course of reconstituting our field, forced by the exigencies of rapidly changing ideas of the Americas, and because we have a heritage of challenging established academic procedures. But to achieve any part of what I have described in the preceding paragraphs, we will have to bring about fundamental changes in the way most modern universities educate.

However sweeping such changes may seem when described in this general manner, they may be realized in many small steps. First, we should not rush to defend American studies as a program or department, especially against emerging programs in ethnic, women's, and gender and sexual studies that often devote much of their curricula to topics relevant to the study of the United States, the Americas, and the borders or contact zones I have described above. As part of the work of our research group at the University of California's Humanities Research Institute in the fall and winter quarters of 1996–1997, we met with faculty in American studies and related programs on the different campuses of the University of California system. On every campus, important curricular changes were underway in the several fields relevant to American studies, most of those changes reflecting various intellectual and educational responses to the issues discussed above. Each campus had very different ideas about the future of American studies as a formal program on that campus, and it was instructive to discover how important local institutional and political factors were in shaping these attitudes. Whereas established American studies programs at UC Davis and UC Santa Cruz are working to help focus and organize curricular changes in their own and collateral disciplines, there were no plans to revive UC Riverside's program, which was discontinued in the late 1970s, or UC Irvine's Comparative Cultures program, which was discontinued in 1993, or to expand a small, primarily instructional undergraduate American studies program at UCLA to include a graduate (and thus more research-intensive) component.

Open forums we held at the 1996 American Studies Association Convention in Kansas City and the 1997 California American Studies Association Convention in Berkeley confirmed our sense that there can be no general model for the institutional future of American studies in U.S. universities, even when interested faculty agree generally with the aims of the new American studies I have outlined in this essay. Different local issues, both specific to the university and its surrounding community, affect institutional arrangements in ways that can only be generalized in terms of a new intellectual regionalism that must be taken into account as we discuss the multiple futures of American studies and the established and emerging disciplines with which American studies must collaborate in the coming decades. This intellectual regionalism is often inflected by the new regionalisms established by the different demographies, ethnicities, and global economic and cultural affiliations characterizing such important border or contact zones as Southern California's relation to Asia, Mexico, Central America, and the Caribbean; greater Houston's relation to Mexico and the Caribbean; Atlanta and the Southeast's relation to the Black Atlantic; Miami's relation to Cuba, Haiti, and Latin America.[18] Universities ought to mediate between local and international knowledges, and the new regionalisms (not to be confused with older, more discrete regional identities), even those shaped in the major period of European immigration, ought to be taken into account by academics reconstituting American studies and related fields on their different campuses.

Our consideration of the academic implications of these new regionalisms should also inform the internationalizing of American studies I discussed above—an internationalizing that should avoid the one-sided, often neo-imperialist cosmopolitanism of an earlier American studies but that should instead complement established international relations (cultural, economic, political) already shaping the college or university's local community.[19] Because new sources of academic funding, especially in support of the sciences, are following the channels of this new regionalism, there will be growing pressure from academic administrators for us to follow such leads. Properly vigilant and often resistant as American studies scholars have been to the ideological consequences of certain academic funds—a vigilance as important in today's private funding situation as when the Department of Defense was our secret source—we should make serious efforts to direct some of this funding to cultural understanding and criticism, as well as to the expansion of foreign language instruction. Regard for these new regionalisms should, of course, avoid provincialisms of their own; University of California, Irvine students need to know about the Black Atlantic as well as the Pacific Rim,

Mexico, and Latin America. In short, our consideration of these local conditions should be contextualized in a larger understanding of the United States in the comparative contexts of Western hemispheric and, finally, global study I have described earlier.

Colleges and universities continue to operate in a state of fiscal crisis as a means of justifying the downsizing that includes drastic transformations of the research mission, especially in the humanities, and the "consolidation" of academic programs. Smaller, newer, underfunded programs are, of course, at the greatest risk, even though the overall savings they offer most universities have little impact on the total budget picture of the institution. In this academic climate, established American studies programs should work cooperatively with traditionally allied programs in ethnic, women's, gender and sexual, and cultural studies and critical theory by spelling out protocols for sharing courses, existing faculty, and the definition and recruitment of new faculty positions. Successful American studies programs should be aware of inclinations by administrators to use them to consolidate different programs those administrators often view as "fragmented," "incoherent," or "needlessly proliferating," especially when those programs are leading the changes in our understanding of the limitations of traditional knowledge-production and its established disciplines.

As much as those of us at colleges and universities without formal American studies programs might wish to have the opportunity to realize some of the ambitions of the new American studies in established curricula and degree requirements, we ought to work toward those ends in cooperation, rather than competition, with colleagues in African American, Asian American, Latino and Chicano, Native American, women's, gender and sexual, and cultural studies and critical theory.[20] Local, national, and international interests should be worked out in cooperation among such complementary fields. What eventually emerges from such collaborative work may well be different from any of the American studies or women's studies programs we have known before, and this flexibility with respect to the emerging knowledges and institutional means of producing and sharing such knowledges should help us avoid the failed intellectual orthodoxies of the past and perhaps bring about unexpected changes in traditional departments, where many of us working for such ends hold our primary appointments. Just such an openness to emerging fields, whose methods and objects of study are still debated and contested, characterizes the attitudes of many scholars who are in no hurry to revive or inaugurate formal American studies undergraduate or graduate programs at colleges and universities presently lacking them. The absence of formal programs, in other words, need not indicate a lack of vitality on the part of the new American studies, especially when it anticipates its future strength as a consequence of educational coalitions with ethnic, women's, gender and sexual, and cultural studies and critical theory.

Cooperative work of this sort is based on our intellectual experience with the many different fields now involved in American studies and the challenging theoretical questions the coordination of these fields involves. No scholar can claim to command any part of American studies; the field is not just multidisciplinary, it is also a cooperative intellectual venture. No matter how innovatively we design curricula, cross-list courses, bring in visitors to our own classes, we can never approximate this collaborative and collective intellectual enterprise until we transform the classroom from the traditional scene of instruction (often a theater of cruel disciplining or trivial imitation) into a joint venture involving many scholars, including our students as active researchers. Team-teaching, coordinated classes, and other traditional responses to the active/passive and master/servant models of teacher/student can today be considered crude versions of the sorts of alternative learning situations offered by the Internet, distance learning, and other electronic means of instruction. Electronic MUDs (Multi-User Dimensions) and MOOs (Multi-Object Orientations), virtual conferences, and hypertext databases should be used as more than merely tools in traditional classroom education and conventional research; they should be imagined as means of achieving changed ideas of what constitutes education and knowledge in the humanities and social sciences. In these ways, we might also balance our national and international aims with different local interests.

The American Studies Association's support of Randy Bass and Jeff Finlay's "American Crossroads Project" and their "Teaching American Studies" (T-Amstudy) at Georgetown has led the way for many other academic professional organizations in experimenting with education that transcends specific university sites.[21] There are, of course, ideological consequences to the use of the Internet in education that must be recognized; as primarily an English-language medium and a technology often shaped by U.S. information-industry protocols, the Internet is in its own right another topic in the study of U.S. cultural imperialism. Yet as a medium that we can use to put faculty and students from around the world in regular and immediate contact with each other, increasingly in a variety of languages, the Internet can be employed to criticize, resist, and perhaps transform such cultural imperialism. Many virtual research centers already link international faculty and students for a fraction of the cost of IRL conferences. Our work as scholars must also be complemented by academic publishers, who must now take the initiative in defining the directions for the future of the electronic dissemination of scholarly work and assuring that appropriate standards for the quality of publication are met even as such publishers guarantee the variety of different approaches and subjects.[22]

Michael Clough, senior fellow at the Council on Foreign Relations, a research associate at the Institute of International Studies at UC Berkeley, and co-chair of the New American Global Dialogue, wrote recently in an op-ed piece in the *Los Angeles Times*: "For better and worse, it is less and less possible for nationally minded elites, sitting in Washington and New York, to construct policies that simultaneously protect and promote the interests of Los Angeles, San Francisco and other emerging regional metropoles. Instead, a new, much more decentralized model of governance, one capable of accommodating the growing diversity of the American politico-cultural economy, must be developed" (M1). A specialist in international relations, Clough is not thinking about the futures of American studies, but rather about the new American studies that has been developing in its own way in the direction of a more "decentralized model," one that is attentive to the different intellectual regions, or contact zones, that represent more adequately the domestic and foreign determinants of the United States and the Americas than previous American studies. Nationalisms and neonationalisms of all sorts are, of course, very much alive not only in the politically, culturally, and linguistically diverse United States, but around the globe. The persistence and even revival of nationalism need not prevent us from trying to think of social organizations in contexts other than "national consensus" and its stereotypes of "national experience" and "character." Postnationalist thinking about what constitutes the United States and the Americas may well offer us our best chance of learning from, rather than repeating, the past.

Notes

1 Werner Sollors, "For a Multilingual Turn in American Studies," *American Studies Association Newsletter* 20, no. 2 (1997): 13–15. Sollors, Marc Shell, and other scholars are working through the Longfellow Institute at Harvard and with Johns Hopkins University Press to publish the Longfellow Institute Series in American Languages and Literatures, "the first systematic attempt to republish historically, aesthetically, and culturally significant works written

in what is now the United States and published in languages other than English." The Longfellow Anthology has already been published, and it will be followed by bilingual and trilingual translations of individual works. Sollors, "From 'English Only' to 'English-Plus' in American Studies," American Crossroads Project, 2 August 1997, discussion list administered by Jeff Finlay (FINLAYJI@guvax.acc.georgetown.edu). Subsequent references are cited parenthetically in the text.

2 E. D. Hirsch Jr., *Cultural Literacy: What Every American Needs to Know* (Boston: Houghton Mifflin, 1987); Arthur M. Schlesinger Jr., *The Disuniting of America: Reflections on a Multicultural Society* (New York: Norton, 1992).

3 In his response to discussion of his essay on the "American Crossroads" list, Sollors notes: "It is also simply not true that monolingualism reduces illiteracy or technological ineffectiveness. . . . It is a myth that bilingualism lowers language performance in first languages. . . . It seems doubtful to me whether 'English only' education, based on the false myths of a monolingual past and of better language skills of monolingual people, makes for more civic cohesion than would a fuller understanding of the pervasive multilingualism in U.S. history and society" ("From 'English Only' to 'English-Plus' in American Studies").

4 Paul Lauter, in his response to Sollors's essay on July 26, 1997, on "American Crossroads," makes a particularly important point about the need to study the ideological assumptions behind previous foreign-language requirements for graduate programs in American studies. Earlier arguments favoring the so-called tool languages of French and German, usually to the neglect of Spanish, Portuguese, Chinese, Japanese, Korean, Vietnamese, and the many other languages crucial to the history of nations and immigrant populations in the Western hemisphere and the virtual repression of the study of Native American languages, except by specialists, have played their parts not only in reinforcing the monolingual ideology of the United States but also in perpetuating what I would term the heritage of Eurocultural colonialism in the United States.

5 I do not include here rigorous accounts of American pragmatism as a methodology, theory, and philosophy in its own right, rather than a vaguely invoked synonym for *American character*. For an excellent account of American pragmatism in this precise sense, see Mark Bauerlein, *The Pragmatic Mind: Explorations in the Psychology of Belief* (Durham, N.C.: Duke University Press, 1997). For a version of how *American pragmatism* can be used as a substitute for *American (national) character*, see Richard Poirier, *Poetry and Pragmatism* (Cambridge, Mass.: Harvard University Press, 1992); and Poirier, *The Renewal of Literature: Emersonian Reflections* (New York: Random House, 1987).

6 Leo Marx, "Rethinking the American Studies Project," in *American Studies in Germany: European Contexts and Intercultural Relations*, ed. Günter H. Lenz and Klaus J. Milich (New York: St. Martin's, 1995), 54. Subsequent references are cited parenthetically in the text.

7   Cary Nelson provides a concise and relevant manifesto of cultural studies, outlining what cultural studies at their best ought to achieve. Missing from his manifesto, however, is any consideration of nationalism and imperialism as central topics for cultural critics. Cary Nelson, *Manifesto of a Tenured Radical* (New York: New York University Press, 1997), 64–70.

8   I am thinking here of my own recent study, *Literary Culture and U.S. Imperialism: From the Revolution to World War II* (New York: Oxford University Press, 2000), a book that develops just this thesis about U.S. nationalism and imperialism from the first decades of the U.S. republic—the Alien and Sedition Acts, for example—to the 1940s, and the work of Amy Kaplan, who is also writing a book on literature's contribution to U.S. imperialism in the early modern period, from the Spanish-American to the First World wars. There are, of course, many other scholars working in this area, many represented in Amy Kaplan and Donald E. Pease, eds., *Cultures of United States Imperialism* (Durham, N.C.: Duke University Press, 1993), and Donald E. Pease, ed., *National Identities and Post-Americanist Narratives* (Durham, N.C.: Duke University Press, 1994).

9   Richard P. Horwitz, preface to *Exporting America: Essays on American Studies Abroad*, ed. Horwitz (New York: Garland, 1993), xiv. The essays in Horwitz's collection by U.S. and non-U.S. specialists in American studies offer interesting complements and case studies to my argument.

10 Jim Zwick, "Towards Critical Internationalism within U.S.-based American Studies," American Crossroads Project, 18 February 1997; John Carlos Rowe, "Response to Jim Zwick," American Crossroads Project, 18 February 1997.

11 Emory Elliott initiated this work as former Chair of the International Committee of the ASA. Like Paul Lauter, Elliott has visited many international American studies programs and helped bring many international scholars to the United States for extended visits.

12 Giles Gunn has conducted a valuable program for international scholars in American studies at the University of California, Santa Barbara since the summer of 1996, with extramural funding from the U.S. Department of State. The Rockefeller Foundation funded an International Forum for U.S. Studies from 1997–1999 at the University of Iowa. Giles Gunn, Chris Newfield, Elliott Butler-Evans (University of California, Santa Barbara), Jeff Peck (Georgetown), Mark Poster, Gabriele Schwab, and I (University of California, Irvine) have been working with American studies scholars in Europe, led by Günter Lenz at Humboldt University (Berlin), on a transatlantic cooperative research and teaching project since 1995.

13 Reinhold Wagnleitner, *Coca-Colonization and the Cold War: The Cultural Mission of the United States in Austria after the Second World War*, trans. Diana M. Wolf (Chapel Hill: University of North Carolina Press, 1994).

14 John Carlos Rowe, "A Future for American Studies: Comparative U.S. Cultures Model," in *American Studies in Germany*, ed. Lenz and Milich, 262–78.

15 During her participation in the Minority Discourse Project at the University

of California's Humanities Research Institute in 1993–1994, Norma Alarçon took colleagues on a tour of the U.S.-Mexican border, both to familiarize them with an important site of political and social conflict and to remind them that all border studies must be mindful of the actual border zones and their consequences for individual lives. I agree that Alarçon's purpose is an important one for us to keep in mind, but I also think that the U.S.-Mexican border was discursively constructed long before physical barriers were erected (by the Treaty of Guadalupe-Hidalgo, for example) and remains discursively as well as physically policed.

16 Sean Wilentz, "Integrating Ethnicity into American Studies," *Chronicle of Higher Education* 29 November 1996, A56. Lawrence Buell argues that "nation and culture aren't coextensive, but neither are they disjunct." Acknowledging that the "familiar debates about national identity vs. cultural particularism" have been replaced by "the issue of whether a model of cultural identity at any level can hold its ground against a model of cultural hybridization or syncretism," he concludes with a markedly colonialist metaphor for the apocalypse facing American studies scholars who abandon the nationalist and exceptionalist models of the previous generation's work: "The more decentered so-called American literary studies becomes, the more suspect the category of nation as a putative cultural unit, and the more likely United States literature specialists may be to oscillate between clinging to discredited assumptions about national distinctiveness vs. throwing ourselves wholly, *amor fati-like*, on the pyre of postnationalism (in a kind of subdisciplinary suttee)" (emphasis added). It is quite a rhetorical stretch to link postnationalist discussions with the outlawed practice of Hindu suttee, but Buell's choice of metaphors reveals his intention of suggesting thereby the "primitivism" of other cultures—a primitivism American studies must avoid. Buell's orientalism in this instance is interestingly, albeit predictably, complemented by appeals to scientific rationality and the rhetoric of Christian belief: "If we're *truly rigorous* in trying to get to whatever *empirical bedrock underlies* those assumptions while at the same time remaining attentive to the distinction between culture and nation (and with this the promise of border, diaspora, and global culture studies), then we will be *faithful* to our *posts* as post-American Americanists, whatever the outcome of the culture wars." Lawrence Buell, "Are We Post-American Studies?" in *Field Work: Sites in Literary and Cultural Studies*, ed. Marjorie Garber, Paul B. Franklin, and Rebecca L. Walkowitz (New York: Routledge, 1996), 89, 91; emphasis added. It is interesting that the "rigor," "empiricism," and "bedrock" demanded by such an investigation should culminate in a merely rhetorical flourish, redolent of religion (now of the Euroamerican Christian varieties, to be sure): "faithful to our posts as post-American Americanists."

17 For a more general treatment of the problem of the Enlightenment university and the new modes of knowledge, see David Lloyd, "Foundations of Diversity: Thinking the University in a Time of Multiculturalism," in *"Culture" and*

the Problem of the Disciplines, ed. John Carlos Rowe (New York: Columbia University Press, 1998), 15–43.

18 Michael Clough, "Birth of Nations," *Los Angeles Times*, 27 July 1997. Subsequent references are cited parenthetically in the text.

19 Paul Gilroy's notion of the "Black Atlantic" is being used as one model in an international exchange program planned by Southern universities—Miami, Florida, LSU, and Houston, among others—to enable their students to study at European, Caribbean, African, and Latin American universities that will share in this curriculum. Rethinking the educational aims of education abroad programs in terms of the global significance of American studies should thus be one of our tasks. See Paul Gilroy, *The Black Atlantic: Modernity and Double Consciousness* (New York: Verso, 1993).

20 Jesse Vasquez, President of the National Association for Ethnic Studies and professor of Education and Puerto Rican Studies at Queens College, responded to Wilentz's "Integrating Ethnicity into American Studies" in an understandably angry letter to the *Chronicle*, concluding an otherwise sensible critique of Wilentz's arguments by challenging: "It may be that it is ethnic studies that now should consider taking over American studies, and not the other way around." Jesse Vasquez, "Opinion" (letter in response to Sean Wilentz's "Integrating Ethnicity into American Studies"), *Chronicle of Higher Education*, 31 January 1997, B3.

21 Randy Bass and Jeffrey Finlay, *Engines of Inquiry: A Practical Guide for Using Technology to Teach America Culture* (Washington, D.C.: Georgetown University Press, 1997).

22 The Columbia Online Project, which makes available portions of recent scholarly books published by Columbia and Oxford University Presses, and *Literature Online* from Chadwyck-Healey, an electronic publisher, are steps in this direction, but academic presses have been incredibly slow to adapt to the electronic means of scholarly dissemination currently available.

Salesman in Moscow

Dana Heller

Although originally [*Death of a Salesman*] might have been considered to be purely American, now the events depicted there are of great importance to everyone. The problem why people decide to take up trade is very exciting. And now it is especially acute because we are going from the planned economy to the market one, and the transition is accompanied by both good and bad things. First of all we observe a sharp increase in the number of salesmen and traders of all kinds . . . longing for easy money. I am Russian but I perfectly understand the problems with which this play deals. Originally they were peculiar to America, but later they transcended the boundaries and became common in every country.—J. Kulikova

Transcending the Boundaries

In his autobiography, *Timebends: A Life*, Arthur Miller claims that while he remained grateful for the affection with which theater audiences in the former Soviet Union received his plays throughout the twenty years that they were performed there, he was dismayed to learn, during a visit to Moscow in 1965, that a Soviet production of *Death of a Salesman* had undergone some changes "as would undermine criticism of American society. . . . Willy had been caricatured as a total fool, and Charley, who offers him financial help, was rewritten and acted as a clownish idiot, since as a businessman he could not possibly be even slightly altruistic or have a shred of sincerity." And it was in this gap between the openhearted generosity of the Russian people and the strictures of the Communist Party that Miller first glimpsed "the coil of the Russian paradox."[1]

Now that an entirely new era has begun in Russia, paradoxes are no less evident—indeed, if anything, they have multiplied tenfold. However, what is just as evident, as the above excerpt from a Russian undergraduate's essay on Arthur Miller's *Death of a Salesman* suggests, is that Russians' attitudes toward the United States, and their perceptions of themselves as a people and nation apart from the rest of the world, are changing. And the paradox Miller's play dramatizes—the plight of the salesman rendered as obsolete as the unnamed commodities he sells—might be regarded as more than a morbid symptom of America's postwar commodity logic. It stands as a challenge to the very legitimacy of a national literature in a world system in which cultural capital and monetary capital transcend the boundaries of nation. An internationalist framework of the sort currently called for in American studies scholarship is already being constructed outside the purview of most U.S. Americanists, in this particular instance by Russians who are drawn to the study of American culture as they seek to make sense of the paradigm shifts taking place in Russian culture. Their voices, drawn from essays on the cross-cultural relevance of Arthur Miller's *Death of a Salesman*, will be used to demonstrate ways in which issues, questions, and critiques can be reformulated for the purposes of American studies teaching and research.

The current wave of discussion centering on the need to internationalize American studies, along with the growing interest in comparative cultural studies approaches, arises out of the ashes of the Cold War, the decline of the nation-state, as well as the international procession of social upheavals and movements of the 1960s that brought about a number of seismic shifts in the organization of cultural identities, knowledges, and institutions.[2] The current upshot suggests that the future of American studies will proceed from the effort to see ourselves as others see us, an effort requiring no less than a critical decentering of the very concept of Americanness itself. And while most faculty and administration regard this as a worthy and even urgent goal, some participants in the American studies scholarly community caution that the current race to "go forth and internationalize" often does not go far enough. For example, Jane C. Desmond and Virginia R. Dominguez call for a "re-situation" of American studies as an academic site that might "create the conditions for a critical interface between domestic and international perspectives."[3] The authors echo Benjamin Lee's 1995 article in *Public Culture*, which addresses the need for "critical internationalism," "a conceptual orientation that resituates the United States in a global context on a number of planes simultaneously: in terms of the scholarship that gets read, written, and cited and, most importantly, in the ways scholars conceive of new directions for formulating research" (475).[4]

The challenge, at present, is to formulate methods of research that will provide insight into a transnational production of perspectives and develop practices of inquiry that radically decenter preconceptions of self and other. However, I suspect that of all the challenges we face in resituating American studies, the toughest will be to resituate ourselves, cognitively and existentially, as teachers, researchers, and participants in the academic professional managerial class. This process—more painstaking than recruiting foreign faculty and far slower than subscribing to an international e-mail discussion list—requires no less than a reassessment of ourselves as consumers of culture, as agents of new educational technologies, as producers and transmitters of knowledge, and, in a sense, as salesmen within the capital-building technologies of academic institutions where competition for limited material resources is keen and where administrators are increasingly adopting the discourse of consumerism, referring to students as "customers" and the intellectual work of faculty as "product." Such a discursive environment makes the business of internationalizing American studies quite saleable since what is at stake is no longer the preservation of a national culture or service to an idea of the nation-state, but, in Bill Readings's words, service to the university as "another corporation in a world of transnationally exchanged capital."[5] Service of this nature upholds the interests of what Lee calls "liberal internationalism" by seeking principally to secure the university's "position vis-à-vis other universities and contribute to the continuing competitiveness of the United States in a changing world" (573).

But what happens to American cultural capital when exported to Russia— a nation whose long history of isolation from the West, of communist-sponsored anti–United States propaganda, and internal pro-democratic dissidence once produced, among Russian youth particularly, a tendency to idealize the United States and its cultural icons, from Mark Twain to Jim Morrison and Michael Jordan. In post-1991 Moscow, the scene has changed. As David Remnick observes, "a year or two of exposure to American-style commercials has produced what decades of Communist propaganda could not: genuine indignation on the part of honest people against the excesses of capitalism."[6] The monopolization of Russian movie houses by superficial Hollywood blockbusters and the saturation of Russian television with cheaply produced, low-quality American soap operas, serials, and made-for-television films has produced, over the last several years, a sense of American cultural fatigue, as well as a distortion of the true diversity and range of U.S. cultural production. And after the combined shocks of the August 17, 1998, ruble devaluation and the March 24, 1999, launching of United States– led NATO missiles on Kosovo, a sense of profound powerlessness and betrayal has produced among many ordinary Russians—and especially among Russian youth—an intense anti-American hatred and distrust. These sentiments are expressed not only at demonstrations outside the American embassy, but in Russians' day-to-day encounters with the primary symbols of Americanization—symbols that no longer stand for democracy, freedom, and the promise of free markets, but for the interests of those who would, in the words of one student who wishes to remain anonymous, "try to buy our country and turn us all into a bunch of Coca-Cola slurping zombies." While these sentiments, shifts, and developments do not bode well for the immediate future of U.S.–Russian relations, they do indicate that a global critical consciousness is developing in Moscow, albeit painfully, particularly among Russian youth. It is the result of a multiple and contradictory network of resistance and attachment to history, to Russian cultural identity, and a gnawing uncertainty about the future that is woven into the forms and substance of everyday life. My exposure to these forms during the year and a half that I lived and worked in Moscow as a Fulbright Lecturer in American literature and culture at Moscow State University led me to consider the extent to which the so-called Americanization of Russia, and the concomitant Russianization of American cultural exports, is resituating national citizen-subjects across national boundaries.[7]

In my original Fulbright application, I expressed an interest in finding out how the conflicts and contradictions of contemporary American literature—debates over the canon, multiculturalism, race, gender, the entire gamut of concepts and terms that set the tone for academic literary discussion in the United States—might be consonant with the current transformations of Russian cultural life and national consciousness. What I did not anticipate, however, was how my own terms and assumptions would be challenged. This process of defamiliarization extended far beyond the range of cultural differences I encountered daily on the Metro, causing me to experience waves of anxiety and self-doubt about the way I look at—and subsequently create—materials in my classes. And approximately halfway through the semester, when I collected and read my students' midterm essays on Arthur Miller's *Death of a Salesman*, I realized that my understanding of American literature was being radically altered—far beyond what I had imagined as an outcome. My students' responses began to show me how one's understanding of a "classic" American literary work is transformed in the context of a critical interface between U.S. and international perspectives. They compelled me to reconsider the value that descriptions like *quintessentially American* hold in the context of a comparative cultural studies. They begged me to expand the terms of my own reading, to first identify and then put aside my own critical agenda in order to understand what the play might mean in a Russian context. In Moscow, I began to develop a powerful sense of how "imagined communities" reimagine one another, and in the process recreate themselves.[8]

Dreamers of the Dream

I taught *Death of a Salesman* as the first work in a course on contemporary American literature that included selected poems by Adrienne Rich and Allen Ginsberg, stories by Flannery O'Connor and Donald Barthelme, essays by Norman Mailer and James Baldwin, Toni Morrison's *Beloved* and Art Spiegelman's *Maus I*. I began with *Salesman* for reasons having to do with historical chronology, although the play was also intended to establish one of the broader themes of the course: the American writer's translation of historical tensions into personal ones. The introductory lecture included background material on Miller himself, the production history of the play, and a brief overview of the play's critical reception. After three weeks of discussion, we watched the 1985 Volker Schlöndorff teleplay starring Dustin Hoffman. At this point, I asked students to consider whether critics who regard Miller's *Death of a Salesman* as the quintessential twentieth-century American play are correct, or if Miller himself was correct in believing the play capable of transcending national concerns, of reaching to some essential core of human longing. Given that Miller's primary motive in directing the 1983 Beijing production of *Salesman* was "to try to show that there is only one humanity," could the play genuinely engage contemporary Russian readers and contribute to the ways in which they think the changes of their own private and public lives?[9] In this way, I hoped to find out if Willy Loman's crisis corresponded in any way to Russian students' sense of crisis, disillusionment, and emergency in a city where virtually everyone is becoming a salesman. Students' responses to this question were very strong and divided.

So, what does *Death of a Salesman* look like when viewed through a Russian prism? For a moment consider the situation of these students. My contemporary American literature class at Moscow University represented a far more culturally and ethnically homogenous group than my classes at Old Dominion University, the state university in Norfolk, Virginia, where I am an associate professor in the English department. The vast majority of these students were Russian nationals of traditional college age, late teens and early twenties. A portion of them attended the university for free, although most paid at least a percentage of their tuition, determined by their academic records and histories and their performances on entry exams. Despite this extraneous difference, a powerful sense of group cohesion and interreliance defined the class, as is common among Russian college students who typically remain tightly grouped together in classes for the full five-year duration of their studies. Undoubtedly, historical and social factors also play a key role in fostering this sense of cohesion: these students are the generation that would define the "New Russia," and they were very much aware of the unique historical position this placed them in. They were bright, fluent in English, some were multilingual, and a number had already spent some time living or studying abroad. Moreover, they were destined to be credentialed by the oldest and most prestigious institution of higher education in Russia. In 1997, with the economic boom still apparently underway and statistics indicating the slow growth of a middle class, one would have thought they had every reason to be optimistic about finding work and making a decent living in Moscow. Yet when I asked them about their futures, they spoke cautiously, many of them expressing doubt and uncertainty about their prospects, the value of their educations, and the future of the Russian state. They expressed a critical awareness of the price that Russians were paying for their new freedoms. When I asked them what kind of work they imagined themselves doing, most said that they would probably wind up in some form of sales.

Olga Sarkisova related the play to the plight of Russian families struggling to survive in the new Russian free market and to the huge gap that has opened up between generations: "I felt that the conflict of Loman's family is very similar to the situations in many Russian families of post-Soviet Russia. Many people who are older than forty often have great difficulties in finding work. The new generations that were raised on the values of Soviet Union and now live in democratic and capitalist Russia often call themselves 'lost generation': values are changing constantly, money is becoming more important than people, community switched to commodities and so [to its] values. So I am certain that this drama has far reaching, cross-cultural significance."

Comparing Willy to the "lost generation" of middle-aged Russians unable to find work in the new market economy at once establishes his cultural relevance as a hapless victim of social change, but at the same time it registers a distinction between Willy's individual experience of dislocation and the collective dislocation of a generation. This distinction appears frequently in students' responses. Helen Averkulva argues that Willy Loman's failure to achieve the American Dream "is also relevant for Russians because we

Russians survived the same disillusionment and corruption of the Socialist Dream. The whole nation was deceived . . . taken in for seventy years. But while Willy Loman is going through his exhaustion alone, we were going through it together, the whole country, on a much larger scale."

Like Olga Sarkisova, Olesia Fedorova locates the play's universality in its family theme: "I think the aspects connected with the inner family life are especially close to the Russian audience, which has always valued good, close relations within the family and between people in general. That is why Willy's loneliness especially hurts Russian hearts . . . and if you wish I could find millions of Willy Lomans in Moscow."

Her comment raises the question of the play's universality and recalls a particular passage from *Salesman in Beijing* wherein Arthur Miller describes the closing moments of Bill Moyers's television special on the Beijing production of *Salesman*. There is "a close-up of a young Chinese . . . saying something about China being full of Willies, dreamers of the dream" (245). In discussion, I asked my students how we might define the specific content of this avowedly transcendent dream. Here, we turned again to *Timebends*, where Miller claims that Willy Loman represents the universal dream "to excel, to win out over anonymity and meaninglessness, to love and be loved, and above all, perhaps, to *count*" (184). Whereas Miller's notion of universal human longing emphasizes competition, achievement, and recognition, students understood the dream to be more specifically oriented to communal and spiritual bonds, and they read Willy's isolation as his failure to reach beyond the superficial demands of competition and desire. Miller's arrogance, some students indicated, is communicated in his presumption that individual accomplishment and self-realization constitute transcultural values. We concluded that while there are undoubtedly Chinese, Russians, and Americans who share this belief in a universal humanity, a transcendent human longing, definitions of the nature of that longing are local, infinitely variable, and culturally nuanced. This observation set the tone for acknowledging other instances in American literary works where cultural differences and commonalities can be seen to coexist rather than cancel each other out.

A number of students expressed unflinching certainty that the play was appropriate only to American culture and society. Natalia Pavlova writes: "In my opinion there are no relevant aspects of the play for the Russian audience. The mentality of these two nations differ so much. Such a life that Willy Loman leads cannot be observed in Russia. The value of money is not overestimated in Russia and forgetfulness is not typical of the Russians. (By forgetfulness, I mean the disrespect for the people who have made the company prosperous, 'forgetfulness' of their merits.) So, *Death of a Salesman* is a truthful play about American society."[10]

In sharp contrast is Vera Shekerbakova's opinion:

> The play is very actual for Russia, especially nowadays when we try to change our history and many old people who lived for the dream of communism (Soviet dream of 70 years) now understand that they lived for nothing, that all their efforts are not needed anymore. The great Russian drama of '90s, that people who had worked for the profit of the country now have to ask money on the streets and Metro. And young people, who finished 10 classes of school, are the richest people in our country. I think that it is very difficult for old generation to watch how ideals have changed. The same crush of the dream happened in Russia. So, now, there are a lot of Willy Lomans in Russia and I think that very soon a lot of Biff Lomans will appear.

Russia's "new" history, which Shekerbakova refers to, is founded on a largely symbolic attempt to reconnect with a history that was dismantled with the Bolshevik Revolution of 1917. The restoration of prerevolutionary street names and the reconstruction of Russian Orthodox cathedrals destroyed under Stalin creates for many Muscovites, not to mention tourists trying to negotiate their way through the city, a disorienting and peculiarly postmodern sense of moving forward into the past. In *Death of a Salesman*, Miller's formal strategy of "timebends," repeated "dramatic rhythms to connect past and present,"[11] evokes a similar sense of slippage and time warp, although in the play this condition is experienced by Willy alone. Still, the return of the past and its reimagined meanings in the context of the present are formal elements that resonated powerfully for my Russian students who are witnessing the resurrection of Russian history as Russia's future.

Shekerbakova, like many of the students, read *Death of a Salesman* as a drama about aging and the expendability of the elderly in a social economy driven by the valuing of a dollar over human relationship and accountability, a conflict unleashed by Russia's own economic-political transformation, the failure of the state to meet pension payments. Willy Loman became for many of my Russian students a vivid emblem of the current situation of Russia's retired laborers and war veterans.[12] Shekerbakova's response also raises the issue of generational conflict and its relation to such economic and ideological sea changes. In this sense, part of the relevance of *Salesman* for Russian readers is its dramatization of the social dynamic that accelerates generational shifts: Willy becomes aligned with an older generation utterly disenfranchised by the imperatives of the marketplace, the imperatives of new technologies. Biff becomes aligned with an incredulous younger generation that has already begun to register its rebellion against the materialist ethos of the "New Russians," or the aggressive entrepreneurial class who moved quickly in the early years of reform to amass huge fortunes, which they then proceeded to showcase in the most notoriously excessive and ostentatious manners. Indeed, whereas Soviet humor typically took the Communist bureaucracy as its principle dupe, New Russians have recently moved to the fore as the undisputed brunt of popular Russian jokes. The newly rich, such as Happy aspires to become, are now mocked and resented by many Russians who have no indigenous framework for comprehending the unchecked and widening gap between rich and poor.

It is not surprising, then, that my Russian students demonstrated a much stronger inclination to identify with Biff than I have observed among students in the United States, more of whom seem inclined to regard Biff as a hopeless "slacker" and identify with Happy's ambition and swagger, despite their recognition of his moral imperfections. At Old Dominion University, the majority of my undergraduates are from middle-class, blue-collar backgrounds. Many are first-generation college students majoring in English in order to become elementary and secondary school teachers. They balance various combinations of part-time jobs, full-time jobs, and family/childrearing responsibilities with their degree progress. Almost without exception, their eyes are on "The Job," and in that sense their willingness to side with Happy's optimism affirms their own hopes and investments in the American Dream.

In Moscow, on the other hand, a cultural sense of disorientation and exhaustion has spread through the population since the heady days of the democratic movement ended with the failed 1993 putsch. There is a general attitude among Muscovites that the new "democratic" or capitalistic system, although nascent and developing, is currently as corrupt and illusory as the former Soviet system was. The old ideology has been replaced by a grab-it-while-you-can capitalist ideology that is pure Darwinism, survival of the fittest. The political choice of many young Russians is to remain flatly indifferent to it. In a way similar to the Russian intelligentsia of the 1960s, the *shestidesiatniki*, who took jobs as boiler room attendants in order to have more time for personal pursuits, many young people are satisfied with "Mcjobs," or work that provides minimal participation in the system.[13]

Natalia Kuzmina voices a more sympathetic understanding of Happy Loman based on his unromantic acceptance of the brutalities incurred by American capitalism and the inability to position oneself entirely outside its structures:

> The American society, based on money . . . cruelty, produces false dreams that later on shatter people's lives. . . . Willy Loman was wrong in thinking that everyone loved and respected him. His son Happy's beliefs are not so idealistic. He realizes that . . . commercial success is a matter of life and death. He is not afraid to challenge it, he is eager to prove that the dreams of his late father were not senseless. But I think it doesn't occur to him that by doing so he will contribute to this pitiless world. And it may happen so that by joining the competition, due to his young strength, fresh ideas, and the drive, he may cause the death of another aged Willy Loman, somebody's husband and father.

Here Happy is cast as a shortsighted realist in an ironic contest of generational one-upmanship. The irony is rooted in his devotion to the very destructive patterns that killed his father, an irony that strikes again at the incompatibility of human compassion and material competition. Yura Babinkov more specifically considers the conflict of material ambition with Russian spiritual values: "Though Russians have been trying to become businessmen lately, it is still *not* essential for the Russian mind to be aimed at making money only . . . we are not as practical as Americans. *Death of a Salesman* is a play that Russians cannot identify with. Of course, one can say that we also have the motif of a person torn between dream and reality in Russian classical literature. But in our literature a man becomes insane not because of the lack of success in business, but because of moral dilemmas and instability of Russian national character."

Here, again, a recognition of cultural differences within a context of potential regularities within cultural forms was useful in approaching the topic of Willy's dual consciousness. For some students, the duality of Willy's mind seemed relevant to a duality that Russians now face. Lyuba Grakhova writes, "This conflict of two ideas . . . can be fairly applied to the Russian society, where one now has a various range of opportunities to reach prosperity, and, on the other hand, to lose everything in life." Once again, however, while Willy's malaise appears to be one that he alone suffers from, the Russian version of this duality is a collective burden. And the belief that Russia's cultural as well as spiritual greatness lies in its privileging of the latter over the former still remains salient. For example, V. Rastorguev writes:

The Russian national character does not presuppose such an unthinking optimism which the Americans have. In my opinion, Russia, through intense suffering, achieved some spiritual development. That is why, I think, it is somehow unnatural for a Russian to see anything tragic in Willy Loman's tragedy. Fear to lose wealth, to be behind others is perceived as a tragedy because of the absence of real spiritual values. Belief in success is a shallow substitute for real values. Miller's making his protagonist a tragic person is a confirmation of American spiritual exhaustion and weakening of human-being. A Russian proverb says: "Man has on earth no home. But he does have wings to heaven." As a Russian, I do not expect a country to bless me with success, guide me and provide my welfare. I should develop some greatness in my own soul.

Belief in the spiritual depth of Russian life and literature and the superficiality of all things American is an opinion often dismissed by Americans as an essentialist myth that serves as compensation for Russia's massive historical losses. But what I found more problematic were the responses of students who read Miller's play as an affirmation of, rather than a critique of, American shallowness. Why bother searching for something noble in a salesman, they repeatedly asked. This led us to the formal question of the status of Miller's play as tragedy, a genre that most students agreed would admit the "common man." Their resistance to Willy Loman's credibility as a legitimate tragic hero, however, grew out of his ostensibly tragic position as a failed salesman, which is not too surprising in a society that is struggling with moral ambivalence about whether salesmen are at all capable of representing the common Russian folk. I suggested that since Miller never tells us what it is that Willy sells, he might want us to understand salesmanship not as a particular occupation but as a metaphor for public function, which clearly Willy can no longer fulfill, and that within certain social and economic systems most public functions require some salesmanship skills, like teaching, for example. A number of students expressed discomfort with this analogy, which then turned to a comparison between the arts of selling and the arts of instruction. While Russian students were more inclined to view teachers as akin to spiritual or religious leaders, my students in the United States have never voiced discomfort with the analogy of teaching and salesmanship; in fact, the equivalence of a seller who makes you want to buy and a professor who makes you want to learn seems self-evident to them. On the surface it would certainly appear that salesman-as-metaphor circulates within a much broader range of conceivable labors in the classless American imaginary. In Moscow, this possibility led to a discussion of U.S. televangelism and the forms and embodiments of spiritual crisis that one is likely to encounter in societies where evangelical culture and commercial culture have a history of more flagrant codependence.

The gradual restoration of the Russian Orthodox Church to a position of political power, the cultural shift away from xenophobia and isolationism, and Russia's new position on the international stage are causes for optimism among my Russian students. The new freedom of the press, the Internet, cable and satellite television are intensifying their perception of the dissolution of national boundaries and the irrelevancy of former U.S.-Soviet antagonisms. For students such as Kulikova, whose comments appear at the beginning of this essay, history has rewritten *Death of a Salesman*, just as Russia has rewritten its history. Helen Averkulva eloquently elaborates on this point:

> On the one hand, *Death of a Salesman* is a very American play, or I would rather say anti-American play, because Arthur Miller, as a supersensitive writer of his time, perceived, felt, the seamy side of the American dream—the side that isn't advertised in billboards and mass media . . . and isn't taught in schools. This American dream clashes with reality, and in reality not everyone or anyone is destined, or fated, to take the best place under the sun. That is the essence of competitiveness. But the American dream implies that "all men are created equal," that everybody from the holy hills of the American land has the equal opportunity to reach success, luxury, respect of the society. . . . Regarding this aspect of dream we can also state that Miller's drama of an aging salesman, torn between dream and reality, has far-reaching cross-cultural significance. However, I can feel with all my fibers that no one culture besides America has such a doctrine, an ideology for the people, the point, the idea, for the sake of which people live. That's why Willy Loman is a tragic hero no less than Hamlet in his rotten Denmark. This tragedy is not the disappointment or disillusionment of one particular person . . . but it is the tragedy of all Willy Lomans . . . all weak, ordinary people . . . there are millions of them. Only one of the millions becomes Henry Ford, Rockefeller, Bill Gates. They are exceptions. And only the culture of America took these exceptions as an example, as an example for the others, and created an American Dream. . . .
>
> But, on the other hand, this play is also relevant for Russians because we Russians survived the same disillusionment and corruption of the Socialist Dream. The whole nation was deceived . . . taken in for seventy years. But while Willy Loman is going through his exhaustion alone, we were going through it together, the whole country, on a much larger scale. So, what happened further. The high-ups made up an ingenious gimmick . . . they

took another idea to live for—they borrowed the American Dream. So, we are all now blinded by this American dream's light. This Dream becomes the incentive, as well as it was to be when the Pilgrims first stepped on the land on Plymouth, when the founding fathers wrote the Declaration of Independence. I know that American Dream has its roots in the history. But we Russians have no background for this Dream. And now there is a crack, a break of all layers of the society, the transitory period from collective minded people to the individualistic approach to life (the same as the breaking of the community in *Death of a Salesman*). We can notice the same tendencies in our Russian society, neighbors stop talking on the flight of steps, stop discussing spiritual problems on the phone . . . stop helping each other, everybody is afraid to stay behind, everybody is eager to catch up with the others, running ahead—to buy CD players, new Mercedes, to date more girls, earn more and more. Children are working the cars in the streets, newsboys are selling news, traffickers are selling cheap clothes—the history repeats itself—so, we are now following in the American steps. Well, perhaps American dream will modify into Russian dream. Sincerely speaking I am afraid that the consequences of realization as well as collapse of the Russian dream will be more tragic, more frightening, world-shaking because we Russians are very unpredictable, we like going to the extremes. I think we are the greatest extremists of the world. But we are alike, Russia and America, that's why I perceive American literature as mine, ours, Russian. Maybe soon there will exist new play, "The Death of a New Russian." But there is also a possibility that the corrupt disillusionment of the Russian dream won't be very tragic just because we Russians are very tolerant, patient, take our fate with a resignation that traces back to the doctrine of the Russian Orthodox church.

A "Salesman Unaware"

Obviously, these responses are not representative of all Russians, nor are they representative of all young people in all countries of the former Soviet Union. And although it hardly needs saying, let the record show that my interpretations of these responses are neither scientific nor conclusive. But I would argue nevertheless that these responses are clearly indicative of a process of resistance, appropriation, and modification, a process through which my students were able to preserve a sense of cultural distinctiveness and at the same time create links with American themes and concerns. Benjamin Lee addresses this decentering function of a comparative cultural criticism that places "the question of universal values in a different light than that assumed by either radical relativists or universalists." Working from the anthropological assumption that universals can only be grounded in a search for "maximal differences," he concludes that "just as a comparative approach does not presuppose the existence of universals, it also does not presuppose a non-empirical justification of relativism, since comparison may reveal some universal regularities in cultural forms" (578). Reading *Salesman* through the differences and commonalities perceived by my Russian students revealed the limitations of my own structural presuppositions and destabilized my own fixed opposition of "views from somewhere" and "views from nowhere," without precluding the discovery of value in either.

Since our weekly meetings ran for only one and a half hours, time constraints made it impossible for us to address the play from every critical angle. Psychological approaches (which are becoming increasingly popular in contemporary Russia) as well as issues of language and rhetoric took up very little of our attention.[14] I did need to explain the concept of life insurance, which for some of them was an obstacle in understanding Willy's motivation to suicide. Although life insurance is becoming more common in Russia, the very idea of assigning a dollar value to a human life came into conflict with many of my students' most basic values, and some thought the entire concept patently absurd.[15] My attempts to develop a discussion around feminist approaches to the play, addressing the silence and lack of space that defines Miller's female characters, produced not so much discomfort—as I had been warned it would—than polite indifference. Although several students expressed disapproval of Willy's harsh treatment of Linda—taking this as evidence of his overall lack of compassion and spiritual depth—more were inclined to see Linda as weak and partially responsible for Willy's death.[16] My U.S. students often hold Linda responsible as well; however, feminist issues are always guaranteed to evoke interest, debate, and responses ranging from sophisticated critical analysis to obligatory acknowledgment of Miller's marginalization of women. In Russia, Western discourses of liberal feminism, feminist psychoanalytic theory, and gender studies have begun to circulate and take hold, especially among intellectuals and academics in larger cities such as Moscow and St. Petersburg. However, a problem remains insofar as the language of Western feminism could not be farther removed from Russian reality—terms such as *patriarchy* and *womanhood* simply have no equivalents in the Russian language, and terms such as *oppression* and *suppression* are words that repel contemporary Russians because of their lingering association with Marxist ideology (Gessen 89–90). The very notion of a feminist "movement" reeks of an absolutism that Russians are desperately trying to distance themselves from. In contemporary Russia, any *ism* is likely to be met with disdain if not outright hostility.

This was certainly the case with Marxism. In the introductory lecture I spoke about Miller's political commitments and affiliations, the American theater as an agent of social reform, Miller's pro-Soviet stance, and his conflicts with McCarthyism. I told them the story of the woman who allegedly stood up in the audience on the opening night of *Salesman* and called the play "a timebomb under American capitalism," as well as Miller's response, that he "hoped it was" (*Timebends*, 184). I had begun to wonder about the extent to which Miller's defiant social vision had been shaped by the heady days of the American left, its backing of Stalin, and its defense of the Soviet experiment, all culminating in *Death of a Salesman*, where, as Helge Normann Nilsen argues, "Biff becomes the vehicle through which Miller subtly introduces his alternative socialist perceptions and values into his work." My students tended to see Biff as representative of similar alternative impulses and agreed with Nilsen's characterization of him as "the only character . . . who really understands the destructive nature of capitalist priorities and feels pity and concern for his father."[17] But while their viewpoints coincided with Nilsen's study of Marxism's influence on *Salesman*, none of them so much as broached the terms *Marxism* or *socialism* in discussion or in writing. When structuring comparisons and contrasts, their reference points were "classic" Russian authors and literary texts of the prerevolutionary period. There was no mention of the dissident tradition or to post-Glasnost literature. However, virtually all of them registered instant recognition and delight when I screened an episode of *The Simpsons* that parodies Willy's speech to Howard ("A man is not a piece of fruit!"). To invite a Marxist reading of the play, even from a Western perspective, would certainly have been to invite their polite indifference, to feel that slight chill of resistance and detachment overtake the room. Rather, by following their cues, by letting our discussions go in the directions they indicated, I could begin to apprehend *Salesman* as a play that cautions against the destructiveness of a kind of hyperindividualism, or as a play legitimately concerned with religion and spirituality, although U.S. American studies scholarship in general, and literary scholarship on *Salesman* in particular, would not regard this as a relevant topic. Yet one might ask to what extent a longing for spiritual redemption is embedded within structures of American consumerism and competition. Working within the critical paradigms of

U.S. American studies, it is not always easy to see the way these issues inter-twine. However, the comparativist dialogue that my students and I estab-lished in Moscow helped clear a space for the reformulation of the terms of inquiry, and consequently for a complete reevaluation of the very object of American studies—Americanness itself.

These reformulations seemed to me deeply ironic in that the establish-ment of American studies abroad owes so much to the conflicts between the United States and the Soviet Union and over whose national values would dominate in the postwar period.[18] The Marshall Plan, the United States Information Agency, and the Fulbright Exchange Program were all estab-lished as strategic means of addressing these antagonisms through cultural diplomacy.[19] And while opportunities for teaching in Russia through Ful-bright exchanges are far less fraught with political, social, and bureaucratic tensions now than they were twenty years ago, Americanists in Russia are still liable to encounter obstacles to establishing genuine critical interface with academic colleagues.[20] The demands of carving out a basic living for oneself in the contemporary Russian university or institute leave little time for lei-surely discussion or collegial exchanges in hallways and offices, and they leave no time to soothe the egos of visiting Western scholars who may be apt to interpret linguistic and cultural differences as signals that their presence is underappreciated. Indeed, for American Fulbrighters in Russia, especially at larger and more cosmopolitan institutions where foreigners have ceased to be the novelty that they once were, the experience of resituation can be one of isolation.

A further irony is that the most recent wave of interest in internationaliz-ing American studies asserted itself alongside a developing trend of declining enrollments in Russian area and language studies programs in the United States, a steadily progressing trend since the breakup of the Soviet Union. At my own university, Russian studies was entirely dismantled and a tenure-track faculty member released, a casualty of the administratively expedient concurrence of a corporate-style state mandate to downsize and decreased student interest in an area studies program whose critical parameters, not to mention its geopolitical boundaries, suddenly no longer seemed certain or marketable. At the same time, the move toward internationalizing American studies suggests a similar anxiety and questioning impulse with respect to national borders, cultural coherence, and the cost-effective organization of academic disciplines. But underlying these reconfigurations is the fact that for decades the American idea of Russia has often provided us with a detour, an indirect route toward addressing—from a distance—our own national anxieties about America's image abroad, as well as our own domestic conflicts and crises. How do—or can—we see ourselves now, in a new epoch of U.S.-Russian relations? How is Russia's current identity crisis understood by Russians in relation to anti-American sentiments, a minimal investment of U.S. monetary capital in Russia, and a dramatic import of U.S. cultural goods, many of which (like the film *Titanic* or anything with a Nike logo) bestow a symbolic prestige on the viewer or wearer that at once calls up Bourdieu's notion of the relative autonomy of cultural forms *and* insists on an expansion of that notion that would take up, in all respects, questions of convertibility and translatability of symbolic capital across boundaries of nation-states.[21] At such a transitional moment in history, not only does it seem essential to develop comparative analyses of cultural capital that can account for the changing interrelationship between symbolic and monetary forms, but it also seems to be a critical time for the United States to promote Russian area studies and think about Russian and American culture from a comparativist perspective.

Indeed, in the commercially aggressive, albeit uncertain urban environment that is Moscow, American studies appears as less a strong arm of ideological coercion than as one of many suspect commodities among the motor oils, Snickers bars, Happy Meals, and Levi's 501s: commodities that are now available to Russians whose national identity—a contradictory assemblage of traditions and values both ancient and modern—is undergoing a period of radical reconfiguration. Meanwhile, virtual Americanness is a hot commodity on the Russian youth market; it circulates through television and radio programming, cigarette advertisements, toy culture, fashion, tourism, Web page design, automotive culture, cuisine, film, video, and theater. In this dizzying commercial context, a Fulbright lecturer in American culture is no less expected to "represent her country well." But while once that meant serving, in the words of one Fulbright alum, as an "ambassador unaware," in contemporary Russia it is difficult to ignore the sense that one has been sent abroad as a "salesman unaware," a trafficker in the "good stuff," or a sort of pseudo-celebrity endorser of American cultural forms high and low.[22] However, from an American perspective, it is sheer arrogance to assume that the widening circulation of American ideas and cultural artifacts is weakening Russian cultural identity and intensifying Russian identifications with the values of the United States. Rather, I would argue that the responses of Russians to American cultural forms reveal more about their attachments to and struggles with a changing sense of what it means to be Russian than they say about the power of American culture in determining the outcome of these changes.

In *Lenin's Tomb*, David Remnick's account of the events leading up to the collapse of the Soviet Union, the author describes an interview with the Charity Society, a Leningrad protection racket. Comprised of four enterprising young men—among them a former athlete and a veteran of the war in Afghanistan—the Charity Society had found a way to translate their strengths into the idiom of a fledgling free market that some compared to "the Wild West" and others to "Chicago in the thirties." In exchange for a bottle of Johnnie Walker, the Charity Society was happy to talk business, which, they boasted, primarily involved "persuasion" and only occasionally required beatings and torture of a purely professional nature. In the midst of the interview one of the interviewees, Sergei, broke into a crazed giggle that seemed at once familiar to Remnick. In fact, it was the same giggle that Robert DeNiro had developed for his character in the movie *Mean Streets*. Remnick remarked on the similarity and Sergei admitted that he had seen the film. "We learn a lot of what we do that way," he said, also citing *Goodfellas* and *Once upon a Time in America* as films he had studied on the Charity Society's video system (316–17). In the early 1990s, these films could have been added to the list of popular American exports to Russia that included Reeboks and Dale Carnegie's *How to Win Friends and Influence People*.

That American culture is having an influence on the newly democratic Russian state, including its now notorious mafia culture, is far less inconspicuous than the process by which the effects of this influence become reinscribed within American culture as qualities horrifyingly, exotically, and uniquely Russian. A distorted media image of the new Russian metropolis, where danger lurks on every corner, where corruption and amorality drive ordinary men and women to thievery and prostitution, has arisen alongside the Hollywood appearance of a new breed of Russian villain. A style of gangsterism at once as familiar as Boris and Natasha Badanoff yet marked by a uniquely post-Soviet thirst for vengeance against the United States perpetuates the notorious instability of the Russian national character in Hollywood films as recent as *The Saint* and *Air Force One*, both of which rebounded back to Russia where they enjoyed brisk sales on the bootleg video market. Yet even when he or she appears with a Russian accent, we might say that the new Russian mobster is no less hybrid a character, no less the product of a collaborative cross-flow of cultural influence, than Mark Twain's Huckleberry Finn. For in much the same way that Twain's chance encounter with the African American hotel clerk "Jimmy" now appears to have inspired the quintessentially American vernacular of Huck, causing recent critics to ask if perhaps Huck was black, we may ask if the ubiquitous Russian mobster performs our own Hollywood fascination with organized crime, an heir unapparent to American myths that are themselves culturally hybrid, based in narratives of urban immigrant experience.[23]

Remnick's anecdote fits well with Richard Pells's argument that "audiences both in the United States and in Europe have become active participants in determining the effects of American mass culture, constantly reinterpreting its messages to fit their own social or personal circumstances" (280). Pells's apprehension of the ability of Europeans to take what they want from American culture, reinterpreting it to suit their own needs despite a long history of American policy aimed at inspiring Europeans to become "more like us," corroborated with my own observations. By no means passive victims of American cultural imperialism or passive consumers of American cultural hegemony, my Russian students are already internationalizing American literature by interpreting and articulating topics through their own national concerns and issues. Reading and rereading these responses to *Salesman*, and including them in the material that my students in the United States receive in preparation for studying the play, continually suggests ways in which readers reconfigure cultural works to suit their own national concerns and to address anxieties about globalization. In Moscow, while some students reconfigured the play to form links between our cultures, others reconfigured it to draw firm lines of separation between us. However, both reconfigurations are registers of the contradictory commercial and economic shifts currently taking place throughout Eastern Europe and the countries of the former Soviet Union. Moreover, they are registers of how Russians are Russianizing what the United States exports to them at every level of culture. And in that sense one might say that my Russian students are young pioneers in a way that their grandparents never could have imagined. Unlike the scholars and lecturers who were my colleagues at Moscow State University, these students came of age in a time of economic crisis and psychological shock, forming and negotiating their identities amidst debates over Westernization versus Russianization, the superficial glut and blurt of American advertising images, and the increasing visibility and popularity of Western—and predominantly American—styles, slang, and popular culture. The gap that opened with the falling away of Marxist-Leninist ideology and the concern—

voiced by Communist Party members as well as former dissidents such as Aleksandr Solzhenitsyn—that a vulgar American influence is weakening orthodox Russian identity, has supported a resurgence of Russian cultural traditionalism set against an incongruous and chaotic commercial landscape where seemingly overnight everything has gone up for sale and everyone has become a salesman. Given this complex state of affairs, Bill Readings's assertion that "once the notion of national identity loses its political relevance, the notion of culture becomes effectively unthinkable" (89–90), does more to establish grounds for his critique of North American cultural studies than it does in accounting for the recent non-Western trends toward Asianization, Hinduization, re-Islamization, and Russianization, trends that cannot be accurately lumped together as reactionary nationalism since they indicate a transnational rethinking of the terms of cultural unity and nonsecular identity in the face of the nation-state's failure to function as their primary source.

Teaching *Salesman* to students in the United States, I have long presented arguments for interpretations of the work based in the particularities of American historical developments and cultural values of the postwar period: competition, rugged individualism, myths of the family, ideologies of gender, consumer capitalism, the social reformist function of the American theater, changes in structures of American labor and community.[24] In Moscow, these factors became less significant for students insofar as they were perfectly capable of grasping the play without extensive American historical knowledge. But they became more significant factors for me as I realized the extent to which my reliance on them had produced nearsightedness with respect to alternative codings in the text. The actual exposure to different strategies of textual reception, and recognition of the different forms of social and cultural life that determine these strategies, were just some of the factors resulting in my resituation within a context of critical internationalism. This led to my apprehension of how very Russian American literature can seem, and how misleading any assumption of a coherent cultural identity has become.

To be an Americanist in Moscow at the close of the twentieth century is in many ways to irrevocably confront the virtual reality of the American national idea. Teaching there showed me both the far-reaching flow of American cultural engagements and the extent to which American culture no longer really matters as such, which is to say as *American* culture. In large part this is because of the dual role of the discourse of Americanization, on one hand asserting America's economic influence along with its cultural influence, and on the other hand prompting resentment, anxiety, and an intensification of non-Western cultural identity. "A West at the peak of its power confronts non-Wests that increasingly have the desire, the will, and the resources to shape the world in non-Western ways," cautions Samuel B. Huntington.[25] Working from the assumption that transnational capitalism has disintegrated the value of national cultures *tout ensemble*, Bill Readings argues that Americanization (which he takes as a synonym for globalization), rather than bringing about a "clash of civilizations" (of the sort Huntington predicts), or a global culture in which everyone is more alike, instead brings about "a global realization of the contentlessness of the national idea, which shares the emptiness of the cash-nexus and of excellence" (35). Readings offers a persuasive analysis of the current crisis of the Western humanities project; however, by neglecting to distinguish between globalization and Americanization, he runs the risk of resituating North American culture at an imaginary center, a focal point from which a global diffusion of national identities proceeds. Such an equation casually enacts the kind of slippage that critics such as Lee, Desmond, and Dominguez warn American studies scholars against insofar as it retains "a tendency to look outward . . . seeing similarities to our own situation rather than exploring the possibilities that analyses of the United States generated by quite different contexts might reveal fundamentally different readings of our contemporary cultural formations" (Desmond and Dominguez 479). When he turns specifically to the project of American studies, Readings reiterates this tendency: "Despite the enormous energy expended in attempts to isolate and define an 'Americanness' in American studies programs, one might read these efforts as nothing more than an attempt to mask the fundamental anxiety that it in some sense *means nothing* to be American, that 'American culture' is becoming increasingly a structural oxymoron" (35–36).

But what I want to suggest is that a critical internationalism would have to challenge any a priori assumption that the isolation of "Americanness" is what directs American studies energies today. It seems to me that precisely the opposite claim could be made, that our anxieties could be shown to stem from the recognition that American studies practices differ from culture to culture and that the definitions, methods, and perspectives that North American scholars assume are exportable everywhere are, in fact, not. In other words, American studies research can no more assume that the object of inquiry is internally defined and its methods universally applicable than critics of Americanization can assume that its causes and effects emanate from within the United States. Indeed, Americanization signals a critical redeployment of the very concept of culture across a diversity of international public spheres, each one with its own set of sense-making strategies with respect to the phenomenon.

American literary works, like most Americans, live in multiple worlds simultaneously. Similarly, in Russia, being Russian means living with a new sense of oneself as an essentially decentered subject; it means absorbing cultural change while maintaining pride in cultural tradition; it means restoring faith in nation without giving reign to a resurgent nationalism based largely in a supplanting of the national idea with elements of traditional culture— language, customs, religious beliefs, and institutional structures. On a not insignificant level, one could say that the decline and collapse of the Soviet Union has amplified the need for U.S. Americanists to come to grips with the same slippage and tension in understanding the domestic relation between nation and culture. This is demonstrated in our ongoing debates over multiculturalism, public funding for the arts and humanities, and transformations of public tensions into playfully ironic bases for new forms of national-cultural cohesion, forms represented by movements such as Queer Nation. The current impulse toward identifying and implementing various modes of internationalist comparative critique is both a response to and a symptom of these transformations taking place across the domestic as well as the world stage. In Moscow, *Death of a Salesman* provided for both my students and myself a flash point of convergent levels of cultural identity, an exercise in reading without national borders. And it was here that I came to apprehend, in contrast to Readings's insistence on the inability of any cultural product to realize a national meaning, that national meanings can be construed as one of many possible levels of cultural identification, with Huntington's notion of "civilization identification" perhaps constituting the broadest possible level in a new phase of world politics defined by the decline of the nation-state's role in determining the fault lines of future conflict. Indeed, the student who predicts the rise of a generation of Russian Biffs or the conceivable creation of a new play, "Death of a New Russian," suggests at one and the same time the assertion of national meaning *and* a concomitant draining away of hegemonic nationalist discourses in an age of transnational flow. "People can and do redefine their identities," Huntington writes, "and, as a result, the composition and boundaries of civilizations change" (24). Paradoxically, this points to the transformation of *Death of a Salesman* into the very thing it condemns: Miller's dissident critique of postindustrial capitalism becomes yet another cultural product in a world of transnationally exchanged cultural capital. Yet at the same time it retains its status as a "classic" American literary work to which students in Russia and elsewhere turn in order to gather information about what it means to be American and, moreover, what it means not to be one; what it means to inhabit multiple and contradictory subject positions without entirely losing a sense of where you live, where you come from.

While I remain convinced of the need for U.S. Americanists to develop a critical internationalism of the kind Lee, Desmond, and Dominguez call for, I suspect that in our very American rush to internationalize, we may be running to the front of an already advancing army, not of soldiers, but of young Russian salesmen. Global distribution networks as well as local reception strategies are already resituating American cultural studies critically and comparatively, a process grasped by experts and nonexperts, many of whom reside outside of the centers of academic exchange and beyond the locations where even our e-mail can reach. During my last trip to Moscow in January 1998, I went to a new department store, "Global USA," which, like so many of Moscow's popular shopping venues, is immense and has no clear commercial relationship to the United States. As I waited in line to have my fresh roasted coffee beans ground by an attendant whose sole responsibility, it seemed, was to operate the self-service grinder, I was distracted by the surrounding aisles stocked in haphazard Russian fashion with housewares, building supplies, electronics, and imported grocery items, and it occurred to me that *Global USA* refers less to an Americanization of the Russian consumer base than to the potential Russianization of cultural goods whose national value is dereferentialized and opened to redescription in the instance of becoming global. Global USA served as a useful reminder that, if we wish to understand the complex process that we refer to as Americanization, we need a more nuanced understanding of the fundamental differences that make it possible for non-Western cultures to reorganize Western meanings in non-Western ways. Quite decidedly, Russian history is marked by this ability, not the least significant example of which is the appropriation and refashioning of Marxism into Leninism, a distinctive Russian philosophy.

While American studies research no longer proceeds from a self-centeredness that ignores the importance of international perspectives, we should now work to ensure that internationalist approaches do not themselves become written as a new master narrative, or centering myth, within institutions and departments. To neglect this task would be to sustain the illusion that the transformations we wish to bring about—in our institutions and in our self-perceptions—can be achieved simply by working within the borders of the

United States. But in fact the United States has a long history of promoting its self-perceptions, cultural values, and institutions by and through the representation of Russia as other. And although politicians can no longer decry the "evils" of the Soviet Union, Russia continues, perhaps more than any other non-Western nation, to function for the U.S. imaginary as a sort of fun house mirror. The obverse should by now be plainly apparent: as the project of reconstructing Russian culture, history, and national character develops in part from within the cultures of the United States, the project of resituating American culture is developing from within Russia. What is there for an Americanist in Moscow to conclude but that attention must be paid?

Notes

The Russian students whose final exams I have excerpted throughout this essay attended my course in contemporary American literature at Moscow State University, in the International College/Faculty of Foreign Languages, in the spring of 1997. The exam asked them to respond to the following: "Some critics consider Arthur Miller's *Death of a Salesman* to be the quintessential twentieth-century American play. Others argue that Miller's drama of an aging salesman, torn between dream and reality, has far-reaching cross-cultural significance. What is your opinion on this? Do you think that *Death of a Salesman* is a play that Russians, as well as Americans, can identify with? What particular aspects of the play are relevant for Russian audiences?" I would like to express my gratitude to the following students for their thoughtful and articulate responses to this question, and, moreover, for their generosity in allowing me to incorporate their work into my argument: Helen Averkulva, Yura Babinkov, Olesia Fedorova, Lyuba Grakhova, J. Kulikova, Natalia Kuzmina, Natalia Pavlova, V. Rastorguev, Olga Sarkisova, and Vera Shekerbakova.

1 Arthur Miller, *Timebends: A Life* (New York: Grove, 1987), 570. Subsequent references are cited parenthetically in the text.

2 See John R. Leo, "Paradigm Shifts: 'Centers' and 'Margins' in American Studies since the Sixties," in *Fringes at the Centre: Actas do XVIII Encontro da APEAA: Associação Portuguesa de Estudos Anglo-Americanos*, vol. 1 (Guarda: Escola Superior de Tecnologia e Gestão e Instituto Politécnico da Guarda, 1997), 327–46; and Richard P. Horwitz, "The Politics of International American Studies," *American Studies International* 31, no. 1 (1993): 89–116. Subsequent references are cited parenthetically in the text. Leo's essay was originally a keynote lecture for the annual meeting of the Portuguese Anglo-American Studies Association, Guarda, March 1997.

3 Jane C. Desmond and Virginia R. Dominguez, "Resituating American Stud-

ies in a Critical Internationalism," *American Quarterly* 48, no. 3 (1996): 477. Here, Desmond and Dominguez quote from Benjamin Lee, "Critical Internationalism," *Public Culture* 7, no. 3 (1995): 559–92. Subsequent references are cited parenthetically in the text.

4   The authors claim that fostering these conditions means redressing a number of institutional and intellectual limitations, all of which can be achieved, they say, even in times of funding cutbacks and academic downsizing. Their recommendations include: using new online technologies to facilitate transnational discussion and to link students in the United States with peer groups at institutions abroad; encouraging Ph.D. research that places topics in a more expanded international context and makes use of international scholarship; requiring foreign language mastery for the Ph.D.; requiring undergraduate and graduate students in the United States to do at least some of their course work abroad; recruiting foreign language faculty and students through Fulbright exchanges; and encouraging international scholarship by setting aside faculty development funds for competitive fellowships so that faculty can develop expertise abroad (486–87).

5   Bill Readings, *The University in Ruins* (Cambridge, Mass.: Harvard University Press, 1996), 43. Subsequent references are cited parenthetically in the text.

6   David Remnick, *Lenin's Tomb: The Last Days of the Soviet Empire* (New York: Vintage, 1996), 540. Subsequent references are cited parenthetically in the text.

7   In Moscow I taught in the faculty of foreign languages and in the faculty of the International College. These faculties are housed together under the direction of Svetlana Ter-Minosova, a linguist by training, who established them both and now serves as dean. Her program teaches language in the context of culture, and literature in the context of the sort of cultural grammar that could be described as semiotics, although the program has no particular theoretical or methodological orientation as such. These faculties are separate from the faculty of philology and linguistics at Moscow State University, where more "scientific" or formalist approaches to literary studies have traditionally presided.

8   Benedict Anderson, *Imagined Communities: Reflections on the Origin and Spread of Nationalism*, rev. ed. (London: Verso, 1991).

9   Arthur Miller, *Salesman in Beijing* (New York: Viking, 1984), 5. Subsequent references are cited parenthetically in the text. See also *Timebends*. Miller writes, "The Chinese reaction to my Beijing production of *Salesman* would confirm what had become more and more obvious over the decades in the play's hundreds of productions throughout the world: Willy was representative everywhere, in every kind of system, of ourselves in this time" (*Timebends*, 184).

10 Was Natalia forgetting about the Russian government's failure to deliver on pensions owed to the elderly, or about its routine suspension of payment to teachers and miners?

11 Susan C. Haedicke, "Celebrating Stylistic Contradictions: *Death of a Salesman* from a Theatrical Perspective," in *Approaches to Teaching Miller's Death of A Salesman*, ed. Matthew C. Roudané (New York: Modern Language Association of America, 1995), 40.

12 The possibility that Willy Loman might be older for a Russian audience than for a Western audience makes sense in the context of current life expectancy for men in Russia, which is currently fifty-four years of age, having dropped significantly over the course of the last eight years.

13 See Masha Gessen, *Dead Again: The Russian Intelligentsia after Communism* (New York: Verso, 1997), especially the final chapter on "The Bad Generation," for a perceptive report on the new Russian society and values. Subsequent references are cited parenthetically in the text.

14 Willy Loman's 1940s "idiolect of cliches" does not cease to function as cliches for those who have never heard them. Part of my introductory lecture was aimed at getting them to understand the more general circulation of Willy's vocabulary in relation to the historical moment—the extent to which his vocabulary reflects not merely his poor philosophy but also how he has uncritically bought into the lie of his society. Willy's thinking does not make him stand out—rather it makes him a conformist, and a failed conformist at that. This was important to convey to Russian students who exist in a culture where entrenched hierarchy, as opposed to personality, still plays a part in defining social position, and where thinking in common is valued above thinking for oneself.

15 While I was trying to explain life insurance to them, I became acutely aware of the euphemisms that I use to talk about death. "Well, you buy life insurance so that your family, your loved ones, will be provided for should something unexpected happen to you." I was met with mostly blank stares. One student asked, "Happen to you? Well, something is going to happen to everybody, isn't it . . . it's expected, yes?" Suffice it to say that American culture's denial of death differs from the general Russian attitude.

16 One female student approached me privately at the end of one of our sessions to ask me about Willy's cruel treatment of Linda.

17 Helge Normann Nilsen, "From *Honors at Dawn* to *Death of a Salesman*: Marxism and the Early Plays of Arthur Miller," *English Studies* 2 (1994): 154. It is clear that Miller strove to preserve Willy's status as an individual agent. Miller scoffs at the remarks of a Chinese viewer in Beijing who understood Willy's fate as his failure to modernize his way of doing business, as if modernization—a buzz word of Chinese society in the mid-1980s—would have saved him in the same way that the Chinese hoped it would save them. However, Miller insists that Willy be understood as more than a product of social transformation, for while he "is indeed a social product . . . his autonomy as a person remains intact, and this can drive the dialecticians crazy" (*Salesman in Beijing*, 204).

18 Richard P. Horwitz writes that while the USIA has testified that it imposes

no ideological attempts to control the substance of Americanists' activities abroad, it has boasted at budget time that it "helped dismantle the Soviet Union" ("Politics of International American Studies," 100). I reiterate his point not to cast aspersions on USIA or Fulbright or any U.S. academic exchange program, but to emphasize that there is an inescapable political role that Americanists play, wittingly or not, in Russia.

19 U.S. government sponsored academic trade programs in Russia tend to be one-sided. The only Fulbright grants currently available to American scholars in Russia are lecturing awards, while research grants are the only grants available to Russian junior scholars who receive grants to the United States. We go there to teach them, and they come here to learn from us. To a not insignificant degree this logic grows out of the erroneous assumption that Russians want simply to establish a replica of American democracy and capitalism in their own land.

20 Numerous Fulbrighters in Russia have described difficulties making contacts with colleagues at their host institutions for a variety of complex reasons that are simultaneously unique to the regional and institutional locale, and at the same time broadly patterned along lines of cultural, social, economic, and political forces. In contemporary Russia it is not unusual for university professors—whose social prestige has declined in the wake of reform—to hold down several jobs at once, often juggling teaching positions with higher paying employment in private enterprise. Academic salaries are notoriously meager and pay schedules are at best unreliable. State university infrastructures outside the major metropolitan cities are in severe decay—a university I visited in Omsk had been doing without electricity for months—and what limited office space exists is distributed according to hierarchical systems of contact and fealty. It is common for faculty to spend only as much time on campus as is absolutely necessary for the delivery of a lecture.

21 Pierre Bourdieu, *Distinction: A Social Critique of the Judgement of Taste*, trans. Richard Nice (Cambridge: Harvard University Press, 1984). On the question of American studies' translatability see Stacilee Ford and Clyde Haulman, "'To Touch the Trends:' Internationalizing American Studies: Perspectives from Hong Kong and Asia," *American Studies International* 34, no. 2 (October 1996): 42–58.

22 Jeanne J. Smoot, "Ambassador Unaware," in *The Fulbright Experience, 1946– 1986: Encounters and Transformations*, ed. Arthur Power Dudden and Russel R. Dunes (New Brunswick: Transaction Books, 1987), 301–2; quoted in Horwitz, "The Politics of International American Studies," 99. While the Fulbright Program has been hugely successful in positively transforming the personal and professional lives of participants, both in the United States and abroad, the program was a direct product of Cold War politics. An extensive history of the Fulbright program and its relation to American foreign policy is beyond the scope of this paper; however the evolution of its political and financial support, and its administrative framework under the United States

Information Agency, has, according to Richard Pells, shaped it into a "sort of cultural Marshall Plan." The U.S. Government has long regarded American culture as an important tool in the expansion of its interests and in the fight against communism, and in this sense American studies has been regarded as far more than an academic enterprise. As Pells observes, "Although it remained a reciprocal arrangement between the United States and other countries, whereby students, teachers, and researchers were supposed to move back and forth expanding their awareness of how different people lived and thought, the [Fulbright] program was also regarded by Congress and the State Department as a means of increasing worldwide appreciation for American's values and institutions" (Richard Pells, *Not Like Us: How Europeans Have Loved, Hated, and Transformed American Culture Since World War II* [New York: Basic Books, 1997], 61, 62). Subsequent references are cited parenthetically in the text.

23 I refer here to Shelley Fisher Fishkin's study *Was Huck Black?: Mark Twain and African-American Voices* (New York: Oxford University Press, 1993).

24 I have come across many useful sources in teaching the play, including Miller's own account of directing *Death of a Salesman* in China, *Salesman in Beijing*, and his autobiography, *Timebends: a Life*. For critical sources, Matthew C. Roudane, ed., *Approaches to Teaching Miller's Death of a Salesman* (New York: Modern Language Association, 1995) includes a useful bibliography and list of critical studies. The collection, however, includes no essays from an international perspective, and none of the contributors are written by scholars working outside the United States.

25 Samuel P. Huntington, "The Clash of Civilizations?," *Foreign Affairs* 72, no. 3 (summer 1993): 26. Subsequent references are cited parenthetically in the text.

The Humanities in the Age of Expressive Individualism and Cultural Radicalism

Winfried Fluck

I

In one sense, the future of American studies seems to be more promising than ever. Because there are so many contested issues and intellectual challenges in the field, American studies have gained greatly in theoretical interest. On the institutional level, the number of professional positions created after World War II in colleges and universities all over the world is remarkable. At the same time, this successful intellectual and institutional expansion has intensified a problem from which the humanities suffer in general, namely that of a growing proliferation and fragmentation of knowledge.[1] Ironically enough, this development threatens to undermine the very promise underlying the success story of the humanities: the promise of meaning. If an interpretation is to provide more than the projection of a strong image of identification, then it should aim at the integration of a number of other perspectives on the text. However, if there are roughly twenty different theoretical approaches to the interpretation of *The Adventures of Huckleberry Finn* and more than a thousand interpretations of the book, all defining themselves against each other and thus differing from other readings by principle, it is no longer possible to set up relations between them in order to sort out their respective strengths and weaknesses—unless, one wants to thematize this problem itself in a metatheoretical comparison of approaches. But, as we will see, that creates problems of its own.

A paradoxical professional logic is at work here which transforms an indispensable strategy of critical insight and interpretive correction into a source of fragmentation and disorientation. In principle, a plurality of interpretative approaches is useful for helping us gain a critical perspective on an object and thus correct an apparently inescapable dialectic of blindness and insight characterizing all interpretations of world and text. Once plurality becomes endless proliferation, however, the initial gain threatens to become a loss. Because we are overwhelmed by a flood of ever new approaches and interpretive claims, scholarly work begins to lose its power of correction and functions as mere displacement instead. There are simply too many different claims to assess their validity or to establish meaningful connections between them in order to put them into perspective. The full impact of this constantly increasing proliferation of meaning making is demonstrated by the fact that even those who hold a critical perspective on the competitive or disruptive nature of the present social and academic system cannot help but to contribute to this process because they have to work within the same institutional framework. Under present conditions, the institutionalized mode of production of knowledge has therefore gained priority over any ideological position in determining the function and effects of work in the humanities. One could argue, for example, that the recent revisionism in American studies has provided a fundamental and long needed change in perspective. But once this perspective is established, it becomes part of the same formation of knowledge production that characterizes the scholarship it replaces. Another race for professional distinction through difference begins, as, to give but one example, the recent criticism on Kate Chopin and *The Awakening* demonstrates (of which, in contrast to *Huckleberry Finn*, we hardly had any interpretations before 1969). Because the novel was neglected for such a long time, it now attracts a lot of critical attention. But the more interpretations we get, the greater the dispersal of meaning because all of these interpretations must, by definition, correct prior interpretations in order to justify their existence. What started out as a heroic effort to recover a representative work thus leads to an endless flow of ever new claims, which ultimately begin to undermine any basis for a claim of representativeness. In the end, *The Awakening* is "great," because, like *Huckleberry Finn* or *The Scarlet Letter*, it can stimulate and accommodate any number of interpretations. Its cultural significance has been absorbed by its professional usefulness.

No particular approach or position is to blame for this situation because it is produced by historical developments that go beyond the impact of any particular position. My argument should thus not be confused with the conservative criticism of the alleged fragmentation of canons or values brought about by the recent revisionism in literary or American studies and/or by the emergence of cultural studies. Actually, I think that the impact of these developments on the idea of the canon is often exaggerated because, inevitably, these movements merely replace older canons by a new set of preferred and canonized works to which critics return again and again. Thus, in discussions in which challenges to existing canons are blamed for fragmentation, the term *fragmentation* is often used as a code word for value conflicts or political disagreements. The fragmentation of knowledge I am talking about here has been going on before and after such recent revisions and is not tied in any causal or unique way to any of them. It has epistemological, social, and institutional reasons. Its origin lies in historicism and its insistence that sense making and interpretation are historical acts; consequently, each period, generation, and group will feel the need to offer its own interpretation of a phenomenon. This tendency has been accelerated—in fact, institutionalized as a professional practice—by professionalization and the emergence of an "academic criticism." Gradually, but especially after the explosion of higher education after World War II, this professionalization has begun to change the function of reinterpretation and has inverted the priorities. While professionalization originally had the purpose of providing interpretation with a solid institutional and methodological base, it has now tied reinterpretation to professional advancement. While in the past each generation or group had its cause for reinterpretation, now each individual scholar has a reason for reinterpretation. Reinterpretation, in turn, must be defined by disagreement and difference, for otherwise it would not meet professional criteria for qualification. A feminist scholar cannot simply publish an essay praising another feminist's interpretation of Kate Chopin. There has to be, at least to a certain extent, a revision, disagreement, or contradiction in order to justify this intervention professionally.[2] Historicism may thus authorize reinterpretation, but professionalization institutionalizes disagreement and difference as professional necessity.[3] The result is a breathtaking proliferation of work, whether "conservative" or "progressive,"[4] that undermines (and delegitimizes) all interpretations in similar ways because, in a professional culture of institutionalized difference, a text can no longer be taken as representative for anything but the author's professional qualification.[5]

Quantity is not the only problem, or even the major problem, of the current proliferation of meaning production, however. Even if one would have the time, energy, and institutional possibilities to sort out the strengths and weaknesses of diverse approaches and innumerable interpretations through a metatheoretical comparison of methods, there would no longer be any point in doing so because such a metatheoretical comment on their adequacy or inadequacy would be considered "policing." In addition, such a metatheoretical position seems inconceivable now that its foundational premise—the possibility of evaluating interpretive truth claims—would have no consensual basis after the demise of the so-called grand narratives. Thus nowadays methodological discussions go into exactly the opposite direction, namely that of unmasking theoretical or methodological claims for interpretive adequateness as disguised power games. The only consensus remaining seems to be that of a broadly defined antifoundationalism, strong in subverting arguments for general criteria on which claims for interpretive adequateness could be based, but weak in suggesting any criteria that would go beyond a mere performative voluntarism.

The current antifoundationalism reflects the changing institutional and social conditions of a profession that has gone from a self-appointed guardian of cultural values to a white-collar profession with its own pressures for professional distinction.[6] The basic social problem of democracy, already diagnosed perceptively by Tocqueville as that of distinguishing oneself from the mass of others, repeats itself on the professional level and creates an escalating logic of "strong" (over)statements that serve the purpose of standing out from the rest. The more professionals in the humanities, the greater the need for distinction. The more existing interpretations of *Huckleberry Finn*, the greater the pressure and need to outperform them. To say, in this situation, that one of the many influences shaping Huck Finn's remarkably original vernacular voice is the African American speech pattern absorbed by the young Samuel Clemens in the Southern town of Hannibal is an important insight and a valuable addition to our understanding of the novel. But as an interpretive claim, it is too modest and sane to stand out from a voluminous body of scholarship on the many important aspects of the book. If one exaggerates this find, however, to suggest that Huck's voice is really a black voice, then this is a startling statement that catches people's attention.[7] Most Twain scholars may find the first claim valid and few may agree with the second, but in the white-collar race for distinction this does not really matter. What counts is visibility, and this purpose can best and most quickly be achieved by strong overstatement.[8] A well-known representative of the New Historicism recently summarized the situation with unusual frankness in response to the challenge of a historian who had listened to a lecture of his and criticized it on the grounds of weak evidence. He conceded readily that his interpretation of *Hamlet* could be considered far-fetched. But in view of the countless interpretations of *Hamlet* already in existence, it was hard to find a new argument. Thus his primary goal was to find an argument that could be considered new and interesting, even if not immediately evident. Such an argument cannot be validated by traditional forms of evidence but solely by whether the critic manages to convince us of a professional product or not, that is, by means of critical performance. Thus an endless spiral is set in motion. The more critical work exists, the greater the need for difference and interpretative disagreement in order to distinguish oneself. However, the greater the disagreement, the greater the fragmentation. The greater the fragmentation, the greater the need—and opportunity!—for new interpretations. But the more interpretations we get, the greater the tendency to devalue individual interpretations and thus, in turn, the greater the need to stand out by forceful overstatement.

II

For a while, theory seemed to offer the solution to this proliferation of meaning production. Theory was defined as that intellectual discipline in which one reflected systematically about the premises and methodological problems of literary criticism and interpretation. By now, however, theory has been transformed from a systematic philosophical discipline into another area of professional empowerment. In its current use and application, theory has not solved the crisis of orientation in the humanities. On the contrary, it has deepened the crisis, not only by becoming useful symbolic capital in the professional race for distinction, but also by feeding and accelerating this race in entirely new and unforeseen ways. The special usefulness of theory for this purpose lies in two of its aspects. Theory can function as a shortcut because it permits the description and characterization of an interpretive object without long, extended study. This extended study can be avoided because theory, as a rule and for good reasons, aims at general statements (of an often sweeping nature), so that explanatory claims tie the interpretation of cultural material to historical laws, social conditions, human faculties, linguistic or cultural mechanisms of inclusion and exclusion, and so forth. In the appropriation of theory by a new generation of scholars, theory has begun to change its nature, however: it, too, becomes a form of symbolic capital judged not by its systematic range but by its potential for strong statements.

This explains two striking facts about the present theory boom. On the one hand, it has been observed that almost all of the thinkers who have dominated critical theory in literary and cultural studies currently do not fare well in their original disciplines, where their theories and statements are considered too sweeping and undifferentiated. Such bold theories are, on the other hand, exactly the basis for their appropriation by literary studies. The fact that the exchange value of theory as symbolic capital dominates literary and cultural studies also explains why many continental theories, developed over years of patient scholarly work, were imported wholesale into the new American market for theory and used up in rapid succession, now seemingly confronting American scholarship with a lack of imports. The reason for this mode of appropriation again is that theory has become a form of symbolic capital in the white-collar race for distinction and difference. Nobody has refuted the mode of textual analysis practiced by Roland Barthes in *S/Z* or, to give another example, the basic insights and claims of reception theory. They no longer play a role in critical discussions now not because they have been disproved, but because they are no longer on the cutting edge of professional distinction.

However, the most striking aspect about recent developments in the humanities and especially American studies is not their theoretical but their radical nature. The dominant approaches of the last fifteen years, ranging from poststructuralism and deconstruction, new historicism, and cultural materialism to the various versions of race, class, and gender studies, may differ widely in many of their arguments, premises, and procedures. What unites them is a new form of radicalism that I would like to call, in contrast to older forms of political radicalism, *cultural radicalism* because the central source of political domination is no longer attributed to the level of political institutions and economic structures but to culture.[9] This paradigm shift in the definition of power has its origins in the student movement of the late sixties. In response to the puzzling and irritating fact that the "oppressed" did not form coalitions with the students following the lead of, above all, Herbert Marcuse, the repression thesis was replaced by the idea of "structural" or "systemic" power, that is, by a redefinition of power as exerted not by agents or institutions of the state but by the system's cunning ways of constituting "subjects" or ascribing "identities" through cultural forms.[10] Thus recent critical theories, different as they may be in many respects, nevertheless have one basic premise in common (and are amazingly predictable in this one respect): they all take their point of departure from the assumption of an all-pervasive, underlying systemic element that constitutes the system's power in an invisible but highly effective way. The names for this systemic element vary, including *the prison-house of language, ideology redefined as semiotic system, the reality effect, the ideological state apparatus, the cinematic apparatus, the symbolic order, episteme, discursive regime, logocentrism, patriarchy, whiteness,* or *Western thought.*[11] But the basic claim is always the same: the invisible power effect of the systemic structure derives from the fact that it determines meaning and the perception of the world before the individual is even aware of it by constituting the linguistic and cultural patterns through which we make sense of the world.

This redefinition of power has led to a constant pressure to out-radicalize others.[12] If power resides in hitherto unacknowledged aspects of language, discourse, or the symbolic order, then there is literally no limit to ever new and more radical discoveries of power effects. And if it is power that determines cultural meaning, then the major question must be that of the possibility or impossibility of opposition. *Opposition*, however, also changes its nature. In view of the shrewd containment of all resistance by discursive regimes, the only way out lies in radical otherness or difference. Thus the development of cultural radicalism has taken a characteristic course: from neo-Marxism, with its critique of the market (which still implies the possibility of resistance), to Foucauldian neohistoricism (which unmasks this form of resistance as really a hidden form of complicity), to race, class, and gender studies (which revive the possibility of resistance by locating it in difference). Actually, the current umbrella concept "race, class, and gender" is a misnomer because the category of class cannot constitute radical difference. Consequently, class analysis no longer constitutes a genuine theoretical option for the new cultural radicalism, while sexual preference, on the other hand, constitutes elementary, unbridgeable difference and has therefore moved to the center of revisionist approaches.

Putting all hopes for resistance on the category of difference creates another theoretical problem, however, because a term for denoting unbridgeable otherness is used as the basis for a broadly defined group identity that does not account for the possibility of difference within this group. Hence we can observe a constant movement or sliding in the use of the category *difference*. In order to make the concept politically meaningful, it must be used as a comprehensive category of distinction and must be equated with a particular gender, ethnic or racial group, or form of sexual preference. However, such redefinition of difference as, for example, racial or gendered identity runs the danger of re-essentializing identity and works against the very idea of difference. The problem arises from the fact that a category taken from linguistic and semiotic analysis, where it describes an uncontrollable dissemination of meaning, is employed to justify claims for social recognition. In the first context, it is an antirepresentational term, used to deconstruct a belief in the possibility of representation; in the second, the idea of representation is not only revived but becomes the central criterion for judging and classifying cultural texts.[13]

Arguments within race, class, and gender studies constantly oscillate between the two options of the term and arrest them almost at will wherever needed. In accordance with the professional culture of performance, difference is used as a means of self-definition and self-empowerment. This, in fact, is the thrust and net result of the current cultural radicalism in the humanities. Since power is redefined as an effect of systemic structures that are virtually everywhere, the term is no longer a category of political analysis, but a word for all possible barriers to the self. And since the subject is, in principle, constituted by systemic effects or is seen, at best, as the site of conflicting systemic effects, it can only be defined through difference, so that the claim or assertion of difference becomes the supreme form of self-empowerment.[14]

The far-reaching radicalization of the humanities in the United States has been an entirely unforeseen and highly surprising development from a European point of view. More specifically, there were two surprises. For one, radicalism reemerged in the United States after it had just turned dogmatic in Europe and had thereby discredited itself completely. One of the recurring arguments of conservatives during the heyday of the student movement in France, Germany, and other European countries was the charge of ideologization, which was considered a typically European illness and regularly contrasted with Anglo-Saxon "common sense." As it turned out, however, common sense was no match for radicalization. Why? And why was there no consideration of the negative experiences made in Europe?

The explanation, I think, lies in the fact that this new wave of American radicalization is not what it appears (and often claims) to be, namely a critical theory with political goals and a political theory. Although it is constantly pointed out that not only the private aspect but literally every aspect of social life is political, there is no systematic reflection on the structures or procedures through which the claims of difference or the Other could become political reality. One reason surely is that the realization of one claim inevitably runs the danger of violating somebody else's claims. Such violations can only be justified on the basis of a set of normative ideas, but normative ideas violate difference, as the various forms of poststructuralist and neopragmatist antifoundationalism point out again and again. There was nothing to be learned, then, from European political radicalism because the new form of cultural radicalism in the United States has entirely different goals. It pursues a politics of self-empowerment, and thus its analyses need no longer be based on Marxist or other social theories attempting to describe the relation between various groups and members of the political system as a whole. Instead, radicalism can focus on the systemic barriers to self-empowerment while, politically speaking, it remains a form of interest-group politics or, in extreme cases, an untheorized form of radical egalitarianism. The problem, then, is not that the humanities have been instrumentalized by politics, as conservatives have it. As cultural radicalism rightly claims, there is no way around politics. The interesting theoretical problem is that they have been appropriated by what, in following the lead of Robert Bellah and others in *Habits of the Heart*, I would like to call the politics of expressive individualism.[15]

The important point to grasp here is that expressive individualism is not a narcissist deformation but a successful end product of a central project of the humanities; it does not reflect the humanities' crisis but their success. Imaginary self-empowerment through cultural difference is not a pathological distortion of the true goals and function of the humanities but a modern manifestation of a promise of self-empowerment in which the humanities have played a crucial role since their inception. The intellectual justification and support of individual development and self-assertion is a major element of what we call modernity (in the sense of *Neuzeit*). Crucial breakthroughs in Western intellectual development which stand at the center of the humanities—for example, the philosophical "discovery" of the subject, the idea of the Enlightenment, the doctrine of individual rights, the modern understanding of the aesthetic as a non-mimetic mode of experience, or the "reinvention" of literature as a fictive realm to transgress the boundaries of existing worlds—have all contributed to this process of individualization and provided it with both intellectual tools as well as moral justification.[16] My claim is that, contrary to its self-perception, the current cultural radicalism does not stand in opposition to this process, but merely represents a new, radicalized stage of it.

As suggested in *Habits of the Heart*, the process of individualization in Western societies can be divided into two major stages—economic or utilitarian individualism and expressive individualism. Disregarding the nostalgic communitarian context of this argument, I find these terms heuristically useful in drawing attention to two different manifestations of individualism in the modern age, which, going beyond *Habits of the Heart*, can best be distinguished by reference to two different sources of self-definition and self-esteem. In the traditional form of economic individualism, as it has been analyzed by Tocqueville, Weber, and numerous others since then, self-esteem is derived primarily from economic success and social recognition. In order to obtain these, the individual has to go through an often long and painful act of deferred gratification and self-denial. Analogous to the act of saving, the goal is to accumulate a stock of capital, in both economic and social terms, which will eventually yield its profits in the form of increased social approval and a rise in the social hierarchy. The prototypical literary genres of this economic individualism are the autobiographical success story, the bildungsroman, and stories of female education found in the domestic novel. They are teleological in conception, their basic narrative pattern is that of a rise or fall, and their recurring emotional dramas are the experience of injustice and the withholding of just rewards, but also, possibly, a final moment of triumphant retribution. Their ideal is the formation of a character that is strong enough to survive this long ordeal of social apprenticeship.

In contrast, the culture of expressive individualism is not primarily concerned with an individual's rise to social respectability or its (tragic or melodramatic) failure, but with the search for self-realization. Its major issues are no longer economic success or the promise of social recognition, but the assertion of cultural difference, that is, the ability of individuals to assert their own uniqueness and otherness against the powers of cultural convention and encroaching disciplinary regimes. If development and growth are key terms of economic individualism, difference is the key term of expressive individualism.[17] This change in the sources of self-esteem is the logical outcome of an ever intensified process of individualization and, coming along with it, increasingly radical forms of cultural dehierarchization. In this process, individuals have to assert their self-worth in opposition to those forces standing in their way. Initially, these forces were obvious sources of inequality such as caste, class, or patriarchy. With the increasing democratization of Western societies—in itself a result of individualization—these sources of inequality have been undermined in authority and have, in fact, often been dissolved or weakened decisively. Inequality remains, but it can no longer be as easily attributed to social structures. Hence the search for new "systemic effects" of inequality and the increased importance of self-fashioning by means of cultural difference.

If the source of power is cultural, however, then culture must also serve as the source of counterdefinition, and the search for self-realization must become the search for alternate cultural options. It is therefore culture that takes the place of the economy as the major model for self-realization, self-assertion, and self-fashioning, because the realm of culture provides something like an archive or storehouse of different models of self-definition. In contrast to the realm of the economy, where self-discipline and a strong "identity" are the most desirable qualities, culture offers an almost inexhaustible supply of options for role-playing and imaginary self-empowerment. Ironically, it is nowadays not a ritual of consent that absorbs "the radical energies of history," as Sacvan Bercovitch writes, but a new stage of individual self-empowerment, articulated most forcefully by cultural radicalism, that redefines political engagement as cultural self-definition, and thus as one possibility for role-taking among many.[18]

As a form of expressive individualism, radicalism changes its function. Instead of providing an ideological base for political analysis, it becomes an intellectual tool in the radical pursuit of difference. This explains its most striking feature: its focus on, if not obsession with, the question of oppositionalism. The striking fact that cultural radicalism's interest in literature seems almost entirely absorbed by the problem of whether these texts are truly oppositional or not is closely linked with the question of cultural difference: "Opposition is the best way to assert cultural difference, for it is opposition that allows difference to emerge most clearly and pointedly."[19] Thus, cultural radicalism can nowadays be regarded as one of the supreme manifestations of expressive individualism in the realm of the humanities. Although it sees itself as a political turn in literary studies, it really represents, at a closer look, another turn of the screw in the cultural history of individualization. This individualism needs radical dehierarchization to eliminate cultural restrictions on self-empowerment, but it also needs the cultural construction of difference to escape from the consequences of radical equality. In this sense, cultural radicalism does not provide an alternative to individualism, but a more radicalized version of individualization; not a critique of individualism by politics, but a critique based on the politics of expressive individualism.

I think, then, that it is the wide-ranging transition from economic to expressive individualism that stands at the center of recent developments in the humanities, including American studies.[20] The effects of this development have been ambiguous. By turning intellectual work into imaginary role-taking, the attractiveness of literary and cultural studies for the individual has increased, while their importance and social relevance have decreased. The more important and useful the humanities become for the individual in search of imaginary self-empowerment, the more irrelevant single works of art or cultural objects become for society. It is, then, this expressive reconfiguration of individualism that I see as the driving force in the current development of American studies. As long as cultural radicalism uses the category of the political to give its own claims for self-definition authority, this issue is effectively obscured. In this version, the political is opposed to individualism because individualism is regarded as a typical manifestation of capitalism. Actually, however, individualism is a product of modernity whose idea of self-development also provides the basis for cultural radicalism.[21]

To talk about individualism is thus not to pass a moral judgment on "selfishness." It was Tocqueville who noted that individualism was not to be confused with egoism or selfishness. As an integral part of a process of modernization, individualism is a social attitude also attracting those who would distance themselves strongly not only from egoism but from cultural radicalism. To give but one example from my own professional background: in its redefinition of literary meaning as (partly) the result of an actualization through the reader, reception theory has given a theoretical boost to individualization within literary studies—as has literary modernism in general. The reason for this was not selfishness but quite the opposite, namely an antitotalitarian impulse that wanted to strengthen the individual through the perspectivizing potential of fiction, always, however, basing this liberating move on the normative basis of hermeneutic theory. Such interventions on behalf of the individual are recurring events in the history of modernity and are almost always based on the expectation of a new, unconstrained consensus of liberated individuals finally able to realize their true human potential. But it never turns out that way. Individualism gladly welcomes the new opening but soon disregards the norms and values which served as its justification.

III

In many respects, my analysis seems to tie in with what must be considered the most penetrating recent analysis of the state of the humanities, John Guillory's *Cultural Capital*, which, in dealing with the problem of literary canon formation, is also centrally concerned with the major contemporary challenge to the humanities, that of the creation of value. For this, Guillory draws on Bourdieu's theory of symbolic capital. In particular, he provides a penetrating critique of two key arguments of the current literary revisionism. One is the redefinition of literature as the representation of a radically different social identity. As Guillory puts it, the "politics of canon formation has been understood as a politics of representation—the representation or lack of representation of certain groups in the canon" (5). This means that "the work is perceived to be immediately expressive of the author's *experience* as a representative member of some social group" (10) and leads to an approach which "is forbidden in principle from recognizing anything in the work of art but the expression of a particular community's particular values" (28). In this approach, all minority members are tacitly assumed to be alike: "The movement to open the canon to noncanonical authors submits the syllabus to a kind of demographic oversight. Canonical and noncanonical authors are supposed to stand for particular social groups, dominant or subordinate." However, this "spokespersonship" actually presents a form of self-empowerment, because "those members of social minorities who enter the university do not 'represent' the social group to which they belong in the same way in which minority legislators can be said to represent their constituencies" (7).

Guillory's second point is the "antifoundationalist" dismissal of the aesthetic as ideology which, in his view, is based on a faulty conflation of the concept of aesthetics with certain discredited values. This creates the dilemma of having to replace the idea of specifically aesthetic criteria with the notion of a "valuing community": "I have already suggested . . . , in considering Fish's notion of an "interpretive community," that such a logical contradiction fatally afflicts the critique of canon formation, and that in practice there is very little to arrest the disintegrative force breaking communities down into progressively smaller groups precisely in order to confirm a distinct, ideal, and homogeneous social identity as the basis of the solidarity and thus the *values* of the community" (277). What may be even worse than this separatist logic is the tacit elision of the possibility of "creative dissent by means of the aesthetic which is implied in the radical relativism of the concept of the valuing community," as Guillory writes with reference to Barbara Herrnstein Smith's *Contingencies of Value*: "What we are not capable of describing in the terms of this theory is the effect of a value judgment which deliberately disputes the normative judgment of one's own community, unless we can posit at the same time some 'limited population' which would affirm that disputative judgment. In other words, there is no place in Smith's formulation for describing the effects of a dissenting judgment *on the community whose judgment is disputed*" (285).

Seen from the perspective presented here, such a critique confirms and complements a view of cultural radicalism as an unacknowledged manifestation of expressive individualism. Aesthetics is described as a discourse of "universal value" because it is believed to suppress difference. In its place, the representation of a different, marginalized identity becomes the new (re-essentialized) base for interpretation and value judgments which, inevitably however, must project a "personal economy" onto an imagined community and thus expresses "a new improved individualism" (283). But I disagree with Guillory in his explanation for this development.[22] Guillory's book is primarily concerned with the literary curriculum of the school, organized by the category of literature as a historically conditioned one for "the cultural capital of the old bourgeoisie": "From this perspective the issue of 'canonicity' will seem less important than the historical crisis of literature—which gives rise to the canon debate" (x). This argument can be extended to the concept of the humanities, which provide the major organizing principle of college curricula and university programs, so that, for Guillory, the crisis of the humanities signals the fact that, as a form of creating capital, the humanities have become increasingly obsolete. Guillory basically attributes the crisis of the humanities to the emergence of a professional managerial class in the university "which no longer requires the cultural capital of the old bourgeoisie": "The decline of the humanities was never the result of newer non-canonical courses or texts, but of a large-scale 'capital flight' in the domain of culture" (45). In this situation, theory displaces the study of literature, because "the syllabus of theory has the oblique purpose of signifying a rapprochement with the technobureaucratic constraints upon intellectual labor" (253). But if "the career of the college professor is increasingly structured as a mimesis of the bureaucratic career" (253), why are intellectuals all over the world, and especially young people (often, and increasingly so, from marginalized groups) submitting themselves to this regime in the first place and in ever growing numbers, despite an often bleak professional outlook?

In following Pierre Bourdieu's crude sociologist bias, Guillory's explanation is unable to admit any psychic, emotional, or imaginary dimension in the relation between literature and the professors of literature, which may have drawn the latter to this particular subject matter and profession. (I am thinking here, for example, of the role of fiction in processes of self-development and imaginary self-empowerment which can be particularly intense in formative years. It would be quite a reduction to assume that a juvenile reader, an adolescent, or a young intellectual looking for an identity in the "other world" of fiction is only trying to establish cultural capital.)[23] What Guillory talks about is a particular form of appropriation of the work of art by the bourgeoisie (his favorite examples are therefore the "collector" and the "corporate buyer"), which may be perpetuated in the (French) school system but cannot explain the entirely different role literature plays in today's humanities. Similarly, Guillory's analysis of the role of theory suffers from its exclusive ties to de Man's "rigor"—which Guillory needs in order to establish an analogy between literary theory and "the 'technical' quality of the knowledge valued by the professional managerial class" (xii). As a consequence, currently much more influential approaches such as the New Historicism, studies of race, gender, and sexual preference, postcolonial studies, and autobiographical and confessional tendencies in literary studies have to be ignored. Certainly recurring attempts in literary criticism to gain respect by more rigorous procedures have been displaced, by and large, by poststructuralism and its aftermath. What we are witnessing today is therefore not a redefinition of literature on the basis of the needs and values of a new "professional managerial class" with its "technobureaucratic constraints," but a redefinition of literature and culture in terms of the needs of expressive individualism. Those working in the field have to make a choice between wanting to take advantage of this development or wanting to reflect on some of its consequences for their own work.

In Guillory's Marxist view, class analysis remains the best way to comprehend the crisis of the humanities. Since it is the function of the humanities to produce cultural capital, any crisis must signal a social and economic realignment. A new class needs new cultural capital. This argument perpetuates a view in which economic structures shape culture. It may be, however, that the cultural realm has turned into a sphere that is, increasingly, contradicting (not opposing) dominant economic and social structures (and thereby creating problems for them). While the economic and professional sphere may indeed be governed by "technobureaucratic values," the cultural realm is nourishing forms of imaginary self-empowerment that contribute to a growing individualization of society—and, for that matter, to a subversion of "technocratic values." Contrary to what Guillory claims, the "distinction" offered by cultural material nowadays is no longer "based on inequality of access to cultural goods" (339), but on its performative and expressive potential to represent difference. Guillory is right in claiming that literary and cultural studies, despite their official self-image as a disinterested search for meaning and aesthetic value, are seriously affected and transformed by professionalization. But the main pressures—and possibilities—these professional structures exert do not go in the direction of technobureaucratic streamlining but, on the contrary, in that of a proliferation of individual expression. Because it continues to work within these structures of professionalization, the new American studies have not only remained within a characteristic mode of knowledge and value production not so different from traditional forms, but they have actually intensified and radicalized this mode. What I suggest, then, in thinking about the future of American studies, is that more attention be paid to the ways in which knowledge is produced in the field—and for what purpose.

Notes

1   In the following analysis I have often set my arguments in the larger context of the humanities because, in my view, the recent development of American studies reenacts a general trend of the humanities in the postmodern period. To counter a possible misunderstanding right from the start, the following essay is thus not one about the "New Americanists" or other recent developments in American studies. It is an essay about a larger intellectual paradigm in the humanities, called here *cultural radicalism*, and its social foundation, called here *expressive individualism*. As far as the New Americanists or other recent approaches are concerned, my only argument is that, contrary to the self-perception of some of its proponents, they are not exempt from these developments, but are affected by them in ways that we should not consider taboo in the movement. Because I am interested in general tendencies, I have also refrained from referring to specific examples of the new American studies or other approaches—with one exception which I employ to illustrate a structural aspect of professionalization (and not in order to discuss the merits of this particular book). Inevitably, as soon as one goes into the discussion of specific examples, the center of discussion changes to a debate on the adequacy or inadequacy of that interpretation. I think, however, that one might very well disagree with interpretations of certain books or approaches and still find my analysis of the general development convincing or acceptable.

2   This does not mean, of course, that a claim for representativeness cannot be made, but as the history of recent critical approaches demonstrates, such a claim will not survive for long and will immediately become the target of another critical intervention.

3   Of course, there is also the possibility that the scholar has discovered something new, but such discoveries have become increasingly rare. Moreover, as the example of Chopin is supposed to show, as soon as new material or a new topic is discovered or introduced, it becomes subject to the same professional logic I am describing. I would therefore classify most of the work done in the humanities nowadays as reinterpretations.

4   The recent revisionism has further intensified this process, but only in consequent application of historicist premises.

5   Again, there is, in my view, no escape from this development because one cannot ignore the postmodern and poststructuralist critique of the arbitrariness of each act of centering. This, in fact, provides an important theoretical justification for cultural studies, because the less we can privilege certain texts

or interpretations as "representative" sources of insight, the more we need to extend our scope of material. However, the more we extend our scope, the more we accelerate the process of diffusion and proliferation. This problem cannot be solved by taking back the claim of representativeness to a privileged subculture or to one's favorite dissenting voice because, inevitably, the process of diffusion will renew and repeat itself on this level for the institutional reasons described.

6 I have called this development the "Americanization" of literary and cultural studies in a different context. By Americanization I mean an advanced stage of professionalization developed most clearly and strongly in the United States, but setting new standards for scholarship in the humanities all over the world. Again, one should emphasize that this professional structure characterizes and shapes work of the left and the right with equal force. For a more extended discussion of some of the consequences, see my essay "The Americanization of Literary Studies," *American Studies International* 28, no. 2 (1990): 9–22.

7 As the question mark in the title of Shelley Fisher Fishkin's book *Was Huck Black? Mark Twain and African-American Voices* indicates, this claim, in parts of the book, remains on the level of a tantalizing suggestion, while, in other parts where Fishkin tries to rescue the novel from the charge of racism, it goes beyond mere suggestion: "Given our awareness now of the extent to which Huck's voice was black, black students who find themselves identifying with Huck may feel somewhat less ambivalence. After all, they are not identifying 'against' their race: rather, they are choosing which of two black voices in the book they find more appealing." Shelley Fisher Fishkin, *Was Huck Black? Mark Twain and African-American Voices* (New York: Oxford University Press, 1993), 107. The point here is the structure of the argument, the extension of a valuable insight into an overstatement. Again, it is important to point out that this procedure is not tied to any particular political perspective or revisionist aim, as a look at criticism of *Huckleberry Finn* of the fifties and sixties can quickly reveal. Fishkin has only done what innumerable other interpretations of formalist persuasions did when they claimed, for example, to have discovered that a certain motif, theme, or pattern provided the novel with organic unity and thus must be seen as key to the meaning of the novel. For a more detailed analysis of the structure and development of Fishkin's argument, see my review of *Was Huck Black?* in *Amerikastudien/American Studies* 39 (1994): 614–17.

8 American literary criticism has therefore adopted a whole new terminology for assessing the significance of an analysis—employing phrases such as "highly suggestive," "powerful," or "dazzling"—all taken from the culture of performance. This is not to say that just any wild or outrageous claim will succeed. Obviously, the critic has to find the right balance between overstatement and acceptability. But acceptability is no longer a hermeneutically based term but a primarily social one, reflecting professional networks and other power games. What the critic needs in this situation is, above all, a "radar," to use David

Riesman's key term for the other-directed person. David Riesman, with Revel Denney and Nathan Glazer, *The Lonely Crowd: A Study of the Changing American Character* (New Haven, Conn.: Yale University Press, 1950).

9   For a more detailed analysis, see my essay "Literature, Liberalism, and the Current Cultural Radicalism," in *Why Literature Matters: Theories and Functions of Literature*, ed. Rüdiger Ahrens and Laurenz Volkmann (Heidelberg: Winter, 1996), 211–34. In the following analysis, my purpose is not to discredit this new form of radicalism, which has opened up important new perspectives, but to understand the logic of its choices.

10 The concept used by the German student movement for this systemic effect was *strukturelle Gewalt*. This term not only expresses the central idea of a form of power that manifests itself not through an agent or somebody's action (which is the usefulness of the idea of structure), but it also describes this invisible exertion of power through structure as a form of coercion or violence (*Gewalt*).

11 It would be fascinating indeed to compare these categories as different versions of the idea of systemic effect: their range of explanation, their implied definition of the system, their definition of what can constitute resistance, and so on.

12 Again, my goal here is to describe the inner logic of a development and the problems it creates. The redefinition of power as all-pervasive systemic effect provides valuable insights into the manifestation of power effects in seemingly "natural" or "innocent" aspects of social life. But it also creates the problem of where to locate power and how to specify its effects. On this point, see the excellent analysis of Wolfram Schmidgen, "The Principle of Negative Identity and the Crisis of Relationality in Contemporary Literary Criticism," *REAL* 11 (1995): 371–404.

13 In his book *Cultural Capital*, John Guillory speaks of "a confusion between representation in the political sense—the relation of a representative to a constituency—and representation in the rather different sense of the relation between an image and what the image represents." John Guillory, *Cultural Capital: The Problem of Literary Canon Formation* (Chicago: University of Chicago Press, 1993), viii. Subsequent references are cited parenthetically in the text. I think it is more adequate, however, to speak not of a confusion but of a conflation.

14 This cultural self-empowerment is not to be equated with "real" social or political empowerment (although it may have such consequences—witness, for example, the impact of feminism in American studies). The term is understood here as an imaginary construct and refers to the possibility of imagining and fashioning oneself as different—stronger, weaker, nonwhite, and so on— and thereby as distinct and not subject to an all-pervasive systemic effect.

15 Although I do not see a ready alternative, I am aware of the difficulties the term poses. One is the communitarian bias in the use of the term *individualism* in *Habits of the Heart*. As the following paragraph is to show, I do not share this

view. Robert N. Bellah et al., *Habits of the Heart: Individualism and Commitment in American Life*. New York: Harper and Row, 1986.

16 I am deliberately using the term *individual* here, and I am using it in the Tocquevillian sense of the smallest social unit. In this sense, *individual* is not to be confused with *individualist, individualistic,* or an ideology of individualism defined by claims of personal freedom or autonomy. It is also not to be confused and conflated with philosophical conceptualizations of the individual such as *subject* or *self*. Deconstructing the category of the subject does not affect the use of the term *individual* as a sociological category because it only deconstructs a particular philosophical interpretation given to that social unit. The fact that the concept of the subject may be an illusion of Western thought and that, consequently, there are no (unified) subjects, does not mean that there are no individuals. Every scholar in the profession acts as such an individual, no matter what his or her status of self-definition as a subject (illusionary unity, correctly decentered, or happily performative) may be. That such a retreat from the category of the *subject* might be of use for philosophy as well is pointed out by John Smith: "Over the past several years, however, a change has been taking place. The focus in the human sciences has been shifting from denunciations or affirmations of the subject to a 'reconstruction' of the individual in a way that avoids the nostalgia for an undeconstructed self. These new efforts do not strive for a return to or of the (repressed) subject. Rather, they work through the crisis of subjectivity toward a new definition." In this context, subject and individual are defined in the following way: "The 'subject' I shall relegate to a philosophical paradigm culminating in Descartes. That paradigm attempts to define 'self-consciousness,' which I take to be a fact, mistakenly in terms of self-reflection. Moreover, that paradigm tends to limit notions of selfhood to self-conscious subjectivity. I shall argue, in good measure following Manfred Frank's lead, that the concept of the 'individual' is more fruitful for our self-understanding. It allows us to shift attention away from the (historically) limited views of subjectivity and self-reflection without abandoning ontologically, politically, epistemologically, and semiotically necessary notions of particularity (resistance to the universal) and interpretation (dialectic between individual and universal). In short, we can abandon the subject but need the individual to arrive at richer conceptions of meaning, self, consciousness, and action." John H. Smith, "The *Transcendence* of the Individual," *Diacritics* 19, no. 2 (1989): 82.

17 In many of these cases, the poststructuralist notion of *différance* provides a major inspiration, but the conceptualizations of difference go far beyond poststructuralist versions. In historical terms, poststructuralism (including deconstruction) provides only one manifestation of this search for difference and is thus part of a larger trend of cultural and intellectual history. One reason for the growing historical importance of the need to be different can be inferred from Tocqueville's observation that democratic societies take away symbolic distinctions. By doing so, they settle the individual with the task of making up

for this loss. In economic individualism, the possibilities for doing this are still limited in comparison to expressive individualism, where the resources of culture have moved to the forefront.

18 Sacvan Bercovitch, *The Office of The Scarlet Letter* (Baltimore: Johns Hopkins University Press, 1991), 90.

19 Winfried Fluck, "Cultures of Criticism: *Moby-Dick*, Expressive Individualism, and the New Historicism," *REAL* 11 (1995): 222–23.

20 Obviously, these two forms are not neatly separated in their actual historical appearance. There are mixed forms and many forms of coexistence. Benjamin Franklin, mentioned by the authors of *Habits of the Heart* as an exemplary representative of economic individualism, is also a master of self-fashioning. But this talent is still instrumentalized for, and subordinated to, the goal of a social rise to material success and social respectability. On the whole, it seems warranted to say, that (a) the social role of expressive individualism has dramatically increased since its first breakthrough manifestations in the Romantic period; (b) this development was propelled decisively by the growing authority of art and other forms of cultural self-expression, but, especially, by the increased possibilities of imaginary self-empowerment offered through fiction; and (c) this gradually emerging expressive individualism has found a whole new range of options in the era of postindustrialism and postmodernism with its new postmaterialist values of self-realization and radical self-determination. While the Romantic period and the experimental culture of modernism can be seen as avant-garde movements of expressive individualism, the postmodern period has witnessed the broad democratization of their cultural insistence on the right (and need) to be different.

21 For an excellent discussion of the ambiguities of modernity, which could provide a useful basis for a reconsideration of the contribution literary and cultural studies have made to modernity and the process of modernization, see John Tomlinson, *Cultural Imperialism: A Critical Introduction* (Baltimore: Johns Hopkins University Press, 1991), especially chapter 5, in which he draws on the work of Marshall Berman and Cornelius Castoriadis.

22 Guillory claims "that the concept of cultural capital can provide the basis for a new historical account" (viii). In contrast, I argue that it is the use value of this cultural capital that counts, and this use is determined by different stages and needs of individualization. Social actors adapt social roles to their own needs and desires, and the realm of culture has become the exemplary training ground for this flexibility.

23 To claim, for example, that the emergence of aesthetic production (and the concept of the *aesthetic*) as a relatively autonomous sphere is to be attributed to the need to distinguish cultural from material capital must ignore the possibilities the aesthetic offers for the processes of symbolic self-definition and imaginary self-empowerment. It must thereby not only miss a crucial dimension of aesthetic experience but also fail to comprehend the crucial role eighteenth-century fiction and art play for the constitution of the individual in modernity.

Autobiographies of the Ex-White Men:

Why Race Is Not a Social Construction

Walter Benn Michaels

"Music is a universal art," says the rich white man in James Weldon Johnson's *Autobiography of an Ex-Coloured Man*, "anybody's music belongs to everybody; you can't limit it to race or country."[1] The novel itself, however, is skeptical about music's claim to universality, approving the colored man's trip "into the very heart of the South, to live among the people, and drink in [his] inspiration firsthand" (104), but disapproving the white performers who come to Harlem "to get their imitations first hand from the Negro entertainers they saw there" (78). Anybody's music may belong to everybody, but there's a difference between the *imitations* that whites get from blacks and the *inspiration* that blacks get from blacks. "This slave music," the ex-colored man says, "will be the most treasured heritage of the American Negro" (133). Black musicians, listening to the spirituals, are claiming their heritage; white musicians, imitating the spirituals (or ragtime or hip hop or the blues) are, as a contributor to the recent anthology *Race Traitor* puts it, denying blacks the "right to any heritage of their own."[2]

The contributors to *Race Traitor*—a journal devoted to "the abolition of the white race"[3]—are divided on the question of whether white people can or should sing the blues. And, indeed, the terms of this division are crucial to the very project of race treason—the project of abolishing not white racism but the white race. Are white people who "borrow from black culture" (Ignatiev and Garvey, "Introduction," 3) helping to make "white people cease to be"[4] or are they just, like the white performers who go to Harlem, "ripping off" blacks?[5] It's when the colored man in Johnson abandons the sources of his inspiration that he becomes an ex-colored man, which is to say that he becomes an imitation—he passes for white. *Race Traitor* imagines that white men—perhaps (as its editors say) "by some engagement with blackness, perhaps even an identification as 'black' "[6]—can become ex-white men. But are whites who engage blackness just passing for black? The ex-colored man rejects his racial identity by concealing it; the ex-white man wishes not to conceal his racial identity but, by rejecting it, to destroy it. The ex-colored man wants to cease to be identified as a Negro; the race traitor—perhaps by identifying himself as black—wants to cease to *be* white.

The difference between these projects is a difference in the theory of racial identity. Race in Johnson's *Autobiography* is a function of what its narrator calls "blood"; it is because his skin is the color of "ivory" that the narrator can pretend to be white, it is because his "blood" is black that he isn't white. By contrast, the editors of *Race Traitor*, like most contemporary racial theorists, believe that race is a "social," "not a biological" "fact." Because, as Michael Omi and Howard Winant put it, "the concept of race has defied biological definition," we must understand it instead as "a social concept."[7] Indeed, it is only because "race is socially constructed" that the commitment to "the abolition of whiteness" can make nongenocidal sense. To "make white people cease to be" is not, on the model of Nazis exterminating Jews, to kill white people; it is rather, on the model of abolitionists freeing slaves, to destroy the social fact of whiteness. Insofar as whiteness, like slavery, is a social fact, it can, like slavery, be abolished; just as there once were millions of ex-slaves, there may in the future be millions of ex-whites.

Of course, the project of abolishing whiteness is made possible but not inevitable by the redefinition of race as a social construction; the celebration of racial identity and the promotion of racial difference have, in fact, been more characteristic ambitions of contemporary racial theory. To the extent, however, that both these projects—celebrating race and abolishing it—depend on our conceiving of race as a social fact, I want to argue that neither can succeed. I want to argue that we cannot think of race as a social fact, like slavery or, to take the analogy that is even more fundamental to the project of race treason, like class. If, as Ignatiev puts it, "race, like class, is 'something which in fact happens,'" then—and this is the project of race treason—it can be "made to unhappen" ("Immigrants," 21). Race is not like class; it neither happens nor can be made to unhappen. And I will also argue, against those social constructionists who wish to "respect and preserve" rather than abolish race that it makes no more sense to respect racial difference than it does to try to abolish it. Indeed, I suggest that the very impulse toward preservation reveals the degree to which those who imagine that they have substituted "performative" for "essentialist" accounts of race remain in fact committed to racial essentialism.

In criticizing the idea that race is a social construction, however, my point will not be to defend the idea that race is, after all, a natural or biological fact; it will not be to defend an essentialist conception of racial identity against anti-essentialist conceptions of it. My point will be rather to insist that our actual racial practices can be understood only as the expression of our commitment to the idea that race is *not* a social construction and to insist further that if we give up that commitment we must give up the idea of race altogether. Either race is an essence or there is no such thing as race. Either way, there can be no ex-black or ex-white men. If race, to be what it is, *must* be essential, then Johnson's ex-colored man, because he once was black, can never stop being black; if there is no such thing as race, then the race traitors' ex-white men, because they never were white, can never stop being white. Either race is the sort of thing that makes rejecting your racial identity just a kind of passing or passing becomes impossible and there is no such thing as racial identity.

How, then, is passing possible? From the standpoint of anti-essentialism, the question can be put this way: how is it possible to pass for something without becoming what it is you pass for? From the essentialist standpoint, the question must be put slightly differently: how is it possible to pass at all? What must race be in order for it to be the sort of thing that can be concealed? In a racial system where racial identity is a function of physical appearance—where, say, as F. James Davis says of Brazil, it is the color of your skin rather than some fact about your ancestry that determines your racial identity[8]—this may be almost impossible. For if your racial identity is determined by your physical appearance—if being dark-skinned makes you black and being light-skinned makes you white—then obviously the only way to pass is by concealing or somehow altering the color of your skin.

And we might note here that the choice between altering or concealing—or, more precisely, the possibility of concealing by altering—raises a question to which we will have to return—if you do somehow manage to alter the color of your skin, are you passing, which is to say, pretending to belong to one race when you really belong to another, or have you in fact stopped belonging to one race and begun instead to belong to the other? A relevant analogy here would be the transsexual—we probably don't want to say that the transsexual is passing—and if we do say that the transsexual is passing, we are required to come up with some account of how a person's *body* can be changed from one sex to another without the *person's* being changed from one sex to another—of where or what the truth is that's being concealed by the alteration. In *Black Skin, White Masks*, Fanon imagines "a serum for 'denegrification'" designed to make it possible for the Negro "to whiten himself";[9] were there actually to be such a serum, would we want to say that the person who used it was now able to pass for white or would we want to say that the person now was white?

Under the American racial system, however—under the rule that one drop of black blood makes a person black—passing need not demand the kinds of physical transformations required by Davis's account of Brazilian theory or by the transsexual. Given the "ivory whiteness" of his skin, all the ex-colored man does is grow a mustache and change his name. Where physical appearance, in other words, does not determine racial identity but is only a sign of it, you can pass without altering your body in any way (without even covering it up, as if in drag). But to say that the one-drop rule (the rule that you don't have to look like what you are) makes passing possible without requiring physical transformation is not, of course, to say that it makes the body irrelevant—the one-drop rule may make race invisible without thereby making it immaterial. After all, the one drop is one drop of blood, and even if we acknowledge that nowadays the concept of black or white blood has no biological currency, we can still understand the appeal to blood as a metaphor for whatever thing there is in the body that does determine your race—say, black or white genes. Under the one-drop rule, then, for black persons to pass as white is for these persons to conceal whatever it is in their bodies that identifies them as being black. But, since it is possible to pass only because that thing is already invisible (which is to say that no physical alteration is required for it to be concealed), then, on this account, passing is less a matter of hiding something than of refusing or failing to acknowledge something.

Racial identity under the one-drop rule thus emerges as something that is not only embodied (in the sense that the one drop [whatever it's one drop of] is in the body) but must also be represented (since, without representation, the fact that it's in the body cannot be known). And this nonidentity of the truth of one's race and the representation of that truth, opens up—may, indeed, be said to constitute—the entire field of racialized discourse. At the simplest level, it inserts race into the field of ethics—if your racial identity is invisible, it becomes something you can lie about or something you can tell the truth about, conceal or reveal. In itself, however, this possibility is of only limited significance. After all, hair color is also something you can conceal or reveal. But there is an important sense in which hair color, while it can be misrepresented, cannot be represented—if your hair is black, you can dye it blonde and misrepresent its true color. But if you leave it black, you will not represent black hair, you will just have black hair. The invisibility of race, however, means that it can be both misrepresented and represented, indeed, that it must be either misrepresented or represented since to leave it unrepresented will be to misrepresent it. If, in other words, you are invisibly black, either you must find some way to represent your blackness or you must pass for white. This is what I mean by saying that the possibility of passing opens up the whole field of racialized discourse. The discourse of race is the discourse of people who can pass but who do not wish to.

And this is true despite the fact that, even under the one-drop rule, comparatively few people can pass. For it is the mere conceptual possibility of passing (of concealing your identity without altering your body) that proclaims the essential invisibility of race, that takes the color even of people who can't pass (the vast majority) and changes it from the *fact* that constitutes their race into a *representation* of the fact that constitutes their race. This is why a writer like Howard Winant can plausibly say that "race is not a matter of color alone. . . . It is more like a way of life, a way of being."[10] Race is not a matter of color alone because, if color does not determine race, color must be understood as only one way—and not necessarily the most important way—of manifesting race. The possibility of belonging to a race that you don't look like you belong to produces the possibility of manifesting your racial identity in your actions, of not merely looking black or white but of acting black or white—more generally, of acting like what you are. It produces, in other words, the idea that certain actions (and we would wish to include under the rubric of action beliefs and values as well as practices—all those things that might be said to constitute one's culture) properly accompany certain identities. Regardless of skin color, there are ways to act black or white. And once we recognize this, we recognize also that even if you can't pass (even if you can't help but look like what you are), you can still fail to act like what you are.

Thus the conceptual possibility of passing not only makes available—to those whose physical appearance is such that they *can* pass—the option of revealing or concealing their racial identity, it makes available to everyone— regardless of whether they can pass—the option of being loyal or disloyal to their race, of embracing or repudiating the way of life their race makes theirs. Passing is possible because race is invisible, and because race is invisible, all the things that make it visible are reduced to mere representations of a racial identity located elsewhere. At the same time, however, because race is invisible and cannot be reduced to any of its representations, any and everything can be understood as a representation of it. It is only because the thing itself is invisible that everything can be imagined as a way of seeing it.

The invisibility of race thus makes an important contribution to its power, which is no doubt why modern American racial thought at its inception was always tempted to locate a person's racial identity not merely in a part of the person that's hard to see—the blood—but in a part of the person that's impossible to see—the soul. Indeed, locating race in the soul rather than the body makes the body itself only a representation of racial essence; it makes race immune even to the fantasy of the denegrification serum—what is not actually in the body cannot be affected by the alteration of the body. And in recent racial thought—in racial thought at the end of the twentieth century instead of at its beginning—the repudiation of the body as the site of racial identity makes the fantasy of biological denegrification equally irrelevant. But, of course, racial thought today—which is to say, the commitment to race as a social construction—understands itself as anti-essentialist, not as a kind of essentialism.

The claim that race is socially constructed is the claim that race is not a biological entity; in the terms of our discussion so far, it amounts to the claim that there is nothing in people's bodies—visible or invisible—that constitutes their racial identity. There is, in other words, no such thing as black or white blood and no genetic equivalent to it. As one biologist puts it, " 'Race' is simply not a category that biologists and anthropologists still take seriously, although as a social phenomenon race still has a compelling reality."[11] But, if we don't think that race is in the soul and we don't think it's in the body, where do we think it is? What kind of reality is the compelling reality of race today?

One way that we might characterize this reality is as the reality of a mistake. Even if race is not a biological fact, many people have believed in it as a biological fact and some people, no doubt, continue to believe in it as a biological fact. And this belief, mistaken though it may be, has obviously had, and no doubt continues to have, significant consequences. So we might think that the reality of race consists in the fact that, even though most of us now know that there is no such thing as race, the fact that we didn't use to know that there was no such thing as race means that we live in a world that is still organized along racial lines. And the point of our new knowledge—the knowledge that there are no biological races—would be to undo the consequences of our old ignorance—to produce a world in which race was not a compelling reality.

Those who are committed to the social construction of race, however (even the race traitors), clearly do not think of racial reality as a mistake; they do not think of race as the sort of thing which, if it doesn't exist in nature, doesn't exist at all. In a well-known passage in *Anti-Semite and Jew*, Sartre says that, in the eyes of the anti-Semite, what makes the Jew a Jew "is the presence in him of 'Jewishness,' a Jewish principle analogous to phlogiston."[12] But when people stopped believing that phlogiston existed in nature, they didn't start believing that phlogiston was a social construction. Which is only to say that the claim that there are no races in nature—that race is a social construction—is not meant to deny that there is such a thing as race; it is meant to give us a better account of what race is. So if we say that because there are no races in nature, racial thinking is just "an illusion," the social constructionist thinks that we have missed the point. If, on the one hand, as Omi and Winant put it, it is a mistake to "think of race as an *essence*, as something fixed, concrete and objective," it is, on the other hand, also a mistake "to see it as a mere illusion, which an ideal social order would eliminate" (68). Those who think of race as a biological fact make the first mistake; those who think of it as mere ideology and argue for the desirability of a color-blind society, make the second. But race consciousness is not false consciousness; indeed to say that because there are no races in nature, there are no races, must be on this view as much a non sequitur as it would be to say that because there are no classes in nature, there are no classes. And just as the denial of the importance of class is a hallmark of liberalism, the denial of race is a strategy of what is now called "liberal racism."[13]

On this account, then, race is a compelling reality in the way that social class is, and the argument that because there is no racial phlogiston there are no races looks as politically problematic as its converse, the anti-Semite's commitment to the principle of Jewishness. For Sartre too, it is only the liberal, the antisocialist democrat, who says that because there is no Jewish phlogiston, "There are no Jews," and he does so out of his individualist hostility to the very idea of class. Fearing the "great collective forms" that threaten liberal democracy, the democrat seeks "to persuade individuals that they exist in an isolated state": "he fears that the Jew will acquire a consciousness of the Jewish collectivity—just as he fears that a 'class consciousness' may awaken in the worker" (56–57). From this standpoint, then, the mistake of the liberal (who thinks that because there is no Jewish essence there are no Jews) both repeats and corrects the mistake of the anti-Semite (who thinks that there are Jews and that what makes them Jewish is the metaphysical essence of Jewishness); the liberal is wrong to assert the reality of the individual and to deny the reality of the class, but he is right to analogize the consciousness of Jewish identity to the consciousness of class identity, to see, in effect, that if there are Jews, they don't need a Jewish essence any more than, say, the workers need a proletarian essence, or the middle class needs a bourgeois essence.

The proletariat and the bourgeoisie don't need an essence because they are

238 / Walter Benn Michaels

who they are, Sartre says, by virtue of "an ensemble of external factors," "an ensemble of various modes of *behavior*" (37). On the model of class identity, then, racial identity, too, would be (what it is often said to be) "performative."[14] And, of course, it is a truly performative conception of race that would make passing impossible. For the space of passing, as we have already seen, is the space of representation, which is to say that passing is possible because we must in our actions either represent or misrepresent our race. But the possibility of representing or misrepresenting our race depends, as we have also already seen, on the nonidentity of the racial representation and the racial reality. And the idea of race as performative undoes this nonidentity; it eliminates the reality—the one drop or the soul—and thus transforms the actions that *represent* racial identity into the actions that *determine* racial identity. Passing becomes impossible because, in the logic of social constructionism, it is impossible not to be what you are passing for.

This is the dream of what *Race Traitor* calls "crossover"—the dream that by ceasing to act white you can cease to be white—and it is this dream that produces both the distinctive technology and the distinctive anxiety of putative ex-white men: the distinctive technology is what Johnson disparagingly called "imitation," what the race traitors describe more hopefully as "borrowing" from black culture; the distinctive anxiety is about whether and when such borrowing can succeed, which is to say about whether and when white people acting like black people can cease to count as exploiting black people and can begin to count instead as becoming if not black, at least "mulatto." Thus, although the music writer Paul Garon appears in *Race Traitor* as a reproachfully Johnsonian figure, criticizing "white blues" as "a weak and imitative form" (174), the cultural project of race treason will be to reconceive imitation as inspiration and to celebrate in particular those white musicians who, in the words of Albert Murray, "embrace certain Negroes not only as kindred spirits but as ancestral figures." The white performers coming to Harlem, Johnson says, only "imitate" the ex-colored man; Woody Herman, Murray says, was "inspire[d]" by Duke Ellington.[15]

Because the difference between imitation and inspiration depends on the ontological priority of racial identity—you are inspired by what you are, you imitate what you aren't—*Race Traitor*'s "Crossover Dreams" depend on undoing it. They depend, in other words, on the idea that since race is a social construction, there is nothing about the bodies of black people that makes those bodies more suited to playing the blues than white bodies. And since even Garon acknowledges that "neither genes nor race-differentiated experience seem to affect one's ability to form certain chords or play certain melodies" (171), it's hard to see by what criteria the efforts of white people to play the blues can count as more imitative than the efforts of black people or by what criteria the "white blues" can count as a more "imitative form" than the black blues. Indeed, since a formal description of the blues requires no reference to the color of those who perform it (any more than does, say, a formal description of the sonnet), and since the very idea of a musical form is itself dependent on the possibility of imitation, it's hard to see how there can be any formal difference between black and white blues. The white musician who learns to form the chords and play the melodies is, Johnson and Garon to the contrary notwithstanding, no more or less committed to imitation than the black musician.

But, of course, the very same argument that works against the idea that crossovers are somehow imitative and inferior also works against the idea that crossovers are actually crossing over. If, in other words, you needn't *be* black to play the blues, you don't *become* black by playing the blues. Race no more follows music than music follows race—what you become by playing the blues is a blues musician, not a black person. Thus the distinction between white blues and black blues must be understood as a distinction between two kinds of people, not between two kinds of music: what makes the music you are playing black is the fact that you are black; what gives the music its color is the color of the people who are playing it. If, then, it is only the anti-essentialist conception of race that makes the project of crossover possible (because only an anti-essentialist conception makes it possible for you to give up being white by giving up white behavior), it is only an essentialist conception of race that makes it desireable (because only an essentialist conception of race makes your behavior white and thus makes you want to give it up). So, although the goal of the ex-white men (crossing over) is fundamentally opposed to the goal of the ex-colored man (passing), the fact that people want to cross over, like the fact that people can pass, turns out to be a tribute to essentialism.

The anti-essentialist performative is in this sense a version of the essentialist denegrification serum: if race is a biological fact, then to change the color of your skin is to change your race; if race is a mode of behavior, then to change your way of life is to change your race. But because race, as Winant says, is "not a matter of color alone," you can't change your race by changing your skin. And because race, in not being a "matter of color *alone*" must nevertheless still be a matter of color, you can't change your race by changing your way of life either. It must still be a matter of color because, without the appeal to color, there can be nothing distinctively racial about your way of life: the social constructionist commitment to the racial performative, in other words, is only skin-deep. It involves not the choice of behavior over color but the adjustment of behavior to color.

And this is true even if we focus not on racial but on what is today called cultural identity. In the most recent American edition of *Anti-Semite and Jew*, Michael Walzer criticizes Sartre for presenting what he calls an "empty" Jewishness (xiii), one without either religious or cultural content. "The Jews who surround us," Sartre says, "have only a ceremonial and polite contact with their religion" (65); he clearly did not anticipate what Walzer calls "the revival of religious interest" (xxv) that we see today.[16] But, of course, the Jewish religion is irrelevant to Sartre, not only because modern anti-Semitism is racial rather than religious in character but, more importantly, because, insofar as Jewishness is understood as a matter of religious belief and practice, the Jew is a Jew only in the way that, say, a Methodist is a Methodist, or a member of the Elk's Club is an Elk. We don't need anti-essentialist accounts of Elks; their identities are purely performative, which is to say that they are entirely constituted by (rather than represented by) behavior. But a Jew does not become Jewish in the same way that an Elk becomes an Elk, and, of course, a Jew cannot resign as a Jew in the same way that an Elk can resign from the Elk's Club.

Another way to put this is to say that Sartre sees on the one hand that Jewishness is not a matter of biology or a "metaphysical essence" (38) (that's the point of his denial of a Jewish phlogiston), but he also sees, on the other hand, that a "principle of Jewishness" cannot simply be replaced by a set of Jewish practices—the anti-Semite hates what the Jew does only insofar as what the Jew does represents what he is. And we can put this point more generally and more positively by noting that the celebration of difference in contemporary multiculturalism depends entirely on our thinking of people's cultural identities as expressed by (rather than constituted by) their practices. Why else should we not only tolerate but esteem actions that may seem to us wrong and beliefs that may seem to us mistaken? If, for example, we think that male circumcision is cruel and pointless, why should we allow it? If we think that female circumcision is even more cruel and just as pointless, why should we allow it? It seems clear that if we value such practices, we do so not because they seem to us in themselves valuable (the point of the example is that they don't), but because they seem to us to represent identities that, as such, are valuable. So, just as it is only the difference between one's identity and one's actions that makes passing possible, it is only the difference between one's identity and one's actions that makes the celebration of difference plausible. And if, as I have argued above, passing is a kind of tribute to essentialism, so, too, is the celebration of cultural difference—it is indeed only if difference is essential that it can, as such, be celebrated.

Sartre is right, then, to insist not only that the Jew is not a Jew because of his Jewish body or his Jewish soul but also that he cannot be a Jew because he does Jewish things. But if there is no Jewish body and there is no Jewish soul and there are no Jewish things to do, what's left? "We must now," Sartre says, "ask ourselves the question: does the Jew exist?" (58). The liberal, as we have already seen, says no. But the liberal's answer cannot be accepted because the liberal also (and for the same reasons) denies that the worker exists. As we have also already seen, however, the analogy between the Jew and the worker is problematic, if only because the worker who saves a lot of money and buys himself a factory becomes a capitalist and ceases to be a worker while the Jew cannot, by, say, converting to Catholicism, cease to be a Jew. So the fact that workers exist doesn't mean that Jews must also exist. And yet, Sartre insists, the Jew does exist. In what amounts to the *degré zéro* of social constructionism, Sartre famously asserts that the Jew is not someone who has a Jewish body or soul or religion or culture: "The Jew is one whom other men consider a Jew" (69).

It is being considered a Jew that constitutes the Jew's "situation." The Jew, of course, is not alone in being in a situation; on the contrary, everyone is in some situation; some "ensemble of limits and restrictions" "forms" everyone and "decides" everyone's "possibilities." But not everyone's situation is the same and not everyone deals with their situation in the same way. The Jew has two ways of dealing with his. One way is by "running away from it" (92). The "inauthentic Jew" denies his Jewishness, either by denying that he himself is Jewish or by denying that there are such things as Jews, indeed, by espousing "a conception of the world that excludes the very idea of race" (110). Sartre understands the first of these denials as the attempt to conceal from others one's situation as a Jew, and the second as the attempt to conceal one's situation as a Jew from oneself. The authentic Jew, by contrast, not only accepts the Jewishness the world imposes on him, but himself chooses that Jewishness; if inauthenticity is "to deny . . . or attempt to escape from" one's "condition as a Jew," "authenticity . . . is to live [it] to the full" (91). The authentic Jew "asserts his claim" as a Jew.

But what claim does the Jew as Jew have? The inauthentic Jew claims to be a man like other men, but it is precisely this universalism, what Sartre calls his "naive monism," that makes him inauthentic. "The authentic Jew abandons the myth of the universal man" and "for the naive monism of the inauthentic Jew he substitutes a social pluralism" (136). But, as we have already seen, this pluralism cannot be understood along the lines of a pluralism that would value Jewish culture. There is no such thing as Jewish culture, Sartre thinks, which is to say that because the assimilated Jew remains Jewish it cannot be his culture that makes him Jewish—and when the anti-Semite calls you a Jew, it is your essence not your culture that he is naming. So if to be a Jew is only to be called a Jew, one's claim as a Jew—one's claim to be what one is called—cannot be the claim to a culture, it can only be the claim to that essence.

The virtue of Sartre's analysis is thus that it makes clear the irreducibility of the notion of essence to identity. Insofar as it is the "situation" (and only the situation) of the Jew that confers on him his Jewishness, Jewishness is defined without recourse to essence. But the situation in which the Jew finds himself is the situation of having a Jewish essence attributed to him (as it happens, by anti-Semites, but of course the theoretical position would be no different if those who made the Jew a Jew by considering him to be a Jew liked Jews), and insofar as the situation in which the Jew finds himself is the situation of having a Jewish essence attributed to him, and insofar as the authentic Jew makes himself authentic by *choosing* the situation in which the anti-Semite has placed him, the authentic Jew makes himself authentic by choosing essence.

That Sartre himself doesn't quite see this is clear from his renewed consideration of the analogy between Jewish identity and class identity. The analogy had been criticized in its first incarnation on the grounds that class identification was a function of "acts" not "essence." Thus, although it was very unlikely, for example, that "the privileged class" would be "willing to cooperate in the socialist reconstruction," there would be "no valid reason for repulsing it" if it did (42). The privileged class is only prevented from doing so by its "situation as a privileged class," not by "some indefinable interior demon," so it is possible for "portions of this class [to] break away from it" and to be "assimilated to the oppressed class"; "they will be judged by their acts, not by their essence." "Je me fous de votre essence eternelle," the communist Politzer says to Sartre; the communists "don't give a damn about essence" (42). But such an assimilationist breaking away from one's Jewish identity (as opposed to one's bourgeois identity) is impossible precisely because the anti-

Semite, unlike the communist, cares about essence not acts. This is what makes him an anti-Semite.

And this point is further complicated by the fact that the authentic Jew is required not only by the anti-Semite but by Sartre to choose the situation that the socialist member of the privileged class may reject. In the logic of anti-essentialism, it is as if the recognition that the "demon" is really only a "situation" counts not so much as demystification but as legitimation. Thus Sartre goes on at some length in praise of the "courage" of the Jew who chooses Jewishness, and thus Winant thinks that the transformation of racial identity into "much more a matter of choice than of ascription" counts not as its elimination but as its "liberation" (169). But since, as I have argued, the situation is inescapably the situation of demonization, to choose it is necessarily to choose essence. The racial identity that is chosen is no less essential than the racial identity that is ascribed—indeed, it is only because it is exactly the same as the racial identity that is ascribed that it counts as racial and that it counts as an identity. If Jewishness really were nothing more than a situation in the same way that class is, the Jew who imagined a world without race would be no more inauthentic than the socialist who imagined a world without class.

So the analogy between race and class cannot, on Sartre's own terms, really stand. For class really is a social construction, which is just to say that you can defend or oppose class difference without thinking that the question of what class you belong to has a biological answer or without thinking, more generally, that the question of what class you belong to can be answered without recourse to what you believe, what you do, and what you own. Citing Sartre's famous depiction of the *garçon de café* in the opening pages of *Being and Nothingness*, Anthony Appiah has recently pointed out that it makes no sense to ask of the waiter—what it *does* make sense to ask of "the black and the white, the homosexual and the heterosexual"—whether he "really is" a waiter.[17] This is because, to use the terms we have derived from *Anti-Semite and Jew*, being a waiter is more like being a religious Jew (or an Elk) than it is like being the racialized Jew identified by the anti-Semite. Because, as Appiah says, "there can be a gap between what a person . . . is and the racial identity he performs," racial identity—unlike religious or professional identity—cannot be understood simply as the "performance" of a "role." It is this gap, Appiah points out, "that makes passing possible," and if, as we have already seen, the possibility of passing is constitutive of racial identity, racial identity, Appiah says, is "in this way, like all the major forms of identification that are central to contemporary identity politics: female and male; gay, lesbian and straight; black, white, yellow . . . even that most neglected of American identities, class" (79–80).

But to what extent is being gay or straight like being black or white; to what extent is being middle-class or working-class like being black or white? It certainly is true that there is a sense in which gay men can pass as straight, a sense, that is, in which a gay man can act straight without thereby becoming straight. But it is only a very limited sense. A gay man can pass as straight by behaving like a straight man, but a gay man who not only behaved like a straight man but also desired what straight men desire and thought of himself as straight would no longer be passing as straight—he would be straight. Gay behavior does not *represent* one's sexuality, it *determines* it. Ontologically speaking (and despite the fact that sexual behavior may well be biologically determined in a way that religious behavior may not), a gay man is like a religious Jew. And what is true of religion and sexuality is even more obviously true of class. The *garçon de café* who saves his tips and buys the café is not a member of the proletariat passing as a member of the petit bourgeoisie—he *is* petit bourgeois. Although there aren't any ex-white or ex-black men, there may well be ex-straight and ex-gay men, and there definitely are ex-waiters and ex-religious Jews.

Race, then, is not like class, which is to say, in Sartrean terms, race is not really a situation in the same way that class is, and the Jew's reasons for wanting to get rid of race are not the same as the socialist's reasons for wanting to get rid of class: the inauthentic Jew, wishing for an end to racial difference, does so not on the grounds that it is unjust, but on the grounds that it is unreal. What the inauthentic Jew and the socialist do have in common is their hostility to the very idea of identity, their hostility, that is, to the idea that their bodies, beliefs and behavior represent rather than determine what they are. The inauthentic Jew expresses this hostility by denying that he is a Jew—since his body isn't Jewish and he does not believe in Judaism. If there is no Jewish phlogiston, there are no Jews; if there are no essences, there are no identities. And the socialist expresses his hostility in the same way—by dividing the world not into Jews and Aryans and blacks and whites but instead into workers and capitalists. Owning the means of production does not represent your identity; it constitutes that identity.

It makes no sense, then, to require of the capitalist or the worker what Sartre requires of the Jew—that he assert his claim as a Jew, that he demand recognition for what he is. One doesn't have such a claim as a capitalist, or even as a worker—workers' claims are based on what they do (that's the point, after all, of calling them workers). It makes sense, in other words, to think of class as a social construction because it doesn't make sense to think of class as an identity—our class is determined by what we do. And it doesn't make sense to think of race (of Jewishness or blackness or whiteness) as a social construction because racial identity is irreducible to action. The identity that is irreducible to action is essential, not socially constructed, and the identity that is identical to action is not really an identity—it's just the name of the action: worker, capitalist. If, then, we do not believe in racial identity as an essence, we cannot believe in racial identity as a social construction, and we ought to give up the idea of racial identity altogether—we should, like the inauthentic Jew, deny that there are such things as Jews, or blacks, or whites.

acti

But race traitors, denying that they are white, do not deny that there are such things as whites and blacks. On the contrary: " 'I'm black and I'm proud,' " Ignatiev says, is "the modern rendition of 'Workers of all countries, unite!' "[18] Race treason treats race like class by turning class into race, turning one's relation to the means of production into one's identity and turning the abolition of private property into the abolition of whiteness. Where economic inequality is the problem, then socialism may be the solution; where whiteness is the problem, blackness is the solution. Thus the "many failings" of America are now understood to "result largely from the unwillingness of so-called whites to embrace" the "presence of Afro-Americans" without "qualification" (Ignatiev and Garvey, "Introduction," 4). And, as identity replaces ideology, the way to correct these failings is to recognize how much "the distinctive character of America owes . . . to the presence of Afro-Americans." Ignatiev and Garvey note with surprise and approval the columnist George Will's observation that because basketball is the "most American of all sports" and black people are "the most American of all Americans," black people are "the most accomplished of basketball players." They approve Will's remark because it honors the "presence" of blacks; they are surprised by it because Will is "conservative" (4). But if "I'm black and I'm proud" can be "the modern rendition of 'Workers of all countries, unite,' " which is to say, if hostility to private property can be replaced by pride in Michael Jordan, then the sense in which George Will is conservative (or the sense in which race traitors are not) needs to be reassessed.

The "most subversive act I can imagine," Ignatiev says, is "treason to the white race" ("Interview," 292). The failure of political imagination involved here is, perhaps, obvious but, whether it is or not, my point in this essay has

246 / Walter Benn Michaels

not been to emphasize the by now familiar discrepancy between the projects of racial identity and economic equality. My point, in other words, has not been to demonstrate the unpleasant political consequences of seeking to be an ex-white man; it has been instead to demonstrate the impossibility of actually being an ex-white man. If there is such a thing as whiteness and you are white, I have argued, you cannot stop being white; and if there is no such thing as whiteness, you also can't stop being white. Either way, whiteness (in particular and race in general) is not—like class—a social construction; it is instead—like phlogiston—a mistake.

Notes

1 James Weldon Johnson, *The Autobiography of an Ex-Coloured Man*, ed. William L. Andrews (New York: Penguin, 1990), 105. Subsequent references are cited parenthetically in the text.
2 Paul Garon, "White Blues" in *Race Traitor*, ed. Noel Ignatiev and John Garvey (New York: Routledge, 1996), 169. Subsequent references are cited parenthetically in the text.
3 Noel Ignatiev and John Garvey, "Introduction: A Beginning," in *Race Traitor*, ed. Ignatiev and Garvey, 2. Subsequent references are cited parenthetically in the text.
4 Noel Ignatiev, "Immigrants and Whites," in *Race Traitor*, ed. Ignatiev and Garvey, 21. Subsequent references are cited parenthetically in the text.
5 "Interview" (with Noel Ignatiev), in *Race Traitor*, ed. Ignatiev and Garvey, 290. Subsequent references are cited parenthetically in the text.
6 "Editors' Reply," in *Race Traitor*, ed. Ignatiev and Garvey, 279.
7 Michael Omi and Howard Winant, *Racial Formation in the United States: From the 1960s to the 1980s* (New York: Routledge, 1986), 58, 60. Subsequent references are cited parenthetically in the text.
8 F. James Davis, *Who Is Black? One Nation's Definition* (University Park: Pennsylvania State University Press, 1991).
9 Frantz Fanon, *Black Skin, White Masks*, trans. Charles Lam Markmann (New York: Grove, 1967), 111.
10 Howard Winant, *Racial Conditions: Politics, Theory, Comparisons* (Minneapolis: University of Minnesota Press, 1994), 86. Subsequent references are cited parenthetically in the text.
11 Richard C. Lewontin, "Of Genes and Genitals," *Transition* 6, no. 1 (1996): 187.
12 Jean-Paul Sartre, *Anti-Semite and Jew*, trans. George J. Becker (New York: Schocken, 1995), 37. Subsequent references are cited parenthetically in the text.

13 Avery F. Gordon and Christopher Newfield, "White Philosophy" in *Identities*, ed. Kwame Anthony Appiah and Henry Louis Gates Jr. (Chicago: University of Chicago Press, 1995), 399. "White Philosophy" is a response to my own essay "Race into Culture: A Critical Genealogy of Cultural Identity," which appears in the same volume.

14 Winant, for example, invoking Homi Bhabha, calls for greater "appreciation of the *performative* aspect of race" (Winant, *Racial Conditions*, 18).

15 Qtd. in Phil Rubio, "Crossover Dreams: The 'Exceptional White' in Popular Culture," in *Race Traitor*, ed. Ignatiev and Garvey, 153.

16 Walzer is here interested not only, or even primarily, in a distinctively religious revival but rather in what he takes to be the renewed interest of Jews in affirming more generally "the value of their history and culture" (xxiv). For a critique of such an interest in history, see Walter Benn Michaels, " 'You Who Never Was There': Slavery and the New Historicism, Deconstruction and the Holocaust," *Narrative* 4, no. 1 (1996): 1–16; for a critique of such an interest in culture, see Walter Benn Michaels, "Posthistoricism," *Transition* 6, no. 2 (1996): 4–19.

17 Kwame Anthony Appiah and Amy Gutmann, *Color Conscious: The Political Morality of Race* (Princeton, N.J.: Princeton University Press, 1996), 79. Subsequent references are cited parenthetically in the text.

18 Noel Ignatiev, "The American Intifada," in *Race Traitor*, ed. Ignatiev and Garvey, 100.

Color Blindness and Acting Out

Carl Gutiérrez-Jones

A number of cultural and literary critics have recently drawn national attention by arguing that their academic fields have been significantly harmed by a regime of multiculturalism, a regime they consider fundamentally racist.[1] At the same time, the recently formed Association of Literary Scholars and Critics is building on similar sentiments by explicitly offering its members a race-free zone of "serious study."[2] Putting aside the question of whether or not such tendencies will come to dominate American studies, this essay explores the work of color blindness as it is currently constituted, including its claims to hold a certain liberatory power. At issue are the mechanisms of change that presumably allow arguments for color blindness to free us from the burden of race and racism, as well as the specific viability of these mechanisms.

One of the more prominent examples of the color-blind intervention may be found in the rethinking of race and American literary modernism produced by Walter Benn Michaels in his book entitled *Our America: Nativism, Modernism, and Pluralism.* This work expresses a deep-seated suspicion of historical and cultural inquiry—even as it mobilizes these forms of inquiry to make its point. As with many other arguments committed to an unequivocal ethic of color blindness, Michaels animates historical analysis only insofar as it offers exempla of philosophically oriented points.[3] Inasmuch as Michaels believes modern American culture to be defined by a raced and racist imperative, his version of modernism constitutes an example of literature gone wrong. The readings of particular texts by Michaels, in turn, assert the ways race consciousness inevitably produces racism. Ultimately, Michaels insists on a radical break with a whole set of interchangeable, "modern" and historically grounded analytical tools, including concepts of race, identity, and the Holocaust.

What may not be as readily apparent is Michaels's resounding faith in individual agency, and in the individual's ability to thoroughly disassociate from a racist culture. And here I would build on a sense that comes through in much of Michaels's recent work, which is that radical, individualized choice is all-important to his analysis. If believing in race is the same as believing in ghosts, which is how Michaels typifies our current predicament, then the invocation of choice in his arguments carries all the freight of an exorcism. Embracing this liberating notion of choice, after reading Michaels, is something like being born again.

Self-consciously provocative as well as oddly inspirational, Michaels's arguments tap a variety of political and interpretive trends that suggest a sea change of sorts. Michaels's recent writings also seem very much in line with conservative gestures that are now focusing on Justice Harlan's dissent in *Plessy v. Fergusson*, gestures exemplified in works like Andrew Kull's *The Color-Blind Constitution*, Dinesh D'Souza's *The End of Racism*, and William Henry's *In Defense of Elitism*.[4] Among other things, Michaels's political commitment is to a vision of society made up of ultimately transparent, individual (trans)actions. At the same time, attempts to posit and interpret group, and especially minority-majority conflicts, are discounted as fundamentally mistaken because the links supposedly binding such groups are always presumed to be artificial.

However, also working within Michaels's approach is an appeal to a less conservative vision which recognizes that aspects of multicultural and minority discourse have in fact stunted critical dialogues about race and culture, and here he builds on a widespread critique of certain crude forms of identity politics. Although he is reticent to acknowledge this in his works, Michaels's concern in this regard is very much in accord with many critics laboring within multicultural and race studies, though few of these critics have come to the same conclusions as Michaels regarding the benefits of race blindness.

Michaels thus taps distinct modes of skepticism about the political claims of academic and popular race discourse, skepticism that in different ways informs a number of the most significant recent contributions to race theory, including the work of scholars like Robyn Wiegman and Wendy Brown.[5] One issue that immediately distinguishes these authors from Michaels is their position on questions of choice and the contingency of individual agency. Where Michaels answers his concerns about racial discourse by turning to a fundamentally radical act of will and consciousness, critics like Wiegman and Brown extend their skepticism to liberal individualism and its promise of autonomous agency.

Another way to think of the distinctions between these authors would be to contrast Michaels's adoption of a discipline-oriented, cultural logic paradigm with the notions of hegemony explored by the other critics. Though not initially posed as a way to read racial dynamics, hegemony has quickly moved to the fore of race studies analysis, particularly with the groundbreaking essays offered by Stuart Hall in the early 1980s.[6] Avoiding this prominent aspect of race studies, Michaels instead posits an overarching logic that appears to move largely unobstructed among a variety of genres and sites of cultural production. To get a better sense of how this particular commitment to reading through cultural logic conditions Michaels's evaluation of race consciousness, I will turn to his latest book, *Our America*, as well as to two other projects: one on Holocaust studies and one devoted to white studies.[7] Weaving together readings of these texts, I will suggest that Michaels writes himself into a scenario in which his use of cultural logic becomes so rigid that the only recourse left is to make a leap of faith into a transparent political realm evacuated of hegemonic concerns, that is, the realm of liberal individualism.

Walter Benn Michaels's work represents a fully articulated criticism of multiculturalism that is widespread if not necessarily dominant or equally systematic in development; for this reason my analysis of his work is most concerned with situating the arguments in terms of larger, if nascent, trends toward race censorship. Michaels's work also suggests a significant rethinking of tendencies in the theorization of race that have helped set the stage for the attack on race-sensitive analysis, and here I am thinking of Omi and Winant's landmark treatment of racial formation dismissing cultural issues in favor of studying social movement history.[8] One might well add other more contemporary examples, including the critical race studies movement's inability, as of yet, to craft a theory of its work that adequately engages culture; this failure to engage is particularly troubling given the movement's investment in the potentially liberatory qualities of the storytelling it practices.

Walter Benn Michaels works against the grain of literature as a field of study, a field that has been typified for some time as remarkably interdisciplinary. He does this by intricately weaving together tight, philosophically tuned arguments that draw heavily on legal rhetoric. Michaels's goal is to convince a diverse body of scholars that their training in matters of cultural critique and historical analysis has been fundamentally in error. In *Our America*, according to Giles Gunn, Michaels "takes on the question of how cultural identity could have been so drastically racialized" in the 1920s, "a time when in various discourses—literary, sociological, political—race itself was becoming increasingly acknowledged as a limited" and problematic bearer of identity.[9] As Gunn points out in his review of *Our America*, "Michaels' answer is brilliantly and disturbingly, if somewhat deceptively, simple." Gunn sums up Michaels's argument as follows: "What was effected, most notably in the great texts of American literary modernism, was not so much the rearticulation of race as a marker of cultural identity but [rather] the reconceptualization of cultural identity [itself] as inherently racial, even racist" (660). The key here for Michaels is that nativism, modernism, and pluralism become manifestations of a single cultural logic. A regime of identity and culture grows out of the white supremacy of the Progressive movement, and this regime takes root in literary America. American modernism's cultural pluralism thus becomes a rearticulation of the "separate but equal" philosophy, but in this instance the notion of racial difference becomes cathected as a new and pervasive object of public discourse. According to Michaels, this process initiates a heretofore unrecognized form of American racism which lasts right into our present. Among other things, then, Michaels's book offers a genealogy claiming to demonstrate how today's multicultural inquiry came to have essentially racist underpinnings.

At a time when arguments for race censorship are having a notable impact, it is perhaps foreseeable that a book like Michaels's might appear. He is riding a broad wave of distrust regarding race-oriented analysis. But where many advocates of color blindness explain the error of our ways with little or no recourse to questions of method, Michaels's approach calls for a complete rethinking of the methodological trends in his field.

In practice, Michaels focuses on a limited field of less problematic literary texts, works that one after another yield up the same logic by which cultural identity is collapsed into race consciousness, and ultimately racism. Tackling the weakness I am describing from another angle, Gunn has argued that "the chief problems with Michaels' thesis stem from the ideologically seamless and ahistorical notion of culture on which [Michaels] depends. . . . Michaels assumes, without ever demonstrating, that cultural concepts possess a logic all their own that inevitably defines and regulates the sorts of instantiation they achieve in discreet historical moments and practices" (660).

Michaels's skepticism regarding historical analysis defines as well his distrust of identity considerations, and so he asks in *Our America*:

> Why does it matter who we are? The answer can't just be the epistemological truism that our account of the past may be partially determined by our own identity, for, of course, this description of the conditions under which we know the past makes no logical difference to the truth or falsity of what we know. It must be instead the ontological claim that we need to know who we are in order to know which past is ours. The real question, however, is not *which* past should count as ours, but why *any* past should count as ours.

Virtually all the events and actions that we study did not happen to us and were not done by us; it is always the history of people who were in some respects like us and in other respects different. When, however, we claim it as ours, we commit ourselves to the ontology of "the Negro," to the identity of the we and they and the primacy of race. (128)

History, in the sense of a past not experienced by us, may not be "ours" in the philosophically absolute sense Michaels describes here. But does it necessarily follow that people therefore have no other contingent and still significant relations with the past? The presumed question, announced here and elsewhere in the book, is how people apparently lose and acquire their culture, their past and their identity. According to Michaels, the American modernists hypostatized difference itself in a race-bound logic of "separate but equal" that completely refigured American nationalism and left us with the fallacious burden of "being ourselves"—in other words, of being true to some preexisting quality out there, a quality presumably not available to the marginalized immigrant. In passages like the one just cited, the key to the logic being described is the notion of choice—a choice to be, ironically, what we already are. This apparent contradiction becomes a crucial lever for Michaels. Over and against the apparently contradictory bases for choices we might make regarding identity in a world we accept as contingent, Michaels insists on a universal understanding of truth and falsity that tropes on American pragmatism.

The whole scenario I have been describing is striking for the way historical and cultural factors are assumed a priori to matter only insofar as they play a nondeterminant role in one's life choices. Along similar lines, we can also start to see why so many texts treated in *Our America* focus on issues of racial passing. The passing thematic helps Michaels avoid an analysis of the ways racial identification transcends individual control as well as the ways race issues shape U.S. institutions. As with most of his recent work, Michaels here delegitimates historical and cultural contingency by collapsing it with choice, thereby clearing a path for a whole series of bold substitutions. On the one hand, any difference between Arthur Schlesinger Jr. and Toni Morrison on race issues is obliterated because both ultimately submit to the same fantasy deriving from the nativists. On the other hand, there is apparently no difference between Faulkner, the character Reverend Shegog in *The Sound and the Fury*, and virtually every other author working in the 1920s. They all presumably exhibit a wish for transubstantiation twisted into an incarnation of race-

bound identities that are all about keeping the family pure—Quentin Comp-
son being Michaels's paradigmatic figure of this logic.

In an implicit fashion, Michaels offers us an alternative to this incestuous
racism by pointing us toward real standards by which to judge "natives" and
"aliens" alike. How such universal standards will be discovered is not an issue
Michaels seems eager to take up, but early on we do get an indication of who,
or more properly what, he considers the real victim to be in this racist cultural
logic. As Michaels reads his paradigmatic text, *The Sound and the Fury*, what
gets truncated by the incestuous and racist drive to protect the family is the
legal contract that should be codified by exogamous marriage (*Our America*,
6–12).

In Michaels's argument, there is a crucial articulation of race, gender, and
sexuality that belies an ostensible focus on race issues. Ultimately, the legally
sanctioned, heterosexual marriage stands out as a primary institutional alternative to current cultural logic. However, this alternative is all but buried in
Michaels's text, and in this he is again quite consistent with regard to larger
trends animating conservative approaches to affirmative action debates and
curriculum revision. While conservative strategists are crafting laws and policies that will detrimentally affect women, people of color, gays and lesbians,
these strategists are trying hard to play the race card so as to deflect questions
about how the laws and policies actually target more than race consciousness.
One lesson of Proposition 209 in California is that this sleight of hand works.
The failure to build effective coalition in the Proposition 209 election played
a key role in the dismantling of affirmative action in California, and the
rhetorical agenda I have been describing had a great deal to do with that failed
alliance.

With the recourse to state-sanctioned marriage, *Our America* posits legal
practice as a principal means of accessing truth and falsity in an era marked by
racial and racist sophistry. Displacing the debate regarding how to read the
U.S. Constitution that animated much of legal scholarship during the 1980s,
Michaels offers a thoroughly philosophical solution to race issues. According
to Michaels, we can either engage in the folly of choosing a race-bound past
and identity to fit our current needs, or we can accept universal standards free
of history's mock restraints. Michaels thus takes readers through a literary
history in order to disparage historical understanding as an untrustworthy
enterprise.

In Michaels's subsequent work on Holocaust studies, these arguments are
taken a step further as he directly ties together the concept of an American

identity, multiculturalism, and the logic of Holocaust itself. Michaels begins the essay by undertaking an analysis of Art Spiegelman's *Maus*. The question for Michaels with regard to this book is how to categorize the various characters in terms of their apparently systematic representation as different species of animals. After probing possible links between species and race, nationality and religion, Michaels decides that in fact the only wholly consistent way to make sense of Spiegelman's designations is to assume that the mice and other species "are made by their proximate relation to the Holocaust" itself. Putting it another way, Michaels argues that *Maus* "invokes the concept of Holocaust as a mechanism of collective identity" ("Logic of Identity").

Considering various arguments for a distinct and/or "exceptional" American culture and identity, Michaels goes on to claim that all concepts of identity depend exactly on an analogous concept of Holocaust. Unpacking *Holocaust* as a logic, Michaels insists that there is a collapse of physical and cultural concerns in the way critics and historians have mobilized ideas about genocide. This slippage enables a hierarchy in which the loss of a people, of a culture, outweighs murder, which is simply a threat to individual people's lives. As a result, according to Michaels, the Holocaust-oriented regime of cultural identity makes possible the subsequent notion that assimilation is paradigmatically comparable to genocide.

Michaels is particularly concerned with the way in which an almost omnipotent valorization of identity undercuts any pursuit of disagreements. His point is that a reduction of all values to those affecting survival and extinction will displace healthy criticism and debate. This is clearly an important intervention, one that has resonance. Many scholars working in minority discourse and race studies know how some positions, built around threats to group survival, can be used to deny the diversity of particular communities. It is very unfortunate, then, that Michaels ignores the parallel work that has taken place in multicultural studies, especially because he might better situate his claims and their applicability, particularly to cruder forms of identity politics and nationalism.

As it stands, however, Michaels offers an ironic "final solution" for identity that is now being replicated by other scholars in the field.[10] As subtle as his work on Holocaust studies is in terms of its philosophical twists and turns, and in terms of its driving desire for a pure form of consistency, its delegitimation of historical concerns comes with a high price. Consider, for instance, what it means for someone writing about the Holocaust to pose as a solution a value that was a key part of Hitler's mechanism for choosing personnel.

Hitler, of course, sought out and made much use precisely of people with shattered identities.[11]

Although Michaels's essay is not explicit in its engagement of legal practice, the extension of his marriage argument in *Our America* is manifested throughout the Holocaust lecture by subtle references to the question of what constitutes a true crime. In Michaels's view, any critique of American cultural identity per se is treated as a crime by the current multicultural regime. This fundamentally unjust situation will only be remedied, according to Michaels, by completely foregoing the logic of identity.

In a similar argument reprinted in this volume, Michaels maintains that the white studies movement submits to exactly the same sort of cultural logic that defines multicultural study. Here again, Michaels's emphasis falls on the essentially fantasmatic nature of racial affiliations. Purely a matter of choice, such self-imposed racial identification is, according to Michaels, misread by an academy that posits race as a meaningful category only by deceptively adopting an ultimately essentialist position. The proof of the fantastic nature of race is in this essay bound up with the fact that students of race dynamics have confused "actions" and choices with "identities."

Following up his presentation of this argument at Dartmouth in 1997, Michaels offered this "Marxist" interpretation as a contrast: "If a member of the proletariat buys a factory and thereby becomes a member of the bourgeoisie, it is this action that defines the person in the Marxist analysis, not recourse to a tautologically derived identity." How a member of the proletariat gained the resources to buy a factory was not a concern to Michaels. While Marxist interpretation in this instance is seemingly favored by Michaels, his deployment of it is almost a parody. Here I assume that the distinctions *proletariat* and *bourgeoisie* are meaningful to the extent that they engage and articulate a certain relation to historical conditions. Individuals in this sort of Marxist interpretation do not simply choose to participate in one category or the other, and for Michaels to offer an example that so easily ignores this historical conditioning, he has to reduce Marxism to a caricature. This turn of events is not accidental. Once the gate to questions of historical conditioning are open, the horses are out, and Michaels becomes responsible for a much more critical appraisal of choice, individualism, and hegemony. In other words, it is no longer viable to maintain a realm of actions and choices freely distinct from nonindividualistically derived conceptual categories.

Taking these works together, Michaels can be reread as promoting a certain set of rhetorical gestures. First, collective identity is suspect in virtually any form, and in all cases individual actors constitute the preferred reference point. Second, there is a basic transparency in people's actions. This notion allows for the simplistic treatment of motivations and representational issues tied to the authors discussed by Michaels. Third, historical and cultural concerns need to be severely limited in terms of application to decision making. This concept is of course crucial when Michaels disconnects people from any past they have not immediately experienced. Fourth, one's relation to culture and history is posed solely as a matter of choice. Everyone becomes a potential perpetrator; by the same token, questions produced in a results-oriented analysis, or victim-oriented analysis—that is, those results so critical to the development of affirmative action and harassment laws—are radically devalued. And finally, language is taken to be transparent. Issues of representation and linguistic ambiguity that have fueled critical debate about *The Sound and the Fury* and *Maus* and so many other texts are pushed aside as a very mechanical rationalism avoids at all costs issues of translation.

Each of these rhetorical gestures exemplifies a fundamental aspect of legal discourse in this country. Feminist legal critics, as well as critical legal and critical races studies scholars, have built much of their respective enterprises around rethinking and challenging precisely these gestures.[12] While the tools these scholars have developed have the potential to enrich further analysis of Michaels's arguments, we are ultimately left to consider just why it is that one of the more comprehensive literary histories of twentieth-century America reads better as legal rhetoric than it does as literary history.

Michaels's version is certainly not the only way of approaching the notion of cultural logics and the limits of identity politics, and in a similar vein I would make it clear that I am not interested in replacing Michaels's demonization of culture/identity/Holocaust/race with my own demonization of law. Instead, I am suggesting that scholars explore the effect of the intellectual amputation that goes along with the practice of color blindness. Another way to think of the problem is to ask what kind of work is accomplished by embracing the color-blind approach? Michaels has posed the paradigmatic value of multiculturalism as survival, but why, for instance, could not one think of multiculturalism's projects in terms of working through less absolute injuries and the traumas associated with them, rather than the threat of totalizing extinction?

While Michaels posits a race fantasy of national, if not international proportions, could not his recourse to the concepts of psychoanalysis also be turned to suggest that the enormous repression required to unthink race-affiliated injuries simply feeds ongoing pathological responses? Reaching out for connections to studies pursuing similar problems, one might consider the work of Eric Santner and Dominick LaCapra on postwar Germany in this context. In *Stranded Objects: Mourning, Memory, and Film in Postwar Germany*, Santner contends that particular objects can become cathected points of displaced and problematic focus when more viable mechanisms for working through traumas are resisted or repressed.[13] In this vein, Santner reads the reconstruction of Germany as a project which, to an extent, substituted for the work of coming to terms with the trauma of a Nazi past. Inasmuch as this substitution deferred a working through of that trauma, the reconstruction itself could become, according to Santner, a kind of stranded object that cannot adequately address the problem that gave rise to its special status as a project in the first place. Herein lies my speculation: could the myriad substitutions that are being produced by scholars like Michaels—substitutions among concepts like racism, race, culture, identity, and Holocaust, as well as substitutions among real and imagined actors—be themselves a sign of a melancholic exhaustion, an exhaustion demonstrated in a series of "stranded objects," or more properly, "stranded judgments," given the recourse to legal discourse I have been describing? Might Michaels's argument itself indicate just how far we are from adequately addressing racial and other forms of injury?

Approaching similar problems from a more explicitly theoretical stance, Dominick LaCapra's recent works have reexamined historical practice in psychoanalytic terms by exploring problems of transference and the working through of traumatic issues and events. As is the case with Eric Santner's *Stranded Objects*, LaCapra's most recent contributions have considered the representational dynamics engaged by treatments of the Holocaust. However, while Santner's approach is oriented toward theories of object relations (especially those developed by D. W. Winnicott), LaCapra's works, including *Representing the Holocaust*, pursue a more varied mapping of Western engagements with notions of injury. As such, they are open to the play of transitional objects and rigorous linguistic analysis yet are also concerned with registering the broad range of competing modes in which injury may be critically or uncritically recognized and addressed, modes including working through, acting out, and critique.[14] Such approaches offer one way of framing the melancholic condition of the color-blind movement. Specifically, I would suggest that efforts like Michaels's to wrestle with questions of race and racism end up "acting out" rather than working through critical problems associated with understanding either race or racism. At stake in the distinction is the question of whether we can gain a critical distance from and successful engagement with highly conflictual issues. If such critical engagement is truncated because the interpretive process is insufficiently self-conscious, thereby conditioning that process to replicate problems inherent in the object of study, then a form of acting out may be at work. In this context, one need not understand working through and acting out as mutually exclusive concepts, and here LaCapra's treatment of the problem is constructive: "The relation between acting-out and working-through should not be seen in terms of a from/to relationship in which the latter is presented as the dialectical transcendence of the former. . . . particularly in the cases of trauma, acting out may be necessary and perhaps never fully overcome. Indeed, it may be intimately bound up with working through problems. But it should not be isolated, theoretically fixated on, or one-sidedly valorized as the horizon of thought or life" (*Representing*, 205). The final warning has bearing on the principal limitation in Michaels's approach to race issues. The strategic denial of race issues by simply leaving race unspoken is at least as old as the framing of the United States Constitution.[15]

Taking on a parallel problem, Judith Butler has offered a subtle critique of the anti-race hate speech movement, a movement which has attempted to develop policy and laws that would punish injurious references to race:

> That such language carries trauma is not a reason to forbid its use. There is no purifying language of its traumatic residue, and no way to work through trauma except through the arduous effort it takes to direct the course of its repetition. It may be that trauma constitutes a strange kind of resource, and repetition, its vexed but promising instrument. After all, to be named by another is traumatic: it is an act that precedes my will, an act that brings me into a linguistic world in which I might then begin to exercise agency at all. . . . The terms by which we are hailed are rarely the ones we choose . . . but these terms we never really choose are the occasion for something we still might call agency, the repetition of an originary subordination for another purpose, one whose future is partially open.[16]

For Butler, there is something like a constitutive trauma that all people experience as linguistic beings, a trauma that is tapped and exacerbated with the use of racist speech. The question of how to reduce injuries, and productively respond to them, in turn requires a careful consideration of the ways censorship may well act out resentments that are ultimately directed toward the contingency that accompanies our very construction as linguistic beings. Of particular concern for Butler is the sovereign sense of self that would presumably be guaranteed by a person's interpellation into the structure of the state. One result is that legal remedies—like statutes challenging race hate speech—may inadvertently end up fixing the language of racism in an all the more cathected and powerful position. Butler therefore suggests a more wary and imaginative engagement with (and appropriation of) racist language, an engagement that takes a thoroughly critical stance toward the legal mechanisms of blind neutrality.

Writing about the Supreme Court decision *Metro v. FCC* (1990), Patricia Williams takes up similar concerns as she argues that, "racial discrimination is powerful precisely because of its frequent invisibility, its felt neutrality. After all, the original sense of discrimination was one of discernment, of refinement, of choice, of value judgment—of the courteous deflection to the noble rather than to the base. It is this complicated social milieu that must be remembered as the backdrop to what both the majority and dissenters refer to as 'preferences' in this case. Racism inscribes culture with generalized preferences and routinized notions of propriety. It is aspiration as much as condemnation; it is an aesthetic."[17]

Working from the notion that racism can function as an aesthetic, it is the judicial desire to simplify and exclude particular interpretations that comes into question. For both Williams and Butler, a skepticism about the law's predilection toward linguistic fixity and reduction translates into a very wary assessment of the law's ability—as currently practiced—to remedy racial injury. But it is Williams's notion of an aesthetic that I would pursue, because it suggests a way of rethinking Michaels's texts in light of what I would argue are complimentary cultural products. Reading Michaels's texts less as literary history and more as the product of a particular moment in race discourse, we can situate a series of works, including his own, in a particular episode, an episode which, for better or worse, has been typified as the backlash of the "angry white male."

From the outset, the figure and significance of the angry white male was contested as well as loaded with symbolic freight. Largely the product of the mainstream media, the phrase initially gained broad public recognition as an explanation for the November 1994 Republican electoral sweep. By December of 1994, the *Wall Street Journal* had found a poster boy for this newly legitimated movement, forty-nine-year-old lab technician Sidney Tracy of Munford, Tennessee. Reporting that the recently unemployed Tracy blamed his plight "in fair measure on affirmative action" because "the President got up there and did everything for blacks and gays," the journal created a reference point that was explicitly cited by publications across the country.[18] As Linda Hirshman discovered, however, there was one problem; Tracy was a devoted Democrat who was misquoted. He had speculated for the *Wall Street Journal* reporter about the forces behind the Republican sweep, but he blamed his own circumstances on corporate downsizing and, after the article, adamantly protested that his own unemployment had nothing to do with affirmative action (in fact, his entire plant had been closed).

At least in part a product of fantasy from the outset, the angry white male type that Sidney Tracy was forced to model found fertile soil in Hollywood. Two of the more notable films in this vein are *Falling Down*, a film taken by many critics as a bold rejection of multiculturalism, and *Disclosure*, an attack on sexual harassment policies.[19] The former was so definitive as regards the angry white male concept that its lead character, D-Fens (an out-of-work defense industry engineer played by Michael Douglas), graced the cover of numerous publications, including *Time*, as a representative figure of the backlash.

In *Falling Down*, Douglas plays a deranged motorist who sets off on a pedestrian rampage after finding that he can no longer maintain the illusion of driving to the job he lost weeks prior. Abandoning his car in a Los Angeles traffic jam, D-Fens sets out for his ex-wife's home so that he might celebrate his daughter's birthday, but it is quickly apparent that this ex-wife is terrified of her former husband, and with reason. While restoring the nuclear family is this man's ostensible goal, the means is the focus of the film, and hence the audience spends much of its time watching him "cut a swath through the dysfunctional infrastructure, human and architectural, of Los Angeles urban life."[20] During this journey, parallel editing establishes a retiring police detective, Prendergast, as D-Fens's alter ego. A cop wrestling with problems comparable to those faced by D-Fens—troubled home life, rotten job, the same traffic jam—this character seems to have at least as many reasons to go off the deep end; yet he is posed as the more sympathetic of the pair.

While the film builds to a climactic confrontation between the two at the story's conclusion, much of D-Fens's damage is already done as he moves through various parts of the city to get home. Alternately assuming the mantle of victim and vigilante, D-Fens amasses a considerable arsenal of weapons while crossing the city. Although the scattershot destruction that ensues is seemingly dictated by accidental encounters, numerous critics have noted that the casualty rate is hardly distributed evenly. As Tom Doherty notes, the list of wounded offers "a fair sampling of white collar, white male hate objects" (39). All of this violence is embellished with the lead character's nostalgic diatribes expressing a wish for a nonexistent earlier period of un-challenged white male privilege; this point is especially apparent in D-Fens's threats to his wife and in home movies of D-Fens's troubled married life.

A good part of the appeal of the film is the vicarious experience of vigilan-tism it offers the audience. This pleasure is based on the audience's ability to imaginatively identify with D-Fens's acting out, an acting out that repeats with escalating violence. The rampage is sustained in part because D-Fens has lost meaningful contact with the world; his tunnel vision cannot see beyond the choice to return to a (nonexistent) home he has lost. In this way his journey represents his attempt to regain both a lost innocence as well as a pre–civil rights era sense of white entitlement.

J. P. Telotte explores a similar aspect of the film in an essay that draws out *Falling Down*'s debt to Federico Fellini's *8 ½*. Telotte argues that contempo-rary American life is defined by "a complex contest between the real and the fake, between the authentic and the product of our fantasies," a situation which is leading increasingly to the "displacement of the real by its models," and in this way, to a "confusion that threatens to undermine the power lodged in our fantasies . . . for coping and gaining release from the deadening effects of everyday reality."[21] In order to situate *Falling Down* in this American context, Telotte invokes Fellini's *8 ½* as one of the film's inspirations, and as its alter ego. For Telotte, *8 ½* is a paradigm of sorts for the filmic treatment of fantasy and of affirming the "vital, even redemptive powers of the imagina-tion" (20). Its central character, Guido, is a filmmaker, resembling Fellini, who struggles with himself to complete a fantasy film about people escaping earth in a rocket. In the process, *8 ½* "repeatedly, and easily, slips into and out of Guido's fantasies, each of which initially seems to accommodate his con-flicting desires, but eventually only frustrates them and leaves Guido brought down once more" (21). Guido's "falling down" reinforces his engagement with those around him, and ultimately he is able to negotiate this social existence as well as his traffic between fantasy and reality; the film project does progress, and it does so in large part because Guido is not completely possessed by his fantasies.

D-Fens models a different path, a distinction that becomes more clear as we compare the films' openings. Both works invite the audience to identify with the frustrations of being caught in a traffic jam. Guido responds to his

sense of being trapped by flying away from his car and finally over a pictur-
esque beach. Tethered to the earth, he remains symbolically attached, and
when he tries to break the bond, an assistant calls out "definitely down,"
whereupon Guido plunges, only to wake from his dream before crashing. In a
scene that, on numerous levels, mimics Guido's introduction, D-Fens likewise abandons his vehicle, but here the fantasy is not broken; D-Fens lives out
his escape. While Guido fantasizes about various violent acts in *8 ½* (hanging
an argumentative screenwriter, shooting himself), he always falls back into a
social reality.

D-Fens, on the other hand, never appears to awaken, and what's worse, he
insists (in frequently violent ways) that others accept his delusions as well:
"There is no negotiation, no contestation for this character; his fantasy must
be everyone else's—or else" (Telotte 22). In one symbolically loaded encounter after another, D-Fens finds himself playing the role of vigilante,
striking out at a variety of white male hate objects as he moves through
distinct neighborhoods. D-Fens's "progress" is ultimately mapped by Detective Prendergast, a character who bears similarities to Fellini's Guido inasmuch as his fantasies, for instance about his dead daughter, are creatively
invoked during the final confrontation in *Falling Down* in an attempt to
defuse D-Fens's violence. The attempt of course fails, and D-Fens commits
suicide rather than accept the loss of his manufactured innocence.

Recalling LaCapra's complication of the acting out–working through
distinction, my point here is not that *Falling Down* fails to be as faithful to
mimetic demands as *8 ½*. Instead, *Falling Down* is interesting for the ways in
which it represents an aspect of acting out central to the assertion of white
privilege in the 1990s, an assertion that finds unacknowledged expression in
arguments for race blindness that do isolate, theoretically fixate on, and one-
sidedly valorize, acting out. This privilege has never existed unchallenged or
untainted, and thus a certain injury has always accompanied what ultimately
is a supremacist project. As different as they may seem, then, I would suggest
that there is a significant connection between the race censorship being
advocated by critics like Walter Benn Michaels and the representation of
white male anger embodied in D-Fens.

Where D-Fens journeys through various barrios, Michaels tracks through
various fields of multicultural inquiry (identity politics, race studies, Holocaust studies, white studies), repeatedly refusing to acknowledge viable negotiations that he might strike up with the works under examination because
everything he encounters is presumably tainted with a cultural logic that

collapses race and racism. It is, of course, no accident that vigilante D-Fens and Michaels are so heavily imbued in legal dynamics. Both have a crucial investment in turning back the laws of multicultural America. But in the final assessment it may well be that the film—despite its mainstream reception— does the most to critically situate the law, its promise, and its limitations. Detective Prendergast saves the day by playing D-Fens's executioner, and in the process is infected to a degree by some of the same impulses that drive D-Fens (Prendergast "puts his wife in her place" and, in an explicitly Dirty Harry moment, tells his captain to "fuck off"). Yet Prendergast also appears capable of communicating with and understanding others in a manner that is not wholly dependent on invoking state-sanctioned privilege, and in this way he is less the policeman than either D-Fens or Michaels. The key is the kind of nostalgic censorship that I am suggesting aligns both Michaels's and D-Fens's projects. Ultimately these projects offer an account of injury that "forecloses the possibility of a critical response to that injury" (Butler 19), thereby confirming the injury's totalizing effects.

Notes

My thanks to Robyn Wiegman, Donald Pease, Richard Helgerson, and Leslie Gutiérrez-Jones for their comments and questions regarding earlier drafts of this paper.

1 In addition to Walter Benn Michaels's work, which will be discussed below, see also Dinesh D'Souza's *The End of Racism: Principles for a Multiracial Society* (New York: Free Press, 1995), as well as Carl Cohen's *Naked Racial Preference* (Lanham, Md.: Madison, 1995).

2 The Association of Literary Scholars and Critics offers its members an avenue for the serious study of literature, as opposed to the current trend, "the conversion of literature into a mere vehicle for the investigation of race, class and gender." Robert Alter, recruitment letter for Association of Literary Scholars and Critics, 18 August 1997.

3 Walter Benn Michaels, *Our America: Nativism, Modernism, and Pluralism* (Durham, N.C.: Duke University Press, 1995). For a fuller examination of this tendency to use historical analysis "against itself," see my essay, "Injury by Design," *Cultural Critique* 40 (1998): 73–102. Subsequent references are cited parenthetically in the text.

4 Andrew Kull, *The Color-Blind Constitution* (Cambridge, Mass.: Harvard University Press, 1992); William A. Henry III, *In Defense of Elitism* (New York: Anchor, 1995).

5 Robyn Wiegman, *American Anatomies: Theorizing Race and Gender* (Durham, N.C.: Duke University Press, 1995); Wendy Brown, "Injury, Identity, Politics," in *Mapping Multiculturalism*, ed. Avery F. Gordon and Christopher Newfield (Minneapolis: University of Minnesota Press, 1996), 155–64.

6 In particular, see Stuart Hall, "Gramsci's Relevance for the Study of Race and Ethnicity," in *Stuart Hall: Critical Dialogues in Cultural Studies*, ed. David Morley and Kuan-Hsing Chen (New York: Routledge, 1996), 411–40.

7 The Holocaust lecture, "The Logic of Identity," was delivered at the School for Criticism and Theory, Dartmouth College, 22 June 1996. A paper on whiteness studies, "Autobiographies of the Ex-White Men: Why Race Is Not a Social Construction," was delivered as part of the "Futures of American Studies" conference at Dartmouth College, 15 August 1997. A revised version of that paper is reprinted in this collection. Subsequent references are cited parenthetically in the text.

8 See Michael Omi and Howard Winant's treatment of race and culture in *Racial Formation in the United States: From the 1960s to the 1990s* (New York: Routledge, 1994), 65.

9 Giles Gunn, review of *Our America: Nativism, Modernism, and Pluralism*, by Walter Benn Michaels, *Journal of American History* 83, no. 2 (1996): 660. Subsequent references are cited parenthetically in the text.

10 Jonathan Arac, for instance, argued that American studies would be best served if participating scholars completely banished the concept of identity immediately, in part because identity study is a symptom of a collective fantasy. "American Pedagogies," paper presented at "The Futures of American Studies," Dartmouth College, 14 August 1997.

11 Dominick LaCapra noted this irony during an exchange with Michaels at the Dartmouth School for Criticism and Theory, 24 June 1996.

12 See Mark Kelman's *A Guide to Critical Legal Studies* (Cambridge, Mass.: Harvard University Press, 1987), 269–95, for an example of this rhetorical overlap.

13 Eric L. Santner, *Stranded Objects: Mourning, Memory, and Film in Postwar Germany* (Ithaca, N.Y.: Cornell University Press, 1990).

14 For an overview of how these modes address injury, or what LaCapra refers to as "trauma," see especially the conclusion to *Representing the Holocaust: History, Theory, Trauma* (Ithaca, N.Y.: Cornell University Press, 1994), 205–23. See also LaCapra's "History and Psychoanalysis," in *Soundings in Critical Theory* (Ithaca, N.Y.: Cornell University Press, 1989), 30–66; D. W. Winnicott, *Playing and Reality* (London: Tavistock, 1971). Subsequent references are cited parenthetically in the text.

15 For an exploration of this aspect of the Constitution, see Derrick Bell's *And We Are Not Saved: The Elusive Quest for Racial Justice* (New York: Basic Books, 1987).

16 Judith Butler, *Excitable Speech: A Politics of the Performative* (New York: Routledge, 1997), 38. Subsequent references are cited parenthetically in the text.

17 Patricia Williams, "Metro Broadcasting, Inc. v. FCC: Regrouping in Singular

Times," in *Critical Race Theory: The Key Writings That Formed the Movement*, ed. Kimberlé Crenshaw et al. (New York: New Press, 1995), 198.

18 Linda Hirshman, "Angry Rewrite Man," *Extra!* May/June 1995, 11.

19 Joel Schumacher, dir., *Falling Down* (Warner Bros., 1993); Barry Levinson, dir., *Disclosure* (Warner Bros., 1994).

20 Tom Doherty, "Falling Down," *Cineaste* summer 1993, 39. Subsequent references are cited parenthetically in the text.

21 J. P. Telotte, "Definitely Falling Down," *Journal of Popular Film and Television* 24, no. 1 (1996): 19. Federico Fellini, dir. *8 ½* (Cineriz, 1963). Subsequent references are cited parenthetically in the text.

DIFFERENTIAL

✦

Whiteness Studies and

the Paradox of Particularity

Robyn Wiegman

This essay takes a critical look at the way that whiteness studies has come to fasten itself on the question of the anti-racist white subject by thinking about the social contexts that currently shape the production of race discourse inside the academy and out. It contributes to the debates in this volume on the futures of American studies by deliberating on the relationships among identity, embodiment, and knowledge—that triumvirate of terms that are at the heart of nation formation and that have long been central to the critical work of American studies as a field. In particular, it hopes to show that the theoretical claim that whiteness achieves its power through universal disembodiment disavows the constitutive force and structure of universalism, which is not devoid of the particular but configured in contradictory relationship to it.

Let me begin with the story of two museums. In Alabama, the Birmingham Civil Rights Institute is located across from the Sixteenth Street Baptist Church, site of multiple bombings in the 1960s, including the now famous one that killed four black girls. Inside the museum are replicas and remnants from the period of official segregation: public bathrooms marked "white" and "colored," pieces of a yellow school bus, a segregated street scene. In the gift shop, patrons can purchase African American history books, posters, postcards, and T-shirts emblazoned with the image of Dr. Martin Luther King Jr.

In 1996 in Laurens, South Carolina, John Howard built another museum in the old Echo Theater, located, as they say, just a stone's throw away from the County Courthouse in the center of town. "The World's Only Klan Museum," blared the marquee.[1] Inside, there were robes and books, Confederate flags, pocket knives, "White Power" sweatshirts, even T-shirts declaring "It's a White Thing. You Wouldn't Understand." When the local authorities denied Mr. Howard a business license to sell souvenirs in the Redneck Shop, he threatened to take his case to court. Suzanne Coe, lawyer for Shannon Faulkner of the Citadel controversy, became his legal counsel; like that earlier case, she said this one, too, was about civil rights.

For Howard, as for his civil rights lawyer, the existence of the Alabama museum—and the legal protections that enabled it and other such projects to come into being—established the legitimacy of, if not the legal precedent for the Klan Museum, guaranteeing Howard's right, in his terms, to display pride in being white. Many of the characteristics of U.S. racial discourse in the 1990s are exhibited in John Howard's story. Most notably, the language of civil rights is mobilized to protect whiteness, which is cast not only as a minority identity, but as one injured by the denial of public representation.[2] In asking the apparatus of the state to adjudicate this "minority" injury, Howard sought a now familiar "equality" within the public culture of U.S. citizenship, marking himself as racially traumatized in order to secure those rights once sanctioned, even celebrated, by segregation. In theoretical terms, we might say that John Howard claimed to be racially particular in order to reestablish the universal privileges that accrued to white bodies under segregation. His case is thus an interesting one for contemporary critical conversations about whiteness, reversing as it does the overwhelming theoretical assumption that making whiteness visible as a particular racial embodiment works, in Richard Dyer's words, "to dislodge [whites] from the position of power."[3] For John Howard, however, it was precisely the claim to an injured particularity, to the markedness of whiteness, that constituted his attempt to reconstruct civil rights legislation as a protection for white supremacy's display.

Since the case has been settled out of court in Howard's favor, can he still preserve his injury? This might seem like an odd question, but I ask it in order to foreground the three interrelated premises about whiteness that shape my inquiry. The first is historical: that the distinctiveness of southern white supremacist identity since the Civil War hinges on a repeated appeal to the minoritized, injured nature of whiteness.[4] To be injured—by the economic transformations of Emancipation, by the perceived loss of all-white social spaces, by the reformation of a national imaginary of white citizen-subjects— provides the basis of white supremacist collective self-fashioning that has functioned and continues to function by producing the threat of its own extinction as the justification and motivation for violent retaliations.[5] The second premise is theoretical: to the extent that critical race theorists have assumed that the power of whiteness arises from its appropriation of the universal and that the universal is opposed to and hence devoid of the particular, we have failed to interpret the tension between particularity and universality that characterizes not simply the legal discourse of race (where early documents enfranchise the "white person"), but the changing contours of white power and privilege in the last three centuries. Apartheid structures, both slavery and Jim Crow segregation, indeed universalized whiteness through the entitlements of the citizen-subject, but they simultaneously mobilized a vast social geometry of white particularity, as the declarative warning "For Whites Only" ominously suggests. While civil rights reform has been successful in reconstructing segregation and its historically specific deployment of the universal and the particular, we have witnessed in the 1990s the growing legalization of powerful new strategies—think here of California's Proposition 209—that refunction the particular as the vehicle for extending the universal reach of whiteness. How do we account for the fact that, in the popular imaginary, John Howard's act signifies as an attempt to resurrect white racial supremacy, while Proposition 209 and other anti–affirmative action endeavors have been routinely resistant to such signification as a strategy of white supremacist reinvestment? The answer to this question, which entails an analysis of the ways in which white power has reconstructed and continues to reconstruct itself in the context of segregation's demise, leads to my third and final premise. But first, I need to tell you more about John Howard's story.

In Laurens, a multiracial town of about 10,000, Howard was not a popular man. Everyone wanted him and his Redneck Shop out. This was a town with a violent history. "For decades," *New York Times* reporter Rick Bragg writes in covering the story, "a piece of rotted rope dangled from a railroad trestle, just outside this little town, a reminder of the last lynching in Laurens County. It was back in 1913, but people still talk of the black man wrongly accused of rape, and the white mob that hanged him." The lynch rope was not removed until 1986 when the trestle was destroyed, which means that at the time the Klan Museum opened, little more than a decade had gone by without a public reminder of violent white supremacy. It also means that no one was compelled, in the course of seventy-three years, to take the lynch rope down. And yet the resurrection of white supremacy's public display in the downtown Klan Museum met with an outpouring of white alarm. One way to read the difference in white response is through the politics of social space: the museum was located in the center part of town, in the most public of public spaces, while the lynch rope hung outside of town, along the road to and from Laurens's historically black section. The lynch rope thus signified the panoptic power of whiteness—always present but never fully visible. The Klan Museum, on the other hand, embodied whiteness in an open public display, marking its presence and visibility and thereby fixing it in an implicit narrative of both local and national violence. To protest the museum meant, for whites, protesting the particularizing pact between segregationist ideologies and white embodied identity. It also meant participating in—indeed actively forging—a counterwhiteness whose primary characteristic is its disaffiliation from white supremacist practices.

It is this disaffiliation that might be thought of as the pedagogical lesson for whites of civil rights reform, where the transformation from segregation to integration reconstructed not only the materiality of black life in the United States, but the national imaginary of race and race discourse within which white identity since the 1960s has moved. Integration, no matter how failed in its utopian projections of a nation beyond race division, nonetheless powerfully suspended the acceptability of white supremacy's public display, so much so that the hegemonic formation of white identity today must be understood as taking shape in the rhetorical, if not always political register of disaffiliation from white supremacist practices and discourses. The effect of this transformation in the public discourse of white identity formation is double-edged: while it mobilizes the residents of Laurens, as elsewhere, to disaffiliate from Howard and the Klan, it also raises segregation and the Klan as referents for white supremacy in toto, which means that many white Americans can now join efforts to undo civil rights reform without recognizing their activities or opinions as participation in the contemporary reconfiguration of white power and privilege.[6] This split in the white subject—between disaffiliation from white supremacist practices and disavowal of the ongoing reformation of white power and one's benefit from it—is central to my third premise: that the referential elision between segregation and white supremacy today forecloses the construction of a coherent public discourse about the meaning and structure of contemporary white power. Indeed, the idea that segregation and white supremacy are equivalent functions to dispute any claim that white supremacy has a contemporary structure, and, in this, the absence of official segregation comes to stand as the historical evidence that a socially structured system of race inequality has been ended. This is why Proposition 209 is illegible as a reconstructive practice of white racial supremacy.

It is this disarticulation of the social as a set of structured relations that serves as the enabling condition for the emphasis on the personal and private that has come in the 1990s to characterize the discourses of the public sphere. Such an "intimate public sphere," as Lauren Berlant calls it, functions as a sentimentalizing racial project—what I call the project of *liberal whiteness*—by transforming white disaffiliation from segregationist white supremacy into a reinvestment in America as a posttraumatic nation.[7] Representations of liberal whiteness have dominated the popular imaginary in the 1990s in narratives that feature whites as the soldiers of civil rights (such as *Mississippi Burning* and *A Time to Kill* or television's "Fences"), in spectacular fantasies of a postracist United States–based new world order (*Independence Day*), and in sentimental renderings of cross-racial relations (*Boys on the Side*). But nowhere is liberal whiteness more successful in its rhetorical appeal than in *Forrest Gump*, the film that received Best Picture honors in 1994.[8] Here, in a narrative set in the South at a bus stop, with a protagonist who is the descendent of the founder of the Klan, we can read the wholesale dissolution of the national trauma of segregation as the film offers a post–civil rights exchange of contextual social knowledge for Gump's sentimental punch line: "I may not be a smart man, but I know how to love." The film's strategic denial of the historical meaning of its protagonist's white body works to forget a national history that cannot be remembered by remembering in haphazard and incoherent ways the images of racial trauma and social dissent not yet forgotten: the physical violence that attended desegregation, the street protests of the sixties, the bloodbath of the Vietnam War, the murder of national political leaders. Through its use of television images and in the passive construction of our model spectator—Forrest Gump who neither can nor wants to "know"—the film offers an anti-epistemological position for whiteness that deftly defies the trauma of both race and history that the civil rights struggle made visible, quite literally on the evening news.

I am interested in *Forrest Gump* as the specific instance and the popular imaginary as the general context for thinking about the academic emergence of an antiracist knowledge project designed to interrogate and historicize whiteness: whiteness studies.[9] Such a project, it seems to me, must necessarily set itself against, on one hand, the liberal whiteness of the public sphere, which desires to render private and personal our understandings of both the social and the historical and, on the other hand, the protocols of disciplinary knowledge, which have served to reproduce the universal epistemological privileges of the white subject as the scholarly agent of the human sciences. In its response to this epistemological privilege, whiteness studies has sought to reverse the methodological objectification of the racially marked "other" that has underwritten the organization of the modern university, bringing whiteness as an embodied identity and historical process of empowerment into critical view.[10] Whether it is by rethinking the history of working-class struggle as the domain for ethnic whitening (the class solidarity school), advocating the abolition of whiteness through white disaffiliation from race privilege (the race traitor school), or analyzing the racialization of the permanent poor in order to demonstrate the otherness of whiteness within (the white trash school), the dominant critical trajectories of whiteness studies forge for white racial formation a particularized history and a particularizing politics that interrupt the universalizing and essentialist conflation of power and privilege with white skin.[11] As James Baldwin puts it, in a line that has become a banner for whiteness studies as a field, "As long as you think you are white, there's no hope for you."[12] Or, as David Roediger glosses, "James Baldwin's point that Europeans arrived in the U.S. and became white—'by deciding they were white'—powerfully directs our attention to the fact that white ethnics . . . by and large chose whiteness, and even struggled to be recognized as white" (*Abolition*, 185).

Whiteness studies thus hopes to bring consciousness and knowledge to bear on the historical problem of white racial supremacy and, in this, it is a social constructionist project that compellingly counters the antiepistemological stance of liberal whiteness in the public sphere. But to the extent that its antiracist agenda is drawn repeatedly to a white subject now hyperconscious of itself, whiteness studies founds itself on an inescapable contradiction: its project to particularize whiteness partakes in the very structure of the universal that particularization seeks to undo. This is the case because particularization requires an emphasis on the body and on reconstituting the linkage between embodiment and identity that universalism has so powerfully disavowed for the white subject. To particularize is thus to refuse the universal's disembodied effect, and yet the destination of the dominant theoretical trajectories in whiteness studies is not toward the white body but away from it, and away from it in such a way that consciousness emerges as the antithesis to the body. If social construction has been used to de-essentialize the racially minoritized subject—to wrestle subjectivity from its oversaturation, indeed reduction to embodiment—then whiteness studies evinces the anxiety of embodiment on the other side of racial power hierarchies, an anxiety that is itself the consequence of counterhegemonic race discourses that have put pressure not just on what but on how the white body means. It is this visibility of whiteness that whiteness studies purports not to be able to read, which is why so many scholars seem confident in reiterating that "whiteness is everywhere" but "very hard to see."[13] Not to see whiteness disaffiliates the antiracist subject from the material power that has essentialized white bodies—that has made bodies signify as corporeally white—by locating that power elsewhere, which is to say that the self-conscious production of the antiracist subject is contingent on a mastery of the meaning of the body, on the rearticulation of the social construction of the significatory power of white skin.[14]

In its epistemological investment in rational white human agency as the defining locus for antiracist critique, then, whiteness studies hopes to differentiate, in the name of antiracism, the relationship among bodies, identities, and subjectivities that have constituted the universalist privilege of white racial formation in modernity. The contradictions that arise here underlie what George Lipsitz has aptly called "the impossibility of the anti-racist subject," demonstrating the difficulty of any disciplinary enterprise that hopes to undo dominant social structures—epistemological as well as economic—through the lens of an identificatory mobile humanist subject.[15] I say this not to be perversely pessimistic in the face of the political optimism expressed by whiteness studies, but because academic field formations are embedded in structures both economic and epistemological—embedded, that is, in a relation of anxiety and desire to both the publishing industry and its fetishism of the new, and to the knowledge industry, whose indebtedness to capital and the state shapes not only the university as a primary scene of subject formation but the organization of knowledge through which both epistemological and symbolic capital flow.

Given these frameworks—of the particular and the universal, of the popular and the academic, of the economic and the epistemological—how might we approach, as an antiracist political investment, the study of whiteness today? My answer to this question will take shape by exploring the contradictory deployments of an antiracist white subject in both the popular and academic realms. Such deployments are not simply ideological oppositions, but indexes of the mutual, if contradictory critical limits of white particularity as a strategy of antiracist critique in the postsegregation era. This essay thus constitutes a political anatomy of whiteness studies in its present tense.

Back to the Future

At the Civil Rights Institute in Birmingham, Alabama, visitors begin their tour by taking a seat on one of the narrow white benches that fill a darkened room behind the admissions booth. As the lights fade, an entire wall comes to life with documentary footage narrating the history of the state and its long and bloody battle to desegregate. A city founded during Reconstruction, Birmingham played a key role in the civil rights struggle by organizing one of the most successful uses of consumer power to grieve forms of inequality sanctioned by the state in U.S. history.[16] The Birmingham bus boycott drew widespread media attention as African American residents turned to other means, most notably walking, to navigate their city. The Civil Rights Institute thematizes this mass resistance by installing its visitor in a space organized around issues and images of mobility. When the documentary ends and the lights return, the movie screen rises dramatically to reveal the space of the museum on the other side. Every visitor to the museum must walk through the screen, so to speak, into rooms and corridors that contain artifacts of the material culture of segregation and the fight to undo it. At nearly every turn, there are more screens—a mock 1960s storefront where boxy televisions broadcast images of encounters between Freedom Fighters and the police; a video wall where multiple contemporary televisions juxtapose racist commercials, political interviews, and the speeches of Martin Luther King Jr. In a grand gesture where history and the present meet, the visitor is positioned in front of a picture window that looks out onto the Sixteenth Street Baptist Church across the street.

Forrest Gump, you might remember, is set at a bus stop, and one of its main technological innovations is its clever insertion of the protagonist into nationally recognizable television scenes.[17] In the most famous instance, Gump becomes a participant in George Wallace's failed attempt to block black entrance to the University of Alabama following the court order to desegregate. Positioned initially as a member of the crowd, Gump symbolically joins the students when he retrieves one of their dropped books; in the spatializing logic of segregation, Gump is here a race traitor.[18] His movement functions as a symbolic rearticulation of the relationship between mobility and immobility that is a key trope for understanding not only the bus stop as a racial discourse but the racialized organization of social space itself. In founding Gump's disaffiliation from white supremacy on the narrative trope of mobility, the film repeatedly redefines white identity as a product of social scripts of immobility. In the opening scene, for instance, with a black woman serving as witness, Gump remembers his first pair of shoes, or I should say he remembers through his desire for her shoes his own personal history of mobility as a series of restrictions. The first was physical, as Forrest was forced to wear leg braces to correct his curvature of the spine; the second was social, as Forrest endured ridicule and exclusion because of his physical and mental disabilities. If the analogy between segregationist racialization and Forrest's restricted mobility, ostracism, and physical difference isn't clear, the narrative locates the scene of Forrest's social exclusion on a school bus where his classmates eagerly refuse him a seat. (Later in the film, he will again be refused a seat on a bus by his fellow inductees in the army.) These scenes perform two functions: they rewrite segregation as a discourse of injury no longer specific to black bodies, which installs whiteness as injury, and they define that injury as private, motivated not by a social system but by the prejudices and moral lacks of individuals who seem simply not to know better. In these narrative moves, national memory is both privatized and disturbingly de-essentialized, by which I mean that the relationship between identity and politics that underwrote so much sixties dissent is disavowed in order to recast the social meaning of Gump's body—his white masculine heterosexuality—as having no historically contextual meaning at all.

If *Forrest Gump* is a liberal white rendition of the history of segregationist apartheid, if the film can be said to be a walk through the archive of popular national memory, its project does not end with white occupation of injury. That would be a version of John Howard's story. *Forrest Gump* has a more pedagogical mission: to demonstrate that difference and injury, even intellectual deficiency, are not impediments to the American way of life. The plot thus advances through scenes in which Forrest gains mobility, thereby exchanging injury and embodiment for liberation and transcendence. As a kid being chased by his classmates, he magically breaks free of his leg braces; as a teenager being harassed by boys in a truck with a Confederate flag license plate, his flight across a college football field results in a scholarship and an all-American athletic career. In Vietnam, his ability to run saves his life and the lives of others, and in the film's oddest and longest segment devoted to mobility, Gump spends three years running from shore to shore, redrawing the boundaries of the nation's geographic identity and demonstrating that no region (no state, no neighborhood, no city street) is off limits or out of reach. All of this mobility critically recasts the segregationist history of the bus stop, even though that too must be left behind. In the final segments of the film, Forrest discovers that he doesn't need the bus to get where he is going, as he is only blocks away from his destination where marriage, the domestic scenario, and a miraculously completed paternity ("Little Forrest") await. He can easily walk there.

In giving to Gump the power of his own self-directed mobility, the film releases him from the bus stop and its symbolic evocation of racial strife in favor of an insulated private and domestic realm. The mobility of his identifications and his symbolic minoritization thus function as preambles to a retreat from the national, which itself serves as a crucial precondition for the film's ideological resolution of white supremacy as a system of material gain. This resolution begins in the film's opening minutes, as the first flashback narrative, told to the black female witness, features Gump's Confederate hero ancestor, Nathan Bedford Forrest. A man born in poverty who grew rich as a slave trader and planter, this Forrest garnered both fame and shame during the Civil War as a brilliant, unconventional battle tactician who incited his men to massacre surrendering black troops at Fort Pillow. But the film's Nathan Bedford Forrest is ludicrous, not powerful; in Gump's mind, he would "dress up in . . . robes and . . . bed sheets and act like . . . ghosts or spooks or something." Gump's mother chose the name to remind her son that "sometimes people do things that just don't make no sense." The film's parable of naming displaces the intimate family relations that attach Gump to a genealogy of masculine aggression and segregationist white supremacy, and in doing so, it importantly diffuses any feminist reading of the violence of patriarchal forms of inheritance.[19] As if to emphasize this point, the patronymic, Forrest, is shifted to Gump's first name, and the repetition of the line, "My name is Forrest, Forrest Gump," continually reminds us of this foundational displacement. In the liberal white fantasy of *Forrest Gump*, the descendent of the founder of the Klan can emerge at the end of the twentieth century shorn of his damaged patriarchal inheritance, which is to say that the intimacy of familial, personal relations has now been successfully separated from the past and tied instead to a prototypically American future. In the process, white power and privilege are displaced from any inherent relation—historically, ideologically, politically—to white skin.[20]

The liberal whiteness formed from these narrative displacements offers a subtle but telling commentary on one of the most volatile issues of the 1990s, affirmative action. In "Whiteness as Property," Cheryl Harris distinguishes between corrective justice, which seeks "compensation for discrete and 'finished' harm done to minority group members or their ancestors" and distributive justice, which "is the claim an individual or group has to the positions or advantages or benefits they would have been awarded under fair conditions."[21] According to Harris, the goals of affirmative action—to address the harms done to those minoritized by racial (or gendered) oppression—are undermined when corrective justice is the interpretative frame because not only is the harm assumed to be finished here, but the practices through which harm has been done are individualized, confined to the one who perpetrated it and the one who endured it. In this context, whites can claim to be innocent and therefore in need of counterlegislative protection because they have not individually perpetuated harm. Whiteness, in short, carries no significatory privilege. This is the logic of Bakke as well as California's recent Proposition 209, and it is the model of compensation being worked out in *Forrest Gump.* Gump's mother, you might recall, supports her family by running a rooming house out of the old plantation that is the ancestral home in Greensboro, Alabama, a narrative convenience that renders the family's historical connection to the economics of slavery if not deficient, at least not materially advantageous. Whatever harm slavery inflicted is finished, and the privileges of economic gain that garner for white identity a material advantage have been narratively swept away. This does not mean that Gump will have no racial debt to pay, but that his debt is, first, not historical, not about the ongoing economic or psychological privilege of whiteness as a material effect of slavery and segregation, and, second, not collective, not about a social identity enhanced and protected by the law as an economic investment.

What, then, is Gump's debt? To answer this question, we need to consider Gump's accumulation of wealth and to return, in time, to the issue of shoes, specifically the red-and-white Nike running shoes that serve as visual cues of the present time of the film. Gump's accumulation of wealth has two primary forms: shrimp and computers. The shrimping business is borne of an interracial male confederation with Bubba, who gives Forrest a seat in the film's second passage through the scene of the school bus and who also gives to Gump all his knowledge about the shrimping business. When Bubba dies in the Vietnam War, Gump returns to the South and shrimps, only to make it big when a hurricane conveniently destroys every other boat in the black-owned industry. Gump's knowledge is quite literally African American knowledge, but the conversion of that labor, if you will, into accumulation is effected through nature, not society. Any debt to be paid is thus a personal one arising from Gump's friendship with Bubba and not from the material advantages accorded to whiteness as an economic privilege. In this parable of the economics of contemporary black-white relations, the debt to be paid by Gump to Bubba's family—half the profits of the shrimp business—is defined not by hierarchy or history, but as an honor to intimate male friendship.

In separating Bubba's knowledge from his body and evacuating that body from the narrative scene, the film constructs Forrest's antiracist liberal white subjectivity on a strategic denial: that identity, embodiment, and knowledge are historically linked. This denial is especially striking since the other form of debt that the film imagines for Gump is likewise borne of a male friendship: in his relationship with Lt. Dan, whose patriotic family has lost a son in every war since the Revolution, Gump both rescues and redeems the multiply injured white Vietnam veteran. This redemption is thematized through mobility as Lt. Dan, initially disabled by the loss of his legs in the war, comes finally to walk again (albeit with artificial limbs), thereby doubling the film's investment in mobility as the resignification of white masculinity. Importantly, the symbolic reconstruction of Lt. Dan's traumatized white male body is accompanied by his own heterosexual completion, which is demonstrated by the introduction of his fiancée, Susan, the only person of Asian descent in a film that devotes significant narrative time to the Vietnam War and its aftermath. And yet the film's commentary on the war is never able to reverberate beyond the sphere of intimate private relationships among U.S. men, as Susan evokes both a history and racial discourse that the film has no mechanism or motive to speak, even as it requires her presence as both witness and accomplice to Lt. Dan's remasculinization.[22] Her insertion into the scene of heterosexual intimacy privatizes the national narrative of war in Southeast Asia, thereby displacing the economics of accumulation that have followed U.S. interventions in the region. By this, I am referring to the significance of Gump and Lt. Dan's investment in Apple Computers, an industry whose transnational circuits of production and distribution are indelibly linked to postwar capitalist expansion in Southeast Asia. If the Vietnam War cost Lt. Dan his legs, his economic mobility is nonetheless enabled by it, as is Gump's, and yet it is precisely this that the film's thematic focus on segregation, mobility, and the resurrection of a privatized U.S. nation occlude. In moving the sites of the accumulation of wealth from shrimping to computer investments, *Forrest Gump* depicts without commentary capital's contemporary mobility from local, regional forms of industry to transnational practices of production and exchange.

With these circuits in mind, let's return now to the opening scene of the film where a feather floats gently from the sky to land on Gump's red-and-white Nike running shoes.[23] As the first material detail offered of the protagonist, Gump's running shoes are simultaneously his signature and personal trademark, the commodity linkage between embodiment and mobility that inaugurates his memory archive and serves in the end to demonstrate his transcendence not only of the trauma of history, but of the social meaning of his own embodied identity. More than this, however, the Nike shoes ground Gump's magical movement in an unconscious relation to a commodity that has itself become associated in the 1990s with the worst aspects of transnational modes of production. In the context of media revelations about Nike's exploitative working conditions in Southeast Asia, the corporation's commodity presence in *Forrest Gump* seems quite overtly engaged in a project of resignification. Through Gump, Nike can seek the reification of all material relations that is the effect of the protagonist's mode of narration, which means participating in the film's celebration of the detachment of state from nation. This celebration is demonstrated in two moves: first, in the way that the televisual archive Gump moves through works to disavow the power of presidents and other state leaders and hence to undermine not simply the authority but the value of contestation at the level of the state; and second, in the way the film endorses the "shore to shore" logic of nation as geographical entity that underlies Gump's seemingly motiveless three-year run across the United States.[24] With the state represented as the site of traumatic instability, loss of decorum, or simple comic incomprehensibility, the nation arises in illustrious geographical wholeness. Transporting Gump there, beyond the historical problematic of the bus stop, are his Nike running shoes; their resignification as a private commodity relation fulfills Nike's own corporate fantasy of an innocent (that is to say nonexploitative) historicity.

In the figure of the shoes, then, lies the film's investment in the simultaneous transnational accumulation of capital in the aftermath of imperial war and the reinvigoration of a national symbolic, rescued now through the individual's pedagogical identification with the commodity (and conversely, the commodity's identification of the individual). As Gump is marked quite literally first and foremost by the trademark, the trademark becomes the film's earliest mechanism for ascribing to Gump a particularizing identity. It is, importantly, an identity that situates him from the outset beyond the specific national contestations of the bus stop, beyond any recognition or reception of the embodied knowledge of the black woman's utterance, "my feet hurt." Gump's debt, after all, has been paid; compensatory justice, imaginable only at the individual level, has been achieved; all that remains is the telling of the tale. If, in the film's formula, that telling takes shape as a walk through the archive of segregation and black-white racial relations, Gump's innocence, which is to say his rescued whiteness, stands on his inexhaustible and dematerialized relation to the commodity.[25] As Gump declares about his chocolates, "I could eat about a million and a half of these."

Whiteness Studies in Forrest Gump's America

Forrest Gump's celebration of the white race traitor who defies the logic of segregation and the history of Southern racism in order to participate inno-cently in the new order of global capital is certainly a far cry from the ideals of whiteness studies. And yet, even as the popular and the academic move toward different political goals, they both begin their projects of rearticulat-ing a postsegregationist white identity at the site of the historical. In *Forrest Gump*, this entails rendering the history of violent white power incompre-hensible, if not comic—the Klan leader, remember, liked "to dress up in . . . robes and . . . bed sheets and act like . . . ghosts or spooks or something." Thus refunctioning the present as the origin for a new America no longer held in grief or guilt to a violently unredeemable past, the film confirms the ideo-logical architecture of the contemporary anti–affirmative action movement. That is, it offers a white subject who becomes particular through a claim to social injury, thereby affirming not only that all historical racial debts have been paid (and hence that the historical is itself irrelevant), but that there is finally no privileged linkage between the protocols of universality and white racial embodiment. At the same time, of course, Forrest Gump, like John Howard of the Klan, can only be injured as a white (and male) subject from the symbolic location of the universal since it is the negation of the expecta-tion or actuality of privilege that makes social injury for whites conceivable in the first place. By this I mean that only from an implicit and prior claim to the universal can the particularity of white injury (indeed the particularity of white identity itself) ever be articulated. Passing as an injured subject through the non-sense of the historical, the white subject thus reclaims its transcen-dent universality on the far side, we might say, of civil rights reform.

Whiteness studies, in contrast, turns with urgency to the historical to serve as the critical construction site for constituting a postsegregationist antiracist white subject. In four regularly cited texts—David Roediger's *The Wages of Whiteness* and *Towards the Abolition of Whiteness*, Theodore Allen's *The Invention of the White Race*, and Noel Ignatiev's *How the Irish Became White*—social historians chart the effects of industrialization, and with it wage labor, on the racialization of ethnic immigrants in the nineteenth cen-tury. In doing so, they locate whiteness not in the epidermal "reality" of white skin, but in complex economic and political processes and practices. Key to the demonstration of the social construction of whiteness is the story

of the Irish who left their homeland as racialized subjects of British colonial rule to become white in the course of nineteenth-century U.S. life. As
W. E. B. Du Bois diagnosed nearly a century ago in *Black Reconstruction*,
whiteness emerged as the compensatory psychological and public wage that
enabled various groups, especially the so-called black Irish, to negotiate a
social status simultaneously distinct from and opposed to that of the slave or
ex-slave.[26] By paying close attention to the Irish's struggle against the negative symbolics of their lower-class status in the United States, this archive,
in Roediger's words, demonstrates how "working class formation and the
systematic development of a sense of whiteness went hand in hand for the
U.S. white working class," so much so, in fact, that the very meaning of
"worker" would be implicitly understood as "white" by the end of the century (*Wages*, 8).

While some scholars disagree with Roediger's tactic to emphasize the
Irish's active pursuit of white identity—Allen, for instance, says the Irish
were "bamboozled" by the ruling class (199)—much of the work in the
proliferating archive of whiteness studies depends for its political force on
the disciplinary legacy of labor history put into play by Roediger.[27] Taking
conscious political action and the centrality of the subject as an agent and not
simply an object of history, labor history, Roediger explains, "has consistently
stressed the role of workers as creators of their own culture [and therefore] it is
particularly well positioned to understand that white identity is not merely
the product of elites or of discourses" (*Abolition*, 75–76). In this retrieval
of the historical as the site of human agency, labor history jump-starts, we
might say, the critical project of imagining an antiracist white subject in the
present, for if whiteness is historically produced and if its production requires something more than the physical characteristic of skin color, then
whiteness as a form of political identification, if not racial identity, can be
reformulated.

This stress on the active process of unthinking whiteness as a structure of
power and privilege is certainly a compelling counter to the unconscious
white subject celebrated in *Forrest Gump*, and it offers, through the political
project mapped by labor history, a means to refunction working-class struggle as cross-racial alliance. But once the theoretical precepts of labor history become installed as the governing disciplinary apparatus of whiteness
studies—that is, once the historical retrieval of agency and the story of pre-
white ethnics who choose whiteness in the tense interplay between race and
class come to define the possibility of the antiracist white subject—the field

begins to generate a range of contradictory, sometimes startling effects. The most critically important include: (1) an emphasis on agency that situates a theoretically white humanist subject at the center of social constructionist analysis; (2) the use of class as the transfer point between looking white and being white; (3) the production of a particularized and minoritized white subject as vehicle for contemporary critical acts of transference and transcendence, which often produces a white masculine position as discursively minor; and (4) a focus on economically disempowered whites, both working-class and poor, as minoritized white subjects. Each of these effects must be read further in the context of the contemporary academy, where the assault against affirmative action has been aggressively pursued in a climate of employment scarcity and corporate downsizing. Such economic constrictions are crucial to understanding why the critical apparatus being forged in whiteness studies bears the unconscious trace of the liberal whiteness its reclamation of history so strenuously seeks to disavow. For in the particularity of the pre-white ethnic, whiteness studies reverses the historical process of white construction, offering for the contemporary white subject a powerful narrative of discursively black ethnic origins. History, in other words, rescues contemporary whiteness from the transcendent universalism that has been understood as its mode of productive power by providing pre-white particularity, which is cast in various trajectories of whiteness studies as an injured and/or minoritized identity.

To trace the critical turns I have narrated above, I want to return to the issues of embodiment and epistemology that underwrote my discussion of mobility as the governing trope of liberal whiteness in the public sphere. In *Forrest Gump*, the social meaning of white embodiment serves as the chief anxiety that leads to the protagonist's representation as mentally and physically deficient, a convenient mechanism for displacing the way the 1960s brought into national consciousness bodies and knowledges that had been exiled from the domain of official culture. To resignify whiteness, the film produces an analogy between Forrest's social exclusion and black embodiment before generating an anti-epistemological transcendence of the bus stop as the national scene of racial strife. These moves, which are predicated on Forrest's mobility, have no hold on interior subjectivity, as Gump's power to identify either politically or personally is made morally simple by his lack of IQ.

Key texts in whiteness studies, on the other hand, work to resignify whiteness by rendering conscious the meaning of white embodiment and by forg-

ing a politicized epistemology that actively produces antiracist identifications. As Roediger writes in *Towards the Abolition of Whiteness*:

> We cannot *afford* to ignore the political implications [that] . . . whites are
> confessing their confusion about whether it is really *worth* the effort to be
> white. We need to say that it is not *worth* it and that many of us do not want to
> do it. Initiatives [should] . . . expos[e] how whiteness is used to make whites
> settle for hopelessness in politics and misery in everyday life. . . . Our opposi-
> tion should focus on contrasting the *bankruptcy* of white politics with the
> possibilities of nonwhiteness. We should point out not just that whites and
> people of color often have common economic *interests* but that people of
> color currently act on those *interests* far more consistently . . . precisely because
> they are not burdened by whiteness. (16–17; emphasis added)

Casting whiteness as the burden that prevents working-class whites from
identifying their real interests, Roediger differentiates identity from identification in order to redirect the "possessive investment in whiteness" toward
political allegiances with those designated as "nonwhite."[28] Such a conception of identificatory mobility is made possible by his analytic focus on labor,
where white identification with racial hierarchy has functioned historically as
a powerful means for disrupting solidarity based on the material dispossessions of economic class.

As Roediger's critical paradigm begins to travel, however—to itself become mobile—in texts that take their disciplinary shape in cultural studies
and elsewhere, the identificatory mobility that his text heralds is disarticu-
lated from labor struggle as a specific project of social movement and installed instead as the abstract theoretical condition of the antiracist white
subject. By this I mean that identificatory mobility becomes the primary
characteristic of antiracist white subjectivity, thereby defining social construction as the critical counter to what we might think of as the political and
theoretical immobility of an essentialized subject. In the process of this rearticulation we encounter a reversal of the political investment but not the
spatializing logic that accompanies the popularized *race-traitoring* white subject in the postsegregationist era: it is the white subject who crosses the
segregationist boundaries of both knowledge and political identification,
while people of color remain politically identified with the social margins.
The political force of social construction as a theoretical vocabulary thus
becomes located in the identificatory mobility of the white subject, and it
is precisely this mobility that grounds what I am calling the paradox of particularity on which whiteness studies is borne. For in the transportation of

the white subject from the universal to the particular, from an implicit (often unconscious) identification with white skin privilege to the conscious production of an antiracist politics, we witness the epistemological privilege that underwrites white racial formation, a privilege that gives to white people the prerogative of individualized, indeed particularized subjectivity. It is the endurance of this privilege, which de-essentializes by differentiating identity from subjectivity, that must be understood as the constitutive universalism of white racial formation, which means that even as we invest in the disidentificatory mobility of the antiracist white subject, we have not escaped the humanist epistemological structure from which whiteness has long drawn its power.

Roediger's work seeks to counter this reinvestment by paying close attention to the history of labor struggle and by articulating the political project of antiracism as coterminous with a successful challenge to capital's racialized organization of labor. In this regard, his emphasis on the subject is itself a means of transport between the individualism that white racial formation affords to white bodies and the collectivity necessary for any powerful counterhegemonic struggle. But it is his emphasis on consciousness as the means to undo the body's social positionality and the desire to remap racial meaning with class identification that reverberates across the proliferating archive of whiteness studies, and in ways that fail to replicate Roediger's own deft negotiation of labor history's disciplinary limits. This seems to me nowhere more true than in the race traitor school of whiteness studies, which draws from class solidarity a hyperknowing subject whose identificatory mobility serves as the means to transcend the social and political meaning of white skin, but does so by reinvesting in heroic masculinity as the means to save the nation embodied now as black.

In the opening editorial to the Routledge volume that collects the first five issues of the journal, editors Noel Ignatiev and John Garvey describe the *Race Traitor* project: "The existence of the white race depends on the willingness of those assigned to it to place their racial interests above class [or] gender. . . . The defection of enough of its members . . . will set off tremors that will lead to its collapse. *Race Traitor* aims to serve as an intellectual center for those seeking to abolish the white race."[29] Guided by the principle *"treason to whiteness is loyalty to humanity"* (10), *Race Traitor* envisions treason on a number of fronts, from verbal retorts to racist jokes or commentaries to interracial marriage to cross-racial identifications in politics, fashion, and music. "What makes you think I am white?" is the quintessential race traitor question, and its deployment in the face of the police is one of the most heralded abolitionist acts. As Garvey and Ignatiev write in "The New Abolitionism,"

> the cops look at a person and then decide on the basis of color whether that person is loyal to or an enemy of the system they are sworn to serve and protect. . . . the cops don't know for sure if the white person to whom they give a break is loyal to them; they assume it. . . . What if the police couldn't tell a loyal person just by color? What if there were enough people around who looked white but were really enemies of official society so that the cops couldn't tell whom to beat and whom to let off? . . . With color no longer serving as a handy guide for the distribution of penalties and rewards, European-Americans of the downtrodden class would at least be compelled to face with sober sense their real condition of life and their relations with humankind. It would be the end of the white race.[30]

In thus forging a "new minority determined to break up the white race" ("New Abolitionism," 107), *Race Traitor* joins Roediger in constructing a model of the mobile antiracist subject whose conscious political production not only particularizes whiteness by citing its power, but does so in order to craft for economically disenfranchised whites a generative and ultimately antiracist class politics.

If this description of *Race Traitor* suggests a coherent intellectual and activist project, it is important to stress that contributions to the journal vary widely in political content. This is due in part to the collective nature of the journal and to its mediation between activist and academic political sites. It is also a consequence, it seems to me, of the difficulties that abound in transposing nineteenth-century antislavery abolition into the paradigmatic site for constructing a late-twentieth-century antiracist subject. By affirming as heroic and antiwhite the work of such abolitionists as John Brown, leader of the failed slave revolt at Harper's Ferry, *Race Traitor* reinscribes the centrality of white masculine leadership even as it posits such leadership as historical evidence for the abolition of the white race. "How many dissident so-called whites would it take to unsettle the nerves of the white executive board? It is impossible to know. One John Brown—against a background of slave resistance—was enough for Virginia" ("Abolish the White Race," 13). Overly drawn to masculine models of armed retaliation, *Race Traitor* effectively evacuates altogether the feminist trajectory of nineteenth-century abolitionism, reproducing instead the white male rebel as the affirmative subject of antiracist struggle. Such affirmation, situated in the context of essays about the Irish and pre-white immigrants, symptomatically demonstrates the oscillation between universal privilege and minoritized particularity that characterizes not only the history of white subject formation in the United States, but the critical apparatus of whiteness studies itself.

Race Traitor's implicit response to its own critical contradiction of abolishing whiteness in a frame of white masculine heroic narrativity is to situate the African American as the quintessential American. Ignatiev writes, "The adoption of a white identity is the most serious barrier to becoming fully American. . . . the United States is an Afro-American country. . . . Above all, the experience of people from Africa in the New World represent the distillation of the American experience, and this concentration of history finds its expression in the psychology, culture, and national character of the American people."[31] Thus defining the abolition of whiteness as the precondition for becoming American, Ignatiev retrieves an American exceptionalist logic that displaces the historical white subject as the national citizen-subject for a narrative of national origin cast now as black.[32] In doing so, a metaphorical America of national longing supplants the materialist America through which state violence—physical, economic, and ideological—has guaranteed the juridical privileges of whiteness. Leaving aside the many ways this formulation eradicates a range of groups and experiences, it is significant how important the resignification of the nation as part of a reclamation of the "human" is to *Race Traitor*: "It is not black people who have been prevented from drawing upon the full variety of experience that has gone into making up America. Rather, it is those who, in maddened pursuit of the white whale, have cut themselves off from human society" ("Immigrants," 19). The abolition of whiteness reclaims the democratic possibility of human sociality, itself a characteristic of the resignified nation.

My focus on the language of nation and national identity is meant to recall the ideological work of *Forrest Gump* and its mobile protagonist whose fantastic projection of a postsegregationist America entailed the literal and symbolic remapping of the American territorial nation. In Gump's claim to what Berlant calls "the normal," the white male subject reconstructs itself on the grounds of a fabled sentimentality, with all state-based debts paid and a reproductive future of politically uncontaminated subjectivity guaranteed. In *Race Traitor*, the editors seek not so much the normal but the "ordinary" as the contrast to the state: "the ordinary people of no country have ever been so well prepared to rule a society as the Americans of today."[33] This is because, in

Ignatiev's words, "few Americans of any ethnic background take a direct hand in the denial of equality to people of color" ("Immigrants," 16–17). The conscious agency that defines the becoming white of the pre-white ethnic is strategically dissolved in the present where the ordinary person is theoretically divested of taking a committed interest in the perpetuation of white racial privilege. Indeed, whiteness, while the object under investigation and ultimate destruction, is exteriorized to such an extent that the conscious agency heralded as necessary to undo it has no theoretical hold on the interior constitution of the subject. In contrast to Roediger's work, here there is no psychological depth to whiteness as a social construction, merely an interpretative inscription based on skin which can be consciously refused: "The white race is a club, which enrolls certain people at birth, without their consent, and brings them up according to its rules. For the most part the members go through life accepting the benefits of membership, without thinking about the costs. When individuals question the rules, the officers are quick to remind them of all they owe to the club, and warn them of the dangers they will face if they leave it. *Race Traitor* aims to dissolve the club, break it apart, to explode it" ("Abolish the White Race," 10–11). In dissolving the club, in revealing the "costs" of membership as the failure of whites to be fully American, *Race Traitor*'s postsegregationist antiracist subject emerges, against the power of the state, as emblem of a coherent nation.

The construction of the antiracist subject in *Race Traitor* thus goes something like this: whiteness is understood as the consequence of a universalizing pact between white skin color and white club privilege, one that deprives white people of both a positive relation to humanity and to American national identity. White supremacy is less an effect of individual activities and ideologies than the consequence of institutions of state power, which themselves alienate the ordinary citizen who is neither directly nor enthusiastically involved in the oppression of people of color. In this way, *Race Traitor* assumes, as does Roediger, that cross-racial class alliance is the locus of more urgent and identifiable political interests for the majority of whites, though *Race Traitor* is dedicated to the possibility of a "minority" of traitors—not, as in Roediger, a mass class movement—to perform the work of abolishing white supremacy. This work involves making whiteness visible as a racial category by interrupting the "natural" assumption that people who look white are invested in being white. Race traitors must thus mark whiteness as a racialized particular in order to perform their disaffiliation from the universality that underwrites the category, where such performance is understood as the necessary claim to an antiracist subjectivity. This is, it seems to me, the performative force of the race traitor question, "what makes you think I am white?" which simultaneously and paradoxically refuses the position of the universally unmarked by ultimately claiming to no longer be marked by it. In asserting the particularity of white racial identity as preamble to refusing it altogether, the race traitor passes through both the universal and the particular in order to found a new minority of formerly white people. Counting on the power of individual disavowal of the juridical white subject of state power, *Race Traitor* reimagines an empowered humanist and quintessentially masculine subject whose intent to repeal its own whiteness is consecrated as the central practice of antiracist struggle.

These moves that seek to privilege the conscious intentions, practices, and political attachments of the subject over the body evince a desire for mastery not over bodies per se but over the social as the discursive setting in which a white body comes to have material meaning. This constitutes an interesting turn of the social constructionist project, as it mobilizes the language of anti-essentialism to evacuate consciousness from social embodiment altogether, thereby rescuing a humanist subject from the overdeterminations of sociality itself. In *White Trash: Race and Class in America*, Annalee Newitz is especially critical of the abjection of the body that underwrites the conscious production of the antiracist subject in the race traitor school. For her, as for other scholars who turn to the permanent poor as a means for studying whiteness, social construction's de-essentializing project must not abandon the body but resignify it in order to differentiate white identity from the practices and structures of white racial supremacy. As she writes in "White Savagery and Humiliation":

> We are asked [by the abolitionists] to demonize whiteness rather than to deconstruct it. . . . Social problems like unequally distributed resources, class privilege, irrational prejudice, and tyrannical bureaucracy which we associate with whiteness are just that—*associated* with whiteness. . . . They are not essential to whiteness itself, any more than laziness and enslavement are essential to blackness. . . . Informing whites that their identities are the problem, rather than various social practices, makes it sound like whites should die rather than that white racism should. The ideologies of white power which make some white people socially destructive are the symptoms of American inequality and injustice, not its principle causes.[34]

In countering the equation between whiteness and supremacy that inaugurates the race traitor's self-consciously critical move to become "nonwhite,"

Newitz pursues a de-essentialized whiteness that can hold its own, so to speak, in the same grammatical gesture as the anti-essentialist analysis of blackness. In the process, the empowered privileges of whiteness and the stereotypes that degrade blackness take on an analytical equivalency, as whiteness is situated as an identity object in need of the same resignification that has accompanied civil rights and black power struggle over and in the name of blackness. "While whiteness is undeniably linked to a series of oppressive social practices, it is also an identity which can be negotiated on an individual level. It is a diversity of cultures" (148). Such diversity points toward the possibility, as Newitz writes with co-editor Matt Wray in the anthology's introduction, of "a more realistic and fair-minded understanding of whiteness as a specific, racially marked group existing in relation to many other such groups."[35]

The desire for a critical paradigm that can approach both black and white on quite literally the same terms—in a mode of theoretical equal opportunity—shapes *White Trash* at a number of levels, providing a means not to deny the body but to radically resignify the social meaning evoked by and invested in white skin: "Our anthology is intended as an intervention in this field [of whiteness studies], offering a critical understanding of how differences within whiteness—differences marked out by categories like white trash—may serve to undo whiteness as racial supremacy, helping to produce multiple, indeterminate, and anti-racist forms of white identity" (4). But even as white trash writers seek to resurrect the possibility of an antiracist subject who is also white—as opposed to the antiracist subject who has transcended whiteness—the critical apparatus put into play here participates in the fantasy of white injury and minoritization evidenced throughout the 1990s in the popular sphere. When the editors write, for instance, that whiteness is "an oppressive ideological construct that promotes and maintains social inequalities, causing great material and psychological harm to both people of color and whites" (3), they inadvertently construct a mutuality of harm hypothesis that powerfully appends whites to the harmed position of people of color. This move serves as the foundation for rendering white trash "not just [as] a classist slur," but as "a racial epithet that marks out certain whites as a breed apart" (4). The double reading of *white trash* as classist and racist is fundamental to *White Trash*'s articulation of itself as an antiracist project, providing the means to first link poverty to racial minoritization and then produce such minoritization as a racialization of whiteness from within.

But how does one arrive at the notion that the class oppression poor whites experience is also a racial oppression, and further that the very category of white trash can serve as a model of antiracist forms of white identity? Wray and Newitz begin by noting that the term has been traced to African American origins, being deployed by slaves as a mode of insult and differentiation in relation to white servants. This origin story, they write, "in the context of black slavery and white servitude speaks to the racialized roots of the meaning of ['white trash']" (2). Racialized in what sense? As a mechanism of institutional power? As a force of subordination? The authors don't say, and it is in this failure to explore the nexus of power embedded in the origin story that allows *white trash* to be cast as a racialization with minoritizing effects. This becomes fully clear, it seems to me, in the introduction's quick turn to the "Eugenic Family Studies" of the late nineteenth and early twentieth centuries, where poor whites were medically investigated on models of genetic defect previously used to define black inferiority. But the authors do not cite the relationship between eugenics and the long traditions of scientific and medical renderings of biologically based ideas of African and African American racial difference; instead their descriptive language of the consequences of eugenics on the enduring stereotypes of poor whites replicates—and comes to stand in for—stereotypes explicitly connected to racist images of blackness:

> The eugenic family studies . . . [were] used . . . as propaganda . . . [for] call[s] to end all forms of welfare and private giving to the poor. . . . the stereotypes of rural poor whites as incestuous and sexually promiscuous, violent, alcoholic, lazy, and stupid remain with us to this day. Alarmingly, contemporary conservative[s] . . . have resurrected this line of biological determinist thinking, blaming white trash for many of the nation's ills and . . . call[ing] for an end of the welfare state. Indeed, the widespread popularity of Herrnstein and Murray's *The Bell Curve* speaks to a renewed interest in U.S. social Darwinism as an explanation for cultural and class differences. (2–3)

The political valence of *white trash* in a slave economy in which servitude has very different meanings for blacks and whites is compressed under the weight of the eugenics model and *white trash* begins to take on the significatory power of a racialized minority itself: "Because white trash is a classed and racialized identity degraded by dominant whiteness, a white trash position vis-à-vis whiteness might be compared to a 'racial minority' position vis-à-vis whiteness" (5).

The consequences of these critical moves are multiple: the insistence on *white trash* as a minoritizing racialization simultaneously disarticulates racism from institutionalized practices of discrimination based on a group's desig-

nated racial status and crafts for poor whites a position structurally comparable to that of a racial minority. An antiracist project for whites is thus inaugurated at the site of a harmed and discriminated whiteness. As the editors
declare at the outset: "Americans love to hate the poor. Lately, it seems there
is no group of poor folks they like to hate more than white trash" (1).[36]
The psychological wages of whiteness defined by Du Bois and taken up
by Roediger are thus supplanted by emphasizing whiteness as a material
privilege—and one whose security has decidedly lessened: "As the economy
and unemployment figures in the U.S. worsen, more whites are losing jobs to
downsizing and corporate restructuring, or taking pay cuts. While it used to
be that whites gained job security at the expense of other racial groups,
whiteness in itself no longer seems a sure path to a good income" (7).[37] In the
context of the introduction's larger and at times deeply contradictory framework, the above assertion functions to produce the power of whiteness as a
fully (and seemingly only) materialized economic relation. When material
advantage does not exist, one hence becomes a racialized minority, albeit
within whiteness. In measuring the comparable worth of marginality in this
way, *White Trash's* intervention into whiteness studies produces, we might
say, a white identity formation that has no compensatory racial debt to pay.

What generates this compulsion for a minoritized whiteness that is not
expensive to people of color? Or more precisely, why does the production of
a minoritized whiteness become the seemingly necessary precondition for
defining the study of whiteness as an antiracist project? Part of the answer to
this question is lodged, as this essay has been suggesting, in the contradictions
between universality and particularity that characterize contemporary postsegregationist racial formation, especially as particularity has become the
invested sign for the creation of antiracist equalities. But particularity is not
essentially anti-essentialist, nor does it guarantee the white subject's disaffiliation from the powers and pretensions of universality. There is, it seems to me,
no theoretical, historical, or methodological escape from the impossibility of
the antiracist white subject, partly because the very focus on the subject has
far too much of the universal at stake.

Objects of Study in Times of Scarcity

The paradox of particularity that we encounter in the three trajectories of
whiteness studies under examination here is inescapable as long as the question of antiracist struggle is registered as one contingent on the social con-

struction of an antiracist white subject. Let me emphasize the conditional here, which implicitly asks us to consider how and why antiracist struggle has become centered on the white subject in the academic discourse of whiteness studies. Certainly it is not the case that social construction emerged as a project about whiteness; rather its political impulse was tied to a critique of the naturalized status afforded to socially constituted differences in various discourses of identity since the 1960s. In this regard, social construction was concerned with those practices, both discursive and material, that had rendered people into groups and defined those groups as culturally if not corporeally coherent and unequal. Under this imperative, social constructionism was focused on understanding in more nuanced ways the relationship between identity, embodiment, and knowledge, which is to say the relationship between racialization as a particularizing series of corporeal markings and the tacit universalism and disembodiment of knowledge formations that constitute the epistemological prerogative of the Enlightened West. Social construction, in other words, hoped to disaffiliate the racialized subject from its oversaturation as particularized embodiment not by disavowing such embodiment but by understanding its material production. In the process, it hoped to transform into knowledge such domains as ethnic studies and women's studies, which had and continue to be understood as academic mediations for politicized bodies and their experience.[38] Such a reduction of the interventionist projects of both ethnic and women's studies is made possible by the lengthy antithetical relationship between embodiment and knowledge that gives shape and sustenance to identity production in modernity, where the very having of an identity must be understood as the concentrated evidence of social practices through which inequalities have been historically generated.

It is the desire to undo this inequality that defines the political horizon of whiteness studies, but embodying whiteness is rarely the critical destination of its dominant theoretical moves, no matter how much the language of particularity is mobilized to mark whiteness as the rhetorical means for disempowering it. In both the class solidarity and race traitor schools, for instance, where whites are encouraged to become race traitors in order to forge class-based alliances, the self-conscious position of disaffiliation that seeks nonwhiteness is one contingent on escaping the overdetermined social meaning of the white body; in this, the antiracist white subject weds itself to knowledge as a rational production and, with knowledge, to a reclamation of history that raises the instance—in most cases the instance of the Irish—to the level of the episteme. The "fact" of the Irish's originary blackness, in other words, sustains the belief in the transcendent possibility of reversing history, even though the language of race in the United States by the early nineteenth century was tied quite resolutely to an economy of corporeal visibility. Recent critical fascination with passing has functioned to point out the fictional error that the visibility of race inscribes, but it should not be lost on us that the ability of some immigrant groups to become white has more than a little to do with U.S. insistence on race as indexed in the color of skin. The fascination within certain trajectories of whiteness studies with the Irish speaks to the very desire that motivates liberal whiteness in the popular sphere: the desire to liberate ourselves from a corporeal identity that signifies the universal privilege of white skin. Where Forrest Gump claims a transcendent humanism based on the unconsciousness of goodness, much of the scholarship in whiteness studies puts into play, in a far more complex and politically progressive way, a project built on the critical value of consciously antiracist intentions.

While the white trash school of whiteness studies works to resist the split between consciousness and embodiment that I have defined as characteristic of certain critical constructions of the antiracist subject, it does not in the end resist the scene of abjection. Indeed, the permanent white poor come to occupy, as significatory value and social fact, the abject of white racial consciousness. As the abject, white trash are by definition outside the circuits of racial power and privilege, a position that guarantees from the outset their equivalency to a racial minority. In this strategy, the white trash school shares with other modes of inquiry in whiteness studies the use of class as a vehicle for imagining the transcendence of power that whiteness, in social constructionist terms, might be said to mean. To put this another way, economic immobility becomes the necessary index of the racial minoritization of whiteness from within. Such a critical emphasis on immobility returns us to the elaborate resignification of segregation that serves as the opening agenda of *Forrest Gump*, where it is precisely the material necessity of divesting from whiteness as economic power that motivates Gump's occupation of the symbolic space of racialized embodiment.

I want to question this collision, not by flattening the incredible—and incredibly important—difference between liberal whiteness and the academic enterprise of whiteness studies, but by asking why we (white critical race thinkers) find ourselves today so impassioned about the need to fashion, from history or economics, from social theory or personal narrative, a paradigmatic antiracist white subject. This critical investment that seeks to undo the rela-

tionship between embodiment and knowledge—attempting to make whiteness have no relationship to knowledge except when knowledge functions to
disavow whiteness—mistakes the functionality of universalism by assuming
that the universal is the scene of subjective unconsciousness. As a consequence
of this mistake, a good deal of scholarship on whiteness has come to insist, in
contradistinction to the way that social constructionism is mobilized to talk
about racially minoritized subjects, that consciousness and social identity are
not epistemologically linked. And it is this insistence, which hopes to disag-
gregate subjectivity from social identity, that is the universal prerogative not
simply of whiteness but of all dominant identities. This is the case in part
because the very notion of a dominant identity emerges as the effect of social
practices of particularization that refuse the racialized, sexualized, and gendered subject the mobility of a de-essentialized subjectivity.

In this essay, I have tried to think critically about whiteness studies as a field
by addressing its own social construction, which is to say that I have tried to
consider how the various formulations of whiteness (as mobile class identification, as self-conscious becoming, as the minority within itself) are situated within contemporary formations of identity, politics, and knowledge.
For if, in the right's version of the popular realm, white men are rescued from a
narrative of U.S. history contaminated by their privilege, whiteness studies
seems to offer the left's hyperconscious other side, likewise particularizing
whiteness in order to transcend its universality. This is not to suggest a faulty
analogy between whiteness studies and the liberal whiteness of Forrest
Gump's America, nor is it to deny the enabling possibilities of forging a
distinction between having white skin and identifying with white skin privilege. It is neither a dismissal of the significance of reading the historical record
of immigration, labor, and slavery in ways that allow us to seriously define the
social construction of whiteness, nor an endorsement of a monolithic rendering of whiteness that fails to attend to the complicated local practices through
which ethnic identity has been racialized in majoritarian or minoritarian
ways. It is rather an interest in the power of disciplinary knowledge that leads
me to question how the study of whiteness has taken shape and why it hinges
antiracist struggle on the question of the white subject.

I raise these issues not to dismiss the political desire that motivates so much
academic labor on whiteness as an object of study, but to emphasize that the
possessive investment in whiteness, as Lipsitz calls it, has institutional form
and force. Whiteness studies emerges, after all, in the midst of a devastating
lack of employment in the academy, one that many commentators connect to
the denationalization of education that has accompanied the dissolution of

the Cold War. In the downsizing of the university and the proletarianization of its intellectual workforce, many of the privileges that have ensured the white hegemony of the intellectual elite have been called into question. New doctorates, especially in the humanities and social sciences, are finding themselves accepting part-time and non–tenure track appointments, and it is not rare to hear both white faculty and graduate students declare that only people of color have escaped the employment crisis of higher education. In addition, many of the disciplines that have upheld the centrality of the Anglo-European tradition (German, French, and Italian) are now under duress, so much so that a few universities are actually considering the possibility of collapsing these departments into a European area studies program. This, combined with the fact that the academy is leading the way in the institutional dismantling of affirmative action, necessitates not a dismissal of the university as extraneous to the political project of abolishing or transforming whiteness but heightened attention to it.

Such attention begins, as this essay has suggested, by linking the discourses of the academy with the popular public sphere and by tracing the disciplinary discourses and methodological assumptions that have mobilized whiteness studies as an emergent field. A critical perspective on a seemingly new object of study is necessary to disrupt the institutional knowledge investments that accompany every disciplinary gesture—those investments whereby the authority of knowers is established by the reproducibility of a chosen object of study. Legitimate objects are never exhaustible; they do not become knowledge objects as a means for their destruction. To consecrate the study of white racial identity and power as a field formation called whiteness studies (as opposed to its earlier operation within ethnic studies) is not to divest whiteness of its authority and power but to rearticulate the locus of its identity claims from the universal to the particular. It is this rearticulation that I have defined as the project of liberal whiteness in the popular sphere, and it has been its logic of intellectual and identitarian mobility that I have critiqued as the theoretical foundation of whiteness studies as an emergent field. For neither the epistemological status of whiteness as the implicit framework for the organization of what we know as the human sciences nor the epistemological status of white scholars as the authorized agents of institutional knowledge is called into question by a field called whiteness studies.

To render whiteness the object of study from within the province of a humanist subject now hyperconscious of itself thus mistakes the way that even radical traditions within modern knowledge formations are not innocently prior to but decisively and unpredictably implicated in the histories and inequalities of racial asymmetries and oppressions. The political project that generates knowledge formations and the political consequences of their generation cannot be unequivocally coordinated, which is to say that the social construction of white racial identities and ideologies that is the object of study in whiteness studies arises in the context of ongoing historical processes. These processes have reworked the relation between universality and particularity that constitutes the negotiated hegemony of white power and made possible new and powerful attacks on civil rights legislation—all as part of a contradictory reconfiguration of the public discourse of race and white racial identity in the postsegregationist era. Far from operating as the opposite or resistant counter to the universal, then, the particular is the necessary contradiction that affords to white power its historical and political elasticity. In this context, the political project for the study of whiteness entails not simply rendering whiteness particular, but engaging with the ways that being particular will not divest whiteness of its universal epistemological power.

Notes

1 I've drawn my information about the original Laurens controversy over the Klan Museum from Rick Bragg's "In a South Carolina Town, a Klan Museum Opens Old Wounds," *New York Times*, 17 November 1996, 16. Subsequent twists and turns of the story are fascinating. Apparently, John Howard sold the Echo Theater to his Klan protégé, Michael Burden who, through his fiancée, was converted into an antiracist. When Burden sold the theater to the local black preacher, Rev. David Kennedy, Howard was given a lifetime guarantee that he could continue to run, rent-free, his museum. The museum is thus housed now in a building owned by an African American, and it is Kennedy's church that has taken in Burden who has been routinely thwarted in his attempts to find steady employment in Laurens. See "Converted by Love, a Former Klansman Finds Ally at Black Church," *Washington Post*, 27 July 1997, A3.

2 In *States of Injury: Power and Freedom in Late Modernity* (Princeton, N.J.: Princeton University Press, 1995), Wendy Brown discusses the replacement of rights for freedoms in the national political lexicon, which has produced what she means by her title—political inclusion as a state of injury. Analyzing the broad scope in which injury-based claims have come to supplant conversations about freedom, she notes that even leftists have become "disoriented about the project of freedom," concerning themselves "not with democratizing power but with distributing goods, and especially with pressuring the state to buttress the rights and increase the entitlements of the socially vulnerable or disadvantaged" (3).

3 Richard Dyer, *White* (New York: Routledge, 1997), 2. He writes, "white

people—not there as a category and everywhere everything as a fact—are difficult, if not impossible, to analyse *qua* white. The subject seems to fall apart in your hands as soon as you begin. Any instance of white representation is always immediately something more specific—*Brief Encounter* is not about white people, it is about English middle-class people; *The Godfather* is not about white people, it is about Italian-American people; but *The Color Purple* is about black people, before it is about poor, southern U.S. people." Dyer, "White," *Screen* 29, no. 4 (1988): 46. To the extent that Dyer's description of the function of the ideology of whiteness as infinite particularity counters the theoretical assumption grafted from it—that whiteness is the category of invisibility and non-particularity—the theoretical articulation of whiteness has been stalled in the collapse of two registers of analysis: (1) the description of the effect of white identity formation that improperly served as its theoretical formulation and (2) a theoretical formulation that cannot render the historical specificity and material production of its description.

4 In the period of nineteenth-century Reconstruction, the ranks of white supremacy swelled from the shared belief in the ascendancy of a new privileged blackness and with it white injury. See Edward L. Ayers, *Vengeance and Justice: Crime and Punishment in the Nineteenth-Century American South* (New York: Oxford University Press, 1984), especially "The Crisis of the New South," 223–65; and Glenda Elizabeth Gilmore, *Gender and Jim Crow: Women and the Politics of White Supremacy in North Carolina, 1896–1920* (Chapel Hill: University of North Carolina Press, 1996), especially 77–89 and 94–99.

5 Jessie Daniels's *White Lies: Race, Class, Gender, and Sexuality in White Supremacist Discourse* (New York: Routledge, 1997) provides an analysis of the documents of contemporary white supremacist organizations, exploring in particular the language of "victimization." See especially 35–43. Subsequent references are cited parenthetically in the text.

6 Many of the more reactionary reformations of white power and privilege currently go undetected by whites, from white suburban flight and the proliferation of gated communities to the privatization of institutions of higher learning and the growth of the prison industry, from the English-only movement to the resurrection of states' rights, from bans on public welfare for immigrants to pro-capital international trade agreements. Instead, Howard's Klan and its spawn are taken as *the* American practice of white supremacy in total, which is just one of the many ways that the reconstruction of civil rights has been accomplished.

7 Lauren Berlant, *The Queen of America Goes to Washington City: Essays on Sex and Citizenship* (Durham, N.C.: Duke University Press, 1997), 1. Subsequent references are cited parenthetically in the text.

8 Robert Zemeckis, dir., *Forrest Gump* (Paramount, 1994).

9 The study of white racial identity and its political project of domination is not new to academic discourse, but such inquiry has recently been consolidated into a field formation by the academic press, academic publishers, and, to

varying degrees, scholars themselves. It is this phenomenon of claiming a field
formation that I understand as the content and contemporary production of
whiteness studies, and it is toward an analysis of the social construction of this
formation that my essay is aimed. See especially David W. Stowe, "Uncolored
People: The Rise of Whiteness Studies," *Lingua Franca*, September/October
1996, 68–77.

Regardless of the definitional construction of the field—which tends to em-
phasize the self-conscious analysis of whiteness from an antiracist white per-
spective—the contemporary archive of scholarship that seeks to study white
racial formation is lengthy. See Theodore W. Allen, *The Invention of the White
Race*, vol. 1 (New York: Verso, 1994); Valerie Babb, *Whiteness Visible: The
Meaning of Whiteness in American Literature and Culture* (New York: New York
University Press, 1998); Jessie Daniels, *White Lies*; Richard Delgado and Jean
Stefancic, eds., *Critical White Studies: Looking behind the Mirror* (Philadelphia:
Temple University Press, 1997); Michelle Fine et al., eds., *Off White: Readings
on Race, Power, and Society* (New York: Routledge, 1997); Ruth Frankenberg,
White Women, Race Matters: The Social Construction of Whiteness (Minneapo-
lis: University of Minnesota Press, 1993); Ruth Frankenberg, ed., *Displacing
Whiteness: Essays in Social and Cultural Criticism* (Durham, N.C.: Duke Univer-
sity Press, 1997); Mike Hill, ed., *Whiteness: A Critical Reader* (New York: New
York University Press, 1997); Noel Ignatiev, *How the Irish Became White* (New
York: Routledge, 1995); Noel Ignatiev and John Garvey, eds., *Race Traitor*
(New York: Routledge, 1996); George Lipsitz, *The Possessive Investment in
Whiteness: How White People Profit from Identity Politics* (Philadelphia: Temple
University Press, 1998); Ian F. Haney López, *White by Law: The Legal Con-
struction of Race* (New York: New York University Press, 1996); Eric Lott, *Love
and Theft: Blackface Minstrelsy and the American Working Class* (New York:
Oxford University Press, 1993); Dana D. Nelson, *National Manhood: Capitalist
Citizenship and the Imagined Fraternity of White Men* (Durham, N.C.: Duke
University Press, 1998); Fred Pfeil, *White Guys: Studies in Postmodern Domina-
tion and Difference* (New York: Verso, 1995); David R. Roediger, *Towards the
Abolition of Whiteness: Essays on Race, Politics, and Working Class History* (Lon-
don: Verso, 1994); Roediger, *The Wages of Whiteness: Race and the Making of the
American Working Class* (London: Verso, 1991); Alexander Saxton, *The Rise and
Fall of the White Republic: Class Politics and Mass Culture in Nineteenth Century
America* (New York: Verso, 1990); Mab Segrest, *Memoir of a Race Traitor* (Bos-
ton: South End, 1994); Vron Ware, *Beyond the Pale: White Women, Racism, and
History* (New York: Verso, 1992); and Matt Wray and Annalee Newitz, eds.,
White Trash: Race and Class in America (New York: Routledge, 1997). Subse-
quent references are cited parenthetically in the text.

10 In the genealogies of whiteness studies constructed by the academic press, the
emphasis on the epistemological reversal has had a powerful effect in displacing the long history of studying white racial identity and power in Ethnic
Studies. For this reason, David R. Roediger has edited *Black on White: Black
Writers on What It Means to Be White* (New York: Schocken, 1998), an anthol-

ogy of critical analysis by black thinkers about white racial formation. Early feminist work, such as *Yours in Struggle: Three Feminist Perspectives of Anti-Semitism and Racism* by Elly Bulkin, Minnie Bruce Pratt, and Barbara Smith (Brooklyn, N.Y.: Long Haul, 1984), which compellingly addressed white racial formation in relation to black and Jewish identities and political identifications, has also been omitted in formulations of this new field. These moves reconvene the logic of white masculinity as the generic subject of whiteness studies even as the ideological hold of that subject is supposed to be under abolition.

11 For paradigmatic examples of scholarship in each of these trajectories, see Roediger, *The Wages of Whiteness* and *Towards the Abolition of Whiteness* (the class solidarity school); Ignatiev and Garvey, *Race Traitor* (the race traitor school); and Wray and Newitz, *White Trash* (the white trash school).

12 See James Baldwin, "On Being 'White' . . . and Other Lies," *Essence*, April 1984, 90–92.

13 I am quoting Lipsitz here, who is paraphrasing Dyer (*Possessive Investment*, 1).

14 The denial of the power and corporeality of whiteness as a bodily production can be read in the discursive history of the figure of passing in academic criticism. While this figure has long been of import to African American studies precisely because of the way it brings into critical view the contradictions of race as a visible production, it is interesting to note that in the 1990s cultural criticism has emphasized the meaning of the passing figure as white. See, for instance, Michael Bérubé's untitled book review of my *American Anatomies: Theorizing Race and Gender* in *African American Review* 31, no. 2 (1997): 317–20. Arguing that "Homer Plessy was 'white.' And every American historian knows it," Bérubé asserts that the one-drop rule "had nothing whatsoever to do with the register of the visible" (319), as if the visible was not in fact the anxiety-producing framework for the one-drop rule's legal articulation. Bérubé forges this usage of Plessy, who occupies a place in African American studies as the quintessential passing figure, in order to inaugurate an analogic claim: "just as black persons were frequently 'white,' so too were white persons discursively 'black'" (319). The discursive blackness of the Irish, Jewish, and Italians are thus presented as coterminous with legal, state-based definitions of racialization—a conflation of enormous political consequences that reiterates, as much of the work in the proliferating archive of whiteness studies now does, the desire to master the meaning of the body by locating a symbolic black origin for contemporary white people.

15 George Lipsitz, private correspondence with author, 18 August 1997. My thanks to George Lipsitz for his thoughtful and thorough consideration of the issues raised in this essay.

16 For a historical analysis of black resistance to public transportation segregation in Birmingham during World War II, see Robin D. G. Kelley, "Congested Terrain: Resistance on Public Transportation," in *Race Rebels: Culture, Politics, and the Black Working Class* (New York: Free Press, 1994), 55–75.

17 I visited the Civil Rights Institute while in Birmingham to deliver the earliest

version of this piece, which means that the juxtaposition between it and *Forrest Gump* originate in a kind of fruitful accident, as opposed to a definitive intertextual exchange. But it was in that museum, with its window—both a screen and a frame—looking out at the Baptist church, that the implications of the film's technological mastery of television, its use of TV memory as the vehicle for encoding and deflecting national crisis and struggle, and its long incomprehensible narrative deliberation on Gump's running trek across the nation began to make sense as tropes/motifs in the renarrativization of segregation from the vantage point of white masculinity.

18 It is this kind of *race–traitoring* that most characterizes the film, as Gump's movement in personal moral terms not only displaces the necessity of conscious identifications as precursors to collective political action, but consigns the entire realm of the historical to television, installing a consumptive spectator as the ultimate witness—and postracist subject—of political change itself.

19 The two most extensive readings of *Forrest Gump* in the context of feminist analyses of gender are Berlant, *The Queen of America*, 176–86; and Thomas B. Byers, "History Re-membered: *Forrest Gump*, Postfeminist Masculinity, and the Burial of the Counterculture," *Modern Fiction Studies* 42, no. 2 (1996): 420–44.

20 This point is explicitly reinforced in the film through Gump's parodic commentary on the white bed sheets worn by members of the Klan. As the figure of white skin, the bed sheets can be cast off by Klan descendants, which means that the materialization of privilege symbolized by and invested in white skin has itself no necessary historical lineage. My thanks to Eva Cherniavsky for suggesting this reading of white skin.

21 Cheryl Harris, "Whiteness as Property," *Harvard Law Review* 106, no. 8 (1993): 1781. Subsequent references are cited parenthetically in the text.

22 On the broader contexts of the remasculinization of the white Vietnam veteran, see Susan Jeffords, *The Remasculinization of America: Gender and the Vietnam War* (Bloomington: Indiana University Press, 1989).

23 Gump wears other kinds of shoes in the film, but the meditation on shoes that opens the film—and subsequent meditations on his mobility—revolve around the Nike running shoes. Even the advertisements for the film, both in theaters and on video, feature Gump in his Nike running shoes.

24 Gump's run, while denied an explanation in the film, begins the day after July 4—the day after Jenny has "run off" without explanation. In the final moves of the narrative, we will find out that it was their encounter on the fourth of July that created "Little Forrest," thereby reinforcing the relation between paternity and the futurity of the nation.

25 My thanks to Eva Cherniavsky, who offered me an understanding of the material investment in whiteness as a relation of inexhaustability to the commodity, and to Patricia McKee, who discussed with me the way that whiteness needs to be thought of as a process of simultaneous materialization and dematerialization.

26 See W. E. B. Du Bois, *Black Reconstruction: An Essay toward a History of the Part Which Black Folk Played in the Attempt to Reconstruct Democracy in America, 1860–1880* (New York: Atheneum, 1935).

27 Jonathan Scott discusses the differences between Roediger and Allen in his review article, "Inside the White Corral," *Minnesota Review* 47 (1996): 93–103.

28 See Lipsitz, *Possessive Investment*, and "The Possessive Investment in Whiteness: Racialized Social Democracy and the 'White' Problem in American Studies," *American Quarterly* 47, no. 3 (1995): 369–87, for a discussion of how national policies in the twentieth century furthered the political agenda of white racial supremacy. For instance, FHA housing programs funneled money toward white Americans in the suburbs instead of into multiethnic urban neighborhoods, thereby restructuring in more segregated ways the racialization of social space in the second half of the twentieth century. See also George J. Sánchez's useful response to Lipsitz's article in the same issue, "Reading Reginald Denny: The Politics of Whiteness in the Late Twentieth Century," 388–94. In a somewhat different vein, see Cheryl Harris, "Whiteness as Property."

29 Noel Ignatiev and John Garvey, "Abolish the White Race," in *Race Traitor*, ed. Ignatiev and Garvey (New York: Routledge, 1996), 9–10. Subsequent references are cited parenthetically in the text.

30 John Garvey and Noel Ignatiev, "The New Abolitionism," *Minnesota Review* 47 (1996): 105–6. Subsequent references are cited parenthetically in the text.

31 Noel Ignatiev, "Immigrants and Whites," in *Race Traitor*, 18–19. Subsequent references are cited parenthetically in the text.

32 "What is the distinctive element of the American experience?" Ignatiev asks. "It is the shock of being torn from a familiar place and hurled into a new environment, compelled to develop a way of life and culture from the materials at hand. And who more embodies that experience, is more the essential product of that experience, than the descendants of the people from Africa who visited these shores together with the first European explorers . . . and whose first settlers were landed here a year before the Mayflower?" ("Immigrants," 19).

33 Noel Ignatiev and John Garvey, "Introduction," in *Race Traitor*, 4.

34 Annalee Newitz, "White Savagery and Humiliation," in *White Trash: Race and Class in America*, ed. Matt Wray and Newitz (New York: Routledge, 1997), 149–50. Subsequent references are cited parenthetically in the text.

35 Matt Wray and Annalee Newitz, "Introduction," in *White Trash*, 5. Subsequent references are cited parenthetically in the text.

36 In drawing attention to the discourse of injury, I do not mean to discount the importance of analyzing the many ways that the white permanent and working poor are representationally "trashed" in U.S. popular culture. Nor do I mean to obviate the fact that Wray and Newitz remark on the problem of a vulgar multiculturalism that attends to whiteness only as victim. But I do think that the introduction is contradictory enough that these caveats are not consti-

tutively formulated within the project's theorization of the permanent poor; rather the very risks that the authors note seem to be the foundational effects of their discursive practices.

37 In his contribution to *White Trash*, Timothy J. Lockley focuses on non-slaveholding whites in the antebellum period under a similar set of disturbing assumptions: "Whiteness per se was not a ticket to the life of leisure. Living in a society which was based on a system of human bondage, and having little or no part in that particular system, gave non-slaveholding whites a unique social status." Timothy J. Lockley, "Partners in Crime: African Americans and Non-slaveholding Whites in Antebellum Georgia," in *White Trash*, 59.

38 Lisa Lowe's "The International within the National: American Studies and Asian American Critique," *Cultural Critique* 40 (1998): 29–45, offers a crucial rearticulation of the epistemological project of Asian American studies, one that dovetails with my insistence here that the legacy of rational disembodiment for modern knowledge regimes has rendered illegitimate the new knowledges born of identity-based social movements precisely because those knowledges refuse to disavow embodiment for knowledge.

Identities and Identity Studies

READING TONI CADE BAMBARA'S ''THE HAMMER MAN''

Lindon Barrett

In many ways, this essay reiterates critical perspectives championed by feminists of color. As documented, for instance, in the collection *This Bridge
Called My Back*, feminists of color have long led the way in recognizing and
theorizing the manner in which categories of identity, made most salient by
dominant cultural codes, ineluctably intersect, transfigure, and remain co-
implicated in one another. Beverly Smith, in an interview in the volume,
states the matter forthrightly: "In reality, the way women live their lives those
separations just don't work. Women don't live their lives like, Well this part is
race, and this is class, and this part has to do with women's identities, so it's
confusing."[1] Gloria Anzaldúa similarly laments that she lives in a world in
which "they chop me up into little fragments and tag each with a label."[2] It is
well known that feminists of color have for many years attempted to critique
and transform the very category of woman as well as undertake critiques of
the imbricated social categories of sexuality and race.

Nonetheless, widely understood conceptions of ethnicity and race remain
largely untransformed by critical visions sponsored by feminists of color, as
evidenced, for instance, by Werner Sollors's codification in "Ethnicity," an
entry in *Critical Terms of Literary Study*. "Ethnic, racial, or national identifications" writes Sollors, "rest on antitheses, on negativity, or on what the
ethnopsychoanalyst Georges Devereux has termed their 'dissociative character."[3] While it is certainly true that acknowledging this "dissociative" character is indispensable to assessing the psychological, social, and political potency
of ethnicity / race, it is still as incomplete a gesture as it is an enabling one. For,
as much as ethnic / racial formations prove dissociative or diacritical, they are
also profoundly syncretic. An often unconsidered dimension of ethnic / racial
specifications is the masking of the more subtle information ethnicity / race,
gender, and sexuality hold for one another.

Forwarding the notion that the integrity and intersectionality of these
categories often remain underestimated, the following discussion suggests
that, as generally configured, the new academic concerns codified as cultural
studies often miss opportunities to interrogate important imbrications of

what are routinely considered separated categories of identity. This investigation considers the way predominant epistemes of cultural studies, in the very gesture of attempting to foster counterknowledges, display widespread respect for the assumed stability and independence of the rubrics of identity, a state of affairs ironically reflecting—at least on one level—institutional and disciplinary inertia. The alternative perspective offered in this analysis is pursued through a reading of Toni Cade Bambara's short story "The Hammer Man," in which the co-implications of fixed categories of identity are evident in the figure of the central ethnic/racial subject, the narrator. Reading "The Hammer Man" with the predominant configurations of cultural studies in mind, it becomes clear that, in the same way other options and recalcitrant knowledges are foreclosed for the narrator by the conclusion of the narrative, they are foreclosed for cultural critiques, overlooking the fact that it may be misleading to believe that the cultural *doxa* in need of explanation does or would correspond—as a matter of course—to those categories offered by the culture under investigation in the first place. In other words, the template of cultural studies as well as disciplinary alliances to the rubrics of cultural identity form the points of interrogation for the following analysis. The literary reading and ensuing discussion aim to explicate not only the imbrication of cultural identities but also the formation of institutional knowledges in terms of putatively discrete rubrics of identity. The aim is to extend the analysis of cultural identities begun by feminists of color into a consideration of ongoing academic configurations of knowledge.

The claims that, at present, the extent to which these kinds of cultural co-implications remain generally undocumented in the epistemes of cultural studies seems inversely related to their articulation in the crises of Bambara's "The Hammer Man." That is to say, reading this narrative within standard epistemological configuration fails completely to account for the narrator's assumption of imposed gendered and sexual identities through what is foremost a crisis of racialization. By the conclusion of "The Hammer Man," the protagonist comes to "know" and respect the forceful, dissociative nature of ethnicity/race but, in addition, by means of the same trauma, she comes to "desire" and inhabit normative gender and sexual roles and their implied heterosexuality. Normative gender and sexual roles transcend what should be the definitive, racialized cleavage of the text. On both sides of what emerges as a stark narrative (and ethnic/racial) divide, the protagonist is pressed toward identical gendered and sexual postures. This syncretism is exposed in terms of the dynamics of the black/white racial dichotomy in the United States.

Indeed, once the notion that dissociation is the single or preeminent issue defining ethnicity/race is eclipsed, what becomes evident is a more complex, asymmetrical configuration determining ethnic/racial membership. For ethnicity/race depends ultimately on a "heteronormative vision."[4] The ultimate logic of ethnicity/race fixes individuals foremost in a procreative relation to social organization. This relation is intent on cultural transmission and/or the transmission of visible physical characteristics speciously and belatedly guaranteeing what seem self-evident divisions and dissociations. The crisis of ethnicity/race, on close examination, proves libidinal, invested ultimately in a set of fundamental prohibitions on the discharge of sexual energies. Ethnicity/race might be thought of as a series of prohibitions on social desire and sexual practice, prohibitions intent on stabilizing and ensuring the transmission of identifying phenotypical (or cultural) traits from generation to generation. Only by a circuitous route through matters of gender and sexuality do the dynamics of ethnicity/race lodge themselves in the dissociation by which they are most routinely understood. By not attending fully to the circuitousness of these dynamics, cultural studies may unintentionally reiterate ideological systems it often sets out to critique or expose. This is an ironic critical position that the historian Joan Scott, in "The Evidence of Experience," instructively details in the context of social history.[5]

One notable site where imbrications of categories of identification are intuitively comprehended and intuitively play themselves out is that of the family. In consideration of the existential (rather than biological) "reality" of race in the context of the United States, the philosopher Naomi Zack outlines, for example, the "asymmetrical kinship systems" constituting the family as a paramount site of these imbrications. Asymmetrical kinship systems, Zack informs us, comprise the most crucial ground and index of ethnicity/race in the United States because, whereas phenotypical or other evidence may in some cases prove so unreliable as to allow particular individuals to "pass," family membership negotiates more assiduously the tensions between the contingencies of individual circumstance and communal dissociative belonging. Zack, concerned with the particular animus between racial blackness and racial whiteness in the United States, spells out the manner in which family, understood as the primary site of ethnic/racial formation, exposes the cathected ground of ethnicity/race, gender, and sexuality:

> Designated black physical racial characteristics are genetic. The mechanism of human genetics is heterosexual sexual intercourse. That fact alone is enough

to account for much of the obscenity, fear, fascination, lust, scorn, degradation, and both real and pseudo-revulsion with which white people have
considered the sexuality of black people. Individuals who are designated black
have the ability, through the mechanism of their heterosexuality, to destroy
the white identity of families, and because race of kin determines race of
individuals, to destroy the white identity of the relatives of their descendants.
Thus the asymmetrical kinship system of racial inheritance in the United
States not only is intrinsically racist in favor of white people, but it defines
black people as intrinsically threatening and dangerous to white families.[6]

What is evident, then, in the one-drop rule of U.S. "black" and "white"
racial specifications,[7] is the fact that, as much as ethnicity/race is a civic, legal,
and psychological discourse of dissociation, it also operates as a civic, legal,
and psychological discourse of sexual practice and gender specification. The
logic of ethnicity/race demands a heterosexual paradigm with its attendant
instantiations of gender imbalance, and this set of mutual information finds its
principal point of cathexis in the figure of the family.[8] The consequence of
making these recognitions is to obviate to some degree the exhaustiveness of
critical attentions that principally imagine "processes of generating feelings
of dissociative belonging" (Sollors 303). Moreover, it obviates epistemological and institutional agendas based on the more or less conscious reiteration of
discrete concepts of social identity.

It may be somewhat counterproductive to consider the rubrics of eth-
nicity/race, gender, and sexuality as primarily independent sites of psychic
and political subjection, even though it is along these lines that cultural
studies for the most part manages the production of academic knowledges of
identity. The enabling gesture of cultural analysis is most often, as in the larger
culture, one marking these sites as generally discrete (though sometimes
overlapping) categories of identification, instead of pursuing the manner in
which they are articulated through and in one another. In this way, more than
speaking to the broader conditions of subjection and subjectivity, this move
may speak to a recent history of transforming challenges to the unacceptable
"isolation of [academic] ideological analysis from concrete cultural struggles."[9] This is not to say that significant work is not being produced beyond
dominant epistemological and institutional frameworks. The work of Judith
Butler, Kimberlé Crenshaw, Lee Edelman, Phillip Brian Harper, Hortense
Spillers, Kendall Thomas, and Jean Walton, to name randomly only a few,
comes to mind. The work of each in the context of black/white relations in
the United States investigates the circumstance that ethnicity/race, hetero-

sexuality, and gender norms rely on—are actually constituted through—each other in their reproduction. As already noted, it is imperative to acknowledge that in the context of the post-1960s academy, the cultural and literary criticism of feminists of color forms one strand of scholarship that has been insistently aware of these matters and has pursued a more syncretic investigative tact than generally taken or understood in the academy.

African American feminist criticism, in particular, provides a significant antecedent for the type of ongoing critical work now gaining increasing currency. Important exchanges initiated by African American feminist critics with a largely masculinist African American critical institution and a largely white feminist critical institution have produced widespread effects on the post-1960s academy, although these effects are rarely as plainly acknowledged as they are by Cheryl Wall, who states: "Not only has the criticism of black women's writing been transformed over the past two decades; this criticism has transformed other critical discourses as well. . . . The extent to which feminist and African Americanist writing and, yes, even the criticism that claims the center are more inclusive than they were twenty years ago owes much to black women's writing and its critics changing as many words as they pleased."[10] Wall rehearses the fact that research initiatives underwritten by African American feminism have had, in addition to an extraordinary breadth of influence, a powerful transformative effect on the very rudiments of the academic conversation itself, of which one sign is the advent of earnest examinations of the undertheorized intersections of cultural and social identity. By no means can African American feminist criticism singularly claim responsibility for the productive critical syncretism of the recent academy, but it does constitute one of the earliest and most visible scholarly fields insistent on demonstrating the intellectual gains of refusing to conceive of the main categories of modern identity as merely separate and independent. In this way, African American feminist interventions played a crucial role in charting present possibilities for reconceiving what are usually understood as fundamental but separate markers of identity in the modern West or ascendant "New World." Such interventions exposed and, with others, continue to expose some of the most subtle machinations of the potent and oppressive cultural logic of the modern West. In the epilogue to *Things of Darkness*, her study of race and gender in early modern England, Kim Hall traces such a debt as well as its radical consequences for what matters have become "visible" at some institutional sites of inquiry.[11]

It bears emphasizing that the issue is not choosing between competing propositions about ethnicity / race—dissociation or syncretism—but imagining, instead, how these propositions are mutually supplementary. Toni Cade Bambara's short story "The Hammer Man" (from her 1972 collection *Gorilla, My Love*) is a brief, exemplary text in this regard. The play of both dissociation and syncretism is paramount in determining the conflicts and crises of Bambara's unnamed pubescent protagonist, a virtually fearless tomboy who finds herself at odds at the opening of the narrative with a variety of people in her African American community. These tensions internal to the community form the preoccupation of the narrative until, in a climactic showdown, the narrator and Manny (her greatest enemy) are paired off one evening in "Douglass Street park" against two white policemen.[12] This heightened confrontation—bringing the greatest tensions of the story to bear through the prism of racial division—profoundly reshapes the protagonist's relation to both her community and larger environment. Not only in terms of racialization but in terms of gender and sexuality as well, this reorientation holds dramatic consequences for her sense of self.

The narrator's account of these events begin with her characteristic humor and insouciance. She proclaims, "I was glad to hear Manny had fallen off the roof" (35), then proceeds, in her rambling, energetic way, to explain how Manny's fall simplifies her life. Indeed, the first two pages or so of the seven-page story comprise her high-spirited explanation of why Manny lay in murderous wait for her on the stoop of her parents' apartment building, "all day and all night, hardly speaking to the people going in and out . . . with his sister bringing him peanut butter sandwiches and cream sodas" (35). Manny seeks revenge for a verbal attack on him (and his mother) made by the narrator—an arbitrary verbal attack motivated only by her mischievous disregard for Manny's reputation as crazy and therefore not to be messed with. After several days and nights of his vigil, Manny is somehow enticed to the roof of the building, perhaps by "Frankie [who might have] got some nasty girls to go up on the roof with him" (36), and Manny's fall releases the narrator from a supposed bout of yellow fever and, therefore, her self-confinement in her parents' apartment.

The end of Manny's vigil allays tensions that have spread through the neighborhood. The narrator's father, in response to Manny's self-declared intent to kill his daughter, jams the head of Manny's older brother, Bernard—"who was more his size" (37)—into a mailbox which, in turn, elicits angry taunts from an uncle of Manny and Bernard. Similarly, Miss Rose, a friend of the family, confronts Manny's mother several times on the narrator's behalf;

Manny's mother chases Miss Rose into the street several times, and everyone in the neighborhood "would congregate on the window sills or the fire escape" (36–37) to watch the two of them "[commence] to get with it, snatching bottles out of the garbage cans and breaking them on the johnny pumps and stuff like that" (36). Even as they eagerly watch, everyone agrees "that it was still much too cold for this kind of nonsense" (37), and the narrator herself marvels at the sight that one could use "the garbage cans for an arsenal . . . [yielding] sticks and table legs and things . . . [and] scissors blades and bicycle chains" (36).

This world of seemingly bizarre interactions seems natural and normal to the narrator, but she ultimately encounters institutional agents who do not share her view and who, much more harshly, denigrate and violently handle people from this world. Ironically, then, her escape from Manny's wrath brings her into confrontation with greater and more daunting forces than the tenacious Manny. What she begins abruptly and inadvertently to face is the dissociative significance of ethnicity / race—and precisely at one of the many institutional sites both manufacturing and maintaining that dissociation. She is bribed by her mother into going to the neighborhood community center, where her mother hopes that contact with activities organized and prescribed for girls will reform her tomboyish ways. Instead, as unreformed and irreverent as ever, the narrator sneaks into the office of the community center and discovers in "one of those not-quite-white folders . . . that I was from a deviant family in a deviant neighborhood" (38). As she chafes at her cultural positioning as "deviant," the consequences of which she does not yet fully understand, she imagines herself more than equal to the encounter. She claims the word "deviant" for her own, running "it into the ground till one day my father got the strap just to show me how deviant he could get" (38). Decidedly, then, both she and her narrative world remain largely unchanged by this encounter. Dramatic and climactic changes in narrative style, her perceptions, and her behavior are yet to come.

A subsequent and more intense moment of racialization holds very different consequences; the long final episode of the narrative draws the lines of enmity and violence most extremely. One night after she is "thrown out of the center for playing pool when [she] should've been sewing" (39), the narrator and Manny are antagonized by two white policemen, and this second, more intense, more immediate encounter with the dissociative dynamic of ethnicity / race profoundly alters her sense of self, as well as radically divides the narrative itself into two dissociated halves. The apparently ubiquitous violence (or threats of violence) marking the initial environment of the story pales in comparison to the possibilities of much more drastic and arbitrary violence brooding over the latter half of the story. The rambling circuitry that characterizes the initial rehearsal of events is superseded by a rehearsal of events that is, by contrast, starkly linear and tightly paced. The humor, levity, and high-spiritedness of the initial portion of the story dissipate. In deference to the dynamics of the "contrastive identification" (Sollors 288) endemic to ethnicity/race, the tone and trajectory of the narrative become starkly polarized. So much so, in fact, that in the latter half of the narrative, the protagonist finds herself declaring solidarity with the very person who is perceived patently as her enemy at the beginning of the narrative: "Now when somebody says [black boy] like that, I gets warm," she states, as tensions mount in the park, "And crazy or no crazy, Manny was my brother at that moment and the cop was the enemy" (40).

Even as her anger and sense of solidarity with Manny grow, the narrator never entirely imagines the full force of the antagonisms playing themselves out. As the police question the two of them for being in the park so late, Manny mindlessly continues to play basketball until one cop "finally grabbed the ball to get Manny's attention. But that didn't work. Manny just stood there with his arms out waiting for the pass so he could save the [imaginary] game. He wasn't paying no mind to the cop. So, quite naturally, when the cop slapped him upside his head it was a surprise" (40). The stark change in the narrative invites the reader to see that the violent confrontations of the latter half of the story are driven by an institutionally sanctioned animus much more menacing than the "deviant" circle of interactions joining together such community figures as Manny and the narrator, Miss Rose and Manny's mother, the narrator's father and Manny's brother Bernard. By comparison, these earlier interactions seem benign, if vitiated, forms of community converse. For example, in the narration of these earlier events, there is the suggestion that Miss Rose and Manny's mother find in their very public battles an odd measure of relief from their quotidian circumstances. For, when Manny's fall from the roof for the most part settles their disagreement, "Miss Rose went back to her dream books and Manny's mother went back to her tumbled-down kitchen of dirty clothes and bundles and bundles of rags and children" (37). The boisterousness and turbulence of frustrated individuals coming together in the first section of the narrative draw out lines and circuits of community, whereas the violence of the latter section reflects the much more damaging and unhealthy effects of institutionalized processes of polarization and abjection. Of the abject, Judith Butler writes that it designates "precisely those 'unlivable' and 'uninhabitable' zones of social life which are nevertheless densely populated by those who do not enjoy the status of the subject, but whose living under the sign of the 'unlivable' is required to circumscribe the domain of the subject."[13]

The apparently definitive issue of the text—the issue underwriting its climactic confrontation as well as shaping the very presentation of the narrative itself—seems, then, the dissociative intervention of ethnicity/race into the world of the narrator. The upshot of this intervention is to draw together the pairs "abject and subject," "racial blackness and racial whiteness," into a definitive homology. The paramount concerns of the narrative are not so deceptively simple, however. Its collective events suggest, quite differently, that to think, speak, and act in deference to ethnicity/race amounts necessarily and already to thinking, speaking, and acting in terms of gender and sexuality. As patently as the events of the narrative are differentiated into two opposed sections by the polarizing dynamic of ethnicity/race, they are united across the divide by powerful citations of gendered and sexual norms. The interplay of all three sites of identification is most evident in the escalating exchanges between the narrator and the increasingly menacing police. After the police assault Manny and take his basketball away, the narrator exhorts them in her characteristically flippant manner to give it back to him so he can continue practicing to be "Mr. Basketball." She is warned in return by one of her adversaries, who calls her "sister," that if she is not careful she will be "run in" too. To this comment she replies with even greater defiance: "I damn sure can't be your sister seeing how I'm a black girl. Boy, I sure will be glad when you run me in so I can tell everyone about that. You must think you're in the South, mister" (40–41).

Like Naomi Zack's codification of the fundamental intersection of race and kinship systems, the narrator's retort exposes the interest of race in the heterosexual relations on which family structures depend. Inadvertently hitting on the full scope of the cultural significance of ethnicity/race, the narrator reads her adversary's use of "sister" in an impossibly literal and consequently deflating manner. If, in fact, she is his sister, then they must share one or both parents, a circumstance that would efface his racial designation as white, produce him as black and, what is more, place him in a resoundingly ironic (and no doubt dangerous) position, especially at the imaginary moment at which he would be forced to face his former peers. At best, the as yet undisclosed moment of heterosexual intimacy that would render them

immediate blood relations—and, therefore, racially identical (i.e., black)—
would constitute on the part of one or both of "their" parents a reckless
disregard of the racial divide the policemen now strictly reiterate through
their hostile actions. At worst, that undisclosed moment of heterosexual
intimacy would render her adversary's life as a highly effective act of passing
that, on the one hand, betrays family and ethic/racial solidarity and, on the
other, dupes another race. Redacted and acknowledged in the exchange is an
implicit heterosexual paradigm, its gendered roles and responsibilities, as well
as its ability to structure and guarantee the ethnic/racial divide and bellig-
erent interaction central to the episode.

This cathexis is also evident in the exchange that follows. Exasperated, and
calling her "little girl," the officer exhorts the narrator to take Manny, her
"boyfriend," home, and she bristles at the comment, as though it stands as the
point beyond all forbearance. "That really got me," she states. "The 'little girl'
was bad enough but that 'boyfriend' was too much" (41). Highlighted once
again is the fact that gendered and sexual identifications are coincident with
her racial identification. The taunt places her directly within the heterosexual
and gendered configurations that she has rejected throughout the narrative
and that she, only moments before, deployed in her own verbal assault.
Further, it reiterates the normative roles already and uniformly foisted on her
by virtually every adult she has encountered in the narrative—regardless of
the side of the fractured narrative (and ethnic/racial divide) on which they
stand. In negotiating the world of her own racial community, as well as the
belligerence of another more institutionally powerful one, she insistently is
confronted by the fact that "norms of realness by which the subject is produced are racially informed conceptions of 'sex'" (Butler 130). She encounters norms that fix gendered and heterosexual bodies within the culturally
and socially (re)productive categories of ethnicity/race.

From the opening moments of the text, the reader finds the narrator's
mother admonishing her to be more ladylike and to stop consorting with
boys in a manner that supposes she can assume the same roles they do. The
community center attempts to discipline her along the same lines, and even
the unconventional Miss Rose most often calls her by her "brother's name by
mistake" (39). Indeed, as though in culmination of the constant chiding of all
the other adults around her, her proper role and her ideal relation to boys is
prosaically redacted by her racialized foe in the park. His comment reiterates
widespread expectations that situate her squarely within economies of race in
which women are understood foremost as "mothers [who] reproduce bodies

not in a social vacuum but for either a dominant or a subordinate group."[14] These repeated citations force her to recognize—if not reconcile herself to— understood cultural and social assignments.

Summarily put, these exchanges in the park reflect the widely accounted dissociative dynamic of ethnic / racial membership, yet they do so in ways that, rather than being merely dissociative, are ineluctably insinuated in a "heteronormative vision of racial identity," a vision that largely forecloses gender insubordination and thus implicitly also "expression of sexual differ- ence" (Thomas 66). What becomes evident is a highly complex and asym- metrical (re)production of ethnicity / race that contemporary epistemologies of cultural studies largely fall short of clarifying or interrogating. That is, if already consequentially circulating categories of identity—race, gender, sexuality—are, according to Robyn Wiegman, "finally the only constitu- tive ground on which [cultural studies] can base its production of counter- knowledges," then cultural studies mounts only a feeble challenge to hege- monic ways of knowing; these counterknowledges would represent negligi- ble challenges to the powerfully oppressive mechanism, to the "logic of modernity . . . [and] the disciplinarity that has accompanied the human's emergence as both subject and object of knowledge, an emergence through which bodies have been increasingly anatomized. . . . [It] does not dismantle the epistemic force of modernity that we engage in, that engages us."[15] Wieg- man is concerned in particular with contemporary feminisms, but one might claim more generally that current epistemologies merely reiterate rubrics of cultural identification endemic to the modern cultural imagination. Standard estimations of ethnicity / race, gender, and sexuality are merely reconstituted in academic settings by translating them into corresponding fields of African American (or any variety of ethnic and racial designations) studies, femi- nisms(s), and queer theory.

In the post-1960s academy, the emergence of analytical / disciplinary cate- gories along the lines of deeply entrenched cultural battles makes visible constituencies never before treated as worthy of such institutional expendi- tures. It "produce[s] a wealth of new evidence previously ignored about these others and . . . draw[s] attention to dimensions of human life and activity usually deemed unworthy of mention in conventional" intellectual settings and paradigms (Scott 398–99). Decidedly, this is extraordinarily important work, and the point here—as decidedly!—is not to characterize it as wrong- headed, frivolous, inept, or in any way in need of coming to a close. Rather, the point is to consider what might be phrased as the institutional exorbitance by means of which that work seems routinely carried out. The issue is the extent to which the conversion of new academic concerns into fields of knowledge reiterates "rather than contests given ideological systems," as well as the extent to which they preclude "critical examinations of the workings of the ideological system itself, its categories of representation . . . [and] its premises about what these categories mean, and how they operate, and of its notions of subjects, origin, and cause" (Scott 400). By construing the rubrics of ethnicity / race, gender, and sexuality for the most part as discrete and self-evident, this institutional exorbitance creates a situation in which the very protocols for situating newly reckoned lives in academic paradigms and archives may ironically constitute an unconsidered dimension of the larger cultural politics effacing and making these lives abject in the first place. The categories themselves are never called into question.

The criticism is one the historian Joan W. Scott mounts against the orthodox historiographical points of departure taken up by even the most radical fields of social and cultural history. Scott critiques the manner in which historians who excavate "human life and activity usually deemed unworthy of mention" leave undisturbed the enabling assumptions of the discipline (and culture) they are challenging, in that they pursue only "an enlargement of the picture, a correction to oversights resulting from inaccuracies or incomplete vision" (399). These historians, Scott argues, accept uninterrogated assumptions of the difference of their subjects and, therefore, foreclose crucial opportunities for "exploring how difference is established, how it operates, how and in what ways it constitutes subjects who see and act in the world" (399–400). Scott's objection is that these historians leave in place reified terms and indices never taken to task; her countervailing position arises from the observation that "it is not individuals who have experience, but subjects who are constituted by experience" (401). Her corrective is to see that what is unproblematically taken as a *source* (of reckoning a group) may be no more than the already circulating *effect* (of reckoning a group). She proposes an antifoundational moment and critique in the place of foundational ones.

The foundational moves Scott critiques assume a fixity of difference and the notion that members of different groups share an incontrovertible index of collective experience by means of which they may be known or considered. Insofar as cultural studies shares with radical social history the impulse to excavate generally unconsidered lives and communities, to make salient areas of cultural life usually never considered in those terms, it seems that an analogy between the missteps of radical social historians and the epistemological routines of cultural analysis holds. In cultural studies, as with social history, terms of difference which might bear closer examination are reified, so that foundational gestures are made when and where it may not be rewarding to make them.

However, this analogy is only a partial one, since the concern with regard to cultural studies is not truly whether one sees its putatively self-evident categories as a source or effect of cultural representations—cultural critics, it seems, are generally aware of this issue. The concern is the degree to which cultural critics may or may not recognize that the designs and effects of cultural representations extend as far as positing the self-evident independence or discretion of identifying categories. The query is to what extent the epistemologies of cultural studies successfully engage the mutually constitutive characters of ethnicity/race, gender, and sexuality. If routine critical protocols elicit a greater fidelity to the ideological systems of institutional sites and archives inherently hostile to constituencies of cultural studies, then in curious ways these protocols fail to negotiate as adeptly as they might the cultural inequities and disturbances they seek to expose. They repeat in some measure the representational violences they aim to dispute—an observation not made to suggest naively the possibility of a pure gesture from within institutional sites that would completely elude or resolve this issue, but only to suggest one way in which a keener sense of the dilemma might inform a more judicious practice. Critical protocols might be reckoned more closely— if not with an incontrovertible presocial essence—at least with the challenges of making visible the multiple and syncretic nature of actual cultural experience. These protocols, to borrow again from Joan Scott, would not allow routinely stable categories to stand as "the origin of our explanation, but [as] that which we want to explain" (412), always with a mind to their pluralities and complicities.

To return, in further illustration, to Bambara's "The Hammer Man," it is important to recognize that the brash, unrestrained descriptive style that opens the narrative returns briefly at its end to present the narrator's dire concluding fantasy of the racially motivated murders of herself and Manny. This peculiar moment that, by recalling the opening style and tone of the story, in this way marks both opposition and resemblance across the narrative divide, is one of the many facets of the narrative prompting the reader to apprehend the uncommon mechanisms of power at work in the protagonist's crisis. The initial brash set of descriptions in the narrative record her view, rejection, and deft negotiation of a circumscribed external world and community, whereas the second records her unexpected internalization of both her original community and wider community's view, grasp, and negotiation of her:

> And I thought to myself, Oh God here I am trying to change my ways, and not talk back in school, and do like my mother wants, but just have this last fling, and now this—getting shot in the stomach and bleeding to death in Douglas Street park and poor Manny getting pistol whipped by those bastards and whatnot. I could see it all, practically crying too. And it just wasn't no kind of thing to happen to a small child like me with my confirmation picture in the paper next to my weeping parents and schoolmates. I could feel the blood sticking to my shirt and my eyeballs slipping away, and then that confirmation picture again; . . . and Miss Rose heading for the precinct with a shotgun; and my father getting old and feeble with no one to doctor him and all. (42)

It is crucial to recognize that this latter description presents completely fabricated events which, nevertheless, powerfully supersede and overdetermine the reality of the first set of descriptions in the narrative, as well as the narrator's original unmindfulness of a variety of categories of cultural identification. The passage is as breathless and unrestrained as the narrative's opening one, but even though its events are entirely imaginary, its significance is more dire and more consequential. Its imaginary violence marks, for the narrator, capitulation on several counts. Her virtual tears witness the singular rupture of the cool bravado that most characterizes her throughout the narrative. Her self-declared alliance with Manny is equally retracted: "And I wished Manny had fallen off the damn roof and died then and there and saved me all the aggravation of being killed with him by these cops" (42). This phantasm of her brutal death signals acquiescent acknowledgment of the remarkable dissociative force of ethnic/racial identifications as well as her recognition of the daunting power of the overwhelming institutional forces zealously enlisted in the endeavor.

The even more peculiar upshot of the fantasy is her very deliberate acquiescence to gender citations she has long resisted, as well as their implicit heterosexual imperatives at which she had just bristled. Given the narrator's attitudes and actions throughout the story, it is remarkable that the narrative concludes with her eager notation that "me and Violet was in this very boss fashion show at the center. And Miss Rose brought me my first corsage—yellow roses to match my shoes" (42–43). The national academic conversation speaks for the most part past the cathected circumstances of the newly corsaged narrator. In the same way the narrator of "The Hammer Man" is reconciled to a disciplinarity that powerfully forges her vision and actions, independent categories of cultural identity are reconstituted within analytical paradigms claiming revelatory critical distance from cultural doxa. In this particular instance, these paradigms would be unequal to accounting for the appearance of a discourse of homosexuality at the climax of a narrative most seemingly about ethnic/racial division.

In order to admire Manny (even at a crucial moment of ethnic/racial solidarity), the narrator must police and constrain Manny's identity as insistently as it is policed by his adversaries—and, even more ironically, just as insistently as the cultural paradigms she originally flaunts finally police and conscript her: "What makes power hold good, what makes it accepted, is simply the fact that it doesn't only weigh on us as a force that says no, but that it traverses and produces things, it induces pleasure, forms of knowledge, produces discourse. It needs to be considered as a productive network which runs through the whole social body."[16] Michel Foucault's conception of power as "produc[ing] effects at the level of desire—and also at the level of knowledge"[17]—is evident, at the peak of the contest in the park, in the reactions of the narrator to the climactic picture-perfect layup, which precipitates the final tussle between him and the police and, in turn, the narrator's transfiguring fantasy of her death. As she first watches, however, she is not yet terrified: "Manny . . . went right into his gliding thing clear up to the backboard, damn near like he was some kind of very beautiful bird. And then he swooshed that ball in, even if there was no net and you couldn't really hear the swoosh. Something happened to the bones in my chest. It was something. . . . Obviously he had just done about the most beautiful thing a man can do and not be a fag. No cop could swoosh without a net" (41–42).

To the narrator's mind, Manny's achievement is a form of black masculine genius and gracefulness at its most thrilling and, as it turns out, both literally and figuratively, also at its most policed. In the minds of her adversaries, the layup represents a form of black masculinity at its most repulsive or threatening, since in the big "guy [who] watched Manny for a while . . . something must've snapped." He grows immediately "hot for taking Manny to jail or to court or somewhere" (41). His response to Manny's layup is to read it as the sign of Manny's intolerable "deviance" and, hence, the catalyst for his incarceration. This response is diametrically opposed to the narrator's dumbfounded admiration. Nonetheless, the layup remains as policed by her hyperbolic pleasure; although Manny is decidedly not included in their numbers, all "fags" are dismissable. Indeed, it is her assurance that Manny is not a fag that allows her to appreciate his ability to do something beautiful. Her deliberate characterization of him as anything but a "fag" provides her the means to recuperate the beauty and gracefulness of his actions within traditional and recognizable citations of the masculine. In her mind, the beauty and the gracefulness showcased here do not mount an effeminate challenge to normative masculinity and gender roles. This is to say, despite herself, the narrator already fully understands and internalizes the gender and sexual prescriptions and proscriptions of both communities—black and white—against which she chafes for most of the narrative.

Whereas present epistemologies generally do not, this climactic self-betrayal suggests that subjection and subjectivity operate across—more so than respect—analytical partitions separating understood codes of identification in the culture and the academy. There is, however, at least one qualification of this commentary still to be made: a more judicious practice of scholarship does not necessarily presume drastic institutional restructuring *of*—but rather *at*—the current locations of cultural studies. It implies the rethinking of the type of work undertaken at institutional sites of scholarship much more so than administrative reconfigurations of departments and programs (undertakings more strongly wedded to the committed and hierarchical administrative work of institutions). It is not the existence of departments and fields such as English, African American studies, women's studies and queer theory that is so much at issue as the type of scholarly practice predominating under these rubrics. A more judicious practice would reform epistemological paradigms rather than more incidental administrative ones, highlight the fact that identities and identity studies do not exclusively concern fixed and discrete social partitionings, and reveal a more elusive cultural logic that is deeply invested in making various groups visible and divisible in the first place. What set of routine principles underwrite such intuitive partitionings? Given this line of reasoning, it would make little sense, for example, that the agenda of women's studies would entail only investigations of those gendered female, or that African American studies would attend only to the "experiences" of those understood as racially black. These fields must also explore those cultural imperatives defining these designations, as well as ascribing and maintaining their peculiar social valences. This is not to say that exactly this type of work is not already being done by a great number of critics beyond those illustrative few mentioned here, but it is to say that this type of work is not yet understood as definitive to the intellectual fields in question. It is not yet commonly understood as work essential to these fields. It is not yet commonly understood as work essential to the knowledges these disciplines hope to groom and disseminate.

The set of issues broached by "The Hammer Man" reveals that the compelling issue for radical critical thought is not at all the familiar rubrics by which it can be most easily defined. The issue, rather, is the particular type of work undertaken—work that at some level must be suspicious of the limiting categories of widespread doxa or even acute disciplinarity. Of course, these kinds of substantive conversations are always ongoing; new trajectories in critical thought routinely compromise or overwhelm established intellectual boundaries. The commerce, for instance, between women's studies and queer theory is highly productive, even as both fields remain to some extent less responsive to considerations of ethnicity / race. Of the engagement of mainstream feminist literary criticism with African American feminism, for example, the literary critic Elizabeth Abel deftly observes:

> There has been little in white feminism comparable to the detailed reconstruction of black women's literary traditions produced by Barbara Christian, Mary Helen Washington, Deborah E. McDowell, Gloria T. Hull, Nellie Y. McKay or Margaret B. Wilkerson; or to the mapping of this literature's social and discursive contexts produced by Hazel Carby, Barbara Smith, Valerie Smith, bell hooks, Michele Wallace, Audre Lorde, or June Jordan. Instead, we have tended to focus our reading on the "celebrity" texts—preeminently those by Hurston, Walker, and Morrison—rather than on "thick" descriptions of discursive contexts and have typically written articles or chapters (rather than books) representing black women's texts as literary and social paradigms of white readers and writers. In these texts we have found alternative family structures, narrative strategies, and constructions of subjectivity: alternative that is, to the cultural practices of white patriarchy, with which literature by white women has come to seem uncomfortably complicit. The implied audience for this critical venture has been white.[18]

What Abel describes, needless to say, does not constitute an earnest conflation of analytic categories.

Yet, oddly enough, the disregard of intellectual boundaries remains one of the chief characteristics of the new field of cultural studies as it has come to greatly influence the type of work Abel characterizes as well as other work; cultural studies is the "newly emergent academic discipline that redefines the boundaries delineating traditional disciplinarities. Cultural studies not only *reframes* the objects of inquiry, but constructs a broader *framework* within which to pursue alternative modes of inquiry. Cultural studies has shifted, redrawn, and sometimes even dissolved the lines demarcating conventional disciplinary boundaries."[19] It may be useful, however, for such inquiries not only to look beyond the boundaries of traditional disciplines but also to look beyond the traditional sites and boundaries of the counterknowledges (and identity studies). The emergent questions might be as overwhelming to cultural studies as those now often posed to more conventional disciplines, and while all these questions may not arise directly from "The Hammer Man," Bambara's short story is highly suggestive of what might be the purview of such inquiries. One might ask, for instance, to what extent has gender been grasped as an always fundamentally racial and heterosexist specification? In what ways has sexuality been investigated in terms of its equal reliance on indispensable racial and gendered citations? The same might be asked about the responsiveness of the governing paradigms of ethnic/racial studies to women's studies and queer theory. To what extent have these paradigms accounted for ethnicity/race as a gendered and heterosexist concept?

What new questions and answers would emerge from paying earnest attention to the undertheorized nexus of the most salient rubrics "of social and subjective being"? They might look as unfamiliar as they would be energizing. If, for instance, "the sexual emerges as the *jouissance* of exploded limits, as the ecstatic suffering into which the human organism is momentarily plunged when it is 'pressed' beyond a certain threshold of endurance," then to what degree is ethnicity/race implicitly committed or antagonistic to this self-dispersion or *jouissance*?[20] Might ethnicity/race be defined in terms of sexual congress from which all jouissance has been strictly economized and overly rationalized, even to a point of nullification? If sexuality (in any of its forms) necessarily troubles "the self [as] a practical convenience . . . promoted to the status of an ethical ideal" (Bersani 222), do gender specifications in their rationalized (though naturalized) relations to sexuality necessarily exacerbate this trouble? In what ways might race be conceived as a symptom of such trouble? In what specific ways and by what means are these varying productions of and relations to the body (implicit in race, gender, and sexuality) represented as cultural difference and produced as social inequalities?

What would it mean to investigate gay and lesbian sexuality not simply as a breach of normative gender citations but as a breach of, a challenge and antithesis to, racialization itself? What, in other words, would one discover if one investigated whether, or to what extent, the logic of homosexuality defies the premises of racialization? Judith Butler poses one question salient to such an inquiry: "How might we understand homosexuality and mis-cegenation to converge at and as the constitutive outside of a normative heterosexuality that is at once the regulation of a racially pure reproduction" (167)? Is lesbian sexuality more threatening to racialization than gay male sexuality (or vice versa)? In what ways do the performances of homosexuality as well as ethnicity/race historically explode "the rites and rights of gender function"?[21]

What are the uninterrogated commonalties of groups opposed to each other across the divide(s) of ethnicity/race, gender, or sexuality? Do opposed formations—racial blackness and whiteness, for example—share a colluded ground? In what ways, if any, do points of collusion overwhelm opposition? Phillip Brian Harper, in his probing article on media representations of the death of the broadcaster Max Robinson outlines his cultural position as follows:

> The white bourgeois cultural context in which Robinson derived his status as an authoritative figure in the mainstream news media must always keep a vigilant check on black male sexuality, which is perceived to be threatening generally (and is assisted in this task by a moralist black middle class that seeks to explode notions of black hypermasculinity). At the same time, the African-American cultural context to which Robinson appealed for his status as a paragon of black pride and self-determination embodies an ethic which pre-cludes sympathetic discussion of black male homosexuality.[22]

One might ask to what extent the claims of bourgeois subjectivity necessarily insinuate themselves into the formative grounds of ethnicity/race, gender, and sexuality—and the dissociative stances taken up along these lines. Is it productive to imagine their permutations through the figure of prolif-erating bourgeois self-disciplinarity? And one might certainly ask, as does "The Hammer Man," in what ways psychic and social economies dictated by ethnicity/race, gender, and sexuality fracture the individual subjects formed through them.

This critical trajectory clearly concerns measures of interdisciplinarity but, much more so, measures of intersectionality: attentiveness to the inexorable overlapping of the central cultural codes of identification. Even as "The Hammer Man" and its narrative structures reflect the dissociative nature of ethnicity/race, its reader is invited in extraordinary ways to see that there also emerges in the text at least a tripartite complex of subject-formation. The

positions assumed by the protagonist in resolving her crisis certainly correspond to the rubrics of ethnicity/race, sexuality, and gender, as well as the
institutional fields into which they are neatly translated by current epistemologies. She declares ethnicity/race solidarity with Manny: "Manny was
my brother at that moment and the cop was the enemy" (40); she upholds
hegemonic sexual proscriptions and allegiances: "[Manny] had just done
about the most beautiful thing a man can do and not be a fag" (42); she
surrenders to gender citations she has long repudiated: "And me and Violet
was in this very boss fashion show at the center" (42–43). Still, these three
positions considered in their co-implications do not correspond to any easily
recognized cultural or analytical rubric. Not so neatly, all three remain integral elements of the social subject (re)produced at sites of both pleasure and
terror in "The Hammer Man." By means of all these positions, the narrator is
compositely articulated as a subject. Present epistemes do not yet routinely
aspire to confront or explicate the nature and meaning of this congruence.
Even so, if the cause is inertia or blindnesses inherited from institutional (and
culturally pervasive) paradigms, then, one can imagine, as already suggested
by the work of feminists of color, that the obstacles for self-defined critical
and radical thought are far from insurmountable.

Notes

I dedicate this essay to the memory of Toni Cade Bambara. I thank Thelma Foote,
Steve Mailloux, John Carlos Rowe, and Robyn Wiegman for their insights and
conversations concerning this article.

1   Barbara Smith and Beverly Smith, "Across the Kitchen Table: A Sister to
    Sister Dialogue," in *This Bridge Called My Back: Writings by Radical Women of
    Color*, ed. Cherríe Moraga and Gloria Anzaldúa (New York: Kitchen Table,
    1983), 116.
2   Gloria Anzaldúa, "La Prieta," in *This Bridge Called My Back*, ed. Moraga and
    Anzaldúa, 205.
3   Werner Sollors, "Ethnicity," in *Critical Terms of Literary Study*, ed. Frank Len-
    tricchia and Thomas McLaughlin (Chicago: University of Chicago Press,
    1995), 288. Subsequent references are cited parenthetically in the text. In a
    move that may seem somewhat problematic, the distinction between the
    concepts *race* and *ethnicity* are for the most part collapsed in my analysis, in fact,
    much in accordance with the insights of Sollors, who writes, "What is often
    called 'race' in the modern United States is perhaps the country's most viru-
    lent ethnic factor" (289). The hope is that whatever subtleties are neglected

and whatever liabilities are incurred by this move will be compensated by the reconceptualization of these terms offered here.

4   Kendall Thomas, " 'Ain't Nothing Like the Real Thing': Black Masculinity, Gay Sexuality, and the Jargon of Authenticity," in *Representing Black Men*, ed. Marcellus Blount and George P. Cunningham (New York: Routledge, 1996), 66. Subsequent references are cited parenthetically in the text.

5   Joan W. Scott, "The Evidence of Experience," in *The Lesbian and Gay Studies Reader*, ed. Henry Abelove, Michèle Aina Barale, and David M. Halperin (New York: Routledge, 1993), 397–415. Subsequent references are cited parenthetically in the text.

6   Naomi Zack, *Race and Mixed Race* (Philadelphia: Temple University Press, 1993), 27.

7   Zack defines the one-drop rule as "the logic of an infinite regress" entailing that "[a] person is black if she has a black forebear, and that forebear was black if she had a black forebear, and so on" (19).

8   For an extended consideration of the highly consequential co-implications of racial, gendered, sexual, commercial, and moral economies in a cultural context, rather than a literary and institututional context, see my "Black Men in the Mix: Badboys, Heroes, Sequins, and Dennis Rodman," *Callaloo* 20, no. 1 (1997): 106–26.

9   Evan Watkins, *Work Time: English Departments and the Circulation of Cultural Value* (Stanford, Calif.: Stanford University Press, 1989), 24.

10 Cheryl A. Wall, "Introduction: Taking Positions and Changing Words," in *Changing Our Own Words: Essays on Criticism, Theory, and Writing by Black Women*, ed. Wall. (New Brunswick, N.J.: Rutgers University Press, 1989), 15.

11 Kim F. Hall, *Things of Darkness: Economies of Race and Gender in Early Modern England* (Ithaca, N.Y.: Cornell University Press, 1995).

12 Toni Cade Bambara, "The Hammer Man," in *Gorilla, My Love* (New York: Vintage, 1992), 39. Subsequent references are cited parenthetically in the text.

13 Judith Butler, *Bodies That Matter: On the Discursive Limits of "Sex"* (New York: Routledge, 1993), 3. Subsequent references are cited parenthetically in the text.

14 Laura Doyle, *Bordering on the Body: The Racial Matrix of Modern Fiction and Culture* (New York: Oxford University Press, 1994), 5.

15 Robyn Wiegman, *American Anatomies: Theorizing Race and Gender* (Durham, N.C.: Duke University Press, 1995), 190.

16 Michel Foucault, "Truth and Power," in *Power/Knowledge: Selected Interview and Other Writings, 1972–1977*, cd. and trans. Colin Gordon (New York: Pantheon, 1980), 119.

17 Michel Foucault, "Body/Power," in *Power/Knowledge*, 59.

18 Elizabeth Abel, "Black Writing, White Reading: Race and the Politics of Feminist Interpretation," in *Female Subjects in Black and White: Race, Psychoanalysis, Feminism*, ed. Abel, Barbara Christian, and Helene Moglen (Berkeley: University of California Press, 1997), 119.

19 Mae G. Henderson, "Introduction: Borders, Boundaries, and Frame(work)s," in *Borders, Boundaries, and Frames: Essays in Cultural Criticism and Cultural Studies*, ed. Henderson (New York: Routledge, 1995), 23.

20 Leo Bersani, "Is the Rectum a Grave?" *October* 43 (1987): 217. Subsequent references are cited parenthetically in the text.

21 Hortense Spillers, " 'The Permanent Obliquity of an In(pha)llibly Straight': In the Time of the Daughter and the Fathers," in *Changing Our Own Words*, ed. Wall, 129.

22 Phillip Brian Harper, "Eloquence and Epitaph: Black Nationalism and the Homophobic Impulse in Responses to the Death of Max Robinson," in *The Lesbian and Gay Studies Reader*, ed. Abelove, Barale, and Halperin, 165.

Hemispheric Vertigo

CUBA, QUEBEC, AND OTHER PROVISIONAL

RECONFIGURATIONS OF "OUR" NEW AMERICA(S)

Ricardo L. Ortíz

In the same way that . . . transnationalism can be mobilized by the state in the interest of properly nationalist ends, so too can the psychic imaginary—in even its most individuated and privatized instantiations—negotiate the terms of trans-nationalism so as to solidify the identification of the individual "citizen" with the national entity whose hegemony transnationalism itself has been understood to challenge. . . . State-ideological functions can never be conceived apart from the citizen-subjects whose activities and consciousness they call into being, which themselves certainly have not been unmoored from the imperatives of modern state-nationalism. The exact character of the relation between the two, though, is anything but predictable or definitively fixed. . . . It remains crucial to study the contingent factors in any given instance of that relation, since in doing so we might at least achieve some understanding of the means by which ideological functions condition our experiences in everyday life, which otherwise would ap-pear as either completely natural or thoroughly intelligible to "common sense." This seems to me a primary task of American Studies.—Phillip Brian Harper, *Private Affairs*

Going Up to Go Down, Going North to Go South

"Pleasure" would almost always be my response to the question, "And what is your purpose in visiting Montreal?" posed to me by Canadian border guards whenever I crossed into Quebec from Vermont, at the checkpoint where U.S. Interstate 89 became the much smaller Canadian rural highway #133. Having left the San Francisco Bay Area in 1996 to take a teaching job at Dartmouth College in New Hampshire, I spent the following two years rather unsuccessfully trying to adjust to life in a remote New England town;

part of that process entailed frequent visits to more cosmopolitan nearby settings, especially Montreal, which, though an hour further away from Dartmouth than Boston, offered an infinitely more seductive, and satisfying, set of cultural and recreational opportunities to me. While both Boston and Montreal boasted thriving gay communities, and while both certainly exhibited the growing influence of the Latin American diaspora through the very visible, and audible, presence of Spanish-speakers on their streets and in their neighborhoods, Montreal clearly offered a more fascinating and in many ways even intellectually challenging intersection of these sexual and transnational cultures, an intersection further complicated by the presence of Québecois cultural and Canadian national elements in the same scene.

Crossing the border into Quebec was always informed for me by two associations I could never quite divorce from the act: one was always occasioned by a road sign just below the checkpoint that, rather than informing travelers that they are just about to enter Canada, announces instead that they are just crossing the latitudinal line marking the halfway point between the Equator and the North Pole; the other, less tangible but by no means less bewildering, had to do with my own set of memories of past border crossings at an analogous geographical site, the United States/Mexico border at Calexico/Mexicali where, in the course of the 1970s, my family found themselves as they traveled back and forth from suburban Los Angeles, where we lived, to San Felipe, a fishing village and beach town on the Gulf Coast of Baja California. Both associations triggered intense cognitive dislocations, one spatial and the other temporal, but both were also necessarily, and significantly, informed by geographical and historical contexts overlaying, and overwhelming, the presumably more neutral vectors of space and time. Knowing, for example, that the Canadian border marked some halfway point between Ecuador and the Arctic, that as many latitudinal zones crossed Canada as crossed not only the United States and Mexico, but also crossed all of Central and a good portion of South America, not only sparked (thanks to my admitted ignorance of geography) a new respect for the dimensions of the Canadian land mass, but also demanded some serious reconsideration of the presumably descriptive functions of such geographical categories as hemispheres, continents, and regions, especially as they underwrite, in terms of their fictive correspondence to, political, cultural, and other symbolically constituted spaces as nations, states, and even communities.

But if my frequent confrontation of this road sign left me feeling unmapped or remapped in primarily spatial ways, by making me think, as I traveled literally "up" the map, of all that lay to the south (or "below"), my equally frequent, mostly cursory, encounters with border guards plunged me back into my own personal and political past, raising familiar but distant ghosts I never expected to revisit in a place so putatively far from home. My family left Cuba in 1966, when I was five years old, and settled in a working-class neighborhood of Los Angeles County; like many Cuban exiles of their generation, my parents took their time about securing permanent resident status, and certainly citizenship, for us, primarily to indulge the fantasy of returning home to Cuba once Fidel Castro was deposed and his revolution discredited. But by the mid-1970s it became clear that exile would be a longer-term condition than they'd hoped; they gave up the ghost of imminent return, and we became resident aliens. Green cards in hand, my family immediately began driving to Mexico on every possible occasion, as many Cubans in southern California did, both to enjoy the familiarity of Mexico's Latino culture and to enjoy the beaches of the Gulf of California, whose waters, unlike the Pacific's, were warm and reminded them of the Caribbean. But even with proper documentation border crossings were never easy for us, thanks primarily to our coloring, our surname, and my parents' very audible "Spanish" accents; so crossing into Mexico was one thing, but crossing back over to the United States always left us with a feeling of profound illegitimacy. Guests in both the country we lived in and the country we visited, getting back over from the latter to the former always left us feeling at best provisionally situated, not quite at home in either place; perhaps least and most at home at the border itself, where U.S. border guards in particular never failed to be suspicious of the documentation we so readily presented to them, and rarely failed to have us pull over for more thorough searches of our car, and more thorough investigations of our history and our motives for travel.

Crossing into and out of Canada in the period that I lived in New England visited these feelings of illegitimacy back on me in surprising ways; a U.S. citizen since 1983 and a frequent traveler to Europe in the course of my well-financed graduate school days, I thought myself rather worldly and, well, accustomed to the ritual of customs. My sense of unease at this particular border, however, had less to do with my (certainly by now more stabilized) political status and more to do with my sexual status; oftentimes my primary if not exclusive purpose in traveling to Montreal was to immerse myself in the familiarity of the queer urban cultural environment of the city's Village district, a neighborhood that, while very uniquely Québecois in many of its qualities, certainly bears many of the qualities of North American queer, and especially male, culture generally, and quite visibly. My response to the Canadian border guards seemed, to me, the appropriate one: "Pleasure" was for me in part a coded but for that reason no less directly truthful way of saying "Because I'm queer." But the pleasures available to me in Montreal were never simply, or even exclusively, defined by its sexual cultures; whatever unease I felt about disclosing myself, even indirectly, as a sexual tourist to these representatives of Canadian state authority was always counteracted by my equally strong, and in some ways more legitimate feeling, desire to immerse myself in a Latin(o) culture, and one not simply defined by the francophonic elements of Québecois culture, but also by the obvious presence of hispanophone, "Latin" Americans in significant numbers, and hailing from a variety of nations, on the same streets.

I begin this collection of observations with the juxtaposition of the epigraph quoting Phillip Harper's extraordinary conclusion to his most thoughtful essay with my own selection of highly personal anecdotes to underscore the tension Harper so usefully elaborates in that passage. Much of Harper's own argument in "Take Me Home" disorients itself around the affective quality produced so often—especially for those of us Harper describes as "non-normative citizens" marked in a variety of visible if not interchangeable ways by disadvantageous social and other differences—by the new opportunities for border-crossing mobility enabled in part by the "new" transnationalism Harper mostly takes to task in that essay.[1] I hope in the following sections of this discussion to refine the edge of productive critical tension that Harper has begun to hone in "Take Me Home" by offering a series of events, of varying levels of public notoriety, each of which offers in turn an example of what I take to be the challenge the new and highly paradoxical transnationalism poses for North American culture critics, especially for those committed in their work to a liberatory politics, one which tends largely to assume that some (though not just any) transcendence of the authority and power of the nation-state is not only desirable but necessary to the fulfillment of their project. As I juxtapose here localized and often quite ephemeral occurrences with the more generalized analytic they occasion, I remain aware of the necessarily uneasy passage from the local to the general (which is not identical to the trip some take far too easily from the local to the global) which trails such moves, regardless of the clarity or precision of their mapping. That unease I here rename the malaise produced by the vertiginous counterflows against which contemporary transnational subjects must navigate to get virtually (and certainly actually!) anywhere.[2]

Global Gloria

"Latin America" is one of the earliest of the world regional designations, dating back to the middle of the nineteenth century . . . originally defined by military strategists, and our conceptualization of it still bears the taint of imperial thinking. . . . Latin America was deliberately coined by French scholars in the middle of the nineteenth century as a way to refer simultaneously to the Spanish-, Portuguese-, and French-speaking portions of the Americas. At the time, the French government under Napoleon III was plotting to carve out a new empire in the region, and the notion of a "Latin" essence linking French- with Spanish- and Portuguese-speaking American countries had a great appeal as a way to naturalize such a project. . . . by disinterested criteria this "Latin" region of the French imperial imagination never made sense; certainly Haitians have less in common with residents of Argentina than with neighboring Jamaicans, . . . strictly speaking, a linguistic definition would mean that Québec, too, ought to be considered part of Latin America.—Martin W. Lewis and Kären E. Wigen, *The Myth of Continents*

If any one event could serve as the paradigm for my encounter with Latin America, and Latin Americans, in Montreal, it would have to be the evening of September 4, 1996, when I saw Gloria Estefan in concert at Montreal's Molson Center. Part of her *Evolution* world tour, the concert was designed to promote *Destiny*, which was at the time Estefan's first English-language album of original compositions in five years, and that was released in conjunction with Estefan's recording of "Reach," one of the two official anthems of the 1996 Atlanta Olympic Games. It bears mentioning here that the other official anthemic diva of those games was Céline Dion. One can only second-guess the strategy that went into choosing these two singers to represent this particular Olympic moment: while both sing primarily in English now, English is neither one's first language, and while together Estefan and Dion can be said to embody something of a larger "American" inter- or even transnationalism, they only achieve this status by downplaying their specific national, cultural, and linguistic origins, origins which in both their cases situate them in contexts (Cuban, Québecois) where nationalism itself remains not simply contested, but radically, constitutively, undecidable. It also bears mentioning here that Estefan's two Spanish-language albums preceding *Destiny*, *Mi Tierra* [My country] and *Abriendo Puertas* [Opening doors] performed a characteristically Latin American double gesture for these post–Cold War, postcolonial times: while the first celebrates Estefan's specifically Cuban national roots in both the lyrical content and musical forms of most of the songs, the second opens out to include forms indigenous across the rest of Latin America and the Caribbean, and it celebrates in its lyrics a pan-Latinism on the basis of language and culture meant to counteract divisions among nations based on geography, politics, and economics. Both of these Spanish-language albums enjoyed considerably more crossover appeal than Estefan and the Miami Sound Machine's earliest recordings in Spanish because they followed the extraordinary success of her English-language recordings from the mid-1980s on.[3]

So when Estefan invaded Dion's home turf in the late summer of 1996, she came armed with a more varied repertoire than she might have been able to perform at any other time in her career. This in part explains why, for an audience whose members spoke primarily French and/or English, Estefan felt comfortable singing more Spanish-language songs, but also why she gave that audience the choice of having her conduct her banter with them either in Spanish or in English. The audience very volubly, and perhaps predictably, chose Spanish. In the liner notes to *Destiny*, Estefan explicitly describes the project underway in her most recent albums as a "bicultural" endeavor; but given that certainly more than two languages, and more than two cultures, were at play at the Molson Center that evening, the decision to contextualize the music, and to connect directly with her audience, in Spanish did more than reinforce anything like a simple biculturalism in Estefan's work. While certainly a significant number of Canadian Latinos were in attendance that evening, one must presume that the majority of people there had requested that the performer communicate to them in a language they did not understand. While this gesture could be read as an affirmation (or perhaps even fetishization) of the performer's Cuban, and hispanophone, roots, it could also be read as a refusal, one which she actively invited, of her equally strong, though perhaps not equally authenticating, North American and anglophone orientation.

As such, the gesture can also be read doubly as an affirmation and refusal of the various forms of nationalism and national identity circulating in this complex performative space; the cultural and linguistic collusion between performer and audience here produces in effect the de- and reconstruction of the national simultaneously by sacrificing in part an anglophonia that represents not only the presence of the United States and its increasingly global cultural and economic reach, but also the dominance of English as Canada's majority language. By asking Estefan, admittedly at her own behest, to address it in Spanish, this Québecois audience agreed, in effect, to collaborate with her in an elaborate fiction, one predicated on an active, willful denial or forgetting of the actual national configuration defining the moment in favor of an imagined, desired Latin transnation where francophones and hispanophones could, impossibly, communicate with one another without or beyond translation. The collective psychic dynamic operating in this gesture might locate for us the place where, for better or worse, resistance meets repression, where what we take as ideology meets what we suspect to be unconscious in a complex ineraction whose effects are not always predictable, legible, or coherent; one has only to consider the effect on audience members of hearing nonetheless in a Spanish they literally do not understand a message, an articulation, of a desire for some alternative world order that is at once political, cultural, and linguistic.

To render this analysis in more practical, tangible terms, one has only to isolate two gestures in Estefan's performance most directly symptomatic of the paradoxical (il)logics of the inter-, trans- and even just national forces at work, and at play, at the Molson Center that evening. Perhaps the most dramatic, theatrical, moment in the show came when, near its end, Estefan stepped into a spherical cage studded with mirrored tiles, a kind of hollowed-out disco ball, and glided over her audience with the help of wires and pulleys; a gutsy move, to be sure, for a performer who'd famously suffered a serious back injury some years before. But also a punning, and cunning, elaboration of the promises and pitfalls of the too fragile pleasures of a transcendent globalism: as go-go girl Gloria cha-cha'd over her rapt audience, the globe serving as her stage alternately remained transparent, exposing the performer's body within, or blinded that audience at moments when the lights hit the mirrored bars at strategic angles. The literally visual interplay of blindness and insight during this number (the song was the up-tempo "Higher") enjoyed its conceptual analogue in the performance of Estefan's most recognizable Spanish-language anthem, "Mi Tierra," that, for all its explicitly and exclusively Cuban lyrical references, can easily serve as a kind of gestalt of the nation, seemingly anyone's nation, in the opportunity it offers to any audience to celebrate their land simultaneously with Estefan's celebration of hers. With the "Mi Tierra" number, Montreal's Molson Center exploded into its giddiest moment of mass *jouissance* that night; audience members waved the flags of various Latin American nations, representing in part Montreal's own various Latino communities, and in general it was impossible not to take into account how a song like "Mi Tierra" not only would, but must, play in Quebec, whose recent history could be measured by the string of failed plebiscites on the question of national autonomy.

Thus Estefan's performance, on that night and in that place, and presumably on other nights and in other places scattered around the world, reflected, perhaps even asserted, the proposition that a certain transcendent cultural globalism (set to a seductive world music to which so many of us would like to dance) can, for all practical consideration, barely disguise its predication on the very conventional, traditional political and economic nationalisms it so explicitly, and evocatively, desires either to sublate or to overcome. At best, one can only temporarily, and unsuccessfully, repress the other, a point most eloquently made in and by the name of the venue where Estefan's intoxicatingly (and intoxicatedly) transnational, translational jamboree situated itself. Montreal's Molson Center names precisely the event's underwriting by an ever expanding multinational corporation whose prominence in one of a growing number of transnational industries, and international markets, reflects as precisely the complex infrastructural forces that only cynically, and opportunistically, invoke the same nationalism so sentimentally serenaded by Estefan and celebrated by her fans.

Nuestramerica.com: A Historical Aside and a Note on Martí

The geography of social life in the late twentieth century has outgrown not only the particular contours of the postwar world map, but also the very conventions by which we represent spatial patterns in image and text. The cultural territories once confidently mapped by anthropologists are increasingly being crosscut and redefined, by the convulsions of peacetime mobility as well as those of war. Historical border zones in particular have acquired unexpected prominence as sites of cultural innovation. . . . the accelerating diaspora of merchants, migrants, and refugees around the world has jostled peoples together, not only along traditional boundary zones, but deep within every major historical region as well. . . . local conceptions of macro-level identity are mutating rapidly . . . [thus requiring] a new sociospatial lexicon capable of analyzing and representing such developments.—Martin W. Lewis and Kären E. Wigen

In the Fall/Winter 1998 issue of its newsletter, *Cuban Affairs*, the liberal, pro-dialogue Washington- and Miami-based Cuban Committee for Democracy reported that "Ambassador Peter Boehm, Canada's representative to the Organization of American States, delivered the keynote address" at the CCD's annual banquet, where his "message of engaging Cuba in contrast to U.S. policy of isolating the island was well received by . . . the audience." Boehm, reportedly "the first Canadian official ever to speak to Cuban Americans in Miami," symbolized in his very presence before such an audience in this particular city the bewildering rate at which changes in the complexity of the political, economic, and even cultural vectors on the North American scene continue to accelerate, oftentimes more quickly than one might imagine, given their failure to register meaningfully on the popular consciousness in the United States, to say nothing of official U.S. policy toward Cuba.[4] Canada has come to provide, in its remarkably open attitude toward economic and political engagement with Cuba's revolutionary government, a viable alternative model for the imagination of a progressive reconfiguration of North American systems of not only political and economic, but also cultural exchange that orients itself along admittedly incongruous axes defined by not only Ottawa and Havana, but also Montreal and Miami. These axes not only sidestep Washington altogether, but in including Miami and Montreal, themselves important stages of American cultural operations, also reflect the significant generational shift in attitudes toward United States/Cuba relations among Cuban Americans in the core exile community. This shift in part explains the vocally anti-Castro Estefan's willingness to play in a nation with such open ties to Castro's government.

At the same time that the CCD newsletter reported on Ambassador Boehm's talk, *Hemisphere*, published by Florida International University's Latin American and Caribbean Studies Center, reported on Canada's evolving role in determining economic policy across the Americas. In his article, "Canada's Southern Exposure," Canadian political scientist Peter McKenna devoted considerable space in what was primarily a report on Canada's "active role at the April 1998 Summit of the Americas in Santiago, Chile" to Canada's critical relation to Cuba. Canada, McKenna reports, has recently "become Cuba's largest trading partner and greatest source of foreign investment," and Canadians, he adds, "also rank first in terms of hard-currency carrying tourists to the country." That some, admittedly more progressive, Cuban American institutions should begin turning to Canada for a different perspective on, perhaps a different paradigm for, Cuban/American relations, bodes well perhaps for a broadly perceived Cuban/American future, if only in that it offers some alternative to the chokehold that the United States–led trade embargo, and Fidel Castro's intransigence in the face of it, have had on imagining anything positive in store for a more exclusively U.S./Cuban future. Commenting on Canadian Prime Minister Chrétien's controversial visit to Cuba in the same month as the Santiago summit, McKenna observes that, while "the visit allowed Canada to reaffirm its economic relationship with Cuba before the U.S. embargo is rescinded," it also allowed Cuba to "underscore the antiquated and absurd nature of U.S. policy toward the island."[5]

Canada's very recent emergence on the Latin American, and specifically Cuban American, scene also begins to correct a certain geographical, and geopolitical, myopia emanating from the south, and perhaps originating in part from an analysis of hemispheric relations dating back as far as, but also as recently influential as, José Martí's famed essay of 1891, "Nuestra América." In the course of his argument in "Our America," Martí develops both a historical analysis and a future vision involving what he considered the two great partners in Western hemispheric relations: Latin America, the "Our" America Martí saw emerging from the night of Spanish and Portuguese colonial rule to take its place as a conglomeration of politically autonomous states but profoundly interrelated cultures on the political stage alongside, and on an equal footing with, something he calls "North America," the other term completing what Martí calls "the two halves of the continent." But all the qualities that Martí ascribes to this "North America" more than suggest that he means exclusively the United States. His North America is populated by "an enterprising and vigorous people, who scorn and ignore Our America," a people he later terms "vindictive and sordid masses" favoring only their nation's "tradition of expansion" in foreign policy. Martí concludes this passage by admonishing that "its good name as a Republic in the eyes of the world's perceptive nations puts upon North America a restraint that cannot be taken away by childish discords among our American nations."[6] Martí's own perception here leaves, perhaps, something to be desired; the willful absenting of Canada from the geopolitical scene as constituted in and by Martí's rhetoric must certainly be pressed beyond its semantic and geographical inaccuracies in order to underscore a dangerous and willful self-blinding.[7]

Rhetorically at least, Martí's conflation of the United States with North America may reflect nothing more than his desire, a desire shared by many of us still, to correct and critique the United States's willful (and ongoing) identification of itself as, simply, "America." But this is, of course, as easily accomplished by referring to the United States as, well, the United States. Of course, in 1891, conflating the United States and North America may only have reflected something of Canada's actual relative irrelevance to the scene of hemispheric politics, at least as it was perceived by Martí. In either case, such a proposition certainly can no longer hold, and, in turn, neither should the inaccurate, if still strategic, rhetorical uses to which the term *North America* is put when it only, however critically, renames the United States. Finally, I do not mean to call here for any redeployment of *North America* as an umbrella term collapsing into itself the United States and Canada, or even the three nations making up the North America of the infamous Free Trade Agreement. I only mean here to point out the partial responsibility of one eminent Latin American writer in the conventional absenting of Canada from certain powerfully imagined, and powerfully strategic, configurations of continental and hemispheric space, and of the political exchanges possible within them, through the course of the twentieth century.

It may bemuse us to discover that we still need to work to imagine Canada *in* North America, let alone to imagine, meaningfully, a Canada *in* Latin America. But more than either of these crucial realities of the late twentieth century, it might have bemused Martí even more to discover that, of all the emerging Latino communities in the major cosmopolitan cities of this newly reconfigured North America, the one which honors him with a major Web site is Montreal's: Nuestramerica.com, a primarily Spanish-language clearinghouse of information about resources available and cultural events of interest to Montreal's growing Latino population, offers me the opportunity to assert the following truth about movement through at least cultural and virtual spaces in this new *América*: especially from outside Canada, anyone navigating through the Web to reach nuestramerica will have to go, at least by typing the ".ca" abbreviation in its URL, significantly, symbolically, "through" Canada.

Postscript

As recently as October 1999, when U.S. President Bill Clinton visited Canada to dedicate the new U.S. embassy in Ottawa, more reminders emerged of Canada's actual place in all or any of the Americas at play in this discussion. Addressing specifically the question of Quebec's sovereignty at an international conference on federalism held at a resort in the province, President

Clinton had these thoughts to share with his audience: "The suggestion that people of a given ethnic group or tribe or religion can only have a meaningful existence if they have their own independent nation is a questionable assertion. . . . The momentum of history," he added, "is toward political integration, not disintegration."[8] While on its face President Clinton's statement may hint at something of a salutary transculturalism at least in his vision of the relation between cultural and political entities, one must hear in such statements the hum of the globalizing economic machine that is in a sense not only underwriting, but enjoining, this expanding integration. As in the scene I described of Gloria Estefan's concert, one can argue ad infinitum, ad nauseam if it was a "good" night for Cubans, or for Québecois, or even for Canadians or Americans, but it was undeniably a good night for Molson and for Sony (Estefan's label). Also, and in closing, one has only to imagine President Clinton making the same seemingly benign, but ultimately deeply patronizing, speech in Chiapas, or in Peru, or in Puerto Rico, to understand just how emphatically in Latin America the North American popular imaginary actually supposes Quebec, and indeed all of Canada, to be.

Notes

1   Phillip Brian Harper, "'Take Me Home': Location Identity, Transnational Exchange," in *Private Affairs: Critical Ventures in the Culture of Social Relations* (New York: New York University Press, 1999), 125–54. The "funny" chance encounter Harper recounts having in Toronto produces in him feelings he later describes in far more general but consistent terms as "the disorientation characterizing the transnational imaginary in the era of global capitalism" (130) and, later (quoting Gloria Anzaldúa), "the subjective discomfort that marks life in the borderlands" (131).

2   The unease I'll insist on maintaining across these remarks emanates in part from the numerous disciplinary dislocations I feel as I make them; what follows in my reading of a concert by Gloria Estefan, which I attended in Montreal soon after arriving in New England, certainly resonates with "queer" possibilities that I do not take up. A reading of this concert within the disciplinary contexts of queer and performance studies will remain, I'm afraid, to be done, deferred in favor of the transnational/translational reading it more immediately compelled. I do not want, however, to pass up the opportunity here to acknowledge at least the promise of productively queer effects embedded in such a reading, especially one that insists on my more evanescent memory of the concert in Montreal with its complex trilingual interplay, than the more conventionally archived version recorded in Miami weeks later. For a valuable analysis of the relation queer critique must have to the ephemeral register of performance, see

José Esteban Muñoz's introductory essay, "Ephemera as Evidence: Introductory Notes to Queer Acts," *Women and Performance* no. 16 (1996): 5–16.

3 Still the most useful critical account of Estefan and the Miami Sound Machine's work is Gustavo Pérez Firmat's, in "A Salsa for All Seasons," chapter 4 of *Life on the Hyphen: The Cuban-American Way* (Austin: University of Texas Press, 1994), esp. 125–33. Estefan performed the *Evolution* concert in Miami for "live" transmission on HBO just weeks after her appearance in Montreal; HBO, Sony, and Estefan Enterprises coproduced and distributed for sale a videotape with the same title (1996). Remarkable for many reasons, the taped performance begins with Estefan exclaiming her pleasure to be "home" in Miami ("There's no place like home!"), and, needless to say, for the benefit of the "audience at home," she kept mostly to English in her banter at the Miami Arena.

4 Silvia Wilhelm, "The Miami Report," *Cuban Affairs* 4, no. 3–4 (1998): 8.

5 Peter McKenna, "Canada's Southern Exposure," *Hemisphere* 8, no. 3 (1998): 26–29.

6 José Martí, "Our America," in *The José Martí Reader: Writings on the Americas,* ed. Deborah Schnookal and Mirta Muñiz (New York: Ocean, 1999), 118. This is the most recent English translation to appear. A thoughtful discussion of Martí's legacy in very recent U.S. and Western hemispheric transnational and postcolonial studies appears in Hortense J. Spillers's essay "Who Cuts the Borders? Some Readings on 'America,'" which introduces the collection *Comparative American Identities: Race, Sex, and Nationality in the Modern Text,* ed. Spillers (New York: Routledge, 1991), esp. 1–3. That collection also features a fascinating essay by Robert Schwarzwald ("Fear of Féderasty: Québec's Inverted Fictions") with a more than tangential relevance to the discussion I conduct here, especially in the first section, regarding the intricate relation of national to sexual subjectivity.

7 My admittedly cautious and modest disloyalty to Martí feels as anxious as it is necessary; Canada may only have come into being as a nation-state some decades before Martí penned "Our America," but the significance of its role in determining the contours of North America should not have been discounted then and must not be discounted now, especially by those of us practicing the disciplines of either American or U.S. Latino studies. Merely to take up the dialectic between "Our" and "North" America as both imagined and instituted by Martí in that essay exercises the worst kind of countercritical disciplinary mimicry. I thus invoke here Robyn Wiegman's concluding argument in *American Anatomies: Theorizing Race and Gender* (Durham, N.C.: Duke University Press, 1995), 201–2, concerning the "alchemical" productions of her own respectful, critical disloyalties to feminism in fashioning my own disloyalties to the orthodoxies of the disciplines I mostly implicitly claim here.

8 Steven Pearlstein, "Clinton Declares Québec Better Off in Canada," *Washington Post,* 9 October 1999. A year later Pearlstein also reported on the current debate in Canada about the nation's very future as a united confederation; according to Pearlstein, "perhaps no nation feels the effects" of globalization

"more keenly, or is more threatened by them," than Canada. Pearlstein, "O, Canada! A National Swan Song?" *Washington Post*, 5 September 2000. To balance Pearlstein's account of the external forces compromising Canadian national identity, see Michael Ignatieff's account of Québecois nationalism's internally negative effects on the cohesion of the confederation in chapter 6, "Québec," of his *Blood and Belonging: Journeys into the New Nationalism* (New York: Noonday, 1993), esp. 143–63.

Marriage as Treason

POLYGAMY, NATION, AND THE NOVEL

Nancy Bentley

Genres, like people, make assumptions, and the genre of the domestic novel carries in its very bones three related assumptions: that sex requires female consent; that marriage means monogamy (a union of only two people); and that the modern nation is most like the family or home, a place of filial belonging. The possibility of polygamy disturbs all three of these convictions and the novel has never tolerated it, even while other forms of writing in the West (speculative theology, political economy) entertained the idea of polygamy's legitimacy well into the nineteenth century. For Richardson's *Pamela* and Brontë's *Jane Eyre*, for instance, the threat of polygamy unveils an otherwise unseen vulnerability in the power of female consent, a woman's right to contract her own sexual arrangements in an exclusive marriage. When Mr. B., now Pamela's husband, teases her that he will exercise the "prerogative" of practicing polygamy enjoyed by husbands in other lands, Pamela responds, "Polygamy and prerogative! Two very bad words!" Certainly Jane Eyre, after her near miss with bigamy, would have agreed with this domestic credo. And for both Pamela and Jane, the specter of polygamy not only threatens the fundamental ground of consent, it also hints at affiliations that could link the British home with something extra-national, with a territory outside "the laws of one's own country," as Mr. B. puts it. For both women, polygamy calls up vague sexual and marital connections to an imperial hinterland. Once conjured, these disturbing imperial relations make the conceptual boundaries of both the household and the homeland shift in disconcerting ways, until home and nation no longer seem mutually defining. Within the precincts of the novel, then, we could say polygamy is like Bertha: the Other as the other woman who could turn out to be part of your own home.[1]

Bigamy and polygamy may seem like eccentric transgressions for the genre of the domestic novel, and they are. But as these brief glimpses begin to suggest, polygamy holds a marginal but nevertheless structurally important place in the history of the genre. Within the imagined universe of the domestic novel, the idea of polygamy or bigamy represents a greater disturbance to bourgeois marriage than even the most flagrant adultery: adultery breaks the marriage contract, but the specter of polygamy hints that marriage may not really be a contract after all, that free consent in marriage could be an illusion. In these kinds of fleeting allusions to patriarchal polygamy and stories of wives hoodwinked into bigamy, the domestic novel located an exotic reminder of the "barbaric" household that middle-class domesticity was confident it had surpassed. At the same time, even invoking such traces could unsettle the novel's habit of imagining the bourgeois home as the center and source of natural law. For the domestic novel, polygamy could not be a form of marriage (as it was for contemporary anthropology and imperial exploration narratives). Polygamy instead marked the defining limit for marriage, a limit that made marriage coterminous with monogamy, with female consent, and with the securities of law and national feeling.

Of course, polygamy was also, then, a subject that could unbind these mutually terminating concepts. For the novel, the historical appearance of polygamy among the "family of white nations" represented a fundamental shock to the system. Mormon polygamy, practiced openly after 1852 in the U.S. Territory of Utah, threatened to rupture the domestic novel's way of imagining an ideal conjoining of womanhood, family, and nation. The specter of white women apparently choosing to enter polygamous marriages confounded fundamental beliefs of the novel-reading public. As a result, many authors—largely women—were prompted to write passionate anti-polygamy novels as part of a broader national reform movement. In these novels writers confront not only a vexing controversy, Utah polygamy, they can also be said to confront their own genre and its sedimented ideas about female consent, domestic love, and national belonging.

Not everyone, it should be noted, regarded Mormon polygamy as a looming national crisis. Some writers regarded the matter with mere curiosity or indifference, even humor. Artemus Ward and Mark Twain, for instance, found the spectacle of Utah polygamy less a national emergency than a Western mother lode to be mined for derisive quips and racy or misogynous sketches. Still others, though troubled by plural marriage, fretted about any governmental interference in household sovereignty. And most nineteenth-century Mormons, of course, believed their "celestial marriage" a key to the country's redemption, not its destruction. But, in an especially telling episode in the history of what scholars have come to call domestic sentimentalism, such counterviews eventually lost their purchase. The struggle against Mormon plural marriage proved that relatively recent ideas about domesticity had become fundamental, not incidental, to U.S. national symbology. This essay examines the links between marriage and nationhood that made polygamy imaginable—and indeed punishable—as a form of treason, the kind of crime against the republic that regicide is against a monarchy. In the end, anti-polygamy writers established a new common sense: to tolerate such a redefining of "home" meant perforce the undoing of the national polity. "Nothing has cast so great a doubt over the future of this country," wrote one female author, "as the Mormon plague spot." If the government showed a "fatal indifference" to polygamy, wrote another, it "shall have substituted a Mormon saint for Liberty's statue, and wiped out this we proudly call the great republic." This imagined anti-icon, a national Statue of Polygamy, shows just how literally plural marriage was, as one writer put it, a "simply monumental" affront to national meaning.[2]

In telling the history of this sentiment, I shall be tracing the way novelists and lawmakers made polygamy a defining limit of national identity, a move that helped to give American nationalism the structure of a domestic novel. Through the crisis of polygamy, the unity of an American people was explicitly identified with shared family feeling. The currency of domestic fiction—sympathy, communal aversions, the binding knowledge of intimate betrayal and suffering—was converted into political currency, as the court rulings on polygamy cases wed sentimental discourse to national law. The polygamy crisis was pivotal in reimagining the nation as, in Lauren Berlant's words, a "state of feeling." Through this crisis, the interiority of one's affective life, intimacies scripted in novels around heterosexual marriage, emerged as a basic criterion of national identity—indeed, as a literal requirement for statehood: Utah was denied admission to the Union until it admitted the heart truths of the domestic novel.

For all its power to vex, then, the scandal of polygamy was a boon for sentimentalism. The history of antipolygamy is largely a story of sentimentalism's success, of its forcefulness—that is, a story of the power of the sentimentalist project to change people's minds and to redirect the force of law. A metonymy for the "bad word" of male prerogative, polygamy allowed domestic writers to stage the last stand of unreconstructed patriarchy. The defeat of polygamy thus made good on sentimentalists' critique of patriarchal familialism and ushered in measurable advances for women. But this success was not without its costs. Sentimentalism succeeded only by doing damage to what was also its most powerful if equivocal resource: its faith in female consent, in the transformative ability of consent in marriage to make or unmake a new world. It could be said that contemporary feminism has inherited this damage, in the form of radical suspicion of consent as a hollow civil agency.[3] The suspicion is not without good reason, of course. But if the archive of sentimentalist texts rightly invites our doubt about the civil effects of consent, I wish to argue that this archive also holds a potential history through which to recover a more canny and historicized concept of consent, a consent that is at once more constrained and less illusory than its divided theorists have painted it. The archive holds, that is, what antipolygamist novelists could not bring themselves to recognize: a notion of consent that allowed subjects like women not self-sovereignty but a self-subjecting that could direct desire into the creation of alternative worlds.

Slavery, Consent, and Nuptial Insanity

Beginning at mid-century, the polygamy or "plural marriage" practiced openly by Mormons in the Territory of Utah received widespread publicity.[4] The news created a public consternation that lasted for more than five decades. Though the Mormon population was small, their desert city remote, very quickly polygamy was perceived as a national problem, an urgent threat to the state and a danger to millions of American families. Abolishing polygamy became a major plank in the platform of the new Republican Party, and eventually Democrats were no more willing to tolerate it than Republicans. Five successive U.S. presidents denounced the practice in major addresses to the state. The organized reform movement that devoted itself to eradicating polygamy is little remembered today, but historian Sarah Barringer Gordon counts it as possibly the "single most successful nineteenth-century political and legal reform campaign."[5] Activists published a newspaper, *The Anti-Polygamy Standard*, and organized mass demonstrations; one rally in Chicago drew 12,000 participants. According to one estimation, at the height of the opposition over 10,000 antipolygamy meetings were held within a six-month period.[6] Probably the most important force in this grassroots movement, however, was the antipolygamy novel, a popular subgenre that produced upwards of a hundred titles, a number of them bestsellers.

As envisioned by novelists, Utah polygamy resurrected the primal American drama of violent captivity. Antipolygamy novels offered readers innumerable variations on the theme of female bondage. In these pages, almost all women in polygamous unions are coerced into marriage in one way or another, forced to reconstitute on American soil the "harems" of "Oriental concubines, in which the women were near-slaves." Cornelia Paddock's *The Fate of Madame La Tour: A Tale of Great Salt Lake* (1881), which sold over 100,000 copies, begins with Brigham Young blackmailing the widow La Tour into coming to Utah by engineering the abduction of her daughter Louise. The crime is a prelude to every imaginable form of coercion imposed on women in order to enforce or protect Utah polygamy. Before the novel is finished, the story exposes a world of adultery, espionage, blood oaths, secret police, and murders by men who "take life with unheard-of refinements of cruelty."[7]

The pathos and extravagant violence in these novels have led earlier critics to dismiss antipolygamy fiction as a species of Victorian sensationalism feigning the respectability of reform. In an age of repression, critics charged, polygamy stories offered sexual titillation behind the cover of moral indignation and bloodletting detailed in the name of righteous exposure.[8] These novels make an aggressive appeal to affect, to be sure. But the designs on readers' feelings are in fact evidence of political intent. As lurid as it is, antipolygamy fiction cannot be understood apart from its place in a serious reform movement, just as the main currents of nineteenth-century American reform, from abolition to temperance, cannot be understood in isolation from a pervasive cultural poetics of melodrama whose excesses of feeling and of violent spectacle are the very marks of political meaning.

In the 1850s, there was no more politically freighted image than the "scourged body of the bondswoman." As historian Amy Dru Stanley has shown, this antislavery icon, a visual and textual motif in countless documents, helped make the slave woman's dispossession figure a notion of bondage that would resonate far beyond the politics of U.S. slavery—indeed, would partly occlude those politics. "Dishonored, stripped bare, the bondswoman literally embodied the denial of property in the self," Stanley observes, an image that "sanctified, by negation, the ideal of self ownership as the essence of freedom." At once embodied in the conspicuousness of black flesh and abstracted as metaphor, a half-literal conception of bondage eventually circulated widely in debates about wage labor, prostitution, marriage, and divorce.[9] Within the tradition of reformist poetics in the United States, bondage was both sexual and political, its politics gathering affective meaning through sensational evocations of lust-driven abuse and violence.

Yet these evocations, though sensational, were also oddly general. This conception of bondage was a symbolic construct that called up the Southern slave system at the same time that it emptied it of historical specificity. The result was a political sign born of the history it obscured. It is the curiously abstracted signifier of the scourged bondswoman that scripts the melodrama of antipolygamy fiction. The earliest and most influential antipolygamy novels, all written in the mid-1850s, cast Mormon wives as "slaves" trapped in states of sexual bondage, in scenes that replicate the stylized abjection of black women's bodies only to replace them with the bodies of white wives. In Maria Ward's novel, *The Mormon Wife*, a bestseller first published in 1855 (as *Female Life among the Mormons*) and reissued for decades afterward, errant wives are subject to "twenty-five lashes" and dissenters are terrorized through an "almost constant exercise of Lynch law." One woman, the narrative relates, "was taken one night, . . . gagged, carried a mile in the woods, stripped nude, tied to a tree, and scourged until the blood ran from her wounds to the ground, in which condition she was left until the next night when her tormentors visited her again, took her back to her husband's residence, and laid her on the doorstep, where she remained until morning."[10]

In moments such as this, a familiar choreography of bondage is at once expressive and mute, a pantomime of displaced scenes of plantation slavery. The polemics against polygamy offer particularly vivid proof of Lauren Berlant's contention that sentimentalist poetics served "to hardwire the history of slavery into the forms of affect that have long distinguished modes of pain, pleasure, identity, and identification in the American culture industry" and its sentimentalist politics.[11] Polygamy first appears in the sphere of electoral politics as the uncanny double of slavery. The 1856 platform of the new Republican Party devoted a plank to denouncing the "twin relics of barbarism—Slavery and Polygamy."[12] The rhetorical twinning, which persisted long after emancipation, illustrates the way a liberal politics arrayed against a concept of bondage found its force less through an appeal to human rights than to sexual and familial wrongs.

For antipolygamy reformers, the most compelling proof of the barbarism of both slavery and polygamy was the brutal indifference both showed to marriage as the sanctification of a woman's powers of sexual consent. Just as the slave plantation had been a deviant family, a seat of "fornication, adultery, concubinage" (qtd. in Stanley 24), the family under polygamy, its critics charged, was "white slavery." Harriet Beecher Stowe insisted that Mormon polygamy was a "degrading bondage, . . . a cruel slavery whose chains have cut into the very hearts of thousands of our sisters."[13] Like slavery, the institution of polygamy was said to violate the Christian family, or what historians today call the contractual family, whose members are to be bound by affection rather than subordination to the patriarchal head and governed by ideals of consent rather than obedience and corporeal force.[14] Slavery and polygamy were thus conjoined as nearly identical crimes against the family. In Mary Hudson's novel *Esther the Gentile* (1880), the narrator even declares that Mormon wives "suffer as the slave women of the South never did. Slave women were torn from their homes by masters while their husbands mourned; the Mormon women are slaves to their husbands, concubines to their religion, and martyrs to a despotism as immoral as the cursed Sodom of old."[15]

The claim here that polygamy was worse than slavery, however, exposes an underlying rhetorical strain. To be a slave to one's husband might well be worse than being a slave to one's master, but if Mormon women suffered, of course, they suffered as wives and not as slaves. By so plainly overreaching, this version of the analogy might be said to uncover its central flaw, the vexed question of marital consent. "Don't you know a slave can't be married?" asks one of Stowe's anguished characters in *Uncle Tom's Cabin*.[16] Simply by virtue of having married at all, plural wives would seem to have exercised the power that virtually defined freedom in abolitionist thought: the power of marital consent.

Consent is an obsessive theme of antipolygamy fiction. In Metta Victor's bestseller *Mormon Wives* (1856), the heroine Margaret confronts her childhood friend Sarah who has converted to Mormonism and appears willing to accept polygamy: "How could you, with all your pride, consent to occupy an inferior, secondary situation, and have the heart of your husband divided among a dozen others?" (185). Margaret means for this to have the force of a stinging rhetorical question. But just this question—how could a woman possibly consent to polygamy—is in fact the enigma motivating the genre's patterns of plot and imagery. For it was the issue of consent that actually made race slavery *opposed* to polygamy in a fundamental way. At some level, of course, Mormon women clearly did choose to enter polygamous marriages, or at least chose to accept polygamy in a way that no one ever consented to slavery.

To call their consent a choice, of course, is to risk giving plural wives a power of agency they may never have possessed. The pressures of family, faith, and economic need constitute an X-factor that make their choice so opaque as to render the idea of consent all but meaningless—meaningless until, that is, it is juxtaposed with the forced abjection of the slave. In its willful, even fantastical, denial of that difference, the imagining of the plural wife as a "greater slave" bespeaks a cultural distress that hovered about the question of women's marital consent. If the task in antislavery literature was to have readers recognize the slave's horrific lack of consent ("how would you like to have *your* sisters, and *your* wives, and *your* daughters, completely, teetotally, and altogether, in the power of a master?" [qtd. in Stanley 25]), the task of antipolygamy writers was to have readers refuse to recognize polygamy as being in any way consensual, something wives acceded to or (worse yet) even desired. Novelists aimed to make a woman's consent to polygamy almost literally unthinkable.

Their urgency in this task gives a clue to just how much was at stake. As I argue in more detail below, a specific notion of female consent represented a form of social legitimation that had become both indispensable and problematic for the modern nation-state. Indispensable because, as a model for social relations, wifely consent could soften the constraints of law and duty into the joys of love; problematic because the passivity of wifely love made it an inherently equivocal model of political agency. Polygamy exacerbated this dilemma in every way. It made all the sharper the felt need among liberals for an affective mode of consensual citizenship, for an extralegal sphere of uniform moral meaning and feeling ("the American home") that could fuse privacy and nationality. At the same time, polygamy uncannily exposed the enduring tensions in the liberal concept of consent. The dilemma gave rise to the defining features of antipolygamy fiction. The outright denial of wives' consent in the scenes of brutal bondage is accompanied by a repetitious, brooding fixation on the problem of consent itself, a fixation most clearly evident in the topos of the polygamous wedding.

In between their depictions of women's kidnapping and assault, antipolygamy novels often feature a scene in which a woman formally does accept plural marriage, usually an episode in the Mormon temple where a first wife participates in the wedding ceremony of her husband and another wife. "And now comes the strangest phase of those tragedies enacted year after year" in Utah, writes the author of *Madame La Tour*, when Jessie, one of La Tour's other daughters, "for her husband's sake, the man she worshiped, . . . consented at last, to the most barbarous rite enjoined by his religion (not hers) and went to the Endowment House to place his hand in the hand of [another] bride" (193). These marriage ceremonies were the very rituals that real nineteenth-century Mormons underscored as proof not just of wives' consent, but of the thoroughly religious nature of the "celestial marriage" they claimed was protected by the Constitution. But, far from ignoring these nuptials, novelists returned to this "strangest phase" of polygamy, the moment of seeming consent, in order to undo its power of legitimation.

Antipolygamy novelists represent Mormon marriage ceremonies in order to transpose the wife's apparent voluntarism, often beginning with a seeming travesty of the traditional language of matrimonial consent as the officiating Mormon Elder turns to the first wife and asks: "Do you give this woman to this man, to be his lawfully wedded wife?" Though they formally assent, in the conventional resolution to the wedding scene first wives regularly faint after speaking their consent, the first sign of an illness that usually kills or drives them mad after this injury to their womanhood. Soon after Druscilla, a wife in Hudson's *Esther the Gentile*, hears these ritual words (from Brigham Young himself), her dead faint prefigures her sorrowful end "wandering the streets of Salt Lake City, the Sodom of the Occident" (166). For Jessie, a first wife in *Madame La Tour*, the temple ceremony had the "effect of paralyzing her faculties" (64). The rite as imaged here does more than perform the marriage; it also vividly enacts her loss of agency and even her mental stability. For a woman, the genre has it, consenting to polygamy is a form of insanity.

"Nuptial insanity" was actually one of the legal grounds that could annul an existing marriage in the United States. If it was determined that one spouse did not have the mental capacity to give free consent at the time of the wedding, the marriage could be declared void from the start (Grossberg 103–52). What such a legal category reflected, of course, was less the sanity or insanity of a given spouse than the particular rationality of the law, its rule-based logic that defined marital agency through exclusive binary categories of consent and insanity. By ruling on consent, the law rationalized the opacity of the decision to marry, denying as a form of unreason (nuptial insanity) any assent to a marriage it found alien or harmful. More importantly, such ruling sanctified as wholly free and uncoerced the contracting of any marriage it deemed proper. Antipolygamy fiction, it could be said, aspired to the same authority to rule on consent. Entering the "evidence" of its own plot lines for a finding of nuptial insanity, antipolygamy novels pronounced a kind of paralegal judgment that women never did and never could freely consent to plural marriage.

In a direct address to the reader, the narrator of Alva Kerr's *Trean; or, The Mormon's Daughter* (1888) asks, "Could else but a sort of insanity have brought the people of these lovely [Utah] valleys out from all corners of the civilized world" to "make them capable of receiving this . . . distorted imitation of Hebrew barbarism?"[17] Kerr articulates a notion of nuptial insanity writ large, without which the genre would be left with a contradiction in terms: a true woman's willing participation in a "Sodom of the Occident." Mormon polygamy is portrayed as confounding the largest racial and global orders against which confusion writers mobilized a chain of recuperative liberal oppositions: wife and slave, consent and coercion, civilization and barbarism. But, as in contemporary marriage law, the novels' articulation of nuptial consent and nuptial insanity may not describe opposing forms of reason and unreason as much as it rehearses its own polarized resolution of the opacity of a certain species of desire: the unreadable, sometimes unintelligible, and perhaps inextricable confluence of motives that compel (do we desire what is compelling?) the assent to any marriage. The fantastic melodramas of abjection in this fiction—the scenes of mesmerism, madness, imprisonment, rape, and (the genre's endgame) suicide or death—do more than indict the Mormon system of polygamy. These negations purify the consent to monogamy as the surest expression of female will. Polygamy is the bondage that sanctifies marriage as freedom.

Resolutions of Feeling

The category of nuptial insanity, while eminently useful, also registered a certain incoherence, a stress on the counterpart concept of marital consent. John Stuart Mill, after noting in *On Liberty* the "language of downright persecution which breaks out from the press of this country whenever it feels called upon to notice the remarkable phenomenon of Mormonism," reminded readers that "this relation [polygamy] is as much voluntary on the part of the women concerned in it . . . as is the case with any other form of marriage institution."[18] Yet the same reasoning could cast a troubling shadow on the voluntary nature of marriage itself: if women could agree to the seeming unfreedom of polygamy, what then is this thing called consent? How is it possible to say that any woman's marriage is freely chosen if the "degradation" of polygamy is chosen as well?

For some observers, then, Mill's logic was all too easily turned on its head. If plural wives entered their marriage bonds as voluntarily as monogamous wives, it took little recasting to say that monogamous wives were just as enslaved as the wives in Utah. As one cagey writer put it, "We are mistaken in supposing the women of Utah are in any greater bondage than are the women of the United States." Elizabeth Cady Stanton, though far from indifferent to the fact of Mormon polygamy, nevertheless saw its crimes as merely relative. In fact, plural marriage in Utah, Stanton averred, had the virtue of an instructive clarity, for it exposed the essential condition of all wives. Stanton declared that in America there were really three kinds of polygamy: Mormon polygamy, bigamy perpetrated through fraud, and the polygamy "everywhere practiced in the United States" involving one wife and multiple mistresses. For Stanton, the "subjection to man" that defined the institution at its core guaranteed that any marriage relation compromised a woman's free consent (only mistresses, Stanton argued, were capable of exercising true consent precisely because they were outside of the bonds of the marriage). Antipolygamists saw the plural wife as an oxymoron; to Stanton she was a redundancy.[19]

For most antipolygamy novelists, who sought to advance rights and protections for women in monogamy, the edge of this polemical weapon was too keen by half. Where a liberal theorist like Mill insisted on the voluntarism of marriage despite the unpleasing implications posed by polygamy, critics like Stanton saw in polygamy proof of the hollowness of consent in marriage. The novelists, however, were prepared neither to accept polygamy as truly voluntary, nor to call all marriage a form of bondage. Insanity and abjection in their fiction mark the narrowing constraints of a position able neither to discredit the notion of marital consent nor to credit the choices of polygamous wives. Mill, it would seem, traded consent too high, but Stanton sold it too short.[20]

To resolve the dilemma, antipolygamy fiction relied on sentimentalism's developed ideal of female love and its natural expression, the "perfect union" of the monogamous home. In a now impressive body of scholarship, historians and critics have shown the way the languages of sentimental domesticity, with their lyrical if repetitive eloquence, made idealized familial bonds the basis for a powerful code of ethics. States of feeling, more than custom or law, became the guarantors of moral authority. Under the sentimentalist symbology, a woman's love is a figure invoking not subjection but human mutuality, the universalizing bonds of shared affection and empathic pain. Consent in this context is less will than (female) feeling, proof of the absence of domination and a witness of virtue and affective identification as the surest civil bonds.

Within the project of sentimentalism, then, the wife's domestic subjection was eclipsed by a perfect unity of hearts whose best exemplar and brightest hope was female love freely given. But like any ideological unity, this one had its pressure points where exiled ideas or objects threatened to come back into view. Polygamy was such a point of potential interruption. As Pamela announces so succinctly, polygamy is one of the domestic novel's primal "bad words," conjuring for novel readers an order of domestic "prerogative" best ignored if not forgotten. Polygamy pointed to a hierarchy that existed not outside of the home but within it. And that domestic hierarchy implied not just that a wife's will could be disregarded (the point of Mr. B.'s jibe to Pamela), but that it could be disregarded *properly* because authorized by her own consent to marry. More unsettling still, the word polygamy bespoke a female desire and volition that the sentimentalist project could not or would not recognize, a desire different from its own yet equally capable of making a world. What may have shocked readers even more than the stylized violence in these novels were the imagined scenes of Utah home life in which the familiar world of domestic activity has become infernally strange. "Terrible it is," writes the narrator of *Plural Marriage: The Heart-History of Adele Hersch* (1885), "to sit alone during the long evenings, trying to work, while Mabel's light laugh rings out, and my husband's—her husband's—voice, reading to her, comes to my ear."[21] At once strange and all too familiar, polygamy effected a return of all that had been repressed in the creation of a coherent and idealized domestic symbology.

But if polygamy was the genre's tabooed bad word, it also presented a nearly ideal opportunity to exorcise any uncanny similarities to the American home. Within the poetics of the novel, Utah polygamy could be excluded from domestic space altogether—could be unveiled, in fact, as the opposite of the domestic, nothing short of a "home-destroying system" (Kerr 65). As the symbolic negation of an idealized domestic unity, Utah polygamy could draw off every historical and personal ambiguity of wifehood, estranging and finally displacing those ambiguities onto the sins of an occidental Sodom, a collection of "unbelievable crimes in a far-off country" (Kerr 65).

This striking last phrase alerts us to national and territorial dimensions so far not closely explored here, but still crucial to the workings of domestic symbology. By denying that plural wives exercised consent, novelists simultaneously denied Mormons any possible place in American nationhood. This was not just because Mormons violated proper marriage law, although that was the reformers' fervent conviction. The more fundamental reason, for antipolygamists, was that Mormons' alleged violations of female consent perforce meant their exile from a federation of feeling that was the affective life of the nation, its psychic and moral unity. The struggle over polygamy offers one of the most vivid demonstrations of a reformulation of national identity as an imagined state of feeling. Certainly it was one of the most literal, as the struggle against polygamy would eventually play itself out in a struggle over statehood. The "far-off country" of Utah would prove its national belonging only when the "heart history" of the Territory had joined the union of domestic feeling that was America.

Sentimental Constitutionalism

"Is there not in the heart of every human being," asks the narrator of Hudson's *Esther the Gentile*, "born in the effulgent light of the nineteenth century, on American soil, a revelation which tells him that God never commanded absolute wrong to his fellow human beings?" (146). The efficiency of its self-affirming structure makes this statement a sentimentalist pedagogy in miniature. The "yes" it presumes affirms not simply that polygamy is one of the wrongs God surely prohibits. The same assent makes that subjective moral feeling, the good that every good person wishes for fellow humans, bear ineluctable witness to the truth of the nationalist mythology, the vanguard "light" and the sacred "soil" entrusted to the American cause.

Such language is, of course, a variant of patriotism, not to mention chauvinism. It is also a further demonstration of the extraordinary range and versatility of the central nationalist symbol of the United States, the sign of America, to gather to itself almost any strong emotional current. The passage draws on patriotism and Americanism, but it is also something distinct from those two. Both of those structures are psychic investments directing feeling toward the nation itself. But the domestic nationalism revealed in antipolygamy fiction describes not a love for the nation (though such is presumed), but a form of national belonging that is made manifest by the love one feels for others. The revelations of the heart, transparent to the suffering and joy of other hearts, are simultaneously a revelation of what Catharine Beecher called the "blessed influences" of moral sentiment entrusted to America (especially American women) as the "cynosure of nations." Because America reveals itself in the "intellectual and moral character" of its people, citizenship is akin to a certain state of affective responsiveness, a naturalization of the soul.[22] The citizen doesn't choose America so much as America chooses the citizen through a revelation of moral-national feeling not unlike a state of grace. Domestic nationalism effected a shift from female consent as the willing submission to authority into a blessed, almost will-less disposition of the heart.

Sarah Barringer Gordon explores an important dimension of this domes-

tic nationalism in a study of the legal implications of the antipolygamy movement. Analyzing literary sentimentalism as a "form of legal argumentation"
("'National Hearthstone,'" 299), Gordon shows the way Utah constituted
an issue almost tailor-made to help articulate what many liberal reformers
believed to be the threat she calls "moral diversity" (316), the lines of seeming
moral difference across space, class, and religions that those reformers saw
protected by a flawed legal system. Novels, reformers held, were the expert
instruments for diagnosing these fault lines. Gordon reads antipolygamy fiction as a virtual "blueprint for legal reform" that took effect when readers,
moved to identify with the pain of fictional Mormon wives, saw their own
marriages "implicated and threatened by the existence of polygamy" (310)
and were persuaded that only the close regulation of marriage by the state
could protect against the damages of moral diversity. Antipolygamy fiction
was a powerful catalyst, if not a cause, of a broad reorientation of marriage law
in particular and in the state's moral governance more generally. As antipolygamy polemics gave rise to a federal campaign, legislators criminalized
plural marriage, disenfranchised all suspected polygamists, and eventually
abolished the church corporation, forcing the forfeiture of most of its property. By joining "legal structure to emotional structure," antipolygamy law
endowed the state with the power to enforce the fantasy of a homogeneous
sphere of moral feeling, a universal and unchanging affective life that Mormons' plural marriages had disproved by their very existence.

Gordon's history of "sentimental constitutionalism" points to significant
changes both in positive law and in an understanding of what law is, a significant development indeed. But the laws to eliminate moral diversity also
reflect a profound reformulation of national identity itself. The push for legal
reforms rested on a retrospective belief in the founding of the American
polity as an originary moment of unified moral feeling, what Victor calls the
nation's "once proud purity" (vii). Under this notion, the purity of homogeneous sentiment becomes the true dwelling place for national meaning, transcending the errors or law or the contingencies of history. The truest measures of Americanness therefore prove internal: whether you belong depends
on what you feel. Hence the emphasis in antipolygamy fiction on the alien
sentiments everywhere in the Mormon colony. "Among the Mormons,"
declares the narrator of Alfreda Bell's *Boadicea the Mormon Wife* (1855), "it is
held 'unnecessary' to endure the sight of suffering." The proof of this sentimental heresy comes when Boadicea learns about a dying woman and an
Elder informs her that it was "not a good act to assist her, for she talks against

us Mormons." "I hope she'll die," he adds, "and the brat, too."[23] In this perfect demonic inversion of the sentimental death scene, sympathy for a dying mother and child is not only missing but actively forbidden, a censure that recrystallizes in the reader the current of feeling it condemns.

These and a thousand other violations of compassion offer in the pages of novels a fictionalized record of the "heart pollution" (Kerr 65) produced by polygamy. In a world where "woman's consent is thought to be a matter of small importance" (Paddock 123), writers were sure that emotional relations would be monstrously damaged. And where the unifying power of monogamy was absent, depravity was certain to fill the vacuum. Polygamy was a "system which enslaved, taught treachery, rapine, and murder as sacred duties" (Paddock 262). While the novels clearly are written to condemn these cruelties, their subtextual task is to call into existence the collective sympathy for the oppressed that was, under sentimentalism, the purest incarnation of the national polity. That intention is clear, for instance, in the preface to Veronique Petit's *Plural Marriage: The Heart-History of Adele Hersch*. Petit's dual dedication to "my sisters" who "appreciate the agony of heart-wounds" and "to the Congress of our beloved country, who can decree that this crime against womanhood shall cease," is an explicit example of the usually tacit positioning of a oneness of empathic feeling as the "heart" of the national existence, which heart the external offices of governance are entrusted to represent.

The foil of polygamy could not have been better designed for this task. By 1885, when the status of wife became the subject of ever noisier arguments, the crimes of polygamy—sure to "desolate all households" (Victor ii)— proved a powerful means of reconstituting, by way of contrast, the symbolic wholeness that was domesticity's highest value and most useful resource. In a real sense, then, polygamy was indeed "more loathsome than slavery to our social and political purity" (Victor vi): more loathsome because more obviously a form of domestic life, but also proportionally more effective as a figural antithesis giving renewed meaning to the trope of the national home. As Grover Cleveland declared in his first address to Congress, "The strength, the perpetuity, and the destiny of the nation rests upon our homes, established by the law of God. These homes are not the homes of polygamy" (Cannon 61).

The "heart histories" of fictional Mormon wives were simultaneously a fantasy record of the emotional histories of thousands of readers. Its very subjectivity gave it its certainty: there may be no arguing with taste, but there is no need for arguing with pain (the public affirmations of consent from Mormon women notwithstanding).[24] This record of suffering, sure of its universality in all good hearts, gave a particular structure of feeling its claim to national law. To analyze this fiction as a literature of nationalism is not to doubt the authenticity of its personalized passions. On the contrary, it is to recognize the way this strain of nationalism, as a lived disposition, drew its immediacy precisely from readers' deepest convictions and fears. At the same time, though, the example of polygamy shows the way marital consent, understood as the surest mark of the nation's "social and political purity" (Victor vi), connected the intimacies of domestic life to some of the most far-reaching forms of worldly power. The polygamy crisis offers a concrete instance of the links that could join domestic feeling to state power and even imperial force. This connection, too, can be said to turn on the vexed question of female consent, as the lines of imperial difference turn out to have been mapped in advance by the territories of the heart.

False Nationals and Yellow Mormons

Monogamy is to polygamy "as England to India."[25] This syllogism, from historian Hubert Howe Bancroft's *History of Utah* (1889), supplies a distilled expression of the larger (and messier) knot of associations at play in the polygamy issue. The logic here springs from a mode of understanding in which the moral is mutatis mutandis always territorial; in which the marital derives meaning from the racial; and in which a relation of opposition can mean a right of possession. Bancroft condenses all of this in the austere idiom of pure reason. But straining against Bancroft's spare logic is his historical subject, polygamy in Utah, which appears to refute that chaste system of reason, as history so often does. The syllogism's logical contrasts, that is, can be (mis)read as proximities, as near relations, just as easily as oppositions.

   Though it holds to the same first principles, antipolygamy fiction never manages to achieve the fixed stability of Bancroft's syllogism. The fiction is alert to, because so disturbed by, the moments in which global oppositions like the contrast between monogamy and polygamy begin to converge. In the imagination of novelists, the closing down of female consent leads to the seduction of whole institutions, to slippages among sexual, racial, legal, and administrative orders. In one novel, the Mormon prophet's power not only seduced multiple wives but, through the same force of seduction, "enthralled a state legislature" and "a federal jury" (qtd. in Givens 141). Metta Victor, warning readers that Utah had applied for admission to the Union, was repelled by the thought of an "institution with which we are to consort" (321). Such consorting, a commingling of oppositional orders, seemed to promise a dangerous increase in moral diversity.

Another writer in this era, African American author Frances Harper, feared the same spreading of corruption in postbellum federalism, though Harper linked America's problem of moral diversity to its sins of racial exclusion and its increasing taste for imperial adventuring. The heroine of Harper's *Iola Leroy* icily observes that the postwar federalism had created an "aristocracy of race wide enough to include the South with its treason and Utah with its abominations, but too narrow to include the bravest colored man" who fought for the Union.[26] But Iola was wrong here in one respect: polygamy in Utah finally would not be tolerated, and, indeed, would be outlawed as treasonous. Perhaps the most telling sign of that refusal to tolerate plural marriage (and an ironic confirmation of Harper's viewpoint) is the fact that Mormons were refused the status of white people. While Utah Mormons included newly arrived foreigners—one novelist complained that too many had "no other naturalization than a Mormon baptism" (qtd. in Gordon, "'National Hearthstone,'" 326)—the population consisted almost exclusively of white New Englanders and British and European immigrants. But even a white population could fail to count as members of the race if they did not have "white" families. It may have been contemporary cartoonists who translated this proposition most vividly. One political cartoon from this era, for instance, shows a bearded white elder in bed with several caricature pickaninnies. Another shows an Elder standing hand in hand with a multiracial chorus line of children, including a Chinese boy, an African girl, and a little Indian brave.[27] These absurd portraits mocked the Mormon claim to domesticity by giving a pictorial expression of the motley aggregation of offspring that was the mixed issue one might expect of an "occidental Sodom."

Behind the cartoons' comic ridicule of Mormons' failure to reproduce a white home was a more serious racial logic. In other antipolygamy texts, Utah polygamy is described as literally producing a distinct and inferior race. "The Asiatic institution was never meant to flourish on American soil," one critic wrote, and physical degeneration is "but a natural result; for polygamy is tenfold more unnatural to such a climate and race than in southern Asia or Africa."[28] Here monogamy for white wives is approaching something of a racial birthright and a fact of natural history. Two scientists confidently reported that "the yellow, sunken, cadaverous visage [of Mormons]; . . . the thick, protuberant lips; the low forehead; the light, yellowish hair, and the lank angular person, constitute an appearance so characteristic of the new race, the production of polygamy, as to distinguish them at a glance" (qtd. in Cannon 78).

This kind of racialized discourse finally had less to do with convictions about genetic inheritance, however, than it did with an unwillingness to recognize the Mormon-controlled Utah Territory as belonging to "the family of white nations" and their rights of self-sovereignty. Scholars analyzing the close kinship between racism and nationalism have observed the way a national identity is frequently the spoken name for an unspoken racial identity. As Etienne Balibar writes, "the racial-cultural identity of the 'true nationals' remains invisible, but it is inferred from (and assured by) its opposite, the alleged, the quasi-hallucinatory visibility of the 'false nationals': Jews, 'wops,' immigrants, *indios*, natives, blacks."[29] The Mormon case confirms but also complicates this assumed connection between race and national identity. Its example counters the idea that being white is the open secret of American identity and suggests rather that whiteness, *like* nationality, is an idealized insider status that could be withheld even from white populations. In that sense, Mormons could be called the truest of "false nationals," white Americans whose alien marriages and homes made them unassimilable to the national body politic, in an exile from domesticity that endowed Mormons with their own "quasi-hallucinatory visibility" amounting to a race apart. "They ain't white," announces one novel's character, "they're Mormons."[30]

Just as their exclusion from American domesticity made Mormons false nationals, it gave them an ambiguous relation to imperial subjects. Frequently fashioned as a "modern Mohammedanism" and "the Islam of America," Mormonism was seen as importing a "Mohammedan barbarism revolting to the civilized world."[31] Mormon homes were "harems," and the Mormon order of priesthood an "oriental despotism." The "enormities of the Mormon system" (Ward 449) were not just brutalities, but unspeakably strange brutalities, as the ideal of domestic intimacy—love that was spontaneous, mutual, undifferentiated—was inverted in fantasies of ritualized acts of domestic violence: infanticide, marital rape, even domestic cannibalism, as in one imagined case of husbands reduced to "feeding on the flesh of dead wives" (Ward 443). The exoticizing imagery confirms the insights of recent scholars about how closely the "sacred precinct" of the domestic sphere was tied to discourses of global empire. The axiom that "domesticity is the antithesis of heathenism" meant that sentimentalist domestic norms had a world mission and a global reach.[32] It also meant that deviation from those norms could transpose even a U.S. territory, a desert in the American West, into a no-man's-land of "distinctly Oriental appearance" (qtd. in Givens 132). But if the imagining of yellow Mormons and orientalist desert cities is evidence of the power and reach of domestic discourse, those bizarre creations also point up the element of hallucination, willful yet panicked, necessary to preserve the requisite "purity" in the categories of domestic feeling.

The narrator of *The Mormon Wife* complains that in Utah, "outsiders rarely know what sights and sounds the domestic hearth witnesses" (335). For all its resemblance to family privacy, this kind of shield against outside oversight—a defining feature of the traditional household—could not be countenanced by domestic novelists who were authorized by virtue of their genre to serve precisely as the witnesses to the domain of the home. The rise of the domestic novel can be thought of as a reterritorializing of household space, a claiming from traditional male heads the right of representation over the world of wives, children, and family relations. That Mormon elders in antipolygamy fiction are always sequestering wives in dungeons and vaults expresses in spatial terms novelists' suspicions that traditional household sovereignty hid and protected all manner of abuse. And when husbands and leaders in this fiction claim that sovereignty outright, their words approach the level of blasphemy. "The true importance of marriage," Brigham Young proclaims to one young woman in *The Mormon Wife*, "is beyond your comprehension." Emily's return challenge to Brigham (which is also her refusal to marry him) enacts in a single speech the genre's reclamation of marriage under the sign of female consent. When Brigham, incredulous, asks, "And you call the holy state of marriage concubinage?" she refutes both him and his defining authority over the whole domain of home and family: "I do, such as you propose. Without love, without sympathy, without congeniality of mind or appropriateness of age; sensuality on one side and compulsion on the other, what else could it be?" (292).

Distilled in this exchange, then, is a final power of sentimental female consent: the right to define what was concubinage (heathen, coercive) and what was marriage (the "holy state" of consensual feeling). Here the woman's right to accept or refuse a marriage proposal is made perfectly continuous with what we might call a power of imperial discernment, the ability to tell (or, from another perspective, to dictate) marriage from bondage, the civilized from the barbaric. This understanding of marital consent was fictional, an ideal conveyed in storytelling. But by now we should be prepared to recognize in storytelling the potential for enormous worldly power: the sentimentalist notion of female consent was eventually enshrined in the highest court as a constituative principle not only of national law but of the existence of the nation itself. In the Supreme Court ruling in *Reynolds v. United States* (1879), Chief Justice Morrison R. Waite dismissed the Mormons' claim to the Constitutional protection of religious freedom, declaring that there is no meaningful legal distinction between Mormon polygamy, which "sacrifices women to the lusts of men," and the religious sacrifices of "barbarous" peoples in which "the widow mounts the funeral pyre in India," or "helpless infants are sacrificed in the waters of the Ganges." The comparison, echoing as it does the central tropes of antipolygamy fiction, roots the legal principle in contemporary domestic thinking and its pivotal concern with women's powers of consent. Like the author of the fictional *Elder Northfield's Home; Or, Sacrificed on the Mormon Altar* (1882), Waite locates an ineluctable harm to wives in the strong patriarchy of polygamous marriage, the wedding "altar" that sacrifices women. Waite's images of exotic violence are meant to refute the very possibility of effective marital consent in polygamy. Even if a wife enters plural marriage voluntarily, like the widow who "mounts the pyre" as an accepted obligation, it is ultimately an expression of the coercion that permeates the condition of barbarism. In the polygamous family, according to this analogy, a wife is helpless and will-less, someone who, like the Indian widow or child, can have no life apart from the patriarchal head. Only monogamy, by implication, distinguishes and protects the status of wife from that of slave.[33]

The status of consensual wife, in turn, secures the identity of America as a civilized nation. "According as monogamous or polygamous marriages are allowed," Waite declares, so follows the form of government and national life. His point is not simply that the state requires monogamy as its law of marriage; it is that monogamy determines the very nature of the state. In *Reynolds*, marriage is the inner life of the nation, the shared life of feeling that makes home and homeland dual aspects of the same whole. Waite cites the views of philosopher Francis Lieber, who, in his essay decrying Mormon polygamy, defined monogamy "as a law written in the heart of our race . . . one of the elementary distinctions—historical and actual—between European and Asiatic humanity. It is one of the frames of our thoughts, and

moulds [*sic*] of our feelings; it is a psychological condition of our jural consciousness, of our liberty, of our literature, of our aspirations, of our religious
conviction, and of our domestic being and family relation, the foundation of
all that is called polity" (qtd. in Weisbrod and Sheingorn 835). Monogamy
here is much more than a marriage practice; it is a national and racial essence
and a principle of being, an expression of subjectivity itself. Waite based his
ruling against plural marriage not on the grounds that it was sinful or criminal, but because it was alterior, because it lay outside of a collective "domestic
being" that was a new synonym for national life.

Forceful Sentiment

The "triumph for believers in monogamy," as the *Reynolds* decision was
described, was in a real sense the coequal victory of the domestic novel, a
genre "where women's words conspicuously . . . mattered" (Brown 634).
The ruling might be described as the moment when the particular world-
view of the domestic novel, its articulation of domestic relations and feeling,
was elevated to the status of law. The decision's implicit reframing of women's
consent, from the willing submission to a patriarchal head to a constitutive
form of national existence, was coauthored by a long list of unnamed fiction writers.

Antipolygamy reform shows the domestic word as power, in all its ambiguous potential. Ruling that polygamy was nonconsensual imposed a powerful tautology: any polygamists, even white ones, would find themselves outside the protection of the nation and lacking its legitimizing structures of
consent. Invoking Lincoln, critics declared that the "national house" could
not stand "with its marriage system partly Moslem and partly Christian"
(qtd. in Hardy 297). This nationalizing of monogamous marriage established
a new relation between moral feeling and state power. The emancipation of
the "innocent victims of this delusion," as Waite described it, coincided
with the legal denial, through the police powers, of the possibility of consensual plural marriage. The Edmunds Act (1882) effected in law what authors insisted in novels: that polygamous marriage was no marriage at all but
the crime of "unlawful cohabitation" that produced illegitimate kin. Just
as novelists refused to recognize the patriarchal household as an indivisible
whole, the Edmunds Act authorized federal marshals to forcibly enter suspected polygamist homes, arresting the criminals—polygamist husbands—

and requiring their wives, as designated victims, to testify against them. The Edmunds–Tucker Act (1887) went even further, dissolving the church corporation altogether. "Brigham's empire" fell and the "domestic being" of the republic was restored.

The sentimental tropes of antipolygamy reform made this continuity between feeling and force seem inevitable, natural; not to use force would have been the abuse of power. To at least one outsider, however (one for whom America was not synonymous with home), it was the conjoining of moral politics and political force that seemed to threaten abuse. In his travel book *New America*, British writer William H. Dixon queries the "New England politician" who has vowed to "crush the Saints": "[Do you mean to] set about promoting morality with bayonets and bowie-knives?" "[Will you] use force—passively, if they submit, actively if they resist?" " 'That's our notion,' replies our candid host."[34] This "notion," born of fiction, sanctified in sentiment, is part of the complex legacy of the nineteenth-century project of sentimentalism, its ability to make forceful, in every sense, a set of ideals about human compassion and relations. Its notions were forceful enough to persuade large numbers of men to "vote against the immediate interests of their sex as an expression of a higher gender ideal" (qtd. in Gordon, " 'National Hearthstone,' " 344) and to advance the dismantling of male household sovereignty;[35] they were forceful enough to marshal the police powers of the state to subdue a nonconforming society and dissolve a church; and forceful enough, finally, to make domestic feeling a defining difference between belonging to the nation and committing treason.

I summarize these far-reaching consequences not to suggest any disingenuous motives in sentimentalist thought but, on the contrary, to argue just how successful that thought was in making a fiction of consent into a national doctrine. Once the unity of the nation was perceived to be rooted in a moral and emotional unity of monogamous marriage, there is little wonder that Mormons' nonconforming marriage law made them seem to be "teach[ing] treason," in "perpetual enmity to the Government and the people of the United States" (Paddock 263). The direction of American law had dissolved the "petite treason" that a wife could commit against a sovereign husband, but marriage emerged now as a matter of grand treason against the state. Historian Nancy Cott points out that in immigration and naturalization acts of this period, "polygamists were listed as excludable and deportable right next to anarchists, as if (following Waite's logic) those who would overthrow the institution of monogamy were dangerously similar to those who would overthrow the state."[36]

Just as polygamy became commensurate with treason, monogamy offered Mormons the chance for statehood. When Mormon leaders announced in 1890 a revelation that marked the official cessation of polygamous practice, it was not long before Utah was admitted into the Union. This episode may be the closest thing in American history to a national quid pro quo: marital conformity in exchange for U.S. statehood. The shift was profound and the consequences large, nothing less than membership in the national sovereignty. And yet this change did not reflect (as reformers claimed) a wholesale change from a culture of coercion to one of consent, for Mormons' plural marriage had actually mirrored the structure of consent that existed in marriage generally. Polygamy reminded even monogamous wives that their consent coexisted with external male prerogatives, structures of authority they could legitimate but not themselves directly possess or negotiate. At the same time, the new society in Utah had shown, with all the drama inherent in nineteenth-century nation building, that women's consent could indeed bring new worlds into existence.

I do not wish to argue that polygamy was finally no different than mainstream marriage. I am suggesting rather that it was the differences in Utah polygamy (real and imaginary) that conveyed the most profound truths about women's consent in marriage generally: that consent did not produce marital parity, but that it could create a real social unity—though the new social formation might be far different than other citizens could understand or desire. In a court deposition, Mormon President Joseph F. Smith explained under cross-examining the Mormon "law of Sarah" requiring the consent of first wives to their husband's additional marriages.

> Q: Is it not true that . . . if she refuses her consent her husband is exempt from the law which requires her consent?
>
> A: Yes; he is exempt from the law which requires her consent. She is commanded to consent, but if she does not, then he is exempt from the requirement.
>
> Q: Then he is at liberty to proceed without her consent, under the law. In other words, her consent amounts to nothing?
>
> A: It amounts to nothing but her consent (qtd. in Van Wagoner 103).

Smith's response measures the wide distance between marital consent and the ideal reciprocity of contract. Yet from another perspective, Smith's reiteration—consent "amounts to nothing but her consent"—can be said to mark not the essential fraud of consent but its radical power. There is no question that Mormon women did consent to plural marriages. In publications, in public assemblies, and in letters and diaries (where affirmation often co-existed with anguished private expressions of turmoil in their marriages), women expressed their willing assent to the "Principle." Certainly there were women who, like one of Brigham Young's wives, Ann Eliza Young, described their experience in the language of coercion once they had left Mormonism. Young's popular exposé, *Wife No. 19*, was subtitled *The Story of a Life in Bondage*.[37] In Fanny Stenhouse's antipolygamy memoir, *Tell It All*, she struggles to decipher how it was that she had "mentally and verbally assented" to her husband's second wife, and describes in retrospect her state of "madness" (457, 453). But even these dissenters, who left Utah and Mormonism altogether when they rejected plural marriage, can be said to prove in their very negations the world-making potential of marital consent. Once they no longer consented, women like Stenhouse and Young were disenchanted with the totality of the Mormon world they had once embraced, and the familiarity of the Utah home became monstrously strange and repugnant.

Conversely, it was precisely the willingness of most plural wives to call their status a chosen freedom that marked their authorization of a lived world—that marked, in other words, its essential difference from slavery. Amounting, in Smith's words, to "nothing but her consent," this delimited agency was still nothing less than the enabling of a whole way of life. As Helen Mar Whitney, a leading apologist for plural wives, noted, "we know the power we hold to declare polygamy illegal." "If there were any necessity," she adds pointedly, "we could assuredly . . . call upon the United States Army stationed here to protect us."[38] Revealed in this crisis of consent was the truth about consent: that it was neither identical with will nor antithetical to subjection, and yet the act of consent, being other than an enslavement, had the ability to make a world—or to unmake one if that consent were refused civil recognition.

While the fiction of female consent penned by novelists can be said to have represented women's interests as a sex, it was enshrined in Constitutional law as a fantasy of uniform "domestic being," a fantasy that was false not only to the experiential world of Mormon wives but to the variegated experiences of women living under monogamy. But, though banished from the law, the precariousness of marital consent, its risks and discontinuities as well as its power, still haunts the pages of antipolygamy novels. In these stories, Utah is a place where domestic feelings lapse unpredictably into constraints and homes into hierarchies. Antipolygamy novels carry an oblique recognition that one's status was not only protected but could also be imperiled through the language of consent. In *The Mormon Wife*, the New England heroine describes an "unaccountable influence" that draws her to her husband, a Mormon: "I consented to be his wife. I seemed to have been cajoled and brought into the measure rather as a third person than a chief actor" (40). But this marriage is in fact a monogamous marriage; as with most of the genre's heroines, it is only much later that she finds herself facing the dilemma of either submitting to polygamy or throwing off a beloved husband. Romantic love itself emerges as a threat to women in these novels. And even monogamous marriage threatens to hold a moment when women stop being a "chief actor" and begin to find themselves "rather as a third person," an actor without any agency. Pointing to the vulnerability of the status of monogamous wife, the novels also hold an implicit critique of monogamous husbands. If no true woman can consent to polygamy, these novelists were sure that virtually all men would consent if they could. "All men have a passion for variety," announces the narrator of *The Mormon Wife*. "Do you fear this of me?" one man asks his fiancée. Her answer: "I fear this of every man who lives in a state of society where polygamy is possible" (219).

Utah is in this fiction a barbaric territory, but it also becomes a "state of society" latent in the republic where the fundamental institution of marriage begins to look like the erasure of consent that had always defined the status of slave. Metta Victor's heroine Margaret is incredulous when she asks Sarah "how could you consent?" But Margaret's declaration to Sarah about the supreme virtue of monogamy carries its own questions about consent: someday, she assures Sarah, you will meet a man "you cannot help but obey" (29). For a wife, marrying means choosing someone "you cannot help but obey": the phrase, with its involution of consent and compulsion, locates the complex work of the domestic novel. At the moment when desire merges into compulsion, compulsion is converted into something you choose, the sign of love itself.

Antipolygamy fiction thus appears to support theorist Carole Pateman's critique that marriage is the transaction in which sexual subordination is, through the alchemy of contract, ratified as free consent. At the same time, however, this fiction and its history show clearly, if ironically, just how much consent matters—its power as a real material force. The antipolygamy novels achieve almost unwittingly an accurate mimesis of the complex and constrained but ultimately meaningful nature of women's consent in marriage. If the marriage contract magically transforms subordination into the equality of free consent, these antipolygamy novels perform a kind of reverse operation:

an unveiling of marriage as a contract where consent matters most—and is most uncontractlike—because it is the precarious act of assenting to subordination. But consent in marriage also matters because it fulfills (if never completely or forever) the very real, very compelling desire not to be a slave—in America, a desire always entangled with racial and national feeling. In American fiction, the complex desire for the status of wife threads its way through the aversion for the status of slave, and consent does the work.

Notes

This essay has benefited from the responses of audiences at UCLA, Harvard, Northwestern, and Vanderbilt universities, and from the Americanists Study Group at the University of Pennsylvania. Bill Handley, Amy Kaplan, and Donald Pease contributed helpful suggestions, and Martha Schoolman provided expert research assistance. A John D. and Rose H. Jackson Fellowship from the Beinecke Library at Yale University helped support my research for this essay.

1 See Felicity Nussbaum, "The Other Woman: Polygamy, Pamela, and the Prerogative of Empire," in *Women, "Race," and Writing in the Early Modern Period*, ed. Margo Hendricks and Patricia Parker (New York: Routledge, 1994), 138–59.

2 Metta Victoria Fuller Victor, *Mormon Wives: A Narrative of Facts Stranger than Fiction* (New York: Derby and Jackson, 1856), xi; Mary Spencer, *Salt Lake Fruit: A Latter-Day Romance* (Boston: Franklin, 1884), v; qtd. in Charles A. Cannon, "The Awesome Power of Sex: The Polemical Campaign against Mormon Polygamy," *Pacific Historical Review* 43 (1974): 61. Subsequent references are cited parenthetically in the text.

3 Leading feminist critiques of consent and contract include Carole Pateman, *The Sexual Contract* (Stanford, Calif.: Stanford University Press, 1988) and Catherine A. MacKinnon, *Towards a Feminist Theory of the State* (Cambridge, Mass.: Harvard University Press, 1989).

4 The term *Mormons* was the informal name for members of the Church of Jesus Christ of Latter-day Saints; it remains the more familiar appellation today. Though, strictly speaking, Mormons practiced *polygyny* (the marriage of one man to multiple women), Mormons and outside observers used the term *polygamy*, as do most scholars. Two relatively recent studies with extensive bibliographies are Carmon B. Hardy, *Solemn Covenant: The Mormon Polygamous Passage* (Urbana: University of Illinois Press, 1992); and Richard S. Van Wagoner, *Mormon Polygamy: A History* (Salt Lake City: Signature, 1989). Subsequent references are cited parenthetically in the text.

5 Sarah Barringer Gordon, " 'Our National Hearthstone': Anti-Polygamy Fiction and the Sentimental Campaign against Moral Diversity in Antebellum

America," *Yale Journal of Law and the Humanities* 8 (1996): 339. Subsequent references are cited parenthetically in the text.

6 For major studies of the antipolygamy reform movement, see Gordon's " 'The Twin Relic of Barbarism': A Legal History of Anti-Polygamy in Nineteenth-Century America" (Ph.D. diss., Princeton University, 1995), and Joan Smyth Iversen, *The Antipolygamy Controversy in U.S. Women's Movements, 1880–1925: A Debate on the American Home* (New York: Garland, 1997).

7 Cornelia Paddock, *The Fate of Madame La Tour: A Tale of Great Salt Lake* (New York: Fords, Howard, and Hulbert, 1881), 112. Subsequent references are cited parenthetically in the text.

8 See Cannon, "The Awesome Power of Sex"; Leonard Arrington and Jon Haupt, "Intolerable Zion: The Image of Mormonism in Nineteenth-Century American Literature," *Western Humanities Review* 22 (1968): 243–60; and Karen Lynn, "Sensational Virtue: Nineteenth-Century Mormon Fiction and American Popular Taste," *Dialogue: A Journal of Mormon Thought* 14 (1981): 101–12. Terryl L. Givens's more recent study, *The Viper on the Hearth: Mormons, Myths, and the Construction of Heresy* (New York: Oxford University Press, 1997), acknowledges that there were more substantial cultural and political motives in this body of popular fiction than merely titillation, though his claim that antipathy toward Mormons was ultimately an anxiety about religious heresy leads him to slight the importance of polygamy and domestic politics. Gordon, " 'National Hearthstone,' " gives the most perceptive summary and analysis of the domestic conventions in this fiction and their link to central legal and cultural issues. Blake Allmendinger's *Ten Most Wanted: The New Western Literature* (New York: Routledge, 1998) discusses antipolygamy fiction in the context of Western themes and concerns; his analysis of the importance of Native peoples in this fiction and in the Utah controversy more generally addresses a significant topic I was unable to discuss in this essay.

9 Amy Dru Stanley, *From Bondage to Contract: Wage Labor, Marriage, and the Market in the Age of Slave Emancipation* (New York: Cambridge University Press, 1998), 27. Subsequent references are cited parenthetically in the text.

10 Maria Ward, *The Mormon Wife: A Life Story of the Sacrifices, Sorrows and Sufferings of Women* (Hartford: Hartford Press, 1872), 313, 428, 429. "Maria Ward" was a pseudonym; the author may have been Cornelia Ferris, the wife of Benjamin Ferris who was appointed territorial secretary to Utah in the 1850s. Subsequent references are cited parenthetically in the text.

11 Lauren Berlant, "Poor Eliza," *American Literature* 70 (1998): 647.

12 Donald Bruce Johnson and Kirk H. Porter, *National Party Platforms, 1840–1972* (Urbana: University of Illinois Press, 1973), 27.

13 Harriet Beecher Stowe, preface to *Tell It All: The Story of A Life's Experience in Mormonism,* by Fanny Stenhouse (Hartford: Worthington, 1890), vi. Subsequent references are cited parenthetically in the text.

14 On the contractual model of the family, see Michael Grossberg, *Governing the Hearth: Law and the Family in Nineteenth-Century America* (Chapel Hill: Uni-

versity of North Carolina Press, 1985). Subsequent references are cited parenthetically in the text.

15 Mary Hudson, *Esther the Gentile* (Topeka: Crane, 1880), 132. Subsequent references are cited parenthetically in the text.

16 Harriet Beecher Stowe, *Uncle Tom's Cabin*, ed. Kathryn Kish Sklar (New York: Library of America, 1982), 29.

17 Alva Milton Kerr, *Trean; or, The Mormon's Daughter: A Romantic Story of Life among the Latter-Day Saints* (Chicago: Belford, Clarke, 1888), 31. Subsequent references are cited parenthetically in the text.

18 John Stuart Mill, *On Liberty*, ed. David Spitz (1859; New York: Norton, 1975), 85–86.

19 Qtd. in Carol Weisbrod and Pamela Sheingorn, "*Reynolds v. United States*: Nineteenth-Century Forms of Marriage and the Status of Women," *Connecticut Law Review* 10 (1978): 829, 834, 841. Subsequent references are cited parenthetically in the text.

20 The diverging views of Mill and Stanton reflect a historical pressure on the concept of female marital consent. Prior to the nineteenth century, it was precisely the acknowledged resemblance of wifehood to servitude that had long given a woman's marital consent its usefulness as a political trope. John Winthrop's "little speech" on liberty, for instance, made conventional use of the figure when he reminded his audience that "the woman's own choice makes such a man her husband; yet being so chosen, he is her lord, and she is to be subject to him, yet in a way of liberty, not of bondage." The likeness between wifehood and bondage makes female consent a valuable emblem of "civil and federal" bonds because subjection could be avowed as an "honor and freedom" rather than as slavery. *The Journal of John Winthrop, 1630–1649*, ed. Richard S. Dunn, James Savage, and Laetitia Yeandle, vol. 3 (Cambridge, Mass.: Belknap, 1996), 282–83. As Gillian Brown notes, early domestic fiction openly recognized a woman's marital consent as a "form of female subjection," an acquiescence to patriarchal authority that novelists acknowledged even as they tried to reconceive it. "Consent, Coquetry, and Consequences," *American Literary History* 9 (1997): 625. But as the nineteenth century increasingly vested notions of liberty in a doctrine of contract directly opposed to slavery, the wife's subjection became a sometimes disconcerting anomaly rather than a useful emblem. After emancipation, the resemblance between marriage and bondage was a rhetorical liability rather than an asset, as Mill's and Stanton's contending views on female consent make clear. For a close historical analysis of this development, see Stanley, *From Bondage to Contract*. Brown's essay offers helpful references for some of the major studies of the consent doctrine. In "Consent and the Body: Injury, Departure, and Desire," *New Literary History* 21 (1990), Elaine Scarry offers a framework for theorizing the equivocal nature of consent (including marital consent) as both subjection and agency.

21 Veronique Petit, *Plural Marriage: The Heart-History of Adele Hersch* (Ithaca, New York: E. D. Norton, 1885), 75. Subsequent references are cited parenthetically in the text.

22 Catharine Beecher, *A Treatise on Domestic Economy* (Boston: Marsh, Capen, Lyon and Webb, 1841), 12–13.

23 Alfreda Eva Bell, *Boadicea the Mormon Wife* (Baltimore: A. R. Orton, 1855), 32.

24 On Mormon women's public support for plural marriage, see Iversen, *The Antipolygamy Controversy*. Prominent women such as Emmeline B. Wells, the editor of the *Women's Exponent*, Martha Hughes Cannon, a physician and later the first female state senator in the United States, and Susa Young Gates, the daughter of Brigham Young, all defended Mormon polygamy as the institution best able to develop female independence, education, and moral leadership in combating the ills of the nation.

25 Hubert Howe Bancroft, *History of Utah* (San Francisco: History Company, 1889), 371–73.

26 Frances E. W. Harper, *Iola Leroy, or Shadows Uplifted* (1892; reprint, New York: Oxford University Press, 1988), 233.

27 These and other depictions can be found in Gary L. Bunker and Davis Bitton, *The Mormon Graphic Image, 1834–1914: Cartoons, Caricatures, and Illustrations* (Salt Lake City: University of Utah Press, 1983).

28 J. H. Beadle, quoted in Kimball Young, *Isn't One Wife Enough?* (New York: Holt, 1954), 24.

29 Etienne Balibar, "Paradoxes of Universality," trans. Michael Edwards, in *Anatomy of Racism*, ed. David Theo Goldberg (Minneapolis: University of Minnesota Press, 1990), 285.

30 Jack London, *Star Rover*, quoted in Givens, *The Viper on the Hearth*, 135. Givens offers several other examples in fiction that differentiate Mormonism from whiteness.

31 See Givens, *The Viper on the Hearth*, 130, and Justin S. Morrill, *Speech of Hon. Justin S. Morrill, of Vermont, on Utah Territory and Its Law—Polygamy and Its License*, qtd. in Sarah Barringer Gordon, " 'The Liberty of Self-Degradation': Polygamy, Woman Suffrage, and Consent in Nineteenth-Century America," *Journal of American History* 83 (1996): 835. Subsequent references are cited parenthetically in the text.

32 Karen Sánchez-Eppler, "Raising Empires Like Children: Race, Nation, and Religious Education," *American Literary History* 8 (1996): 413. Also see Amy Kaplan, "Manifest Domesticity," reprinted in this volume; Lora Romero, *Home Fronts: Domesticity and Its Critics in the Antebellum United States* (Durham, N.C.: Duke University Press, 1997); and Laura Wexler, "Tender Violence: Literary Eavesdropping, Domestic Fiction, and Educational Reform," in *The Culture of Sentiment: Race, Gender, and Sentimentality in Nineteenth-Century America*, ed. Shirley Samuels (New York: Oxford University Press, 1992), 9–38.

33 *Reynolds v. United States*, 98 US 145 (1879); Jennie Bartlett Switzer, *Elder Northfield's Home; Or, Sacrificed on the Mormon Altar* (New York: Brown, 1882).

34 William H. Dixon, *New America*, vol. 1 (London: Hurst and Blackett, 1867), 351.

35 Gordon, " 'National Hearthstone,' " describes the "reallocation of power" in marriage that made wives visible "as rights-bearers, if not precisely as legal actors" and supported the increasing intervention in marriage by the state (346).

36 Nancy F. Cott, "Giving Character to Our Whole Civil Polity: Marriage and the Public Order in the Late Nineteenth Century," in *U.S. History as Women's History: New Feminist Essays*, ed. Linda K. Kerber, Alice Kessler-Harris, and Kathryn Kish Sklar (Chapel Hill: University of North Carolina Press, 1995), 117.

37 Ann Eliza Young, *Wife No. 19; Or, The Story of a Life in Bondage, Being a Complete Exposé of Mormonism, and Revealing Sorrows, Sacrifices and Sufferings of Women in Polygamy* (Hartford: Dustin, Gilman, 1876).

38 Helen Mar Whitney, *Why We Practice Plural Marriage* (Salt Lake City: Juvenile Instructor Office, 1884), qtd. in Kimball Young, *Isn't One Wife Enough?*, 54.

622.2
Osbourne
Everything when
you are a
kid affects
you later in
life

Litigious Therapeutics

RECOVERING THE RIGHTS OF CHILDREN

Gillian Brown

"If you ever had reason to suspect that you may have been sexually abused [as a child], even if you have no explicit memory of it, the chances are very high that you were"—not remembering, advises Beverly Engel, marriage, family, and child counselor, is itself a symptom of the violation.[1] According to this arresting axiom of contemporary child abuse survival therapy, there is no way of determining that a person was not abused. Thus emerges a portrait of the entire population as, unknown to themselves, victimized children. All experience furnishes evidence of this condition, whether or not memory corroborates it.

So, if you exempt yourself from a history of child abuse, you might do well to consult abuse therapist Renee Fredrickson's all-inclusive list of revelatory signs: if you have difficulty falling or staying asleep, don't take care of your teeth, fear going to the dentist, prefer one position during sex, have had a period of sexual promiscuity in your life, eat too much or too little, have recurring dreams, are usually numb or startle easily, space out or daydream, are hypervigilant or take foolish risks, "you will want to consider the possibility that you have repressed memories." And as Fredrickson writes, "if you have repressed memories of childhood trauma, the memories are undoubtedly about abuse."[2]

The identifying signs of child abuse, which appear on similar lists throughout recovery literature, are, as Fredrickson inventively states, "as varied as the human spirit" (30). There is a place for everyone in the recovery movement that qualifies almost any aspect of being as evidence of abuse. This catholicity of the therapeutic vision of experience offers individuals endless possibilities of identification, identification moored in memory, or more exactly, in a rhetoric of memory. The individuality and fallibility of memory make it a register of both truth and falsity. It is the ingeniousness of the recovery movement to appeal to memory as truth while promoting its unverifiability. Abuse therapeutics assume and rely on the uncertainties, indeed, the irrecoverability, of memory.

For despite the attention abuse therapeutics gives to repressed memory syndrome, and despite the proliferation of personal testimonies of abuse experiences that the movement has generated, memory and testimony actually matter very little in the therapist's determination of a history of abuse. All that matters is that a client feels she has been abused. "You only have to assert your reality," Fredrickson counsels her clients and readers, "even if you are the only one who perceives it" (205). Not only do the memories and testimonies of the accused not count—they of course deny the charge—but the content and verifiability of the accusation does not matter. "External proof of repressed memories" of childhood sexual abuse "is elusive," and, indeed, "does not help much if you do get it" (Fredrickson 162). The importance of repressed memories lies in the telling, for as Harvard psychiatrist Judith Herman stresses, "in the telling, the trauma story becomes a testimony . . . giving a new and larger dimension to the patient's individual experience."[3]

Substantiating evidence is unimportant and unnecessary to abuse declarations because they rely on and promote the force of the validity of personal perspective, a perspective that an individual can develop or acquire. Thus the feeling of having been abused need not even originate in the client; the presentation of strong feelings of unhappiness occasions a formulaic interpretation of abuse, an interpretation suggested by the therapist or by some other source—a friend, a book, a newspaper article, a lecture, a TV program. The very therapeutic process of memory recovery often generates and manufactures memories, as social critics Richard Ofshe and Ethan Watters note:

> As the therapist pushes to find more hidden memories, the client, who is already trained in the process, often comes up with still more accounts of having been abused. A vicious cycle is established. When the new set of memories again do nothing to "cure" the client, most likely leaving him or her even more distraught, the therapist can suggest that even worse memories lie in the unconscious. Once the patient and the therapist become fully adept at the alchemy that turns imagination into memory-belief, the process often continues until the client's worst fears are forged into memories. What could be more psychologically damaging than being raped by one's father? Having to have his baby. What could be worse than having to give birth to your father's child? Having to kill the child. What could be worse than having to kill a baby? Having to eat the baby after you've killed it. What could be worse than all this? Having to do these things during ritualized worship of the Devil.[4]

In the case of the 1988 satanic ritual abuse scandals in Olympia, Washington, two sisters recovered memories of abuse after their family watched Geraldo

Rivera's special report entitled "Devil Worship: Exposing Satan's Underground."[5]

Almost as a parody of historicism, the insubstantiality of sources and evidence in abuse memories and accusations allows for—as it affirms—the testimonies of those whose voices have historically counted least. Psychotherapist Alice Miller's dictum that "the child is always innocent," a pronouncement clearly aimed to promote the advocacy of abused children, formally establishes the reality of sexual abuse as it generally stipulates the purity and veracity of the victim's perspective.[6] If the child is always innocent, what the child reports—or what a client remembers or recovers about childhood experience—must be true. Recognition of abuse thus has served as affirmation of the voices of other traditionally underrepresented or disadvantaged persons in modern American society, especially women. So it is not surprising that other narratives of abuse—accounts of the terrible effects of racism or domestic violence, for example—have gained a legal and social status in recent years, have attained a validity as explanations if not justifications for certain individual acts and behaviors. The sexual abuse explanation, moreover, has become a compelling metaphor for whatever forms of abuse and suffering that women (and others) have experienced; it furnishes a mode of making sense of personal experience and pain.[7]

Yet sense is not the only thing accusers seek. When they go public with their accusations and seek reparation through the legal system, they are developing more than a metaphor: they are asserting the actuality of abuse and naming the abuser or abusers. In doing so, they indict parents or parental figures. What the abuse story offers is the most powerful justification for severance of filial relations with parents. Abuse therapists encourage this disaffiliation, which they call detachment or divorce, as an act of self-determination, a fundamental exercise and expression of what they term the "right to recovery."[8]

The term *detachment* also aptly describes the actual indifference to the rights of children that continues amidst the contemporary rhetoric of concern about them. For example, a recent *New York Times* editorial observes that "New York City's child welfare program is still in shambles, failing to perform even routine tasks that would make victims of abuse or neglect less vulnerable."[9] That children, especially poor and minority children, regularly suffer from inadequate social services, medical care, and education, remains conspicuously absent from the drama of the abuse recovery movement's vindication of the wrongs of children—that is, of primarily white, middle-class, female children. A much older and continuous narrative of childhood sexual abuse, recorded in slave narratives and black American autobiographies, significantly remains offstage.[10]

While the contemporary popularity of the abuse narrative registers a new validation of hitherto disregarded personal perspectives, a crucial respect for the testimonies and psychologies of victimized individuals, vindication generally operates as a private affair, independent of the public policies affecting the lives of children. Not surprisingly, the portrait of abusive family relations comes into relief and wide circulation at a time when Americans, or at least the representations of American sentiment, appear most hostile to social welfare programs. It is therefore important to consider how the current affirmation of previously discounted testimonies, clearly a critical benefit to the many who have suffered abuse, operates to restrict rather than extend entitlements.

Foregrounding the rights of children, the abuse recovery movement draws on, and reconfigures, a crucial concept of the liberal tradition: the long-standing identification of individual entitlement with children.[11] Since Locke, the politicization and sexualization of children has served to define and protect identity. Invoking the vividness of childhood—vivid because relayed in registers of adult experience (namely, politics and sexuality)—summons what Judith Herman calls a sense of "commonality" (214–36), indeed, a common fact of experience. This unrepressed memory of childhood is what the abuse survivor movement depends on for substantiating evidence. The fact that an individual can adopt and agree to a narrative of her past that she doesn't remember—to a circumstantial account that cultural agencies such as therapy and the media furnish and endorse—suggests the crucial role of external formal corroboration and credit in sustaining the individual's sense of abuse.[12] From the now acceptable chronology that abuse narratives represent, persons can discover a standard of their personal histories. For while the truth of abuse doesn't require direct testimony and corroboration, it does enlist a common heritage as its irrefutable proof. By common heritage, I mean both the liberal rhetorical tradition of the entitled child and the genealogical vision of contemporary abuse therapeutics.

The Liberal Tradition of the Entitled Child

Locke notably endowed children with the faculty of self-determination, with consent. Proponents of monarchy regularly had argued that the natural subordination of children to parents exemplified the natural order of the subject's relation to the monarch. To advance the claims of present generations against the arbitrary rule of monarchy, Locke's political theory and psychology crucially revised the idea of the child's subordinate position. Far from signifying a natural order of subjection, the dependent condition of a person's minority is defined by Locke as the child's "express or tacit consent" to necessary parental governance.[13] Even though children initially lack reason and will—the necessary components of self-direction—they are born with property in themselves, property which is merely held in trust by the parents until the children can manage their own property, that is, themselves.

Since parental dominion extends no further than the minority of the children, the latter naturally check the extent of their own subjection. The children's consent, then, ratifies their dependence on the parent as well as their future independence from the parent. Recognizing and protecting an embryonic form of agency in the child, Locke welds consent to natural sequence. The eventuality of childhood's end in adulthood aligns individual freedom with futurity, an expectation granted by birthright. Independent agency is postponed but certain, indeed certain by virtue of its postponement. In the provisionality of childhood, Locke finds a paradigm of freedom, which he defines as the suspended state before the determination and implementation of an act. It is in the mind's "power to suspend the execution and satisfaction of any of its desires" that Locke situates "the source of all liberty." "For during this suspension of any desire before the will be determined to action, and the action (which follows that determination) done, we have opportunity to examine, view, and judge of the good or evil of what we are going to do."[14]

Agency thus does not simply reside in the body, naturally developing with it, but inheres in the process of measuring what a body might do against some standard—in Locke's words, "good or evil." Law, whether religious or secular, supplies the standards of measurement, the horizons in which consent operates. It is law as well as bodily state that determines the span of childhood, stipulating the age of majority and the age of consent. Like childhood, consent is both natural and statutory, a faculty and right originating from birth, defined and protected by law. In consent, persons appear forever filial, suspended between their desires and whatever cultural authority they do or will embody. With the entitlement of the child, childhood becomes an integral aspect and continuous component of adulthood.

The Lockean formulation of the rights of individuals charges parents or governors with a natural and legal duty to protect and respect children, just as it licenses government to serve and protect citizens. Violation of parental duty toward children accordingly figures prominently in justificatory rhetorics of early modern republican revolutions. It is this eighteenth-century alignment of rights with children that made stories of Marie Antoinette's incest with her son effective antimonarchical polemics.[15] Similarly, to rally American colonists to revolt from the rule of Great Britain, Tom Paine's *Common Sense* characterized Americans as children fleeing from a tyrannical parent, "not from the tender embraces of the mother, but from the cruelty of the monster," the mother turned monstrous.[16] Paine's image of child abuse, which clearly remains potent in the American imagination of identity, draws on an iconography of abusive or insensitive parenthood familiar from widely read novels as well as from political philosophy and educational theories.[17]

The eighteenth-century emergence of the figure of the wronged child—exemplified most dramatically by the story of the Children in the Wood, known today as Hansel and Gretel, whose parents desert them, or in some versions of the story, murder them—supplies political discourse with a new rhetorical tool. With the image of the wronged child, the case for individual rights gains a powerful affective appeal. In stories of children's suffering, the most extreme forms of affliction—starvation, imprisonment, violence, and death—foreground bodily harms feared by everyone. Children's greater vulnerability to harm and helplessness to overcome it summon an urgency to the redress of their conditions, an urgency that Paine musters in his portrayal of American colonists as suffering children.

Along with the figure of the wronged child emerges the figure of the empowered child. In the popular stories of Jack the Giantkiller and retellings of the ancient tale of Tom Thumb, tiny children manage amazing feats of courage, strength, and ingenuity. And in the less fantastic new stories invented by eighteenth-century writers, poor children such as Goody Two-Shoes and Giles Gingerbread display an industriousness that makes them successful and respected adults. The victimized child—or the underprivileged child—often becomes, like Goody and other virtuous heroines and heroes of children's literature, the capable child who skillfully negotiates the circumstances of life.[18] At the heart of the appeal for suffering children thus lies a confidence in the ability of children to make it on their own: the faith that Paine urges Americans to attach to their independence. But first he projects the vulnerability of the American situation.

To make the revolutionary cause common sense, Paine appeals to what he conceives of as universal feelings about injury and redress, "those feelings and affections which nature justifies" (89). Everyone, because "sensible of injuries," can imagine what it feels like to be driven from house and home, to have property destroyed and circumstances ruined. Everyone can and should make the sufferers' case their own. For, as Paine reasons, "the social compact would dissolve, and justice be extirpated the earth, or have only a casual existence were we callous to the touches of affection. The robber and the murderer, would often escape unpunished, did not the injuries which our tempers sustain, provoke us into justice" (100).

Making his case for the injured colonial subjects, Paine developed the Lockean figure of the child-citizen into the figure of crime victim. In urging the "common cause" of redressing the wrongs suffered by the American colonists, Paine recalls his readers to their social affections, the common concern epitomized by parental sentiment for children. His repeated exhortations to remember the children and their future children expand the population of sufferers under England's rule and thereby widen the sympathy that would relieve such suffering. Breaking from England—the abusive parent— therefore " 'tis not the concern of a day, a year, or an age; posterity are virtually involved in the contest, and will be more or less affected, even to the end of time, by the proceedings now" (82). To avoid the break, Paine stresses, only would defer this act to the next generation, and therefore would burden them with sufferings that could be prevented: "Wherefore since nothing but blows will do, for God's sake, let us come to a final separation, and not leave the next generation to be cutting throats, under the violated unmeaning names of parent and child" (90).

After "the fatal nineteenth of April 1775," when the English troops massacred Americans at Lexington, King George can only be disdained as "the wretch, that with the pretended title of FATHER OF HIS PEOPLE can unfeelingly hear of their slaughter, and composedly sleep with their blood upon his soul" (92). And because such abusive and illegitimate authority "sooner or later must have an end," "as parents, we [Americans] can have no joy, knowing that this government is not sufficiently lasting to ensure any thing which we may bequeath to posterity" (87). So "the precariousness with which all

American property is possessed" threatens present and future persons. The effects of Britain's injuries against Americans appear permanent and perpetual. Marked and forever altered by these injuries, Americans must halt any continued affiliation with England. Indeed, "the last cord now is broken" for "as well as the lover can forgive the ravisher of his mistress" can "the continent forgive the murders of Britain" (99). "There are injuries which nature cannot forgive," Paine declares; the injuries that the American colonists have suffered from the British government appear as assaults on persons which amount to robberies of their former conditions. Because violence invades and irrevocably alters bodies, it interrupts the natural courses of persons—it robs them of time as they have known it. Thus Paine puts the American complaint in the form of a lament: "Can ye restore to us the time that is past? Can ye give to prostitution its former innocence?" (99). In the image of the ravished mistress, as well as in the image of the prostitute whose "former innocence" can never be restored, Paine represents colonial Americans as permeable bodies, bodies now altered beyond the innocent state of childhood, bodies which must be protected by separating them from their former relations. And the offspring who represent the future of these bodies, their generative, affective, and economic capacities, will also be protected by the break from Britain. Paine thus envisions the reformation of the North American colonies into an independent nation as the establishment of an "asylum for mankind" (100), no less than a protective act for the future of humanity.[19]

The Genealogical Vision of Abuse Therapeutics

From the reparative model of sociopolitical relations envisioned by Paine, we can trace the therapeutic pattern through which Americans have characteristically defined their rights, a pattern perhaps most familiarly evident in tort law, and now manifest in the media and counseling practices whereby the suffering seek solace. An extreme version of Paine's notion of reparative sympathy, the abuse recovery movement literalizes his recommendation to make the sufferer's case one's own. Invoking the universal experience of childhood, abuse therapeutics suggest that anyone may in fact be an abuse victim. By virtue of having been children, all persons are potential casualties of abuse. As in the case of minors protected by the laws of statutory rape, an arbitrary rule invents and defines crime and victim.

But because, in another turn of the screw in this vision of victimage, the abusers themselves very likely were also abused as children (or, as is also sometimes claimed, in a prior life), we are left with a strange panorama of victimization and victims without perpetrators, or rather, with perpetrators infinitely receding into the past (Edmundson 57–58). Abuse strangely operates as both a crime and a defense of the same crime. This protean facility of abuse—its availability as an accusation to anyone of whatever age—would appear to undermine the prosecutorial force of the abuse charge. A statutory refuge open to everyone doesn't maintain the distinctions a statute works to define and maintain. By the account of abuse therapeutics, everyone is entitled to the protection of the statutory: everyone needs advocacy and compensation because everyone is a victim. Abuse therapeutics thus extend the formalism of statutory protection to apply to the entire population.

Perhaps it is only fitting that the perspective of abused children eliminates adulthood altogether. As adult perpetrators of abuse readily turn into (as they turn out to be) abused children, parental authority withers away. At the same time, the parent's defensive application of the abuse charge extends the logic of the victim's claims and confirms it. In this weird rehabilitation of parents / perpetrators into victimized children, parents come to resemble and reiterate their children—they are the best imaginable advocates and corroborators of their children's perspectives. The point of the vision of ubiquitous child abuse is thus to establish an identity between parent and child, to remake the parent in the child's image. Furnished with both a historical source and precedent, the abuse assertion gains the authority of numbers and agreement.

As if following Aristotle's recommendation to rhetoricians that "if you have no witnesses on your side," you should "argue that the judges must decide from what is probable," abuse therapeutics devise a means of meeting the qualifications of probability.[20] Probability, as Locke recognized, in fact does not operate independently of witnesses because it is an agreement based on two fallible forms of proof: conformity with our own experience and the testimony of others' experience (*Human Understanding*, 2: 365–66). Taking a cue from Locke's delineation of judgment as a process of measuring internal and external accounts, abuse therapeutics conjure an external testimony. To this end, the retrospective line of victimage in the narrative of abuse creates the semblance of a corroborating witness. In effect, then, the figure of the abused-abusive parent provides a testimony of experience that conforms with the child's alleged experience. From this concurrence of others' experience with the individual's own experience emerges the probability of abuse.

By marshaling hypothetical witnesses from the population pool of the victimized—which includes everyone—abuse therapeutics garner credibility for an otherwise purely circumstantial narrative.[21] The probability of having been abused produces probable confirming testimonies of abuse, a concocted standard by which the assertion of abuse gains not specific corroboration but general reasonability. Whereas the evidentiary project of the Lockean self is a continual task of measurement and judgment, the evidentiary project of abuse therapeutics is to make identity literally self-evident, beyond questions of proof. The individual experience of abuse is made manifest in and as a standard experience of the population. Abuse therapeutics thereby relieve the self from the very evidentiary task that for Locke constitutes and manifests individual freedom. The substance and verifiability of individual memory, then, don't matter for the truth of abuse because that truth is everyone's heritage. More precisely, the concept of memory attains an authoritative status. Memory can be assigned to persons, as in the film *Bladerunner*, thereby formally constituting their identities. In this employment of memory, memory stands as a formal truth, uncomplicated by the numerous factors of time, age, perspective, vocabulary, education, fantasy, and desire that usually attend and shape it. The work of memory, which is the usual task of the therapy of traumatized individuals, disappears in abuse therapeutics, which instead supplies the individual with a ready-made memory and identity. Thus the work of abuse therapeutics is to encourage individuals to claim their heritage, to recover identity through common sense: to find their memories to be in conformity with their heritage.[22]

Directed against the heritability of power, liberalism (as Locke conceived it and Paine elaborated it in *Common Sense* and later in *The Rights of Man*) eschews appeals to heritage, any invocations of the priority of the past. Indeed, obligation to the future, to the unborn, is what haunts liberalism since the eighteenth century.[23] The past, of course, does not disappear with the appearance of each new generation. Rather, all children develop and ideally help define their relation to external measures, including the measure of history. History thus provides one of the corroborative sources of the individual. But it is a source subject to questioning, a testimony that can be stricken or repudiated or discredited or simply ignored.

Making family history bear witness to a certain account of individual experience, abuse therapeutics heed the evidentiary imperative of liberal individualism to substantiate oneself but significantly alter the status of supporting evidence. That is, the recovery movement constructs a form of literally unquestionable evidence. Substituting heritage for history, as the movement does, stipulates the past of the individual. Heritage is an authoritative and venerable account of the individual that does not need remembering: it can simply be claimed. Thus, as abuse therapeutics invoke and employ the liberal tradition of individual rights, they display the appeal of making claims to heritage that continues to complicate the operation of liberalism to counteract heritability.

In Paine's vindication of the wrongs of children, sympathy for the suffering child operates to redirect Americans from a sense of obligation to the past (embodied in monarchy) to a sense of obligation to the future. Contrary to the late twentieth-century rhetoric of children and national debt, Paine strikingly imagines national debt as the "national bond" (102) that will sustain the affective relations between present and future. As the sign of Americans' obligation to their children, debt will remind them of what their revolutionary ancestors have done for them. Indeed, not to establish independence from Britain, according to Paine, "is using posterity with the utmost cruelty; because it is leaving them with the great work to do, and a debt upon their backs from which they derive no advantage" (101). As a British colony, America has to pay Britain's considerable national debts. By allowing this situation to continue, "we [Americans] are running the next generation into debt" (87). If future Americans are to be obligated to a debt, it should be a debt made by Americans: "we ought to do the work of it, otherwise we use [posterity] meanly and pitifully" (87). The work of present Americans in contracting a national debt—the work of revolution and nation building—therefore will save and serve future Americans. And, Paine stresses, "whatever we may contract on this account will serve as a glorious memento of our virtue. Can we but leave posterity with a settled form of government, an independent constitution of its own, the purchase at any price will be cheap" (101).

Testament to a new social compact—the formation of an independent American nation—the debt in Paine's view enables and benefits the generations who inherit it. The documentation of commitment to the future, debt conveys to posterity their own right to manage their relation to the past and to look forward. And, as Paine's fellow proponents of an American republic immediately recognized, posterity might choose to relinquish or reorganize their relation to the past.[24] For the sake of this cause, which affects the fate of posterity "even to the end of time" (82), Paine realigns American colonists from their ties to the past to their duties to the future. In one of the most memorable of the many striking images in *Common Sense*, Paine envisions how the revolution will inhabit the landscape of distant generations to come: "The least fracture now will be like a name engraved with the point of a pin on the tender rind of a young oak; the wound will enlarge with the tree, and posterity read it in full grown letters" (81). Enacting revolution and contracting a new national debt will transform the world. The event will leave its mark, significantly in the process of natural growth, to be seen, traced, and appreciated. Time will enhance the magnitude of the message that present acts can convey as these acts accrue in the age and girth of the oak.

To counter and repair the image of Americans as wounded children, an image sustained in the description of the impressionable "tender rind of a young oak," Paine imagines their revolution as a healing incision. The revolutionary "fracture" operates not to injure or destroy, but to furnish the future with a record of commitment to it. Paine describes this wounding as a form of writing, the engraving of a name, a process that succeeds and memorializes the present. The pain and suffering ascribed to the injured colonists are thus relieved and replaced by the activities of working, rebelling, fighting, contracting, and building. It is not enough for Americans to think of themselves as injured children: they have to become rescuers and guardians of themselves and of those children yet to come. The prosthetics of revolution, debt, manufacture, and trade that Paine prescribes thus also invoke the figures of heroic children which accompany the eighteenth-century figures of suffering children. Significantly, as Paine envisions the future in *Common Sense*, the image of abused children gives way to lists and enumerations of potential American prosperity, to representations of possibilities awaiting incorporation rather than of permanently injured bodies.

To the third edition of the pamphlet, Paine appended a list of calculations of the cost of building an American navy for the national defense and commerce. The numbers by which Paine tallies the expense of this enterprise, for which he recommends contracting a national debt, promise security and comfort. Rather than concluding with the imagery of criminally altered bodies—such as the ravished mistress or the ruined prostitute or the hurt child—Paine supplements the all too vulnerable and evanescent location of the body with written figures that measure (or at least predict) the accumulation of resources that will sustain bodies. The safety and welfare of bodies requires metaphysical operations to forward them. Thus for Paine, the measures of statistics and future history (itself a statistical conjecture) crucially function in the liberal rhetoric of individual rights to record what persons have done and can do. The scarred oak survives; its marks of injury become both the sign of its healing and the register of something more: the realization of growth that the future can bring. Paine's imagery of pain gives way to an imagery of the gains that can succeed pain.

Childhood's End

In contemporary abuse therapeutics, the spectacle of pain doesn't disappear but instead perpetually recurs. In taking up Paine's powerful rhetoric, his descendants in the abuse recovery movement redirect it from the future into an undocumentable and omnipresent past. The undocumentable past of abuse therapeutics often partakes of the fantastic or supernatural, issuing in accounts of abuse conducted by satanic cults.[25] Cults immediately suggest a frightening numerousness: numbers of perpetrators and numbers of crimes to which satanic allegiances continually and regularly incite their members. The seemingly irrational alignment of abuse narratives with satanism makes sense when we consider how the pervasiveness of Satan suggests both numerousness and immeasureability: a spectral ordination in place of verifiable numbers to which accusations can be tied. By this connection to the ancient tradition of Satan stories, abuse narratives attain a potentially even more authoritative status; they take on mythic proportions. As a common heritage to which individuals tether their memories, the contemporary abuse narrative forms and furnishes an originary myth of our most recent social compact. This myth tells Americans a story through which they confirm the establishment and continuation of therapeutic authority, an authority now accorded not just to the health professions but to media, government, religion, and education. The current vogue in victimage stories thus cannot be reduced simply to the legal defense tactic Alan Dershowitz calls "the abuse excuse."[26] Members of a culture founded on Paine's prototype of the abuse excuse, Americans continue to regard their rights as forms of self-defense against an external authority perceived as abusive. And as the recent events of Waco, the Oklahoma City Federal Building bombing, and Texas secession attest, Americans often regard their own government as the abusive authority, an operation of intrusive and illegitimate power to be repudiated and even eliminated.

For Paine and early Americans, however, the principle of the entitled child crucially depends on the ephemerality of childhood and the formal exemptions and protections granted that temporary state: on the courses of natural and cultural history. Contrary to this recognition of the potentiality and inevitability of change, the genealogical vision of the abuse recovery movement binds the child to an eternal past. Abuse therapeutics insist on history as a continual repetition of the same events, on personal experience as an unremitting common sense. The change to which childhood is inextricably bound in the liberal tradition disappears in the recovery movement's representation of American heritage. To recover the connection of childhood with change may require yet another rewriting of the social compact in which individuals revoke the charter of therapeutic authority.

Notes

1   Beverly Engel, *The Right to Innocence: Healing the Trauma of Childhood Sexual Abuse* (New York: Ivy Books, 1989), 2. Subsequent references are cited parenthetically in the text.

2   Renee Fredrickson, *Repressed Memories: A Journey to Recovery from Sexual Abuse* (New York: Simon and Schuster, 1992), 48–51, 23. Subsequent references are cited parenthetically in the text.

3   Judith Lewis Herman, *Trauma and Recovery* (New York: Basic Books, 1992), 181. Subsequent references are cited parenthetically in the text.

4   Richard Ofshe and Ethan Watters, *Making Monsters: False Memories, Psychotherapy, and Sexual Hysteria* (New York: Scribner's, 1994), 177. Subsequent references are cited parenthetically in the text.

5   Mark Edmundson, *Nightmare on Main Street: Angels, Sadomasochism, and the Culture of Gothic* (Cambridge, Mass.: Harvard University Press, 1997), 39. Subsequent references are cited parenthetically in the text.

6   Alice Miller, *Thou Shalt Not Be Aware: Society's Betrayal of the Child*, trans. Hildegarde Hannum and Hunter Hannum (New York: Meridian, 1986), 314.

7   For a critique of feminist claims for and of the recovery movement, see Wendy Kaminer, *I'm Dysfunctional, You're Dysfunctional: The Recovery Movement and Other Self-Help Fashions* (Reading, Mass.: Addison-Wesley, 1992), esp. 87–100.

8   Engel, *Right to Innocence*, 199–200; Ellen Bass and Laura Davis, *The Courage to Heal: A Guide for Women Survivors of Child Sexual Abuse* (New York: Harper and Row, 1988).

9   "Little Progress on Child Abuse," *New York Times*, 17 August 1997, 14.

10 Since the nineteenth century, a narrative of childhood sexual abuse course also exists in court records and social work reports. In her pioneering study *Heroes of Their Own Lives*, Linda Gordon has usefully initiated the investigation of the historical and political construction of family violence. As Gordon writes, "to insist that family violence is a political issue is not to deny its material reality as

a problem for individuals—a painful, often terrifying reality." Linda Gordon, *Heroes of Their Own Lives: The Politics and History of Family Violence: Boston 1880–1960* (New York: Penguin, 1989), 5. As this essay will show, the rhetorics and therapies addressing abusive family relations also operate to construct the realities and significance of individual experience.

11 Since Philippe Ariès's study *Centuries of Childhood: A Social History of Family Life*, trans. Robert Baldick (New York: Vintage, 1962) established the key role of late seventeenth- and early eighteenth-century changing conceptions of childhood in the rise of modernity, scholars have noted the connection between rhetorics of individual rights and rhetorics of childhood. David Archard informatively tracks the coupling of childhood with issues of rights in recent studies in *Children: Rights and Childhood* (New York: Routledge, 1993), 178–84. Exploring this coupling in the literary realm, Jacqueline Rose sees children's fiction, which first emerged in written and widely available forms in the eighteenth century, as promoting and maintaining "the sexual and political mystification of the child" through which adults define identity. Jacqueline Rose, *The Case of Peter Pan, Or, The Impossibility of Children's Fiction* (Philadelphia: University of Pennsylvania Press, 1992), 11.

12 Alexander Welsh has demonstrated the changing status of circumstantial evidence in the Anglo-American legal and literary imaginations, revealing how respect for this form of evidence historically has served prosecutorial purposes—just as it is now serving the prosecutorial projects of abuse victims. See Alexander Welsh, *Strong Representations: Narrative and Circumstantial Evidence in England* (Baltimore: Johns Hopkins University Press, 1992), esp. 1–62.

13 John Locke, *Two Treatises of Government*, ed. Peter Laslett (1690; Cambridge: Cambridge University Press, 1960), 335.

14 Locke, *An Essay Concerning Human Understanding*, 2 vols., ed. Alexander Campbell Fraser (1690; New York: Dover, 1959), 1:345. Subsequent references are cited parenthetically in the text.

15 See Lynn Hunt, "The Many Bodies of Marie Antoinette: Political Pornography and the Problem of the Feminine in the French Revolution," in *Eroticism and the Body Politic*, ed. Hunt (Baltimore: Johns Hopkins University Press, 1991), 108–30.

16 Thomas Paine, *Common Sense* (1776; New York: Penguin, 1982), 84. Subsequent references are cited parenthetically in the text.

17 See Jay Fliegelman, *Prodigals and Pilgrims: The American Revolution against Patriarchal Authority, 1750–1800* (Cambridge: Cambridge University Press, 1982), 9–194.

18 See Gillian Avery, *Behold the Child: American Children and Their Books, 1621–1922* (Baltimore: Johns Hopkins University Press, 1994), 36–62.

19 Eric Foner has pointed out that Paine always considered the larger republican argument of *Common Sense* more important than the local call for American independence. Paine himself wrote in 1806 that "my motive and object in all my political works, beginning with *Common Sense*, have been to rescue man

from tyranny and false systems and false principles of government, and enable him to be free." Eric Foner, *Tom Paine and Revolutionary America* (New York: Oxford University Press, 1976), 75.

20   Aristotle, *Rhetoric*, trans. W. Rhys Roberts (New York: Modern Library, 1954), 86.

21   Ian Hacking's study *The Emergence of Probability* reminds us that probability and statistics historically had to attain their status as registers of reality. Mary Poovey has recently explored fictive possibilities and pitfalls of the statistical in early nineteenth-century scientific discourse. Ian Hacking, *The Emergence of Probability: A Philosophical Study of Early Ideas about Probability, Induction, and Statistical Inference* (Cambridge: Cambridge University Press, 1975); Mary Poovey, "Figures of Arithmetic, Figures of Speech: The Discourse of Statistics in the 1830s," *Critical Inquiry* 19, no. 2 (1993): 256–76.

22   Steven Knapp provocatively raises the question, "Why should it ever matter, if it does, that an authoritative narrative correspond to, or have anything much to do with, historical actuality?" Steven Knapp, "Collective Memory and the Actual Past," in *Literary Interest: The Limits of Anti-Formalism* (Cambridge, Mass.: Harvard University Press, 1993), 107. While consideration of this question is beyond the scope of my essay, I would suggest that the cooperative association delineated in Knapp's question is precisely what the recovery movement is trying to establish when it encourages individuals to accept and identify with an account of experience that purports to be a pervasive historical reality.

23   Present American debates and energies surrounding abortion thus can be seen as a locus for late twentieth-century concerns about whether the ideal of obligation to the future serves the needs of Americans now.

24   Debt does not worry Paine and other republican defenders of the sovereignty of the people because even though debt may commit future generations to repayment, it only does so if those generations choose to continue the political system into which they are born, if they choose to identify themselves with their revolutionary ancestors. As Noah Webster put it in 1787, people "have no right to make laws for those who are not in existence"; making debts confers responsibility on those who are not in existence only if they accept the authority of their government and therefore authorize that government to assume debts, old or new. Qtd. in Gordon S. Wood, *The Creation of the American Republic, 1776–1787* (New York: Norton, 1972), 378–79.

25   See Ofshe and Watters, *Making Monsters*; Lawrence Wright, *Remembering Satan* (New York: Knopf, 1994); and Richard A. Gardner, *True and False Accusations of Child Sex Abuse* (Cresskill, N.J.: Creative Therapeutics, 1992).

26   Alan M. Dershowitz, *The Abuse Excuse and Other Cop-Outs, Sob Stories, and Evasions of Responsibility* (New York: Little, Brown, 1994).

American Studies in

the "Age of the World Picture"

THINKING THE QUESTION OF LANGUAGE

William V. Spanos

The trouble with Eichmann was precisely that so many were like him, and that the many were neither perverted nor sadistic, that they were, and still are, terribly and terrifyingly normal. From the viewpoint of our legal institutions and of our moral standards of judgment, this normality was much more terrifying than all the atrocities put together, for it implied . . . that this new type of criminal, who is in actual fact *hostis generis humani*, commits his crimes under circumstances that make it well-nigh impossible for him to know or to feel that he is doing wrong.
—Hannah Arendt, *Eichmann in Jerusalem*

We had to destroy Ben Tre in order to save it.—an American colonel in Vietnam, as reported by Michael Herr

I

One of the major achievements of the emergent New Americanist studies—and I think here of the brilliant inaugural work of Sacvan Bercovitch and especially of Donald Pease—has been its exposure not simply of the imperial Cold War logic informing the American canon established by the Old Americanists—Perry Miller, F. O. Matthiessen, Lionel Trilling, Richard Chase, Quentin Anderson, and so on—but also of that undeviating logic's origins in the founding moment of the powerful ideology of American exceptionalism: the perennial belief in America's unique ameliorative global mission in the world. I am, of course, referring to the American Puritans' representation of their physical and spiritual departure from Europe and the plantation of their colony in the "New World" as their providentially ordained "errand into the wilderness" to build a "City on the Hill," a (self)representation, as Bercovitch has shown, that has been endorsed and perpetuated in secularized form by the nationalistic custodians, both high and low, of the American cultural memory ever since that founding moment of American history.[1]

This genealogical New Americanist discourse has been salutary because, in destructuring the American canon incumbent on the invention of the American Renaissance, it has released, or, better, decolonized, a multiplicity of American "Others" from the bondage of the imperialist structure imposed on them by the Old Americanists' commitment to the nationalist/ exceptionalist project. To put this achievement another way, the genealogical project of the New Americanists has reenergized American studies by making visible those constituencies of the American polis that were hitherto rendered invisible by the dominant culture—native Americans, blacks, women, gays, ethnic minorities, and so forth. In so doing, it has contributed significantly to the establishment of a cultural context enabling these silenced constituencies to answer back to the dominant culture that had spoken for them in the past.

Despite this achievement, however, the New Americanist initiative has not, in my mind, adequately thought that which its oppositional discourse has decolonized, rendered visible, and given voice to. And this, I submit, is because it remains vestigially inscribed by the ideology of American exceptionalism even as it criticizes it and tries to transcend its confining parameters. In thus focusing on this vestigial adherence to the exceptionalist problematic, despite its impulse toward expanding and diversifying the horizon of American studies, the New Americanist discourse has remained too local—too American—in scope; it has failed to adequately think the global implications of its critique of exceptionalism. And this is because, in tracing the American canon established by the Old Americanists back through the Cold War to the founding moment of American exceptionalism, the New Americanists' genealogical project has not penetrated to the ontological ground of this relay between the canon and the Cold War, to its deepest, most deeply backgrounded, and most invisible ideological structure. I am not simply referring to America's tenacious historical privileging of the imperial metaphysical perspective as the agent of knowledge production, that perspective, synchronous with the founding of the idea and practices of Europe, which, in perceiving time from after or above its disseminations, enables the spatialization of being and subjugation or accommodation of the differences it disseminates to the identical, self-present, and plenary (global/planetary) whole. I am also referring to America's obsessive and systematic refinement and fulfillment of the panoptic logic of this old world perspective in an indissolubly related relay of worldly imperial practices, the intrinsic goal of which is not simply the domination of global space but also of thinking itself. In the wake of the massive critique of the destructive or deconstructive initiative of the 1970s—its interrogation of the Western ontotheological tradition, meaning logocentrism—in the 1980s, the New Americanists' genealogical project, in other words, has all too hastily rejected theory for practice, or, rather, has reduced them to a binary opposition that privileges practice over theory. In so doing, this initiative "against theory"[2] has failed to attend to the fact that the American imperial project has entailed not simply the colonization of the planet but also, and above all, the reification and colonization of thinking and language.

The critique of deconstructive theory was justifiable insofar as its early practitioners overdetermined the question of being. (I contributed to that project in a chapter on the indifference of *différance* in my book *Heidegger and Criticism*.[3]) But, I submit, it has blinded itself to the indissoluble, however unevenly practiced, relationship between metaphysical thinking and global domination, what I have elsewhere called the *Pax Metaphysica* and the *Pax Americana*.[4] It is a blindness borne witness to by the indifference of New Americanist criticism—indeed, as in the synecdochal case of Richard Rorty's recent book *Achieving Our Country*,[5] of virtually all posttheoretical discourses—to the simultaneous announcement by the deputies of the dominant American culture (and the media that transmits its "American" vision) of the "end of history" and the advent of "the New World Order." I am not simply referring to Francis Fukuyama, whose highly mediatized book *The End of History and the Last Man* can all too easily, but mistakenly, be refuted by reference to global events since the Gulf War,[6] but also to Richard Haass, who, in his resonantly entitled book, *The Reluctant Sheriff*, accommodates these contradictory contemporary events to the discourse of the new world order.[7] This announcement of the end of history, it should be underscored, not only asserts its continuity with and fulfillment of the positive global promise of American democracy announced by Alexis de Tocqueville in 1835: "The gradual development of the principle of equality is . . . a providential fact. It has all the characteristics of such a fact: it is universal, it is lasting. It constantly eludes all human interference, and all events as well as all men contribute to its progress."[8] It also blatantly recuperates the Hegelian dialectical Universal History (and the metaphysical thinking endemic to it), albeit in the latter's highly developed instrumentalist allotrope, and appropriates it to the global post–Cold War context. And this despite their apparently decisive delegitimation by theory in the 1970s. "What is emerging victorious," Fukuyama writes, "is not so much liberal practice, as the liberal *idea*. That is to say, for a very large part of the world, there is now no ideology with pretensions to universality that is in a position to challenge liberal democracy, and no universal principle of legitimacy other than the sovereignty of the people." And, in a way that predicts the response to the end of the Cold War by oppositional critics, he adds: "Even non-democrats will have to speak the language of democracy in order to justify their deviation from the single universal standard" (45).

And that is precisely my point. The universalist-instrumentalist discourse that frames the triumphalist American vision of the brave new post–Cold War world rings hollow in the wake of its self-destruction during the Vietnam War and of the postmodern thinking that has tacitly theorized the violence inherent in its saying. Nevertheless, New Americanists continue unthinkly to use this language even when it opposes the violence of its practices, thus becoming unwitting accomplices of the very regime of truth it would delegitimate. This complicity, for example, is manifest, as Paul Bové has decisively shown, in Bercovitch's "reformist" mode of dealing with problems confronting the Americanist seeking for alternatives to the consensus-producing imperatives of the American jeremiadic discourse, specifically, his disabling delimitation of critical options to those made available by that discourse: "The option [for American critics] is not multiplicity or consensus. It is whether to make use of the categories of the culture or to be used by them."[9]

To generalize Bové's critique of Bercovitch in the current global terms I am interested in, like the scientists in Heidegger's paradigm in "What Is Metaphysics?"—who willfully "wish to know nothing about [the nothing]" on which the discourse of the technological "age of the world picture" is constructed[10]—the New Americanists have failed to respond to the claim of the silent and spectral hollowness that haunts the triumphalist post–Cold War discourse of the dominant culture. Which is to say, they fail to hear its call to rethink the thinking of the global regime of (American) truth. And in so doing, they become unwitting accomplices of a Euro-American global momentum that current neo-Marxist discourse identifies as the commodification of the planet, but, for reasons that will become clearer later, I prefer, after Heidegger, to put as the reduction of the being of being to "standing [disposable] reserve" (*Bestand*).[11]

II

Although recent New Americanist genealogies of the American exceptionalist cultural and political tradition have traced its origins back to the violence
informing the Puritan errand into the wilderness, it has not been adequately
noticed that the Puritan project, not only in its practices, but also and above
all in its theoretical justification of its violence, especially against the Native
Americans, was not exceptionalist in any radical sense. It did not constitute a
fundamental break from the idea of Europe. The Puritans represented the old
world as having betrayed the Word of God, his imperative to sow that Word
throughout the *orbis terrarum* and beyond its frontiers into the *terra incognita*.
They did not view themselves as radical revolutionaries, but, as the rhetoric
of the Puritan jeremiadic discourse everywhere implies, as a "saving remnant" in the face of Europe's corruption of the Word and the disintegration of
the *Civitas Terrena*. Far from breaking with the old world, the Puritans in fact
appropriated its providential theology and the prefigurative method of Biblical exegesis of the Patristic Fathers (an appropriation that Bercovitch leaves
unsaid in his otherwise enabling analysis of Puritan typological interpretation
in *The American Jeremiad*) to represent their historical moment in global,
indeed, cosmological terms. They thus represented themselves not simply as
the divinely ordained contemporary type of those Israelites who would lead
the people out of captivity into the promised land (Isa. 10:12), but, tellingly,
as in the instance of Cotton Mather's *Magnalia Christi Americana*,[12] of those
Trojans—Aeneas and his small band of exiles—whose founding of Rome,
according to medieval Christian exegetes, prefigured the rebuilding of the
Civitas Terrena (the Holy Roman Empire). In this the Puritans were essentially, if not specifically, repeating in America a pattern of nation and empire building that became fundamental to European peoples—most notably
the British, the French, and the Portuguese, all of whom claimed Trojan
ancestry—since the fall of the Roman Empire.[13]

To put it in a way that foregrounds what usually is left unattended by
Americanists, the Puritans, like the Europeans of earlier agrarian societies,
represented themselves as the protagonists of a providential or promise/
fulfillment metanarrative, as a small dissenting community of word- or Seed-
bearers elected and ordained by God to plant the word/Seed in the new
world wilderness and thus to fulfill the promise that the old world in its self-
indulgent decadence had turned away from and forgotten, if not entirely

abandoned. Thus despite the historically specific differences in their comportment toward being, the Puritans' errand was not exceptionalist in essence. They did not inaugurate something radically new in the "New World." As the title of Cotton Mather's history of the Puritans suggests, their mission, rather, like that of the Trojan remnant under Aeneas, was to renew the old world: to achieve the *Pax Theologica* in America that had been previously assigned by God to Christian Europe. Their mission, that is, was to fulfill the providential logic of the Christic Word by establishing the Pax Americana.

What needs to be emphasized in the face of a tendency of Americanists, both Old and New, to overlook it, is that this Adamic Puritan errand is not simply an imperialist project restricted to the domination and pacification of a physical space; it is also and simultaneously an imperialist project intended to dominate and pacify—to colonize—thinking itself. This is in part why I have invoked and related the terms *Pax Metaphysica* and *Pax Americana* in the context of the present post–Cold War occasion: they are terms that echo the perennial global dream, inaugurated by the promise/fulfillment structure of *The Aeneid*, Virgil's metaphysical justification of the Roman empire and its *Pax Romana*, of the European nation-states. The other reason for so doing is to render visible not simply the negation by exclusion or accommodation of the Other that is endemic to the Pax Americana, but the resonant silence to which the saying of the Other is reduced by the global fulfillment of the logical economy of American thinking, by the Pax Metaphysica, as it were, that justifies the establishment of the Pax Americana.

This global vision of America's mission in the world, in which a totalizing ontological representation justifies a totalizing or imperial sociopolitical practice, underlies the differential history of America from its Puritan origins, and it is European and Eurocentric in essence. Though it assumes different names in the process of this history, it has always functioned in the same way, as inaugural New Americanist texts such as Richard Drinnon's *Facing West: The Metaphysics of Indian-Hating and Empire Building*, Richard Slotkin's *Regeneration through Violence*, *Fatal Environment*, and *Gunfighter Nation*, and Sacvan Bercovich's *American Jeremiad* suggest, if only symptomatically.[14] The ontological representation precedes and justifies a sociopolitical practice that, whatever its locus, is global in scope.

In the post-Revolutionary nineteenth century, for example, the Puritan *theologos*, as de Tocqueville's *Democracy in America* bears witness, became history per se, and the providentially ordained Puritan errand into the wilderness was secularized as the idea of Manifest Destiny, the universalist binary logic of which transformed the American continent into a space divided between the "domiciliated" and nomadic, the improved and unimproved, culture and wilderness, civilization and savagery.[15] This transformation thus precipitated the perennially enabling American culture and politics of the frontier, which justified the violence of westward expansion, "Indian" removal, and the war against Mexico. In the twentieth century, after that continental space had been colonized and the westward momentum had reached the "last frontier," it was this same binarist ontological representation of being at large that ordained the invasion of the Phillipines,[16] and, later, as John Hellman's *American Myth and the Legacy of the Vietnam War* suggests without saying so, the American intervention in Southeast Asia in the name of the Kennedy administration's "New Frontier."[17]

What differentiates the ontological thinking informing and driving these global imperial practices is not simply the increasing naturalization of the supernatural *logos*, but the decreasing visibility of the determinative role this metaphysical principle of principles plays in these practices; that is, the increasing efficacy of that ontological thinking vis-à-vis the domination of the Other all along the continuum of being enabled by the technologization and instrumentalization of the word. I am referring to the transformation of metaphysical knowledge production in the period of the Enlightenment, brilliantly and decisively thematized by Michel Foucault, that precipitated the panoptic microphysics of the inclusive classificatory table and the instrumental thinking that reduces being in all its living variety to docile and useful objects that take their proper place within a larger (global) identical whole, or, to recall Heidegger's apt phrase, into standing and disposable reserve.

Finally, the ontological justification of America's global errand blatantly resurfaces in the post–Cold War period, despite the self-destruction of the instrumentalist version of metaphysical American thinking that was the consequence of the genocidal violence its quantitative measure enabled. Following the collapse of Soviet communism and the surgically executed victory in the Gulf War, the deputies of the dominant political order, facilitated by the culture industry's sustained incremental project to forget Vietnam by representing it, announced "the end of history" and "the advent of the New World Order" under the aegis of liberal capitalist democracy. Given the depth to which the eschatological structure has been inscribed in the collective American identity, it was inevitable, despite the resistance of actual history, that this announcement of the Pax Americana should invoke a metaphysical concept of historical temporality, in this case a Hegelian version of de Tocqueville's Universal History and, as Derrida has pointed out, that it should articulate the coming to be of this epochal event in the language of last things: in the biblical rhetoric of "good news" (Fukuyama xiii).[18] What needs to be emphasized in the light of my earlier criticism of Bercovitch's containment of opposition within the discourse of America is that this post–Cold War announcement of the global scope of American thinking in effect accomplishes the reduction of the "truth" of any other, radically different and differential, way of thinking, past, present, or future, to the status of a vehicle of the untruth, of nonbeing, of the outrageous phantasmic, which is to say, of the utterly unsayable.

This, despite his canonization, was the proleptic testimony of Herman Melville, especially in "Bartleby the Scrivener" and in *Pierre*, which address the hegemonization and banalization of the discourse of "revolutionary" America. Melville was acutely aware of the unexceptionalist character of antebellum America (an awareness enabled in part by his profoundly resistant comparative reading of European philosophy and that of "Young America"). And in the wake of his unhoming—his "extraordinary emergency" out of America and into the decentered global domain of ontological ambiguity (*die Unheimlichkeit*)[19]—Melville recognized the urgent need not simply to attend to the silence to which the deputies of the dominant American culture had reduced recalcitrant American voices like his, but to think this negative unsayable positively. I mean, to quote Melville, the appropriation and total inscription of the imperial logos—"the Talismanic Secret" of that "guild of [old world] self-imposters," "Plato, Spinoza, Goethe"—by their unexceptional American ephebes: that "preposterous rabble of Muggletonian Scots and Yankees, whose vile brogue still the more bestreaks the stripedness of their Greek or German Neoplatonical originals" (*Pierre*, 208). It is also the testimony, however unwittingly, of both his outraged contemporary critics— those like George Washington Peck, who, identifying Melville's fantastic saying as a madness that menaced the American way of life and its promise, would "turn our critical Aegis" on him and "freeze him into silence"[20]—and of all those sympathetic post-Revivalists after him who, in remembering Melville, accomplished the same silencing by accommodating his ec-centric antinationalist nationalist *poiesis* to the American canon, which is to say by turning this anxiety-provoking solicitor of American exceptionalist certainty into a national monument.

But this proleptic witness to the bereavement of a viable critical language was not limited to Melville. It was also the testimony of Henry Adams, another American who, like Melville, was driven into silence and the awareness of the urgency to think differently and differentially in the face of the impending global conquest and colonization of thought by an Americanism that had fulfilled the reifying logical economy of the European end-of-history thinking.[21] It is, furthermore, and not incidentally, this spectral silence, precipitated by the globalization of the polyvalently imperial discourse of America, that resonates, if only symptomatically, in the work of white modern and postmodern American writers: in the beatific ravings of Jack Kerouac and Allen Ginsberg; the minimalism of Robert Creeley; the irreverently garrulous retrieval of the preterited in Thomas Pynchon; the obsession with the literature of exhaustion in John Barth; the celebration of waste in Donald Barthelme; the defiant vulgarization of the phallic-driven, American high seriousness in Kathy Acker. Even more tellingly, it can also be heard in the visible invisibility of modern and postmodern black American writers such as Richard Wright, Ralph Ellison, James Baldwin, and Ishmael Reed; in the unspeakable rage of Malcolm X and Eldrige Cleaver; in the preoccupation with the "veil" in W. E. B. Du Bois; in the deliberately provocative nonviolence of Martin Luther King; and, not least, in the retrieval of the specter of blackness from white writing in Toni Morrison. Instigated by the fulfillment of a pragmatist tradition in an instrumentalism that has banalized thought and routinized violence, what all these alienated writers have in common with Melville and Adams is a symptomatic, if unevenly thought, awareness of another ontology, another way of comporting oneself toward being that would retrieve the nonbeing that the dominant American discourse, in its commitment to decidability, will, like the discourse of modern science Heidegger interrogates, have nothing to do with. What, in short, affiliates these otherwise different American writers is, to invoke Melville again, the symptomatic desire to get a "voice out of Silence."

It is, I submit, this pervasive spectral silence precipitated by the globalization of the idea of American liberal capitalist democracy—this dislocating awareness of the unsayable in the face of the colonization of thinking, the restriction of what is permitted to be said to the simulacrum, and the reduction of being to a technological disposable reserve—that resonates all across the continuum of being, from the subject and language through gender and race, to the international sphere, that Americanists, old and new, have failed to hear, let alone think, in their continuing preoccupation with the local.

III

In criticizing New Americanist studies for its vestigial adherence to the myth of American exceptionalism, I do not want to give the impression that I entirely endorse an unequivocal abandonment of the national focus of American literary and cultural studies in favor of the global perspective that late postmodernists as diverse as Fredric Jameson, Michael Hardt, Paul Bové, Masao Miyoshi, Ronald Judy, and Bill Readings, among others, claim has superseded traditional national boundaries and, in the case of Readings, the idea of the university whose origins lie in the Enlightenment with Kant and Humboldt. This is the international perspective incumbent on the decline of the nation-state and the idea of the university as the site of the reproduction and maintenance of its national culture in the wake of the triumph of transnational or late capitalism:

> The current shift in the role of the university is, above all, determined by the decline of the national cultural mission that has up to now provided its *raison d'etre*. . . . In short, the University is becoming a different kind of institution, one that is no longer linked to the destiny of the nation-state by virtue of its role as producer, protector, and inculcator of an idea of national culture. The process of economic globalization brings with it the relative decline of the nation-state as the prime instant of the production of capital around the world. For its part, the University is becoming a transnational bureaucratic corporation, either tied to transnational instances of government such as the European Union or functioning independently, by analogy with a transnational corporation.[22]

In identifying postmodernism with the logic of late capitalism and, especially in the case of Readings, the postnational university with a commodified principle of performative "excellence" that is devoid of content, these late postmodernist advocates of a global perspective claim that the model of the center and periphery that had hitherto determined oppositional criticism of imperialism is no longer viable in an age characterized by the free-flowing movement of global capital. They thus represent the idea and power of the United States as anachronistic and recommend instead a critique that bypasses the site of America understood as a nation-state in favor of a decentered one that critically addresses the centerless and untethered structures and functioning of transnational capital.

This reorientation of critique from the local to the global, for example, was epitomized by the interventions of some of the members of the *boundary 2* editorial collective at a colloquium with a number of Tunisian intellectuals from the academic and business communities, sponsored by the Bourguiba Institute in Tunisia, on the question of the Tunisian government's massive intitiative to substitute English for French (the language of North African colonialism) as a second language in March 1998 as a means of integrating into the global economy. In that dialogue both parties of the Tunisian contingency were generally in favor of this initiative, but they disagreed strongly about the context in which English should be taught. Although the academics professed a postcolonial Arab nationalist perspective, they nevertheless believed that such an initiative could best be fulfilled by incorporating the teaching of English into the humanities, specifically courses in American and especially British literature, which, like the Leavisites they apparently were trained by, they identified with "civilization." On the other hand, the representatives of the business and financial community, dissatisfied by the results vis-à-vis English proficiency of such a humanist education, were committed to the teaching of English as a skill adequate to the global marketplace. The members of the *boundary 2* editorial collective, particularly Paul Bové, Ronald Judy, and Wlad Godzich, were critical of both these perspectives. Assuming transnational capitalism as a fait accompli and thus the obsolescence of the nation-state, each in their own way argued that, in addressing the problem posed by the apparent incommensurability between the initiative to nationalize their country and the initiative to integrate its economy into a world market dominated by North America, postcolonial countries like Tunisia should abandon the obsolete notion, persistently held by academics, that the English language is identical with Americanization. As Ronald Judy put it proleptically in a memorandom to the *boundary 2* collective analyzing the forthcoming context of the colloquium:

> It would be a serious error to imagine that because of [the Tunisian government's obvious initiative to embrace the North American concept of a free market economy and the English-language education that is a requisite of successful integration] Tunisia is necessarily undergoing what we might call Americanization. . . . The rapid growth of English-language education around the world, in conjunction with a global telecommunications dominated by North American interests notwithstanding, it is extremely hasty and in error to identify English with Americanization, or, for that matter, with anything like Anglo-American, or even Anglo-Saxon, culture. In the confu-

sion that characterizes our times, and that is still far from being fathomed, one thing is clear. For all the reinvigorated movements of nationalism around the globe that identify cultural authenticity with linguistic identity, there is no such culture that can even hope to claim global dominance. In this regard, Global English poses a most vexing problem precisely because it does not indicate any particular national culture. . . . We simply have no idea what Global English stands for except the global market, which is to say, we have no idea what it stands for culturally.[23]

Instead, these members of the *boundary 2* collective offered a third alternative, one which they claimed would not only avoid the neocolonialist consequences of both the Tunisian humanists' and the businessmen's projects. Like Bill Readings's recommendation to American oppositional intellectuals vis-à-vis "the University in ruins," they advised our Tunisian colleagues to acknowledge the irreversible reality of the planetary scope of transnational capital and the free market and to resist the anachronistic notion that English in the post–Cold War era was fraught with a cultural ideology. Put positively, if too briefly, they recommended that the task of intellectuals in postcolonial nations like Tunisia seeking integration into the global economy is to realize that the Global English of transnational capital is a concept that, like Readings's "University of excellence," is a global vehicle of communication empty of ideological cultural content, and that this "neutral" English is an essential agent of transnational capitalism's project to reduce historical reality at large to the simulacrum. Only by such an understanding of the hyperrealist language of the global economy, they claimed, can such countries learn to think and resist—to rethink—the negative effects of this disappearance of content in Global English. To appropriate the language Readings uses to characterize the oppositional strategy he claims is essential in the wake of what he sees as the accomplished commodification and transnationalization of the North American university in the posthistorical era, only by "an engagement with and transvaluation of this epochal shift," which, "for heuristic purposes," he subsumes "under the name 'dereferentialization'" (166–67) can postcolonial countries that have been compelled to integrate their economies into the global marketplace attune themselves to the power of the market-induced deculturalization of English and enable themselves to gain immunity from the disastrous economic, cultural, and sociopolitical consequences that are now manifesting themselves in the postcolonial Southeast Asian countries that have blindly embraced the global free market.

This analysis of the rush toward Global English by postcolonial nations and the concomitant recommendation to undertake "an endless *detournement* of the spaces willed to us by a history whose temporality we no longer inhabit" (Readings 129) are powerfully persuasive, and they must be part of the consciousness of any New Americanist concerned about the future of American studies.[24] But the argument is somewhat disabled by a curious blindness to what Readings refers to as the "pragmatist" problematic that enables them (167–68). It fails, in its reliance on global oversight, to perceive the role that Western metaphysics, in its developed, instrumentalized—meaning Americanized—allotrope, continues to play in the transformation of cultural English into Global English. Whatever the degree of denationalization induced by the free market of transnational capital, the English of the global marketplace remains, pace Judy and Readings, referential and cultural. However stripped of specific cultural reference, that is, this so-called Global English, "dominated by North American interests," as Judy puts it, remains a metaphysical/representational language that is generally Western, but specifically American, colonialist, and dominant insofar as it has been, since its origins, informed by an imperial ontology that represents being from after or above temporality or history. Insofar, that is, as this global language is informed by a white mythology, specifically by a binary metaphorics that privileges the relay of tropes circulating around panoptic vision—light, space, the center, and the phallic seed over darkness, time, periphery, and fallow (feminine) earth—that enables the colonization and pacification of time's disseminations. It may be that the center endemic to the Western imperial project has been indeed decentered in the postmodern age. The center may have become, under the aegis of late capitalism, a free-floating center, a center that is simultaneously nowhere and everywhere. But, however more invisible and thus beyond the reach of freeplay than it was in the age of modernity, it is still an occidental center that is informed by the will to power and thus is capable of accommodating and reducing all alterity within its totalizing circumference.

To translate this ontological paradigm, this center which is nowhere and everywhere, into the context of the present global scene being established by late capitalism, what we are bearing witness to in this post–Cold War conjuncture is not the irreversible demise of the cultural referent America and the advent of posthistory, as Readings and my *boundary 2* colleagues all too hastily affirm. Rather, as Heidegger observed a long time ago when he identified the triumph of technological thinking in modernity—of the enframement (*Ge-stell*) of the time of being endemic to advanced metaphysical thinking—as the "Age of the World Picture," we are being witness to the transformation of the United States, the self-appointed heir of European culture, into Americanism. I mean, with Heidegger among many others, a Europeanization (under the name of *America*) of thinking "carried so far that any thinking which rejects the claim of reason as not originary, simply has to be maligned today as unreason."[25] It is a global way of perceiving being whose logic indeed culminates in the end of history, but in an end of history understood not as a utopian condition, but as a universal death: the utter annulment of the living differential force of being in all its bodily manifestations—language, culture, race, gender, polis, nation, and world. Put alternatively, what we are witnessing by way of the globalization of the Americanism that has assumed the failed European burden of light is the complete Americanization of the earth and man. And this means the reduction of thinking at large to a universal instrumentalism and of the being to which it refers to disposable reserve.

IV

My intention in thus expressing reservations about this now characteristic posthistorical version of the historical shift from the nation-state to the global scene is not to exonerate Americanists for not adequately engaging the global context. For, as I have said, however critical of the negative consequences of the doctrine of American exceptionalism, American studies as a field of inquiry remains, as the inordinate focus of its criticism on the literature and culture of the United States suggests, vestigially inscribed by the exceptionalist code. Or to put it in Readings's terms, it continues in its disciplinary parochialism to adhere symptomatically, even in its reiterated call for a community of dissensus, to the now patently anachronistic German Enlightenment notion that the university exists to fulfill the cultural potentialities of the national state. Despite a certain hesitation related to my reservations about a full endorsement of transnational capital as a fait accompli, I am in agreement with Paul Bové's critical assessment of contemporary American studies in his strong essay, "Notes toward a Politics of 'American' Criticism," especially if his invocation of the exilic consciousness as a fundamental imperative of the contemporary occasion is understood not simply as a political or cultural but also as an ontological referent:

> While honoring the values of distance and the experience of exile that theorize it as a critical necessity, one must also wonder if the study of culture does not require an even more complex and difficult position: being in and of one's locale while understanding its needs and hence one's own projects in terms of

a global or transnationalist set of interlocking perspectives. The best critical emblem for our time might be what Gayatri Spivak has taught us to call the "post-colonial subject," that is, the gendered intellectual engaged in agonistic analysis of global issues central to regional and national concerns and always motivated by an understanding of the complex position that any citizen of a postmodern cultural multiplicity must occupy.

I want to suggest too crudely that "American Studies" taken as a field in its "theoretical fullness"—I realize this formulation occludes specific differences—has not yet reached that point of "exile" in relation to itself and its nationalist projects. (63)

I cannot in this brief space provide the evidence to support my claim that the field of New Americanist studies remains vestigially and disablingly local in scope. But symptoms abound besides the relative indifference to the global issues that have been fundamental to the making of the American national identity and that now, in the post–Cold War occasion, when the deputies of the dominant American culture are overtly proclaiming the advent of the American peace, have come irreversibly to the fore. I am referring, for example, to its practitioners' tendency to overdetermine the New Historicism; to restrict their discursive references to others within the hermetic field imaginary of American studies, that is to other prominent Americanists, mostly white; to be relatively indifferent to continental, African, Asian, and Latin American thinkers and critics who contextualize the neoimperial practices of the postcolonial occasion in terms of the increasingly central and unilateral role of America; to articulate opposition in the terms laid down by the American discourse it would resist; and, not least, to eschew or to reduce and accommodate to the literary discipline the radically antimetaphysical interpretations of being—such as those of Heidegger, Derrida, Lyotard, Deleuze, Bhabha, Lacoue-Labarthe, Nancy, Agamben—in favor of the empirical/pragmatist perspective that, in its origins, is simultaneous with the secularization of the Puritan theologos. (A cursory glance at the indexes of the several volumes of *The Cambridge History of American Literature* edited by Sacvan Bercovitch will bear this last tendency out.) And even when the interpretive strategies of these antimetaphysical theorists are acknowledged by Americanists as viable instruments of criticism, as in the case of Gerald Graff's and Gregory Jay's defense of Derridian deconstruction, they are invoked to "teach the conflicts."[26] Whatever their intention, this means tacitly the reduction of the very real imbalances of power that exist in this world to equally weighted and free-floating abstract positions to be negotiated, that is to a humanistic pluralism that occurs outside of history, beyond the specific place and time where power relations are always already imbalanced and so must be construed as relations of injustice. In other words, "teaching the conflicts" means accommodating them to the metaphysical framework of liberal American democratic thought.

It is, of course, not easy for an American academic who is not a woman, a black, a homosexual, or a member of an ethnic minority to feel the anguish and indignation of social and political exile even though, as Bové observes, our exilic condition—"the multipositionality of the [American critics]"— "has already been partly theorized within criticism in the work not only of Spivak, but Foucault, Gramsci and others" ("Notes Toward a Politics," 69). But, to put this condition in Spivak's phrase, it is even more difficult to be "outside in the teaching machine"[27] at the more rarified but indissolubly related sites of thinking and language. The fact is, however, that American academics—at least those who have acknowledged the decentering of the onto-, theo-, and anthropo-*logos*—are, like Melville and Adams, all ontological exiles, which means that they are bereft of a language positively capable of saying that which the dominant mode of thinking renders unsayable. This, even though we feel it only symptomatically, is especially the case in the post– Cold War occasion which has borne witness to the announcement by the dominant American culture of the global triumph of liberal capitalist democracy, of the metaphysical principles informing this polity, and of the instrumental thinking and language that constitute its agent.

I mean by this that sense of alienation from the "real world" that is incumbent on the global colonization of thinking by American instrumentalism or rather by the Americanization of thinking, that sense of futility that comes over us when we realize that even our criticism of America must be carried out in—must be answerable to—the language of America, that sense, in other words, that we have been compelled into tacit, frustrating silence in the face of the triumph of a banal instrumental thinking that routinizes violence. The difference between most contemporary Americanists and Melville and Adams is that, unlike the latter, the former locate the cause of their alienation and their bereavement elsewhere than at the original site of thinking and language. Melville and Adams were driven by crises of American history that exposed the aporias informing the truth discourse of American exceptionalism to attend to the spectral shadow of—that belongs to and haunts—the imperial light of metaphysical reason and to inaugurate or at least to call for a rethinking of American thinking that reconstellated America into the global scene. Despite the ontological directives made available by the epistemic catastrophe of the Vietnam War and a certain spirit of postmetaphysical continental theory, Americanist thinking remains locked within the light of American pragmatic rationality. It continues to address the crisis of America at ontic or second-order sites such as American politics, or history, or cultural institutions, blind to the fact, even as its discourse everywhere symptomatically announces it, that these are derivatives of the original American appropriation and fulfillment of the European ontological representation of the being of being.

As I see it, then, the project of American studies in the age of the world picture is to transform a symptomatic sense of the exilic condition into a fully knowing one. And, I suggest, following the inaugurative directives of Melville and Adams, this can be done by reconstellating the national focus of American studies inscribed by the invention of the American Renaissance into the contemporary global matrix, that is, by dis-locating the sedimented constellation into which American criticism has hitherto been imbedded, the post–Cold War world now being represented as "the end of history" and "the New World Order." At this reconstellated site, we take our place as Americanists with those early postmetaphysical European thinkers who, profoundly dissatisfied with the restricted economy of the thought and language prevailing in the world of modernity, not least in America, have, each in their own way, attempted to thematize that metaphysically induced condition of silence: the nothing that it is the task of the *Abgeschiedene*—the estranged thinker unhomed by the planetary triumph of technological thought in the age of the world picture—to think (Heidegger); the *différance* or trace (Derrida); the *aporia* (de Man); the *differend* (Lyotard), and so forth.

In so doing, furthermore, we also discover our solidarity as American intellectuals with those various constituencies of the human community at large that the predatory global project of Western colonialism, facilitated by what Edward Said has called "the textual attitude,"[28] has displaced and unhomed in the name of civilization. I am referring to those invisible and voiceless people whom Hannah Arendt identified as "pariahs," and Frantz Fanon, "the wretched of the earth" and, more recently, whom Said has called "emigrés," Deleuze and Guattari, "nomads," Homi Bhabha, "hybrids" ("the minus in the origin"),[29] and Spivak, the "catachrestic remainder." For it is this initiative to reconstellate the relatively pure ontological disclosures of the unsayable of those early postmetaphysical thinkers into the postcolonial context that distinguishes the thought of these later, more politically oriented theorists and renders their work valuable for Americanists in the post–Cold War occasion.

What all these postmetaphysical thinkers symptomatically, if not explicitly, bear witness to is the global scope of Americanism, and—much more to the point—the globalization of its utter banality and the routinization of the violent praxis intrinsic to it. Each in their own way, that is, testify not simply to the historical fulfillment of the logical economy of Western metaphysics— the perception of being *meta ta physika*—in a planetary American instrumentalism that is utterly indifferent to the differences that the be-ing of being disseminates, but also to the concomitant justification of a kind of practice that reduces these differences to disposable reserve on a global scale. Despite certain symptomatic gestures in that direction, especially Donald Pease's important initiative to reconstellate the Old Americanist's literary history into the Cold War context,[30] it is this deadly double globalization that the New Americanists have failed adequately to attend to in their preoccupations with American literature understood as national enterprise.

V

This failure is especially difficult to understand because it is precisely this double globalization—this momentum toward the absolutization of instrumental thinking and the practical Americanization of the planet—and its deadly consequences that were proleptically disclosed in the process of America's aggressive intervention in Vietnam. I am not simply referring to the United States' unexceptional exceptionalism that assumed the "burden" of saving Southeast Asia for the "free world" from the decadent old world colonialism of France. I am also, and above all, referring to the way its executioners thought and conducted the war in Vietnam. That first postmodern war was not only fought by a powerful "can-do" military army, but also, as in the case of Napoleon's invasion of Egypt in 1798, by a powerful army of can-do cultural experts—"orientalists," as it were—in the Pentagon and in Saigon, the "best and the brightest," as David Halberstam puts it, of a generation of young Americans educated to think in those quantitative global terms in elite American universities, most notably Harvard.[31] The difference is that this army of American cultural experts brought to bear on the recalcitrant Vietnamese "wilderness" a kind of "objective" thinking that was infinitely more sophisticated, efficient, and deadly than the Enlightenment thinking of the army of savants that accompanied Napoleon's imperial legions to Egypt.

As Richard Ohmann's brilliant analysis of the appallingly banal inhumanity of the language of the *Pentagon Papers* demonstrated a quarter of a century ago (only to be forgotten), it was an unrelenting "problem solving" or instrumentalist rationality—the fulfilled allotrope of the American pragmatist tradition that based its projections on a preestablished but unacknowledged narrative scenario—that was, in its commitment to a purely quantitative measure, absolutely stripped of any consciousness of particularity, especially human particularity.[32] We must not make the mistake of reading the logic of these memoranda as simply a conscious strategy, cynical or otherwise, intended to render the conduct of the war more efficient by obliterating from view the particularities of that historical occasion that would complicate and impede its progress. This kind of liberal reading attributes the American intervention in Vietnam and its conduct of the war to a "betrayal" or "mistaken" application of the fundamental principles of American democracy and thus deflects critical attention from where it belongs. On the contrary, the logic of these Pentagon thinkers was the logic of common sense. Those who practiced it were not unique conspirators, misguided or evil men in the conventional sense of the word; they were Americans whose thought was consonant with the truth as most Americans understood it. That is the real horror of these inhuman documents: they show no evidence whatsoever of their authors' consciousness of the reality they were indiscriminately obliterating. As Ohmann says, "The main point to make [in the context of the effects of the cost/benefit rhetorical framework of this problem solving thinking] is that since the suffering of the Vietnamese didn't impinge on the consciousness of the policy-makers as a cost, it had virtually no existence for them" (202).[33] And the army of soldiers, who were the executioners of these thinkers' "errand in the [Vietnamese] wilderness," waged the war according to the unexceptional exceptionalist truth of this unerring terrorist logic and its preestablished scenario. I am referring, of course, to the horrific strategy euphemistically called "attrition," but more accurately, the "body count" that, in its purely quantitative measure, indiscriminately killed and maimed countless innocent peasants—women, men, and children—as well as enemy soldiers, wasted the Vietnamese landscape by means of the most advanced technology of mass destruction, and irreversibly transformed a deeply rooted rice culture into a population of displaced persons, all in the name of saving Vietnam for the free world. To put this unspeakable horror synecdochically, the logical economy of the representative American thinking that informs *The Pentagon Papers* had as its practical end the monomaniacal, I am tempted to say Ahabian, rationality of the American colonel who, after a "successful" search-and-destroy mission, said in response to a reporter's expression of dismay over the absoluteness of the carnage, "We had to destroy Ben Tre in order to save it."[34]

This reduction of thinking to quantification and the accompanying routinization of violence such problem-solving thinking entails is "the banality of evil," as I understand Hannah Arendt's controversial—and thus marginalized—analysis of the language Adolph Eichmann used to justify his practice as the coordinator of the "Final Solution" at his trial in Jerusalem in 1961.[35] It will no doubt be objected to by many Americanists that Arendt did not intend the phrase to be applied to the thinking and practice of the "Free [Western] World"—especially America. But such an objection, I would respond, would be symptomatic of the exceptionalist thinking that continues to disable both the dominant and oppositional Americanist discourses. Arendt, at some point between *Eichmann in Jerusalem* and the end of her life, recognized the banality of Eichmann's evil as symptomatic of a larger global momentum of Western, if not specifically American, thinking/practice. This is clearly suggested by her pointed assertion that it was the utter commonplaceness of this Nazi functionary's language that instigated her monumental effort to rethink the "Life of the Mind" in her last great unfinished book in the 1970s:

> The immediate impulse [for "my preoccupation with mental activities" in *The Life of the Mind*] came from my attending the Eichmann trial in Jerusalem. In my report of it I spoke of "the banality of evil." Behind that phrase, I held no thesis or doctrine, although I was dimly aware of the fact that it went counter to our tradition of thought—literary, theological, or philosophical—about the phenomenon of evil. Evil, we have learned, is something demonic. . . . However, what I was confronted with was utterly different and still undeniably factual. I was struck by a manifest shallowness in the doer of his deeds that made it impossible to trace the uncontestable evil of his deeds to any deeper level of roots or motives. The deeds were monstrous, but the doer . . . was quite ordinary, commonplace, and neither demonic nor monstrous. There was no sign in him of firm ideological convictions or of specific evil motives, and the only notable characteristic one could detect in his past behavior as well as in his behavior during the trial . . . was something entirely negative: it was not stupidity but *thoughtlessness*.[36]

Thought in the light of the raison d'être for Arendt's project to rethink thinking, though she admittedly did not make this connection, the instrumentalist thinking/language of the memoranda of *The Pentagon Papers* assumes a dark significance that, one would suppose, calls urgently for thinking.

It would not be an exaggeration to conclude that there is a clear continuity between the terrible banality of this Nazi functionary's thought and practice and the utterly dehumanized mindlessness of the representative problem-solving thinking and practice of the highly educated Washington bureaucrats who planned and conducted the war against the Vietnamese people and their earth in the name of America's global mission on behalf of the truth of the free world. This is to say that Americanists must cease, once and for all, to think liberal democratic America in the metanarrative terms of American exceptionalism, which, in the particular analogy I have invoked by way of Arendt's resonant phrase, means to differentiate the synecdochical banality of Eichmann's instrumentalist language from that of the American authors of the memoranda of *The Pentagon Papers*.

Americanists, both Old and New, have, of course, always been critically conscious of the dehumanizing effects incumbent on the valorization of technology as such. But I am less certain that they have been attentive to the inordinate degree to which the dominant American culture has appropriated and assimilated technology into the American language, the degree to which this instrumentalist culture of artisans and merchants has incorporated in its *episteme*, via John Locke and other British empiricists, the momentous spirit-crippling recommendations offered by Bishop Thomas Spratt in his *History of the Royal Society* to British intellectuals of his day concerning the use of language:

> They [the members of the Royal Society] have therefore been most rigorous in putting into execution, the only Remedy that can be found for this extravagance [of the poetic discourse that gives "the mind a motion too changeable, and bewitching, to consist with right practice"]: and that has been, a constant Resolution, to reject all the amplifications, digressions, and swellings of style: *to return to the primitive purity, and shortness*, when men deliver'd so many things, almost in an equal number of words. *They have exacted from their members, a close, naked, natural way of speaking; positive expressions, clear senses; a native easiness; bringing all things as near the Mathematical plainness, as they can: and preferring the language of Artizans, Countrymen, and Merchants, before that, of Wits, or Scholars.*[37]

To merely acknowledge the dangers of technology without referring to the far more dangerous technologization of the American language and its reduction to a cybernetic instrument is, to put it mildly, inadequate. This is especially the case if we are cognizant of the fact that American English has

assumed global status in the post–Cold War era, the era I have called, after
Heidegger, the age of the world picture.

As a consequence of their failure to attend to this technologization of language, in other words, Americanists have failed to recognize, despite the dis-
localizing evidence of such delegitimating aporetic events as the Vietnam
War, the complicity between American instrumental thinking and an invisible and elusive, but no less life-destroying, neoimperial American instrumentalism. Equally telling, they have also been blinded by their relative indifference to the question of language, to the threat that the fulfillment of its
paranoid end-oriented logical economy poses to the differential being of
being at large, especially at the present conjuncture, which the intellectual
deputies of the dominant culture are heralding as tidings of good news and
representing as the end of history presided over by liberal capitalist democracy.

If, however, as Americanists, we reconstellate the American exceptionalist
myth into this global post–Cold War context, we are forewarned of a different end of history from that euphorically announced by these imperial
prophets. The promised end they announce in the eschatological language of
good news undergoes a solicitation that discloses this *eschatos* to be not the
annulment of desire and conflict in an achieved plenary City on the Hill, but
the death of consciousness, the negation of our awareness of the fragile but
intensely life-affirming essence of our mortality. And so of our sense of the
dignity and worth of the indissoluble relay of Others that, in our radical
finiteness, we are always already in the condition of being-with.

In his highly mediatized recent book, provocatively entitled *Achieving
Our Country*, Richard Rorty, the heir of the American pragmatist tradition,
castigates the New Left that emerged during the Vietnam War for its disparagement of the positive social and political potentialities of democratic institutions, indeed, of its blatant anti-Americanism. And he calls for "a mor-
atorium" on the theory that, he claims, has nourished negativity into a fully
fledged defeatist doctrine of original sin (91) and for a resurgence of "national pride" within a revitalized leftist politics that has its origins in the
"civic religion" (15, 38, 101) of Walt Whitman, John Dewey, William James,
and its practical manifestation in the political initiatives of such social reformers as Eugene Debs, A. Philip Randolph, John L. Lewis, and Lyndon Baynes
Johnson.

For Rorty, it was the 1960s—the decade of the protest movement against
the Vietnam War—that spawned what, in a strange reversal of actuality, he
calls this disabling "spectatorial" (35) anti-American "new academic" or

"Cultural Left" and marginalized what, adapting the Emersonian tradition to his exceptionalist project, he calls "the party of hope" (14, 107),[38] the traditional "reformist Left," which "dated back to the Progressive Era" (1900–64) and "struggled within the framework of constitutional democracy to protect the weak from the strong" (43). Despite his avowed antipathy toward the Vietnam War, Rorty, who was a committed advocate of the Cold War, is compelled by his "national pride" to interpret the American government's intervention in Vietnam and its brutal conduct of the war as a mistake or betrayal of America's benign democratic principles. Refusing to entertain the possibility that these constituted a disclosure of a radical break in its episteme, he would, ironically, like the politically conservative prophets of the dominant culture and the culture industry that serves it, tacitly have us forget the Vietnam witnessed by the New Left—"kick the Vietnam Syndrome," as it were—on behalf of fulfilling what he calls, after the progressivist Herbert Croly, "the promise of American life" (46, 97).

But what that jeremiadic recommendation means, as I have been suggesting, is not simply the forgetting of an unfortunate but remediable mistake in the progressive history of liberal America. As the studied absence in his book of any reference to the exceptionalist ontological justification of the United States' intervention in Southeast Asia—and his sustained disparagement of anti-American continental philosophers, such as Heidegger, Derrida, and Foucault—emphatically make clear, it also, and above all, means the forgetting of the terrible and dislocating lesson concerning the imperial global pretentions of American problem-solving thinking synecdochically disclosed in the dreadful banality of the instrumentalist language of the memoranda comprising *The Pentagon Papers*. It would not simply obliterate from our consciousness the history-ordained provenance of the American exceptionalist mission in the wilderness of Vietnam that informs these memoranda. It would also obliterate the threat that the instrumental American thinking, which is the agent of this exceptionalist mission, poses to the very humanity of humanity in achieving planetary domination.

In criticizing the "hopelessness" (37) of the post-Vietnam cultural left, Rorty no doubt means to include the New Americanists. But insofar as the New Americanist initiative has failed to think the question of being and language adequately, specifically the globalization of American English, to hear the reiterative symptomatic call of continental philosophers to attend to the specter of instrumental reason and to recognize the need for a way of thinking that is not answerable to America, it is not only not immune to his criticism; it is, as in the examples of Bercovitch's, Graff's, and Jay's continued adherence to "the categories of [American] culture" in their oppositional criticism, complicitous with his retrogressive prophetic nationalist project.

All of which is to say that the first task of American studies in the age of the world picture, in which being at large has been reduced to disposable reserve, is to dislocate itself from the national context in which it continues, however vestigially, to be embedded into the global frame that from the exceptionalist beginning has determined America's cultural identity. Such a reconstellation would not only disclose the European, that is metaphysical provenance of the myth of American exceptionalism, but it would also foreground the fulfillment of its logical economy—its promise/fulfillment narrative structure—in a global Americanism that renders all thinking and practice answerable to its imperial instrumental imperatives. Only by way of such a reconstellation, I submit, will American studies be positively capable of transforming its practitioners' symptomatic sense of exile from the discursive homeland into conscious and effective knowledge. That is to say, only by such a reconstellation will Americanists be enabled to perceive the urgency of its second and integrally related task: to think their exilic condition not simply as a consequence of the fulfillment of the prophetic American narrative implicit in the metaphysically exceptionalist errand, but as the resonantly contradictory—and potentially activist—silence precipitated by this end, the silence that haunts, indeed, menaces the logic of the triumphant discourse of the American homeland. To invoke the proleptic witness of Melville and Adams once more, only by way of such a reconstellation will Americanists be enabled to hear this spectral voice of silence to which the global Americanization of any other kind of saying has been reduced and thus to think the positive possibilities latent in its radical otherness. Not least, such a reconstellation will enable them to recognize their solidarity with the estranged thinkers—the Abgeschiedene—of the nothing, the aporia, the différance, the catachrestic remainder, the differand, the rhizome, the minus in the origin, and with all those nomadic political constituencies of the human community that have been unhomed by the depredations of the polyvalent Western/American imperial project.

For the oppositional American intellectual, the age of the world picture is an interregnum. It is a time that has borne witness to the global triumph of the ontological principles of liberal capitalist democracy and the spatialized or reified language of *homo faber* that, according to Hannah Arendt, is intrinsic to the human condition of this kind of polity.[39] What this means is, in fact, the exhaustion and demise of those categories of emancipatory thought and practice celebrated by Richard Rorty and the reformist saving remnant he represents—and adhered to by Bercovitch and all too many New Americanists. In this in-between—this "destitute time," to appropriate Heidegger's apt Hölderlinian description of the Americanization of the planet[40]—the critical intellectual has ostensibly no other option available than to think and say according to the imperatives of the dominant American discourse. Thus those intellectuals who, in the phrase Donald Pease appropriates from Noam Chomsky, would "deter democracy"[41] and the momentum toward the devastation of the planet must rethink thinking itself. That is to say, they must think positively that which the globalization of Americanism has rendered unsayable: the shadow of—that is that belongs to—the light of instrumental reason and that haunts its death-oriented, promissory banality.

Notes

1   Sacvan Bercovitch, *The American Jeremiad* (Madison: University of Wisconsin Press, 1978). Subsequent references are cited parenthetically in the text.

2   See Steven Knapp and Walter Benn Michaels, "Against Theory," in *Against Theory: Literary Studies and the New Pragmatism*, ed. W. J. T. Mitchell (Chicago: University of Chicago Press, 1985), 11–30. For a powerful critique of the ahistorical history of these new pragmatists, see Paul A. Bové, "Introduction: In the Wake of Theory," in *In the Wake of Theory* (Middletown, Conn.: Wesleyan University Press, 1992), 48–66.

3   William V. Spanos, *Heidegger and Criticism: Retrieving the Cultural Politics of Destruction* (Minneapolis: University of Minnesota Press, 1993), 81–131.

4   William V. Spanos, *America's Shadow: An Anatomy of Empire* (Minneapolis: University of Minnesota Press, 2000).

5   Richard Rorty, *Achieving Our Country: Leftist Thought in Twentieth-Century America* (Cambridge, Mass.: Harvard University Press, 1998). Subsequent references are cited parenthetically in the text.

6   Francis Fukuyama, *The End of History and the Last Man* (New York: Free Press, 1992). Subsequent references are cited parenthetically in the text.

7   Richard Haass, *The Reluctant Sheriff: The United States after the Cold War* (Washington, D.C.: Institute of Foreign Affairs, 1997).

8   Alexis de Tocqueville, *Democracy in America*, vol. 1, trans. Henry Reeve, rev. Francis Bowen, ed. Phillips Bradley (New York: Vintage, 1990), 6. That Fukuyama himself understands his end-of-history discourse as the fulfillment of de Tocqueville's prophecy is suggested by the fact that the former invokes the latter fourteen times in his book.

9   Sacvan Bercovitch, afterword to *Ideology and Classic American Literature*, ed. Bercovitch and Myra Jehlen (Cambridge: Cambridge University Press, 1986), 438. Bové's critique appears in "Notes toward a Politics of 'American' Criticism," in *In the Wake of Theory*, 52–60. Subsequent references are cited parenthetically in the text.

10 Martin Heidegger, "What Is Metaphysics?" in *Basic Writings from Being and Time (1927) to The Task of Thinking (1964)*, ed. David Farrell Krell (New York: Harper Collins, 1993), 96. See also "The Age of the World Picture," in *The Question Concerning Technology and Other Essays*, trans. William Lovitt (New York: Harper and Row, 1977), 115–54. Subsequent references are cited parenthetically in the text.

11 Martin Heidegger, "The Question Concerning Technology," in *The Question Concerning Technology*, 17.

12 The pervasive motif of the "saving remnant" that conflates the Israelites and Aeneas' Trojan exiles in Mather's typological representation of the Puritan errand is introduced in the "General Introduction" of the *Magnalia*:

> The Reader will doubtless desire to know, what it was that
> —*tot Volvere casus*
> *Insignes Pietate Viros, tot adire Labores,*
> *Impulerit.*

As Mather's editors note, this is an adaptation of Virgil's *Aeneid* 1.9–11, which they translate: "Did drive men of such wondrous goodness to traverse so many perils, to face so many trials." *Magnalia Christi Americanam*, book 1, ed. Kenneth B. Murdoch with Elizabeth W. Miller (1702; Cambridge, Mass.: Belknap, 1977), 90. See also, Bercovitch, *American Jeremiad*, 87.

13 See Richard Waswo, *The Founding Legend of Western Civilization: From Virgil to Vietnam* (Hanover, N.H.: University Press of New England, 1997).

14 Richard Drinnon, *Facing West: The Metaphysics of Indian-Hating and Empire Building* (Minneapolis: University of Minnesota Press, 1980); Richard Slotkin, *Regeneration through Violence: The Mythology of the American Frontier, 1600–1860* (Middletown, Conn.: Wesleyan University Press, 1973); Slotkin, *The Fatal Environment: The Myth of the Frontier in the Age of Industrialization, 1800–1890* (New York: Atheneum, 1985); Slotkin, *Gunfighter Nation: The Myth of the Frontier in Twentieth-Century America* (New York: Atheneum, 1992).

15 This post-Enlightenment European binarism—and its rhetoric—for example, pervades the narratives of the French and Indian wars of the American historian Francis Parkman. See especially, *The Conspiracy of Pontiac* (1851; New York: Library of America, 1991).

16 See Frank Lentricchia, "Anatomy of a Jar," in *Ariel and the Police: Michel Foucault, William James, Wallace Stevens* (Madison: University of Wisconsin Press, 1988), 3–27.

17 John Hellman, *American Myth and the Legacy of Vietnam* (New York: Columbia University Press, 1986).

18 For Derrida's analysis and critique of this eschatological rhetoric, see *Specters of Marx: The State of the Debt, the Work of Mourning, and the New International*, trans. Peggy Kamuf (New York: Routledge, 1994), 56–64.

19 "She [Pierre's mother] was a noble creature, but formed chiefly for the gilded prosperities of life, and hitherto mostly used to its unruffled serenities bred and expanded, in all developments, under the sole influence of hereditary forms and world-usages. Not his refined, courtly, loving, equable mother, Pierre felt, could unreservedly, and like a heaven's heroine, meet the shock of his extraordinary emergency, and applaud his heart's echo, a sublime resolve, whose execution should call down the astonishment and jeers of the world." Herman Melville, *Pierre; Or, The Ambiguities*, ed. Harrison Hayford, Hershel Parker, and G. Thomas Tanselle (1852; Chicago: Northwestern University Press, 1971), 88. Subsequent references are cited parenthetically in the text.

20 George Washington Peck, review of *Pierre*, by Herman Melville, *American Whig Review*, 16 (November 1852); reprinted in *Herman Melville: The Contemporary Reviews*, ed. Brian Higgins and Hershel Parker (Cambridge: Cambridge University Press, 1995), 443.

21 See Paul A. Bové, "Abandoning Knowledge: Disciplines, Discourse, Dogma," *New Literary History* 25 (1994): 601–19; Bové, "Giving Thought to America: Intellect and *The Education of Henry Adams*," *Critical Inquiry* 23 (1996): 80–108.

22 Bill Readings, *The University in Ruins* (Cambridge, Mass.: Harvard University Press, 1996), 3. Subsequent references are cited parenthetically in the text.

23 Ronald Judy to *boundary 2* collective, memorandum, 5 February 1998. See also Readings, *University in Ruins*: "One can understand the point that I have already made concerning the status of 'globalization' as a kind of 'Americanization.' Global 'Americanization' today (unlike during the period of the Cold War, Korea, and Vietnam) does not mean American national predominance but a global realization of the contentlessness of the American national idea, which shares the emptiness of the cash-nexus and of excellence. Despite the enormous energy expended in attempts to isolate and define an 'Americanness' in American studies programs, one might read these efforts as nothing more than an attempt to mask the fundamental anxiety that it in some sense *means nothing* to be American, that American 'culture' is becoming increasingly a structural oxymoron" (35–36).

24 The term *detournement* (diversion) derives from Guy Debord: "As a proponent of the replacement of subject by predicate, following Feuerbach's systematic practice of it, the young Marx achieved the most cogent use of this *insurrectional style*: thus the philosophy of poverty became the poverty of philosophy. The device of detournement restores all the subversive qualities to past critical judgments that have congealed into respectable truths—or, in other words, that have been transformed into lies." Debord, *The Society of the Spectacle*, trans. Donald Nicholson-Smith (New York: Zone, 1994), 144–45.

25 Martin Heidegger, "A Dialogue on Language," in *On the Way to Language*, trans. Peter D. Hertz (New York: Harper and Row, 1971), 15. See also, "The

Age of the World Picture," where he writes: "'Americanism' is something European. It is an as-yet-uncomprehended species of the gigantic, the gigantic that is itself still inchoate and does not as yet originate at all out of the complete and gathered metaphysical essence of the modern age" (153).

26 Gerald Graff, *Beyond the Culture Wars: How Teaching the Conflicts Can Revitalize American Education* (New York: Norton, 1992); Graff, "Teach the Conflicts," *South Atlantic Quarterly* 89 (1990): 51–68; Gregory S. Jay, *American Literature and the Culture Wars* (Ithaca, N.Y.: Cornell University Press, 1997).

27 Gayatri Chakravorty Spivak, "Marginality in the Teaching Machine," in *Outside in the Teaching Machine* (New York: Routledge, 1993), 53–76.

28 Edward W. Said, *Orientalism* (New York: Vintage, 1979), 92.

29 See Hannah Arendt, "The Jew as Pariah," in *The Jew as Pariah: Jewish Identity and Politics in the Modern Age*, ed. Ron H. Feldman (New York: Grove, 1978), 67–90; Franz Fanon, *The Wretched of the Earth*, trans. Constance Farrington (New York: Grove, 1963); Edward W. Said, *Culture and Imperialism* (New York: Knopf, 1993), 332–36; Gilles Deleuze and Félix Guattari, "Treatise on Nomadology—The War Machine," in *A Thousand Plateaus: Capitalism and Schizophrenia*, trans. Brian Massumi (Minneapolis: University of Minnesota Press, 1987), 351–423; Homi K. Bhabha, "Signs Taken as Wonders," in *The Location of Culture* (New York: Routledge, 1994), 102–22; Bhabha, "DissemiNation: Time, Narrative, and the Margins of the Modern Nation," in *Nation and Narration*, ed. Bhabha (New York: Routledge, 1990), 312; and Spivak, "Marginality in the Teaching Machine."

30 See especially Donald E. Pease, "New Americanists: Revisionist Interventions into the Canon," *boundary 2* 17 (1990): 1–37, which appeared in a special issue of *boundary 2*, entitled "New Americanists," edited by Pease.

31 David Halberstam, *The Best and the Brightest* (New York: Random House, 1972).

32 Richard Ohmann, *English in America: A Radical View of the Profession* (New York: Oxford University Press, 1976), 190–206.

33 One of the saddest and most telling ironies of the war's aftermath is that the intellectual deputies of America who planned the war in Vietnam learned virtually nothing about American thinking from the defeat of the United States. This is synecdochically borne witness to by the highly mediatized memoirs of Robert S. McNamara, *In Retrospect: The Tragedy and Lessons of Vietnam* (New York: Times Books, 1995), in which McNamara carries out his confession of guilt according to the dictates of the very kind of instrumentalist thinking that determined his and his Pentagon colleagues' planning of the Vietnam War. Recalling, for example, the Johnson administration's fateful decision to escalate the war on the basis of General Westmoreland's assessment of the military conditions in Vietnam in 1965, McNamara writes: "Although I questioned these fundamental assumptions during my meetings with Westy and his staff, the discussions proved to be superficial. Looking back, I clearly erred by not forcing—then or later, in either Saigon or Washington—a knock-

down, drag-out debate over the loose assumptions, unasked questions, and thin analyses underlying our military strategy in Vietnam. I spent twenty years as a manager identifying problems and forcing organizations—often against their will—to think deeply and realistically about alternative courses of action and their consequences. I doubt I will ever fully understand why I did not do so here" (202). After leaving the Johnson administration in 1968, McNamara became the director of the World Bank, where he reorganized its functioning in the third world according to the quantitative imperial logic he brought to bear on the problems posed by Vietnam. See Susan George and Fabrizio Sabelli, *Faith and Credit: The World Bank's Secular Empire* (Boulder, Colo.: Westview, 1994), 37–57.

34 Michael Herr, *Dispatches* (New York: Vintage, 1991), 71.

35 Hannah Arendt, *Eichmann in Jerusalem: A Report on the Banality of Evil* (New York: Penguin, 1977).

36 Hannah Arendt, *The Life of the Mind* (New York: Harcourt Brace Jovanovich, 1978), 3–4.

37 Bishop Thomas Spratt, *History of the Royal Society* (1702), qtd. in Basil Willey, *The Seventeenth Century Background: Studies in the Thought of the Age in Relation to Poetry and Religion* (London: Chatto and Windus, 1949), 212.

38 In invoking Emerson's phrase, Rorty tacitly identifies his project with the exceptionalist American Adamic tradition thematized by R. W. B. Lewis in *The American Adam: Innocence, Tragedy, and Tradition in the Nineteenth Century* (Chicago: University of Chicago Press, 1955).

39 As Arendt writes: "Among the outstanding characteristics of the modern age from its beginning to our time we find the typical attitudes of *homo faber*: his instrumentalization of the world, his confidence in tools and in the productivity of the maker of artificial objects; his trust in the all-comprehensive range of the means-end category, his conviction that every issue can be solved and every human motivation reduced to the principle of utility; his sovereignty, which regards everything given as material and thinks of the whole of nature as of 'an immense fabric from which we can cut out whatever we want to resew it however we like'; his equation of intelligence with ingenuity, that is, his contempt for all thought which cannot be considered to be "the first step . . . for the fabrication of artificial objects, particularly of tools to make tools, and to vary their fabrication indefinitely; finally, his matter-of-course identification of fabrication with action." Hannah Arendt, *The Human Condition* (Chicago: University of Chicago Press, 1958), 306. The quotations are from Henri Bergson, *L'Evolution creatrice* (Paris: Presses universitaires de France, 1948), 157, 140.

40 Martin Heidegger, "What are Poets For?" in *Poetry, Language, Thought*, trans. Albert Hofstadter (New York: Harper and Row, 1971), 91.

41 Donald Pease, *Visionary Compacts: American Renaissance Writings in Cultural Context* (Madison: University of Wisconsin Press, 1987), 274. See Noam Chomsky, *Deterring Democracy* (New York: Hill and Wang, 1992).

COUNTERHEGEMONIC

✧

Work and Culture in American Studies

Michael Denning

Perhaps the central concept in the revival of American studies over the last two decades has been that of culture. The linguistic turn of the 1960s and 1970s was displaced by a cultural turn in the 1980s and 1990s. Raymond Williams, who was as responsible as anyone for the revival of the term, once told an interviewer that sometimes he wished he had never heard the damn word; I know the feeling. After looking around my office, a student once joked that every book in it had the word culture in its title—an exaggeration, but not by much. However, since the present situation of American studies is closely tied to the notion of culture, thinking about the futures of American studies might be helped by a reflection on culture.

Updating the History of the Concept of Culture

The history of the definitions of culture is an old genre that goes back at least to 1782. Culture is a word of Latin origin which, it seems, the English adopted from the Germans who had adopted it from the French who there-upon abandoned it totally: E. B. Tylor's *Primitive Culture* was translated as *La Civilisation primitive* in 1876–78, and as late as 1950 Ruth Benedict's *Patterns of Culture* was translated as *Echantillons de civilisations*. Let me pick up the story at mid-century. Some readers may recognize T. S. Eliot's once canonic and now more rarely cited opening of 1948: "My purpose in writing the following chapters is not, as might appear from a casual inspection of the table of contents, to outline a social or political philosophy; nor is the book intended to be merely a vehicle for my observations on a variety of topics. My aim is to help define a word, the word *culture*." Others may recognize A. L. Kroeber and Clyde Kluckhohn's equally if differently canonic opening from 1952: "The 'culture concept of the anthropologists and sociologists is coming to be regarded as the foundation stone of the social sciences.' . . . few intellectuals will challenge the statement that the idea of culture, in the technical an-thropological sense, is one of the key notions of contemporary American thought. In explanatory importance and in generality of application it is comparable to such categories as gravity in physics, disease in medicine, evolution in biology." Between Eliot's modestly titled *Notes towards the Definition of Culture* and Kroeber and Kluckhohn's confident and encyclopedic *Culture: A Critical Review of Concepts and Definitions* stood the mid-century culture concept.[1]

My opening question is simple: how did a term which was almost entirely the property of mainstream scholarship and conservative criticism in 1950 become the slogan of the left, the postmodern, the avant-garde in 2002? There is little doubt that the concept of culture was generally conservative at mid-century, tied to notions of consensus and organicism. As Warren Susman has argued, the "general and even popular 'discovery' of the concept of culture" in the 1930s "could and did have results far more conservative than radical, no matter what the intentions of those who orginally championed some of the ideas and efforts."[2] However, if Eliot and Kroeber and Kluckhohn epitomize this tendency, they now seem more an end than a beginning.

Both Eliot and Kroeber and Kluckhohn look back eighty years and find the same landmarks: Matthew Arnold's *Culture and Anarchy* of 1869 and E. B. Tylor's *Primitive Culture* of 1871. Between Arnold and Eliot, Tylor and Kroeber and Kluckhohn, we see what we might broadly call the modernist conceptions of culture: the literary and humanistic notion of culture as an ideal, the arts and letters, the "study and pursuit of perfection," combining "sweetness and light" with "fire and strength," to use Arnold's words; and, on the other hand, the anthropological notion of culture as a whole way of life, the "complex whole," in Tylor's words, of "knowledge, belief, art, law, morals, custom" and other capabilities and habits. Though aspects of Arnold and Tylor seem more Victorian than modern, their concepts of culture come to prominence in the modern era. Kroeber and Kluckhohn argue that Tylor's sense of culture does not come into widespread use until after 1920; similarly Raymond Williams's *Culture and Society* jumps quickly from Arnold over an "interregnum" to the clearly modernist figures of Eliot, Richards, and Leavis. Moreover, though the modern concept of culture has some roots in mid-nineteenth-century Germany, neither Marx nor Engels used it (although in 1857 Marx notes that he should not forget "so-called cultural history").[3]

These modernist conceptions of culture dominated the first half of the twentieth century, until, beginning in the 1950s, new postmodern definitions of culture emerged that broke decisively from both the Arnoldian sweetness and light and the anthropological customs and morals, giving both Eliot and Kroeber and Kluckhohn their retrospective air. *Culture and Society,*

Raymond Williams's key intervention in the history of the culture concept, stands as a vanishing mediator; it borrowed from the Arnoldian and Tylorian traditions while burying them.[4]

How do we account for this history? Why did the concept of culture appear, and why did its meaning change? In a classic analysis of the meaning of the abstraction *labor*, Marx argued that the concept of a generalized, unspecified labor did not emerge until certain social relations created an equivalence between the many different activities that henceforth became labor: "It was a prodigious advance of Adam Smith," Marx wrote, "to throw away any specificity in wealth-producing activity—labor pure and simple, neither manufacturing nor commercial nor agricultural labor, but the one as much as the other." "The most general abstractions," Marx suggested, "generally develop only with the richest concrete development, where one [abstraction] appears common to many, common to all" ("Introduction," 149–50; translator's brackets). One might pursue a similar inquiry about the concept of culture. What concrete development enabled the general abstraction of culture? What allowed the reduction of a wide range of human activities to the peculiar common denominator we call culture? We often forget the strangeness of the category, a strangeness that led Adorno and Horkheimer to refuse it: "To speak of culture was always contrary to culture. Culture as a common denominator already contains in embryo that schematization and process of cataloguing and classification which bring culture within the sphere of administration."[5] Why did the modernist concept of culture emerge in 1870? And why did it undergo a sea change in 1950?

A rereading of Arnold and Eliot, Tylor and Kroeber and Kluckhohn, offers a plausible hypothesis: the modernist notion of culture is largely the product of a crisis in religious thinking. For both Arnold and Eliot, culture was less a canon of great books than the historic dialectic between Hellenism and Hebraism, classical antiquity and biblical revelation. Moreover, both Arnold and Eliot understood culture in relation to the battles between the established church and the dissenting sects. Sharing the peculiarities of Anglicanism—a Catholicism without a pope, a Protestantism without a sect—they both imagined culture as an ideal whole that incorporates the social cement of religion without its doctrinal controversies. The two errors, Eliot tells us, are either to see religion and culture as identical, or to see a relation between religion and culture. Searching to solve this conundrum, he arrives at a metaphor: culture is the "incarnation" of religion (*Notes*, 105).

Similarly, the anthropological science of culture emerged largely as the

imperial encounter with "savage" religion, the recoding of religious difference—which is to say paganism—as "primitive culture." Though the science of culture, like the Arnoldian tradition, continued to draw a line between the sacred and the profane, culture, the science of the complex whole
no less than the study of perfection, was able to cross that line with relative
ease, seeing all the particular forms of worship as means, not ends.

These two modernist notions of culture had remarkable success and influence in the first half of the twentieth century, particularly, as Kroeber
and Kluckhohn noted, in the societies of the European semiperiphery, the
United States, and Russia. The Marxist tradition adopted aspects of both the
anthropological definition, particularly in theorizing the "national" question, and the high culture definition, particularly in the social democratic
tradition of appropriating and popularizing the classics: this was the cultural
history that was the object of Walter Benjamin's brilliant critique in his essay
on Eduard Fuchs. It offers as its major addition the concept of cultural revolution, which comes out of the Russian Marxist tradition, particularly the
work of Lenin and Trotsky; this will deeply influence Lukács, particularly in
his pathbreaking essay, "The Old Culture and the New Culture" of 1920,
and Gramsci. Nevertheless, by 1950, it would be odd to think of a specifically
Marxist theory of culture the way there was, from Mehring and Plekhanov
to Christopher Caudwell and Ernst Fischer, a Marxist aesthetics.

Once we reach the work of Raymond Williams, *culture* emerges as a
very different kind of abstraction. Williams's carefully constructed index of
"Words, Themes, and Persons" in *Culture and Society* has entries for "Ideology" and "Panopticon," but none for "Religion." Arnold and Eliot's concern for the controversies of establishment—the disestablishment of the Irish
church, Arnold's thoughts on the "great sexual insurrection of our Anglo-
Teutonic race" figured by the Shakers and the Mormons, or Eliot's use of the
term "sub-culture" to refer to the divided parts of Christendom, to Roman
Catholics in England—are replaced in Williams's *The Long Revolution* by the
grand chapters on education, the growth of the reading public, and the rise
of the popular press. Culture becomes a new kind of abstraction with the
dramatic explosion throughout the world of what was called at the time
"mass culture"—a culture that seemed as far from customs and morals as from
the pursuit of perfection, as far from folk culture as from elite culture. The
change is even registered in the difference between Arnold and Eliot. If
Arnold's culture of 1869 was still optimistic and expanding—"culture, or the
study of perfection, leads us to conceive of no perfection as being real which
is not a *general* perfection, embracing all our fellow-men" (with only a small

caveat about the popular literature which condescended to the masses)—
Eliot's culture of 1948 was a shrinking terrain caught between the market
and the state (*Culture and Anarchy*, 174).

The shape of this new postmodern culture concept—the culture of the
cultural industries and the cultural state—can be seen in the essays of the
1940s and 1950s that have lasted longer than those of Eliot or Kroeber and
Kluckhohn: Adorno and Horkheimer's "The Culture Industry," Dwight
Macdonald's "Theory of Popular Culture," later revised as "Theory of Mass
Culture" and then as "Masscult and Midcult" (it is interesting to note that
Eliot himself wrote that "Macdonald's theory strikes me as the best *alternative*
to my own that I have seen" [*Notes*, 83]), Roland Barthes's *Mythologies*,
Richard Hoggart's *The Uses of Literacy*, C. Wright Mills's unfinished book on
The Cultural Apparatus, Williams's own *The Long Revolution*, C. L. R. James's
turn from an Arnoldian Trotskyist cultural politics to a new engagement
with popular or mass culture in *American Civilization* and *Beyond a Boundary*,
and the American studies movement associated with figures like Leo Marx,
whose "Notes on the Culture of the New Capitalism" was published in
Monthly Review in 1959. It is perhaps not an accident that one of the first uses
of the term *postmodern* appears in the landmark anthology *Mass Culture* of
1957, which collected essays by Adorno and Macdonald, among others. By
1959, Daniel Bell was noting that the new journals of the left, *Dissent* and
Universities and Left Review (soon to become *New Left Review*) "are full of
attacks against advertising, the debaucheries of mass culture and the like. . . .
these problems are essentially cultural and not political," he argued, "and
the problem of radical thought today is to reconsider the relationship of
culture to society."[6]

The four decades since Bell wrote have seen an extended reconsideration
of the relationship of culture to society, as both Arnoldian cultural criticism
and Tylorian cultural anthropology have been displaced by versions of cultural studies that one might call, borrowing from Robert Heilbroner, socioanalytic theories of culture.[7]

The Antinomies of Cultural Studies

One could begin to sort out the kinds of socioanalytic theories of culture by
intellectual histories and national traditions—British cultural studies, French
structuralism and poststructuralism, German critical theory, North American theory, canon revision, and new historicism, Latin American depen-

dency theory, Indian subaltern studies, and others. No term captures all of these trends: postmodern theory is too broad, cultural Marxism misses the often antagonistic relation to the Marxist tradition, New Left theory sounds too narrowly political. Nevertheless, a generation of New Left intellectuals around the globe, figures who came of age in the 1940s and 1950s, did seem to turn to culture in order to reshape radical thought (see Table 1). In retrospect, it was a generation as striking as the classic modernist generation of Western Marxists—the generation of Lukács, Gramsci, Benjamin, Sartre, de Beauvoir, and C. L. R. James.

The turn to culture was not a turn back to Arnold or Tylor; rather it was, as Bell put it, a turn to "advertising" and the "debaucheries of mass culture," the very aspects of the "new capitalism," as Leo Marx called it, that generated this new abstraction *culture* and seemed to leave both arts and customs behind. The most visible manifestation, the phenomenal appearance, of this new world lay in the new means of communication. I use this phrase—means of communication—in part because the word *communication* proved a key one for this generation. (Perhaps, as Kenneth Burke suggested in the early 1950s, the word was a displacement, carrying some of the libidinal energies invested in the now disgraced master concept *communism*.[8]) *Communications* was the title of Raymond Williams's major programmatic work. I also use the phrase because it captures the first key antinomy of cultural studies, the hesitation between the means of communication as the mass media and the means of communication as the forms and codes by which communication takes place. On the one hand, the means of communication understood as a set of instruments and technologies—the mass media—constantly tempted us toward versions of technological determinism, from McLuhan's *The Mechanical Bride* and *Understanding Media* to the enormous prestige of Benjamin's rediscovered "The Work of Art in the Age of Mechanical Reproduction." This line culminates in Armand Mattelart's genealogy of communications, *Mapping World Communication*, which is both an "itinerary of . . . technical object[s]" and a history of the theories that accounted for them.[9]

On the other hand, the means of communication understood as the forms and codes of symbolic action led to a resurrection of the ancient sciences of rhetoric and hermeneutics, with their concern for the tropes and allegories of social discourse, and the invention of the new sciences of signs and sign systems, semiology and semiotics. Both sides could be seen in the influential work of Roland Barthes: the playful decodings of detergents and plastics, of the brain of Einstein and a photograph of a saluting black soldier in *My-*

TABLE 1: Selected New Left Intellectuals

The year they turned 20 (a *Culture and Society* trick)

Roland Barthes 1935	Samir Amin 1951
C. Wright Mills 1936	Stuart Hall 1952
Louis Althusser 1938	Alexander Kluge 1952
Leo Marx 1939	Tony Negri 1953
Doris Lessing 1939	Susan Sontag 1953
Renato Constantino 1939	Stanley Aronowitz 1953
Harry Braverman 1940	Fredric Jameson 1954
Raymond Williams 1941	Enrique Dussel 1954
Betty Friedan 1941	Amiri Baraka 1954
Ernest Mandel 1943	Edward Said 1955
E. P. Thompson 1944	Ernesto Laclau 1955
Amilcar Cabral 1944	Armand Mattelart 1956
André Gorz 1944	Nicos Poulantzas 1956
Lucio Colletti 1944	Wolfgang Haug 1956
Frantz Fanon 1945	Frigga Haug 1957
Michel Foucault 1946	Perry Anderson 1958
John Berger 1946	Ngugi wa Thiong'o 1958
Gustavo Gutiérrez 1948	E. San Juan 1958
Jürgen Habermas 1949	Juliet Mitchell 1960
Noam Chomsky 1949	Regis Debray 1960
Hans Magnus Enzensberger 1949	Christine Delphy 1961
Andre Gunder Frank 1949	Julia Kristeva 1961
Jean Baudrillard 1949	Etienne Balibar 1962
Immanuel Wallerstein 1950	Walter Rodney 1962
Pierre Bourdieu 1950	Gayatri Spivak 1962
Jacques Derrida 1950	Ariel Dorfman 1962
Guy Debord 1951	Terry Eagleton 1963
Roberto Fernández Retamar 1951	Sheila Rowbotham 1963
Nawal el Saadawi 1951	Tariq Ali 1963
Richard Ohmann 1951	Angela Davis 1964

thologies, set along the quasi-mathematical rigor and forbidding jargon of *Elements of Semiology*. The last half-century has seen the rise and fall of several of these new "sciences," including deconstruction and discourse analysis; nevertheless, their central object—what Stuart Hall has called the "relations of representation"—remains at the heart of cultural studies.[10]

These new analyses of the means of communication, of what came to be

660

called mass culture, were not simply added to an already established social or political theory. Rather, as is implied by the echo between means of communication and means of production, the mass media often appeared as the central terrain, the dominant level, of a "postindustrial," "consumer" order. The new cultural materialisms did not simply constitute a reassertion of the importance of the superstructure, but a rethinking of economy and politics in cultural terms. One can see this even in the least cultural of the New Left Marxists, the *Monthly Review* tendency, who placed a powerful explanatory emphasis on the role of advertising and the "sales effort" in monopoly capitalism.

In a way, this was not surprising, for the new mass culture, the means of communication, was itself closely tied to the power of the market and the state. The division between market and state echoes throughout the postwar years, and it shapes the second fundamental antinomy of cultural studies— spectacle or surveillance, shopping mall or prison. Let me begin with the market. The great conundrum facing the 1960s New Left was how to invent a Marxism without class; how to maintain the insights and political drive of historical materialism in an epoch when left, right, and center generally agreed that the classes of Fordist capitalism were passing from the stage of world history, when the "labor metaphysic," as C. Wright Mills put it in his influential "Letter to the New Left" (published in New Left magazines on both sides of the Atlantic), seemed irrelevant.[11]

The solution lay in the resurrection of the secret history of the commodity, from Lukács's long forgotten *History and Class Consciousness* with its analysis of reification, to Benjamin's archaeology of the "universe of commodities" in the arcades and world exhibitions of nineteenth-century Paris, to Adorno and Horkheimer's account of the "Culture Industry" where the commodity form reduces all art to the eternal sameness of radio jingles, to the "sexual sell" that lay at the heart of the emptiness Betty Friedan called "the problem that has no name," the "feminine mystique." It was a short step from Benjamin's Paris arcades to Fredric Jameson's Bonaventure Hotel; and one can take Guy Debord's Situationist pamphlet of 1968, *The Society of the Spectacle*, as the quintessential denunciation of a world where we don 3-D glasses in the cinema of daily life. In Latin America, where political independence coincided with economic and cultural domination, cultural imperialism was also cast in commodity terms, as in the 1971 Chilean classic by Armand Mattelart and Ariel Dorfman, *How to Read Donald Duck: Imperialist Ideology in the Disney Comic.*[12]

The contradictions of this commodity Marxism are well known, as we veered from advertising dystopias to rock and rap utopias. Few of us have been immune to either the despair induced by more and more genuinely mindless entertainment or the hopes inspired by the occasional eruption of a genuinely popular and liberatory art. As long as capitalist culture presents itself as an immense accumulation of commodities—displayed in the multimedia emporia of Barnes and Noble, Tower Records, and Blockbuster Video—no escape from the antinomies of consumer culture is likely. And Jameson's dialectic of reification and utopia stands as one of the richest, if necessarily failed, imaginary resolutions of that contradiction.[13]

Moreover, it is worth recalling that the power of commodity theories of culture goes beyond the analysis of popular cultural commodities themselves. Together the theory of reification—the transformation of relations between people into relations between things as a result of the generalization of the commodity form—and the inverse but complementary theory of the fetishism of commodities and the fetishism of capital—the transformation of the products of human labor into godlike creatures with the power to dictate the terms of daily work—constitute an entire aesthetic: a theory of the history of the senses in which those aspects of daily life that had formed a "complex whole"—food, worship, art, song, sport—are divided and taylorized into the disconnected jargons, subcultures, and specializations of postmodern daily life. The results of this instrumentalization of human culture are powerfully analyzed in the work of Pierre Bourdieu, where culture emerges not simply as consumption but as productive consumption; that is to say, as an investment in the creation of a specifically cultural capital. It is a small capital, to be sure, always dominated by economic capital; nevertheless, in the symbolic violence of the fields and habituses of capitalism, human choices in food, clothing, and the arts become badges of distinction, the stakes and weapons in class struggle.

The major alternatives to these commodity theories of culture have been those that begin from the state rather than the market, from the exercise of power and domination rather than the buying and selling of goods and labor, from theories of ideology rather than theories of fetishism.[14] "Our society is one not of spectacle, but of surveillance," Michel Foucault wrote in *Discipline and Punish*, and he implicitly replaced the nineteenth-century Parisian arcades of Benjamin with the nineteenth-century French penitentiaries, as Mike Davis would later replace Jameson's Bonaventure Hotel with the Metropolitan Detention Center as the emblem of postmodern Los Angeles. The prison—or what Foucault called the "carceral archipelago," the network of prison, police, and delinquent—held a central place in New Left politics and imagination: "Sometimes I think this whole world / Is one big prison yard / Some of us are prisoners, / The rest of us are guards," Bob Dylan sang after the shooting of George Jackson. *Discipline and Punish* itself had its origins in the prison revolt at Attica, New York. However, the power of *Discipline and Punish* lay not in the horrifying if static diptychs of premodern and modern punishment—the torture of the regicide juxtaposed to the timetable of the house of young prisoners, the chain gang set against the police carriage—nor even in its alleged theory of power. Rather it lay in the long digression of part 3 which outlined the formation of a disciplinary society and what we might call a discipline theory of culture. Discipline became another name for culture itself, now defined as the articulation of knowledge and power; discipline produces docile and useful bodies through elaborate techniques. Discipline indeed has the same productive double meaning we saw in "means of communication": the disciplines are at once the institutions and apparatuses of cultural knowledge, the human sciences, and the particular forms and codes by which that knowledge is transmitted. Just as Marx dissected the simple forms of value, so Foucault anatomized the simple forms of discipline: hierarchical observation, normalization, examination.[15]

The analysis of these articulations of power and knowledge, these disciplines, offers a remarkable contrast to the commodity theories of culture. The fascinating world of consumer desire—the fetishism and fashion of world's fairs and shopping malls, what Benjamin called the "sex-appeal of the inorganic"[16]—fades before the relentless surveillance and policing of desire by what are the state and quasi-state institutions of the Western social democracies and the Eastern people's democracies: prisons, armies, schools, hospitals—and, as elaborated in Edward Said's *Orientalism* and *Culture and Imperialism*, in the disciplines, discourses, and apparatuses of the colonial state.

For if the New Left was in part a rebellion against the consumer capitalism of the affluent society, it was also a revolt against the institutions of what Louis Althusser called, in his most influential essay, the "ideological state apparatuses," the ISAs. The ISAs were, one might say, the state counterpart to Adorno and Horkheimer's culture industry. Like the disciplines, the ideological state apparatuses created—interpellated, in Althusser's jargon—subjects; we recognize who we are in being addressed by the institutions we live in. However, though the discipline / apparatus theories of culture depended on the double meaning of subject—one was subjected to power and domination, but one was also a subject, an agent capable of action—for the most part the docile body overshadowed the useful body. The disciplines and the apparatus were like the Borg on *Star Trek*: resistance was futile.

The other major political, or state-oriented, theory of culture—what I will call the hegemony theory of culture—developed as a response to the imprisonment of the subaltern in the disciplines and apparatuses of the state. Like the discipline theory, the hegemony theory stressed the complexity of the modern state, a state which is, in Gramsci's words, educative, ethical, cultural: it "plans, urges, incites, solicits, punishes." But the source of the hegemony argument was not the epochal history writing that underwrote the formation of a disciplinary or commodity society. Rather it was the conjunctural analyses found in Marx's famous pamphlet on the defeat of the revolutions of 1848 and the rise of Louis Napoleon, *The Eighteenth Brumaire*, those found in Gramsci's notes on the defeat of the Italian factory councils and the rise of Mussolini, and those in Stuart Hall's brilliant articles on the defeat of social democracy and the New Left and the rise of Margaret Thatcher. All three "pamphlets" set the economic narrative in the background, insisting on the relative autonomy of state and social movement politics; however, all three were less interested in "power" or "domination" than in the "relations of force" of particular moments. The argument of all three was, in essence, that politics worked like poetry, that the relations of force were intertwined with the relations of representation. The struggle for hegemony was not merely the disciplining of docile / useful bodies, nor was it simply the cheap bread and circuses of a McDonald's Happy Meal; rather, it depended on the work of representation, the summoning up of the ghosts and costumes of the past to revolutionize the present. Just as Marx called Louis Napoleon an artist in his own right, a comedian who took "his comedy for world history," so Hall argued that Thatcher, "our most-beloved Good Housekeeper," succeeded by representing—depicting and speaking for—the Thatcherite man and woman in us all.[17]

"The question of hegemony," Hall wrote, "is always the question of a new cultural order. . . . Cultural power [is] the power to define, to 'make things mean'" (170). This politics of representation extended beyond the state and political parties to what Gramsci called "the forms of cultural organisation"— schools, churches, newspapers, theaters, literary quarterlies, serial novels, and the intellectuals who staffed these institutions. Neither shopping mall nor prison, culture appeared as a giant school system, its product less spectacle or surveillance than the school recital of the Pledge of Allegiance, the articulation of that hybrid of nationalism and populism that Hall, following Gramsci, called the "national popular." The emergence of this hegemony theory of culture was closely connected to the upheavals in mass education, which ranged from the formation of the postwar U.S. "multiversity" and the Labour-oriented adult education at the base of British cultural studies, to the international student revolts of 1968, to the past two decades' battles over affirmative action and curricular reform.

Hall's attention to the national popular, and to the place of racisms in its formation, was part of a dramatic shift in the relations of force in cultural studies generally, a shift that took place in the late 1970s and early 1980s. The post–World War II fascination with mass culture, with culture as the means of communication, began to be displaced by the notion of culture as communities, as peoples. Cultural theory increasingly took up the question of how peoples are produced: it focused on people-producing concepts—*nation, race, ethnicity, colony, color, minority, region, diaspora, migrant, postcolonial*—and the national and imperial discourses that underlay these fantasies of racial and ethnic identity.

The transformation had many symptoms and markers: the great debate about the "canon," which proved not to be about high and low culture, but about the lineaments of a national language, literature, and education system; the trajectory of the poststructuralists Gayatri Spivak and Edward Said from their early meditations on *différance* and beginnings to their critiques of the discourses of colonial and postcolonial regimes; the remarkable success in the humanities of Benedict Anderson's little book of 1983, *Imagined Communities*; the relative waning of Raymond Williams as the emblem of British cultural studies largely because of his apparent blindness to questions of nation, race, and empire; the emergence of the leading intellectuals of the decolonizing national liberation movements, figures like Du Bois, Fanon, and C. L. R. James, into the mainstream of North Atlantic cultural theory; the reemergence of Etienne Balibar, an architect of the Althusserian rereading of *Capital*, as a theorist of racism and nationalism; and the revival of American studies, the original identity discipline, itself.

One could see this "national turn" in cultural theory as the resurrection of the pluralist anthropological notion of culture as the ways of life of particular peoples, the foundation for the studies of national character. Indeed, both defenders and critics of multiculturalism have seen this as an "identity theory of culture," implicitly adopting Immanuel Wallerstein's definition of culture: "when we talk of traits which are neither universal nor idiosyncratic we often use the term 'culture.' . . . Culture is a way of summarizing the ways in which groups distinguish themselves from other groups." For me, this definition misses precisely those aspects of postmodernity that had rendered the "mores and customs" notion of culture inadequate: the mass culture of market and state. Actually, the radical core of so-called identity theories of culture lies in the fact that they are not pluralist group or ethnic theories, but what I will call, borrowing from Nancy Fraser's recent book, "recognition theories of culture."[18] They find their inspiration in the Hegelian/existentialist theories of culture that emerged alongside the mass culture debates of the 1950s in Sartre's *Anti-Semite and Jew*, de Beauvoir's *The Second Sex*, Fanon's *Black Skin, White Masks*, and even, I think, in Hoggart's *The Uses of Literacy*. In all of these works, the culture of the subaltern is a product of a dialectic of self and other, where the self is objectified as the other and denied any reciprocity of recognition. The politics of recognition range from Fanon's attack on the illusions of any national or identity culture and his defense of the cleansing violence of the colonial subject in *The Wretched of the Earth*, to the consciousness-raising that sought to exorcise the ideologies of inferiority and inessentiality inscribed on the self, to the claim—on the state and the market—for cultural justice, for "affirmative action" in the woeful bureaucratic language we must defend. A recognition theory of culture is *not* built on the plurality of a multiculture, but on what Gayatri Spivak has seen as the radical emptiness of the category of the subaltern, the "underother" to translate it from one English to another. Nevertheless, any recognition theory of culture remains caught within the antinomies of self and other, identity and difference, center and margin.

From Text to Work: Toward a Labor Theory of Culture

If the New Left's postwar socioanalytic theories of culture—cultural studies for short—were the product of a new attention to the means of communication dominated by the forces of the market and the state, it is not surprising that they resurrected Marx's theories of fetishism and ideology. But cultural studies also resurrected Marx's analysis of the labor process, and much of its most interesting work developed out of a creative tension between the analysis of the labor process and the analysis of mass culture. This was the dialectic around which Stanley Aronowitz's classic *False Promises* was built— "Colonized Leisure, Trivialized Work" was the title of a central essay.[19] In the Birmingham Cultural Studies Centre of the 1970s, the work of Stuart Hall and others on the media developed in a vital tension with the work of Paul Willis and others on the labor process. And the early works of socialist-feminist cultural critique, like those of Barbara Ehrenreich, tied the labor processes of housework, of feminized occupations, and of birth itself to the mass culture addressed to women. Indeed, the catchphrase of contemporary cultural studies, "contested terrain," originated in the studies of the labor process.

The landmark study of the labor process—and a central, if sometimes overlooked, work of postwar cultural studies—was Harry Braverman's *Labor and Monopoly Capital*.[20] If Foucault began from the prison, Braverman began from the factory and the office; what Foucault called discipline, "movement in a resistant medium," Braverman called by two names: management and craft. Against the scientific management of Taylorism, he defended a scientific workmanship. A reconsideration of Braverman's account of the labor process offers another way of approaching the antinomies of contemporary cultural studies, the lineaments of a labor theory of culture.

This return to a labor metaphysic may seem odd, even perverse. If anything remains of Marxism in our post-Fordist, postindustrial cybereconomy, one would not think that it was its emphasis on work and production. Capitalism, we are told, is not about work but about the market; none of us really work, we simply sell our weekdays in order to buy our weekends. The capitalist dream of complete automation never dies—robotic assembly lines, desktop publishing, and money breeding money on an eternally rising stock exchange. Bill Gates's Microsoft mansion is the latest rewiring of a utopia without work. Virtually all of liberal and radical thought is, as Harry Braverman once noted, a critique of capitalism as a mode of distribution rather than as a mode of production. Moreover, even many radical anthropologists, ecologists, and feminists have argued that Marxism is, in Baudrillard's famous phrase, a "mirror of production," a captive of the nineteenth-century desire to dominate nature with a spiraling and self-destructive exploitation of energy and resources.[21]

In addition, work and culture seem to be opposites in a number of ways. Culture is seen as the equivalent of leisure, not labor; the symbolic, not the material; shopping and tourism, not jobs; sex, desire, and fantasy, not work. It is a commonplace to note our reluctance to represent work in our popular stories; a martian who hijacked the stock of the average video store would reasonably conclude that humans spent far more of their time engaged in sex than in work. And most work remains invisible: we have all seen more different places of consumption than places of production—The Gap in the mall, not the garment sweatshops; the Honda showroom, not the auto factory; Perdue chickens in Stop and Shop, not the chicken processing plants. These places of consumption are of course places of work; but it is not an accident that we tend to see frontline service workers—the UPS drivers in the 1997 strike, for example—as the most characteristic kinds of workers.

However, Braverman reminds us that work and culture are synonyms, not antonyms. Culture is the product and result of labor, part of the same process. Quoting the famous passage in *Capital* where Marx distinguished the spider from the weaver, the bee from the architect—"what distinguishes the worst architect from the best of bees is this, that the architect raises the structure in imagination before he erects it in reality. At the end of every labor process we get a result that had already existed in the imagination of the laborer at its commencement"[22]—he notes how Marx's definition of human labor echoes Aristotle's definition of art. Human work and culture is purposive, conscious, and directed by conceptual thought.

Thus, the fundamental divide in this theory of culture is not that between labor and leisure, nor that between self and other, men and women, Jews and Goyim, Greeks and barbarians, cowboys and Indians. Rather it is the line between conception and execution, between, to use a musical example, composition and performance. The fundamental aspect of human labor, Braverman argues, is that the unity of conception and execution can be broken in time, space, and motive force; it is this that produces human culture. One person can conceive and another execute. This is both the power and tragedy of human labor. A conception can be communicated from one place and time to another by sophisticated means of communication: writing and the means of mechanical and electronic reproduction. It can be saved in a variety of means of storage—books, blueprints, machines, computer programs—to be executed later, even centuries later, as we stage new productions of Shakespeare's plays and Beethoven's symphonies. The great attraction of the improvisatory arts—particularly jazz—lies in their promise to reunite composition and performance.

Thus art and culture are not the opposite of labor, but forms of labor. And the history of culture is the history of works become texts, of the labor process and occupations in a variety of industries. The unity and division between mental and manual labor is the starting point of any labor theory of culture. Of course, we are more aware of their separation than their unity, since, as Braverman argued, "the separation of hand and brain is the most decisive single step taken in the division of labor by the capitalist mode of production. . . . The unity of thought and action, conception and execution, hand and mind, which capitalism threatened from its beginnings, is now attacked by a systematic dissolution employing all the resources of science and the various engineering disciplines based upon it" (126, 174). Though there remains a mental element to all manual labor, and a manual element to all mental labor—even Lt. Troi in *Star Trek* gets exhausted exercising her Beta-zoid telepathy as the ship's counselor—the illusion of their separation is a real one. All people are intellectuals, Gramsci writes in a classic version of this theory, but not all have the function of intellectuals in a given society. Thus culture appears simultaneously as something we all have (unlike the Arnoldian culture) and as something in which a few are specialists. Culture appears to us as a vast store of accumulated mental labor—the history of consciousness as one metaphor puts it. This accumulated mental labor appears to be the property of separate classes—leisured or cultured or intellectual classes—or of a separate time, a leisure time: hence the centrality of the struggles for the eight-hour day, the weekend, the paid vacation, the rights to adolescent education and adult retirement.

Just as the antinomies of public and private, liberty and equality, haunt liberal thought, the paradoxical unity and division of mental and manual labor haunts all socialist theories of culture. It lies behind a number of classic debates that liberal thinkers rarely if ever even enter: the relation between base and superstructure in social thought; the relation between workers and intellectuals in political organization. It is not suprising that many of the most powerful utopian images in the socialist tradition are images of the union of mental and manual labor: Marx's somewhat humorous vision of a society where one may "hunt in the morning, fish in the afternoon, rear cattle in the evening, criticize after dinner . . . without ever becoming hunter, fisherman, shepherd or critic"; William Morris's craft ideal; the slogan of worker's self-management; and the various communitarian experiments from Brook Farm to Dorothy Day's Catholic Worker.[23]

All very well, you may say, but what are the consequences of such a definition of culture? Let me conclude by first saying that I don't wish to eliminate the other conceptions of culture I have outlined. We live in a divided and reified culture, and I find that all of the socioanalytic theories of culture I have outlined—commodity, investment, discipline, hegemony, recognition—have their interpretive power and, as we used to say, their relative autonomy. However, a labor theory of culture does address a number of weaknesses and false problems in these other conceptions.

First, a labor theory of culture can take us beyond the noisy sphere of the market in the analysis of mass culture, reminding us that the apparent confrontation between cultural commodities and cultural consumers—with its valorization of resistant or subversive readings—obscures the laborers in the culture industry. If no reading is uncontested, neither is any composition or performance; the fundamental contradiction in the culture industries is that they are not automatons, but depend on the sale of the products of particular labor powers. As a result, as I argued at length in *The Cultural Front*, the struggles of the hacks and stars of the culture industries are fundamental to any understanding of mass culture. With the digitization of cultural skills— think of the effect of synthesized and sampled musics on contemporary instrumentalists—Braverman's model grows more and more relevant to cultural studies. Moreover, by reminding us of the important analytic distinction between the labor process and the valorization process, between the material content of purposive human activity and the specific form labor takes under capitalism, a labor theory of culture guards against the reduction of culture to commodification.

Second, a labor theory of culture avoids a fundamental weakness of the political theories of culture—again, using *political* in the narrow sense. One reason I hold on to the concept of culture rather than switching to the classical concept of ideology—there are many days when I would be happy to call what I do ideological studies rather than cultural studies—is that the concept of ideology remains a political term, having to do with power, domination, and legitimation. And a fundamental weakness of both the discipline and hegemony theories of culture is the tendency to see all of culture as first and foremost a weapon, a tool for constructing subjects of one sort or another. This has led some in cultural studies, including Eric Lott, to call for a revival of the aesthetic. Lott's own early work was a brilliant example of, in his words, "the definition of culture as 'a whole way of conflict,'" looking at "the role of culture in . . . political development."[24] I think that what Lott wants is less the aesthetic than a sense that culture is a kind of work, rooted in our senses as well as our politics, and in its own materials and instruments; it thus always goes beyond the ideological functions emphasized in the political definitions of culture.

In this way, a labor theory of culture also enriches Fredric Jameson's influential argument for the utopian elements of cultural productions. For

Jameson, utopia is represented not by private desire and pleasure but by collective wish fulfillment, the imagination of community. But one needs to add to this a legacy of classical German aesthetics, the promise of play, of unalienated labor. How does labor get turned into beauty, particularly since we usually don't want to look at it? Performance is always tied to a strict economy of when and when not to show them that you're sweating. How do the rhythms of work become the rhythms of art? The hypothesis of a *labor unconscious* would mean that cultural historians and interpreters ought to explore the relations between forms of work and forms of art not only in those classic "folk" genres—quilts, sea chanteys, and field hollers—where the connections seem immediate, but in the arts and entertainments that seem most distant from the world of work.

Finally, the labor theory of culture reminds us that the cultures of the subaltern, the underothers, which demand recognition and cultural justice are not simply the expression of some preexisting identity; their unities and divisions are the mediated products of the forms of labor—childbirth, slavery, sweatshop, assembly line—to which subalterns have been subjected. It is worth recalling that one of the most powerful works in what I have called the recognition theory of culture—Tillie Olsen's *Silences* of 1978—was also an expression of a labor theory of culture, seeing work and art as two sides of the same reality. "For our silenced people," the dedication of *Silences* reads, "century after century their beings consumed in the hard, everyday essential work of maintaining human life. Their art, which still they made—as their other contributions—anonymous; refused respect, recognition; lost."[25]

If the revolutionary explosion of the means of communication—the vast culture industries and state cultural apparatuses—set the agenda for cultural studies in the second half of the twentieth century, perhaps their very ordinariness today can lead us back to their place in daily life, to a sense of culture not simply as the peculiar ways of life of small and distinctive communities of identity nor as the new high arts of the studios of Disney or Nintendo, but as the means of subsistence of mobile and migrant global workers. In the circuit of labor-power, the working day is the moment of consumption; culture is the labor that produces labor-power. For labor-power remains a curious commodity in that it, unlike other commodities, is not produced as a commodity. Culture is a name for that habitus that forms, subjects, disciplines, entertains, and qualifies labor-power; in it lies the very resistance to becoming labor-power. It is the contradictory realm of work in the shadow of value, the unpaid and "unproductive" labor of the household, what the

autonomous Marxists called the "social factory"; but it is also the contradictory realm of the arts of daily life, of what Marx called "the pleasures of the
labourer," the "social needs and social pleasures" that are called forth by the
"rapid growth of productive capital." It was, curiously, the story that was not
told in *Capital*, what David Harvey calls "Marx's rather surprising failure to
undertake any systematic study of the processes governing the production
and reproduction of labor power itself." "This omission is," Harvey remarks,
"one of the most serious of all the gaps in Marx's own theory, and one that is
proving extremely difficult to plug if only because the relations between
accumulation and the social processes of reproduction of labor power are
hidden in such a maze of complexity that they seem to defy analysis." That
maze of complexity—the labyrinth of capital, labor, and culture—remains
the challenge of an emancipatory cultural studies.[26]

Notes

I was particularly happy to give the keynote address at the 1998 Dartmouth Institute on "The Futures of American Studies"—on which this essay is based—
because I am a graduate of Dartmouth, and it was an opportunity to thank my
undergraduate teachers: Don Pease, who first suggested I read Althusser; Jim
Heffernan, who advised my senior essay on Blake; Peter Bien, a draft counselor in
those last years of the Vietnam War and extraordinary guide to Joyce and modernism; Marlene Fried, a model to those of us in the Dartmouth Radical Union and
teacher of my first course in Marxism; and particularly Lou Renza, a mentor or,
more accurately, antimentor.

1   T. S. Eliot, *Notes towards the Definition of Culture*, reprinted in Eliot, *Christianity
    and Culture: The Idea of a Christian Society and Notes towards the Definition of Cul-
    ture* (San Diego: Harcourt, Brace, 1976), 85; A. L. Kroeber and Clyde Kluck-
    hohn, *Culture: A Critical Review of Concepts and Definitions* (New York: Vin-
    tage, 1952), 3. Kroeber and Kluckhohn are quoting Stuart Chase, *The Proper
    Study of Mankind* (New York: Harper, 1948), 59. See also Denys Cuche, *La
    notion de culture dans les sciences sociales* (Paris: Editions La Découverte, 1996).
    Subsequent references are cited parenthetically in the text.
2   Warren I. Susman, *Culture as History: The Transformation of American Society in
    the Twentieth Century* (New York: Pantheon, 1984), 153, 164.
3   Matthew Arnold, *Culture and Anarchy and Other Writings*, ed. Stefan Collini
    (Cambridge: Cambridge University Press, 1993), 81, 141; E. B. Tylor, *Primi-
    tive Culture*, vol. 3 of *Collected Works* (London: Routledge, 1994), 1; Raymond
    Williams, *Culture and Society, 1780–1950* (New York: Columbia University
    Press, 1983); Karl Marx, "Introduction to the *Grundrisse*," in *Marx: Later Politi-*

cal Writings, ed. and trans. Terrell Carver (Cambridge: Cambridge University Press, 1996), 154. See also Raymond Williams, "Marx on Culture," in his *What I Came to Say* (London: Hutchinson Radius, 1989). Subsequent references are cited parenthetically in the text.

4   "*Culture and Society*," Williams noted twenty years later, "served as a bridge . . . but a bridge is something that people pass over. Still today many American readers say, oh yes, we agree with your position, we read *Culture and Society*. . . . And I say that is not my position. . . . I read this book as I might read a book by somebody else. It is a work most distant from me . . . ironically . . . the very success of the book . . . has created the conditions for its critique." Raymond Williams, *Politics and Letters: Interviews with New Left Review* (London: Verso, 1981), 110, 107, 100.

5   Max Horkheimer and Theodor W. Adorno, *Dialectic of Enlightenment*, trans. John Cumming (New York: Seabury Press, 1972), 131.

6   Daniel Bell, *The End of Ideology: On the Exhaustion of Political Ideas in the Fifties* (New York: Free Press, 1962), 313.

7   Robert L. Heilbroner, *Marxism, For and Against* (New York: Norton, 1980).

8   Kenneth Burke, "Curriculum Criticum," in *Counter-Statement* (Los Altos, Calif.: Hermes Publications, 1953), 215.

9   Armand Mattelart, *Mapping World Communication: War, Progress, Culture*, trans. Susan Emanuel and James A. Cohen (Minneapolis: University of Minnesota Press, 1994), ix.

10   Stuart Hall, "New Ethnicities," in *Stuart Hall: Critical Dialogues in Cultural Studies*, ed. David Morley and Kuan-Hsing Chen (New York: Routledge, 1996), 442.

11   C. Wright Mills, "The New Left," in *Power, Politics, and People: The Collected Essays of C. Wright Mills*, ed. Irving Louis Horowitz (New York: Ballantine, 1963), 256. Originally published as "Letter to the New Left," *New Left Review* 5 (1960): 18–23; and "On the New Left," *Studies on the Left* 2, no. 1 (1961): 63–72.

12   Georg Lukács, *History and Class Consciousness: Studies in Marxist Dialectics*, trans. Rodney Livingstone (Cambridge, Mass.: MIT Press, 1971); Walter Benjamin, "Paris, Capital of the Nineteenth Century," in *Reflections: Essays, Aphorisms, Autobiographical Writings*, ed. Peter Demetz (New York: Schocken, 1986), 153; Max Horkheimer and Theodor Adorno, "The Culture Industry: Enlightenment as Mass Deception," in *Dialectic of Enlightenment*, trans. John Cumming (New York: Continuum, 1976), 120–67; Betty Friedan, *The Feminine Mystique* (New York: Norton, 1963), 15–32, 206–32; Fredric Jameson, "The Cultural Logic of Late Capitalism," in *Postmodernism: Or, the Cultural Logic of Late Capitalism* (Durham, N.C.: Duke University Press, 1991), 39–44; Guy Debord, *The Society of the Spectacle*, trans. Donald Nicholson-Smith (New York: Zone, 1994); Ariel Dorfman and Armand Mattelart, *How to Read Donald Duck: Imperialist Ideology in the Disney Comic*, trans. David Kunzle (New York: International General, 1975). The critical theory of the German New

Left included several powerful elaborations of the Frankfurt themes which, however, were not that well known in English. See Hans Magnus Enzensberger, *The Consciousness Industry: On Literature, Politics, and the Media* (New York: Seabury, 1974); Wolfgang Fritz Haug, *Critique of Commodity Aesthetics: Appearance, Sexuality, and Advertising in Capitalist Society*, trans. Robert Bock (Minneapolis: University of Minnesota Press, 1986); and Oskar Negt and Alexander Kluge, *Public Sphere and Experience: Toward an Analysis of the Bourgeois and Proletarian Public Sphere*, trans. Peter Labanyi, Jamie Owen Daniel, and Assenka Oksiloff (Minneapolis: University of Minnesota Press, 1993).

13 Fredric Jameson, "Reification and Utopia in Mass Culture," in his *Signatures of the Visible* (New York: Routledge, 1992), 9–34.

14 Etienne Balibar argues that ideology and fetishism are not two halves of the same theory but two different theories: "The theory of ideology is fundamentally a *theory of the State* (by which we mean the mode of domination inherent in the State), whereas that of fetishism is fundamentally a *theory of the market* (the mode of subjection or constitution of the 'world' of subjects and objects inherent in the organization of society as market and its domination by market forces)." The first, he suggests, develops out of Marx's critique of Hegel on the state; the second out of Marx's critique of political economy. Etienne Balibar, *The Philosophy of Marx*, trans. Chris Turner (London: Verso, 1995), 77–78.

15 Michel Foucault, *Discipline and Punish: The Birth of the Prison*, trans. Alan Sheridan (New York: Pantheon, 1977), 217.

16 Walter Benjamin, *Charles Baudelaire: A Lyric Poet in the Era of High Capitalism*, trans. Harry Zohn (London: New Left Books, 1973), 166.

17 Gramsci quoted in Stuart Hall, "Gramsci's Relevance for the Study of Race and Ethnicity," in *Stuart Hall: Critical Dialogues in Cultural Studies*, ed. David Morley and Kuan-Hsing Chen (New York: Routledge, 1996), 429; Karl Marx, *The Eighteenth Brumaire of Louis Bonaparte* (New York: International Publishers, 1963), 77; Stuart Hall, *The Hard Road to Renewal: Thatcherism and the Crisis of the Left* (London: Verso, 1988), 71. Subsequent references are cited parenthetically in the text.

18 Immanuel Wallerstein, *Geopolitics and Geoculture: Essays on the Changing World-System* (Cambridge: Cambridge University Press, 1991), 158; Nancy Fraser, *Justice Interruptus: Critical Reflections on the "Postsocialist" Condition* (New York: Routledge, 1997).

19 Stanley Aronowitz, *False Promises: The Shaping of American Working Class Consciousness* (New York: McGraw-Hill, 1973).

20 Harry Braverman, *Labor and Monopoly Capital: The Degradation of Work in the Twentieth Century* (New York: Monthly Review, 1974). Subsequent references are cited parenthetically in the text.

21 Jean Baudrillard, *The Mirror of Production* (St. Louis: Telos, 1975).

22 Karl Marx, *Capital: A Critique of Political Economy*, vol. 1, trans. Ben Fowkes (Harmondsworth, U.K.: Penguin, 1976), 284.

23 Karl Marx and Frederick Engels, *The German Ideology* (New York: International Publishers, 1970), 53.

24 Eric Lott, "The Aesthetic Ante: Pleasure, Pop Culture, and the Middle Passage," *Callaloo* 17, no. 2 (1994): 545–55; Lott, *Love and Theft: Blackface Minstrelsy and the American Working Class* (New York: Oxford University Press, 1993), 10–11.

25 Tillie Olsen, *Silences* (New York: Delta, 1978), ix.

26 Karl Marx, *Wage-Labour and Capital* (New York: International Publishers, 1976), 33; David Harvey, *The Limits to Capital* (Chicago: University of Chicago Press, 1982), 163.

"Sent for You Yesterday, Here You Come Today"

AMERICAN STUDIES SCHOLARSHIP AND

THE NEW SOCIAL MOVEMENTS

George Lipsitz

The broad rubric of American studies now conceals more from us than it reveals. This is not because researchers in American studies are incompetent or uninformed. On the contrary, the field constitutes a lively, productive, and important site for contemporary cultural criticism and academic inquiry. It is just that in our efforts to remain inclusive, interdisciplinary, and open-minded, we have not done enough to define the conditions that bring us together, the historical trajectories that we inherit, and the forces that connect our work as researchers and teachers to broader social formations. Particularly at this moment in history when the globalization of economic activity, the emergence of new technologies, and the seeming disintegration of oppositional social movements radically disrupts our understanding of the connections linking culture to place while calling into question unproblematized assumptions about the nation-state as the logical and inevitable unit of study, it is important for us to move toward greater consensus about the purpose and potential of American studies scholarship.[1]

We live in a time when a handful of transnational corporations control one third of the productive private sector assets in the world. More than 800 million workers—nearly 30 percent of the global labor force—work for subsistence wages or less. In Africa, Asia, and Latin America close to 500,000 children die every year from malnutrition or from completely preventable diseases. The richest fifth of the world's population receives 150 times as much income as the poorest fifth, and in Southern hemisphere countries alone during the 1980s, the gap between the rich and the poor doubled.[2] United Nations figures disclosed the existence of two million refugees in 1970; by 1992 that number had grown to 44 million people, and the organization's high commissioner for refugees estimated an increase of 10,000 refugees per day in that year alone.[3]

The United States now houses the fifth largest Spanish-speaking population in the world, and if current population trends in Colombia and Argentina continue, the United States will have the third largest group of Spanish-speakers within ten years.[4] New York City is now the largest Caribbean city in the world, housing a Caribbean population larger than the combined populations of Kingston (Jamaica), San Juan (Puerto Rico), and Port-of-Spain (Trinidad). More people from the Caribbean island of Nevis live in New York City than live in Nevis. Nearly 40 percent of the population of Puerto Ricans now dwells on the North American mainland.[5] Anywhere from 300,000 to 500,000 Salvadorans reside in Los Angeles, while more than 300,000 Dominicans live in New York City.[6]

Children in the Los Angeles Unified School District come from families that speak at least 120 different languages and dialects. The population of Los Angeles makes it the second largest Mexican city, the second largest Guatemalan, and the third largest Canadian city in the world. Los Angeles is home to the largest concentration of Koreans outside of Korea, of Iranians outside of Iran, and of Garifuna Indians outside of Belize. More Samoans reside in Los Angeles than in American Samoa.[7]

The movement of products and people across the globe affects everything in North American society from the identity of babies available for adoption to the price of drugs on the streets, from the identities of clerks in convenience stores to the ownership of downtown real estate. The "Pocahontas" pajamas worn by some of our most affluent children are made under sweatshop conditions by low-wage women workers in Haiti. The "Air Jordan" athletic shoes that serve as symbols of inner-city African American culture all around the globe are assembled by low-paid women workers in Indonesia. These new realities express only a small measure of the larger discontinuities and ruptures of our time, but they underscore one of the most important aspects of the current moment for American studies, that is, a radical disturbance in the links between culture and place.

Efforts to address the unique or singular qualities of national culture in the United States no longer seem as relevant as they once did when citizens of the United States could more easily ignore their links with the rest of the world. Scholarship in American studies under contemporary conditions evokes the tension in the words that Little Jimmy Rushing used to sing in the 1930s as the vocalist for Count Basie's Band—"sent for you yesterday, here you come today." Just as we have become more and more expert about defining national culture, the question of national culture itself must now undergo revision and critique.

Yet discontinuity between the past and present can also serve as a generative source of insight and understanding. In times of crisis we often see that
we need a new understanding of the past as well as of the present, that
developments that might strike us as fundamentally new and unexpected also
have a long history of their own. In addition, the current crises instigated by
globalization make matters of locality and place even more important in the
present because we feel the effects of globalization most fully when they call
our attention to the distinctly national and local inflections of processes that
take place everywhere. Rather than being obsolete, American studies scholarship might help us understand the ways in which better knowledge about
suppressed elements of the past might make us better prepared for the present
and the future that we face from the effects of globalization.

In his provocative and profoundly important book, *The Cultural Front*,
Michael Denning reminds us of the origins of the American studies project in
responses by intellectuals to the social upheavals of the 1930s and 1940s.
Denning establishes a lineage of enormous importance for contemporary
academic practitioners of American studies by uncovering a hidden history
of the field replete with surprising linkages between professional academics
and social movement institutions. He demonstrates the ways in which cultural production, consumption, and criticism enabled academics, artists, and
activists to work together in a variety of institutional sites, ranging from
college classrooms to evening adult education courses, from literary magazines to trade union leafleting, from Hollywood film studios to amateur
camera clubs, from mass circulation magazines to discussion groups at neighborhood bookstores. His research recovers important international, interethnic, and antiracist elements of the original American studies project in a
way that offers important lessons for the present and the future.

Most importantly, Denning compels us to think of American studies not
just in terms of academic inquiry and arguments, but also in terms of social
movements, spaces, and institutions. In a time when nascent social movements are articulating some of the most important cultural, economic, and
political critiques of globalization, scholarship connecting academic research
to the work of social movements holds great promise for the generation of
new knowledge, as well as for the development of resistance against the
increasingly indecent global social order.

Denning reminds us that at the very time that Charles Beard served as
professor of history at Columbia University and secured a professional and
popular following through arguments that identified the antagonism between democracy and capitalism as the core contradiction within the U.S.

national narrative, he also taught evening adult education classes sponsored by the International Ladies' Garment Workers Union at the Workers University in New York. F. O. Matthiessen not only defined the American Renaissance of the nineteenth century through his work as a professor of literature at Harvard University, but he also served as a founder, trustee, and teacher at the trade union–sponsored Samuel Adams School for evening adult education in Boston. Kenneth MacGowan established his scholarly reputation during the 1930s at UCLA as one of the first academic analysts of cinema, but in the evenings he taught at the ILGWU's Los Angeles and Hollywood adult education schools along with screenwriter John Howard Lawson, composer Earl Robinson, and People's Songs activist Harry Hay.[8] Associating themselves with trade union night schools enabled these scholars and artists to secure a broader audience for their work, but it also offered them opportunities to learn from workers whose cultural tastes, political allegiances, and social activities played a crucial role in the "discovery" and "invention" of something called "American Culture" during the New Deal and World War II eras.[9]

In some cases intellectual work and artistic production emerged directly out of activism. Novelist H. T. Tsiang and other Chinatown writers in New York participated enthusiastically in mobilizing support for the Chinese Hand Laundry Alliance (Denning, *Cultural Front*, 237). In 1941, filmmaker Orson Welles joined with F. O. Mathiessen and music producer John Hammond as co-chairs of a citizens' committee protesting the deportation of Harry Bridges, the Australian-born leader of the International Longshore Workers' Union. Filipino Labor Union organizers Chris Mensalvas and Carlos Bulosan worked together as labor activists and as co-publishers of a literary magazine, *The New Tide*, in the 1930s. Twenty years later, as president of a local cannery workers' union in Seattle, Mensalvas hired Bulosan to edit the union yearbook (Denning, *Cultural Front*, 273, 281). After receiving a doctorate in economics from Columbia University, Ernesto Galarza worked with Luisa Moreno throughout the Southwest as an organizer for the Pan American Union in the mid-1930s, and in 1937 became editor of a picture magazine dedicated to telling the story of CIO organizing to a mass audience (Denning, *Cultural Front*, 277). The Socialist Party's Rebel Arts Group in New York City included dancers, musicians, writers, and artists. It sponsored a drama club, chess club, camera club, and a puppet group, while also broadcasting dramas on radio station WEVD (a station that selected the initials of Eugene Victor Debs as its call letters). In Carmel, California, the John Reed

Club, supported by the Communist Party, brought together photographer Edward Weston, sculptor Jo Davidson, playwright Orrick Johns, writers Ella Winter, Lincoln Steffens, and (for a time) Langston Hughes to sponsor lectures by radical intellectuals and labor leaders, while at the same time mobilizing support for trade union struggles by farm workers, cannery employees, and longshoremen (Denning, *Cultural Front*, 208).

The story of Depression-era activism, Popular Front art, and the political culture of the 1930s and 1940s has been told many times, but in his carefully researched and wide-ranging account, Denning develops original interpretations of four key relationships that contain extraordinary import for our understanding of the problems and possibilities within contemporary American studies scholarship.[10] Although he does not always develop fully the theoretical implications of the issues he raises, Denning's evidence and analysis leads logically to a reconsideration and re-theorization of the relationships between politics and culture, between ethnic identity and class consciousness, between the myth of American exceptionalism and the always international identities of the U.S. nation-state and its inhabitants, and between cultural practice and cultural theory.

Denning moves the discussion of links between politics and culture in the 1930s and 1940s beyond sectarian disputes about the Communist Party and its enemies into a broader and more productive exploration of the ways in which social crises create new cultures and foment new forms of cultural expression. He locates sectarian rivalries and strategic contestation among Stalinists, Trotskyists, socialists, and liberals within a broader context that he describes as "the age of the CIO," a designation designed to demonstrate the power of social movements, to show how social movements shake up social life and create the conditions that make new forms of cultural production and cultural criticism both necessary and inevitable. Working from concepts developed by Raymond Williams and Antonio Gramsci, Denning depicts the America and the American studies created in the 1930s and 1940s as a product of new ways of "feeling and seeing reality" brought into being by the egalitarian and inclusionary social movements that emerged in the age of the CIO. He calls attention to the argument advanced by Gramsci that "[a] new social group that enters history with a hegemonic attitude, with a self-confidence which it initially did not have, cannot but stir up from deep within it personalities who would not previously have found sufficient strength to express themselves fully in a particular direction."[11] Thus, for Denning, the Popular Front during the New Deal and World War II is not so much the creation of the Communist Party and its front organizations, but rather the visible mani-festation of a new popular imagination provoked by the experiences of every-day life, labor, politics, and culture in a time of turmoil and transformation.

Denning's second major contribution to our understanding of the origins of Depression-era Americanism and the rise of American studies comes from his recuperation of ethnicity as a powerful independent generator of radical politics during the 1930s and 1940s, rather than as simply one site where class consciousness emerged. American studies scholars in recent years have em-phasized the extraordinary energy unleashed by the affirmation of ethnicity in that era through events as diverse as the interethnic electoral coalitions that secured Fiorello LaGuardia's election as mayor of New York and Anton Cermak's election as mayor of Chicago, the culture of unity celebrating ethnic difference within CIO organizing drives, the radical journalism of Louis Adamic that campaigned to make the Statue of Liberty a sacred symbol of national inclusion, and ethnic festivals that portrayed immigrants and their children as "redemptive outsiders" rather than unwanted aliens.[12] Denning delineates the broad base developed for an inclusionary and pluralistic vision of the American nation through the extraordinary self-activity of ethnic American organizations and individuals, including the Japanese Proletarian Artists' League and the Japanese Workers' Camera Club in Los Angeles; magazines, including Louis Adamic's *Common Ground*, Ralph Ellison's *Negro Quarterly*, Dorothy West's *Challenge*, and the League of American Writers' *The Clipper*; and the efforts of a broad range of artists and writers includ-ing Mine Okubo, Jacob Lawrence, Ollie Harrington, Mario Suarez, Mari Tomasi, Toshiro Mori, Hisaye Yamamoto, Gwendolyn Brooks, Paule Mar-shall, Milton Murayama, Zora Neale Hurston, Roshio Mori, Carlos Bulo-san, Arna Bontemps, and Younghill Kang among others (*Cultural Front*, 65, 217, 222, 225, 235, 447).

One of Denning's distinct contributions to our knowledge about these expressions of ethnicity comes from his ability to analyze them as part of a common class experience rather than as solely ethnic developments. Den-ning shows that what united these diverse expressions of ethnic identity and affiliation was a shared historical experience with "ethnic formation" pro-duced by "the restructuring of the American peoples" by labor migrations ranging from the movement of Asian immigrants across the Pacific to the journeys across the Atlantic by people from southern and eastern Europe, from the exodus enacted by the Mexican Revolution and the development of railroads in the U.S. Southwest to the great migration of African Americans from the sharecropping South to the industrialized North and West (*Cultural Front*, 239). While not reducible to class, the identities formed through these processes of ethnic formation contained powerful working-class inflections. As Denning explains, by the 1930s "ethnicity and race had become the modality through which working-class peoples experienced their lives and mapped their communities. . . . The invention of ethnicity was a central form of class consciousness in the United States" (*Cultural Front*, 239). Consequently, no atomized class consciousness completely independent of ethnic identity could exist in the United States, but at the same time many seemingly discrete ethnic identities contained a sedimented class content.

Yet affirmation of ethnic identity during the 1930s and 1940s—as part of strategies for addressing and redressing the humiliating subordinations of working-class life and inverting the ideological formulations that rendered immigrants and their children as unworthy and unwelcome participants in American politics—eventually evolved into an uncritical cultural pluralism after World War II. European Americans secured a significant measure of ethnic inclusion for themselves at the price of becoming complicit in the racialized exclusion of communities of color through the exclusionary policies of trade unions, New Deal social welfare agencies, immigration officials, and private realtors, lenders, and employers.[13] The militaristic and expansionist commitments of the U.S. government during the Cold War transformed the egalitarian nationalism of the Popular Front into jingoistic expansionism, setting the stage for anticommunist purges of progressives from public and private institutions as well as for an imperialist foreign policy that exported the class antagonisms of U.S. society to countries all around the globe.[14] Consequently, it has been tempting for scholars to view the politics and the culture of the Popular Front as innately assimilationist, xenophobic, and nationalistic.[15] American studies itself has been implicated in this project because of its inattention to the role of imperialism in U.S. history and because its core questions about "what is an American" have assumed the existence of an unproblematized, undifferentiated, and distinctly national "American" identity that differs from the identities open to individuals from other national contexts.

Denning offers some cautionary obstacles to these readings through his third major contribution in *The Cultural Front*, his recuperation of the expressly internationalist content of the cultural politics of the Popular Front. He shows how the literary journal *Front* printed articles in three languages and featured contributions by Peruvian Marxist theoretician José Carlos Mariátegui as well as Japanese proletarian poet Kei Mariyama. A trip to Haiti in 1931 energized Langston Hughes and initiated his commitment to blending art and activism in works that included his play *Emperor in Haiti* and his collaboration with composer William Grant Still on the opera *Troubled Island*. African American units of the Federal Theatre Project produced works set in Haiti, including *Black Empire* performed in Los Angeles, and *Haiti* in New York. Jacob Lawrence painted a series of historical paintings about Toussaint L'Ouverture, while Arna Bontemps set his novel *Drums at Dusk* in Haiti. Young Filipinos in Hollywood managed to publish one issue of *The New Tide*, a literary magazine that featured a prose poem about leaving the Philippines by Chris Mensalvas and a story by Filipino American writer José Garcia Villa, along with a story protesting against lynching and a poem by William Carlos Williams. Emigré Japanese writer and feminist Ayako Ishigaki published the autobiography *Restless Wave* under the pen name Haru Matsui with the left-wing Modern Age Books (Denning, *Cultural Front*, 145, 217, 222, 396). Joseph Freeman argued that the interest in national identity among Popular Front writers did not originate in an uncritical and unproblematic nationalism and cultural pluralism, but from the converse. "If you lose an arm, you are likely to think a great deal about arms," Freeman opined, "and if you are born into an oppressed nationality you are likely to think a great deal about oppression and nationalism." Freeman went on to contend that "the native-born American takes his Americanism for granted; the 'alien' absorbing America into his heart, being absorbed into its culture, thinks about the meaning of America day and night" (qtd. in Denning, *Cultural Front*, 130).

Denning demonstrates that this internationalist presence not only added a global dimension to the better-known regionalist and nationalist cultural expressions of the Popular Front, but that it also served as an independent site for theorizing about the antagonisms and affinities emerging from questions of citizenship, nationality, culture, and class. For example, he shows how Carey McWilliams's location in Los Angeles encouraged him to view race relations from a West Coast perspective that contained profound consequences for his understanding of the United States as an always international entity. Confronted with the internment of Japanese Americans and the "zoot suit riots" with their violence against Mexican Americans, McWilliams in 1943 saw the United States as increasingly oriented toward Central America, South America, and the Pacific. This understanding provoked him to rethink U.S. history and to propose a new periodization, one that traced the origins of the modern era to 1876 and its aftermath—the time when the United

States abandoned African Americans through the end of Reconstruction, excluded Asians through the Chinese Exclusion Act of 1882, began to place Native Americans on reservations, and set the stage for global expansion through successive moves to secure control over Hawai'i, Cuba, the Philippines, and Puerto Rico (*Cultural Front*, 450). Similarly, African American sociologist Oliver C. Cox traced the unequal life chances confronting African Americans to the participation by the United States in a world capitalist system "in which racialization is a fundamental economic and political process" (Denning, *Cultural Front*, 453). Even the discovery of U.S. ethnicities often had an international dimension. Denning notes that Joseph Freeman and Richard Wright first became interested in Marxism because they felt that the writing of Lenin and Stalin on oppressed nationalities helped them understand their ethnic experiences as a Jewish American and as an African American (*Cultural Front*, 131).

Denning's fourth major contribution comes from his extraordinary success in using evidence about cultural expressions to advance our understanding of culture as a social force. Rather than representing either transparent truths about social relations or functioning as transmission belts to disseminate the unmediated ideology of the owners of the commercial culture industry, Popular Front culture constituted a complex site where a variety of social identities could be arbitrated and negotiated. Denning explains, for example, how critics Kenneth Burke and C. L. R. James interpreted the prevalence of brutality, violence, and sadism in 1930s fiction and film as a register of a historically specific kind of crisis brought on by the Depression— in Burke's words, a time when "the perception of discordance is perceived without smile or laughter."[16] Drawing on Burke's formulation, Denning calls our attention to the importance of a genre of films and fictional tales that he characterizes as "ghetto pastorals" and as examples of "the proletarian grotesque." He identifies these allegorical stories of urban terror—often dismissed by previous critics as middle-class misrepresentations of working-class life—as important expressions of a social reality aimed less at direct descriptions of social class than at attempts to represent a "cityscape composed in a pidgin of American slang and ghetto dialect, with traces of old country tongues" (*Cultural Front*, 231). Aiming neither for socialist realism nor for bourgeois romanticism, the ghetto pastorals in Denning's view attempted to rebuild and transcend modernism through a contradictory blend of the magic and the real, of the allegorical and the empirical. They relied on "the proletarian grotesque" to interrupt the ideological closures enacted by traditional narrative form and ideologies about the autonomy of art, as well as to reflect and shape the resentments of their audiences.

Denning also shows how difficult it can be for intellectuals to understand their own social location in an era of intense class conflict. The age of the CIO not only involved mass mobilizations by workers on issues important to their class, but it provoked as well a broader identity crisis about the relationships between people from different classes and strata. Denning makes productive use of ruminations by John Dos Passos in a 1930 article about the nature of intellectual work, where the author described the similarities between his social role as a writer and the work performed by engineers, scientists, independent manual craftsmen, artists, actors, and " 'technicians of one sort or another.' " Dos Passos observed that this group of people tended to belong to their jobs regardless of their individual ideas, that their lives were defined by a core contradiction emanating from " 'the fact that along with the technical education that makes them valuable to the community they have taken in a subconscious political education that makes them servants of the owners.' " Denning builds on this argument made by Dos Passos in his nonfiction writing to analyze the author's emphasis in the U.S.A. trilogy on "the contradictory lives of those who traded in the speech of the people" (Cultural Front, 179, 180). More than a site for choosing sides in an already declared class war, responsible intellectual work emerges in this analysis as an effort to understand the problems and the potential of their contradictory allegiances characterizing the lives of intellectuals.

In our time, when the social role of intellectuals remains undertheorized and when images of the grotesque play a central role in cultural expressions of all kinds, Denning's discussions of the cultural front contain compelling insights about the present as well as about the past. It makes a difference for our work in the present when we acknowledge that the origins of American studies lie both inside and outside the academy, that the social movements of the 1930s were both an inspirational stimulus and an empirical site for the construction of the field. It makes a difference for our work in the present when we understand that class and ethnicity have always been linked in the United States, that each identity is experienced through the other—as well as through gender, sexuality, religion and many other social identities—and that there can be no valid mutually exclusive opposition between ethnic studies and American studies. It makes a difference for our work in the present when we enable ourselves to see that globalization is not new, that a long history of labor migration, imperial expansion, and international solidarity have shaped the American nation in ways that cannot be reversed by political, cultural, or intellectual projects remaining purely national in scope. It makes a difference for our work in the present when we encounter the evidence Denning offers about the power of the ghetto pastoral and the proletarian grotesque in the 1930s and how difficult, yet how necessary it was for intellectuals to theorize their relationship to social movements and oppressed populations in that era. For these reasons and many more, it is impossible to overestimate the importance of Michael Denning's achievements in *The Cultural Front*; it is a book certain to transform American studies in significant and lasting ways.

Yet the same qualities that make Denning's fine work so compelling require us to ask how the rich and full past that he describes has become the impoverished present for those of us working within American studies today. What has happened to divide specialized academic inquiry from social movement activism? Why do desires for ethnic inclusion and empowerment now seem so divorced from concerns about social class? How did the inclusionary nationalism and international solidarity of the Depression and World War II eras become transformed into the imperial expansionism of the Cold War? Which elements of Popular Front culture continue to inform and inspire egalitarian social movements and which ones now serve other purposes? What price did the Popular Front culture pay for its association with the Communist Party, not just through the impact of anticommunism in the postwar period, but also through the internal deficiencies of the vanguard party model as a stimulus for effective social change? Most importantly, why were the emancipatory visions of the Popular Front so concentrated on redemptive views of America as an island of virtue in a degraded and corrupt world?

Not all of these questions can be answered here, but we can make a good start by asking about the causes and consequences of the emphasis on "American" identity by the Popular Front. Certainly the long history of anti-immigrant nativism in America, the stigmatization of outsiders, and the countersubversive hysterias deployed against communities of color had something to do with the desire among aggrieved groups to escape the terms by which they had been stigmatized and, instead, to claim insider status for themselves; all of these factors account for some of the emphasis on national identity within the Popular Front. Anton Cermak's opponent in the Chicago mayoralty race in 1932 bragged that he could trace his own ancestry back to the landing of the Mayflower in Massachusetts in 1620, deriding Cermak as "Pushcart Tony, the son of immigrants." Cermak scored a great public relations victory by replying that he regretted that his ancestors had not come over on the Mayflower, but assured his listeners that "they got here as fast as they could."[17] With this quip, Cermak inverted the terms of the debate by presenting immigrants as more deserving than the native-born because they came to America by choice rather than by the accident of birth. In addition, as Denning points out, by associating themselves with the "Lincoln Republic"—the republican-era America before the dawn of corporate capitalism—Popular Front patriots could deploy the contrast between a producer democracy and a parasitical capitalism for their own purposes and could present their mostly white, Anglo-Saxon, and Protestant enemies as interlopers and radicals betraying the "true American" mission (*Cultural Front*, 163–99).

Yet for all its utility, it was precisely the invocation of an ideal America that set the stage for the defeat of the Popular Front and for the inversion of its icons and symbols in the Cold War era. Coupled with the crippling vanguardism of the Communist Party which, as often as not, repressed rather than released the egalitarian energies erupting from the grass roots in the age of the CIO, the effort to "let America be America again" (in the words of Langston Hughes) contained contradictions that allowed for the transformation of the Popular Front into the Cold War.

Denning's identification of the origins of America and American studies within the Popular Front of the 1930s needs to be placed in a broader context of American exceptionalism. In her original and generative introduction to her co-edited book, *Cultures of United States Imperialism*, Amy Kaplan constructs another genealogy of American studies, one that identifies the construction of an exceptionalist America as part of a project intended to evade responsibility for the nation's imperial practices and ambitions. Kaplan points to Perry Miller's 1956 preface to his pathbreaking study of Puritan intellectual history, *Errand into the Wilderness*, where Miller traces the origins of his thinking about the Puritans to his experiences in the 1920s as a college dropout, unloading drums of oil on the banks of the Congo River in Africa. He testifies to an "epiphany" about the coherence and uniqueness of American identity because of his encounter with what he perceived as the "blankness" of Africa and the difference between its "jungle" landscape and the early American frontier. Kaplan notes that the binary opposition between a blank jungle and a noble frontier provides the conditions of possibility for the core narrative of American exceptionalism—the belief in America as an island of virtue in a corrupt world and the contrast between the inevitable decline of

European empires and the "illimitable capacity for self-renewal and expansion" of the United States.[18]

Kaplan's categories help us discern the hidden contradictions within some of the Popular Front politics celebrated by Denning. She observes that the American exceptionalism articulated by Perry Miller (and I would argue embraced by the Popular Front) depends on the occlusion of America's role in the world. It proceeds on the assumption of American nationality as what Kaplan describes as "a monolithic and self-contained whole" (15). Consequently, the progressive celebration of the nation's diverse national origins also works conservatively to endorse the building of an American nationality as an atomized identity detached from its own history of conquest, slavery, and genocide, as well as from its role in denying the national aspirations of people in the Caribbean, Latin America, Africa, and Asia. Thus even the progressive multiculturalism and polyvocality of the Popular Front contains the seeds for an imperial consensus capable of reconciling diverse groups into a common national project through shared participation in warfare. This reconciliation of diverse national groups into a unified totality forms the subtext of an astounding range of war novels and motion pictures from World War II through the Gulf War, and it helps explain how the Popular Front of the New Deal eventually became incorporated into World War II and then the Cold War.

Kaplan's emphasis on American exceptionalism helps us understand the limits of the Popular Front version of American studies, especially in respect to its organic links with an uninterrogated emphasis on the nation-state as the logical object of intellectual and political activity, its ultimately conservative racial and gender politics, and its inadequacy as a basis for re-theorizing American studies in an age of globalization. It was the reliance on the Lincoln Republic as the lost ideal erased by contemporary capitalism that prevented the Popular Front from addressing adequately the legacies of slavery, conquest, and overseas imperialism in the American past and present. It was the reliance on a masculinized vision of class struggle that occluded the feminist possibilities implicit in the actions of radical women activists and artists in the 1930s. Perhaps most importantly, it was the emphasis on ethnic unity and the incorporation of racialized minorities into an ethnic paradigm that made the Popular Front at one and the same time a focal point for class unity and an instrument for increasing the privileges and power of whiteness and masculinity, an indisputably important moment in the history of American egalitarianism and an impediment to genuinely global and postnational politics.

Attempts to separate progressive articulations of America and American studies from their history as building blocks for hierarchical, exploitative, and imperial projects need to reckon with the ideological origins of American exceptionalism and their conflation of culture and place. David W. Noble provides the best analysis of American exceptionalism to date in his 1986 book, *The End of American History*.[19] In this book, Noble locates the origins of American exceptionalism in the metaphor of two worlds, in the identification of an innocent and virtuous America (the new world) alone and embattled against the forces of European corruption.

Ironically enough, this metaphor of two worlds was a European rather than an American invention. Drawing on the scholarship of Sacvan Bercovitch and J. G. A. Pocock, Noble explains that classical republican theorists in England viewed their own country as corrupt because they felt that the rise of capitalism had elevated the private, particularistic, and selfish interests of a few over the public universal interest needed to preserve the social contract. They discerned their loss of freedom in many ways, but especially through the introduction of a particular kind of time. They perceived that, previous to the capitalist era, time had belonged to God—that the days and nights, seasons, and years marked a temporal flow ordained by the deity. But the emergence of capitalism gave time a different meaning. Capitalists could divide the day into hours, minutes, and seconds of labor that could be bought and sold. Even worse in the republican view, interest-bearing loans and investments made time itself a commodity; capitalist time forced them to mortgage the future, to trade time they did not yet have in return for resources they needed. To classical republicans, feudalism had been ruled by space, by the land one tilled or the community in which one lived, but capitalism was ruled by time.

Dreams of escape to America not only aimed at a change of spaces, but also at an escape from time. Classical republicans (and generations of republican theorists who followed them) believed that European space had been corrupted by time, but that a producer-oriented yeoman democracy was still possible in America. They saw the American space as sacred because it might be a place where one could escape the corruptions of time by living within the timeless physical space of American nature. Even though the trading companies that financed British settlement in the colonies clearly sought profitable returns on their investments, the ideologies of commercial property and capitalist time coexisted uneasily in North America with a republican ideology that became more powerful in the colonies than it had ever been in England.

When skilled artisans and landowning farmers resisted the eclipse of the Lincoln Republic by the rise of industrial capitalism after the Civil War, they often justified their anticapitalism through republican ideology.[20] Owning land (and the tools with which to work it) seemed to ensure economic and political independence through control over space, while working for wages or incurring debts brought dependency and obligation in the arenas of time. Frederick Jackson Turner's articulation of the Frontier Thesis in the 1890s predicted a threat to American freedom from the closing of western lands (which limited access to space); as Noble explains, Turner believed that the escape from European time to American space had been temporary and that the closing of the frontier proved that, in the long run, time had been more powerful than space.

Noble's work provides an important context for the anticapitalism of Denning's Popular Front. Activists of the 1930s could draw on several centuries of anticapitalist and antimonopoly republicanism that argued that American space had to remain free of European time. Charles Beard's conception of American history as a struggle between democracy and capitalism rested on a belief that democracy emerged out of agrarian life in America and that capitalism's corruption came from Europe. Beard objected to the dynamism of capitalism, arguing that it was the enemy of tradition, that it brought immigrants from Europe to work in America as a way of replacing free Americans with subservient Europeans accustomed to domination. Beard changed his mind many times—about industrialization, about the New Deal, about overseas expansion and imperialism—but his many changes all stemmed from a consistent search for a way to escape the tyranny of capitalist time. Despite his participation in ILGWU evening education courses, Beard cannot be confused with the entire Popular Front, but his premises help explain the nationalism within the Popular Front that made "America" such a powerful symbol. By associating themselves with the American landscape, literally and figuratively, Popular Front artists and intellectuals activated powerful symbols of freedom. Yet by maintaining a Manichaean split between an innocent American space and a corrupt European time, they simply inverted, rather than superseded, the nationalist sense of American exceptionalism held by their capitalist opponents as well as their anticapitalist allies.

Noble's study revolves around the search by historians for a national narrative that might fulfill republican hopes for a free space outside of the corruptions of time. But historians by definition deal with change over time, with competition over scarce resources, with political conflicts that endlessly indicate the futility of a universal or national narrative capable of expressing the interests of all. The five historians whom Noble examines—Frederick Jackson Turner, Charles Beard, Reinhold Niebuhr, Richard Hofstadter, and William Appleman Williams—all fail to one degree or another, but the nature of their failures has much to teach us about the core questions in Denning's book.

Turner and Beard distrusted capitalism deeply, but they could not envision any actual social group capable of acting unselfishly and universally. Turner accepted that Native Americans should be conquered in the name of freedom, but admitted that European settlement from the east coast and Europe soon overwhelmed free spaces with the considerations of capitalist time. It should not be surprising that Turner's Frontier Thesis struck many capitalists as decidedly in their interests because it could justify overseas expansion as necessary to American freedom, as the moral equivalent of the settling of the West, which Turner considered the crucible of American freedom.

The historical writings by Turner and Beard attempted to call an oppositional constituency into being through prophecy, through warnings about the impending loss of freedom that Americans faced, and through appeals to the creation of a powerful national identity capable of overcoming selfish divisions. Turner died during the Progressive era, but Beard became an important figure in the era of the CIO, although not always in alignment with its dominant political forces. Hofstadter and Niebuhr participated in Popular Front politics and pursued anticapitalist stances in the 1930s. But World War II convinced them that most of the ideals of republicanism were impractical, that an imperfect capitalism was more desirable than fascism or communism, and they became virulent anticommunist and enthusiastic advocates of Cold War militarism and expansion in the postwar era. Yet even here, they drew on residual elements of republicanism. The very same features of republicanism that lauded America's isolation from the rest of the world also contained impulses toward imperialism. Because they viewed America's differences from the rest of the world as both the source of the nation's virtue and its peril, some republican thinkers from the early nineteenth through the twentieth century concluded that the only way to preserve freedom would be to make the American system universal, to spread its political and economic systems to the rest of the world. Although they resigned themselves to the inevitability of inequality and injustice in the world, Hofstadter and Niebuhr drew on the Manichaean oppositions between innocence and evil at the heart of republicanism in their support for U.S. foreign policy during the Cold War era.

William Appleman Williams was the only one of the historians studied by Noble who experienced at least partial success in reconciling anticapitalist goals with historical methods, but he did so only through a radical critique of the core categories of space and time so central to both historians and republican theorists. Williams argued that the capitalists and the anticapitalists (or at least the Marxist left) shared the same false premises—that affiliations to particular places had to proceed at the level of the nation-state, that time had to be defined as the present as it would look to the future, that the spaces in which humans acted embraced the whole world. Williams believed that many different kinds of places could be created as social units that would be superior to the nation-state; that definitions of time should evade both stasis or simplistic narratives of progress, but favor conceptions of time that united the past, present, and future into an ongoing dialogue; and that the scale of global trade and global profits led inevitably to totalitarianism and war. Williams objected to the Cold War because he thought both the United States and the Soviet Union believed that their particular systems had to become universal—an error that he viewed as common to capitalism, Marxism, and republicanism.

Williams came to these conclusions at a time when many veterans of the age of the CIO had become corporate liberals, anticommunist conservatives, and cold warriors. But his insights did not belong to him alone; they emerged from antiwar, feminist, and Native American social movement groups of the 1970s and 1980s whose perspectives drew Williams's attention.

Noble argues that the search for a unified national narrative lies at the heart of American exceptionalism, that human freedom depends on an unpredictable creativity that cannot be found within historical narratives of nation. This does not mean that the nation-state is irrelevant to political or intellectual action, only that it cannot provide the ultimate terrain for imagination and contestation. The age of the CIO has much to teach us within American studies, but so does our own era. In social movement struggles in the United States and around the world, a new historical formation can teach us lessons about culture and politics that are both old and new at the same time. The important victories of the Popular Front came through the power of social movements and their institutions, through unexpected alliances and affiliations across and within social categories, through the ability of culture to reflect and shape past, present, and future social relations, and through an understanding of the always international aspects of U.S. identity. But the social movements of the age of the CIO also suffered from uninterrogated assumptions, from their inherited vocabulary about time, space, and the nation-state, from the limits of the political vanguard and the artistic avant-garde, from an underestimation of the importance of direct democracy and continuous cultural renewal, and from their embeddedness in a kind of time with too little room for unpredictable creativity.

Our time is a time of unpredictable creativity. New social movements and American studies scholars confront the same forces in different ways as we try to imagine and enact more decent social relations. Scholars who work through social movement institutions as well as academic institutions, who refuse to separate social identities into mutually exclusive realms, who understand the always international dimensions of U.S. culture and the connections linking low-wage labor and racialization to sexism and citizenship, and who embrace the ways in which new eras demand both new forms of cultural expression and new methods of cultural criticism, will be prepared for the demands of the future in a way that does honor to our past without getting trapped by its contradictions and shortcomings.

Notes

1 In this respect, I think the field stands at essentially the same place that it did a decade ago when Giles Gunn proposed "that a field, no less than a discipline, defines itself—as, say, a subject area alone does not—chiefly in relation to the questions it asks, the problems it poses, the arguments it encourages; while none of these matters can be contemplated in isolation from actual research, the research that is actually produced within any field ultimately matters, in the sense of being susceptible to definition and assessment, only in relation to such things—only by virtue of the way it refines the questions, clarifies the problems, and deepens the argument. The field of American Studies has not possessed this clear sense of itself at least since the 1950s and early 1960s." Giles Gunn, *Culture of Criticism and the Criticism of Culture* (New York: Oxford University Press, 1987), 148.
2 Dan Gallin, "Inside the New World Order," *New Politics* 5, no. 1 (1994): 106, 114; Robin Wright, "A Revolution at Work," *Los Angeles Times* 7 March 1995; Davison Budhoo, "IMF/World Bank Wreak Havoc on the Third World," in *50 Years Is Enough: The Case against the World Bank and the International Monetary Fund*, ed. Kevin Danaher (Boston: South End, 1994), 21–22.
3 Walden Bello, "Global Economic Counterrevolution: How Northern Economic Warfare Devastates the South," in *50 Years Is Enough*, ed. Danaher, 19.
4 John Beverley, *Against Literature* (Minneapolis: University of Minnesota Press, 1993), 121–22.
5 Winston James, "Migration, Racism, and Identity: The Caribbean Experi-

ence in Britain," *New Left Review* 193 (1992): 36–37; Jorge Duany, "Popular Music in Puerto Rico: Toward an Anthropology of Salsa," *Revista de música latino americana* 5, no. 2 (1985): 195; Peter Manuel, *Caribbean Currents: Caribbean Music from Rumba to Reggae* (Philadelphia: Temple University Press, 1995), 241.

6 Norma Chinchilla, Nora Hamilton, and James Loucky, "Central Americans in Los Angeles: An Immigrant Community in Transition," in *In The Barrios: Latinos and the Underclass Debate*, ed. Joan Moore and Raquel Pinderhughes (New York: Russell Sage Foundation, 1993), 53; Patricia R. Pessar, *A Visa for a Dream: Dominicans in the United States* (Boston: Allyn and Bacon, 1995), 22.

7 Manuel, *Caribbean Currents*, 241; Georges Sabagh and Mehdi Bozogmehr, "Population Changes: Immigration and Ethnic Transformation," in *Ethnic Los Angeles*, ed. Roger Waldinger and Bozorgmehr (New York: Russel Sage Foundation, 1996), 79–107.

8 Michael Denning, *The Cultural Front: The Laboring of American Culture in the Twentieth Century* (London: Verso, 1996), 69–70. Subsequent references are cited parenthetically in the text.

9 Denning prefigured this argument more than a decade ago in " 'The Special American Conditions': Marxism and American Studies," *American Quarterly* 38, no. 3 (1986): 356–80. Journalist Louis Adamic played a key role during the 1930s in mobilizing immigrants and their children to think of themselves as "redemptive outsiders" rather than as unwanted aliens, while the visual art of Thomas Hart Benton, the photographs of the Farm Security Administration photographers, the musical compositions of Virgil Thompson and Aaron Copeland, the folklore of B. A. Botkin, and the literary creations of Langston Hughes and John Dos Passos among others celebrated a new sense of national unity. David Peeler identifies the iconography of the "common man" as the common currency of New Deal culture, while Lizabeth Cohen emphasizes the importance of the "culture of unity" fashioned through the activist efforts of the CIO. Denning fuses these arguments together by delineating the ways in which what he calls "the age of the CIO" forced a fundamental reformulation within U.S. culture and politics. David P. Peeler, *Hope among Us Yet: Social Criticism and Social Solace in Depression America* (Athens: University of Georgia Press, 1987); Lizabeth Cohen, *Making a New Deal: Industrial Workers in Chicago, 1919–1939* (New York: Cambridge University Press, 1990). Subsequent references are cited parenthetically in the text.

10 Among the best previously written accounts are Paula Rabinowitz, *Labor and Desire: Women's Revolutionary Fiction in Depression America* (Chapel Hill: University of North Carolina Press, 1991); Alan Wald, *Writing from the Left: New Essays on Radical Culture and Politics* (London: Verso, 1994); Douglas Wixson, *Worker-Writer in America: Jack Conroy and the Tradition of Midwestern Literary Radicalism, 1898–1990* (Urbana: University of Illinois Press, 1994); Robin D. G. Kelley, *Hammer and Hoe: Alabama Communists during the Great Depression* (Chapel Hill: University of North Carolina Press, 1990); and Paul

Buhle, *Marxism in the United States: Remapping the History of the American Left* (London: Verso, 1991).

11 Antonio Gramsci, *Selections from Cultural Writings*, ed. David Forgacs and Geoffrey Nowell-Smith, trans. William Boelhower (Cambridge, Mass.: Harvard University Press, 1985), 98. Qtd. in Denning, *Cultural Front*, 135.

12 See Cohen, *Making a New Deal*; George J. Sánchez, *Becoming Mexican American: Ethnicity, Culture, and Identity in Chicano Los Angeles, 1900–1945* (New York: Oxford University Press, 1991); April R. Schultz, *Ethnicity on Parade: Inventing the Norwegian American through Celebration* (Amherst: University of Massachusetts Press, 1994); John Higham, *Send These to Me: Immigrants in Urban America* (Baltimore: Johns Hopkins University Press, 1984).

13 See Jill Quadagno, *The Color of Welfare: How Racism Undermined the War on Poverty* (New York: Oxford University Press, 1994); and George Lipsitz, *The Possessive Investment in Whiteness: How White People Profit from Identity Politics* (Philadelphia: Temple University Press, 1998).

14 George Lipsitz, *Rainbow at Midnight: Labor and Culture in the 1940s* (Urbana: University of Illinois Press, 1994).

15 See Gary Gerstle, *Working-Class Americanism: The Politics of Labor in a Textile City, 1941–1960* (Cambridge: Cambridge University Press, 1989), for an uncritical embrace of this caricature. See Amy Kaplan and Donald E. Pease, eds., *Cultures of United States Imperialism* (Durham, N.C.: Duke University Press, 1993); and Jonathan Arac, *Critical Genealogies: Historical Situations for Postmodern Literary Studies* (New York: Columbia University Press, 1987) for more sophisticated and useful critiques.

16 Kenneth Burke, *Permanence and Change: An Anatomy of Purpose* (New York: New Republic, 1935), 145–46; C. L. R. James, *American Civilization*, ed. Anna Grimshaw and Keith Hart (Cambridge, Mass.: Blackwell, 1993), 127, 148, 158. Qtd. in Denning, *Cultural Front*, 122.

17 Roger Daniels, *Coming to America: A History of Immigration and Ethnicity in American Life* (New York: HarperCollins, 1990), 282.

18 Amy Kaplan, "Left Alone with America: The Absence of Empire in the Study of American Culture," in *Cultures of United States Imperialism*, ed. Kaplan and Pease, 9. Subsequent references are cited parenthetically in the text.

19 David W. Noble, *The End of American History: Democracy, Capitalism, and the Metaphor of Two Worlds in Anglo-American Historical Writing, 1880–1980* (Minneapolis: University of Minnesota Press, 1985).

20 Eric Foner, *Free Soil, Free Labor, Free Men: The Ideology of the Republican Party before the Civil War* (New York: Oxford University Press, 1970); David Montgomery, *Beyond Equality: Labor and the Radical Republicans, 1862–1872* (New York: Knopf, 1967); Lawrence Goodwyn, *The Populist Moment: A Short History of the Agrarian Revolt in America* (New York: Oxford University Press, 1978).

Toward a Dialogics of

International American Culture Studies

TRANSNATIONALITY, BORDER DISCOURSES,

AND PUBLIC CULTURE(S)

Günter H. Lenz

American Studies and British Cultural Studies

In the late 1960s, American studies were in a deep crisis. They were declared intellectually bankrupt, politically reactionary, a handmaiden of American imperialism during the Cold War era, and a failure in their effort to offer an interdisciplinary understanding of American culture as a whole, past and present. The various redefinitions that were given during the 1970s and early 1980s usually replaced key terms or critical approaches that had characterized the field by their opposites without seriously reconceptualizing the formative principles and objectives of American studies in a rapidly changing cultural and theoretical context. American studies as an integrative study of American culture fell apart and were replaced by a sequence of politically engendered and committed interdisciplinary programs such as African American studies, women's studies, urban studies, popular culture studies, Native American studies, Chicano/a studies, Asian American studies, queer studies, and so on, that, however, often seemed to have to face methodological and institutional problems similar to those of the American studies programs they rejected. Anyway, American studies did not seem any longer to work anywhere near the frontiers of contemporary scholarship.

Thus it did not come as a surprise that when British cultural studies were widely discovered during the second half of the 1980s and the famous "Cultural Studies Now and in the Future" conference at the University of Illinois at Urbana-Champaign in 1990 provided the defining moment for a triumphal success of cultural studies in the United States during the 1990s, they were received as another wave of traveling theory from Europe. Cultural studies from the Birmingham Centre seemed to offer new answers to the political and theoretical questions that deconstruction, poststructuralism, and the various modes of literary theory had posed, provoked, and left unsolved in a period of postmodernity, post-Fordism, postcolonialism, and of the demise of state socialism. Again, the rage for European theory entailed a complete dismissal of earlier American projects and programs of cultural critique. In his book, *Crusoe's Footprints: Cultural Studies in Britain and America*, Patrick Brantlinger dismisses American studies in one paragraph as a negative example not to be followed. The "sacred text" for cultural studies in the United States, the 1990 conference proceedings published as *Cultural Studies* in 1992, does not mention American studies at all in its 778 pages, with one exception. The exception is philosopher Cornel West who, in his contribution "The Postmodern Crisis of the Black Intellectuals," asks for a critical reception of British cultural studies and a careful analysis of how they can be "related to the U.S. context." For West this means that American cultural studies scholars have critically to reconstruct and reclaim a "tradition of very important left cultural reflection" in the United States and of "American studies" as a "site upon which cross-fertilizations with the best of [British cultural studies] can take place in the U.S. context." In West's assessment this is absolutely vital, as he sees the very reason for the eventual serious impasse of deconstruction in the United States in the critics' failure to transculturate philosophical theories developed in very different political, social, and cultural contexts and relate them to "native" traditions of thought.[1]

The pertinence of Cornel West's warnings seems to have been borne out. Cultural studies have been tremendously successful in the United States during the 1990s. Many new cultural studies programs have been institutionalized. Cultural studies have dominated the field of communication theory and broken new ground in the study of cultural production in mass media and popular culture. The cultural studies approach had been seen as a threat by many traditional departments, especially in anthropology and in English, but also in sociology and history, but it is now widely accepted as an important partner in a dialogue that has deeply changed scholarly work in these disciplines. Ironically, however, the wide-ranging success of cultural studies in the United States is now seen by its foremost spokesman and practitioner, Lawrence Grossberg, as an indication of a serious crisis that manifests itself in "a certain theoretical exhaustion, . . . a failure on the part of cultural studies to theorize in response to its project/context," as he puts it in the introduction to the collection of his essays on cultural studies, *Bringing It all Back Home: Essays on Cultural Studies*.[2] In a 1996 essay he writes: "The state of cultural studies [in the United States] demands attention. In fact, cultural studies has never been in a more precarious and ambivalent position than it is now in the U.S. academy." Cultural studies has become an umbrella term for all kinds of activities without any clear sense of direction. However, "the troubled state of cultural studies in the U.S. cannot simply be attributed to its institutional-ization and its commodification." To Grossberg an adequate explanation asks for a radically contextualist and historical approach: "We must begin the impossible but necessary task of narrating the history—the formation, re-ception, articulation, distribution, and proliferation—of cultural studies in the U.S."[3]

Now, if for Grossberg cultural studies are not about "theory," but about "finding theoretical resources that allow you to redescribe the context that has posed a political challenge" (*Bringing*, 291), if they are "one way . . . of politicizing theory and theorizing politics" and distinguished by "a radi-cal contextuality which affects its every aspect and dimension" ("Toward a Genealogy," 142–43), what are the shortcomings of cultural studies in the United States? Grossberg refutes several recurrent charges against cultural studies—for example, that they overemphasize class over race or that they ignore economics—by pointing to the contested nature of these terms in cultural studies discourses and their changing function in contemporary so-ciety. But he criticizes cultural studies as practiced in the United States for a reductionist notion of culture in the predominant approaches in mass com-munication studies, a conflation of cultural studies with their "instantiation as a question about the constitution and politics of textuality" ("Toward a Ge-nealogy," 139). He also worries about their overengagement with issues of cultural identity, an insufficient understanding of the workings of power and of the cultural implications and repercussions of globalization processes. Cul-tural studies as practiced in the United States have also been, as Benjamin Lee has pointed out, "relatively Eurocentric and uncomparative," lacking any "comparative or cross-cultural perspective" in their dealing with the issues of multiculturalism and the canon.[4] One could add that they not only have virtually ignored work done in American studies, but that they also have failed to elaborate the implications of the challenging theoretical and highly politically charged work in minority discourses and new interdisciplinary studies programs developed in the United States since the 1960s and their implications for a more penetrating understanding of American culture as a multiculture.

Grossberg outlines some crucial political, social, cultural, institutional, and ideological parameters for a successful transculturation of British cultural studies into the U.S. academic and public context, but he also is suspicious about the widespread critical demands for an "Americanization" of cultural studies. Yet recontextualizing cultural studies in the United States cannot and does not mean to look for and claim something "uniquely" or "essentially" "American," as this would only reconfirm American exceptionalism or be American identity politics writ large, as there is no homogeneous and isolated unified American culture as such. If for Grossberg, "cultural studies is built upon a conflicted and conflictual theory of culture" (*Bringing*, 294), on the awareness of the manifold interrelationships among the various dimensions of cultural difference, its concept of culture is necessarily—and in many productive ways—"ambiguous" ("Towards a Genealogy," 138), its theory is always ambivalent, hybrid, and strategic. Therefore, the history of cultural studies in the United States cannot be characterized by an evolutionary process toward a "disciplinary" or "interdisciplinary" "paradigm" achieving maturity, but will be, as Grossberg writes, "as discontinuous, uneven, fragmentary, and contradictory as contemporary culture itself" ("Towards a Genealogy," 134).

If these suggestions indicate the direction the "impossible but necessary task of narrating the history . . . of cultural studies in the U.S." should take, the demand of "radically contextualizing" ("Towards a Genealogy," 143) cultural studies in a spatial sense, of relocating, transculturating British cultural studies in the United States has to be defined in a new way. It is not the question of relating a body of scholarly theories and practices to a stable, culturally unique space, of fetishizing the local as a coherent, independent, bounded field, of the "spatial specificity of American cultural studies," of geographical "identities" (*Bringing*, 288). Instead, the multiple interactions of the new communication networks, global migrations, and spatial and cultural de- and reterritorializations have made the old notion of spatially defined communities and cultures obsolete, or highly questionable. This new sense of place as flexible, permeable, and interconnected recognizes the globalizing processes of contemporary culture that transcend any fixed space, but, at the same time, produce and rearticulate new kinds of localizing discourses and modes of cultural production and consumption. Therefore, seen in this perspective, the task of "radically contextualizing" cultural studies in the United States in their inter- and transcultural implications and dimensions turns out to be even more formidable and urgent.

If American studies was in crisis in the decades following the late 1960s and virtually ignored by the new cultural studies movement appropriated from Great Britain, today the situation seems to be somewhat reversed. Cultural studies is said to be in "deep trouble," whereas American studies has seen a remarkable "revival" in its professional activities, as Michael Denning writes in a recent article: "American Studies has once again become a site of 'radical critique,' and this is in large part due to the 'national' turn in cultural studies. For American studies, with its obsessional concern for the character of America, was the original 'identity politics.' "[5] Seen before the background of the debate about the need for a "radical contextualization" of cultural studies in the United States and the redefinition of cultural space, Denning's observations about the "revival" of American studies as a "space" for radical cultural critique are obviously ambiguous, intertwining a positive assessment of the "radical" potential of new developments in American studies with an implicit warning about their possibly crippling focus on specifically American "identities" and the national frame of reference. Even though George Lipsitz's statement of 1990 in the *American Quarterly* that "we are facing a crisis in American studies scholarship as we enter the 1990s" seems to offer the opposite assessment of the state of American studies, it concurs in Denning's remarks about their revival.[6] Lipsitz points out shortcomings and misdirections in American studies scholarship, but for him the "crisis" of American studies in the 1990s is a healthy sign for their activities in a time of challenge by European cultural theory that potentially can result in an innovative and productive reconstitution of American studies. I think it is no accident that Michael Denning and George Lipsitz, who have extensively worked on the whole range of popular culture in the United States, are leading figures in attempts to negotiate British cultural studies with the tradition of American (culture) studies in the United States.

The New Americanists: Toward Postnational Narratives

In recent years, a number of new efforts to redefine the objectives and the scope and methods of American studies in response to the challenges of critical theory of the 1970s and 1980s have been made. Also, American studies have become much more aware of their international and comparative dimensions. For years, the American Studies Association has emphasized the "internationalization of American Studies" by initiating and supporting new American studies programs in all parts of the world, by inviting international scholars to its conventions (some of which have been co-organized

with other national American studies associations), and by featuring an increasing number of sessions of the convention program that explicitly deal
with the problems and the potential of pursuing American studies in an international perspective.[7] *American Studies International* has for decades brought
attention to the development of American studies abroad and provided a
forum to international and American scholars for discussing the complex
issues of international American studies. Since 1989 the European Association for American Studies has expanded its geographical scope to include
Eastern European and other countries and gained a new strength. Responding to the pressures and possibilities of a much closer economic and political
cooperation in the European Community, the EAAS has begun to raise the
question of the future of national American studies associations and of the
specific potential of something like European American studies.[8]

However, do these new directions and revisionist theoretical redefinitions
of the project of American (culture) studies and their internationalizing visions provide answers to the questions of contextualization, historicization,
and a comparative and cross-cultural perspective that the recent critique of
the cultural studies movement in the United States has raised?

A critical look at the most prominent recent programmatic statements
analyzing the work of a new generation of scholars in American studies and
projecting their objectives for the future confirms Denning's implicitly ambivalent assessment of the current state of the field. In his introduction to
the volume *The New American Studies*—a collection of essays from the journal *Representations* that display the rich variety of approaches and materials
treated in the study of American culture in response to the analytical and
rhetorical strategies and the aims of the New Historicism—Philip Fisher
offers a version of "New American Studies" that strongly reconfirms American exceptionalism. His account of the history of American studies does not
find much (or anything) of redeeming value in the past. He reduces the
various alternative minority discourses and interdisciplinary studies programs
to political "identity movements" that have affected our understanding of the
unity of American culture in times of crisis, but are not seen as inherently
characterizing the dynamics of American culture as a multiculture with its
various conflicting dimensions and fault lines of cultural difference and social
heterogeneity. Fisher uses his (suggestive) concept of the plurality and openness of rhetorics to introduce the notion of the "civil war within representation" as the central, "normative" experience in and of American culture
that makes the (European) notion of the state and of "ideology" as a "cul-

tural mechanism of stabilization and transmission" inapplicable to the United States. The United States as an "Emersonian or speculative society" is celebrated in its benign uniqueness (and in its isolation from the rest of the world). American studies are restricted to the national frame of reference of a unique American culture that turns all dissent and oppositional differences into a reaffirmation of its underlying fundamental consensus. In conclusion Fisher writes: "We have rhetorics because we have no ideology, and we have no ideology because we lack the apparatus of ideology: a national religion, a unitary system of education under the control of the state, a cultural life and media monopolized by the state by means of ownership or subsidy."[9]

It is here that the second project of reconceptualizing American studies critically situates itself. Donald E. Pease, in his introductions to the two volumes of essays of the *New Americanists* (first published in *boundary 2*, later as *New Americanists: Revisionist Interventions into the Canon* and *National Identities and Postnational Narratives*), strongly argues the inescapably ideological implications of literary and cultural production in the United States, and he explicitly asks American studies to redefine the meaning of "America" and to write postnational narratives. He finds the American New Historicism important for its reconstruction of "the relations between public and cultural matters previously denied," for its reading strategies that "construct relations between otherwise unrelated political, economic, and historical materials and the meta-texts of American Studies," and for—potentially—returning "questions of class, race, and gender from the political unconscious of American Studies."[10] But he rejects the versions of American New Historicism that argue in terms of homologies and the notion of culture as a closed system that reduces conflicts and dissent to a form of dissensus that, in the end, only reconfirms a preestablished unity.[11] Pease also replaces the common, rather mechanistic understanding of the workings of "ideology" by a much more dynamic and complex Gramscian notion of "hegemony" and sets the New Americanists the task of conceiving a "counterhegemony" that succeeds in linking "repressed sociopolitical contexts *within* literary works to the sociopolitical issues *external* to the academic field" ("New Americanists," 23, 29, 32).

The introduction to *New Americanists: Revisionist Interventions into the Canon* does not fully elaborate the implications of Pease's project. He writes near the end of his essay that the "political unconscious of the primal scene of [the New Americanists'] New Historicist readings embodies *both* the *repressed* relationships between the literary and the political and the *disenfran-*

chised groups previously unrepresentable in this relationship." But when he continues, "New Americanists have a responsibility to make these absent subjects representable in this field's past and present" ("New Americanists," 31) he, again, constructs the cultural representation of the "disenfranchised groups" in a more or less monological way, making them "representable," and integrates them into a new kind of "national metanarrative," as he acknowledges in his introduction to the second volume, *National Identities and Postnational Narratives.*[12] What is not pursued in the first volume is recognizing these groups' own voices, social movements, and forms of representing themselves as a challenge to the revisionary "counterhegemonic" national New Americanists project. In his second introductory essay Pease concludes: "Instead of accepting this assumption as the basis for their social identities, the socially disenfranchised figures within emancipatory political movements understand that the universality of the national identity depends on their externality for its integrity. In the wake of this recognition, these movement figures offered themselves up not for integration within the national narrative but, by way of what I am calling postnational narratives, actively contested its social arrangements" ("National Identities," 3).

This notion of "*post*national narratives" is crucial for American studies of the future. It points to a reconceptualization of the national context, of national identities, of intracultural differences and conflicts within U.S. American (multi)culture. It is in these processes that what Pease calls the "national subject peoples, figures of race, class, and gender" claim agency, articulate their potentially counterhegemonic social and cultural power, and dismantle the coherence of a national cultural narrative that had been built on placing them in a subordinate position and/or reading them out of the "universally" valid synthesis of the national culture. Yet the "performative power" of these "postnational forces for social change" (Pease, "National Identities," 4–5) in redefining a program for American studies that reconstitutes the politics of U.S. American culture as a multiculture of many conflicting, asymmetrical, as well as overlapping fault lines of difference can only be fully perceived and made productive if cultural critique transcends the limitations of more or less isolated minority discourses and articulates in its analytical strategies their multiply ambivalent positionings, their internal differences, and their interrelationships.

Donald Pease's project for postnational New Americanists is permeated by a "conflicted and conflictual theory of culture," to refer back to Lawrence Grossberg's phrase. For him, New Americanists must understand themselves as "multiply interpellated—within social movements as well as academic fields," and he highlights their positioning at "intranational boundar[ies]" ("National Identities," 5). Yet I think that his introduction and the essays collected in the volume *National Identities and Postnational Narratives* have to be supplemented in two ways. The analytical strategies of U.S. American multicultural critique have to be elaborated in their complex implications more fully, and the postnational project of the New Americanists has to become more explicitly dialogical in order to transcend the self-critical and self-reflective stance of white intellectuals that again resituate the counterhegemonic articulations of those "figures of race, class, and gender" in the complex and expansive dramatizations of their own discourses.

American Multicultural Critique and the Dialectics of Border Discourses

If multiculturalism is not taken as a "liberal" version of cultural diversity or a pluralism of (more or less) independent group cultures, but in its radical, transformative version as being characterized by contested and provisional negotiations of the various, conflicting dimensions of cultural difference and of the organization and institutionalization of social heterogeneity, its critical cultural practices have most powerfully been articulated in the border discourses that have been worked out in their intercultural as well as trans- and postnational dynamics mostly by critics positioned and positioning themselves at the boundaries of cultures, in cultural "contact zones," at defining moments of the clash, the mixing, and the reconstitution of cultures.[13] These border discourses that explore the analytical and political potential of concepts such as cultural translation, transculturation, border cultures, *mestizaje* consciousness, cultural hybridity, creolization, and diaspora address the processes of the construction of cultural difference and otherness in the encounters of cultures and elaborate the various dimensions of inter- and intracultural difference in the constitution and reconstitution of multiple, plurivocal cultural identities and communities. All of them point to the effects of power, of imperialism and (post)colonialism, but they also can—and do—dramatize the dialectical processes of the de- and reconstruction of cultures of resistance, of provisional cultural identities and communities in the postmodern age. A critical study of the uses border discourses have made of these concepts shows that they have to be radically contextualized and historicized in U.S. American cultural critique. The notion of cultural hybridity, for example, as developed by Homi Bhabha in his analysis of the discursive dialectic in the India of the British Empire, cannot simply be applied to an analysis of culture(s) in the United States.

All of these border discourses have been conceived in specific material and discursive contexts. They have been elaborated in very different, often conflicting ways and should not be used interchangeably as metaphors for describing cultural difference and otherness. None of them can be used as the master trope or new synthesis for the analysis of cultural differences and cultures of difference in a postmodern, globalizing, increasingly postnational world. In their different ways, they conceptualize and dramatize cultural heterogeneity and versions of cultural "impurity" and fragmentation, but these discourses of cultural difference and "impure mixtures" are also energized by reference to their invisible Other, to the visions of a lost or a utopian unity or the (deceptive) vision of an earlier state of purity. If these border concepts represented the negative Other in earlier dominant discourses, marks of oppression or victimization and, in some cases, of the dubious claims of biologistic essentialism, minority and border discourses today have radically deconstructed the so-called positive Other of these terms and de-essentialized, revalorized, reterritorialized, and transculturated their negative meanings and attempted to reassert cultural practices and discursive strategies of their own. However, it is crucial to realize that these border discourses do not only address problems and perspectives of specific minorities and marginalized positionalities. They are *not* identical with minority discourses in the sense of giving direct expression and voice to the experience and the perspectives of ethnic or cultural minorities themselves. Instead, they are always doubly encoded, also functioning as counterdiscourses, counter-readings through an active decentering, displacement, deterritorialization of "master discourses" and the competing discourses in society.[14] All of them engage important dimensions and problems of contemporary societies and rearticulate the complex intercultural and intracultural dynamics of difference and otherness of their cultures at large. These border discourses and their central analytical concepts are not in isolation constitutive of the various politically engendered interdisciplinary programs in academia such as African American studies, Asian American studies, Chicano/a studies, Native American studies, women's studies, or queer studies. On the contrary, they deconstruct in their complex interactive dynamics the tendency toward a monocausal essentialism or identity politics in terms of race, ethnicity, gender, sex, or territory that has often been characteristic of these programs, and reengage them in recognizing and exploring their multiple interactions. If most of these border discourses seem to be based on spatial metaphors and visions, they also address the defining moments in time, the cultural processes of the encounter and the reconstitution of cultures and thus displace and replace the epistemology of vision and objectification by a dialogics and dialectics of discursive practices.

Cultures of U.S. Imperialism and the Internationalization of American Studies

The border discourses in their inherent hybridity also pose the questions of the meaning of "America" in American studies and of the intercultural, transnational interrelationships that have characterized U.S. American culture. The final concept of the border discourses I mentioned, the concept of *diaspora* and *diasporic discourses*, can return us to the project of the New Americanists. This notion can activate a powerful analytical potential, as it can be seen as one way of explicitly addressing the tenuous, changing relations of cultures and territories or spaces and, in the perspective of time, the manifold processes of globalization and reassertions of localisms as they have become characteristic in the contemporary world. Paul Gilroy's *The Black Atlantic: Modernity and Double Consciousness* and Lisa Lowe's *Immigrant Acts: On Asian American Cultural Politics* are two different, but equally compelling studies that explore the implications of different diasporic cultures and their multiperspectival, transformative interactions for understanding the transnational dynamics of U.S. multiculture and exploring the relational definitions of African American, black British, and African cultures or the intricate intercultural networks of Asian American and American Asian cultures.[15]

Raising the question of postnational narratives cannot only refer to a reconceptualization of the workings of national identity and counter-identities in the United States, but it also means asking for a much more elaborated critical redefinition of the meaning of America and of the transnational effects and entanglements of United States culture(s) on a global scale. Richard P. Horwitz and several contributors to the volume *Exporting America: Essays on American Studies Abroad* have scrutinized the "politics of international American Studies" and critically debated the ideological premises and different strategies by the federal government and other agencies of "exporting the American Dream" during the Cold War era.[16] Yet, important as this critique of the imperial "politics of international American Studies" is, it has to be extended to a more radical investigation of the mutual implications of the construction of American culture(s) at home and the dynamics of transnational cultural critique. It is not sufficient in a time of globalization to trace the cultural impact of the United States on other nations all over the world in order to reintroduce the history of American imperialism into the debates about postcolonialism; it is also a matter of showing how the global processes of American (cultural) imperialism have had a formative impact on the political organization and the academic institutionalization of United States cultures of difference and the study of American multiculture at large.

In their introductory essays to their co-edited volume *Cultures of United States Imperialism*, Amy Kaplan and Donald E. Pease pursue the consequences of their insight that the emphasis on "multicultural diversity and scholarly 'dissensus'"—on "internal differences and conflicts, structured around the relations of race, gender, ethnicity, and class" in contemporary American studies—runs the risk, as Amy Kaplan puts it, "of being bound by the old paradigm of unity if it concentrates on the internal lineaments of American culture and leaves national borders intact instead of interrogating their formation." The essays collected in the book, instead, set out to contribute, as Kaplan writes, to

> the multicultural critique of American ethnocentrism, not by supplanting heterogeneity with a new synthesis of empire, but by relating those internal categories of gender, race, and ethnicity to the global dynamics of empire-building. *Cultures of United States Imperialism* explores how such diverse identities cohere, fragment, and change in relation to one another and to ideologies of nationhood through the crucible of international power relations, and how, conversely, imperialism as a political or economic process abroad is inseparable from the social relations and cultural discourses of race, gender, ethnicity, and class at home.[17]

The volume's focus on the "interconnections between internal and external colonization in the imperial constitution of American national culture" has several important consequences for American studies. First, it reopens the question of the genealogy of American studies, in Kaplan's reinterpretation of the repressed imperialist dimensions of the "primal scene" (what Pease calls its "inaugural moment")[18] in Perry Miller's preface to *Errand Into the Wilderness* about his epiphany on the river Congo, his decision to pursue in his

scholarship the explanation of the "meaning of America," but also in Donald
Pease's sketch of four periods in the history of American studies. However, I
think that the earlier period of American studies is still seen too much in the
light (or darkness) of the reductive polemical construction of the so-called
myth-symbol school. Particularly, if we widen the scope of our rereading of
American cultural studies from the 1930s to the 1960s beyond the limits of
academic American studies departments to include cultural, historical, and
social critics from other departments and from outside academia, we can
rediscover and reclaim important and challenging strategies of radical cultural
critique. These strategies anticipated in specific ways many—clearly not all—
of the self-reflective and deconstructive approaches of European poststructuralist theory as well as of the New Historicism and enable us to recontextualize the recent critical discourses in cultural studies and of the New
Americanists in a rehistoricized understanding of the complex earlier dynamics of American multiculture(s).[19]

A second crucial consequence of the focus on the interrelations of intracultural differences and the global dynamics of empire building is the rigorously transnational, intercultural, and comparative reconstitution of American studies.[20] Amy Kaplan puts strong emphasis on showing "the absence of
culture from the history of U.S. imperialism; the absence of empire from the
study of American culture; and the absence of the United States from the
postcolonial study of imperialism" ("Left Alone," 11).[21] For Donald Pease, in
the context of global imperialism, "U.S. cultural formations manifest themselves as heterogeneous and unevenly developed modes of *internal colonization*
in complex relations with the Second and Third World nations"—heterogeneous cultural histories that are to be restored through an "uncovering of
reciprocal interanimations of U.S. cultures and U.S. imperialism" ("New
Perspectives," 23; emphasis added). Grasping these reciprocal interanimations
of internally heterogeneous and divided U.S. cultures and the forces and
effects of transnational U.S. cultural imperialism is crucial to reconceiving the
dynamics of power in postnational and transnational American studies. If the
heterogeneity of cultures at home asks for an assertion of a common national
culture by way of the construction of cultural difference and alterity abroad,
the imperialist appropriation of other cultures also predetermines the terms
and perspectives used in defining the contours and fault lines of difference
that in the common understanding of multiculturalism have displaced histories by myths and social conflicts by the rituals of cultural dissent and diversity.

Kaplan and Pease's program for the study of the repercussions of U.S.

cultural imperialism, and, more generally, of the cultures of United States imperialism is very sophisticated, provocative, and exploratory. They have complemented and reconfigured in a more radically political way what in recent years has established itself as the "discourse of global localism" (Pease, "New Perspectives," 26). However, the focus on the workings of U.S. imperialism in American studies should not lead to a one-directional approach in which the more recent insight into the inherent self-difference of a multicultural U.S American society is transferred to a global perspective and that explores the interrelations between cultures only from the perspective of the influence or impact of a politically and economically more powerful culture on other cultures and limits itself to studying the repercussions of imperialist adventures on the reconstitution of U.S. cultures at home. If modernization turns out to have been, and to be, not identical with Americanization, as many foreign observers had claimed earlier during this "American Century," the more recent globalization processes are also not to be seen simply as processes of Americanization of a new post-Fordist capitalism of the one remaining world power, but as happening and being conceived in different ways in a multicentered world.

What is needed is a genuinely dialogic notion of cultural critique and of inter- and postnational American culture studies in order to bring into view the always two-directional processes of transculturation and rearticulation of the political role of American media, of the products of popular/mass culture in various parts of the world, and of the cultural repercussions and preconditions of the different processes of what is summarily called globalization. *Dialogic* in this context is to be understood in the vein of the Bakhtinian notions of dialogism, heteroglossia, and hybridization, of the intertextual relations between discourses, or of the internal dialogization and differentiation of discourses in their specific historical and social contexts, as well as referring to the encounter, confrontation, or clash of different cultures enacted in the critical debates between representatives of these different perspectives and discursive positions. The call for a comparative approach often is motivated by the desire, fully justified, of enlarging and revising the scope of the American literary and cultural canon and of reintroducing cultural difference and diversity, but the way the manifestations of cultural difference in the United States are appropriated tends to cut them off from their intercultural, transnational dimensions and interrelationships. Obviously, comparative analyses can no longer consist in putting side by side "independent," "stable," "unified" cultures and judging them according to common, seemingly objective and universal criteria and standards. Cultural identities and communities are never stable, unified, isolated, or continuous, but are always multiple, contested, discontinuous, and changing, as recent anthropology and minority discourses have shown. Cultures are always hybridized, multi-cultural, and intercultural, and they work and function less through a consensus on shared values and a common core culture, than through debate, controversies, and negotiations. In a time of globalization (and the concomitant processes of relocalizations) in the economy and in communication, the very notion and the public role(s) of the realm(s) of culture have undergone fundamental changes, and there are no "objective" "outsider" positions from which critics could conduct a comparative survey. In this sense, any critical non-American disourse is always already implicated in U.S. American culture, but in spite of its impressive power, what is called, or contructed as, "American culture" is never omnipresent and is always in contested relationships with other cultures. Also, there is no global culture, there are only cultural products and practices that can be found in more and more parts of the world, yet are recodified and refunctionalized differently in different contexts.

These critical reflections ask for a redefinition of *comparative* in terms of interculturality, cultural encounters, and "contact zones."[22] Comparative American culture studies have to be reconceived in a dialogic manner in the context of what Jane C. Desmond and Virginia R. Dominguez call, following Benjamin Lee, a "shared critical internationalism" that in its work and its directions in research and teaching "resituates the United States in a global context" (Desmond and Dominguez 475).[23]

The Dialogics of International American Culture Studies

Therefore, comparative and international American culture studies in a new sense should, first, explore the agency of other, non-American cultures in responding to and recodifying the increasing presence of U.S. American mass media and products of popular culture, and, second, recognize and explore—in critical cross-cultural dialogues of U.S. American cultural studies scholars with representatives of other cultures, drawing on the work of cultural critics, travelers, immigrants, migrants, and exiles—how these other cultures articulate alternative modes of cultural representation and alternative cultural practices, interactive and transformative processes that have been changing their own cultures as well as U.S. American cultures.

My elaboration of the potential of border discourses and of intercultural, comparative approaches for defining the project of American studies in the future has, obviously, important consequences for a reconceptualization of the question of inter- or transdisciplinarity, for the pedagogy and curriculum development of American studies. These approaches also help in redefining the role of American studies scholars and scholarship in the reconstitution and rearticulation of public cultures and the meaning of citizenship that are no longer based on the notions of the normative power of a common national culture, and of citizenship in a nation-state as that exclusionary "identity which subordinates and coordinates all other identities—of religion, estate, family, gender, ethnicity, region, and the like—to its framework of a uniform body of law."[24] Border discourses, conceived from an intracultural as well as an intercultural perspective by American radical, feminist, and minority critics or by foreign American studies scholars, address in a self-critical, self-reflective manner the question of authoring, of authorizing cultural critique, the problem of speaking for others or for your own group, the logic of multiple subjects, the dialogics of competing critical discourses.[25] What distinguishes these border discourses, as I understand them, is that they cannot be contained in traditional scholarly disciplines and that they do not allow the creation of disembodied inter- or transdisciplinary synthesizing cultural studies programs, but force American studies scholars radically to contextualize their cultural theory, their teaching, and their public role.

Border discourses achieve their critical power by being and remaining hybridized discourses that cross disciplinary lines in order to define and explore the analytical and political questions and projects posed in and for American culture(s). Moving beyond the old notion of interdisciplinarity as the (re-)combination of methods from several academic disciplines in the pursuit of an overarching research project, is to confront what Clifford Geertz has called the "blurring of genres."[26] This means that we recognize that cultures are not so much static, closed networks of meanings, or "texts," but most of all force fields of open, contested, transgressive, transnational "cultural flows" that are articulated and negotiated in specific local situations and that ask for "hybrid," "creolized," and "creolizing" discourses and a dialogical, multifocal reorganization of knowledge.[27] American studies—and here they can learn from British cultural studies—should not attempt to replace traditional scholarly disciplines or look for a new totalizing meta-theory or metadisciplinarity or acquiesce in a noncommitted dispersion and fragmentation of the field in the vein of diffuse postmodern or postnational social and cultural processes of globalization seen as something like an uncontrollable natural force. They should transcend the parochialism of many multiculturalist debates on cultural difference that often lack an explicitly comparative, intercultural perspective. American studies should provide, instead—and this I consider vitally important—a forum and force field for explicitly addressing the workings of American public culture as a dialogue of competing discourses under conditions of unequal power and for studying the interrelations between the various, politically authorized minority discourses and interdisciplinary studies programs that are engaged in, as well as transcend, U.S. national culture(s). American studies should, at the same time, be conceived and organized in their institutional and professional activities as a site for the interchange of cultural critique articulated from different and conflicting comparative positionings, for inter- and transdisciplinary projects, realized from local and global, American and non-American, national and postnational perspectives of cultures as cultures of difference. The pedagogical potential of border discourses and comparative intercultural approaches has been addressed in a creative and suggestive manner by Henry Giroux, Paul Lauter, and especially in John Carlos Rowe's "comparative U.S. Cultures Model."[28] They have—in different ways—reopened the question of the role American studies and American studies scholars as public intellectuals can play in constructing notions of cultural politics and public spheres in the contemporary world.

This is a project that has to be pursued not only in the United States but equally urgently among the international community of American studies scholars. Foreign scholars who work outside the United States and confront the problem of understanding how national U.S. American (multi)culture is constituted and reconstitutes itself in the interplay of heterogeneous local cultures or subcultures and is made and remade in different intercultural and transnational discourses, can play a productive and challenging role in exploring the impact of U.S. American culture and society on cultures and societies all over the world and of how the processes of resistance, transculturation, and articulation of alternative visions have worked. But they also confront the question of how a heterogeneous multicultural and transnational society like the United States has constituted and reconstituted itself as a national (not necessarily a "common") culture and state that even in an era of globalization still has to confront the problems, and perhaps the opportunities, of cultural difference and social heterogeneity in its borders.[29] However, foreign scholars can make an important contribution to dialogical inter- and postnational American studies only when they move beyond the common—mostly justified—complaint that their work has more or less consistently been ignored by their colleagues in the United States or confined to studies of immigration and of direct intellectual influences, or that they are immediately identified and marked in the U.S. American acedemic contexts by way of their national, ethnic, or racial origin as specialists in their fields of minority studies and discourses in various ethnic studies or other interdisciplinary programs. Foreign American studies scholars have to investigate and articulate more rigorously than they have done in the past their own positionings in the interchanges between U.S. American cultures and their (and other) cultures and to define clearly the political and cultural role and function of conceptualizing and institutionalizing interdisciplinary American studies programs in their own national or transnational contexts. Let me indicate some directions and projects, seen from a European, particularly German, perspective.

Too often charges of "Americanization" have functioned for scholars abroad as strategies of displacement, of othering unwanted processes and effects of social change, of economic and social modernization or globalization happening in countries all over the world as the result of the impact of outside forces, of the powerful United States, instead of exploring the specific complex and contradictory historical dynamics of their own countries. In the case of (Western) Europe, the continuing charges of an almost total "Americanization," of U.S. "cultural imperialism," or of politically diverse versions of so-called anti-Americanism have for a long time prevented us from seeing how strikingly different cultural and social developments in various European countries, especially after World War II, have been. If we compare the debates on multiculturalism in the United States (or in Canada) and in European countries, we realize that they emphasize different dimensions of multiculturalism and that their notions of "cultural difference" are differently encoded and politically charged, as Berndt Ostendorf has pointed out in his essays on the politics of multiculturalism in the United States and Germany.[30] They are grounded in different historical experiences of, and dealings with, ethnic and cultural heterogeneity (for example, the increasing heterogeneity of multicultural European nation-states due to mass migrations from former colonies, immigration, people seeking asylum, or, in the case of Germany, of so-called repatriated nationals) and based on different notions and legal constructions of citizenship and different culture concepts. In the case of Germany, citizenship is still based on *ius sanguinis*, on a closed culture concept (*Volksnation*) that has repressed alternative traditions of cultural pluralism. Confronting multicultural differences, social heterogeneity, and transnational interrelations in the United States forces foreign American studies scholars, particularly in Europe, to revise radically their traditional visions and ideological constructions of a homogeneous culture as the basis for their own nation-states that, as it is argued, has only recently inceasingly come under attack from outside by forces of heterogeneity and cultural difference. In the public debate in Germany, multiculturalism has often been reduced to diversity of lifestyles and a plurality of "exotic" customs, or to the "*Ausländer-problematik*," the "integration" of foreigners into German society, but not with full citizen rights. However, in spite of the embarrassing distortions of the implications and the potential of multiculturalism in official government proclamations—positions the new federal government set out to relinquish— Germany seems to me to present a challenging case study in the politics of multiculturalism as it forces us to come to terms with the legacies of the Cold War in the country most exposed to its confrontational ideological politics and to reconceive the consequences and problems of reunification after 1989 as a special and unprecedented project of multiculturalism.[31] What this can tell us is that the very differences that permeate and motivate the discourses of multiculturalism in the United States, Canada, and in various European countries demand a mutually critical dialogic engagement that can contribute to correcting and reassessing the objectives and the organization of cultures and societies today.

The charges of Americanization have also obscured the complex dialectics of the modes of intercultural understanding, of the constructions, deconstructions, and reconstructions of competing metaphors, visions, and ideologies (often going back to earlier centuries) of America and Europe (or the West), and of their cultural functions and political repercussions. The media of communication and the products of U.S. American (mass) culture may be "everywhere," and some Western European countries may (deceptively) look like being totally "Americanized," but its products and performative modes have always been, as Rob Kroes puts it in his book *If You've Seen One, You've Seen the Mall: Europeans and American Mass Culture*, "creatively manipulate[d], reinterpret[ed], and recontextualize[ed]."[32] American culture is not the homogenized powerful, imperializing or globalizing Other, but it is in itself multiplicitous, inherently differentiated and conflicted, and always changing in active responses to alternative, multicultural, and intercultural experiences and discourses.

Two of the key terms describing these processes are transculturation and traveling theory. The impact of American modernist culture, including popular and mass culture, was not only, or, was not so much, part of the American postwar reeducation program or of American cultural imperialism, but had a liberating effect on the reconstitution of modernism in West Germany after World War II and helped to redefine the elitist, closed concept of high culture (*Kultur* with a capital "K") of the German tradition. Yet American modernism was not only transformed and appropriated in the different German/European contexts. It was also, in some places, reinterpreted—against the grain of so-called (white) classic Anglo-American modernism dominant at the time—as multiplicitous and multicultural (as we would put it today), as a fascinating (non-European) way of encompassing and interrelating, for example, the radical avant-garde in the arts, Hollywood film genres, and black music, especially modern jazz, or, to use Hans Magnus Enzensberger's example, Faulkner and the Katzenjammer Kids.[33] If transculturation is always a two- or multi-directional process, the same is true for what Edward W. Said has called "traveling theory."[34] If Said emphasizes the "deradicalization" of European critical theories, such as neo-Marxism, poststructuralism, or, we could add, British cultural studies, in the American context, the same could be argued, for example, for the fate of American multiculturalist and minority discourses and of feminist theory in Germany. Yet the question is less one of misunderstanding or perversion, but of processes of recodification and refunctionalization in different contexts. These intercultural encounters do not happen, however, between two more or less unified national bodies of theory, but in the frame of a multicentered, transnational world of competing discourses. It is the role of wide-ranging, often vaguely defined theoretical concepts such as postmodernism, postcolonialism, or multiculturalism to remind us of the need to approach questions of traveling theory and of intercultural relationships in the wider contemporary horizon of the dynamics of the global and the local that are addressed in the various border discourses of hybridity, creolization, and diaspora referred to above.

In a time of the redefinition of the political relations of the U.S. government with Europe after the end of the Cold War and of the effects of unifying the countries of the European Community and extending its borders to include other, especially Eastern European states (where the repercussions of Americanization processes had worked in fundamentally different ways), the scope, the objectives, and the organization of American culture studies have to be reconceived. The task of scholars in American studies outside the United States is to scrutinize and reassess the problematic, the structure, and the forms of institutionalization of American studies, especially as the teaching of a foreign culture, society, and language, and of cultural studies programs in their own countries. If American studies outside the United States can vitally contribute to a dialogical critique of the intricate and highly charged workings of U.S. cultural imperialism and of the "cultures of U.S. imperialism," they also have to pursue the question of how far their own American studies programs, often founded as "area studies programs" in the period of the Cold War, have been implicated in, and actively supportive of, these imperial politics. The vicissitudes of the limited potential of a critical self-consciousness based on a critical attitude of interdisciplinary work in American studies toward the limiting paradigms of the traditional disciplines and on the claim of early American studies of combining the activities of the scholar and the citizen in a critical manner can be overcome by decentering their own historical and political positioning, engaging in dialogues with scholars from other countries, and resituating their work in the more general dialectical processes of globalization and relocalization of transnational cultures and their discursive representations. Certainly, American studies, even when they are internationalized, or internationalizing, in the ways suggested, cannot claim priority in studying the dynamics of the global/local processes of cultural change and the changing role of culture, but they can reflect on the political implications of the current call for the internationalization of cultural studies in the post–Cold War period of a globalizing American capitalism and provide crucially important models for future intercultural studies. Seen in this way, American studies of the future offer a chance and a vision of turning their work and their programs into contact zones of the encounter, the interactions, and the study of cultures as a critical response to the changes in a globalizing world of, but certainly not exclusively, the transnational corporations.

Notes

1 Patrick Brantlinger, *Crusoe's Footprints: Cultural Studies in Britain and America* (New York: Routledge, 1990), 26–27; Cornel West, "The Postmodern Crisis of the Black Intellectuals," in *Cultural Studies*, ed. Lawrence Grossberg, Cary Nelson, and Paula A. Treichler (New York: Routledge, 1992), 693. See West's own study *The American Evasion of Philosophy: A Genealogy of Pragmatism* (Madison: University of Wisconsin Press, 1989).

2 Lawrence Grossberg, *Bringing It All Back Home: Essays on Cultural Studies*

(Durham, N.C.: Duke University Press, 1997), 19. Subsequent references are cited parenthetically in the text.

3   Lawrence Grossberg, "Toward a Genealogy of the State of Cultural Studies: The Discipline of Communication and the Reception of Cultural Studies in the United States," in *Disciplinarity and Dissent in Cultural Studies*, ed. Cary Nelson and Dilip Parameshwar Gaonkar (New York: Routledge, 1996), 131, 133. Subsequent references are cited parenthetically in the text.

4   Benjamin Lee, "Between Nations and Disciplines," in *Disciplinarity and Dissent in Cultural Studies*, ed. Nelson and Gaonkar, 220.

5   Michael Denning, "Culture and the Crisis: The Political and Intellectual Origins of Cultural Studies in the United States," in *Disciplinarity and Dissent in Cultural Studies*, ed. Nelson and Gaonkar, 273. See also Paul Lauter's comment that "American Studies as a field is quite healthy"; however, he continues, "still, the situation for its graduate students is not." Paul Lauter, "A Call for (at Least a Little) American Studies Chauvinism," *American Studies Newsletter* 18 (1995): 1. Subsequent references are cited parenthetically in the text.

6   George Lipsitz, "Listening to Learn, Learning to Listen: Popular Culture, Cultural Theory, and American Studies," *American Quarterly* 42, no. 4 (1990): 616.

7   Robert Walker, "The Internationalization of American Studies," *American Studies International* 26, no. 1 (1988): 67–71.

8   See, for example, Rob Kroes, "National American Studies in Europe, Transnational American Studies in America?" in *American Studies in Germany: European Contexts and Intercultural Relations*, ed. Günter H. Lenz and Klaus J. Milich (New York: St. Martin's, 1995), 147–58. Subsequent references are cited parenthetically in the text.

9   Philip Fisher, "Introduction : The New American Studies," in *The New American Studies: Essays from Representations*, ed. Fisher (Berkeley: University of California Press, 1991), xxii.

10 Donald E. Pease, "New Americanists: Revisionist Interventions into the Canon," *boundary 2* 17, no. 1 (1990): 16, 19. Subsequent references are cited parenthetically in the text.

11 See Pease's critique of Sacvan Bercovitch's work, "New Americanists," 23, 29.

12 Donald E. Pease, "National Identities, Postmodern Artifacts, and Postnational Narratives," *boundary 2* 19, no. 1 (1992): 2. Subsequent references are cited parenthetically in the text.

13 See my essay "Transnational American Studies: Negotiating Cultures of Difference—Multicultural Identities, Communities, and Border Discourses," in *Multiculturalism in Transit: A German-American Exchange*, ed. Klaus J. Milich and Jeffrey M. Peck (New York: Berghahn, 1998), 129–66. For a perceptive and challenging account of a "strong" version of a "transformative" multiculturalism, see Christopher Newfield and Avery F. Gordon, "Multiculturalism's Unfinished Business," in *Mapping Multiculturalism*, ed. Gordon and Newfield (Minneapolis: University of Minnesota Press, 1996), 76–115.

14 Gilles Deleuze and Félix Guattari, *Kafka: Toward a Minor Literature*, trans. Dana Polan (Minneapolis: University of Minnesota Press, 1986).

15 Paul Gilroy, *The Black Atlantic: Modernity and Double Consciousness* (New York: Verso, 1993); Lisa Lowe, *Immigrant Acts: On Asian American Cultural Politics* (Durham, N.C.: Duke University Press, 1996).

16 See Richard P. Horwitz, "The Politics of International American Studies," in *Exporting America: Essays on American Studies Abroad*, ed. Horwitz (New York: Garland, 1993), 377–418.

17 Amy Kaplan, " 'Left Alone with America': The Absence of Empire in the Study of American Culture," in *Cultures of United States Imperialism*, ed. Kaplan and Donald E. Pease (Durham, N.C.: Duke University Press, 1993), 15–16. Subsequent references are cited parenthetically in the text.

18 Donald E. Pease, "New Perspectives on U.S. Cultures and Imperialism," in *Cultures of United States Imperialism*, ed. Kaplan and Pease, 23. Subsequent references are cited parenthetically in the text.

19 See, for example, my earlier essays "American Studies and the Radical Tradition," *Prospects* 12 (1987): 21–58; and "The Radical Imagination: Revisionary Modes of Radical Cultural Criticism in Thirties America," in *Looking Inward—Looking Outward: From the 1930s through the 1940s*, ed. Steve Ickringill (Amsterdam: VU University Press, 1990), 94–126; and, particularly for the wider cultural context, Michael Denning, " 'The Special American Conditions': Marxism and American Studies," *American Quarterly* 38, no. 3 (1986): 356–80; his essay "Culture and the Crisis"; and his recent book *The Cultural Front: The Laboring of American Culture in the Twentieth Century* (London: Verso, 1996).

20 For recent essays emphasizing the need for American studies to become more international and more comparative, see Jane C. Desmond and Virginia R. Domínguez, "Resituating American Studies in a Critical Internationalism," *American Quarterly* 48, no. 3 (1996): 475–90; from Great Britain, Paul Giles, "Reconstructing American Studies: Transnational Paradoxes, Comparative Perspectives," *Journal of American Studies* 28 (1994): 335–58; and Giles, "Virtual Americas: The Internationalization of American Studies and the Ideology of Exchange," *American Quarterly* 50, no. 3 (1998): 523–47; from the Netherlands, Mel van Elteren, "American Studies in Europe: Its Vital Role in Internationalizing the Field," *Journal of American Culture* 20, no. 4 (1997): 87–96; and Kroes, "National American Studies in Europe." (See also the other essays in Lenz and Milich, eds., *American Studies in Germany*). Subsequent references are cited parenthetically in the text.

21 The "absence of the United States from the postcolonial study of imperialism" certainly accounts for the widespread readiness in cultural studies in the United States to adopt with little, if any qualifications models of postcolonial criticism developed in other parts of the world.

22 See John Carlos Rowe, "A Future for 'American Studies': The Comparative U.S. Cultures Model," in *American Studies in Germany*, ed. Lenz and Milich,

262–78; and Mary Louise Pratt, "Arts of the Contact Zone," *Profession* (1991): 33–40.

23 For a "more international model of cultural studies," see also the Chicago Critical Studies Group, "Critical Multiculturalism," *Critical Inquiry* 18 (1992): 530–55; Benjamin Lee, "Critical Internationalism," *Public Culture* 7, no. 3 (1995): 559–92; and Lee, "Between Nations and Disciplines."

24 See James Holston and Arjun Appadurai's suggestive essay "Cities and Citizenship," *Public Culture* 8, no. 2 (1996): 187.

25 See the contributions to *Who Can Speak? Authority and Critical Identity*, ed. Judith Roof and Robyn Wiegman (Urbana: University of Illinois Press, 1995).

26 Clifford Geertz, "Blurred Genres: The Refiguration of Social Thought," in *Local Knowledge: Further Essays in Interpretive Anthropology* (New York: Basic Books, 1983), 19–35.

27 See Ulf Hannerz, *Cultural Complexity: Studies in the Social Organization of Meaning* (New York: Columbia University Press, 1992); and Hannerz, *Transnational Connnections: Culture, People, Places* (New York: Routledge, 1996).

28 Henry Giroux, *Border Crossings: Cultural Workers and the Politics of Education* (New York: Routledge, 1992); Stanley Aronowitz and Henry A. Giroux, *Postmodern Education: Politics, Culture, and Social Criticism* (Minneapolis: University of Minnesota Press, 1991); Paul Lauter, "The Literatures of America: A Comparative Discipline," in *Redefining American Literary History*, ed. A. LaVonne Brown Ruoff and Jerry W. Ward Jr. (New York: Modern Language Association of America, 1990), 9–34; Rowe, "A Future for 'American Studies.' "

29 See Kwame Anthony Appiah's important reflections on distinguishing between "nation" and "state," between "common culture" and "dominant culture," and between "common culture" ("I am inclined to say that there is not now and there has never been a common culture in the United States") and "citizens committed to common institutions" or a shared "political culture" ("What I think we really need"). Kwame Anthony Appiah, "Against National Culture," in *Text and Nation: Cross-Disciplinary Essays on Cultural and National Identities*, ed. Laura García-Moreno and Peter C. Pfeiffer (Columbia, S.C.: Camden House, 1996), 184, 186. See also Appiah, *Identity against Culture: Understandings of Multiculturalism* (Berkeley: Doreen B. Townsend Center for the Humanities, University of California, 1994).

30 See, for example, Berndt Ostendorf, "The Costs of Multiculturalism," working paper no. 50 (Berlin: John F. Kennedy-Institut für Nordamerikastudien der Freien Universität, 1992), 1–30; and Ostendorf, "Inclusion, Exclusion and the Politics of Cultural Difference," in *Fusion of Cultures?* ed. Peter O. Stummer and Christopher Balme (Amsterdam: Rodopi, 1996), 205–23.

31 For a first effort of dealing with the problems of a "German-German multiculturalism," see Dieter Thomä, "Multikulturalismus, Demokratie, Nation: Zur Philosophe der deutschen Einheit," *Deutsche Zeitschrift für Philosophie* 43 (1995): 349–63.

32 Rob Kroes, *If You've Seen One, You've Seen the Mall: Europeans and American Mass Culture* (Urbana: University of Illinois Press, 1996), 156.

33 See my essay "Refractions of Modernity—Reconstituting Modernism in West Germany after World War II: Jackson Pollock, Ezra Pound, and Charlie Parker," in *Living with America, 1946–1996*, ed. Cristina Giorcelli and Rob Kroes (Amsterdam: VU University Press, 1997), 139–70.

34 Edward W. Said, "Traveling Theory," in *The World, the Text, and the Critic* (Cambridge, Mass.: Harvard University Press, 1983), 226–47.

American Studies, American Politics,

and the Reinvention of Class

Paul Lauter

On May 28, 1996, five or six thousand people gathered on the New Haven Green, across from Yale's Old Campus, the site of the university's commencement exercises. Many wore paper caps announcing their affiliation with local unions of carpenters, warehousemen, miners, janitors, drug and hospital workers. They carried placards demanding that Yale University really negotiate with its clerical, dining hall, and custodial unions, and that it recognize the Graduate Employees and Students Organization (GESO), the teaching assistants' union. Ralph Fassanella signed copies of his prints to raise money for a strike fund. Richard Trumka, secretary-treasurer of the AFL-CIO, demanded movement on the stalled negotiations. Representatives of locals 34 and 35 asked why the second wealthiest university in the world's richest country, with an endowment then up to $4.7 billion, could not, or would not, provide ordinary workers in the nation's seventh poorest city with a living wage—not to speak of any reasonable share of local taxes. At a signal, the crowd formed into ranks and, led by Jesse Jackson and officials of the AFL-CIO, marched out onto Chapel Street, from whence it proceeded to circle the Old Campus wherein was taking place Yale's annual commencement. The walls did not fall, as we know.

Why memorialize this scene, even so briefly, and what has it to do with the future of American studies? Were I in a prophetic mode, I might claim that American studies has little future unless or until what that demonstration expressed marches fully into the Old Campus, Sterling Library, and most of all, the Hall of Graduate Studies and similar venues around the nation. But being of more moderate disposition, I wish only to remark that, at least for me, the future of American studies is inextricably bound up with the social forces that, in the recent history of the United States, inhabit the Green, the streets, the kitchens, and jails of New Haven and other cities and towns, but rarely their classrooms. Our problem as students of American studies is to understand why, to be sure; but more than that, in a well-known phrase, it is to change that reality. Understanding the forces now reshaping American higher education is no easy task, and I will not pretend to draw a definitive picture. Contradictory policy proposals, shifting alliances, and wide discrepancies between aspiration and reality abound. I will suggest, however, that a form of class analysis provides a peculiarly useful lens through which to interpret these forces. More importantly, perhaps, a class perspective may offer certain tools helpful to those desiring to analyze, contest, and, it may be, to change the directions in which American higher education seems now to be moving.

The directions now being set for American higher education will mean the transformation of that institution. Are such transformations desirable? Or rather, as a class perspective leads me to ask, for whom might they be desired goals and for whom would they be problems, and why? We need to consider a quite varied set of recent and ongoing events in order to ask what, if any, patterns begin to emerge from them: the recent and unlamented culture wars; the Yale TA, clerical, and groundskeeper strikes; the rapidly expanding organizations of TAs, adjuncts, and other university professionals; the efforts to eliminate or restrict tenure at places like Bennington, Minnesota, and the Arizona International Campus, or to hire only to term contracts and not to tenure lines; reports like that of the Council for Aid to Education, called *Breaking the Social Contract*, and that of a congressionally inspired National Commission on the Cost of Higher Education;[1] the still more recent ending of affirmative action policies in Texas and California, and of student development courses at the four-year colleges of the City University of New York. Are there discernable patterns in such miscellaneous data? Why might they make advocates of certain well-established ideas about higher education nervous? And, a preliminary but fundamental question, why fret at all about the futures of colleges and universities, much less of American studies?

One might, after all, argue that the American academy has become little more than a training ground for consumption. When he was president of Brown University, Vartan Gregorian pointed with pride to the fact that colleges offer their clientele relatively reasonable accommodations, abundant food, trained security, endless entertainment and special events, with even some educational opportunities thrown in—all for about $125 per day, or less, cheap at the price. Less even than the antiunion Marriott corporation can provide. Gregorian's account is true, of course. I will acknowledge, too, the self-seeking and pettiness, the excesses of specialization, the nesting of privilege that characterize academic life. And, as I will say later, academic institutions are, in many respects, training students to be comfortable and compliant inhabitants of a selfish order. But it is still a terrain worth struggling over. The

U.S. academy remains among the rather few institutions still receptive to efforts to resist the gospel of the bottom line now virtually uncontested as the proof of value in American democracy. It is not that academies are in some meanings of the term essentially subversive; but I do think they provide spaces within which ways of thinking about societies and cultures alternative to accepted or imposed wisdoms can grow, and perhaps even flourish. Know-nothings the world over have devoted considerable attention to preventing people from being educated. That seems to me one meaning of the savage attacks on educators and students in places from Cambodia to Algeria to Eastern Germany to Iran, and many in-between. And of certain events like the recent "culture wars" closer to home.

But even if one does not share my attachment to the academic enterprise, I think one might well be alarmed by present trends, or, rather, the conjunction of the policies and events on which I shall touch. In response to these, I wish to ask what the role of those of us in American studies might be in contesting the ongoing transformations of higher education and in offering alternative visions, policies, and forms of work, particularly by bringing class more fully into the discussion.

I

The spectrum of current policy initiatives ranges, like most political discourse in the United States, from what might be called the most right to the less right. The most right has made the withdrawal of public support from higher education, the privatization of its costs, and the consequent shrinking of the educational sector—especially in terms of its access to disadvantaged students—central to its program. The logic of this strategy is not hard to follow: by making higher education an increasingly dear commodity, one restricts access to it to those able to pay the freight; or, more accurately, in the old Selective Service metaphor, one "channels" potential students into different institutions supposedly more "suitable" for them. Those who can pay, to Dartmouth and Yale; those who can pay less, to Michigan and Texas; less still, to Kent State and Potsdam; and least, to Borough of Manhattan and Isothermal community colleges. And then there are other institutions, Soledad for example, to gather in the altogether unwashed—or unwashable. This is, of course, a formula for reproducing privilege and managing discontent. Still, one does not often see thoroughgoing most right proposals for reforming educational institutions for two reasons: first, the desired model already exists, at least in imagination, in the elite institutions of the 1950s. More important, however, is that most right ideas are grounded on the view of the world articulated by Elliott Abrams; "where liberals see 'problems,' " he wrote, "neo-conservatives see 'conditions.' "[2] That is to say, certain conditions of poverty, intelligence, inequity are not amenable to amelioration, certainly not by mere educational programs; it doesn't pay to try educating some people, for, as *The Bell Curve* seems to argue, discrepancies in IQ and other measures of intellect seem genetic. Designing inclusive educational programs would therefore be a labor lost. Indeed, the underlying assumption here is that too many students who cannot profit from it are now enrolled in higher education, straining institutional resources, pushing down standards, and contributing to the creation of an overeducated and thus restive workforce.[3]

Lest one think that this strategy is merely a rhetorical exercise among conservatives, one might consider recent developments in Texas and California and at the City University of New York. The clear design of Governor Pataki, of Mayor Giuliani, and of their appointees and trolls has been to cut back on the number of students, particularly those from minority, recent immigrant, and working-class populations attending CUNY, especially the four-year institutions. By ending remedial course work at such colleges, the CUNY trustees do not bar anyone from attending—that would be undemocratic! No, they only make it less likely that poor and minority students will surmount the new hurdles to admission; thus the policy has the practical effect of reversing the purpose of "open admissions," that is, to open wider the gates to educational opportunity for poor, working-class, and minority aspirants.[4]

Likewise, in California and Texas, the ending of affirmative action programs does not reinstate the de facto segregation of those states' flagship institutions that largely obtained thirty and more years ago. That would be politically inexpedient. But the objective impact is once more to place barriers in the way of less well-prepared and in practice often minority and working-class students. In both cases the method is that made familiar by the Selective Service's infamous "Channeling" memorandum of the 1960s, which extolled the "American or indirect way of achieving what is done by direction in foreign countries where choice is not permitted. Here, choice is limited but not denied."[5] In this case, the workforce is "indirectly" being channeled or, more simply, divided by seeming to push decisions onto individuals about how much of one's young life to invest in an educational enterprise.[6]

The less right, a.k.a. liberal, strategy maintains that access to higher education is increasingly important, necessary both to individual advancement and for maintaining the American economy in a competitive world. But money is short, universities are wasteful, and professors are fatally unbusinesslike. What's needed, then, are the kinds of reorganizations characteristic of competitive American businesses. These would, presumably, make colleges more cost-effective without abrogating the implicit social contract underwriting upward mobility through access to educational resources. Reforms would also encourage continuing support for higher education by states and localities instead of pushing, as with most right proposals, toward privatization of such costs.

This all sounds reasonable . . . until one looks more closely at the implications of such ideas for those who attend and those who work in colleges and universities. For example, one exemplary, businesslike reform has to do with what is called "role differentiation." So as not to "duplicate" curricula, undesirable on fiscal grounds, anthropology and film study, say, might disappear from Keene State University's menu since these might not fit the role laid out for such a "state undergraduate institution," as *Breaking the Social Contract* puts it: that is, taking "the lead in teacher training and areas related to regional economic development." For, after all, "the liberal arts undergraduate mission" in such a structure would be the role of "the independent college sector"—that is to say, Dartmouth (20). In that direction lies a system even more stratified along class lines than the systems of our European colleagues. Where most right proposals would track students largely on the basis of their ability to pay, less right proposals would accomplish much the same end by differentiating institutions, not individual pocket books. But stratification, like baloney, is stratification, no matter how you slice it.

Similarly, built into less right proposals for financing colleges and universities are ideas for reorganizing the work of teaching that would not only significantly speed up and disempower educational workers in the name of productivity, but which would even more deeply institutionalize the present three-tiered system of the academic workforce. That consists of a relatively privileged but smaller and smaller professoriat at one end, which increasingly identifies socially and culturally with its managerial peers; a larger and larger army of the underemployed—graduate students, adjuncts, and temporaries—at the other end, rightfully enraged at the disparity between their hopes and desires and the debased professional world they inhabit; and between them an anxious set of younger faculty aspiring to permanence but terrified lest a step to the wrong drummer cast them forever into the bottom ranks. That is a formula, as Yale has demonstrated, for keeping workers divided, always an important consideration for managers and those to whom they report. In such a context, for example, an attack from the right on tenure, which primarily protects established professors, could win, if not support, at least strategic silence or casual assent from those on the bottom, against whose job prospects the existing tenure system seems to incline.[7] Similarly, efforts by full-time faculty to roll back the exploitative use of adjuncts can be experienced by part-timers as an attempt to eliminate the fragile livelihood of those trying to maintain their tenuous hold at the fringes of the profession. Furthermore, as the 1998 debate within the National Education Association (NEA) over joining ranks with the American Federation of Teachers (AFT) indicated, the ideology of professionalism still prevents many teachers from discovering themselves as labor having more interests in common with other workers, including those who clean and serve and type, than with managerial bureaucrats who never enter a classroom, whether to teach in it, clean it, or learn in it. The managerial strategy should be clear from other industries, like the airlines, in which long employed workers, especially privileged ones like pilots, possess benefits and salary schedules not available to new hires, especially those in less skilled categories. The point is fundamentally to keep the workers divided, by crafts when available, by seniority where feasible, by culture if possible. The relatively successful UPS strike of 1997, in which full-time workers supported the demands of part-timers, and in which very different categories of employees stood together, demonstrates why maintaining divisions among workers continues to be such a central managerial objective.

Furthermore, at the institutional level, different ranks of colleges have already found themselves with distinct, and sometimes contradictory, objectives: for example, increases in funding to community colleges, as in New York, have entailed cutbacks at other kinds of institutions. The mandate to eliminate skills courses at CUNY's four-year colleges will inevitably shift a large student population to the community colleges; the likely impact is, on one hand, to overburden the two-year institutions and, on the other, to undermine the current budgets of the soon-to-be-smaller senior colleges. Thus maintaining any kind of unified front in relationship, for example, to state or city authorities becomes more and more difficult. Indeed, the very concept of a higher education community seems to me altogether anach-ronistic as different interest groups within the "industry" vie with one an-other for lebensraum.

Thus what is at contest is not, to my mind, some minor set of reforms of the higher education system designed to increase its efficiency at a time when state funds have increasingly flowed into prisons and profits. The assaults of the culture wars, the antiunion policies of New Haven's biggest employer, the systematic attacks on tenure, affirmative action, and remedial courses, and the new policy initiatives—they all seem to me parts of a typically decentered but broadscale effort to reshape the institutions of higher education to fit the agenda of triumphant global capitalism.

But what of American studies? We have, alas, significantly contributed to the processes of obscuring certain class realities at the center of American experi-ence. I want to illustrate that by propounding Lauter's "Frontier Thesis." Frederick Jackson Turner's "Frontier Thesis" has, of course, been destroyed as a credible intellectual construct by scholars,[8] but it continues to live a kind of unnatural afterlife in the social and political culture of the United States. His idea that the presence of the "frontier," whatever precisely that was taken to mean, fundamentally marked American experience, remains alive in slo-gan, in image, and in popular fancy. Indeed, his notion that the "closing" of the frontier distinguished the earlier period of eighteenth- and nineteenth-century America from the modern world stimulated historians of his school, and politicians of many persuasions, to search out or to reenact conjectural versions of the frontier and the pioneer to affirm the equally suppositional values of that earlier time. Criticisms of Turner's ideas and those of later historians like Ray Billington have focused on the ambiguities of the term *frontier*, a concept so fluid and ill-defined as to be practically meaningless; on the lack of empirical evidence to support Turner's underlying historical accounts of American development; on the implicit ethnocentrism of the notion that, at a frontier, something called civilization confronted something other; and on the American exceptionalism functionally underwritten by the Frontier Thesis. But few mainstream or even revisionist historians have asked why the concept continues to hold a place in the popular imagination, or the role it has played in helping sustain fundamental American ideological structures.

Turner was, in part, trying to account for a phenomenon widely observable on this continent, certainly since the advent of Europeans: the willingness of many Europeans to pull up stakes when things got bad and move on. Turner conceptualized that process within a geographical framework: while there was a frontier, people were able to take the role of pioneer and move into the supposedly lightly inhabited territory ahead. Geography was, in this sense, destiny. But the phenomenon of moving on continues to this day, without anything faintly resembling the frontier of Turner's or anyone else's thesis. What the geographical framework obscures is the cultural work of individualism as an ideology; or, rather, it insists on glorifying a largely individualistic response to broader social and economic changes. Turner's argument structures a drama in which the individual hardy pioneer takes on himself responsibility for moving on when things aren't working right in the current settlement. Implicitly, those who try to stick it out at home aren't pioneers, don't share the great adventure of the newest frontier, are themselves responsible for being stuck in the traps of "sivilization." So if Youngstown Sheet and Tube leaves their city in the lurch, or if General Motors wrecks Flint, it's up to individual workers and their families to pull up stakes, pack the wagon, hit the road, and seek out their fortunes on the frontiers of the Sun Belt.

I would not make too much of Lauter's frontier thesis except as a way of suggesting how an excessive focus on the idea of the frontier in American studies—as compared, say, with a more class-inflected concept of urbanization—has been a factor in how our discipline has over the years helped rationalize American individualism. So the question for me comes back to our role in bringing such self-serving ideologies under scrutiny and in illuminating alternatives. Historically, American studies practitioners had a long tradition, particularly before the field took on academic garb in the post–World War II period, of efforts to participate in working-class institutions. To cite one of the more obvious examples: at Yale in the 1920s, F. O. Matthiessen had taught English to a group of men at the New Haven Hungarian Club and had discovered "a kind of comradeship" with them he "never wanted to lose."[9] Later, he became an activist in the Harvard Teachers' Union—its founding vice-president, later president, as well as delegate to the American Federation of Teachers and to the Boston Central Labor Council.[10] In 1944, he helped to found the Sam Adams Labor School in Boston, served as one of its trustees, and taught a course there on the subjects with which he had dealt in *American Renaissance* ("Labor," 73–74). Matthiessen had also written about the persecution of miners in Gallup, New Mexico,[11] actively supported the left-wing Harvard Student Union, fought against the deportation of West Coast longshoremen's leader Harry Bridges, and canvassed working-class districts for the Progressive Party in 1948, among other activities. To be sure, Matthiessen's is an ambiguous and therefore instructive case: he never seemed able to reconcile his socialist convictions with his patrician aesthetic preferences (for Henry James, for example) nor the concern of the left in which he participated about issues of race and gender with the white and male American literary canon he helped so forcefully to establish (as in the *Oxford Book of American Verse*). What was taken to be his sentimental and Stalinist fellow traveling was excoriated by critics like Irving Howe and Lionel Trilling even as he was being condemned as politically mushy by the *New Masses*.[12] His ironic self-description, "an outdated middle-class intellectual," no doubt haunts the political dreams of many an academic. There is a good deal to be learned, I think, precisely from the unresolved contradictions of Matthiessen's career, probably unresolvable given the social position of those embedded in the academy, even today.

What might be useful contemporary equivalents of such out-of-classroom-and-library (I do not want to say off-campus) American studies practice? Here I want to emphasize one central to Matthiessen—unions. I would not pretend that unions offer a one-size-fits-all solution to the kinds of problems now faced by an opposition to the corporatization of colleges and universities. In fact, as is well known, unions have also often been part of the problem rather than part of the solution. In the United States particularly, they have acted as mechanisms to discipline and control the workforce, to deflect working-class militance, and to shift attention from fundamental issues like who bakes the economic pie and what's in it to the question of how large a slice the boss will cut you. Teachers' unions have, unfortunately, too often shrunk themselves to fit this narrow view of working people's organizations. Yet unions are among the most basic of the forms of working-class institutions, even in America.

In the beginning—the 1950s and before—the American Federation of Teachers represented in many respects a progressive force. It insisted, on one hand, that public employees had the right to organize, an idea not widely accepted (then or now) in the United States. Moreover, it opposed the collaborationist strategy of the National Education Association, which included in its membership not only rank-and-file teachers, but the very managers who controlled their work lives. To be sure, some AFT locals suffered from endemic and organizationally crippling anticommunism, not to speak of the kind of racism that set them against the very communities teachers were supposed to be serving. But on the whole, one had good reason to be proud of one's union card—I've kept my first one, in fact, ever since 1959.

Over time, however, two problems developed. In the first place, teachers' unions—like some others—came in practice increasingly to represent only a narrow, and usually privileged, fraction of the workforce: the tenured faculty. My own union at SUNY, for example, once in a burst of democratic enthusiasm negotiated a salary increase in the form of a flat sum rather than a percentage. The full professors—especially the doctors—were outraged, and that was the last time such an arrangement was even seriously considered. Percentage increases obviously benefit most those at the top of the scale and, more to my point, increasingly divide those at the top from those at the bottom. But that was no new thing, for few teachers' unions really tried to organize, or do much to serve, those on the bottom—not just the untenured faculty but the adjuncts, the other part-timers, the TAs, the lab assistants, in short, the increasing army of those mostly being exploited by colleges and universities, including, sadly, by their unionized bosses. In virtually every case in which part-timers were seriously organized, the efforts were made not by existing unions of full-timers but by newly developed organizations. And even when that was not the case, the unions were dominated by full-timers whose interests—in terms of compensation, loads, and even course content—differed substantially from those of part-timers or the untenured, much less TAs or other employees.

The second problem, widespread in the labor movement generally, had to do with the basically defensive outlook of American labor. A kind of social settlement, advantageous to some groups—particularly white, ethnic, northern, and originally urban—had been consolidated during the Cold War. Union members could then count on decent pension plans, reasonable security, meaningful health plans, secure and economical suburban housing, educational opportunities for their children, and the like. The price, of course, apart from the infectious spread of Cold War ideology, was the increasing impoverishment of the cities and of most of those, largely unorganized, stuck in them.[13] But that was not of major concern to most unions, which saw their job as servicing the members, not organizing the unorganized, forget caring for the clients. There were, to be sure, honorable exceptions to such generalizations, like the Farm Workers, the Meat Cutters, the Furriers, and Local 1199, Drug and Hospital Workers. But teachers' unions were, for all their social democratic rhetoric, not generally to be counted among the militants, much less the progressives.

In saying that, I do not mean to denigrate the real efforts of unions to hold the line against attacks on tenure, retrenchment provisions, and arbitrary layoffs. Nor do I want to forget the significant efforts of the NEA and some AFT locals to implement affirmative action plans, often against administrative intransigence and manipulation. But unions proved to be weak reeds when push came to shove, and shove to assault, as was often the case in recent decades. Most particularly, unions were seldom able to act forcefully in the interests of the least-privileged members of the academic enterprise, the teaching assistants, groundskeepers, secretaries, and dining hall employees, for example.

But that has, I think, been changing, and unions now—or so my opening vignette suggests—are going to be increasingly important not just in the struggle against academic downsizing but in the wider contests over power and direction in the academy. Why? First of all, the logic of downsizing has led many institutions to offer desirable retirement incentives—bronze parachutes—to large numbers of senior faculty. Meantime, the bull market has increased pension benefits to unprecedented heights: the value of CREF stocks, for example, shot up over 19 percent during 1997. Thus a significant number of senior faculty, even in the humanities, find themselves with retirement packages close to and sometimes exceeding a cool million. Retirement beckons. In many places, therefore, the ranks of the privileged have been significantly thinned. Meanwhile, the ranks of the unprivileged swell daily. The balance of power within unions has been shifting in significant ways, and it is no longer visionary to imagine many of them being taken over by younger, more militant, and also more socially progressive groups and caucuses. Furthermore, in situations where that seems unlikely, those struggling to organize have—like the Wisconsin TAs of the 1960s—turned away from existing teachers' associations to other workers' organizations which, in some cases, can bring greater pressure to bear on recalcitrant institutions. Such is the case, for example, of the Union of Student Employees, which is affiliated with the United Auto Workers, or the Iowa Committee to Organize Graduate Students, affiliated with the United Electrical Workers, just as in the 1960s the Wisconsin TAs had been affiliated with the Teamsters. There is, too, a fresh sense of urgency about organizing beginning to be displayed by the labor movement more broadly, as well as an increased readiness to seek common ground with academics, long viewed with suspicion by older trade unionists. Some of these elements underlay the Yale commencement demonstration as well as the formation of an organization like Scholars, Artists, and Writers for Social Justice (SAWSJ), which has developed a series of teach-ins and a variety of other projects linking the academy to progressive forces within the labor movement.

Finally, however, I do have to say that unions continue to be the most likely forms through which struggles against the corporate transformations of higher education can be contested. This has little to do with ideology, but with the internal logic of capitalism. The sanctity of contractual relationships is central to that logic. And while individual capitalists, like individual managers, are forever violating contractual relationships, every one of them would insist on the truism that national polity is based on "the rule of law, not of men." Contracts are rules of law; collegiality is the rule of men—and generally, still, "men" in the generic sense too. Whatever else they are, unions are mechanisms for enforcing, or at least pursuing, rules of law. To me, then, a major tool in the struggle with downsizing, educational corporatization, and managerial control has to do with finding ways to build into enforceable contracts enforceable goals. So far, most academic organizations have been too bound in by the economist precepts of business unionism. We do not, in fact, begin to know what it would be possible to negotiate, even within the accepted rubrics of wages, working conditions, and job security. For example, can a contract provide for goals and timetables—terrible words!—for instituting equitable pay, benefits, and other rights for part-timers? Can the struggle to institute such contractual provisions, as in the recent UPS strike, be used to organize workers and communities behind them? Can such struggles become the means for teaching students and colleagues about class?

Class? Well, after all, what I am talking about really involves the reinvigoration of class struggle on the campus. Saying it that way sounds, I know, like an opera libretto by Leonid Brezhnev. In fact, what I am suggesting is not nearly as remote or as monumental as the archaic phrasing: it involves bringing into the campus mix a greater presence of working-class institutions and of class-focused curricula, and real efforts to carry the resources of the campus and faculty to public teaching opportunities. These are dialectically related. To the extent that working people have a stake—rather than an enemy—in the academy, they support and in fact invigorate a class-conscious curriculum. Likewise, efforts to connect campus and communities force on academics a discourse to which a wider constituency has access, as well as greater clarity about conceptualizing class. What this amounts to is a kind of challenge to respond to changes in the political economy, among them the greater presence of working-class students on many campuses, the increasingly uneven distribution of income and wealth in the United States, and the ever new institutional forms and ideologies that mask class conflict in this country. Such are, to me, the fundamental challenges facing American studies.

III

Others have anticipated that direction in practice. It is striking to me that at Yale and elsewhere, a significant number of graduate students from American studies were among the leaders of TA unions and other forms of organizing. So far as faculty at Yale were concerned, almost all the militant support for the students came from those in the American studies program. I don't see that as accidental. Kathy Newman's article in *Will Teach for Food* suggests some reasons why. She points out that "graduate students are increasingly unhappy about material issues, such as TA compensation, teacher training, professional development, health benefits, and the collapsed job market. But the greatest controversies are over issues of representation and power."[14] What two terms could better characterize the preoccupations of American studies folk? Further, as Newman's article illustrates, the tools developed in this discipline for analyzing patterns of representation are wonderfully adaptable to political struggles, like those over the unionization of graduate students. Newman examines, on the one hand, the largely negative representations of graduate students not only in the popular media but in Yale's own press in an effort to understand the cultural dynamics central to winning people to your side. At the same time, she demonstrates how such an understanding can usefully enable participants in the struggle to generate images and arguments with the power to persuade. As she puts it: "When we explain our role in the university as teachers, rather than as subsidized consumers, we generate more sympathy and understanding. Moreover, by framing our union drives in the larger context of academic downsizing, we link our issues to the issues of the average working American—in almost any profession. These days, everyone is getting downsized. But not everyone is organizing to fight it" (121).

In these and other respects American studies can provide what Corey Robin and Michelle Stephens, in another article from *Will Teach for Food*, present as a necessary ingredient to a successful organizing campaign. "Organizers assume," they write, "that while people do not need to subscribe to a radical ideology in order to join a union, they do need an analysis of their experience as individual graduate students that enables them to see what they share with their fellow students."[15] In other words, the practical experiences of real class struggle generate understanding of how the world and its institutions, including the academy, actually operate in class terms. No surprise. Or as H. H. Lewis put it, in a poem resurrected by Cary Nelson:

> Here I am
> Hunkered over the cow-donick,
> Earning my one dollar per
> And realizing,
> With the goo upon overalls,
> How environment works up a feller's pants-legs
>   to govern his thought.[16]

Obviously, such understandings do not emerge only from organizing or from participating in unions. In fact, American studies practitioners have only begun to test out ways in which our work as intellectuals can usefully be integrated with the variety of working-class organizations, on campus and off. The American Studies Association has long had a Minority Scholars Committee, a Women's Committee, a Students' Committee, and has even changed the structure of its International Committee so that it will represent the international members. But it has until recently had no committee to address issues of work, workers, or even—whisper the word—class, or a real institutional mechanism for carrying out themes such as that of the 1997 convention, "Going Public." Now, an association task force is addressing issues of part-time employment and labor organization, while a working-class caucus and other groupings have developed panels and discussions at conventions. Both developments could be of value in helping teachers alter what, how, and where we teach, especially about class.[17]

Why class remains the unaddressed item in the familiar trio race, gender, and class is at one level quite obvious, but in other ways very complex.[18] Clearly, class analysis flies in the face of America's predominant ideology of individualism and has long been associated with communism and other presumably foreign ways of thinking. But many other issues sharply inhibit discussion of class in (and out) of the classroom: the embarrassed reluctance of most students to acknowledge, much less discuss, class identity; the tendency to "study down," and thus to assume that class is a phenomenon associated with workers rather than a set of relationships helping define all of us; the often confusing intersections of class with other markers of identity, like gender and race; perhaps above all the ways in which patterns of consumption both manifest and obscure class relationships. In any event, a critical part of initiating a curriculum that takes class seriously is understanding more fully what has stood in the way of such study. Equally important is examining the variety of definitions of class with at least as much intellectual energy as has been devoted to analyzing other conceptual frameworks like race, gender, and sexuality. Left intellectuals have obviously been pursuing this inquiry for decades, but their analyses have made surprisingly little impact on curricula in the United States. In what ways is that related to the tiny proportion of the American labor force that is unionized? Or to the tinier proportion of organized academics? Or to the systemic and long-standing alienation of the academy from the labor movement?

The development of a class-conscious, much less a working-class conscious, curriculum will not, I suspect, take the forms that feminist and minority scholarship and teaching have produced, in part because the connections between campus and a class-conscious community are so attenuated. We do not have very good contemporary models for the practice of linking American studies intellectual work and working-class organizing and social projects. But more such models exist than most academics realize. It may well be the case that new institutional structures, hybrids of campus and community or workplace educational programs, will have to be devised.[19] Curricular forms will, I suspect, emerge as connections begin to be developed between academic intellectuals and working-class organizations. We may even in the process learn to speak together.

IV

Of course, communication is not the primary issue; it is power. Moreover, the lessons taught by educational institutions are not always, or even primarily, those communicated by the talk of teachers, even the most inspired. Lessons, powerful lessons, are taught by how things are managed, and thus by the managers, however unfamiliar they may be with the inside of a classroom.

Indeed, the lessons of power are often those modeled by how classrooms are organized, employees managed, decisions executed—and how a college interfaces with the community it often dominates and always shapes. In a sense, the demonstration with which I began this chapter can be seen as dramatizing a great and increasing divide between undergraduate Yale students, who learn every day that they are powerful behind their walls of privilege, and most of those who tend to them in the dining halls, classrooms, buildings, and libraries. To be sure, some students and a few faculty wore buttons and armbands stating their affiliation with those outside the walls. And it was no doubt true that more sympathized with the demonstrators than news reports, which concentrated on parental anger at "interference" with the commencement ceremony, would have led one to believe. Still, the issue is not generalized sympathy with the cause of two or three small unions. It is, rather, what an institution teaches day by day and year by year about class norms and expectations; those things it teaches not by its generally liberal rhetoric but by the force of example, by what it countenances and what it does not. One remembers Karl Shapiro's poem "University": "To hurt the Negro and avoid the Jew / Is the curriculum."[20]

What, then, is taught by what we might, after Jules Henry, call the "noise," the "hidden curriculum," of university education?[21] I want to emphasize three areas: relations between gown and town, those between people who study in academe and people who serve them, and the question of truth, that ambiguous tabernacle theoretically at the center of the university. I should preface these remarks by emphasizing that they are speculative and impressionistic rather than based in ethnography or survey research of students at Yale or elsewhere. I offer them as a kind of challenge to those better situated and able than I to apply such social science tools to the issue of what students actually learn in the school.

The first lesson, I think, is that large corporate entities have no meaningful responsibility to the communities in which they exist. To be sure, there have always been primarily student organizations like PIRGs, as well as numbers of individual students involved in community-focused tutorial projects. I do not wish in any sense to demean these. But part of the problem is precisely what is taught by the contrast between what are constituted as individual actions, joining a PIRG or doing tutoring, which of course are based on ethical values, and corporate actions—far more formidable—overwhelmingly rooted in bottom-line factors. The university argument that policy must be based on what managers interpret as the institution's responsibility to students is the equivalent to the corporate canard that it necessarily answers (more accurately, "they necessarily answer") only to shareholders. That is a disingenuous argument, first, because it leaves out the self-interested role of managers and, second, because it places communities, and ultimately employees as well, outside the processes by which decisions affecting such peoples' lives are made. Thus Yale was able to rationalize its efforts not only to outsource food services and cut down the number of jobs available in New Haven, but also to deny its dining hall workers the year-round employment of which they had previously been assured. Outsourcing, cutbacks, speedups, and the like are familiar, of course; the claim I am raising, however, is that the naturalization of a division between ethical individual behavior and venal corporate actions is an essential part of higher education's hidden curriculum today. Lesson one.

The second, linked lesson has to do with the divide between those who are served at the university and those who serve. Of course, there has always been a certain potential for class tension between them, rooted, in the case of faculty-student interactions, in their differing relations to that form of cultural capital called grades. But today more and more of the students at state and larger private universities are taught by part-timers, temporaries, teaching associates, and the like, whose job status, pay, and working conditions are rather more like those of the groundskeepers than those to which students, particularly at fancy private institutions, look forward. A subtle shift in the balance of authority has taken place, abetted by what was, in the 1960s, a progressive innovation, student evaluations of faculty performance.[22] Abetted, too, by the consumerist philosophy fostered by managers claiming the necessity to make their institutions competitive. In such an environment, undergraduate students expect to be waited on, amused, stimulated, but not too challenged—they are, after all, paying clients, and faculty among the service personnel are easily intimidated by the threat of complaint or withdrawal to a more accommodating venue.[23] What is being naturalized here is the lesson of class separation, increasingly important to learn as divisions of income and wealth widen in the United States, and as more and more people are forced to accommodate themselves to pervasively antidemocratic economic and social arrangements.

The third issue concerns truth. Here it is useful to recollect the ardent columns and letters produced by Yale faculty in support of the proposition that teaching assistants were not employees but apprentices benignly supervised by their senior mentors.[24] Did anyone believe this stuff? Certainly not the Yale administration and legal staff, who jettisoned the argument and

acknowledged that TAs were, indeed, workers when it became legally convenient to do so. But no one should be surprised: as Micaela di Leonardo has
pointed out, books and articles which utterly falsify the political and social
history of New Haven have continued to be taught at Yale to generations of
students.[25] Does anyone think undergraduates are stupid and don't perceive
reality? Perhaps. But what is at stake here is not truth but ideology, what is
being defended is not the idea of a university but the basis of privilege, and
what is being taught is a lesson popular in '90s America: spin it hard enough,
and people will believe a lemon is a coconut.

It is against such lessons—and one could describe others—that, it seems to
me, the best of American studies scholarship needs to be deployed. For that,
we have some excellent models, among them the work of Sandra Patton, of
Richard Flacks and Scott Thomas, and of Micaela di Leonardo cited earlier.
What characterizes such work? First of all, it is based on empirical study:
Flacks and Thomas use surveys of students at the University of California,
Santa Barbara and elsewhere; di Leonardo employs ethnographic tools to
examine in detail the New Haven neighborhood in which she lived. Patton
uses the work of Michael Agar to argue "that the boundaries of ethnographic
study can be usefully reconceptualized to include a focus on the relationships
between individuals, social institutions, and the State, rather than solely considering relationships between members of a particular cultural group."[26] By
pointing to such fundamentally social science approaches, am I promoting a
direction away from the cultural turn of American studies, projecting an
announcement akin to Stanley Fish's that the moment of theory in literary
study had passed? Of course, I am not Stanley Fish, nor was meant to be, and I
am not predicting the demise of cultural study as central to the enterprise to
which this book is devoted, American studies. I would argue, however, that
such empirical research will, and should, play a substantially larger role in
American studies than it has in the last decade or more. The reasons have to
do with a second quality in the work I have cited: it is directed to questions
informing fundamental policy decisions in the United States. Di Leonardo
attacks the "'underclass' concept," exemplified in books like William Julius
Wilson's *When Work Disappears*, which bases its analysis of American urban
problems "on passive-verb, ahistorical political economy and 'blame the victim' sociology" ("Patterns," 319). Her object is to replace the hegemony of
ideas about defective "others" with "carefully historicized empirical work"
that can locate the sources of American poverty in specific government
policies—like those which shifted resources out of cities and into suburbs—
and in uncontrolled forms of capital movement—of the sort continually

disputed between General Motors and the United Auto Workers. Her point is not that knowledge of the truth about capital will make any of us free, but that such knowledge will arm those contesting policies and legislation based on false models of urban poverty.[27] Similarly, Patton analyzes the ways in which right-wing social scientists like Charles Murray and David Murray construct a "salvation narrative, in which White families, bearing the torch of 'family values' in popular representations, are the only families—or even mothers—who can save Black children."[28] Such narratives, Patton argues, locate the cause of American social problems not in poverty, deindustrialization, and the upward flow of wealth, but in the "immorality" of black mothers, which leads to illegitimacy, poor parenting, and other forms of social pathology—an analysis used to underwrite the policy initiatives that led to passage of bills fostering transracial adoption and virtually eliminating AFDC.

The research of Flacks and Thomas emerges in the wake of increasingly successful efforts to roll back affirmative action procedures in hiring and, particularly, in college admissions. The underlying argument behind affirmative action in admissions was that earlier unfairness needed to be redressed by providing a leg up to populations—the "historically by-passed"—who had been cheated of truly equal opportunity. However historically just, that argument has proved politically vulnerable to the charges of fostering quotas and of cheating whites who themselves were supposedly guiltless of harming the victims of earlier forms of discrimination. Flacks and Thomas begin from a different set of questions. They ask not who has been previously injured, but who is now in fact better using the social resource offered by higher educational institutions. Their evidence suggests that

> *the students most likely to be disposed to academic values and demands and to make use of the resources available on campus for their own development are today students for whom university attendance involves both sacrifice and risk—students usually regarded as "disadvantaged" because of race and class backgrounds.* Students who are supported by their parents, unburdened by debt and work demands, and raised by college educated parents are, paradoxically, more likely to be distanced from the values and opportunities provided by the institution. From a historical perspective we might say that the old "collegiate" hedonistic subcultural pattern has returned—and it is largely constituted by white students, particularly white males from relatively advantaged backgrounds.[29]

The policy implication one might draw from their research, if its conclusions are sustained, to put it in brutal instrumental terms mimicked from the studies with which this article began, is that, in a period of economic constraint, an opportunity like obtaining a college education cannot continue to be squandered on students who systematically disregard what can be seen as a privilege and, in so doing, hog educational space better made available to those who will make the most constructive use of it. Or again, the higher education industry cannot afford to squander its resources on those who rely primarily on social networks preestablished by class, race, and gender rather than on mastering the intellectual content of colleges. I have used this bureaucratic phrasing to call attention to a fundamental irony of studies like *Breaking the Social Contract: The Fiscal Crisis in Higher Education* and *Straight Talk about College Costs and Prices*. Because they never ask who goes to college, who might go, who ought to go, or how that could be decided, they beg the fundamental economic issues they are theoretically designed to address. No surprise: those are the issues of the American class system.

Now I am neither utopian nor optimistic enough to imagine that American universities will ever be transformed into engines of working-class insurgency. But they can become instruments, as they have been in varied measure before, for helping level the playing field rather than, as too often now, tilting it further. That objective, it seems to me, is a goal both of progressive faculty and of working-class, minority, and immigrant communities, and thus an intellectual and policy basis for alliances between such groups. If the political force of open admissions, affirmative action, bilingual education, and similar initiatives is spent or fatally blocked, it seems to me that our job is to reconceive the grounds for struggling toward "a free university in a free society" (to recycle a brilliant SDS slogan). Besides, as I said at the outset, I do not think that a disobedient discipline like American studies has much of a future in a corporatized university. Self-interest, then, as well as idealism prompt us to apply what we know, what we learn, and what we teach to the project of sustaining in the academy the possibilities of democracy.

Notes

1 Council for Aid to Education, *Breaking the Social Contract: The Fiscal Crisis in Higher Education* (Santa Monica, Calif.: Rand, 1997); National Commission on the Cost of Higher Education, *Straight Talk about College Costs and Prices* (Phoenix: Oryx, 1998). Subsequent references are cited parenthetically in the text.

2 Elliott Abrams, "Why Are There Neoconservatives?" *American Spectator*, November 1979, 10–11.

3 Here, for example, is George F. Will on the subject: "But, then, the market for college graduates is saturated: an estimated 20 percent work in jobs that do not really require a degree. Says [Anne] Matthews [in *Bright College Years: Inside the American Campus Today*], 'A third of Domino's pizza-delivery drivers in the Washington, D.C., area have BAs.' A help wanted ad seeking a warehouse supervisor for The Gap reads: 'Bachelor's degree required, and the ability to lift 50 pounds.' Matthews's book refutes the premise of President Clinton's plan for tuition tax credits and deductions." George Will, "The Education Bubble," *Washington Post*, 30 March 1997, C7.

4 The 1999 report of the Mayor's commission on CUNY included in an appendix information indicating that New York State's funding had, in constant dollars, decreased by 40 percent since 1980, while New York City's funds had been cut by 90 percent! See Nathan Glazer, "What the CUNY-Bashers Overlook," *New York Times*, 11 July 1999. It has not been unusual for students to be closed out of required courses, to register in courses where they must sit in the aisles of lecture halls, or for whole categories of curricular offerings to be cycled down to a once-in-three-years basis.

5 "Channeling," in *The Conspiracy of the Young*, eds. Paul Lauter and Florence Howe (New York: World Publishing, 1970), 189.

6 Not incidentally, the reduction in minority student participation in higher education also serves the cultural interests of the right. In the late 1960s, the increasing presence of unprecedented numbers of black, Latino, and other minority students, as well as a new generation of activist women, provided the impetus, the urgency, and the political muscle crucial to the development of black studies, women's studies, multiculturalism, and similar academic innovations. Removing significant numbers of such students may have the effect of undercutting the base of student support for such programs and thus their rationale for existence—a long-term goal of right-wingers. The logic of that strategy is revealed in the attacks by Ward Connerly, leader of the antiaffirmative action initiative, on ethnic and minority studies programs in the University of California. Removing such programs, or even occupying them with self-defense, would further strip away institutions' support of what we once called historically by-passed students on campuses that they already experience as chilly, if not downright hostile. Moreover, as the recent efforts by CUNY trustees to impose a Western civilization requirement suggest, one goal of most right efforts is to foster a traditional culture by resuscitating a traditional curriculum.

7 A lively debate on the subject took place on the American studies listserv H-AMSTDY, 7–14 August 1997 (H-net.msu.edu).

8 For a succinct example, see the entry on the "Frontier" by Patricia Nelson Limerick in *A Companion to American Thought*, ed. Richard Wightman Fox and James T. Kloppenberg (Oxford: Blackwell, 1995), 255–59.

9   "The Education of a Socialist," in *F. O. Matthiessen, 1902–1950: A Collective Portrait*, ed. Paul M. Sweezy and Leo Huberman (New York: Schuman, 1950), 5. This piece is excerpted from Matthiessen's *From the Heart of Europe* (New York: Oxford, 1948).

10   Paul M. Sweezy, "Labor and Political Activities," in *F. O. Matthiessen*, 61–63. Subsequent references are cited parenthetically in the text.

11   F. O. Matthiessen, "The New Mexican Workers' Case," *New Republic*, 8 May 1935, 361–63.

12   The best account of the virtues and contradictions in Matthiessen's political activities and cultural writings is, I think, to be found in William E. Cain, *F. O. Matthiessen and the Politics of Criticism* (Madison: University of Wisconsin Press, 1988), especially chapter 4 and the conclusion.

13   A trenchant analysis is provided by Micaela di Leonardo in "White Lies, Black Myths: Rape, Race, and the Black 'Underclass,'" in *The Gender/Sexuality Reader: Culture, History, Political Economy*, ed. Roger N. Lancaster and Micaela di Leonardo (New York: Routledge, 1997), 53–68.

14   Kathy M. Newman, "Poor, Hungry, and Desperate? Or, Privileged, Histrionic, and Demanding? In Search of the True Meaning of 'Ph.D.,'" in *Will Teach for Food: Academic Labor in Crisis*, ed. Cary Nelson (Minneapolis: University of Minnesota Press, 1997), 88. Subsequent references are cited parenthetically in the text.

15   Corey Robin and Michelle Stephens, "Against the Grain: Organizing TAs at Yale," in *Will Teach for Food*, ed. Nelson, 59.

16   From Lewis's book, *Thinking of Russia* (1932), reprinted by Nelson in *Repression and Recovery: Modern American Poetry and the Politics of Cultural Memory, 1910–1945* (Madison: University of Wisconsin Press, 1989), 49.

17   Here's a simple idea: drawing a lesson from the early days of women's studies, such a group could collect and issue a volume of syllabi and essays that address class questions and the difficult problems of teaching about class in American educational institutions.

18   See Paul Lauter and Ann Fitzgerald, introduction to *Literature, Class, and Culture*, ed. Lauter and Fitzgerald (New York: Longman, 2001).

19   An interesting instance may be provided by the program for UAW workers in the big three auto manufacturing companies being developed at the University of Michigan-Dearborn, and being delivered online.

20   Karl Shapiro, *Collected Poems, 1940–1978* (New York: Random House, 1978), 10.

21   Jules Henry, *Culture Against Man* (New York: Random House, 1963), 289–90.

22   A useful and easily accessible analysis of some of the negative policy implications of student evaluations is to be found in Robert E. Haskell, "Academic Freedom, Tenure, and Student Evaluation of Faculty: Galloping Polls in the 21st Century," *Education Policy Analysis Archives* (a peer-reviewed electronic journal) 5 (1997), located at: ⟨http://www.bus.lsu.edu/accounting/faculty/

lcrumbley/educpoly.htm⟩. Haskell's article is primarily concerned with the issue of academic freedom, but he cites a number of other studies dealing with the impact of student evaluations, particularly on job retention decisions. See also, Robin Wilson, "New Research Casts Doubt on Value of Student Evaluations of Professors," *Chronicle of Higher Education*, 16 January 1998, A12. This article summarizes studies published, among other places, in *Change Magazine* (Wendy M. Williams and Stephen J. Ceci, " 'How'm I Doing?' Problems with Student Ratings of Instructors and Courses," September–October 1997, 12–23) and *American Psychologist* (Anthony G. Greenwal and Gerald M. Gillmore, "Grading Leniency Is a Removable Contaminant of Student Ratings," *American Psychologist* 52, no. 11 [1997]: 1209–17).

23 On the *New York Times* op-ed page, Sheila Schwartz, a retired professor of English education at SUNY, New Paltz, related how one of her unhappy students arrived at her office with a West Point husband decked out in full uniform, including a galaxy of medals. Schwartz, of course, laughed, but for a younger faculty member or a part-timer such a display, and an assistant dean's complaint about her hard standards, would be no laughing matter but the preliminary to joblessness. Sheila Schwartz, "Teaching's Unlettered Future," *New York Times*, 6 August 1998, 23.

24 The locus classicus of this swill is probably to be found in Peter Brooks's endpaper "Graduate Learning as Apprenticeship," *Chronicle of Higher Education*, 20 December 1996, A52. I remember coming on a book when I was an undergraduate titled, as I recall it, *How to Lie with Statistics*. I suppose a collection of these paeans to mentoring could be collected in a volume called "How to Lie with Panache." While the Brooks article would no doubt be a star attraction, form letters, written in the wake of the TAs grade strike, from Yale's president Richard Levin and from senior members of its English department would no doubt provide excellent filler.

25 Micaela di Leonardo, "Patterns of Culture Wars: Place, Modernity, and the Contemporary Political Economy of Difference," in *Exotics at Home: Anthropologies, Others, American Modernity* (Chicago: University of Chicago Press, 1998), esp. 319–24.

26 Sandra Patton, "Producing '(Il)Legitimate' Citizens: An Interdisciplinary Ethnographic Approach to Public Policy," paper presented at the American Studies Association convention, Kansas City, 1996. A fuller version of this paper is incorporated into Patton's book *Birthmarks: Transracial Adoption in Contemporary America* (New York: New York University Press, 2000).

27 It is interesting to speculate in this connection what combination of informed testimony and political pressure apparently moved the National Commission on the Cost of Higher Education from what initially appeared to be a very conservative agenda to its relatively restrained report.

28 The articles referred to include Charles Murray, "The Coming White Underclass," *Wall Street Journal*, 29 October 1993, A14; David W. Murray, "Poor

Suffering Bastards: An Anthropologist Looks at Illegitimacy," *Policy Review* 68 (1994): 9–15.

29 Richard Flacks and Scott L. Thomas, "Students in the Nineties: Report on a Project in Progress," unpublished paper. Flacks and Thomas are careful to qualify these generalizations by pointing out, first, that the majority of white students do not "identify with the party culture," and that they need to conduct more research to clarify the outlooks and behaviors of such students as well as of Asian American students since their sample contained too few of the last to draw meaningful conclusions.

The End of Academia

THE FUTURE OF AMERICAN STUDIES

Eric Cheyfitz

> The bourgeois apparatus of production and publication can assimilate astonishing quantities of revolutionary themes . . . without calling its own existence, and the existence of the class that owns it, seriously into question.
> —Walter Benjamin, "The Author as Producer"

I

The quote from Benjamin makes a distinction not between form and content or even between form and function, but, crucially, between form and action. It describes all too perfectly the current state of American studies specifically, and of all the humanities in general. A progressive agenda, focused on issues of inclusion (race, gender, class, and sexuality), informs the content of the currently central work of American studies, while the fundamental structure of the university becomes increasingly exclusive or regressive because of the fundamental disjunction between the form of multicultural curricula and social action. While the American studies curriculum represents the redistribution of a certain cultural capital (the opening of the canon to previously excluded voices), the university represents the increasing concentration of capital itself and thus, ironically, the control of that redistributed cultural capital in fewer and fewer hands.

According to a front page story in the *New York Times* for Sunday, June 21, 1998, "Universities" are "Giving Less Financial Aid On Basis Of Need": "We are experiencing a heaping on of greater privilege to wealthy and middle-class kids," said Morton Schapiro, an economics professor and dean at the University of Southern California and coauthor of *The Student Aid Game* (Princeton University Press, 1997). "Will institutions meet the needs of lower-income students?" Professor Schapiro asked. "These days, almost the entire enrollment rate increase is from the middle income and above. The gaps between whites and non-whites going to college is greater than it was in 1980. The poor are increasingly restricted to community colleges, even being squeezed out of four-year public institutions."[1]

We should remember in this context that, according to the 2000 Current Population Survey (CPS) of the Bureau of the Census, only 26 percent of Americans twenty-five years and older have a bachelor's degree or higher in the first place, and that, also according to the CPS, income level is a direct correlation of educational attainment. In 1999 (the last year for which we have statistics), the average yearly earnings of a high school graduate, based on a population of those eighteen years and older, was $24,572, while the earnings for those holding bachelor's degrees was $45,678. People holding advanced degrees (master's, doctorate, and professional) averaged $81,154.[2] It should also be noted that the income gap between these categories has widened markedly since 1996, when the average yearly earnings of a high school graduate, based on a population of those eighteen years and older, was $22,154, while the earnings for those holding bachelor's degrees was $38,112, and people holding advanced degrees averaged $61,317. All of these statistics are significantly inflected negatively for race and gender. The category of class is implicit in these demographics as well. The CPS tells us that educational attainment is highly concentrated in the professional and managerial classes; and as its statistics show, race and gender divisions create their own classes within a class.[3]

My primary point is, then, that there is no point in talking about the future of American studies without talking about its institutional arrangements; and, I am arguing, the distribution of cultural and economic capital detailed in the CPS are the inescapable context for these arrangements. Further, the survey tells us that these two kinds of capital are part and parcel of one another.

But how we talk about these institutional arrangements is necessarily crucial, so that our discourses are not simply contained or, to use Benjamin's terms, "assimilated" by these arrangements. The kind of assimilated discourse that I have in mind, one that announces itself as a radical critique of the institutional arrangements of the university (and the discipline of English in particular) but remains comfortably contained by these arrangements, is Cary Nelson's book *Manifesto of a Tenured Radical*.[4] The allusion to Roger Kimball's right-wing diatribe against university academics *Tenured Radicals* lends Nelson's discourse a touch of irony, but the overwhelming tone of the book is that of the jeremiad.

Nelson's book, while certainly seriously concerned with a complex of issues that go under the name of the "current crisis of the university in the United States," remains substantially at home, that is to say settled, in both the university and the America from which and at which Nelson positions his critique. A primary sign of Nelson's settlement is that he appears to believe that, in and of itself, a certain kind of university teaching, marked by a multiculturalism engaging the historic conflicts of race, gender, class, and sexuality, and that he relates emphatically to the social conflicts of the present moment, constitutes a radical act. In this belief in a curriculum of cultural studies as social action, Nelson makes the mistake of severing culture from politics, precisely at the point where he believes to be politicizing culture. The mistake, though, is common enough to particular "cutting-edge" academic discourses that fetishize the realm of culture so that it appears to assume an autonomous function in and of itself.

The discourses that fetishize culture function synechdochally, taking the part (their version of disciplinary dynamics) for the whole (societal dynamics). The result is hallucinatory. To take another example and expand on it somewhat, in his *American Literature and the Culture Wars*, Gregory Jay peppers his book with references to the redistribution of resources, but he never offers a sustained critique of American capitalism per se or the university's place in it. Detaching culture from politics or, what amounts to the same thing, conflating political representation with representation in cultural forms (in this case the curriculum), Jay appears reasonably comfortable with the university's redistributive mechanisms: "From the evidence, I can only conclude that it is precisely because higher education has done so much (though not enough) to redistribute access to representation that colleges and universities have come under such vitriolic attack."[5]

Both Nelson and Jay believe that the university system can be reformed sui generis. In Jay this attitude contrives a vision of the class-conscious, multicultural classroom as the site of transformation: "In the setting of the classroom, students should be given an opportunity to use class analysis to cross the borders between identity categories, to explore common class experiences with students of very different racial or ethnic communities, or, perhaps more explosively, to confront students from the dominant class with an analysis that targets their economic privilege rather than their skin color" (125). But the question is: how does Jay's vision of a classroom diverse enough in terms of class and race to allow for the kind of transformative dialogue he imagines jibe with the current institutional realities of postsecondary education.

The demographics presented by Schapiro cited above point to the ideal nature of Jay's vision of the multicultural university, a vision offered by Michael Bérubé who writes of "the arrival at universities of *vastly* more diverse student populations (particularly more diverse with regard to class origins) beginning in the late 1960s."[6] In fact, the heterogeneous classroom and university that Jay, Bérubé, and others proclaim as reality is an ideal that can only be achieved if there is an actual transformation of the socioeconomic inequalities that are part and parcel of the U.S. institutional arrangements of which the university is an integral part.

While there was a "democratizing of college which began with the GI bill after the Second World War [and] continued throughout the 1970s until almost every community had a publicly funded college or a university where tuition was inexpensive and admission standards were permissive for resident high school graduates,"[7] in the last twenty years this democratizing process has been reversed, and in its place we find an increasingly class-stratified, class-segregated system of higher education. Linda Ray Pratt posits the university's adoption of the corporate model as a significant cause of this stratification:

> When education becomes essentially a component in the efficiency of a performance-measured economy, the question of who is worth the investment also becomes sharper, and meaner. The use of community colleges to train the mass of skilled workers, and the restriction of university enrollments to these workers' future managers and directors, makes good business sense. Education programmed in this way will inevitably favor the white economic elites and result in aggregating nonwhites in second-tier institutions that prepare them to fill jobs that others will supervise. Such controls on access to knowledge serve one conception of social cohesion. Educating the elite for leadership was the traditional function of higher education, and dividing institutions and students into distinct tiers preserves the class division while pretending to make education more democratic. (39)

In order to forge his educational ideal, Jay must abstract the university from these arrangements of race and class segregation by kind of institution. Jay's multicultural classroom, where transformative dialogue can take place across race and class boundaries, is a fiction composed by collapsing the actual hierarchies of dispersed institutional spaces into a single mythic multicultural space. Here is Lawrence Levine in a particularly dazzling moment of such abstraction:

> the real fragmentation confronting this society has *nothing to do* with the university, which is one of the more successfully integrated and heterogeneous institutions in the United States, and everything to do with the reality that forms of fragmentation—social, ethnic, racial, religious, regional, eco-

nomic—have been endemic in the United States from the outset. In our own time this historic fragmentation has been exacerbated because a significant part of our population has been removed from the economy and turned into a permanent underclass with no ladders leading out of its predicament and consequently little hope.[8]

Notice Levine's use of the passive mode ("has been removed"), so that all agency for the creation of a "permanent underclass" that, not incidentally, is marked by the fact that it has historically relatively little access ("no ladders") to the university, is obscured. This rhetorical strategy absolves Levine from discussing the university's involvement in corporate capitalism and hence its involvement in the maintenance of the underclass.

Texts like Levine's *The Opening of the American Mind*, and Bérubé's trendy "It's Renaissance Time: New Historicism, American Studies, and American Identity" from his book *Public Access*, give us histories of the humanities that deinstitutionalize the disciplines and thus dehistoricize and depoliticize them even as they claim to be doing the opposite. Such texts are prime examples of the displacement of politics and history by an understanding of culture that disarticulates it from history and politics. Thus Bérubé can make the following claim as if it had historical force: "Politically activist cultural criticism (together with politically critical cultural activism) got women and minorities into faculty positions in American universities in the first place; from that space, among others, feminism and multiculturalism retheorizes the American cultural heritage that has begotten them."[9]

Bérubé's version of history raises a question: how does the civil rights movement of the 1950s and 1960s, with its legislative victories in the area of affirmative action, victories now in the process of reversal, fit into this closed circuit of cultural critics and "cultural heritage," where culture itself is, logically, the only causative force? Bérubé's through-the-looking-glass historical logic implicitly posits ethnic and women's studies programs as the forerunners of the civil rights and women's movements, rather than as the result. In and of itself, expressive culture has no particular political force (look at the ease with which mass advertising absorbs popular music), thus Bérubé's phrases "activist cultural criticism" and "cultural activism," besides reversing the cause-and-effect relationship between the civil rights and women's movements in the United States and postsecondary curricula, seem oxymoronic.

Work like that of the texts by Jay, Nelson, Levine, and Bérubé conflates theory with practice (culture with politics), as does Gerald Graff's *Beyond the*

Culture Wars: How Teaching the Conflicts Can Revitalize American Education.
"Teaching the conflicts," to take a particularly egregious example, will clearly
not "revitalize American education," which can only be revitalized by a
revolutionary redistribution of resources to currently impoverished groups.
Graff's wildly inflationary claim, which appears to conflate American higher
education with all education in America, is theater of the absurd when juxtaposed to the social realities of these groups. It projects an exceptionally local
example (Graff's classroom practice, to be exact) about how to teach elite
university students the liberal arts into a global solution for a world of radical
inequalities. Let me give two examples of such inequality that I know something about both in theory and in practice:

Since 1997, while I was on an NEH fellowship in the Southwest, I have
worked with members of the Navajo community who live on Big Mountain
on the Navajo reservation, which like the rest of "Indian Country" (the
legal designation for federally controlled tribes and tribal lands) has the highest unemployment and poverty rates, and, consequently, lowest levels of
educational achievement in the United States.[10] At the end of 1996, the
Navajo Nation Division of Economic Development reported that 76.18 percent of all Navajo personal income was spent off reservation, a sure sign of
the federal government's colonial policies that have historically resulted in
the present radical underdevelopment of Indian Country. I work with a
group of Navajos impacted by the so-called Navajo-Hopi Land Dispute, a
government-mandated division of traditional Indian lands, fueled by corporate mineral interests, that is ongoing and has resulted since 1974 in the
removal of approximately 12,000 Navajos from their ancestral homes.[11] Minimal as it is at this point, my work takes as its model the redistribution of
cultural capital (legal and historical knowledge necessary to make critical
judgments) and economic capital (the money and know-how to build infrastructure in a place where there is no running water, electricity, or roads)
from privileged sites of accumulation (universities, foundations, corporations, the government) into a site of particular need, in this case Navajos who
are struggling to stay on their land in the face of a combine of governmental
and corporate power.

At West Philadelphia High School, with a 98 percent black enrollment,
where 85 percent of the 1800 students are low-income—45 percent of the
students were on welfare in 1994—Farah Griffin and I, with the crucial help
of two former graduate students, Giselle Anatol and Kendall Johnson, taught
a course, *The American Literature of Social Action and Social Vision*, in the fall of

1995, which we repeated in the spring of 1999, that brought together ten West Philadelphia juniors and seniors and ten Penn undergraduates to explore issues of the distribution of capital both locally and globally. The course was enabled by West teachers Carol Merrill, John Skeif, and Alan Teplitski and sponsored and funded through the Center for Community Partnerships, under the directorship of Ira Harkavy, at the University of Pennsylvania, which is, after the city government, the largest employer in Philadelphia. Penn has a commitment through the center to redistributing some of its capital (faculty, students, material, funds) to the schools of West Philadelphia, which are part of the exceptionally poor Philadelphia school district (the state is currently considering taking the district over). Not surprisingly, the poverty of the district—its families and schools—has a major impact on academic achievement. Of the 10,000 students who entered their freshman year in high school in 1989, only 45 percent graduated four years later.[12]

Penn's intervention in this situation, however relatively substantial, is inconsequential on the systemic (as opposed to the personal) level precisely because it is the curricular exception, not the norm, as it should be. Farah and I found that the course we taught was effective in raising the critical literacy of both Penn and West students, which included improving the skill levels of the West students, and in energizing all the students by bringing them together to do research on the issues of social justice that impact the West Philadelphia community where Penn is located and where we all live and/or work, although in vastly different circumstances of class. Crucial to any success we had was the radically reduced teacher/student ratio that structured the class: twenty students, four instructors, with the ten Penn students, who were paired in research teams with the West students, able to act implicitly as mentors in the area of skills, while the West students implicitly mentored the Penn students in certain areas of reality. The average class size at West is thirty-three with one teacher ("Report Card," P13).

For this model, and the one I have suggested for Navajo, to become the norm rather than the exception, we would, of course, need a revolution in our current social agenda that mandated a radical redistribution of capital from privileged communities to communities of need. Without such a revolution, we will move increasingly toward a society dominated by an oligarchy of wealth, with increasingly disastrous sociopolitical results.

In his famous definition, Louis Althusser defines *ideology* as the representation of "the imaginary relationship of individuals to their real conditions of existence."[13] The conditions of existence in West Philadelphia and at Navajo that I have been sketching are the real conditions of our existence, the base-line of social, political, economic, and cultural life in the United States, to which the discourses of Graff, Nelson, Jay, Bérubé, and Levine (the discourses of cultural fetishism) bear an imaginary relationship, an ideological relationship in which the privileged class, as in the pastoral, dress up in the costumes of the dispossessed and perform a play we call "multiculturalism."

In contradistinction to those discourses, Paul Lauter in *Canons and Contexts* does an excellent political job of detailing the corporatization of the university under the rubric of "retrenchment," which he dates from the early 1970s.[14] Lauter makes it clear that academic and larger social agendas are necessarily linked: "No coherent educational program can be mounted unless an academic community first comes to share a set of social goals that informs and shapes schooling. A transitional program for education, in short, requires a transitional program for society" (233). But Lauter's program for university reform consists only of a very general set of guidelines; and though he notes, crucially, that "reforms must help reconnect schooling with the work needed to eliminate the fundamental social problems of America" (237), and asks the essential question of "how academic institutions can creatively interact with poor and minority communities" (220), he makes no suggestions in this essay about how this should be accomplished or even if he thinks it can be accomplished within the present capitalist system for which, as he understands so cogently, the university labors, a system in which, as Lauter notes, "colleges and universities have replaced secondary schools as primary mechanisms for sorting people on the basis, mainly, of their class origins."[15]

One key value of Lauter's work is that it raises implicitly the question of reform or revolution in relation to the "market-driven ideology of today's college managers" (*Canons*, 206). Its advocacy seems to hover between the two: advocating an incremental struggle for power (between administrators and faculty) within the institution (214), while recognizing that such a struggle is already being determined by market forces that require transinstitutional organizational ties of resistance between progressive forces in the university and the community to struggle for a redistribution of resources.

It is my argument that such a significant redistribution cannot take place within what I have termed in other work "the limits of capitalism's imagination."[16] That is, such redistribution will ultimately require revolution, not reform, a redistribution of the means of production as the necessary condition for a redistribution of resources. But, it should be emphasized, in a transitional stage reform and revolution are not necessarily mutually exclusive: one can work for local reforms, while one builds structures of revolutionary consciousness—structures that look forward to revolution. Such a productive relationship between reform and revolution is predicated, however, on a historical consciousness aware of the convergences and divergences of liberalism and the left.

Classic liberalism, a product of the Enlightenment, is not simply based in a theory of individual rights protected from state power (emblematized in a document like the Declaration of Independence), but also crucially in a theory of the natural inequalities of property that it is, according to U.S. constitutional theory as articulated in Federalist X, "the first object of government" to protect.[17] If, as Eric Foner argues, it is the basis of classic liberalism in individual rights that marks its convergence with the historic left,[18] it is the basis of classic liberalism in naturalized inequalities of property, defining the limits of capitalism's imagination, that marks its divergence from the historic left, which constitutes itself on an equalizing of property through the state mechanism of redistribution.

Foner makes an important distinction between "classical liberalism" and "modern liberalism or social liberalism. . . . [which] is geared more to the so-called welfare state and inequalities of economic power, and is not as worried about the state interfering with individual rights. Indeed, it often sees the national government as the protector of liberties against local majorities" (6), a protection that is itself enshrined in Federalist X, where, ironically, the minority that posed itself as beleaguered were the property-holding "founding fathers," who worried strenuously about a debt-ridden majority demanding a redistribution of wealth (411); hence, its call for government to protect minority rights from what it oddly terms majority "faction" (407–8).

What we term today *liberalism* and *conservatism* both have their origins in classical liberalism: both in the fear of governmental power overwhelming individual rights and, importantly, in a certain naturalization of market forces that we term *capitalism*. Clearly, at some point, and this point certainly comes into visibility in the Progressive era, classical liberalism splits into modern liberalism and conservatism, and modern liberalism becomes inflected with the left ideology of redistribution, which it understands as being possible through reform, not revolution. Jane Addams is a fine example of this modern liberalism. As Foner points out, there are today "political theorists" who "argue" that "a more egalitarian distribution of wealth and power . . . can be developed on strictly liberal grounds" (7).

The words "more egalitarian" trouble me because they imply an already relatively egalitarian distribution of wealth and power within the capitalist democracy of the United States. My understanding contradicts this, both immediately and historically. But beyond that, the question posed here is whether liberalism can within this democracy sufficiently denaturalize capitalist ideology so that significant redistribution can take place through a program of reform, or whether in order to effect such redistribution a revolutionary break of some kind will be required. It is my understanding that liberalism, classical and modern, by definition naturalizes the market; that in order for significant redistribution to take place the market must be utterly denaturalized in the Marxist sense (defetishized) and that therefore liberal reform by definition cannot accomplish a program of significant redistribution. This leaves revolution, of a kind to be imagined, as the only course with which to achieve social justice, defined as the equal distribution of capital of all kinds, and all the kinds, as I have been stressing, are inseparably interwoven.

For university professionals such a revolution would mean the end of academia as we know it. But the academia we know or thought we knew or imagined, the academia grounded in the liberal arts and professional autonomy, is already at an end through the mechanisms of capitalist power as represented for us by the modern, transnational corporation. For Veblen (see note 14) this academia's end was virtually in its beginning. So we can continue to work for this power or we can begin to resist it, or, more precisely I suppose, we can continue to work for it as we resist it.

Issues of work and resistance lie at the ideological center of Nelson's *Manifesto of a Tenured Radical*. Within Nelson's imaginary and buttressing it is the equation of graduate students, working on Ph.Ds in English and the other humanities and facing what certainly appears to be a permanently depressed job market, with the exploited working classes: those people who because of radically limited educational opportunities (no college and sometimes no high school degrees either) have virtually no job options in today's labor market where relatively high-paying unskilled jobs have disappeared because of the shift from an industrial to a service economy (and within the industrial sphere from a Fordist to a post-Fordist mode of production) in conjunction with the government-sponsored, corporate-inspired weakening of the labor movement. Thus Nelson's cultural studies, which claims an interest in teaching class conflict, effectively erases the category of class in his analysis of the academic job market by erasing the relations of this market to the larger labor markets with which it is imbricated but to which it is not simply equivalent.

In the process, Nelson, who otherwise gives clear evidence of being aware of the relations of the university to society, not only erases crucial class differences in American labor markets but takes all political agency away from the actual and potential graduate students he champions, implicitly characterizing them, in the figures of his discourse in *Manifesto*, as passive dupes of an academic bait-and-switch game that cons them into Ph.D. programs with promises of jobs that never materialize and then abandons them there, teaching-slaves of a system from which there is apparently no escape. "Trainees at McDonalds now have better opportunities for advancement than many graduate students" (201), Nelson tells us. Intentional hyperbole, perhaps, though in his 1998 candidate's statement for a position on the MLA Executive Council (Nelson was representing the Graduate Student Caucus), Nelson, apparently without irony, calls college teaching "the lowest-paid legal job in America."[19] If Nelson is being hyperbolic, the figures for average earnings relative to educational attainment already cited from the CPS survey tells us just how inflated this hyperbole is.

Nelson's discourse of exploited graduate student labor is, indeed, a melodrama (villainous faculty and administrators oppressing downtrodden but noble grad students). And as in those nineteenth-century melodramas of beset womanhood, with which it seems to share a certain generic affinity, Nelson's solution to the despair of his "heroine" is union, not literal marriage, of course, in Nelson's narrative, but labor union: a happy merger of graduate students and working classes, in which a bond of mutual support is formed around an agenda of common labor interests. But a question is implied in this narrative of union: what are the actual, as distinct from fantasized, common interests of a class that has the privilege of attending graduate school and, crucially, of leaving it for other opportunities should it prove burdensome, the privilege, that is, of the widest degree of career choice, and a class that as a class has been historically locked in the lower economic levels of U.S. society?

In analyzing the 1995–96 graduate student grade strike at Yale, Nelson at one point alludes in passing to the affiliation of the GESO (the Graduate Employees and Student Organization) with locals 34 (clerical and technical workers) and 35 (service and maintenance workers) of the Hotel Employees and Restaurant Employees International Union. He then remarks that "alliances with union leaders are easier to create and sustain than alliances with the rank-and-file membership" (*Manifesto*, 208). But he does not elaborate on this crucial if passing remark in either *Manifesto of a Tenured Radical* or in the book he edited as well in 1997, on the Yale graduate student strike and the "crisis" in "Academic labor," the egregiously titled *Will Teach for Food: Academic Labor in Crisis*. In implicitly comparing elite Yale graduate students to

the homeless, the title trumps the hyperbole of Nelson's McDonald's metaphor, if it is indeed intended as figurative (Nelson's MLA candidate's statement
suggests it isn't), and, even allowing for intended irony, occupies the area of
the fantastic.

Questions arise. Was the strike, which "collapsed" (*Manifesto*, 207) early in
1996 when the graduate students under punitive pressure from the Yale
administration decided to turn in their grades, supported in any material
ways (funds, work slowdowns or walk-outs, etc.) by the rank and file of these
locals, which did not have extensive strike funds in the first place? What was
the attitude of the rank and file toward the strike? None of the essays in *Will
Teach for Food* answer these questions or take up in any but the most cursory
ways the relationship between the GESO and locals 34 and 35, which were
then organized in what appeared to be the loosest of alliances, the FUE (Federation of University Employees at Yale University; now the FHUE, Federation of Hospital and University Employees).

Nor for that matter do these essays discuss the relationship between 34 and
35, which represent different classes of workers (white- and blue-collar respectively) and have different race/gender compositions (34 is largely white
and female; 35 is largely male, with a higher concentration of blacks and
Latinos). All of the sixteen essays, including Nelson's introduction, in *Will
Teach for Food* are written by either Yale graduate students (two of the essays)
or academics (only two of whom are part-timers), with the exception of a
piece that gives a brief history of the unionization of nonacademic employees
at Yale, written by John Wilhelm, a 1967 Yale graduate, who is now president
and was then general secretary-treasurer of the Hotel Employees and Restaurant Employees International Union. In addition, Barbara Ehrenreich provides a very brief foreword.

There are no rank-and-file voices from the membership of 34 and 35 in
this volume, nor are their any voices from graduate students at so-called
second-tier universities who typically, unlike Yale graduate students, are the
first generation of college students (of any level) in their families and who,
also unlike Yale graduate students in the humanities, are compelled from day
one in order to receive their fellowships to teach composition courses. Many
of these students, under what they perceive rightly as the pressures of the job
market, now take their doctorates in composition and rhetoric; but this, according to the class hierarchies of the profession, places them automatically in
the underclass of academic workers, many of whom will find jobs in fourth-
tier institutions (community colleges and two-year technical schools).[20]

This raises the question of how Yale graduate students, who protested having to teach classes of twenty students while their counterparts at Princeton only had classes of fifteen and who "criticize[d]" Yale "for not providing enough resources to meet the educational needs of both the undergraduates and the graduate students,"[21] came to represent the crisis in academic labor in the first place. What is the force of this demand for resources in relation to situations of actual deprivation? I think here not only of the range of poorly funded postsecondary institutions but also of Navajo and of what the students at West Philadelphia High School, where the average class size is thirty-three, could do in classes of only twenty students with the resources that Yale provides its students.

Not surprisingly, in an environment where the material issues of class difference are basically elided, the two essays by the GESO members mirror and are mirrored by the melodrama of union that Nelson unfolds in *Manifesto*. This narrative is grounded in both a bourgeois narcissism and a nostalgia for a pastoral academic past, located by these graduate students in their undergraduate experiences, that erases the fundamental class conflict, both inflected and obscured by forces of gender, race, and sexuality, historically driving the divisions in U.S. Society. The failed irony of Nelson's comparison of McDonald's workers to graduate students is perfectly mirrored in the words of GESO member Kathy M. Newman, commenting on the career choices in the "culture industry" for Yale Ph.D.s in a downsized academic market: "These days, getting a job in Hollywood might be easier than getting tenure."[22] Can the workers of locals 34 and 35 imagine, can they afford to imagine, a career trajectory that has as its bottom work at McDonald's and at its top university tenure, possibly, or, if not that, a lucrative career in the culture industry? Newman's example of Yale-grad-student-turned-culture-worker is *X-Files* star David Duchovny.

Whatever the value of certain individual essays in *Will Teach for Food*, its fundamental format—its exclusion of working-class voices and mediation of the issues involved by, mostly, the voices of academic celebrity—ensures that it will have a settling effect on the status quo it wants to disturb.

In the now no longer extant 1998 Web pages posted by the Federation of University Employees at Yale—which discussed the GESO strike with its legitimate demands for higher pay and better health benefits and the 1996 strike by locals 34 and 35 focused on crucial economic issues involving two-tier pay systems, outsourcing/subcontracting, the use of nonunion "casual" workers by Yale, and the reduction of worker retirement benefits—the only mention of support by the two locals for the GESO (and the two locals contributed to each other's strike funds) is a demonstration, attended by workers from the union, at a university hearing on January 13, 1996, for three graduate students charged with violations of academic conduct for their part in the grade strike (the charges were subsequently dismissed in the context of an Unfair Labor Practice complaint by the General Counsel of the NLRB on behalf of the GESO). Moreover, when on February 8, 1996, Local 34, representing its 2600 members (secretaries, librarians, lab technicians, and health care workers) went out on strike, Gordon Lafer, a Yale Ph.D. and then Research Director of the Federation of University Employees, e-mailed a letter "To Friends of the Yale Unions" that, while asserting common interests, suggested a certain lack, beyond an unspecified "formal" affiliation, of those interests between a class of academics and the working class at Yale and elsewhere:

> I know that many of you on this e-mail list initially became interested in the particular issues surrounding the graduate teachers' strike here, and may feel less interested in a conflict which doesn't directly involve teaching staff or questions of academic freedom. For those of us here, however, the TA strike and today's strike are part of the same struggle. The three unions here—GESO, Local 34, and Local 35 (service and maintenance workers)—are formally allied together. More important, we all face the same kind of bullying and threats, and the same attempts by administrators to prevent others from sharing in Yale's wealth or having a meaningful say over their work conditions here.[23]

Granted the justness of their claims for better health benefits and more pay (claims that Yale subsequently met), the graduate students were not then and are not now not at all in the same relation to "Yale's wealth" as the workers, a relation Lafer's e-mail elides. In the first place, the students are not dependent on Yale's wealth for their survival because of their level of educational attainment, they are mobile in terms of other professional opportunities. In the second place, this wealth, in the form of tuition wavers and fellowship support, is being put at the student's disposal so that they can improve their already highly credentialed positions, while they do work of their own choosing that, presumably, they find fulfilling.

I share Nelson's bleak view of the job market and the current structure of the university, appreciating in particular his analysis of the overproduction of Ph.D.s and its subversion of the tenure system, while I support the right of graduate students to organize/unionize for better pay and benefits, and while

I support unionization in general (though not without an awareness of how U.S. unions have helped to weaken themselves historically both through racism, sexism, and a failure, particularly after World War II, to construct a theory and a practice to oppose international capitalism and its quest for ever cheaper labor), my vision of social change is opposite to his. That is, my sense is that unless we change the corporate dynamic of America to one of redistribution of all kinds of capital, we cannot change the institutional arrangements of the university, which is, after all, no more than a corporation among corporations, albeit one that contains a certain kind of countercorporate discourse.

Indeed, in a frank if unguarded moment toward the end of *Manifesto of a Tenured Radical*, Nelson, in chiding the Yale faculty and administrators for their hysterical reaction to the unionization of graduate students and the strike, reassures them that they would really have "risk[ed]" very little in recognizing the GESO. For "if GESO is recognized as a bargaining agent, Yale's massive $4 billion endowment will *grow* [Nelson's emphasis] at a somewhat slower rate, and graduate student teachers will receive somewhat better salaries and benefits. . . . *[but] [n]othing else will change*" (206; emphasis added). Nelson makes my point exactly and reveals his agenda as at best marginally reformist rather than radical. That is, if graduate students along with sympathetic faculty and administrators do not organize around issues of redistribution beginning *not* with their immediate material needs but with the needs for the cultural capital of radically undereducated communities, in which many universities and four-year colleges are situated that the university controls, then the current situation of the academic job market will never change. We will only have, and this seems to me to be the unconsciously cynical tack of Nelson's book, slightly higher paid and benefited teaching assistants and adjunct labor to support an increasingly diminishing class of privileged, tenured positions, of which both Nelson and I are current beneficiaries. In an essay in *Will Teach for Food*, Andrew Ross, in broad terms, makes the claim I am elaborating here: "For if there is going to be a graduate union at universities like Yale, why not aim for an expansive, utopian union with a broad intellectual role to play on and off campus? Don't settle for a technocratic bargaining unit, whose only mandate is the protection of its students' material concerns."[24]

I must emphasize here that the support of the GESO and other students and faculty both then and now for the agendas of locals 34 and 35 appears in part to be an example of the kind of organization to which I and Ross refer, though it was not clear from any of the materials that I reviewed, including the Web pages of the GESO as they stood in 1998, how and to what extent this support took specific shape. And this remains the case with the current Web pages. I understand that at one time GESO was involved in the summer in educational and recreational community outreach in conjunction with 34 and 35, but that this has been discontinued; and there is no mention on the current Web pages of such an educational agenda, which one might think would be a central concern of progressive educators seeking a community-based labor movement. There are links on the current Web pages to Social Justice Network at Yale and SAWSJ (Scholars, Artists, and Writers for Social Justice), and the GESO is involved with diversity issues at the University. But its organizational statement (http://www.yaleunions.org/geso/works.htm) remains contained within the limited material concerns of its constituents.

Locals 34 and 35 won most of their fundamental demands in the 1996 strike, defeating Yale's agenda to outsource dining hall work and abolish summer work, which keeps its workers employed all year, while gaining recognition of "casual workers'" right to join the union. The GESO Web pages in 1998 reported that while Yale continued to refuse to recognize the GESO, the union had gained free health care for all graduate students and reduced payments for dependents. I understand as well that GESO attained significant concessions from Yale on important issues, including pay raises for TAs. Even as it awaited the final outcome of the Unfair Labor Practice complaint against Yale, a complaint that Yale settled in March 2000, agreeing to post signs recognizing its employees' right to unionize, the GESO was making steady gains. The remaining legal question, whether or not graduate student teachers are employees, appears to have been settled in an October 2000 ruling by the NLRB that NYU graduate students are to be considered as such. The ongoing history of these issues suggests quite a different narrative than Nelson's melodrama of union provides.

Central to Nelson's narrative, to my own, and to the reasons for the formation of the GESO and other graduate teaching unions around the country, is the collapse of the academic job market and the relation of this collapse to the radical shifts that have been occurring since the 1970s and before (see Aronowitz and particularly Veblen) in the socioeconomic structure of the United States and the world. There is a lot of full-time teaching that needs to be done in the United States, but the current institutional arrangements of higher education in relation to primary and secondary education, and of all formal education to community needs, interdicts the creation of what could be a full-employment job market for teachers of all kinds.

In what follows, I sketch a possible future for American studies, what I have termed for some time *Americas Cultural Studies*,[25] based in a curriculum geared to both social vision and social action that redistributes the capital of the university throughout communities of need.

II

Clearly, the profession of university and college teaching is marked today by an increase in the adjunct labor force: part-time and year-to-year full-time instructors with Ph.D.s as well as graduate students, who form a special part of this force because they are still in training and thus have not yet entered the doctoral job market. In a recent "Report," Jane Buck, the president of the AAUP notes: "The increasing use of contingent academic labor threatens shared governance, academic freedom, and the quality of our students' education. Data provided by the U.S. Department of Education indicate that 33 percent of the faculty were part-time in 1987. The figure rose to 43 percent in 1998, and some estimates put the current figure at 46 percent."[26]

The increase in adjunct teaching is accompanied by the reduction in tenured faculty (those who can claim any institutional power: living wages, benefits, and a say in governance) and a simultaneous increase in a class of professional administrators whose primary allegiance is to a corporate agenda of profit and loss, marked by the historically recent but now familiar discourse of downsizing and outsourcing. Thus within the university, while its multicultural curricula insinuate community, structural alienation increasingly prevails: tenured and tenure-track faculty are alienated both from adjunct faculty, including their graduate students, who face a job market that is shrinking in terms of tenure-track appointments, and those administrative and maintenance workers who are threatened with downsizing and outsourcing; and all faculty and staff are alienated from the upper administration by issues of governance.

Within the ranks of the tenured and tenure-track faculty there is also a structural alienation, not only the traditional one between those who have tenure and those who are working for it in a system of increasing scarcity of tenured positions, but within the tenured ranks themselves, where a system of celebrity has taken hold, linked to factors of location and publication; factors, that is, of visibility and invisibility. Based on the concentration of capital (significant salaries and grants) and cultural capital (visibility of publication and the consequent commanding of lecture circuits) in fewer and fewer hands, celebrity, which gives the appearance of being free from conventions in its speculative energy, is actually, in direct proportion to the brilliance of its aura, at the mercy of the speculative conventions of capital—the limits of capitalism's imagination.

The aura of celebrity radiates what Benjamin terms in "The Work of Art in the Age of Mechanical Reproduction" "the phony spell of a commodity."[27] That is, celebrity is the commodity fetish par excellence, mystifying the actual relations of production through the staging of academic autonomy. Take, for example, a performance in the *New Yorker* of the academic celebrity Henry Louis Gates Jr., writing about that celebrity of celebrities, Michael Jordan. Gates's job in this piece that passes for cultural criticism, which displays him chatting comfortably with the superstar in the inner sanctum of Jordan's office in his Chicago restaurant, is, under the auspices of the political celebrity of Jesse Jackson, to rationalize Jordan's public indifference to the exploitation of Asian workers abroad and the working-class black community at home by Nike, a company, as we know, in which Jordan has a sizeable investment.

Gates begins part of his essay with a spurious question: "Should athletes be required to serve as political spokesman?"[28] The question is spurious because, employing the language of coercion ("required"), it begs the question of every citizen's social responsibility in a democracy, denying in the process the fact that, as a corporate spokesman, Jordan is already acting as a political spokesman. By way of answering the question, Gates then allows Jackson to step forward and absolve Jordan from the social responsibilities that all citizens in a democracy are enjoined to exercise, particularly a citizen who is an owner of property inflicting social damage. "Michael has not succumbed to that temptation" (to be a "sociopolitical analyst"), Jackson responds (58), thereby transforming the abdication of civic responsibility into a positive act of self-denial, inflected with the figures of religious asceticism ("not succumbed to . . . temptation"), the figures of sainthood, implicitly conferred here by a prominent religious figure, the Reverend Jackson himself.

It is but a short step from this piece of crude mystification for Gates to announce that, indeed, Jordan "does have a strong social conscience" (58) because some comments the athlete makes in the interview demonstrate he is aware of the destructive force that sports celebrity, projected into the black working-class community as career ideal, has on the future of that community. That social awareness here is completely alienated from social action of any kind is apparently of no concern to Gates, who completely conflates private conversation, where talk is very cheap, with costly public action in his analysis of Jordan.

The system of academic celebrity helps ensure the corporate containment of academic discourse. In an age when theory stresses the anonymity of writing, those writing theory are passionately bound to a system of celebrity where people may be encouraged to theorize anonymity, the dispersal of the subject in the community of signifiers, but not to practice it. The subject as a force of the ideological state apparatus, the author-function, is more dominant than ever. Put in another way, egomania, the founding neurosis of the Protestant ethic and the spirit of capitalism, not community, rules the day.

This rule has a precise historical trajectory to which Americanists in particular should be sensitive: the founding narratives of Protestant America lament the fall from a putative Christian community modeled on the communism of Christ and his disciples to the agon of possessive individualism, even as they recognize and violently oppose—a violence born of the ambivalence of nostalgia—the kinship-based communal economies of Native America. In the Southwest, to take a significant counter-example, the Pueblo and Navajo founding narratives do not begin with a fall from community but with an ascent to it, an emergence from the earth, and a communal will to maintain the ties of extended kinship that balance all relationships in the face of the constant crisis of community.

In the controversial Warren Beatty film *Bulworth*, there is a scene where Senator Bulworth sits down to face a panel of journalists for a televised question-and-answer session. The first thing the senator points out is that the corporate capital that is financing his campaign is the same capital that is paying the journalists before him. Thus what is staged as critical discourse and open debate is no more than a closed circuit of celebrity. This scene, it seems to me, is an apt figure for the possible future of American studies and for the political structures in which this future will take place. I suppose there is no need to remark that the future is now. And so the question for American studies at the present moment, as it imagines its future, is very much: how can we open up this closed circuit of capital in order to redistribute it to communities of need that are the foundation of both the discipline and the nation?

III

The national ideology of the United States at the present moment, which is emphatically governed by this closed circuit, the limits of capitalism's imagination, might be encapsulated in the credo: Granted that development is uneven, and parts of the world still require cultivation, everything is, nevertheless, essentially settled. History is over. Capitalism (also known as the free market, also known as democracy) is virtually triumphant, with its corollary that Marxism / communism / socialism(s) is dead.

The conflation in the national ideology of capitalism and democracy is crucial. The citizenry is not meant to think the possible contradictions between the two terms, because to recognize contradictions is to begin to think historically. In describing this ideology, I use the word *settled* because of its special resonance in the rhetoric of American ideology: the notion of settlement, in the sense of settling a "wilderness," creating plantations, which in the formative seventeenth century meant establishing a colony: Jamestown, Santa Fe, Plymouth, Massachusetts Bay. So, ideologically, the nation measures its currently settled state against this primal moment of settlement, before which it can only imagine the abyss of the unsettling, the darkness of "savagery," which typically takes communal forms, Native American kinship or socialist economies, for example.

This primal moment of settlement is grounded in two facts that the national ideology of settlement cannot contain and has persistently refused to address (of course that is the job of ideology, precisely not to address the crucial or to address it in a way that does not address it): the fact that U.S. settlement was and continues to be based on land stolen from Indians; the fact that U.S. settlement could not proceed without the slave labor of Africans. Today just as Indian lands are still engrossed by the federal government through a complex colonial legal system, and Indian tribes remain oxymoronically defined within this system as "domestic dependent nations," so black labor, liberated by the Civil War for the free market, continues to be exploited: undereducated, underpayed, ill-nourished and ill-housed. It is, of course, not the only exploited labor in this country; but it is the model for all exploited labor, just as the underdevelopment of Indian Country through the reservation system is the model for all underdevelopment. The inner city is a kind of reservation. This exploitation of Indian lands and black labor, not only in the United States but throughout the Americas, where indigenous labor has and continues to be exploited as well, finds its correlatives historically in the growing inequalities of wealth that are the principal product, nationally and internationally, of the free market.

The situation of primary and secondary education in the United States, and thus inescapably of postsecondary education as well, is a particular local expression of this global context of lack: the result, except on Indian reservations where the underfunding of education is a federal issue, of a radically discrepant property tax base, which is maintained through the persistent underdevelopment of particular urban and rural spaces, marked by boundaries of race and class. This underdevelopment is rationalized by a free market ideology, enforced by law, that separates issues of social justice from those of economy.

This separation, which interdicts a national discussion on the central issue of redistribution, is inscribed in the classic liberal ideology that underwrites the U.S. Constitution and is theorized so cogently in the Federalist Papers of Madison, Jay, and Hamilton, where the classic Federalist X argues, as noted, that "the first object of government" is to protect the natural "diversity" in "the faculties of men" that leads to an "unequal distribution of property." The paper condemns at its end as a "wicked project" the call for "an equal distribution of property" (411). Thus formative U.S. constitutional theory enshrines at once a system of political justice based on economic injustice. "We, the people" have not been able to think coherently about social justice since that time. The remarkable current similarity between the Democratic and Republican parties in their enthusiastic endorsement of corporate America and the free market—where, to reference two figureheads, does Ronald Reagan end and Bill Clinton begin?—is inscribed in the Lockean naturalization of property rights, the naturalization of the market, that Federalist X endorses. This endorsement amounts to the naturalization of fundamental inequality.

If we refuse to freeze the facts of stolen Indian land and exploited black labor in an ideological past (of the end of slavery, the fulfillment of civil rights, of most Americans' utter ignorance of the history or current state of Indian/U.S. relations) or in a dehistoricized multiculturalism, then we should find them profoundly unsettling. For they are here with us in that other nation in which we actually live. That nation in which nothing is settled. An Americas Cultural Studies program needs to address *that* unsettled nation, which I will now refer to as *this* nation. This nation, or, more precisely, inter-nation (to mark the imbrication of national boundaries with international entanglements), is framed by the central question that Fanon poses in *The Wretched of the Earth* in 1961: "What counts today, the question which is looming on the horizon, is the need for a redistribution of wealth. Humanity must reply to this question, or be shaken to pieces by it."[29] The horizon is here and the tremors have long since begun.

I am in the first place, then, suggesting the need for complex linkages around the issue of redistribution between certain disciplines within the university: African American studies, women's studies, Native American studies, and other ethnic, area, and regional studies, groups and programs, under the umbrella of Americas cultural studies. The common topic for dialogue, I would suggest, should be versions of community. For the idea of redistribution and its dynamic is communal, and what is lacking in this inter-nation is the theory and practice of a just community, though there are various communities within the inter-nation that have historically had such a theory and such a practice. Traditional American Indian communities, for example, where the basis of wealth, the land, has always been communal or kin-based, that is, the antithesis of property, which is inherently individu-alized and thus exclusive, come to mind immediately.

The curriculum that develops from such linkages would need to be one based in theory *and*, crucially, practice, not, I want to emphasize, the con-flation of theory *with* practice. Currently, to return to the beginnings of this essay, like the economic capital with which it is inseparably linked, cul-tural capital (knowledge) is in the hands of an elite and circulates exclusively through the interconnected channels of elite institutions, in which network the university occupies a key position. Because of material constraints, the Navajos with whom I work, for example, cannot, literally, gain independent access to the historical and legal documents that are dislocating their lives. Because of the impoverishment of their neighborhood, the students at West Philadelphia High School confront a radical lack of materials. We spent our grant money on buying books and subscribing to newspapers that the stu-dents could own.

The increasing corporatization of the university bears clear witness to this dynamic of power. An Americas cultural studies program, then, based in the university and supported by the corporate capital of the university, must nevertheless find ways to resist the corporatization of the university, which includes finding transformative ways of redistributing the cultural capital of the university to the community. The two examples of work at Navajo and in West Philadelphia High School are partial examples or figures for the kind of

Americas cultural studies program I have in mind: one that moves cultural capital out of the closed circuit of the university.

It is exceptionally important that this work not be conceived of as philanthropic or as a special part of the curriculum, as it is now, but that it be conceived of as political, as a model for the whole curriculum, which would have as its goal a transformation of fundamental relationships between all schools—primary, secondary, and postsecondary—in the community and between the community and its schools. There is no reason that research, its tools, and the leisure to do it should be the exclusive province of university academics; and, indeed, given the structures of alienation within academia that I have sketched, of a relatively small percentage of university academics at that. In a model of just community, the ability to do research must be redistributed throughout the community.

It is also exceptionally important in developing a community curriculum for an Americas cultural studies program that this curriculum not be dictated by the university to the community, but that it be developed by the community in dialogue with the university. The danger of traditional power taking over this dialogue and turning it into one more monologue of the rich to the poor is clear and present. Let me quote Hazel Carby here:

> We need to ask ourselves some serious questions about our culture and our politics. Is the emphasis on cultural diversity making invisible the politics of race in this increasingly segregated nation, and is the language of cultural diversity a convenient substitute for the political action needed to desegregate? . . . While the attention of faculty and administrators has been directed toward increasing the representation of different social groups in the curriculum or the college handbook, few alliances have been forged with substantial forces across this society that will significantly halt and reverse the declining numbers of black, working-class, and poor people among university student bodies or faculty.[30]

To emphasize a fundamental point, then: a great majority of the people represented in the academic discourses of multiculturalism, because of the unequal distribution of capital of all kinds that structures the inter-nation, cannot gain entry to the institutions, to the discourses, which are representing them. If these theories of multiculturalism do not turn themselves into praxis, then they will simply become what they already have in most cases—the newest academic formalism, the latest academic fashion, the discourses of celebrity.

I take it, then, that the future of American studies, if it is to have a future worth participating in, is to work for the entry of these constituencies into the university. But, decidedly, not the university as it is presently constituted as an arm of corporate capital; rather, the university radically redistributed throughout the community in forms that an Americas cultural studies curriculum must work to imagine and implement.

Notes

1   Ethan Bronner, "Universities Giving Less Financial Aid on Basis of Need," *New York Times*, 21 June 1998, 1.
2   Andrea Curry and Eric Newburger, "Educational Attainment in the United States (Update): March 2000," in *Current Population Reports*, ed. Bureau of the Census (Washington, D.C.: GPO, 2000).
3   Andrea Curry and Jennifer Day, "Educational Attainment in the United States: March 1997," in *Current Population Reports*, ed. Bureau of the Census (Washington, D.C.: GPO, 1998).
4   Cary Nelson, *Manifesto of a Tenured Radical* (New York: New York University Press, 1997). Subsequent references are cited parenthetically in the text.
5   Gregory S. Jay, *American Literature and the Culture Wars* (Ithaca, N.Y.: Cornell University Press, 1997), 57. Subsequent references are cited parenthetically in the text.
6   Michael Bérubé, *The Employment of English: Theory, Jobs, and the Future of Literary Studies* (New York: New York University Press, 1998), 22; emphasis added.
7   Linda Ray Pratt, "Going Public: Political Discourse and the Faculty Voice," in *Higher Education under Fire: Politics, Economics, and the Crisis of the Humanities*, ed. Michael Bérubé and Cary Nelson (New York: Routledge, 1995), 36. Subsequent references are cited parenthetically in the text.
8   Lawrence W. Levine, *The Opening of the American Mind: Canons, Culture, and History* (Boston: Beacon, 1996), 32; emphasis added.
9   Michael Bérubé, "It's Renaissance Time: New Historicism, American Studies, and American Identity," in *Public Access: Literary Theory and American Cultural Politics* (London: Verso, 1994), 219.
10 Darrell Watchman, ed., *Navajo Nation 1997 Close-Up Program* (Window Rock, Ariz.: Navajo Nation, Division of Education, 1997); Bureau of the Census, *We, the First Americans* prepared by U.S. Dept. of Commerce, Economics and Statistics Administration, Bureau of the Census (Washington, D.C.: GPO, 1993).
11 Eric Cheyfitz, "The Navajo-Hopi Land Dispute: A Brief History," *Interventions: International Journal of Postcolonial Studies* 2, no. 2 (2000): 248–75.

12 "Report Card on the Schools," *Philadelphia Enquirer*, 20 September 1998; "A District in Distress," *Philadelphia Enquirer*, 23 October 1994. Subsequent references are cited parenthetically in the text.

13 Louis Althusser, "Ideology and Ideological State Apparatuses (Notes towards an Investigation)," in *Essays on Ideology* (London: Verso, 1971), 36.

14 Paul Lauter, *Canons and Contexts* (New York: Oxford University Press, 1991), 230. Subsequent references are cited parenthetically in the text. Stanley Aronowitz suggests that what we term the *corporatization* of the university has its beginnings in the first part of the twentieth century, marked by Thorstein Veblen's *The Higher Learning in America: A Memorandum on the Conduct of Universities by Businessmen* (1918; New Brunswick, N.J.: Transaction, 1993). Aronowitz, "Academic Unionism and the Future of Higher Education," in *Will Teach for Food: Academic Labor in Crisis*, ed. Cary Nelson (Minneapolis: University of Minnesota Press, 1997), 194–95. The Veblen is decidedly prescient and reminds us that the corporatization of the university begins with the development of the modern (late nineteenth-century) university itself. Indeed, Bill Readings's *The University in Ruins* (Cambridge, Mass.: Harvard University Press, 1996), while cogent in certain ways, could have benefited from Veblen's historical understanding, a component Readings's analysis lacks.

15 Paul Lauter, " 'Political Correctness' and the Attack on American Colleges," in *Higher Education under Fire*, ed. Bérubé and Nelson, 80.

16 Eric Cheyfitz, "Redistribution and the Transformation of American Studies," in *Critical Theory and the Teaching of Literature: Politics, Curriculum, Pedagogy*, ed. James F. Slevin and Art Young (Urbana, Ill.: National Council of Teachers of English, 1996), 116–17.

17 James Madison, "The Federalist X," in *The Debate on the Constitution: Federalist and Antifederalist Speeches, Articles, and Letters during the Struggle over Ratification*, ed. Bernard Bailyn (New York: Library of America, 1993), 405–6. Subsequent references are cited parenthetically in the text.

18 Eric Foner, "Common Origins, Different Paths," *Radical History Review* 71 (1998): 7. Subsequent references are cited parenthetically in the text.

19 Nelson appears to be referring to adjunct teaching; but even if he is, and his syntax is ambiguous (perhaps intentionally so), his statement remains outlandish. Nelson's candidate statement was forwarded to me through e-mail on September 16, 1998. The originating address is: hjulien@email.GC.Cuny.edu.

20 I want to thank Paula Bennett for providing me with this description of conditions at second-tier schools. My understanding of the tier system in higher education comes from Stanley Aronowitz, "Academic Unionism," 188–89.

21 Corey Robin and Michelle Stephens, "Against the Grain: Organizing TAs at Yale," in *Will Teach for Food*, ed. Nelson, 53.

22 Kathy M. Newman, "Poor, Hungry, and Desperate? Or, Privileged, Histrionic, and Demanding? In Search of the True Meaning of 'Ph.D.,' " in *Will Teach for Food*, ed. Nelson, 120.

23 In 1998 I referenced this e-mail at http://kuhttp.cc.ukans.edu/cwis/organi-
    zations/aegis/public__html/yaleinf2.html, which is no longer extant.

24 Andrew Ross, "The Labor behind the Cult of Work," in *Will Teach for Food*,
    ed. Nelson, 142.

25 Eric Cheyfitz, "What Work Is There for Us to Do? American Literary Study
    or Americas Cultural Studies?" *American Literature* 67 (1995): 843–53.

26 Jane Buck, "The President's Report: Successes, Setbacks, and Contingent
    Labor," *Academe: Bulletin of the American Association of University Professors* 87,
    no. 5 (2001): 18–21.

27 Walter Benjamin, "The Work of Art in the Age of Mechanical Reproduc-
    tion," in *Illuminations*, ed. Hannah Arendt, trans. Harry Zohn (New York:
    Schocken, 1969), 231.

28 Henry Louis Gates Jr., "Net Worth," *New Yorker*, 1 June 1998, 57–58. Subse-
    quent references are cited parenthetically in the text.

29 Frantz Fanon, *The Wretched of the Earth*, trans. Constance Farrington (New
    York: Grove, 1963), 98.

30 Hazel V. Carby, "The Multicultural Wars," *Radical History Review* 54 (1992):
    13–14.

Nation dot com

AMERICAN STUDIES AND THE PRODUCTION

OF THE CORPORATIST CITIZEN

Russ Castronovo

Thinking about Futures

With at least some of its origins in a folksy research practice that encouraged scholars to pause before tombstones in rural graveyards, to finger cotton fabrics spun long ago at textile mills, in short, to examine the materials of history, American studies has lent important institutional and intellectual support to textured, and often thickly descriptive cultural investigations of the national past. In part because of this strength, however, American studies has not always excelled in understanding the future, particularly its own futures as a discipline. Though the price of articulating analyses of America that attend to popular knowledges, countermemories, and nontraditional practices need not entail the sacrifice of metacritical reflection about the organizing principles central to this interdisciplinary field, critics have charged that American studies tends to operate with theoretical blindness. An undiscriminating humanism, according to Jeffrey Louis Decker, "has been the primary theoretical presupposition in American Studies."[1] For Michael Denning, this ascendancy impoverishes the impact that other theoretical perspectives—most notably ones informed by Marxist analysis—can have on the field.[2] Such objections, in essence, are not new; as Paul Giles contends, the "complaint about an apparent absence of theoretical self-consciousness has been a long-standing issue within the American Studies World."[3]

The essays collected in this volume implicitly engage this critique by presenting readings that inevitably invite varying degrees of self-critical reflection about the futures of American studies as a professional, pedagogical, and intellectual enterprise. For the moment, however, I would like to consider this endeavor within the framework of commodities speculation such as when we invest in livestock futures, hoping that pork bellies purchased for twenty-five dollars will soon fetch thirty dollars. What, then, does it mean for us as academic professionals to trade in American studies futures? Given the current state of the humanities in higher education, even the most sanguine teachers and scholars among us might be wise to search for intellectual invest- ments with better track records than American studies. But such thinking overlooks the way in which the interdisciplinary character of American stud- ies offers the university a corporate model that recombines departmental divisions and maximizes faculty resources in unexpected and highly produc- tive ways. Those who do not see American studies futures as a sound, diversi- fied opportunity in these days of a bearish humanities market fail to recognize that student-consumers have been gobbling up seats in American studies courses. From modest projections of student enrollments, we can conclude that college administrators are likely to continue their support of American studies programs. Portfolios from around the country provide encouraging data: enrollments in American studies at DePaul University have experi- enced dramatic increase; Berkeley's recently inaugurated American cultures program already boasts three hundred majors; American studies at UC Santa Cruz, which first became a major in 1987, had become the most popular undergraduate major by 1992; Washington State University has built a stead- ily growing American studies program, especially at the graduate level.[4] The futures of American studies look good.

Although American studies may be performing above market expecta- tions in the humanities, we need to assess the sociopolitical impact that these commodities futures have on the intellectual landscape of higher learning, especially in its most public representations and uses. In this regard Richard Dienst's analysis of the futures market and globalized capital has particular relevance for American studies: if "axioms of 'productivity' and 'competi- tiveness' are more than just keywords of economic success" and "have now been enshrined as the only abiding civic virtues," what then do we make of the institutional and academic success of American studies?[5] This ques- tion becomes even more pointed when we consider that the discipline has achieved this success, in part, by fostering investigations that critically address the role of U.S. nationalism in the Americas. Are cultural studies of national- ism, especially as it impacts women, ethnic minorities, indigenous peoples, and the working classes, the resource that have made American studies pro- ductive and competitive? The success of American studies is not a purely academic matter; rather, it is a trend that emerges as part of the university's deepening corporate consciousness. Superadded to significant material sup- port that the private sector lends to science and technology research on college campuses, the university has studiously retooled the humanities as a site of preprofessional training. American studies, especially in its self-advertisement in college catalog statements and program descriptions, leads the way to this new educational frontier by promising to teach students the stuff "first-world" workers and consumers need to know about the global reach of national culture.

Within a corporatist conception of liberal education, American studies operates as a practical wing of a humanities curriculum often derided as having little connection to the real world. This business sense allows American studies to represent itself as a competitive university division, skilled in producing students able to reconcile national citizenship with the pressures of globalism. At first glance, this tension between the "America" of American studies and globalism seems both innovative and salutary. Attention to border crossings, minority cultures, and international contexts have unsettled and displaced once ascendant narratives of scholarship and teaching that had structured American studies as a place of exceptionalism, Cold War consensus, and boundary regulation. And yet, has the death of the nation been exaggerated? An American studies for the twenty-first century invites cross-cultural challenges in our curricula, teaching, and research, but does it do so at the risk of ignoring the abiding force of the nation? Critical senses of nationalism—including trans-, post-, and international perspectives—integrated into American studies represent significant contributions in the field for thinking beyond the geopolitical culture of the United States. But in terms of the administrative and public representation of American studies, these perspectives also dutifully align with the economic and integrationist objectives of the nation-state.

Decades before Clark Kerr spoke of higher education in the United States as "a prime instrument of national purpose," the university had long seemed the ideal propagator and storehouse of national pedagogy.[6] According to Richard Ohmann, Harvard's president held in 1869 that academia had a certain "utility to the state," while later down the road at Princeton, Woodrow Wilson "called for universities to serve the nation" (298, 286). This line of ideological justification remained intact at least until 1976 when Ohmann published *English in America*, a polemic that hinges in part on the contention that even courses as politically innocuous as freshman English provide a preprofessional setting where students acquire habits and skills deemed useful "to needs of the industrial state and its governing class" (94).[7] But in an era when capital has become increasingly global and when national identity has become in part increasingly postnational, can we still be assured that the university is the handmaiden of the nation-state? In his provocatively entitled *The University in Ruins* (1996), Bill Readings responds with an emphatic "no" as he considers this question: "The economics of globalization mean that the University is no longer called upon to train citizen subjects, while the politics of the end of the Cold War mean that the University is no longer called upon to uphold national prestige by producing and legitimating national culture. . . . the University is no longer primarily an ideological arm of the nation-state but an autonomous bureaucratic corporation."[8] It is indeed difficult to identify the precise moment during the twenty years that separate Ohmann's critique from Readings's when the university found the moribund form of the nation-state obsolete to its mission and purpose. This difficulty arises from the fact that no such moment exists because no such death has occurred. Rather, the nation has been displaced, not in the sense of being outmoded, but in the sense of shedding its restrictive connection to place and adapting to economic conditions and cultural influences that no longer stop at borders.

The nation—and most especially the educational apparatus of the American nation—remains central to globalization. "After I studied in the States," said Hasung Jang, a professor of finance at Korea University, "I saw that there was no other way. I accept free markets. There is only one way to organize an economy and it will dominate the world."[9] Coming in the context of a 1998 *New York Times Magazine* piece about the crisis in Asian markets, Jang's comments are used to suggest that this "one way" will be the American way. Entitled "The World's Biggest Out-of-Business Sale," the essay unabashedly gloats over the sluggish economies of the Asian "tigers" and heralds the decline as a golden opportunity to infuse the Pacific Rim with American capital and ideologies. Laden with appreciation for mythic individualism and sharp Yankee business dealings, the national rhetoric here underscores Tom Nairn's observation that a "transnational market economy finally captured the globe, but no accompanying metamorphosis of nations was permitted."[10] It is at this level of rhetoric that we witness the articulation of asymmetrical connections between economy and academic discipline: as with global markets that know no borders but still depend on nation-states to provide frames of law and stability, so, too, American studies fails to confine its inquiries to the geographic limits of the United States, even as it depends on "America" as an organizing methodological principle. At a discursive level, American studies practice resonates with the cross-cultural and fluid style of American business practice. Implicit in this orientation is an awareness of the nation's recrudescence in a global guise, and it is this recognition that most profoundly accounts for the success and popularity of an interdisciplinary field that teaches students how to behave as national citizens in a global era.

"A certain 'Americanization,' " comments Readings, "moves the University further away from direct ties to the nation-state" (4). This argument enables us to understand why the nation may not matter to the university as it once did in the bicentennial year that saw the publication of Ohmann's *English in America*. Even so, I want to argue that the case of American studies demonstrates that the nation still matters to the university—but in ways that now seem to have little stake in either promoting or questioning the well-worn parameters of U.S. exceptionalism. For within movements of transnational capital and multinational business concerns, the United States cannot afford to think of itself as an exception. Instead its citizens have to recognize that, like markets, they, too, are international. Nevertheless, this incipient cosmopolitanism is offset by persistent senses of national attachment; as Pheng Cheah observes, "economic transnationalism . . . is often U.S. economic nationalism in global guise."[11] The nation, despite Readings's claims to the contrary, has not become anachronistic to the university's mission, though it has been estranged and dislocated, forced to compete under global pressures.

Here's where American studies enters the picture, a picture redrawn in much more ambiguous ways by international contexts and multicultural affiliations. As a field that lacks firm disciplinary borders, American studies fosters senses of dislocated national identity produced and demanded by global markets. At the public and administrative levels of interdisciplinary justification, American studies suggests that it educates national citizens for international settings by teaching them that American identities are not exceptional but instead are always enmeshed, not in a corporate society, but in a corporate world. While American studies addresses issues of community, ethnicity, marginalization, and pluralism, it is also always implicitly talking about incorporation as a mode of belonging that makes us feel at home within the workplace, the nation-state, and the world at large—all at the same time. This simultaneity of comfort shapes the utopian paradox of American studies as a boundaryless discipline where cross-cultural study and postnational impulses remain underwritten by the nation-state.[12]

Promises of utopian futures rest very much on a technology of incorporation that privileges a flexible community of adaptable citizens. Nathaniel Hawthorne's novel of one such utopian community, *The Blithedale Romance*, acts as a critical prehistory of an American studies future that I want to address. But first it is necessary to examine the not so critical prehistories of open, porous, interdisciplinary community that colleges and universities tell in their presentations of American studies to prospective students. Especially in program and departmental descriptions found along the World Wide Web, American studies self-consciously portrays itself as an arena of instant, universal access that as a field of study reconciles feelings of national belonging with the realities of border traffic, global commerce, and transnational identity.

A Prehistory of the Future

As American studies proclaims itself a porous and flexible multidiscipline resistant to academic border patrols, it nonetheless remains consistent with ideals of national incorporation. Consider this passage from Patricia Nelson Limerick's 1996 presidential address to the ASA: "Thank heavens, then, for American studies: the place of refuge for those who cannot find a home in the more conventional neighborhood, the sanctuary for displaced hearts and minds, the place where *no one* is fully at ease. And here is the glory of the ASA: since *no one* feels fully at ease, no one has the right or the power to make anyone else feel *less* at ease. . . . The joy of American studies is precisely in its lack of firm limits and borders."[13] Limerick offers a post–Cold War narrative: disciplinary curtains that once legitimated standoffs between academic departments as well as sustained professional hierarchies are, like the Berlin Wall, crumbling in the face of a benign onslaught of Whitmanesque inclusivity. In the wake of this chilly academic détente, American studies arises as a Statue of Liberty of higher education offering "sanctuary" for the "displaced" and "refuge" for the intellectually homeless. Beneath these rhapsodic tones, however, lies an entrenched narrative of national administration. American studies prepares us for a boundaryless world by offering scholars, in Limerick's terms, a type of migrant identity, but it does so in ways that remain perfectly consistent with Americanist rhetoric. The utopian impulse that lies within promises of academic equality and a professional kindness toward strangers privileges a rootlessness that gives way to incorporation. Utopia is generally a nice aim, but too often in U.S. contexts utopia has proven coincident with the goal of articulating the community as a state where all belong because all are forced to belong. The "glory" of American studies is that it has a pedagogy directed to the future; its agenda is to educate our students how to identify as citizens of the nation-state.

No doubt this pedagogy, as I'm describing it, seems the relic of an earlier era—like some deserted factory from the Rust Belt—when the U.S. economy still seemed to enjoy vitality and strength at home. Thus one could well object at this point and argue, quite correctly, that significant scholarship in American studies has challenged precisely this narrative, aggressively resituating this field in a "global context" informed by "critical internationalism," as Jane Desmond and Virginia Dominguez have done.[14] Prompted by Donald Pease's injunction to reconfigure "the national narrative" as a "*post*national" set of stories, Carolyn Porter stresses the need to interrogate assumptions that "the nation itself is the basic unit of, and frame for, analysis."[15] Yet even as research and course curricula disperse the field among Asian, African, Native American studies as well as among discourses of Latin America and the Pacific Rim, much of the official apparatus of American studies clings to ideologies of the nation-state. Certainly the narrative has been modernized but has it been un-imagined, not so that it has a different future but so that it has an alternative prehistory? Can American studies operate beneath or before the impulse to incorporate? At a time before utopian project and national ultimatum converge, at a space beneath the linkage of multinational capital with liberal conceptions of citizenship, we need a prehistory of American studies that addresses the corporatist pedagogy that encourages belonging. This prehistory, notably, might examine the material effects of American studies 101 as a venture that seeks to retool students as national citizens able to compete in a postindustrial world of globalized capital.

Although projects to make American studies transnational reveal this generic introductory course as antiquated, such efforts often underestimate the enduring links between corporate capital, national incorporation, and education. In its most public guises, American studies imagines corporatist citizens with the desire to belong. The World Wide Web—by its very name— would seem hostile to this regressive narrative of American studies as national discipline. When I went out voyaging along the Web, however, I came back laden with imperatives of the nation-state. By double-clicking on home pages for American studies programs, browsers of this public yet corporate medium learn that, while an interdisciplinary curriculum tests the borders of the nation, it also expands that nation in order to produce citizens adaptable to changing economic conditions. In my travels along the Web I found two disjunctures. First, American studies on the Web is not the same as American studies in the classroom. The research and teaching that many of us perform, radically conflict with public representations of American studies transmitted via computer technology. Second, though the Web may be worldwide, it is also provincial, always returning the user to a bureaucratic pluralism that explains why the multicultural nature of American studies coheres to national pedagogy. While such disjunctures might appear as evidence that what Pease calls the "field-imaginary" or "disciplinary unconscious" of American studies is deeply split, they more accurately point to the regulatory existence of a disciplinary conscious, of an administrative imaginary out of step with the field-imaginary.[16] That is, what we imagine about the field of American studies, specifically in our classrooms and scholarship, conflicts with institutional and administrative priorities found in public representations of American studies. Still the term *administrative imaginary* is imprecise, not simply because we may doubt whether administrators have imaginations, but because administration justifies intellectual pursuits and curricular innovations as moments of national pedagogy, a strategy that has the material consequence of repressing the disciplinary unconscious. Instead of an administrative imaginary, we need to speak of an *administrative materiality* that governs the field-imaginary of American studies.[17]

College and university home pages on the World Wide Web neatly package the administrative materiality of American studies. "What does it mean to be an American?"—this is the question that leads off the program description at DePaul University. The answer lies not in the question Crèvecoeur first posed in 1782. Nor does integrative attention to "literature, history, geography, and politics" that is the stock in trade of interdisciplinary methodology provide an answer. Both responses are insufficient because this question is not so much a question as it as an advertisement for "an excellent major" that provides skills and training for professional life in a diversified workplace. Pondering the meaning of Americanness makes good business sense and thus American studies appeals to "students seeking careers . . . [in] public relations, advertising and marketing, public policy administration, law . . . historic preservation, business, teaching, or public policy."[18] San Diego State University adds to this list, identifying "international business," "law enforcement," and "government service" as career pathways blazed by this interdisciplinary major.[19] Denaturalizing national narratives have opened our field to complex questions that sever "America" from the United States by encouraging cross-cultural investigations that traverse national borders. At the same time, this critical perspective has also opened an array of new opportunities in the global marketplace for students destined to become workers. In an essay on making American studies transnational, Paul Giles writes that "the increasingly unstable nature of national identities may create its own opportunities for the future development of American Studies" (339). Administrative materiality, however, has no problem with this instability because it reads the demand in American studies futures as a matter of economic development: thus San Diego State's home page informs browsers that "business and teaching professions in foreign countries welcome American studies majors who can help them understand the way business and social life are conducted in the United States." National pedagogy prepares citizens for a globalism whose purpose is not to decenter and ideologically remap the United States but to make the rest of the unstable world understand American business better.

"What Can You Do with an American Studies Degree" is the title of one page at the University of Alabama Web site. After offering a range of job opportunities that includes "corporate consultants" and "old-fashioned entrepreneurs," the authors admit that they have asked the wrong question: "The real question is this: what can't you do with an American Studies major?" The accompanying photograph of smiling, tasseled graduates at May 1997 graduation doesn't offer an explicit answer, but the beaming faces suggest that these American studies majors have followed tips on how "to increase your marketability" provided on this page, and now face a future of limitless possibility and promotion.[20] While this question appears so rich as to defy a simple answer of three or four career choices, I want to suggest that quite possibly one thing you can't do with an American studies major is not be a national citizen. Can we un-imagine American studies so that we can have identities beneath and before that of citizen? I am not advocating disenfranchisements that would make us noncitizens; instead, I am wondering if we can become non-national citizens. Instead of narrow senses of citizenship tied to the linkages between financial corporations and the nation-state, I would like to see an American studies that proliferates citizenship across multiple levels (the local, regional, activist, social, pan-national, cosmopolitan) so as to offer strategic identities for confronting pedagogies of incorporation.[21]

Although I want to reiterate that these Web site narratives do not correspond to the work we see ourselves performing as teachers and scholars, this thinking about American studies futures as a national economic question underpins some of the broader ideological justifications for the cross-cultural study of America. For Patricia Nelson Limerick, the focus that our discipline brings to the struggles of racial, ethnic, and sexual minorities becomes a prime resource of U.S. postindustrial society: "In our times, developed nations may not be doing too well in industrial productivity, but their productivity in ethnogenesis is extraordinary. If only we could include new cultures and new ethnicities in the Gross National Product, the American GNP would gain a new vitality" (465). Clearly Limerick's fanciful scenario is not meant to be taken seriously, though her desire to see aliens and outsiders valued represents an important political commitment. Still, her statement hinges on a rhetoric of interpellation that accepts the nation as the ultimate collective arena for citizenship. The administrative materiality that privileges economic evidence and marketplace metaphors bolsters utopian visions of a nation able to respond to the entropic fragmentation of diversity, of a nation able to integrate as much *pluribus* as possible into the *unum* of the state. According to Sean Wilentz in an essay entitled "Integrating Ethnicity into American Studies," the field helps combat the "fear . . . that a fixation on ethnic differences presents a distorted picture of the United States as a country that is all 'pluribus' and no 'unum.' "[22] Interdisciplinarity thus becomes an ideal strategy for articulating the utopian dimensions of national pedagogy spelled out along the Web. As one college home page puts it, "Programs in American Studies rest on the belief that a nation's culture is a unified whole, so that the student's studies must not be restricted to the boundaries of any one discipline."[23] Methodology serves as ideology: the contradiction of studying national culture in an era of transnationalism becomes a coherent endeavor as American studies enables the humanities and its students to enter the discourse of global markets without sacrificing identities tied to state apparatuses.

And what makes ideological sense can turn a profit. The integrative pluralism found in Limerick's presidential address and Wilentz's essay, wonderfully echoed by descriptions of integrative methodology along the World Wide Web, accounts for the competitive edge that American studies brings to the university. American studies is the sign that liberal education keeps pace with the corporate world. Not simply a matter of intellectual position, scholarly attention to diversity mirrors corporate attention to racial, ethnic, and gender identities as desirable assets. "For the business world it's multiculturalism or die," writes Stanley Fish.[24] Though diversity in academic culture certainly differs from diversity in corporate culture, we should not ignore associations of multiculturalism with flexibility, broadened horizons, and unity in each context. Nor should we overlook the fact that the university is tied to and even structured like a corporation. At the University of

Minnesota, critical concern and respect for "pluralist cultures" is precisely what makes American studies one of the "strongest and most well-known *assets* in the humanities."[25] As part of what Avery Gordon calls "diversity management," the U.S. workplace values multicultural identity as a means of managing difference and producing unity among employees. "If you thought you had to leave your cultural identity at home," explains Gordon, "now you're expected to contribute it generously to the corporate mission."[26] Thus when home pages for American studies programs speak of the necessity of approaching "American culture as a whole" and studying "the core values of American culture," the World Wide Web is advertising the ability of this multidiscipline to teach a consensual and unifying ethic that is so highly prized by corporate culture.[27] Talk of intellectual investment, educational capital, and national belonging that pervades academic Web sites, not to mention Limerick's presidential address, predicts bright days for American studies by reading the academic future as an economic forecast and evaluating interdisciplinary learning as a market strategy where the humanities are the commodity that is being traded.

Even programs that explicitly situate curricula in non-national contexts return to pedagogies of the nation-state. My home university stresses how proximity to the Caribbean and Latin America demands an orientation geared toward consideration of "the United States in the wider context of the Americas." But on scrolling down, one finds that a national focus reasserts itself by listing courses in the American presidency and American movie genres as the backbone of the major.[28] In similar fashion, the University of Hawai'i states that its "cross-cultural dimension" reaches out to the Pacific and Asia and thus "differentiates it significantly from most other programs in the field." And yet we read that this "cross-cultural dimension" prepares students for a range of careers including "business administration," "government service," and "travel industry management." Here, administrative material reality seems ignorant of other nationalisms and excessive to U.S. nationalism, most notably the Hawaiian nationalism of University of Hawai'i faculty member Haunani Kay Trask whose scathing critiques of the tourism industry underpin demands for island sovereignty.[29] On the World Wide Web, administrative materiality triumphs over the field-imaginary.

Dead Citizens of Past Utopias

In the face of the insistent narratives of the nation-state, critics such as Michael Cowan, Amy Kaplan, Carolyn Porter, and Virginia Dominguez and Jane Desmond advocate approaches and methodologies that discard the nation as the organizing principle. Porter, for instance, calls for "cultural work [that] invites us to join in developing a field-imaginary that might enable us and our students to see beyond 'Our America' to that other America 'which is not ours'" (521).[30] Significantly, this effort to shape the field-imaginary can structure administrative materiality; the home page for American culture at UC Berkeley "recognizes that political, cultural and economic patterns do not stop at national borders" but are instead framed by "larger world systems."[31] Such critiques imagine a perhaps radically different future for American studies, suggesting how the field can implement a pedagogy resistant to economic and administrative imperatives that structure public representations of the discipline. I want to take a different tack, however, working backward to the origins of this academic community as part of a paradoxical search for non-national citizenship within a scholarly paradigm oriented around the nation-state. At "www.brown.edu" we learn that the "Department of American Civilization . . . was founded in 1945."[32] This chronology, however, locates the birth of institutional American studies at a moment when nuclear weaponry confirmed the worldwide hegemony of the American state in ghastly terms. Reaching still further back, in 1942, Princeton established American studies "in response to the perception among faculty and students that (in their own words) 'many educated Americans have in their education been cut off from a clear understanding of the traditions of their country.'"[33] Chronology provides cohesion and continuity: in this case, "www.princeton.edu" supplies the foundational narrative that interdepartmental study offers an answer to disintegrating national identity.

Dissatisfied with these actual origins, I found myself in pursuit of more mythic—but no less real—beginnings of a utopian project called American studies. This fictional department has a diverse faculty with interests in African American and Native American studies, regionalism and religion, Puritanism and women's studies. Or, in the terms Nathaniel Hawthorne uses in *The Blithedale Romance* to describe this interdisciplinary gathering bent on twin ideals of pluralism and homogeneity: "Among them was an Indian chief . . . a Bavarian broom-girl, a negro of the Jim Crow order, one or two foresters of the middle-ages, a Kentucky woodsman in trimmed hunting-shirt and deerskin leggings, and a Shaker elder, quaint, demure, broad-brimmed, and square-skirted. . . . Arm in arm, or otherwise huddled to-gether, in strange discrepancy, stood Puritans, gay Cavaliers, and Revolution-ary officers . . . [and a] renowned old witch of Lynn broomstick in hand."[34] Diversity on Blithedale Farm is only simulacra in which members from a white leisure class dress up in this garb of the historically marginalized as easily as they wear their own costumes of the enfranchised. The masquerade at the heart of this scene anticipates the critique of American studies as a place where white students can "do" ethnic studies. Furthermore, the peaceful cooperation that finds Puritans and Cavaliers "arm in arm" and indigenous peoples lounging alongside white settlers marks a prototypical rendition of the worldwide narrative of American studies in which increased economic opportunity reconciles the antagonistic diversity among us all. Only by for-getting historical specificity can this version of American studies promote interdisciplinary community; only by theatricalizing material differences can Blithedale script a unified social drama.

Undoubtedly, my implementation of *The Blithedale Romance* adheres to traditional disciplinary hierarchies within interdisciplinarity that continue to privilege the literary artifact, and even returns us to early formations of American studies that took New England as the extent of America. But because it offers commentary on social and economic techniques that foster belonging, specifically in the formation and fragmentation of one utopian community, Hawthorne's novel enables an analysis of the primordial obses-sion with incorporation that continues to pervade the future of American studies. After all, in this representation of a utopian collective Hawthorne is writing about a joint-stock company, a subject that allows him to unveil resonant overlaps between incorporation as the coming together of citizens and corporations as business entities. This overlap is felt as much on Blithe-dale Farm as it is in American studies: in each context, the capacity to labor, whether it is to perform agricultural tasks that enrich the rural collective or to find a career that takes part in the economy of the nation-state, guarantees citizenship. Using *Blithedale* as a critical lens to evaluate the stress that Ameri-can studies places on the multiple senses of incorporation suggests the need for articulating an interdisciplinary methodology that includes possibilities of non-national citizenship. This project, then, may help those of us caught within the web of public, administrative, and technological representations of American studies to recognize the importance of declaring, along with Hawthorne's narrator at the end of "The Custom-House," that "I am a citizen of somewhere else."[35]

The imagined community of Blithedale, according to Hawthorne's narrator, Miles Coverdale, is designed to give voice to "blithe tones of brotherhood" by breaking with "the weary tread-mill of the established system" (12, 19). While "brotherhood" is hardly a nefarious project, Coverdale's catachrestic use of a "tread-mill" to represent society betrays how the utopian goal is antithetical to contexts of work and labor. The reformers seek "brotherhood" by forgetting, rather than addressing, any conditions that inevitably clash with such idealistic "tones." They pretend that class differences do not exist, even though the first common meal that seats dandies from town next to laborers from the field creates an "oppressive" awkwardness (25). This affected annihilation of class consciousness surfaces in the history of Brook Farm, the socialist community that Hawthorne joined and later took as a model for Blithedale. In an invitation for Emerson to buy into this endeavor at collective reform, Brook Farm's founder, George Ripley, drew attention to inequities of labor only to resolve these by subtly forgetting them: "Our objects, as you know, are to insure a more natural union between intellectual and manual labor than now exists; to combine the thinker and the worker, as far as possible, in the same individual; to guarantee the highest mental freedom, adapted to their tastes and talents . . . to do away with the necessity of menial services. . . . Thought would preside over the operations of labor, and labor would contribute to the expansion of thought; we should have industry without drudgery, and true equality without vulgarity."[36] Although Ripley desires to bridge a social gulf, his language remains elitist, suspicious of the physicality of labor, or, as he calls it, "drudgery" and "vulgarity." Couched in terms that continue to reify humans on the basis of work, Ripley's vision adheres to typical assumptions about workers who do not think and intellectuals who do not work. Citizens tethered to a "tread-mill" have no time to meditate on "brotherhood." When Brook Farm drafted a constitution in 1844, the language of universalism made the forgetting of class consciousness and economic grievances complete: "from this document . . . we propose a radical and universal reform, rather to redress any particular wrong or remove the sufferings of any single class of human beings" (qtd. in Sams 96). Transcending the material particulars of oppressed groups, the associationists sought to ignore difference and obviate historically based inequities that cause a "single class" to be singled out as an unequal sharer in the circulation of goods, resources, and social justice.

At first glance, American studies defies narratives of the universal. Its interdisciplinary soul is often taken as evidence of an innovative approach that provides multiple angles on particulars of race, gender, ethnicity, and class. On closer inspection, however, this aim and methodology resemble the universalist objectives promulgated at Brook Farm. The attention to diversity within American studies congeals into the utopian promise of corporate culture. By studying difference, our students can all become the same in at least one respect—they will all have the opportunity to become employed. American studies teaches students how to manage diversity so that, in the words of Gordon, "individual differences are, like the market itself, assets for growth if not for liberation itself" (5). Such potentially profitable invocations of difference may perhaps revitalize the American GNP as Limerick suggests, adding to the cultural capital of the nation while preparing students for the challenges and resources of a multiethnic professional class. But what remains in question is the degree to which a workplace utopia impoverishes history.

Utopia allows only a thin, anemic past. At Blithedale, pluralism is possible only because the "Indian chief" and the "negro of the Jim Crow order" lack corporeal, historical depth since they are in actuality well-to-do white citizens assuming identities of white working-class people pretending to be marginalized figures in American history. Within this doubly mediated facade, Blithedale orchestrates the image of an egalitarian theater where the equal opportunity to work at producing fictive identities makes hierarchies of race and class irrelevant. There is more than enough work to go around, especially when the work itself is sublimated, in Hawthorne's words, as "the spiritualization of labor" (65). All can find jobs; employment provides the collective grist that manages the community's diversity. Blithedale thus anticipates the powerful promise of unity that's at the heart of American studies on the Web, where a range of career options equally awaits students. No matter the particular path—literature, history, ethnic studies, film—that students pursue in this interdisciplinary major, regardless of one's intellectual (or corporeal) history, all are marketable. Pluralism becomes a matter of economic opportunity. As one university Web page states, "A degree in American Studies is an *investment* that will serve your interests well. . . . Do what you love and the money will follow."[37] Incorporation (in a communal sense) depends on corporations (in a business sense). Student-consumers emerge as student-products, assuming the role of corporatist citizens. Though enmeshed in a metaphoric economic-statist body, the corporatist citizen suffers a loss of body, particularly the experiences, connections, and memories of what Marx called "species-being." As Robyn Wiegman argues, only through "dis-corporation" do subjects become citizens.[38]

Equally important in this context are Wiegman's remarks about an integrationist strategy that substitutes the veneer of representation for the plenitude of embodied history. In other words, "a negro of the Jim Crow order" stands in for the more complex presence of African bodies and labor in the United States. As Wiegman explains, an "integrationist aesthetic works by apprehending political equality as coterminous with representational presence, thereby undermining political analyses that pivot on the exclusion, silence, or invisibility of various groups and their histories" (117). Erasure of one's history—especially as it recalls identities compromised by contexts of poverty and sexuality—stands as the only entrance requirement to the Blithedale American studies program. Priscilla, for instance, is incorporated into the community because she refuses to manifest any corporeal history. The Blithedalers accept her precisely on the condition that none inquire about her past. As a spirit-medium, her disdain for the earthly permits her to chat with the dead; in political terms, her disembodiment identifies her as what Lauren Berlant describes as the "unhistorical little girl" who enjoys a life of dead citizenship. "Dead citizenship" Berlant explains, "haunts the shadow-land of national culture. . . . In the fantasy world of national culture, citizens aspire to dead identities—constitutional personhood in its public-sphere abstraction."[39] Coverdale has so fallen in love with dead citizenship that his political thoughts border on a type of necro-ideology. He seeks to make Zenobia iconic, nullifying the specificity that lends depth to her grievances, desires, and betrayals. "She is reduced by Coverdale to a disembodied idea—woman incarnate, the enigma of femininity," writes Elisabeth Bronfen.[40] Coverdale desires to see this woman humbled, attending to her soul's enfranchisement rather than her body's empowerment. When he pulls her drowned corpse from the river, he quickly interprets her appearance, musculature, and posture—all her corporeal attributes—as proof that even a person committed to cultural criticism, as is Zenobia, will abandon social agitation and at last find repose and harmony. His hope is that in death Zenobia will transcend the need to act politically. In life she protests women's circumscribed roles, but now as a frozen icon she conveys a very different message: "Her arms had grown rigid in the act of struggling, and were bent before her, with clenched hands; her knees, too, were bent, and—thank God for it!—in the attitude of prayer. Ah, that rigidity! It is impossible to bear the terror of it. . . . She knelt, as if in prayer. With the last, choking consciousness, her soul, bubbling out through her lips, it may be, had given itself up to the Father, reconciled and penitent" (235). The poet's description calms her: thrown into a trance of death and rescued from "nervous" meditations on gender inequality, Zenobia ceases her "act of struggling" against the social current. In Coverdale's narrative, she finds incorporation.

Yet the repressed returns: historical traces of her resistance to being a good citizen or a good girl like Priscilla erupt from within the very posture Coverdale at first finds so reassuring. Her body accepts death but not dematerialization, as Coverdale is forced to acknowledge: "But her arms! They were bent before her, as if she struggled against Providence in never-ending hostility. Her hands! They were clenched in immitigable defiance. Away with the hideous thought" (235). Zenobia's recalcitrant materiality overcomes Coverdale's desire for a passive female subject, for one who works well within the community, for a body forgetful of its contempt for prevailing social hierarchies. Her motionless, statuesque body expresses history if not accusation. Zenobia is the citizen who will not suffer amnesia; her body chooses the ghastly over the sentimental, memory over transcendence. Her wounded, combative body becomes a memorial whose physicality recalls the historical past to a community that only thinks about a utopian future. Coverdale attempts to smooth over this conflict and antagonism by encouraging amnesia, by banishing "the hideous thought" of a body animated by opposition to inegalitarian social conditions. Her dead body bears memory of the very real discord in a community that was supposed to have none.

In the most final ways, then, the recalcitrant materiality of Zenobia's body objects to the future of Blithedale farm as mythic American studies department. The corpse resists incorporation. Her dead body offers a contradictory strategy of gauging whether American studies, especially in terms of the material effects of public representation on the Web, makes us dead or live citizens. The dead body has no future in a community that substitutes images of harmony for histories of social opposition; its rigid musculature and insistent memory permit no escape into the rituals of discorporation that legislate the forgetting of species-being so essential to liberal pluralism. Remembering Zenobia's corpse is crucial in the context of American studies where successful enrollment in an increasingly global business field prepares a more encompassing corporate body: a citizenry versed in lessons of the nation-state. By evaluating the material effects of American studies on the Web in terms of *The Blithedale Romance*, we witness that this interdiscipline sits amid a rhetorical collapse that renders the student's future allegiance to economic corporations as a badge of successful incorporation in national community. Against this backdrop of employment as enfranchisement, a noncorporatist stance, such as Zenobia's, may help us to un-imagine community and recover non-national citizenship.

The multiple of levels of citizenship—activist, local, global—that appear in the wake of the nation-state nonetheless resound with privilege. In order to discuss the troubling inequities of who is enabled to incorporate or disincorporate, I want to turn to Hawthorne's novel one last time. Even before her suicide, Zenobia leaves Blithedale because she can, and takes up a lavish residence in town. The obviousness of her wealth and sexuality speak to her privilege; the social resources she commands reveals that her decision to abandon this prototypical American studies community—like her willingness to join the collective enterprise in the first place—is a luxury not everyone shares. Only for the already represented is a noncorporatist identity an attractive role; only for the already enfranchised is non-national citizenship a viable political choice. As a cross-cultural American studies examines nationalism and citizenship, indeed, as an American studies of the future endeavors to uncouple these terms, the field also needs to speak about the ways in which its constitution and foundational assumptions depend on unspoken privileges of the nation-state. Even as we un-imagine the communities that require corporatist citizens, we need to recognize this thinking as a luxury. Non-national citizenship derives from social resources to which not everyone has equal claim or equal access.[41] In a climate where a public, technological American studies links economic success and belonging to the nation-state, where incorporation fuels a desire for highly profitable forms of amnesia, we need to work toward the redistribution of citizenship. But without awareness that the diversification of citizenship along registers other than that of the nation involves the unequal allocation of belonging, bodies, and corporation, this project is likely to replicate the nation in other guises, in new and improved forms.

Notes

This article is indebted to generous criticism from Leslie Bow, Michael Cowan, Joel Pfister, and Michael Rothberg. I am also grateful to the Humanities Colloquium at the University of Miami, which provided a forum to discuss connections between higher education and the nation-state.

1   Jeffrey Louis Decker, "Dis-assembling the Machine in the Garden: Anti-humanism and the Critique of American Studies," *New Literary History* 23 (1992): 282.

2   Michael Denning, " 'The Special American Conditions': Marxism and American Studies," *American Quarterly* 38, no. 3 (1986): 360.

3   Paul Giles, "Reconstructing American Studies: Transnational Paradoxes, Comparative Perspectives," *Journal of American Studies* 28 (1994): 336. Subsequent references are cited parenthetically in the text.

4   I would like to thank Carol Cyganowski (DePaul University), Kathleen Moran (UC Berkeley), Michael Cowan (UC Santa Cruz), and T. V. Reed (Washington State University) for providing me with this information.

5   Richard Dienst, "The Futures Market: Global Economics and Cultural Studies," in *Reading the Shape of the World: Toward an International Cultural Studies*, ed. Henry Schwarz and Richard Dienst (Boulder, Colo.: Westview, 1996), 78.

6   Richard Ohmann, *English in America: A Radical View of the Profession* (New York: Oxford University Press, 1976), 300. Subsequent references are cited parenthetically in the text. Here one could also think of Althusser's claim that the most effective ideological state apparatus is the school. Louis Althusser, "Ideology and Ideological State Apparatuses (Notes towards an Investigation)," in *For Marx*, trans. Ben Brewster (New York: Pantheon, 1969), 156.

7   For more recent critiques of the links between academia and the interests of U.S. capital, see *Social Text* 44 (1995), a special issue devoted to "corporate culture" as well as Christopher Newfield, "What Was Political Correctness? Race, the Right, and Managerial Democracy in the Humanities," *Critical Inquiry* 19 (1993): 308–36; and Gary Rhoades and Sheila Slaughter, "Academic Capitalism, Managed Professionals, and Supply-Side Higher Education," *Social Text* 51 (1997): 9–38.

8   Bill Readings, *The University in Ruins* (Cambridge, Mass.: Harvard University Press, 1996), 14, 40. Subsequent references are cited parenthetically in the text.

9   Michael Lewis, "The World's Biggest Out-of-Business Sale," *New York Times Magazine*, 31 May 1998, 53.

10 Tom Nairn, "Breakwaters of 2000: From Ethnic to Civic Nationalism," *New Left Review* 214 (1995): 94. Subsequent references are cited parenthetically in the text.

11 Pheng Cheah, "Introduction Part II: The Cosmopolitical—Today," *Cosmopolitics: Thinking and Feeling beyond the Nation*, ed. Pheng Cheah and Bruce Robbins (Minneapolis: University of Minnesota Press, 1998), 31. Bruce Robbins also observes the enduring force of nationalism within the cosmopolitan, and speaks of "the large extent to which multinational and transnational corporations remain rooted in their nations of origin." Bruce Robbins, "Introduction Part I: Actually Existing Cosmopolitanism," in *Cosmopolitics*, ed. Cheah and Robbins, 13. For the continuing role nationalism plays in global economies, see also Nairn, "Breakwaters"; Gopal Balakrishnan, "The National Imagination," *New Left Review* 211 (1995): 56–69; and Joel Reed, "Nationalisms in a

Global Economy," in *Reading the Shape of the World*, ed. Schwarz and Dienst, 30–49.

12 On the formatting of utopia as a boundaryless horizon, see Louis Marin, "Frontiers of Utopia: Past and Present," *Critical Inquiry* 19 (1993): 403.

13 Patricia Nelson Limerick, "Insiders and Outsiders: The Borders of the USA and the Limits of the ASA: Presidential Address to the American Studies Association, 31 October 1996," *American Quarterly* 49, no. 3 (1997): 452, 455. Subsequent references are cited parenthetically in the text.

14 Jane C. Desmond and Virginia R. Dominguez, "Resituating American Studies in a Critical Internationalism," *American Quarterly* 48, no. 3 (1996): 475. Subsequent references are cited parenthetically in the text.

15 Donald Pease, "National Identities, Postmodern Artifacts, and Postnational Narratives," *boundary 2* 19, no. 1 (1992): 7; Carolyn Porter, "What We Know That We Don't Know: Remapping American Literary Studies," *American Literary History* 6 (1994): 470. Subsequent references are cited parenthetically in the text.

16 Donald Pease, "New Americanists: Revisionist Interventions into the Canon," *boundary 2* 17, no. 1 (1990): 11.

17 While this materiality frequently orders the imaginary of American studies, it is important to keep in mind that Web pages are also creating an imaginary, projecting an ideal vision of a department's or program's mission.

18 DePaul University, "American Studies Program Description," http://condor. depaul.edu/~american/descript.html.

19 San Diego State University, "SDSU American Studies," http://www.sdsu. edu/academicprog/american.html#program.

20 University of Alabama, "What Can You Do with an American Studies Degree? American Studies at UA," http://www.as.ua.edu/american__studies/ what.html.

21 For explorations of some of these different registers of citizenship, see the various essays in Gershon Shafir, ed., *The Citizenship Debates: A Reader* (Minneapolis: University of Minnesota Press, 1998). See also the caution implicit in Gayatri Spivak's description of "hot peace" as a climate in which identities appearing in the gaps between nation and state can take on a reactionary and extremist character. Gayatri Chakravorty Spivak, "Cultural Talks in the Hot Peace: Revisiting the 'Global Village,' " in *Cosmopolitics*, ed. Cheah and Robbins, 334.

22 Sean Wilentz, "Integrating Ethnicity into American Studies," *Chronicle of Higher Education*, 29 November 1996, A56.

23 College of Staten Island, CUNY, "American Studies Program," http://www. library.csi.cuny.edu/dept/americanstudies.

24 Stanley Fish, "Boutique Multiculturalism, or Why Liberals Are Incapable of Thinking about Hate Speech," *Critical Inquiry* 23 (1997): 386.

25 University of Minnesota, "American Studies Program History," http://www. cla.umn.edu/american/programain.html. Emphasis added.

26   Avery F. Gordon, "The Work of Corporate Culture: Diversity Management," *Social Text* 44 (1995): 18. Subsequent references are cited parenthetically in the text.

27   University of Southern Maine, "American & New England Studies," http://www.usm.maine.edu/~anes/overview.html; Eckerd College, "American Studies," http://www.eckerd.edu/cgi-bin/w3-msql/catlas/ msdec.html?/ temp=AM.

28   University of Miami, "American Studies," http://www.as.miami.edu/old sas/as.html.

29   University of Hawai'i, "American Studies," http://www.hawaii.edu/cata log/a%26s/amst.html.

30   Porter, "What We Know That We Don't Know," Michael Cowan, "Boundary as Center: Inventing an American Studies Culture," *Prospects: An Annual of American Cultural Studies* 12 (1987): 1–20; Amy Kaplan, " 'Left Alone with America': The Absence of Empire in the Study of American Culture," in *Cultures of United States Imperialism*, ed. Kaplan and Donald E. Pease (Durham, N.C.: Duke University Press, 1993), 3–21; Desmond and Dominguez, "Re-situating American Studies."

31   University of California, Berkeley, "American Studies at UC Berkeley," http://ls.berkeley.edu/dept/as/AS-home.html#majorinfo.

32   Brown University, "The American Civilization Department," http://www. brown.edu/Departments/AmCiv/intro.html.

33   Princeton University, "Program in American Studies," http://www.prince ton.edu/~ams/program.html.

34   Nathaniel Hawthorne, *The Blithedale Romance* (1852; New York: Penguin, 1984), 209–10. Subsequent references are cited parenthetically in the text.

35   Hawthorne, Nathaniel, *The Scarlet Letter: A Romance* (1850; New York: Penguin, 1983), 74.

36   Qtd. in Henry W. Sams, *Autobiography of Brook Farm* (Englewood Cliffs, N.J.: Prentice-Hall, 1958), 6. Subsequent references are cited parenthetically in the text.

37   University of Alabama, "What Can You Do with an American Studies Degree? American Studies at UA"; emphasis added.

38   Robyn Wiegman, *American Anatomies: Theorizing Race and Gender* (Durham, N.C.: Duke University Press, 1995), 50. Subsequent references are cited parenthetically in the text.

39   Lauren Berlant, *The Queen of America Goes to Washington City: Essays on Sex and Citizenship* (Durham, N.C.: Duke University Press, 1997), 59–60.

40   Elisabeth Bronfen, *Over Her Dead Body: Death, Femininity, and the Aesthetic* (New York: Routledge, 1992), 247.

41   On the social resources necessary to citizenship, see J. M. Barbalet, *Citizenship: Rights, Struggle, and Class Inequality* (Minneapolis: University of Minnesota Press, 1988), 1.

AFTERWORD

✧

ConsterNation

Dana D. Nelson

I've been thinking about democracy lately, and specifically about what kinds of things work to block and reroute the democratic imaginary. I've been working from the compellingly simple definitions of political (anti)theorist C. Douglas Lummis in his book *Radical Democracy*.[1] There, he talks about the immediacy of democracy, its antiexpert and extra-institutional nature. And he talks about several modes of belief that contain and block democratic energies for the present, like sentimentalism, cynicism, and faith in the future. He describes two modes of futurity: faith in a redemptive, sacred afterlife, or in scientific progress. In both realms, injustices and disagreements will miraculously be solved. Both these futuristic modes refer us back to sentimentalism or cynicism, for now.

Lummis's analysis was in my mind as I read through many of the articles that have been produced under the framework of the Futures of American Studies, preparing for a paper for a Dartmouth Futures Institute in 1999 that formed the basis for this essay.[2] Contemplating these many different and worthwhile arguments, I began to wonder if our hope for these futures has more to do with a blockage in our relation to democracy than it does with any deficit in imagined directions for our disciplinary futures. And I began to pay attention to the way *nation* has been loaded up to bear the burden of and take the name for that blockage in our democratic imaginary. Rebutting American studies Cold War exceptionalism, recent scholars have been rethinking and retheorizing nation as an essentially antimulticultural formation. This compelling school of analysis has productively deterritorialized (United States of) American studies without necessarily formulating a coherent alternative identification. And so a great deal of the recent writing about futures has been devoted to projecting international, transnational, antinational, and postnational models for what for some time has been a nationally grounded interdiscipline.

These counter-nationalist schools of historical analysis and cultural theory have been absolutely central to the current vitality of American studies. Yet I want both to historicize and to rethink our focus on the political value of *nation*. I'll be suggesting here that even the resisting ways we think about nation are conditioned by a very particular, durably antidemocratic false choice entailed within the nation logic of the U.S. Constitution. Because of this, and despite our best efforts, our American studies futures remain in thrall to the fate of the U.S. nation-state. As we search for futuristic alternatives to a theoretically overstabilized concept of nation, we stay inside Constitutionalism's strongly antipolitical logic, collaborating with its desire for a realm ultimately freed from political struggle.

As Sheldon Wolin argued some time ago, we have failed to pay enough attention to the way that the Constitution created a new, abstracted, and antipolitical national identity that worked to sublate what it cast as the confusions, unpredictability, and inefficiency of local democracy. The Constitutional formulation of nation, Wolin insists, suppressed the proliferating political vitality of democracy in the name of nation. Its construction of political unity encouraged citizens to look away from and even to fear democracy's enormous potential for changing their relation to the concept and the practice of nation. Instead, the Constitutional nation persistently draws our attention toward its containment promise, its promise to manage democracy for us, toward a better future. Insofar as it is effective at this containment, it keeps our best energy and even our desires directed away from democratic practice and its always open, uncontainable possibilities for social change now.

I will be arguing here, following Wolin, that we would do well to stop vesting so much of our energy in imagined (anti)nationalist futures. Democratic politicalism is the way out of the false choices proffered by nationalism, not in the future, but right now.[3] We might productively sidestep questions of nation, and reinvigorate ourselves for the work of democratization: *Mars Attacks!* provides a fun gloss of some of the constitutionally false choices that circulate around the multiculturalist being of nation, one that seems germane to our present academic moment.

Mars Attacks! Nationalism, Multiculturalism, and a False Choice

Mars Attacks! opens with a classic scene of multiculturalism and its discontents, what filmmakers have been exploiting for years in narratives of *alien-Nation.* "Four miles outside of Lockjaw, Kentucky," a man of Asian descent walks out of his wood-frame, white-shuttered farmhouse, carrying his trash to the corner. Just as he deposits it, a red tractor and its rednecked driver arrive on the scene to query whether Mr. Lee is preparing for "Filipino New Years." "Why you say dat?" returns the apparently vexed Mr. Lee. "'Cuz," explains the white Kentuckian, whose accent is as thick as the inflected English of Mr. Lee, "ye're cookin' up a feast—I smelt it all the way from the inter-stite. Whadiz that? Bar-be-kew?" This scene is our first encounter with the disturbing alien: it turns out that Martians have fired up a whole herd of cattle who come blazing down the road just as a spaceship rises up from behind the Lees' house.[4]

As its opening scene indicates, *Mars Attacks!* plays on all the usual slippages stock in alien invasion movies: where brown and green aliens refract white national anxieties about legal and illegal immigration; where the United States "we" is synecdochically the imperiled world. Recent movies have always worked to ease the tension of these (bad-faith) politics, with multiracial guy teams banding forces to save the United States/world (as in, for instance, the movies *Independence Day* or *Men in Black*). But *Mars Attacks!* makes the battle between multiculturalist tolerance and nationalist/universalist protectionism explicit. When President Dale must decide how to respond to the thousands of Martian spacecraft surrounding the planet, he consults with two experts, Professor Donald Kessler and General Decker. Kessler represents the case for academic multiculturalism, insisting that the Martians' "extremely advanced technology suggests that they are peaceful: advanced civilization is by definition not barbaric." He urges that "we need a welcome mat, not a row of tanks." Quite differently, General Decker sees the spaceships as warships and urges immediate nuclear recourse. Barely able to contain his impatience with "liberals . . . peacemongers . . . IDIOTS!" Decker and his nationally protectionist conservatism are apparently exonerated when the Martians obliterate their welcoming committee in the desert of Nevada, taking the fashion model talk show hostess Nathalie Lake and her little dog Poppy alive for experiments in hybridity that do not seem to promise much in the way of "getting along."

Though the scales apparently now tip toward militant nationalism, the movie won't let us forget multiculturalism's critical possibilities. After this, the president's daughter Taffy draws on a cultural relativism model to hypothesize an explanation for the Martians' vicious barbecuing of their hosts: perhaps they were alarmed by the dove let go by one of the onlookers in response to the Martian message that "we come in peace." President Dale adopts this multiculturalist theory when he radios the Martians that night, expressing his hope that the first event was "a cultural misunderstanding."

Exultantly he accepts the Martian ambassador's request to address Congress with a formal apology: his multiculturalist diplomatic success is a "triumph," he gloats, "for my administration." The next day, without apology, the Martians fry Congress. Soon they are back for the Washington Monument and the White House, and, following that, viewers are treated to a montage of toppling national treasures: Big Ben, the Eiffel Tower, the Taj Mahal, Stonehenge. But later, it becomes clear that Taffy was at least partly right: birds do drive the Martians nuts. So maybe the whole thing was not preplanned; maybe it *was* a cultural misunderstanding. Dangling that prospect, Burton offers lots of pleasure for antinationalist proponents. First, there is the libidinal satisfaction of the gray-suits in Congress getting zapped, then the warmongering General Decker gets shrunk and squashed, and finally the president gets impaled by a handshake while standing on a supposed Pentagon command center's situation map (a literal jab at U.S. cultures of imperialism). Then there is the weirdly resonant message that gets sent when Slim Whitman's "Indian Love Call" explodes Martian brains and thwarts their apparently genocidal invasion.

The movie gives two faces to multiculturalism: the first a PMC-engineered and managed multiculturalism in scientist Kessler (President of the American Academy of Astronautics), and the second, a boozy, feel-good multiculturalist anarchy in the person of Barbara Land, the Las Vegas millionaire's wife. Kessler initially seems to be the "better" version, a qualified professional ready to manage a galactic crisis. Kessler's confident expertise on Nathalie Lake's talk show—and her sycophantic response—underscores the antipolitical drive of his multiculturalism, an ethos Peter Euben analyzes in recent academic culture, where "more and more of political life is being claimed as the eminent domain of professional experts and professors who reappropriate knowledge while forming a caste of initiates."[5] In case viewers might think that the movie supports the managed version, Kessler gets zapped along with Congress. By the end of *Mars Attacks!* only the laissez-faire (if not quite anarchist) multiculturalism is left standing. The loosely coherent new ager Barbara Land makes it to the postapocalypse Tahoe nature celebration with Tommy Lee Jones. And doughnut fry boy Richie takes the occasion of his Congressional medal of honor for saving the world to elaborate on his ideas for rebuilding America: "Now we just have to start over and start rebuilding everything, like our houses. But I was thinking, instead of houses we could live in tepees, because it's better in a lot of ways. Okay, that's all."

Tim Burton's zany, retro-futuristic alien invasion spoof plays on a wide and contradictory range of multiculturalist and (post–) Cold War culturalist fears and desires. It symptomatizes a false choice that nationalism poses for multiculturalist investments in U.S. global politics. The movie poses a critical dilemma between multiculturalism and militarized nationalism (cum globalism). We can see the suggested stakes of this choice when the president is impaled right after sentimentally deploying one of multiculturalism's most loaded and patently antipolitical lines: "can't we just . . . get along?" The humor that circulates around this supposed impasse can help us reflect on the way American studies scholarship gets bamboozled by a false argument—one that curtails our ability to claim politicalness in the moment we engage it. This argument is roughly that multiculturalism's success will be determined by America's ability to "just get along." Alternatively, multiculturalism's failure to ensure intercultural harmony either indicates the bankruptcy of the U.S. political structure and historical legacy (we cannot get along because "they" ruined our ability to do so), or the rightness of conservative attempts to enforce English-only, "cultural literacy" norms onto the United States' diverse populations (we will all get along if we talk the same language and share the same values).

The false choice is that we must either get along or agree to be internally and externally policed for our own good. We should notice here that both options idealize a political harmony that has never come to pass, quite simply because it is unrealistic. Of course we cannot just get along. "We" never will, no matter how long we wait or educate. The question that is open in this debate is always and only whether we try to disappear difference by fixing, reorienting, and tolerating, or just by bombing the hell out of it. This formulation of the question in fact disappears the possibility of difference (not just identity difference but political difference) as an ongoing fact, neither good nor bad, one that must always and forever be negotiated and could be embraced—even cultivated—for the purposes of a functional and even vital political disunity. Our ability politically to triumph in the zero-sum game presented by this false choice leaves us waiting for the moment when the battle is finally over, that moment after the war when we get to be the de facto (if exhausted) multiculturalist remainder. Exhausted multiculturalist remainder is what Richie's suggestion for tepees sounds like, for sure. If that is the best articulation of multiculturalism kids like Richie can come up with after the war, we planners in academia have got to be worrying that our multicultural postnationalist future is not going to get off to a very good start.

We have been planning for the end of nation or at least its diminished importance for lo these past many years in American studies. We have all kinds of multicultural, antistate visions for the moment of rebuilding. But no one has zapped our congressional and executive branches yet, let alone the Supreme Court or the Federal Treasury, and I'm not holding my breath on being put in charge if someone did. I'm finding that I want to think not so much about the future, but what is going on when we think about the future now.

American★Studies★Nation★Thing

Discussions of possibilities for American studies futures in the last decade of the millennium often concentrate on versions of two key questions: how to find an ethically multiculturalist American studies relation to the (NAFTA) Americas and the global-corporate new world order, and how productively to reorient American studies away from the destructive history of U.S. (white, New England–grown, bourgeois, masculinist) nationalism in particular and the essential racist tendencies of modern nationalism more generally.[6] Both approaches take U.S. nationalism as a problem, but there seems to be little consensus around how to develop American studies outside a national(ist) denominative.

Janice Radway detailed several scenes for such collective ambivalence in her important 1998 ASA presidential address, a version of which opens this current volume. Radway's address surveys the possibilities for cultural and academic change invoked in recent scholarship. She outlines these works' "collective force" in challenging the unity and consensus narratives that block our ability to think outside the national unity narrative, a narrative she labels the "American democratic idea."[7] In Radway's view, the accumulating force of this recent scholarship teaches us that from any vantage—"nationalism, race, culture, ethnicity, identity, sex, and gender" (10)—"culture," and particularly U.S. culture, cannot adequately be "conceived as a unitary, uniform thing." She describes the ideal that this body of work collectively outlines: "intricate interdependency" (15, 10). Radway explores, problematizes, and ultimately rejects three institutional alternatives to our current American studies paradigm: international United States studies, inter-Americas studies, and intercultural studies. She ultimately suggests that the American studies restructuring that could come in response to questions of difference raised within American studies scholarship may not be "adequately done in the current historical context . . . [of] rapidly advancing global neo-colonialism that specifically benefits the United States" (8).

This address indexes an American studies immobility at the site of nation and its complex interrelation with expanding capital. Radway provides a powerful overview of the diverse scholarship that has been helping us imagine powerful alternatives to a current immobility. For Radway, this scholarship shows us what might occur, but only when the current aggressive proliferation of U.S. "neo-colonial" capitalist expansionism is somehow stopped. Her desires for a postnational politics of "intricate interdependency" are ones that cannot be realized now: we must wait for saner governments, or a global redistribution of capital and power (or maybe just a stock market crash). And by equating the problematic neoimperialist capitalist nation—this America— *with* democracy (the "American democratic idea"), she seems to surrender from the start the political possibilities *of* democracy.

That surrender is what I want to question. Democracy can supply the political agency for Radway's project, the ideal and the means by which to act on and in the "intricate interdependency" in difference that radical scholarship has described, analyzed, and made both tangible and desirable. *Intricate interdependency*—made political—describes precisely the radical democratic project. *Intricate interdependency*—politically realized—would constitute an ongoing, proliferating, empowering, and always risky democratic struggle that would touch on every aspect of our personal and public ways of being. *Intricate interdependency*—not a delivered fact but a political project—is another way of describing radical democracy's vitality, "the vital source of energy at the center of all living politics" (Lummis 25). The realization of Radway's desire for the political generalization of intricate interdependency depends on retaking democratic practice from its national containment structures. Allowing democracy, the American democratic idea, to collapse with the very force designed to contain it, the monolith of nation, Radway has nowhere to put her hope but in the future.

Another important essay, by Nikhil Singh, takes a more historicist approach to the same set of issues. Singh proposes holding onto one of the terms that Radway's analysis suggests we repudiate—nation—but his differently oppositional and valuable project again highlights the way a focus on the future of nation can function to divert us from politically engaging the present. In "Culture/Wars," Singh outlines the value of retaking nation for a differently conceptualized universalism, a multiculturalist universalism. In Singh's words, his theoretical project combines "a hermeneutics of suspicion about . . . historically determinate claims to universality . . . with a sense that universalism is absolutely indispensable as an *ideal* and a *symbol*."[8] Highlighting Martin Luther King Jr.'s "paradigmatic" embrace of "the fictive universalism of the American nation state," Singh names this tradition of "black worldliness" as the most viable countertradition for the resuscitation of an ideal of nation that could democratically enhance multiculturalism through anti-imperialist universalism (509, 514). He posits this democratically aimed universalism as indispensable to an American (studies) future.[9]

Singh formulates his argument through an impressive mixture of careful historicism and theoretical idealism: "What it has actually meant in recent history (and what it might mean in the future) to rely on the U.S. nation state *as a stable container of social antagonisms, and as the necessary horizon of our hopes for justice*" (472). I want to dwell momentarily not on Singh's reclaiming of nation as an aim for our hope but on the temporal lacunae that emerge as he articulates his critical hope ("to assess . . . what [nation] has actually meant and what it might mean"), a gap that lingers between his analytic critique of the imperialism of U.S. Cold War culturalism and his historicist reorientation of "black worldliness" toward an equivocally specified, more hopeful national/world future. We can name that gap "the present." The present in Singh's essay is the time of "culture wars" and not the time at which we aim our hope. This is the time where the meaning of the "harshest and most enduring and intractable divisions within American life" (471) are exhaustively argued and helpfully analyzed, but not altered. In this present, we are stuck in seemingly endless and unwinnable conflict between the bureaucratic/ideological forces of managed consensus versus competing arguments and confusion about the political value of multiculturalist agendas.

The present in these two essays as in much American studies work is the place where we are too bogged in conflict to lodge our hope. Our ideas about democracy correlate factually with this tedious and disappointing present; our (lack of) ideas and optimism about now indexes not just our political impatience, but also our political fatigue. American studies radical thinkers surrender hope for a democratic present because democracy feels too exhausting and even more than a little frightening when we factor in how we almost always feel as though we are losing too many important battles these days. Talk of democracy usually puts us in a bad mood—especially after the November 2000 "election" debacle. We do not want to trust our future to the unenlightened majority in politics—national, local, or departmental. Indeed, department meetings are usually our most immediate measure for the banality and intractability of political negotiation: we have to fight too hard for too little, and compromise with opponents feels too much like consorting with the enemy. Our gains feel like tokens. Even within our academic and local political communities, the maintenance of alliance is hard work and we can all count too many dispiriting disagreements that led to the disintegration of coalitions large and small. These local battles provide the affective template for national political issues that we care about, like setbacks in affirmative action and gay rights, and feminist backlash. We put our hopes in future chairs and deans and presidents and shrug with cynicism if not real disgust at our current slate of candidates.

We feel blocked, without and within. Thinking about politics now fatigues us with the maddingly petty and the overwhelmingly important. This exhaustion is what we want to escape in turning to our work; we are comforted by shaping visions of a world free of the frictions of substantial disagreement, where the annoying messiness of all today's disagreement can be replaced by tolerance and respect. We know up close and personal that we do not live in that world now, and so we spin out comforting visions for (cleaned-up) American studies futures. Since it is obviously going to take some time (who knows how long?) to arrive at that antistate of full enlightenment, this desire keeps us oriented toward an intellectually miraculated, interdisplinarily converging future. This counternational, multicultural America functions as the site for futuristically clarified political investments that paradoxically cement our contemporary political disinvestment. Lummis puts it this way: "Faith in the humans [or the American studies] of the future is faith in an abstraction; it is trust that cannot be reciprocated or grounded in any real promise. It is an evasion of the real task, the one thing needful, which is to work for a world founded on real trust among real humans, now" (151). The real task, Lummis implies, would come in developing our willingness to work with and in a full range of difference, now. Not just differences we find intriguing, but also the ones we find utterly grating. Paradoxically, as we use our scholarship to denounce the homogenizing drives of the nation-state in favor of an extra- or transnational multiculturalist future, we solidify our own desires to avoid implication in the irreducibly heterogeneous mess of the contemporary democratic space.

This desire on the part of politically invested intellectuals to eradicate the messiness of politics from the future is one that Bonnie Honig has usefully mapped. The works of the political theorists she analyzes, like much counternationalist American studies scholarship, project multicultural democratic "success" as the "elimination . . . of dissonance, conflict or struggle" (2), the place where, fully recognizing and appreciating difference, we will at last be able to "get along." We have roundly and rightfully rejected liberal consensus—but we seem nevertheless to equate theoretical and political success with a world where difference no longer results in conflict, an accepting dissensus that looks and works pretty much like consensus.

This allergy to ongoing, contingent, irresolvable political struggle, the way it figures as a threat to our schemes, not an ultimate goal for them, implicates us in the *Mars Attacks!* dilemma. The movie's sheer silliness refracts an obdurate and serious political trap: the idea that there are only two choices, just getting along or total war. This false choice keeps us locked in an antidemocratic mode; it prevents us from embracing conflictual politics fully as a healthy, absolutely necessary, and even occasionally enjoyable feature of multicultural, national democracy; it keeps us from understanding and especially from taking any pleasure in the way that disagreement—and not just difference and interdependency—is also another word for democracy.

Our bad mood about democracy (-as-disagreement) too often keeps us from enjoying and later remembering moments of successful disagreement, successful collaborations and reciprocity, or just flat-out peacefulness in the moments where we are not currently in disagreement with habitual opponents. Our affective register for democracy (-as-disagreement) both inside and outside the academy is "war" where the threatened outcome is diminishment at best and disintegration at worst. But here is my point: we are letting the antidemocratic bent of national and academic institutionalism train and limit our democratic energy and imagination. Democracy's battles sometimes feel as devastating as we might know or imagine war to be. Democratic compromise and reciprocity feels like failure when we compare it to what things might have looked like if we had won on every point. But democracy also feels like the deep satisfactions we get from coalitions and political relationships effectively built across time and vastly diverging life circumstances. Important, changeable, life-sustaining. We know and treasure those feelings of connection and success and hold them against the hard moments when we disagree with our colleagues and political allies, when their changes and differences infuriate us unbearably. Those thick, messy, good feelings—the loaded joy we feel when we have worked out the alliance again even in the midst of compromises we still do not exactly like—they are about democracy too. They should stand alongside the feelings we have about connections we could not or did not sustain. It is worth our political present to remember this fuller range of democratic feeling, and in fact to remember that democracy will always feel, often simultaneously, both good and bad.

Let me frame this point historically. The Constitution promised to replace the messiness of political negotiation with a politically clarifying structure that would result in repeating and functional enactments of political unity.[10] Constitutionalism offered scientifically and expertly to manage the local excesses of democracy; it tapped into unnecessarily rigid desires for unity, wholeness, sameness, and stability. In this, it cultivated citizenship around desires that make us scared of democracy. Constitutionalism's formula for political identity abjected not just identity difference in its construction of an implicitly white, male, property-holding "universal" citizen, but also political disagreement and what Wolin terms our "birthright of politicalness." I'm suggesting that the move to reclaim identity difference while trying to ward off political conflict keeps us stuck in a very particularly U.S. nation logic. Standing inside Constitutionalism's false and antidemocratic abjection of disagreement and political messiness, we continue to experience and project the surrender of our politicalness not as a loss but as a relief, doing it now in the name of American studies futures as an antidote to the current United States of American nationalism.[11]

Democratic Politicalness

We do not have to buy into the logic that disagreement is something we must aim ultimately to solve; we do not have to participate in the closure of the very political space that a more agentic, participatory democracy requires. But cultivating politicalness will require a kind of engagement with our workspace that Constitutionalism as well as intellectual moralism and PMC entitlement has trained us to avoid and dislike.[12]

In his analysis of the place of the intellectual in "modern democratic society," Jeffrey Goldfarb identifies academic/intellectual habits that disable our contributions to the "consequential democratic politics of general society."[13] He points out that many postmodern and culturalist academics have substituted academic politics for public democratic engagement, and he calls for us to stop confusing the two. He insists that too many intellectuals on the academic left confuse ideology (by which he means politically aimed analyses) for politics, imagining that political problems can be solved with the right political theory. In their determined search for "correct interpretation," they imagine wrongly that "political action simply involves bringing their dis-covered truth to the people" (14–15). This false idea of political process unfits such intellectuals for the necessarily tangled conflict and complicated process of compromise of democratic politics, where ideally intellectuals' thinking should inform deliberative processes. But the perceived relevance of intellec-tuals within those deliberations depends at least in part on the ability to understand that, in Goldfarb's summary, "the worlds of intellectual inquiry and political action are separate though problematically related" (15).

Attending to such critiques does not mean we should forget that the contributions of cultural studies in American studies have been enormously important to redeveloping the politics of our interdiscipline. Patrick McGee recently and elegantly described that influence: "Cultural studies is the meth-odology of hope. . . . [It is] an inflection of intellectual work with the re-sponsibilities of desire. It has a transformative effect on every theory and discipline that comes into contact with it because it insists on taking into account *real* human desires and the *other* voices that are both constituted and repressed by disciplinary and theoretical discourses. Like deconstruction and psychoanalysis, it unlocks . . . closed meaning; but it also constructs meaning as a form of political responsibility."[14] My aspirations for reclaiming demo-cratic politicalness now depend on us working at bringing the best of our political hopes to our daily interactions in our workaday world, even as we might also be trying to develop ways to transform our critical insights into some kind of political action outside of academia. Whether we are able to find routes for political action outside academia, we have plenty within the academy now.[15] I think of the kind of work at democratic politicalness I'm describing as being something like the humility of a yoga practice, taking in the air where we are and looking to find more space—both inside and around us—for expanding democratic politicalness, relaxing into the discomfort that comes with self-governance and disagreement to find the difference between pain that promotes health and pain that signals injury. This would be a demo-cratic practice where we would seek daily to find ways of helping ourselves and others remember, believe in, and articulate our/their (probably dif-ferent) hopes; to find ways of keeping our political hopes going in the midst of setbacks, disappointments, and compromises. This would be a democratic practice of getting over our (anti)political melancholy for the good old past that locates the conditions for change always in the future, those days when we felt we could trust progress for the establishment of tolerance and social justice.[16]

Cultivating our politicalness and our commitment to living democracy will mean increasing our ability to operate and implement in disagreement, not just outside academia but also within our workspaces. It might also help us develop the tolerance for consociational compromise—theoretically and practically—that could leverage us more institutional agency in what Wahneema Lubiano recently summarized as "the incredibly powerful . . . relationship between the university system, the primary and secondary educational system in the United States, and a military and international global economy."[17] Recognizing that our work operates within the state complex and the neocolonial global economy should not be the grounds for our political resignation. In Wahneema Lubiano's pithy summary, if the "water is being poisoned right here at the well . . . [i]t is important to make a stand right here at the well" (75). If our visions for American studies futures are going to be recognizable as something other than what Marcuse described as "mere utopias," then we have to work at finding the conditions for and practices of those futures in the lives, interactions, and affective repertoires of our colleagues, students, and own selves, now.[18] And we may well begin by developing and sharing democratic strategies for repoliticizing our workplace interactions and our pedagogy, two subjects that radical American studies thinkers too often overlook in their discussion of futures.

Cultivating our own politicalness will help us deal more effectively and fully within a radically changed and still morphing econo-academic setting. Politicalness could help us move beyond just kvetching about accelerated public/private preparation divides, about the new obsession with outside funding, about constant-jeopardy program "re-prioritization." Politicalness would carry us to challenge our dead citizenship in the so-called shared governance structures of our undemocratic universities and to fight effectively for more self-management. Humanities academics have long been sniffily dismissive about business management practices and philosophy. Politicalness tells us we can no longer afford this pose, that we give up too much democratic space by striking it. As Christopher Newfield argues: "We should not just critique but *redefine* academic business—that is, we should reexamine and revise the business model. This could lead to collaborations with management writers and trainers, people who surpass most academics in coping with managerial roadblocks and who could also learn from academic experience. We should go beyond critique to achieving real *managerial power* for the nonprofit approaches to human development that drew most of us into higher education in the first place."[19] Politicalness with respect to academic self-management will require that we politicize university *economicalness*, an exercise that might allow us, for instance, to interact politically, proactively, and productively within college budgetary environments, with large business, and small and big donors to forward our not-for-profit goals.

As immediately and democratically important as engagements within our academic workplace is the pedagogical work we do. Let me hark back to Richie Norris's plans for rebuilding America with tepees: our own theoretical focus on social movement and identity politics as an alternative to politics of the nation-state may be leaving our students in a lurch of imagined citizenship. Acculturated to the stale icons of dead citizenship, and schooled to look toward a multicultural global future, they have few live references for conceptualizing their own functional politicalness in the theoretically bankrupt but actually existing nation-state.[20] Our students need politicalness, perhaps even more than we do. After all, those of us who have jobs are versed in hiding in the cracks of the interdisciplinary strategizing of our administrations. But our students face, for the most part, a brave new world without TIAA-CREFF.

We can empower them not just by teaching them oppositional histories, but by helping them rethink democratic citizenship through a politicalness that does not take nation but democracy as its telos. We can help them claim a politicalness that would proliferate ideas about and spaces for democracy in national and non-national sites. This conception of politicalness is a different citizenship, one that, to paraphrase Bonnie Honig, is not a juridical *status* granted by the state, but a *practice* built from the belief that everyone has a right to participate in and create access to self-governance, in and outside official spaces of U.S. governance.[21]

If we are serious about using our classrooms and subject expertise to help our students gain ways to proliferate politicalness in their own lives, we need to think and write more about American studies pedagogical models. This means a renewed engagement with questions of democracy and teaching in American studies practice, vexing questions about the politics of our pedagogy, and queries into whether our political desires coordinate with democratic practice. As Peter Euben warns, this is a complicated undertaking, one that asks us to interrogate our pedagogical aims in the context of our ideals for democratic politicality—an interrogation that we may never stabilize with a clear solution:

> While education implies a hierarchy between teacher and student or parent and teacher, politics presupposes the equality of political adults. This is a useful warning against vanguardism and the pretensions of what Foucault calls

"general intellectuals." But it is not conclusive if democratic political education is done democratically, if it is democratic in text and subject, in substance and process. For Socrates, that requires "genuine" dialogue rather than a covert monologue. But since dialogues involve complex negotiations of power at the moment of a dialogue's establishment and re-negotiations thereafter, "real" dialogue is only possible when philosophers converse with and are part of an activist citizenry able to talk freely to power because it exercises it and understands its dynamics. (72)

And it is not, perhaps, just our students who need to be able to speak to our power but also we who need to work at respecting their desires and goals—and not just reforming them—as a crucial part of fashioning this democratic pedagogical polytonality. Jeff Smith puts it this way: "The academy is not a family. It is an *intentional community*, comprised of people who are nearly all voting-age adult citizens. Taking such people seriously—as presumably we all mean to do—means honoring the choices they make, and indeed, deferring to those choices if at all possible. To do otherwise is undemocratic at best, if not infantalizing and frankly oppressive. It is to treat others instrumentally, as means to *our* ends, rather than as ends in themselves."[22] This respect will be hard to achieve if we calculate the immediate way our hopes for the political future rub hard against our students' purchase into the individualist tide of global capital and for-profit modes of knowledge that seem likeliest to help them ride it successfully.

So at least some of this pedagogical work will mean interrogating our socially constructed feelings—and not just the feelings of our students—about democracy and disagreement. How good are we at letting our students disagree with us and have life goals politically, socially, economically different from ours? How do we use the subjects of American studies to make a classroom experience and a learning culture that would cultivate an increased level of tolerance in ourselves and for our students to develop the political work of disagreement—disagreements we may never resolve and do not even need to resolve in order to stay in political practice together? How do we conceptualize a pedagogy for democratic disagreement that does not make agreement its goal? What does a pedagogy that fosters consociational disunity, community without unity, look like?[23] How are we shaping the nationally oriented subject of American studies to develop our students' ability to identify venues beyond the now more meaningless than ever "vote" for practices of politicality and the growth of democracy in a way that does not look to nation for reference or antireference?

I'm not sure I have good answers yet to these multiplying pedagogical questions. I have been experimenting for years to find decent strategies to politicalize classroom learning for democratic expansion. I keep searching for models that provide a demanding, yet supportive, intellectually rigorous but nonjudgmental (by this I do not mean nonevaluative) environment. I want my students to understand that I expect hard work, analytic rigor, and commitment to the interpersonal work of learning. I strive to convey my own passion for critical thinking and my own equally passionate interest in helping them learn how to think critically, if that is what they want to do. I try to foster these aims through pedagogy that positions students to understand texts both in their historical context and in terms of their current relevance to contemporary issues. Most importantly, while I model for them the results of my own thinking processes about contemporary issues, acknowledging their often political implications, I work to make clear at every turn that I judge them neither for agreeing nor disagreeing with my reasoned opinions about the literature or about contemporary issues raised in discussion: the aim is that they learn to think carefully and own their opinions, no matter whether we see eye to eye. This posture frustrates them more and more, trained as they are by the vo-teching of state universities to want definite, usable answers. It frustrates me too, because I spent my graduate training and early years in the profession believing it was my job to convert them to my more humane and compassionate way of thinking, the way of thinking that felt so emancipatory to me in my own undergraduate conversion. Surrendering this goal makes me constantly worried that I've given up too much.

But my pedagogical experiment with dialogue in place of conversion is one I'm going to keep up until I am convinced that it's wrong. Here's what I try to do in this experiment. I emphasize to my students that democratic dialogue is a process of critical engagement in civic issues that entails together the skills they develop in critical thinking, the principle of intellectual work, and an abiding, ethically based commitment to listening to the ideas, opinions, and agendas of others, no matter how fully we might disagree with them. I encourage them to think of democracy not as a thing or a product, but as a dynamic that depends on their labor—articulating their opinions and participating in an exchange that entails listening to those with whom they might disagree. Democracy, in my classrooms, is an immediate, ongoing and long-term process, one that functions through and as dialogue. Its achievement is measured in how well it brings humans together in their present differences, always to learn from each other if never fully to persuade.

Of course, we're not running the nation or even a neighborhood in my classrooms: we don't have to figure out how to live together, but how to learn about a particular topic together. Are the skills we develop in my classrooms transferable? I don't feel sure that I know this yet. All I'm running on is my sense that the conversion model—even the conversion model that is about converting to tolerance—doesn't teach us useful democratic strategies for those times when tolerance is not in place. I'm running on the register of my own ongoing discomfort with disagreement, those moments when I deeply want students who disagree with me to drop the class, or do something so awful that I get to fail them. I'm running on my own impatience with the state of political rhetoric in the United States among our supposed brightest and best, as for instance when Trent Lott joked, at the news of Hilary Clinton's election to the Senate, "maybe she'll get struck by lightning before January," or jokes that circulated in the election aftermath among my lefty friends that fantasized funny scenarios where we could watch George W. Bush die a "tragic" death. These jokes, I thought, invoked an antipolitical and antidemocratic desire for the end of disagreement. As political statements, they performed the renunciation of democratic engagement. Some of my friends thought I was overreading these moments. I think that's possible, but I feel comfortable in asserting that, in general, we are as a nation and as a profession in need of some better resources when it comes to tolerating and thinking past the political disagreements of our own moment.

Conclusion

I have been urging us to step outside the depoliticizing logic of U.S. Constitutional nationalism and have argued that our habit of developing frameworks that counterpose nation with the post-/inter-/trans-/antinational future is not helping us in the present. I have argued for the importance of reclaiming democratic politicalness now, for removing the blinkers of a singular orientation toward or against nation, and for proliferating space for democratic feelings and actions in the places most familiar to us. These are often the places where we feel most frustrated and where it is hardest to imagine good change happening. Part of this is our fault. The pedagogy we offer too infrequently works to explain or expand democratic citizenship now in the places where we work and teach, and our scholarship tends to document antidemocratic longing for the place where the political work of disagreement ends. We need to experiment with embracing disagreement practically and emotionally in order to reorient our energy toward democracy. We do not have to wait either to be recognized as public intellectuals or for the collapse of global-nationalist capital to start working at having a democratizing and political impact now.

Let me at last take up my title: The Constitutional formula redirected political energy for self-governance away from local culture and replaced it with a seductively powerful abstraction—"people's sovereignty"—which it promised to provide the nation structure for administrating. This particular hegemonic national articulation worked to displace people's solidly developing sense of their own political agency by, in Wolin's words, obscuring "questions of power and authority," severing "political activity from specific localities," and "producing an abstract category, 'participation'" (5). This particular formulation of nation does the work of consterNation. ConsterNation is feeling helpless and confused as we look to America—or its alternative future—to grant us the sensation of democratic power and the promise of political rescue. The choice it formulates for us is to join its power via patriotism or to stand in helpless dismay—or to put this another way, to love it or leave it. That is a false choice, and my point is simple: we need to step outside its bribe of cleanliness. There are no clean choices when it comes to the work of democracy. There is just the risk and the mess and the temporal rewards of proliferating politicalness. This is, as I have been trying to inspire my readers to feel, a complicated and smaller package—that is also a real and good alternative now to the hopelessly stalled, singular offer of "the future."

Notes

I'd like to thank several colleague friends who helped me think about this article as I was writing it to present at the Futures Institute and as I was revising it later: Dale Bauer, Russ Castronovo, Richard Morrison, and Chris Newfield. Don Pease and Robyn Wiegman both asked helpful questions at the institute and gave me great editorial suggestions later. The 1999 institute participants gave me wonderful ideas for further developing that afternoon. Ivy Schweitzer, as always, is a fabulous interlocutor and her passions and ideas I hope made their way into my last draft here.

1 C. Douglas Lummis, *Radical Democracy* (Ithaca, N.Y.: Cornell University Press, 1996). Subsequent references are cited parenthetically in the text.
2 See for instance, Robyn Wiegman's special issue of *Cultural Critique*, "The Futures of American Studies," 40 (1998); Jane C. Desmond and Virginia R. Dominguez, "Resituating American Studies in a Critical Internationalism," *American Quarterly* 48, no. 3 (1996): 475–90; Eric Cheyfitz, "What Work Is There for Us to Do? American Literary Studies or Americas Cultural Stud-

ies?" *American Literature* 67, no. 4 (1995): 843–53; Betsy Erkkila, "Ethnicity, Literary Theory, and the Grounds of Resistance," *American Quarterly* 47, no. 4 (1995): 563–94; Carolyn Porter, "What We Know That We Don't Know: Remapping American Literary Studies," *American Literary History* 6 (1994): 467–526; Paul Giles, "Reconstructing American Studies: Transnational Paradoxes, Comparative Perspectives," *Journal of American Studies* 28 (1994): 335–58; Donald E. Pease, "National Identities, Postmodern Artifacts, and Postnational Narratives," *boundary 2* 19, no. 1 (1992): 1–13; and any recent American Studies presidential address.

3   Sheldon Wolin describes politicalness as "our capacity for developing into beings who know and value what it means to participate in and be responsible for the care and improvement of our common and collective life." Sheldon S. Wolin, *The Presence of the Past: Essays on the State and the Constitution* (Baltimore: Johns Hopkins University Press, 1989), 139. Subsequent references are cited parenthetically in the text. It is a definition incomplete in its gentle optimism, one that might usefully be supplemented by Bonnie Honig's affirmation of the value of embracing political struggle for the health of democracy: "To affirm the perpetuity of contest is not to celebrate a world without points of stabilization; it is to affirm the reality of perpetual contest, even within an ordered setting, and to identify the affirmative dimensions of contestation. It is to see that the always-imperfect closure of political space tends to engender remainders and that, if those remainders are not engaged, they may return to haunt and destabilize the very closures that deny their existence. It is to treat rights and laws as part of a political contest rather than as the instrument of its closure. It is to see that attempts to shut down the agon perpetually fail, that the best (or worst) they do is displace politics onto other sites and topics, where the struggle of identity and difference, resistance and closure, is then repeated." Honig, *Political Theory and the Displacement of Politics* (Ithaca, N.Y.: Cornell University Press, 1993), 15–16. Subsequent references are cited parenthetically in the text.

4   Tim Burton, dir., *Mars Attacks!* (Warner Bros., 1996).

5   Peter Euben, "Taking It to the Streets: Radical Democracy and Radicalizing Theory," in *Radical Democracy: Identity, Citizenship, and the State*, ed. David Trend (New York: Routledge, 1996), 64. Subsequent references are cited parenthetically in the text.

6   See, for instance, Etienne Balibar, "The Nation Form: History and Ideology," *Review, Fernand Braudel Center* 13, no. 3 (1990): 329–61; and Slavoj Žižek, "Eastern Europe's Republics of Gilead," *New Left Review* 183 (1990): 50–62.

7   Janice Radway, "What's in a Name? Presidential Address to the American Studies Association, 20 November, 1998," *American Quarterly* 51, no. 1 (1999): 8. Subsequent references are cited parenthetically in the text.

8   Nikhil Pal Singh, "Culture/Wars: Recoding Empire in an Age of Democracy," *American Quarterly* 50, no. 3 (1998): 514. Subsequent references are cited parenthetically in the text.

9   Democratic in the sense that this universalism comes to us from "the insurrectionary, republican demand for liberty and equality derived from a long, revolutionary, democratic tradition thought to precede and exceed the social institution of modern states" (481–82). Singh does not here attempt to define democracy. He does seem to suggest it deserves the kind of analytic complication that he offers for the notion of universalism.

10   I detail this argument in the first chapter of my book *National Manhood: Capitalist Citizenship and the Imagined Fraternity of White Men* (Durham, N.C.: Duke University Press, 1998).

11   In a different context, Laura Kipnis has described the antipolitical energy of planning for the future, where "children" might well stand in for the "next generation" of American studies: "Investing futurity and optimism in your children is always a good displacement; they make convenient prostheses for any surplus hopefulness you find yourself burdened with, as well as tidy explanations for your inertia should you be called on to explain it." "Adultery," *Critical Inquiry* 24 (1998): 326.

12   Wendy Brown, in her forthcoming essay, "Toward a Genealogy of Contemporary Political Moralism" (in *Materializing Democracy*, ed. Russ Castronovo and Dana D. Nelson [Durham, N.C.: Duke University Press, 2002]), talks about moralism in this way: "As leftists are not free of attachment to total critique and total transformation, liberals are not free of attachment to ontological and political universalism and hence to assimilationism. Neither leftists nor liberals are free of attachment to progress in history. The consequence of living these attachments as ungrievable losses (ungrievable because not fully avowed as attachments and hence as losses) is theoretical as well as political impotence and rage, which converts discursively to reproachful political moralism. Put differently, the righteous moralism that so many have registered as the characteristic political discourse of our time—as the tiresome tonality and uninspiring spirit of right, center and left—I want to consider as a *symptom* of a certain kind of loss."

13   Jeffrey C. Goldfarb, *Civility and Subversion: The Intellectual in Democratic Society* (New York: Cambridge University Press, 1998), 74. Subsequent references are cited parenthetically in the text.

14   Patrick McGee, *Cinema, Theory, and Political Responsibility in Contemporary Culture* (New York: Cambridge University Press, 1997), 36.

15   It is not at all clear to me that the best political use of our energy does come in being a "public intellectual," nor is it clear to me that our deciding to contribute to public debates will lead unproblematically to a forum for our ideas that we will feel satisfied by. For an interesting argument about "the ways in which academics' presumptions of intellectual authority (however well deserved) are sometimes at odds with our civic desires," see Elizabeth Ervin's "Academics and the Negotiation of Local Knowledge," *College English* 61, no. 4 (1999): 448–70.

16   As Wendy Brown describes it, "The irony of melancholia, of course, is that

attachment to the object of one's sorrowful loss supersedes any desire to recover from this loss, to live free of it in the present, to be unburdened by it." "Resisting Left Melancholy," *boundary 2* 26, no. 3 (1999): 20.

17 Wahneema Lubiano, "Like Being Mugged by a Metaphor: Multiculturalism and State Narratives," in *Mapping Multiculturalism*, ed. Avery F. Gordon and Christopher Newfield (Minneapolis: University of Minnesota Press, 1996), 69. Subsequent references are cited parenthetically in the text.

18 Herbert Marcuse, "Philosophy and Critical Theory," in *Negations: Essays in Critical Theory*, trans. Jeremy J. Shapiro (Boston: Beacon, 1968), 143. Avery Gordon's work "On Utopian Thinking" brought my attention back to this passage and boosted my hopefulness about the present in important ways. Finding these conditions will mean risking a fuller commitment to a democracy that happens not "out there" but with us. It will perhaps mean, as Lummis suggests, falling in love with it, not idealistically, but with open eyes: "Given its muddled meaning in contemporary discourse, to say that you are for democracy suggests silliness, to say that you are *interested* in it, at least in so-called democratic countries, may be taken as a sign of bad taste, especially in academic circles. 'Democracy' is, of course, a word everyone is willing to use, but to fall in love with it is another matter. As for political philosophies of liberation, we are today in a kind of Hundred Flowers period. We are surrounded by a profusion of schools of thought, many of which are brilliantly sophisticated and terribly difficult, requiring years of study to understand. In this context to choose democracy as the issue to be interested in is hardly stylish. It is rather like entering a society of gourmet cooks and announcing that you like the taste of plain water" (19–20).

19 Christopher Newfield, "Recapturing Academic Business," in *Chalk Lines: The Politics of Work in the Managed University*, ed. Randy Martin (Durham, N.C.: Duke University Press, 1998), 71.

20 What they have is more like what Lauren Berlant has described as "dead citizenship": "I use the word 'dead' . . . in the rhetorical sense designated by the phrase 'dead metaphor.' . . . In the fantasy world of national culture, citizens aspire to dead identities—constitutional personhood in its public-sphere abstractions and suprahistoricity; reproductive heterosexuality in the zone of privacy." Lauren Berlant, *The Queen of America Goes to Washington City: Essays on Sex and Citizenship* (Durham, N.C.: Duke University Press, 1997), 60.

21 See Bonnie Honig's "Immigrant America? How Foreignness 'Solves' Democracy's Problems," *Social Text* 16, no. 3 (1998): 19.

22 Jeff Smith, "Student Goals, Gatekeeping, and Some Questions of Ethics," *College English* 59, no. 3 (1997): 317.

23 I take this phrase from political philosopher William Corlett's provocative book, *Community without Unity: A Politics of Derridean Extravagance* (Durham, N.C.: Duke University Press, 1989).

Bibliography

Abel, Elizabeth. "Black Writing, White Reading: Race and the Politics of Feminist Interpretation." In *Female Subjects in Black and White: Race, Psychoanalysis, Feminism*, ed. Elizabeth Abel, Barbara Christian, and Helene Moglen, 102–31. Berkeley: University of California Press, 1997.

Abelove, Henry, Michèle Aina Barale, and David M. Halperin, eds. *The Lesbian and Gay Studies Reader*. New York: Routledge, 1993.

Adorno, Theodor W. *Critical Models: Interventions and Catchwords*. Trans. Henry W. Pickford. New York: Columbia University Press, 1998.

Agamben, Giorgio. *Homo Sacer: Sovereign Power and Bare Life*. Trans. Daniel Heller-Roazen. Stanford, Calif.: Stanford University Press, 1998.

Allen, Theodore W. *The Invention of the White Race*. Vol. 1. New York: Verso, 1994.

Allmendinger, Blake. *Ten Most Wanted: The New Western Literature*. New York: Routledge, 1998.

Althusser, Louis. "Ideology and Ideological State Apparatuses (Notes towards an Investigation)." In *For Marx*. Trans. Ben Brewster. New York: Pantheon, 1969. 127–160.

Anderson, Benedict. *Imagined Communities: Reflections on the Origin and Spread of Nationalism*. Rev. ed. London: Verso, 1991.

Appiah, Kwame Anthony. "Against National Culture." In *Text and Nation: Cross-Disciplinary Essays on Cultural and National Identities*, ed. Laura García-Moreno and Peter C. Pfeiffer, 175–90. Columbia, S.C.: Camden House, 1996.

———. *Identity against Culture: Understandings of Multiculturalism*. Berkeley: Doreen B. Townsend Center for the Humanities, University of California, 1994.

Appiah, Kwame Anthony, and Henry Louis Gates Jr., eds. *Identities*. Chicago: University of Chicago Press, 1995.

Appiah, Kwame Anthony, and Amy Gutmann. *Color Conscious: The Political Morality of Race*. Princeton, N.J.: Princeton UP, 1996.

Appleby, Joyce. "Recovering America's Historical Diversity: Beyond Exceptionalism." *Journal of American History* 79, no. 2 (1992): 419–31.

Arac, Jonathan. "American Pedagogies." Paper presented at The Futures of American Studies Conference, Dartmouth College, 14 August 1997.

———. *Critical Genealogies: Historical Situations for Postmodern Literary Studies*. New York: Columbia University Press, 1987.

Archard, David. *Children: Rights and Childhood*. New York: Routledge, 1993.

Arendt, Hannah. *Eichmann in Jerusalem: A Report on the Banality of Evil*. New York: Penguin, 1977.

———. *The Human Condition*. Chicago: University of Chicago Press, 1958.

———. "The Jew as Pariah." In *The Jew as Pariah: Jewish Identity and Politics in the Modern Age*, ed. Ron H. Feldman, 67–90. New York: Grove, 1978.

———. *The Life of the Mind*. New York: Harcourt Brace Jovanovich, 1978.

Aries, Philippe. *Centuries of Childhood: A Social History of Family Life*. Trans. Robert Baldick. New York: Vintage, 1962.

Aristotle. *Rhetoric*. Trans. W. Rhys Roberts. New York: Modern Library, 1954.

Armstrong, Nancy. *Desire and Domestic Fiction: A Political History of the Novel*. New York: Oxford University Press, 1987.

Arnold, Matthew. *Culture and Anarchy and Other Writings*. Ed. Stefan Collini. Cambridge: Cambridge University Press, 1993.

Aronowitz, Stanley. *False Promises: The Shaping of American Working Class Consciousness*. New York: McGraw-Hill, 1973.

Aronowitz, Stanley, and Henry A. Giroux. *Postmodern Education: Politics, Culture, and Social Criticism*. Minneapolis: University of Minnesota Press, 1991.

Arrington, Leonard, and Jon Haupt. "Intolerable Zion: The Image of Mormonism in Nineteenth-Century American Literature." *Western Humanities Review* 22 (1968): 243–60.

Avery, Gillian. *Behold the Child: American Children and Their Books, 1621–1922*. Baltimore: Johns Hopkins University Press, 1994.

Ayers, Edward L. *Vengeance and Justice: Crime and Punishment in the Nineteenth-Century American South*. New York: Oxford University Press, 1984.

Babb, Valerie. *Whiteness Visible: The Meaning of Whiteness in American Literature and Culture*. New York: New York University Press, 1998.

Balakrishnan, Gopal. "The National Imagination." *New Left Review* 211 (1995): 56–69.

Baldwin, James. "On Being 'White' . . . and Other Lies." *Essence*, April 1984, 90–92.

Balibar, Etienne. "The Nation Form: History and Ideology." *Review, Fernand Braudel Center* 13, no. 3 (1990): 329–61.

——. "Paradoxes of Universality." Trans. Michael Edwards. In *Anatomy of Racism*, ed. David Theo Goldberg, 283–94. Minneapolis: University of Minnesota Press, 1990.

——. *The Philosophy of Marx*. Trans. Chris Turner. London: Verso, 1995.

Balibar, Etienne, and Immanuel Wallerstein. *Race, Nation, Class: Ambiguous Identities*. London: Verso, 1991.

Bambara, Toni Cade. "The Hammer Man." In *Gorilla, My Love*, 33–43. 1972. New York: Vintage, 1992.

Bancroft, Hubert Howe. *History of Utah*. San Francisco: History Company, 1889.

Banta, Martha. "Working the Levees: Building Them Up or Knocking Them Down?" *American Quarterly* 43, no. 3 (1991): 375–91.

Barbalet, J. M. *Citizenship: Rights, Struggle, and Class Inequality*. Minneapolis: University of Minnesota Press, 1988.

Barrett, Lindon. "Black Men in the Mix: Badboys, Heroes, Sequins, and Dennis Rodman." *Callaloo* 20, no. 1 (1997): 106–26.

Bass, Ellen, and Laura Davis. *The Courage to Heal: A Guide for Women Survivors of Child Sexual Abuse*. New York: Harper and Row, 1988.

Bass, Randy, and Jeffrey Finlay. *Engines of Inquiry: A Practical Guide for Using Technol-*

ogy to Teach America Studies. Washington, D.C.: Georgetown University Press, 1997.

Baudrillard, Jean. *The Mirror of Production*. St. Louis: Telos, 1975.

Bauerlein, Mark. *The Pragmatic Mind: Explorations in the Psychology of Belief*. Durham, N.C.: Duke University Press, 1997.

Bawer, Bruce. *A Place at the Table: The Gay Individual in American Society*. New York: Touchstone, 1994.

Baym, Nina. "Melodramas of Beset Manhood: How Theories of American Fiction Exclude Women Authors." *American Quarterly* 33, no. 2 (1981): 123–39.

——. "Onward Christian Women: Sarah J. Hale's History of the World." *New England Quarterly* 63 (1990): 249–70.

——. *Woman's Fiction: A Guide to Novels by and about Women in America, 1820–1870*. Ithaca, N.Y.: Cornell University Press, 1978.

Beecher, Catharine. *A Treatise on Domestic Economy*. Boston: Marsh, Capen, Lyon and Webb, 1841.

Beecher, Catharine, and Harriet Beecher Stowe. *The American Woman's Home*. Hartford: Ford, 1869.

Bell, Alfreda Eva. *Boadicea the Mormon Wife*. Baltimore: A. R. Orton, 1855.

Bell, Daniel. *The End of Ideology: On the Exhaustion of Political Ideas in the Fifties*. New York: Free Press, 1962.

Bell, Derrick. *And We Are Not Saved: The Elusive Quest for Racial Justice*. New York: Basic Books, 1987.

Bellah, Robert N., et al. *Habits of the Heart: Individualism and Commitment in American Life*. New York: Harper and Row, 1986.

Benjamin, Walter. *Charles Baudelaire: A Lyric Poet in the Era of High Capitalism*. Trans. Harry Zohn. London: New Left Books, 1973.

——. *Illuminations*. Ed. Hannah Arendt. Trans. Harry Zohn. New York: Schocken, 1969.

——. *Reflections: Essays, Aphorisms, Autobiographical Writings*, ed. Peter Demetz, trans. Edmund Jephcott. New York: Schocken, 1986.

Bercovitch, Sacvan. Afterword to *Ideology and Classic American Literature*, ed. Bercovitch and Myra Jehlen, 418–42. Cambridge: Cambridge University Press, 1986.

——. *The American Jeremiad*. Madison: University of Wisconsin Press, 1978.

——. *The Office of The Scarlet Letter*. Baltimore: Johns Hopkins University Press, 1991.

——. *The Rites of Assent: Transformations in the Symbolic Construction of America*. New York: Routledge, 1993.

Bergson, Henri. *L'Evolution créatrice*. Paris: Presses universitaires de France, 1948.

Berlant, Lauren. "Live Sex Acts (Parental Advisory: Explicit Material)." *Feminist Studies* 21, no. 2 (1995): 379–404.

——. "Poor Eliza." *American Literature* 70, no. 3 (1998): 635–68.

——. *The Queen of America Goes to Washington City: Essays on Sex and Citizenship*. Durham, N.C.: Duke University Press, 1997.

Bersani, Leo. "Is the Rectum a Grave?" *October* 43 (1987): 197–222.

Bérubé, Michael. *The Employment of English: Theory, Jobs, and the Future of Literary Studies*. New York: New York University Press, 1998.

——. "It's Renaissance Time: New Historicism, American Studies, and American Identity." In *Public Access: Literary Theory and American Cultural Politics*, 203–24. London: Verso, 1994.

——. Review of *American Anatomies: Theorizing Race and Gender*, by Robyn Wiegman. *African American Review* 31, no. 2 (1997): 317–20.

Bérubé, Michael, and Cary Nelson, eds. *Higher Education under Fire: Politics, Economics, and the Crisis of the Humanities*. New York: Routledge, 1995.

Beverley, John. *Against Literature*. Minneapolis: University of Minnesota Press, 1993.

Bhabha, Homi K. "DissemiNation: Time, Narrative, and the Margins of the Modern Nation." In *Nation and Narration*, ed. Homi Bhabha, 291–322. New York: Routledge, 1990.

——. *The Location of Culture*. New York: Routledge, 1994.

Bloch, Ernst. *The Utopian Function of Art and Literature: Selected Essays*. Trans. Jack Zipes and Frank Mecklenburg. Cambridge, Mass.: MIT Press, 1988.

Bode, Carl. "The Start of the ASA." *American Quarterly* 31, no. 3 (1979): 345–54.

Bourdieu, Pierre. *Distinction: A Social Critique of the Judgement of Taste*. Trans. Richard Nice. Cambridge, Mass.: Harvard University Press, 1984.

Bové, Paul A. "Abandoning Knowledge: Disciplines, Discourse, Dogma." *New Literary History* 25 (1994): 601–19.

——. "Giving Thought to America: Intellect and *The Education of Henry Adams*." *Critical Inquiry* 23, no. 1 (1996): 80–108.

——. *In the Wake of Theory*. Middletown, Conn.: Wesleyan University Press, 1992.

——. "Policing Thought: On Learning How to Read Henry Adams." *Critical Inquiry* 23, no. 4 (1997): 939–46.

Brantlinger, Patrick. *Crusoe's Footprints: Cultural Studies in Britain and America*. New York: Routledge, 1990.

Braverman, Harry. *Labor and Monopoly Capital: The Degradation of Work in the Twentieth Century*. New York: Monthly Review, 1974.

Bronfen, Elisabeth. *Over Her Dead Body: Death, Femininity, and the Aesthetic*. New York: Routledge, 1992.

Brown, Gillian. "Consent, Coquetry, and Consequences." *American Literary History* 9 (1997): 625–52.

——. *Domestic Individualism: Imagining Self in Nineteenth-Century America*. Berkeley: University of California Press, 1990.

Brown, Wendy. "Resisting Left Melancholy." *boundary 2* 26, no. 3 (1999): 19–27.

——. *States of Injury: Power and Freedom in Late Modernity*. Princeton, N.J.: Princeton University Press, 1995.

——. "Toward a Genealogy of Contemporary Political Moralism." In *Materializing Democracy*, ed. Russ Castronovo and Dana D. Nelson. Durham, N.C.: Duke University Press, forthcoming.

Buell, Lawrence. "Are We Post-American Studies?" In *Field Work: Sites in Literary and Cultural Studies*, ed. Marjorie Garber, Paul B. Franklin, and Rebecca L. Walkowitz, 87–93. New York: Routledge, 1996.

Buhle, Paul. *Marxism in the United States: Remapping the History of the American Left*. London: Verso, 1991.

Bulkin, Elly, Minnie Bruce Pratt, and Barbara Smith. *Yours in Struggle: Three Feminist Perspectives of Anti-Semitism and Racism*. Brooklyn, N.Y.: Long Haul, 1984.

Bunker, Gary L., and Davis Bitton. *The Mormon Graphic Image, 1834–1914: Cartoons, Caricatures, and Illustrations*. Salt Lake City: University of Utah Press, 1983.

Burke, Kenneth. *Counter-Statement*. Los Altos, Calif.: Hermes Publications, 1953.

———. *Permanence and Change: An Anatomy of Purpose*. New York: New Republic, 1935.

Burton, Tim, dir. *Mars Attacks!* Warner Bros., 1996.

Butler, Judith. *Bodies That Matter: On the Discursive Limits of "Sex."* New York: Routledge, 1993.

———. *Excitable Speech: A Politics of the Performative*. New York: Routledge, 1997.

Byers, Thomas B. "History Re-membered: *Forrest Gump*, Postfeminist Masculinity, and the Burial of the Counterculture." *Modern Fiction Studies* 42, no. 2 (1996): 420–44.

Cain, William E. *F. O. Matthiessen and the Politics of Criticism*. Madison: University of Wisconsin Press, 1988.

Campbell, David. "Political Prosaics, Transversal Politics, and the Anarchical World." In *Challenging Boundaries: Global Flows, Territorial Identities*, Ed. Michael J. Shapiro and Hayward R. Alker, 7–32. Minneapolis: University of Minnesota Press, 1996.

Cannon, Charles A. "The Awesome Power of Sex: The Polemical Campaign against Mormon Polygamy." *Pacific Historical Review* 43 (1974): 61–82.

Carby, Hazel V. "The Multicultural Wars." *Radical History Review* 54 (1992): 7–18.

Carnoy, Martin. "Education, State, and Culture in American Society." In *Critical Pedagogy, the State, and Cultural Struggle*, Ed. Henry A. Giroux and Peter L. McLaren, 3–23. Albany: State University of New York Press, 1989.

Castellanos, Susan. "Masculine Sentimentalism and the Project of Nation-Building." Paper presented at the Nineteenth-Century Women Writers in the Twenty-First Century Conference, Trinity College, May–June 1996.

Castoriadis, Cornelius. *The Imaginary Institution of Society*. Cambridge, Mass.: MIT Press, 1987.

Chan, Sucheng. *Asian Americans: An Interpretive History*. Boston: Twayne, 1991.

"Channeling." *The Conspiracy of the Young*, ed. Paul Lauter and Florence Howe, 184–91. New York: World Publishing, 1970.

Chase, Richard Volney. *Herman Melville: A Critical Study*. New York: Macmillan, 1949.

Chatterjee, Partha. *The Nation and Its Fragments: Colonial and Postcolonial Histories*. Princeton, N.J.: Princeton University Press, 1993.

Cheah, Pheng, and Bruce Robbins, eds. *Cosmopolitics: Thinking and Feeling beyond the Nation*. Minneapolis: University of Minnesota Press, 1998.

Cheyfitz, Eric. "The Navajo-Hopi Land Dispute: A Brief History." *Interventions: International Journal of Postcolonial Studies* 2, no. 2 (2000): 248–75.

——. "Redistribution and the Transformation of American Studies." In *Critical Theory and the Teaching of Literature: Politics, Curriculum, Pedagogy*, ed. James F. Slevin and Art Young, 93–122. Urbana, Ill.: National Council of Teachers of English, 1996.

——. "What Work Is There for Us to Do? American Literary Study or Americas Cultural Studies?" *American Literature* 67, no. 4 (1995): 843–53.

Chicago Critical Studies Group. "Critical Multiculturalism." *Critical Inquiry* 18, no. 3 (1992): 530–55.

Chinchilla, Norma, Nora Hamilton, and James Loucky. "Central Americans in Los Angeles: An Immigrant Community in Transition." In *In The Barrios: Latinos and the Underclass Debate*, ed. Joan Moore and Raquel Pinderhughes, 51–78. New York: Russell Sage Foundation, 1993.

Chomsky, Noam. *Deterring Democracy*. New York: Hill and Wang, 1992.

Clifford, James. *Routes: Travel and Translation in the Late Twentieth Century*. Cambridge, Mass.: Harvard University Press, 1997.

Cohen, Carl. *Naked Racial Preference*. Lanham, Md.: Madison, 1995.

Cohen, Lizabeth. *Making a New Deal: Industrial Workers in Chicago, 1919–1939*. New York: Cambridge University Press, 1990.

Connolly, William E. *The Ethos of Pluralization*. Minneapolis: University of Minnesota Press, 1995.

Corlett, William. *Community without Unity: A Politics of Derridean Extravagance*. Durham, N.C.: Duke University Press, 1989.

"Corporate Culture." Special issue of *Social Text* 44 (1995).

Cott, Nancy F. *The Bonds of Womanhood: "Woman's Sphere" in New England, 1780–1835*. New Haven, Conn.: Yale University Press, 1977.

——. "Giving Character to Our Whole Civil Polity: Marriage and the Public Order in the Late Nineteenth Century." In *U.S. History as Women's History: New Feminist Essays*, ed. Linda K. Kerber, Alice Kessler-Harris, and Kathryn Kish Sklar, 107–21. Chapel Hill: University of North Carolina Press, 1995.

Council for Aid to Education. *Breaking the Social Contract: The Fiscal Crisis in Higher Education*. Santa Monica, Calif.: Rand, 1997.

Cowan, Michael. "Boundary as Center: Inventing an American Studies Culture." *Prospects: An Annual of American Cultural Studies* 12 (1987): 1–20.

Crenshaw, Kimberlé. "Demarginalizing the Intersection of Race and Sex: A Black Feminist Critique of Antidiscrimination Doctrine, Feminist Theory, and Antiracist Politics." *University of Chicago Legal Forum* 139 (1989): 139–67.

Crenshaw, Kimberlé, et al., eds. *Critical Race Theory: The Key Writings That Formed the Movement*. New York: New Press, 1995.

Cuche, Denys. *La notion de culture dans les sciences sociales*. Paris: Editions La Découverte, 1996.

Cumings, Bruce. *The Origins of the Korean War*. Princeton, N.J.: Princeton University Press, 1981–1990.

Cummins, Maria Susanna. *The Lamplighter*. 1854. New Brunswick, N.J.: Rutgers University Press, 1988.

Dallal, Jenine Abboushi. "The Beauty of Imperialism: Emerson, Melville, Flaubert, and Al-Shidyac." Ph.D. diss., Harvard University, 1996.

Danaher, Kevin, ed. *50 Years Is Enough: The Case against the World Bank and the International Monetary Fund*. Boston: South End, 1994.

Daniels, Jessie. *White Lies: Race, Class, Gender, and Sexuality in White Supremacist Discourse*. New York: Routledge, 1997.

Daniels, Roger. *Coming to America: A History of Immigration and Ethnicity in American Life*. New York: HarperCollins, 1990.

Davidson, Cathy. "Loose Change." *American Quarterly* 46, no. 2 (1996): 123–38.

Davis, Allen F. "The Politics of American Studies." *American Quarterly* 42, no. 3 (1990): 353–74.

Davis, F. James. *Who Is Black? One Nation's Definition*. University Park: Pennsylvania State University Press, 1991.

Debord, Guy. *The Society of the Spectacle*. Trans. Donald Nicholson-Smith. New York: Zone, 1994.

Decker, Jeffrey Louis. "Dis-assembling the Machine in the Garden: Antihumanism and the Critique of American Studies." *New Literary History* 23 (1992): 281–306.

Delany, Samuel R. *The Motion of Light in Water: Sex and Science Fiction Writing in the East Village: 1960–1965*. London: Paladin, 1988.

———. *Times Square Red, Times Square Blue*. New York: New York University Press, 1999.

Deleuze, Gilles, and Félix Guattari. *Kafka: Toward a Minor Literature*. Trans. Dana Polan. Minneapolis: University of Minnesota Press, 1986.

———. *A Thousand Plateaus: Capitalism and Schizophrenia*. Trans. Brian Massumi. Minneapolis: University of Minnesota Press, 1987.

Delgado, Richard, ed. *Critical Race Theory: The Cutting Edge*. Philadelphia: Temple University Press, 1995.

Delgado, Richard, and Jean Stefancic, eds. *Critical White Studies: Looking behind the Mirror*. Philadelphia: Temple University Press, 1997.

Denning, Michael. *The Cultural Front: The Laboring of American Culture in the Twentieth Century*. London: Verso, 1996.

———. " 'The Special American Conditions': Marxism and American Studies." *American Quarterly* 38, no. 3 (1986): 356–80.

Derrida, Jacques. "Declarations of Independence." Trans. Tom Keenan and Tom Pepper. *New Political Science* 15 (1976): 7–15.

———. *Of Grammatology*. Trans. Gayatri Chakravorty Spivak. Baltimore: Johns Hopkins University Press, 1976.

———. *Specters of Marx: The State of the Debt, the Work of Mourning, and the New International*. Trans. Peggy Kamuf. New York: Routledge, 1994.

Dershowitz, Alan M. *The Abuse Excuse and Other Cop-Outs, Sob Stories, and Evasions of Responsibility*. New York: Little, Brown, 1994.

Desmond, Jane C., and Virginia R. Dominguez. "Resituating American Studies in a Critical Internationalism." *American Quarterly* 48, no. 3 (1996): 475–90.

di Leonardo, Micaela. *Exotics at Home: Anthropologies, Others, American Modernity.* Chicago: University of Chicago Press, 1998.

———."White Lies, Black Myths: Rape, Race, and the Black 'Underclass.' " In *The Gender/Sexuality Reader: Culture, History, Political Economy*, ed. Roger N. Lancaster and di Leonardo, 53–68. New York: Routledge, 1997.

Dixon, William H. *New America.* 2 vols. London: Hurst and Blackett, 1867.

Dortman, Ariel, and Armand Mattelart. *How to Read Donald Duck: Imperialist Ideology in the Disney Comic.* Trans. David Kunzle. New York: International General, 1975.

Douglas, Ann. *The Feminization of American Culture.* New York: Knopf, 1977.

Douzinas, Costas, and Ronnie Warrington. " 'A Well-Founded Fear of Justice': Law and Ethics in Postmodernity." In *Legal Studies as Cultural Studies: A Reader in (Post)Modern Critical Theory*, ed. Jerry Leonard, 197–229. Albany: State University of New York Press, 1995.

Doyle, Laura. *Bordering on the Body: The Racial Matrix of Modern Fiction and Culture.* New York: Oxford University Press, 1994.

Drinnon, Richard. *Facing West: The Metaphysics of Indian-Hating and Empire Building.* Minneapolis: University of Minnesota Press, 1980.

D'Souza, Dinesh. *The End of Racism: Principles for a Multiracial Society.* New York: Free Press, 1995.

Duany, Jorge. "Popular Music in Puerto Rico: Toward an Anthropology of Salsa." *Revista de música latino americana* 5, no. 2 (1985): 186–216.

Du Bois, W. E. B. *Black Reconstruction: An Essay toward a History of the Part which Black Folk Played in the Attempt to Reconstruct Democracy in America, 1860–1880.* New York: Atheneum, 1935.

Duggan, Lisa. "The Discipline Problem: Queer Theory Meets Lesbian and Gay History." *GLQ: A Journal of Lesbian and Gay Studies* 2, no. 3 (1995): 179–91.

———. *The Incredibly Shrinking Public Sphere.* Boston: Beacon Press, 2002.

———. "Queering the State." *Social Text* 39 (1994): 1–14.

Dyer, Richard. *White.* New York: Routledge, 1997.

———. "White." *Screen* 29, no. 4 (1988): 44–64.

Edmundson, Mark. *Nightmare on Main Street: Angels, Sadomasochism, and the Culture of Gothic.* Cambridge, Mass.: Harvard University Press, 1997.

Eliot, T. S. *Christianity and Culture: The Idea of a Christian Society and Notes towards the Definition of Culture.* San Diego, Calif.: Harcourt, Brace, 1976.

Elteren, Melvan. "American Studies in Europe: Its Vital Role in Internationalizing the Field." *Journal of American Culture* 20, no. 4 (1997): 87–96.

Eng, David L. "Out Here and Over There: Queerness and Diaspora in Asian American Studies." *Social Text* 52–53 (1997): 31–52.

Engel, Beverly. *The Right to Innocence: Healing the Trauma of Childhood Sexual Abuse.* New York: Ivy Books, 1989.

Enzensberger, Hans Magnus. *The Consciousness Industry: On Literature, Politics, and the Media*. New York: Seabury, 1974.

Erkkila, Betsy. "Ethnicity, Literary Theory, and the Grounds of Resistance." *American Quarterly* 47, no. 4 (1995): 563–94.

Ervin, Elizabeth. "Academics and the Negotiation of Local Knowledge." *College English* 61, no. 4 (1999): 448–70.

Euben, Peter. "Taking It to the Streets: Radical Democracy and Radicalizing Theory." In *Radical Democracy: Identity, Citizenship, and the State*, ed. David Trend, 62–77. New York: Routledge, 1996.

Fanon, Frantz. *Black Skin, White Masks*. Trans. Charles Lam Markmann. New York: Grove, 1967.

———. *The Wretched of the Earth*. Trans. Constance Farrington. New York: Grove, 1963.

Fellini, Federico, dir., *8 1/2*. Cinerz, 1963.

Fine, Michelle, et al., eds. *Off White: Readings on Race, Power, and Society*. New York: Routledge, 1997.

Finley, Ruth E. *The Lady of Godey's: Sarah Josepha Hale*. Philadelphia: Lippincott, 1931.

Fish, Stanley. "Boutique Multiculturalism, or Why Liberals Are Incapable of Thinking about Hate Speech." *Critical Inquiry* 23, no. 2 (1997): 378–95.

Fisher, Philip, ed. *The New American Studies: Essays from Representations*. Berkeley: University of California Press, 1991.

Fishkin, Shelley Fisher. *Was Huck Black? Mark Twain and African-American Voices*. New York: Oxford University Press, 1993.

Flacks, Richard, and Scott L. Thomas. "Students in the Nineties: Report on a Project in Progress." Unpublished essay.

Fliegelman, Jay. *Prodigals and Pilgrims: The American Revolution against Patriarchal Authority, 1750–1800*. Cambridge: Cambridge University Press, 1982.

Fluck, Winfried. "The Americanization of Literary Studies." *American Studies International* 28, no. 2 (1990): 9–22.

———. "Cultures of Criticism: *Moby-Dick*, Expressive Individualism, and the New Historicism." *REAL* 11 (1995): 207–28.

———. "Literature, Liberalism, and the Current Cultural Radicalism." In *Why Literature Matters: Theories and Functions of Literature*, ed. Rüdiger Ahrens and Laurenz Volkmann, 211–34. Heidelberg: Winter, 1996.

———. Review of *Was Huck Black?*, by Shelley Fisher Fishkin. *Amerikastudien/American Studies* 39 (1994): 614–17.

Foner, Eric. "Common Origins, Different Paths." *Radical History Review* 71 (1998): 6–10.

———. *Free Soil, Free Labor, Free Men: The Ideology of the Republican Party before the Civil War*. New York: Oxford University Press, 1970.

———. *Tom Paine and Revolutionary America*. New York: Oxford University Press, 1976.

Ford, Stacilee, and Clyde Haulman. " 'To Touch the Trends': Internationalizing

American Studies: Perspectives from Hong Kong and Asia," *American Studies International* 34, no. 2 (1996): 42–58.

Forgie, George B. *Patricide in the House Divided: A Psychological Interpretation of Lincoln and His Age*. New York: Norton, 1979.

Foucault, Michel. *Discipline and Punish: The Birth of the Prison*. Trans. Alan Sheridan. New York: Pantheon, 1977.

——. *History of Sexuality*, vol. 1. Trans. Robert Hurley. New York: Vintage, 1990.

——. "Of Other Spaces," *Diacritics* 16, no. 1 (1986): 22–27.

——. *Power/Knowledge: Selected Interviews and Other Writings, 1972–1977*. Ed. and trans. Colin Gordon. New York: Pantheon, 1980.

Frankenberg, Ruth. *White Women, Race Matters: The Social Construction of Whiteness*. Minneapolis: University of Minnesota Press, 1993.

——, ed. *Displacing Whiteness: Essays in Social and Cultural Criticism*. Durham, N.C.: Duke University Press, 1997.

Fraser, Nancy. *Justice Interruptus: Critical Reflections on the "Postsocialist" Condition*. New York: Routledge, 1997.

Fredrickson, George M. *The Black Image in the White Mind: The Debate on Afro-American Character and Destiny, 1817–1914*. New York: Harper and Row, 1971.

Fredrickson, Renee. *Repressed Memories: A Journey to Recovery from Sexual Abuse*. New York: Simon and Schuster, 1992.

Fregoso, Rosa Linda. "Recycling Colonialist Fantasies on the Texas Borderlands." In *Home, Exile, Homeland: Film, Media, and the Politics of Place*, ed. Hamid Nacify, 169–92. New York: Routledge, 1999.

Friedan, Betty. *The Feminine Mystique*. New York: Norton, 1963.

Fukuyama, Francis. *The End of History and the Last Man*. New York: Free Press, 1992.

Gallin, Dan. "Inside the New World Order." *New Politics* 5, no. 1 (1994): 106–23.

Gardner, Richard A. *True and False Accusations of Child Sex Abuse*. Cresskill, N.J.: Creative Therapeutics, 1992.

Garvey, John, and Noel Ignatiev. "The New Abolitionism," *Minnesota Review* 47 (1996): 105–8.

Geertz, Clifford. "Blurred Genres: The Refiguration of Social Thought." In *Local Knowledge: Further Essays in Interpretive Anthropology*, 19–35. New York: Basic Books, 1983.

George, Susan, and Fabrizio Sabelli. *Faith and Credit: The World Bank's Secular Empire*. Boulder, Colo.: Westview Press, 1994.

Gerstle, Gary. *Working-Class Americanism: The Politics of Labor in a Textile City, 1941–1960*. Cambridge: Cambridge University Press, 1989.

Gessen, Masha. *Dead Again: The Russian Intelligentsia after Communism*. New York: Verso, 1997.

Giles, Paul. "Reconstructing American Studies: Transnational Paradoxes, Comparative Perspectives." *Journal of American Studies* 28 (1994): 335–58.

——. "Virtual Americas: The Internationalization of American Studies and the Ideology of Exchange." *American Quarterly* 50, no. 3 (1998): 523–47.

Gilmore, Glenda Elizabeth. *Gender and Jim Crow: Women and the Politics of White Supremacy in North Carolina, 1896–1920*. Chapel Hill: University of North Carolina Press, 1996.

Gilroy, Paul. *The Black Atlantic: Modernity and Double Consciousness*. New York: Verso, 1993.

Ginsberg, Allen. "America." In *Howl: And Other Poems*, 31–34. San Francisco: City Lights, 1956.

Giroux, Henry. *Border Crossings: Cultural Workers and the Politics of Education*. New York: Routledge, 1992.

Givens, Terryl L. *The Viper on the Hearth: Mormons, Myths, and the Construction of Heresy*. New York: Oxford University Press, 1997.

Glenn, Evelyn Nakano. "Racial Ethnic Women's Labor: The Intersection of Race, Gender, and Class Oppression." *Review of Radical Political Economics* 17, no. 3 (1983): 86–108.

Goldfarb, Jeffrey C. *Civility and Subversion: The Intellectual in Democratic Society*. New York: Cambridge University Press, 1998.

Goodwyn, Lawrence. *The Populist Moment: A Short History of the Agrarian Revolt in America*. New York: Oxford University Press, 1978.

Gopinath, Gayatri. "Nostalgia, Desire, Diaspora: South Asian Sexualities in Motion." *positions: east asia cultures critique* 5, no. 2 (1997): 467–89.

Gordon, Avery F., and Christopher Newfield, eds. *Mapping Multiculturalism*. Minneapolis: University of Minnesota Press, 1996.

Gordon, Linda. *Heroes of Their Own Lives: The Politics and History of Family Violence: Boston 1880–1960*. New York: Penguin, 1989.

Gordon, Sarah Barringer. " 'The Liberty of Self-Degradation': Polygamy, Woman Suffrage, and Consent in Nineteenth-Century America." *Journal of American History* 83, no. 3 (1996): 815–47.

——. " 'Our National Hearthstone': Anti-polygamy Fiction and the Sentimental Campaign against Moral Diversity in Antebellum America." *Yale Journal of Law and the Humanities* 8 (1996): 295–350.

——. " 'The Twin Relic of Barbarism': A Legal History of Anti-polygamy in Nineteenth-Century America." Ph.D. diss., Princeton University, 1995.

Gossett, Thomas F. *Uncle Tom's Cabin and American Culture*. Dallas: Southern Methodist University Press, 1985.

Gotanda, Neil. "Towards Repeal of Asian Exclusion: The Magnuson Act of 1943, the Act of July 2, 1946, the Presidential Proclamation of July 4, 1946, the Act of August 9, 1949, and the Act of August 1, 1950." In *Asian Americans in Congress: A Documentary History*, ed. Hyung Chan Kim, 309–28. Westport, Conn.: Greenwood, 1995.

Graff, Gerald. *Beyond the Culture Wars: How Teaching the Conflicts Can Revitalize American Education*. New York: Norton, 1992.

——. "Teach the Conflicts." *South Atlantic Quarterly* 89 (1990): 51–68.

Gramsci, Antonio. *Selections from Cultural Writings*. Ed. David Forgacs and Geoffrey

Nowell-Smith. Trans. William Boelhower. Cambridge, Mass.: Harvard University Press, 1985.

Grimshaw, Patricia. *Paths of Duty: American Missionary Wives in Nineteenth-Century Hawaii*. Honolulu: University of Hawaii Press, 1989.

Grossberg, Lawrence. *Bringing It All Back Home: Essays on Cultural Studies*. Durham, N.C.: Duke University Press, 1997.

Grossberg, Michael. *Governing the Hearth: Law and the Family in Nineteenth-Century America*. Chapel Hill: University of North Carolina Press, 1985.

Guillory, John. *Cultural Capital: The Problem of Literary Canon Formation*. Chicago: University of Chicago Press, 1993.

Gunn, Giles. *Culture of Criticism and the Criticism of Culture*. New York: Oxford University Press, 1987.

———. Review of *Our America: Nativism, Modernism and Pluralism*, by Walter Benn Michaels. *Journal of American History* 82, no. 2 (1996): 660.

Gupta, Akhil, and James Ferguson, eds. *Culture, Power, Place: Explorations in Critical Anthropology*. Durham, N.C.: Duke University Press, 1997.

Gutiérrez-Jones, Carl. "Injury by Design." *Cultural Critique* 40 (1998): 73–102.

Hale, Sarah J. *Liberia; Or Mr. Peyton's Experiments*. 1853. Upper Saddle River, N.J.: Gregg, 1968.

———. *Northwood; Or, Life North and South: Showing the True Character of Both*. New York: Long and Brother, 1852.

———. *Woman's Record*. New York: Harper, 1853.

Hall, Kim. In *Things of Darkness: Economies of Race and Gender in Early Modern England*. Ithaca, N.Y.: Cornell University Press, 1995.

Hall, Stuart. *The Hard Road to Renewal: Thatcherism and the Crisis of the Left*. London: Verso, 1988.

———. "Notes on Deconstructing the Popular." In *People's History and Socialist Theory*, ed. Raphael Samuel, 226–39. London: Routledge and Kegan Paul, 1981.

Hannerz, Ulf. *Cultural Complexity: Studies in the Social Organization of Meaning*. New York: Columbia University Press, 1992.

———. *Transnational Connections: Culture, People, Places*. New York: Routledge, 1996.

Hansen, Karen Tranberg, ed. *African Encounters with Domesticity*. New Brunswick, N.J.: Rutgers University Press, 1992.

Hardy, Carmon B. *Solemn Covenant: The Mormon Polygamous Passage*. Urbana: University of Illinois Press, 1992.

Harper, Frances E. W. *Iola Leroy, or Shadows Uplifted*. 1892. New York: Oxford University Press, 1988.

Harper, Phillip Brian. *Private Affairs: Critical Ventures in the Culture of Social Relations*. New York: New York University Press, 1999.

Harris, Cheryl. "Whiteness as Property." *Harvard Law Review* 106, no. 8 (1993): 1710–91.

Hartz, Louis. *The Liberal Tradition in America: An Interpretation of American Political Thought since the Revolution*. New York: Harcourt, Brace, 1955.

Harvey, David. *The Limits to Capital*. Chicago: University of Chicago Press, 1982.

Haskell, Robert E. "Academic Freedom, Tenure, and Student Evaluation of Faculty: Galloping Polls in the Twenty-First Century." *Education Policy Analysis Archives*, 12 February 1997. ⟨http://www.bus.lsu.edu/accounting/faculty/lcrumbley/educpoly.htm⟩.

Haug, Wolfgang Fritz. *Critique of Commodity Aesthetics: Appearance, Sexuality, and Advertising in Capitalist Society*. Trans. Robert Bock. Minneapolis: University of Minnesota Press, 1986.

Hawthorne, Nathaniel. *The Blithedale Romance*. 1852. New York: Penguin, 1984.

——. *The Scarlet Letter: A Romance*. 1850. New York: Penguin, 1983.

Heidegger, Martin. "A Dialogue on Language." In *On the Way to Language*, trans. Peter D. Hertz, 1–54. New York: Harper and Row, 1971.

——. *The Question Concerning Technology and Other Essays*. Trans. William Lovitt. New York: Harper and Row, 1977.

——. "What Are Poets For?" In *Poetry, Language, Thought*, trans. Albert Hofstadter, 89–142. New York: Harper and Row, 1971.

——. "What Is Metaphysics?" In *Basic Writings from Being and Time (1927) to The Task of Thinking (1964)*, ed. David Farrell Krell, 89–100. New York: Harper Collins, 1993.

Heilbroner, Robert L. *Marxism, For and Against*. New York: Norton, 1980.

Hellman, John. *American Myth and the Legacy of Vietnam*. New York: Columbia University Press, 1986.

Henderson, Mae G. "Introduction: Borders, Boundaries, and Frame(work)s." In *Borders, Boundaries, and Frames: Essays in Cultural Criticism and Cultural Studies*, ed. Henderson, 1–30. New York: Routledge, 1995.

Henry, Jules. *Culture Against Man*. New York: Random House, 1963.

Henry, Paget, and Paul Buhle, eds. *C. L. R. James's Caribbean*. Durham, N.C.: Duke University Press, 1992.

Henry, William A., III. *In Defense of Elitism*. New York: Anchor, 1995.

Herman, Judith Lewis. *Trauma and Recovery*. New York: Basic Books, 1992.

Herr, Michael. *Dispatches*. New York: Vintage, 1991.

Hietala, Thomas R. *Manifest Design: Anxious Aggrandizement in Late Jacksonian America*. Ithaca, N.Y.: Cornell University Press, 1985.

Higham, John. *Send These to Me: Immigrants in Urban America*. Baltimore: Johns Hopkins University Press, 1984.

Hill, Mike, ed. *Whiteness: A Critical Reader*. New York: New York University Press, 1997.

Hirsch, E. D., Jr. *Cultural Literacy: What Every American Needs to Know*. Boston: Houghton Mifflin, 1987.

Holston, James, and Arjun Appadurai. "Cities and Citizenship." *Public Culture* 8, no. 2 (1996): 187–204.

Hong, Grace Kyungwon. " '. . . Something Forgotten Which Should Have Been Remembered': Private Property and Cross-Racial Solidarity in the Work of Hisaye Yamamoto." *American Literature* 71, no. 2 (1999): 291–310.

Honig, Bonnie. "Immigrant America? How Foreignness 'Solves' Democracy's Problems." *Social Text* 16, no. 3 (1998): 1–27.

———. *Political Theory and the Displacement of Politics*. Ithaca, N.Y.: Cornell University Press, 1993.

Horkheimer, Max, and Theodor W. Adorno. *Dialectic of Enlightenment*. Trans. John Cumming. New York: Seabury, 1972.

Horsman, Reginald. *Race and Manifest Destiny: The Origins of American Racial Anglo-Saxonism*. Cambridge, Mass.: Harvard University Press, 1981.

Horwitz, Richard P. "The Politics of International American Studies." In *Exporting America: Essays on American Studies Abroad*, ed. Richard P. Horwitz, 377–418. New York: Garland, 1993.

Hudson, Mary. *Esther the Gentile*. Topeka: Crane, 1880.

Hunt, Lynn. "The Many Bodies of Marie Antoinette: Political Pornography and the Problem of the Feminine in the French Revolution." In *Eroticism and the Body Politic*, ed. Hunt, 108–30. Baltimore: Johns Hopkins University Press, 1991.

Huntington, Samuel P. "The Clash of Civilizations?" *Foreign Affairs* 72, no. 3 (1993): 22–49.

Ignatieff, Michael. *Blood and Belonging: Journeys into the New Nationalism*. New York: Noonday, 1993.

Ignatiev, Noel. *How the Irish Became White*. New York: Routledge, 1995.

Ignatiev, Noel, and John Garvey, eds. *Race Traitor*. New York: Routledge, 1996.

Iversen, Joan Smyth. *The Antipolygamy Controversy in U.S. Women's Movements, 1880–1925: A Debate on the American Home*. New York: Garland, 1997.

Jaluague, Eleanor M. "Race, Immigration, and Contradiction in Carlos Bulosan's *American Is in the Heart*." *Hitting Critical Mass*, forthcoming.

James, C. L. R. *American Civilization*. Ed. Anna Grimshaw and Keith Hart. Cambridge, Mass.: Blackwell, 1993.

———. *Beyond a Boundary*. London: Hutchinson, 1963.

———. *The Future in the Present: Selected Writings*. Westport, Conn.: Lawrence Hill, 1977.

———. *Mariners, Renegades, and Castaways: The Story of Herman Melville and the World We Live In*. New York: n.p., 1953.

James, C. L. R., Grace Lee, and Pierre Chaulieu. *Facing Reality*. Detroit: Bewick, 1974.

James, Winston. "Migration, Racism, and Identity: The Caribbean Experience in Britain." *New Left Review* 193 (1992): 14–56.

Jameson, Fredric. *Postmodernism; Or, the Cultural Logic of Late Capitalism*. Durham, N.C.: Duke University Press, 1991.

———. *Signatures of the Visible*. New York: Routledge, 1992.

Jay, Gregory S. *American Literature and the Culture Wars*. Ithaca, N.Y.: Cornell University Press, 1997.

Jeffords, Susan. *The Remasculinization of America: Gender and the Vietnam War*. Bloomington: Indiana University Press, 1989.

Johannsen, Robert W. *To the Halls of the Montezumas: The Mexican War in the American Imagination*. New York: Oxford University Press, 1985.

Johnson, Donald Bruce, and Kirk H. Porter, comp. *National Party Platforms, 1840–1972.* Urbana: University of Illinois Press, 1973.

Johnson, James Weldon. *The Autobiography of an Ex-Coloured Man.* Ed. William L. Andrews. New York: Penguin, 1990.

Jun, Helen Heran. "Race For Citizenship: African Americans and Asian Americans." Ph.D. diss., University of California, San Diego, in progress.

Kaminer, Wendy. *I'm Dysfunctional, You're Dysfunctional: The Recovery Movement and Other Self-Help Fashions.* Reading, Mass.: Addison-Wesley, 1992.

Kammen, Michael. "The Problem of American Exceptionalism: A Reconsideration." *American Quarterly* 45, no. 1 (1993): 1–43.

Kaplan, Amy, and Donald E. Pease, eds. *Cultures of United States Imperialism.* Durham, N.C.: Duke University Press, 1993.

Kelley, Mary. *Private Woman, Public Stage: Literary Domesticity in Nineteenth-Century America.* New York: Oxford University Press, 1984.

Kelley, Robin D. G. *Hammer and Hoe: Alabama Communists during the Great Depression.* Chapel Hill: University of North Carolina Press, 1990.

———. *Race Rebels: Culture, Politics, and the Black Working Class.* New York: Free Press, 1994.

Kelman, Mark. *A Guide to Critical Legal Studies.* Cambridge, Mass.: Harvard University Press, 1987.

Kerber, Linda K. "Diversity and the Transformation of American Studies." *American Quarterly* 41, no. 3 (1989): 415–31.

———. "Separate Spheres, Female Worlds, Woman's Place: The Rhetoric of Women's History." *Journal of American History* 75, no. 1 (1988): 9–39.

———. *Women of the Republic: Intellect and Ideology in Revolutionary America.* Chapel Hill: University of North Carolina Press, 1980.

Kerr, Alva Milton. *Trean; or, The Mormon's Daughter: A Romantic Story of Life among the Latter-Day Saints.* Chicago: Belford, Clarke, 1888.

Kessler-Harris, Alice. "Cultural Locations: Positioning American Studies in the Great Debate." *American Quarterly* 44, no. 3 (1992): 299–312.

Kipnis, Laura. "Adultery." *Critical Inquiry* 24, no. 2 (1998): 289–327.

Knapp, Steven. "Collective Memory and the Actual Past." In *Literary Interest: The Limits of Anti-formalism,* 106–40. Cambridge, Mass.: Harvard University Press, 1993.

Knapp, Steven, and Walter Benn Michaels. "Against Theory." In *Against Theory: Literary Studies and the New Pragmatism,* ed. W. J. T. Mitchell, 11–30. Chicago: University of Chicago Press, 1985.

Kolodny, Annette. *The Land before Her: Fantasy and Experience of the American Frontiers, 1630–1860.* Chapel Hill: University of North Carolina Press, 1984.

Kroeber, A. L., and Clyde Kluckhohn. *Culture: A Critical Review of Concepts and Definitions.* New York: Vintage, 1952.

Kroes, Rob. *If You've Seen One, You've Seen the Mall: Europeans and American Mass Culture.* Urbana: University of Illinois Press, 1996.

Kull, Andrew. *The Color-Blind Constitution.* Cambridge, Mass.: Harvard University Press, 1992.

LaCapra, Dominick. "History and Psychoanalysis." In *Soundings in Critical Theory*, 30–66. Ithaca, N.Y.: Cornell University Press, 1989.

——. *Representing the Holocaust: History, Theory, Trauma*. Ithaca, N.Y.: Cornell University Press, 1994.

LaFeber, Walter. *The American Age: United States Foreign Policy at Home and Abroad Since 1750*. New York: Norton, 1989.

Lasch, Christopher. "The Cultural Cold War: A Short History of the Congress for Cultural Freedom." In *Towards a New Past: Dissenting Essays in American History*, ed. Barton J. Bernstein, 322–59. New York: Pantheon, 1968.

Lauter, Paul. "A Call for (at Least a Little) American Studies Chauvinism." *American Studies Newsletter* 18 (1995): 1–3.

——. *Canons and Contexts*. New York: Oxford University Press, 1991.

——. *From Walden Pond to Jurassic Park: Activism, Culture, and American Studies*. Durham, N.C.: Duke University Press, 2001.

——. "The Literatures of America: A Comparative Discipline." In *Redefining American Literary History*, ed. A. LaVonne Brown Ruoff and Jerry W. Ward Jr., 9–34. New York: Modern Language Association of America, 1990.

——. "Versions of Nashville, Visions of American Studies." *American Quarterly* 47, no. 2 (1995): 185–203.

Lauter, Paul, and Ann Fitzgerald, eds. *Literature, Class, and Culture*. New York: Longman, 2001.

Lee, Benjamin. "Critical Internationalism," *Public Culture* 7, no. 3 (1995): 559–92.

Lentricchia, Frank. "Anatomy of a Jar." In *Ariel and the Police: Michel Foucault, William James, Wallace Stevens*, 3–27. Madison: University of Wisonsin Press, 1988.

Lenz, Günter. "American Studies and the Radical Tradition." *Prospects* 12 (1987): 21–58.

——. "The Radical Imagination: Revisionary Modes of Radical Cultural Criticism in Thirties America." In *Looking Inward—Looking Outward: From the 1930s through the 1940s*, ed. Steve Ickringill, 94–126. Amersterdam: VU University Press, 1990.

——. "Refractions of Modernity—Reconstituting Modernism in West Germany after World War II: Jackson Pollock, Ezra Pound, and Charlie Parker." In *Living with America, 1946–1996*, ed. Cristina Giorcelli and Rob Kroes, 139–70. Amsterdam: VU University Press, 1997.

——. "Transnational American Studies: Negotiating Cultures of Difference—Multicultural Identities, Communities, and Border Discourses." In *Multiculturalism in Transit: A German-American Exchange*, ed. Klaus J. Milich and Jeffrey M. Peck, 129–66. New York: Berghahn, 1998.

Lenz, Günter H., and Klaus J. Milich, eds. *American Studies in Germany: European Contexts and Intercultural Relations*. New York: St. Martin's, 1995.

Leo, John R. "Paradigm Shifts: 'Centers' and 'Margins' in American Studies since the Sixties." In *Fringes at the Centre: Actas do XVIII Encontro da APEAA: Associoação Portuguesa de Estudos Anglo-Americanos*, vol. 1. 327–46. Guarda: Escola Superior de Tecnologia e Gestão e Instituto Politécnico da Guarda, 1997.

Levine, Lawrence W. *The Opening of the American Mind: Canons, Culture, and History*. Boston: Beacon, 1996.

Levinson, Barry, dir. *Disclosure*. Warner Bros., 1994.

Lewis, Martin W., and Kären E. Wigen, *The Myth of Continents: A Critique of Metageography*. Berkeley: University of California Press, 1997.

Lewis, R. W. B. *The American Adam: Innocence, Tragedy, and Tradition in the Nineteenth Century*. Chicago: University of Chicago Press, 1955.

Lewontin, Richard C. "Of Genes and Genitals." *Transition* 6, no. 1 (1996): 178–93.

Limerick, Patricia Nelson. "Frontier." In *A Companion to American Thought*, ed. Richard Wightman Fox and James T. Kloppenberg, 255–59. Oxford: Blackwell, 1995.

——. "Insiders and Outsiders: The Borders of the USA and the Limits of the ASA: Presidential Address to the American Studies Association, 31 October 1996." *American Quarterly* 49, no. 3 (1997): 449–69.

Lipsitz, George. "Listening to Learn, Learning to Listen: Popular Culture, Cultural Theory, and American Studies." *American Quarterly* 42, no. 4 (1990): 615–36.

——. *The Possessive Investment in Whiteness: How White People Profit from Identity Politics*. Philadelphia: Temple University Press, 1998.

——. "The Possessive Investment in Whiteness: Racialized Social Democracy and the 'White' Problem in American Studies." *American Quarterly* 47, no. 3 (1995): 369–87.

——. *Rainbow at Midnight: Labor and Culture in the 1940s*. Urbana: University of Illinois Press, 1994.

——. " 'Sent For You Yesterday, Here You Come Today': American Studies Scholarship and the New Social Movements." *Cultural Critique* 40 (1998): 203–25.

——. *Time Passages: Collective Memory and American Popular Culture*. Minneapolis: University of Minnesota Press, 1990.

Lloyd, David. "Foundations of Diversity: Thinking the University in a Time of Multiculturalism." In *"Culture" and the Problem of the Disciplines*, ed. John Carlos Rowe, 15–43. New York: Columbia University Press, 1998.

Locke, John. *An Essay Concerning Human Understanding*. 1690. 2 vols. Ed. Alexander Campbell Fraser. New York: Dover, 1959.

——. *Two Treatises of Government*. 1690. Ed. Peter Laslett. Cambridge: Cambridge University Press, 1960.

López, Ian F. Haney. *White by Law: The Legal Construction of Race*. New York: New York University Press, 1996.

Lott, Eric. "The Aesthetic Ante: Pleasure, Pop Culture, and the Middle Passage." *Callaloo* 17, no. 2 (1994): 545–55.

——. *Love and Theft: Blackface Minstrelsy and the American Working Class*. New York: Oxford University Press, 1993.

Lowe, Lisa. *Immigrant Acts: On Asian American Cultural Politics*. Durham, N.C.: Duke University Press, 1996.

——. "The International within the National: American Studies and Asian American Critique." *Cultural Critique* 40 (1998): 29–45.

Lowe, Lisa, and David Lloyd, eds. *The Politics of Culture in the Shadow of Capital.* Durham, N.C.: Duke University Press, 1997.

Lubiano, Wahneema, ed. *The House that Race Built: Black Americans, U.S. Terrain.* New York: Pantheon, 1997.

Lukács, Georg. *History and Class Consciousness: Studies in Marxist Dialectics.* Trans. Rodney Livingstone. Cambridge, Mass.: MIT Press, 1971.

Lummis, C. Douglas. *Radical Democracy.* Ithaca, N.Y.: Cornell University Press, 1996.

Maddox, Lucy, ed. *Locating American Studies: The Evolution of a Discipline.* Baltimore: Johns Hopkins University Press, 1999.

Madison, James. "The Federalist X." In *The Debate on the Constitution: Federalist and Antifederalist Speeches, Articles, and Letters during the Struggle over Ratification,* ed. Bernard Bailyn, 404–11. New York: Library of America, 1993.

Manuel, Peter. *Caribbean Currents: Caribbean Music from Rumba to Reggae.* Philadelphia: Temple University Press, 1995.

Marable, Manning. *Race, Reform, and Rebellion: The Second Reconstruction in Black America, 1945–1990.* 2d ed. Jackson: University Press of Mississippi, 1991.

Marcuse, Herbert. "Philosophy and Critical Theory." In *Negations: Essays in Critical Theory,* trans. Jeremy J. Shapiro, 134–58. Boston: Beacon, 1968.

Marin, Louis. "Frontiers of Utopia: Past and Present." *Critical Inquiry* 19, no. 3 (1993): 397–420.

Martí, José. "Our America." In *Our America: Writings on Latin America and the Struggle for Cuban Independence,* ed. Philip S. Foner, trans. Elinor Randall, 84–94. New York: Monthly Review, 1977.

Marx, Karl. *Capital: A Critique of Political Economy.* Vol. 1. Trans. Ben Fowkes. Harmondsworth, U.K.: Penguin, 1976.

——. *The Eighteenth Brumaire of Louis Bonaparte.* New York: International Publishers, 1963.

——. "Introduction to the *Grundrisse.*" In *Marx: Later Political Writings,* ed. and trans. Terrell Carver, 128–57. Cambridge: Cambridge University Press, 1996.

——. *Wage-Labour and Capital.* New York: International Publishers, 1976.

Marx, Karl, and Frederick Engels. *The German Ideology.* New York: International Publishers, 1970.

Massey, Doreen. "Spaces of Politics." In *Human Geography Today,* ed. Massey, John Allen, and Philip Sarre, 279–94. Cambridge: Polity Press, 1999.

Mather, Cotton. *Magnalia Christi Americana.* 1702. Ed. Kenneth B. Murdoch with Elizabeth W. Miller. Cambridge, Mass.: Belknap, 1977.

Mattelart, Armand. *Mapping World Communication: War, Progress, Culture.* Trans. Susan Emanuel and James A. Cohen. Minneapolis: University of Minnesota Press, 1994.

May, Elaine Tyler. "The Radical Roots of American Studies." *American Quarterly* 48, no. 2 (1996): 179–200.

McClintock, Anne. *Imperial Leather: Race, Gender, and Sexuality in the Colonial Conquest.* New York: Routledge, 1995.

McGee, Patrick. *Cinema, Theory, and Political Responsibility in Contemporary Culture.* New York: Cambridge University Press, 1997.

McNamara, Robert S. *In Retrospect: The Tragedy and Lessons of Vietnam.* New York: Times Books, 1995.

Michaels, Walter Benn. "Autobiographies of the Ex-White Men: Why Race Is Not a Social Construction." Paper presented at The Futures of American Studies Conference, Dartmouth College, 15 August 1997.

———. "The Logic of Identity." Paper presented at the School for Criticism and Theory, Dartmouth College, July 1996.

———. *Our America: Nativism, Modernism, and Pluralism.* Durham, N.C.: Duke University Press, 1995.

———. "Posthistoricism." *Transition* 6, no. 2 (1996): 4–19.

———. " 'You Who Never Was There': Slavery and the New Historicism, Deconstruction and the Holocaust." *Narrative* 4, no. 1 (1996): 1–16.

Mill, John Stuart. *On Liberty.* 1859. Ed. David Spitz. New York: Norton, 1975.

Miller, Alice. *Thou Shalt Not Be Aware: Society's Betrayal of the Child.* Trans. Hildegarde Hannum and Hunter Hannum. New York: Meridian, 1986.

Miller, Arthur. *Salesman in Beijing.* New York: Viking, 1984.

———. *Timebends: A Life.* New York: Grove, 1987.

Mills, C. Wright. "The New Left." In *Power, Politics, and People: The Collected Essays of C. Wright Mills,* ed. Irving Louis Horowitz, 247–59. New York: Ballantine, 1963.

Mohanty, Chandra Talpade. "Women Workers and Capitalist Scripts: Ideologies of Domination, Common Interests, and the Politics of Solidarity." In *Feminist Genealogies, Colonial Legacies, Democratic Futures,* ed. M. Jacqui Alexander and Mohanty, 3–29. New York: Routledge, 1997.

Montgomery, David. *Beyond Equality: Labor and the Radical Republicans, 1862–1872.* New York: Knopf, 1967.

Moraga, Cherríe, and Gloria Anzaldúa, eds. *This Bridge Called My Back: Writings by Radical Women of Color.* New York: Kitchen Table, 1983.

Morley, David, and Kuan-Hsing Chen, eds. *Stuart Hall: Critical Dialogues in Cultural Studies.* New York: Routledge, 1996.

Morris, Meaghan. "Future Fear." In *Mapping the Futures: Local Cultures, Global Change,* ed. Jon Bird et al., 30–46. New York: Routledge, 1993.

Morrison, Toni. *Playing in the Dark: Whiteness and the Literary Imagination.* Cambridge, Mass.: Harvard University Press, 1992.

Muñoz, José Esteban. "Dead White: Notes on the Whiteness of the Queer Screen." *GLQ: A Journal of Lesbian and Gay Studies* 4, no. 1 (1998): 127–38.

———. *Disidentifications: Queers of Color and the Performance of Politics.* Minneapolis: University of Minnesota Press, 1999.

———. "Ephemera as Evidence: Introductory Notes to Queer Acts." *Women and Performance* no. 16 (1996): 5–16.

Nairn, Tom. "Breakwaters of 2000: From Ethnic to Civic Nationalism." *New Left Review* 214 (1995): 91–103.

National Commission on the Cost of Higher Education. *Straight Talk about College Costs and Prices*. Phoenix: Oryx, 1998.

Negt, Oskar, and Alexander Kluge. *Public Sphere and Experience: Toward an Analysis of the Bourgeois and Proletarian Public Sphere*. Trans. Peter Labanyi, Jamie Owen Daniel, and Assenka Oksiloff. Minneapolis: University of Minnesota Press, 1993.

Nelson, Cary. *Manifesto of a Tenured Radical*. New York: New York University Press, 1997.

———, ed. *Will Teach for Food: Academic Labor in Crisis*. Minneapolis: University of Minnesota Press, 1997.

Nelson, Cary, and Dilip Parameshwar Gaonkar, eds. *Disciplinarity and Dissent in Cultural Studies*. New York: Routledge, 1996.

Nelson, Dana D. *National Manhood: Capitalist Citizenship and the Imagined Fraternity of White Men*. Durham, N.C.: Duke University Press, 1998.

Newfield, Christopher. "Recapturing Academic Business." In *Chalk Lines: The Politics of Work in the Managed University*, ed. Randy Martin, 69–102. Durham, N.C.: Duke University Press, 1998.

———. "What Was Political Correctness? Race, the Right, and Managerial Democracy in the Humanities." *Critical Inquiry* 19, no. 2 (1993): 308–36.

Newitz, Annalee, and Matt Wray. "What is 'White Trash'?" *Minnesota Review* 47 (1996): 57–72.

Nilsen, Helge Normann. "From *Honors at Dawn* to *Death of a Salesman*: Marxism and the Early Plays of Arthur Miller." *English Studies* 2 (1994): 157–65.

Noble, David W. *The End of American History: Democracy, Capitalism, and the Metaphor of Two Worlds in Anglo-American Historical Writing, 1880–1980*. Minneapolis: University of Minnesota Press, 1985.

Nussbaum, Felicity. "The Other Woman: Polygamy, Pamela, and the Prerogative of Empire." In *Women, "Race," and Writing in the Early Modern Period*, ed. Margo Hendricks and Patricia Parker, 138–59. New York: Routledge, 1994.

Ofshe, Richard, and Ethan Watters. *Making Monsters: False Memories, Psychotherapy, and Sexual Hysteria*. New York: Scribner's, 1994.

Ohmann, Richard. *English in America: A Radical View of the Profession*. New York: Oxford University Press, 1976.

Okihiro, Gary Y. *Margins and Mainstreams: Asians in American History and Culture*. Seattle: University of Washington Press, 1994.

Olsen, Tillie. *Silences*. New York: Delta, 1978.

Omi, Michael, and Howard Winant. *Racial Formation in the United States: From the 1960s to the 1990s*. New York: Routledge, 1994.

Ong, Paul, Edna Bonacich, and Lucie Cheng, eds. *The New Asian Immigration in Los Angeles and Global Restructuring*. Philadelphia: Temple University Press, 1994.

Ostendorf, Berndt. "The Costs of Multiculturalism." Working paper no. 50. Berlin: John F. Kennedy-Institut für Nordamerikastudien der Freien Universität, 1992.

———. "Inclusion, Exclusion, and the Politics of Cultural Difference." In *Fusion of Cultures?* ed. Peter O. Stummer and Christopher Balme, 205–23. Amsterdam: Rodopi, 1996.

Paddock, Cornelia. *The Fate of Madame La Tour: A Tale of Great Salt Lake*. New York: Fords, Howard, and Hulbert, 1881.

Paine, Thomas. *Common Sense*. 1776. New York: Penguin, 1982.

Paredes, Américo. *George Washington Gómez: A Mexicotexan Novel*. Houston: Arte Publico, 1990.

———. *"With His Pistol in His Hand": A Border Ballad and Its Hero*. Austin: University of Texas Press, 1958.

Parkman, Francis. *The Conspiracy of Pontiac*. 1851. New York: Library of America, 1991.

Pascoe, Peggy. *Relations of Rescue: The Search for Female Moral Authority in the American West, 1874–1939*. New York: Oxford University Press, 1990.

Pateman, Carole. *The Sexual Contract*. Stanford, Calif.: Stanford University Press, 1988.

Paterson, Thomas G., ed. *Major Problems in American Foreign Policy: Documents and Essays*. 2 vols. Lexington, Mass.: Heath, 1989.

Patton, Sandra. "Producing '(Il)Legitimate' Citizens: An Interdisciplinary Ethnographic Approach to Public Policy." Paper presented at American Studies Association. Kansas City, 1996.

Pease, Donald E. "*Moby Dick* and the Cold War." In *The American Renaissance Reconsidered*, ed. Walter Benn Michaels and Pease, 113–154. Baltimore: Johns Hopkins University Press, 1985.

———. "National Identities, Postmodern Artifacts, and Postnational Narratives." *boundary 2* 19, no. 1 (1992): 1–13.

———. "New Americanists: Revisionist Interventions into the Canon." *boundary 2* 17, no. 1 (1990): 1–37.

———. *Visionary Compacts: American Renaissance Writings in Cultural Context*. Madison: University of Wisconsin Press, 1987.

———, ed. *National Identities and Post-Americanist Narratives*. Durham, N.C.: Duke University Press, 1994.

Peeler, David P. *Hope among Us Yet: Social Criticism and Social Solace in Depression America*. Athens: University of Georgia Press, 1987.

Pells, Richard. *Not Like Us: How Europeans Have Loved, Hated, and Transformed American Culture since World War II*. New York: Basic Books, 1997.

Pérez Firmat, Gustavo. *Life on the Hyphen: The Cuban-American Way*. Austin: University of Texas Press, 1994.

Pessar, Patricia R. *A Visa for a Dream: Dominicans in the United States*. Boston: Allyn and Bacon, 1995.

Petit, Veronique. *Plural Marriage: The Heart-History of Adele Hersch*. Ithaca: New York: E. D. Norton, 1885.

Pfeil, Fred. *White Guys: Studies in Postmodern Domination and Difference*. New York: Verso, 1995.

Poirier, Richard. *Poetry and Pragmatism*. Cambridge, Mass.: Harvard University Press, 1992.

———. *The Renewal of Literature: Emersonian Reflections*. New York: Random House, 1987.

Poovey, Mary. "Figures of Arithmetic, Figures of Speech: The Discourse of Statistics in the 1830s." *Critical Inquiry* 19, no. 2 (1993): 256–76.

Porter, Carolyn. "What We Know That We Don't Know: Remapping American Literary Studies." *American Literary History* 6 (1994): 467–526.

Pratt, Mary Louise. "Arts of the Contact Zone." *Profession* 91 (1991): 33–40.

Quadagno, Jill. *The Color of Welfare: How Racism Undermined the War on Poverty.* New York: Oxford University Press, 1994.

Rabinowitz, Paula. *Labor and Desire: Women's Revolutionary Fiction in Depression America.* Chapel Hill: University of North Carolina Press, 1991.

Radway, Janice. "What's in a Name? Presidential Address to the American Studies Association, 20 November 1998." *American Quarterly* 51, no. 1 (1999): 1–32.

Readings, Bill. *The University in Ruins.* Cambridge, Mass.: Harvard University Press, 1996.

Reddy, Chandan. "Home, Houses, Non-identity: Paris Is Burning." In *Burning Down the House: Recycling Domesticity*, ed. Rosemary Marangoly George, 355–79. Boulder, Colo.: Westview, 1998.

Remnick, David. *Lenin's Tomb: The Last Days of the Soviet Empire.* New York: Vintage, 1996.

Rhoades, Gary, and Sheila Slaughter. "Academic Capitalism, Managed Professionals, and Supply-Side Higher Education." *Social Text* 51 (1997): 9–38.

Ricoeur, Paul. "The Political Paradox." In *Legitimacy and the State*, ed. William Connolly, 250–72. New York: New York University Press, 1984.

Riesman, David, Revel Denny and Nathan Glazer. *The Lonely Crowd: A Study of the Changing American Character.* New Haven, Conn.: Yale University Press, 1950.

Riley, Denise. *"Am I That Name?": Feminism and the Category of 'Women' in History.* Minneapolis: University of Minnesota Press, 1988.

Robinson, Cedric. "C. L. R. James and the World-System." In *C. L. R. James: His Intellectual Legacies*, ed. Selwyn R. Cudjoe and William E. Cain, 244–59. Amherst: University of Massachusetts Press, 1995.

Roediger, David R. *Towards the Abolition of Whiteness: Essays on Race, Politics, and Working Class History.* London: Verso, 1994.

———. *The Wages of Whiteness: Race and the Making of the American Working Class.* London: Verso, 1991.

———, ed. *Black on White: Black Writers on What It Means to Be White.* New York: Schocken, 1998.

Romero, Lora. *Home Fronts: Domesticity and Its Critics in the Antebellum United States.* Durham, N.C.: Duke University Press, 1997.

Roof, Judith, and Robyn Wiegman, eds. *Who Can Speak? Authority and Critical Identity.* Urbana: University of Illinois Press, 1995.

Rorty, Richard. *Achieving Our Country: Leftist Thought in Twentieth-Century America.* Cambridge, Mass.: Harvard University Press, 1998.

Rose, Jacqueline. *The Case of Peter Pan, Or, The Impossibility of Children's Fiction.* 1984. Philadelphia: University of Pennsylvania Press, 1992.

Roudané, Matthew C., ed. *Approaches to Teaching Miller's Death of a Salesman.* New York: Modern Language Association of America, 1995.

Rowe, John Carlos. *Literary Culture and U.S. Imperialism: From the Revolution to World War II.* New York: Oxford University Press, 2000.

Ryan, Mary P. *Cradle of the Middle Class: The Family in Oneida County, New York, 1790–1865.* Cambridge: Cambridge University Press, 1981.

———. *The Empire of the Mother: American Writing about Domesticity, 1830 to 1860.* New York: Haworth, 1982.

Ryan, Susan M. "Errand into Africa: Colonization and Nation Building in Sarah J. Hale's Liberia." *New England Quarterly* 68 (1995): 558–83.

Sabagh, Georges, and Mehdi Bozogmehr. "Population Changes: Immigration and Ethnic Transformation." In *Ethnic Los Angeles*, ed. Roger Waldinger and Bozorgmehr, 79–107. New York: Russell Sage Foundation, 1996.

Said, Edward W. *Culture and Imperialism.* New York: Knopf, 1993.

———. *Orientalism.* New York: Vintage, 1979.

———. "Traveling Theory." In *The World, the Text, and the Critic*, 226–47. Cambridge, Mass.: Harvard University Press, 1983.

Saldívar, José David. *Border Matters: Remapping American Cultural Studies.* Berkeley: University of California Press, 1997.

———. *The Dialectics of Our America: Genealogy, Cultural Critique, and Literary History.* Durham, N.C.: Duke University Press, 1991.

Sams, Henry W. *Autobiography of Brook Farm.* Englewood Cliffs, N.J.: Prentice-Hall, 1958.

Samuels, Shirley, ed. *The Culture of Sentiment: Race, Gender, and Sentimentality in Nineteenth-Century America.* New York: Oxford University Press, 1992.

Sánchez, George J. *Becoming Mexican American: Ethnicity, Culture, and Identity in Chicano Los Angeles, 1900–1945.* New York: Oxford University Press, 1991.

———. "Reading Reginald Denny: The Politics of Whiteness in the Late Twentieth Century." *American Quarterly* 47, no. 3 (1995): 388–94.

Sánchez-Eppler, Karen. "Raising Empires Like Children: Race, Nation, and Religious Education." *American Literary History* 8 (1996): 399–425.

Sandford, Mariellen R., ed. *Happenings and Other Acts.* New York: Routledge, 1994.

Santner, Eric L. *Stranded Objects: Mourning, Memory, and Film in Postwar Germany.* Ithaca, N.Y.: Cornell University Press, 1990.

Sartre, Jean-Paul. *Anti-Semite and Jew.* Trans. George J. Becker. New York: Schocken, 1995.

Saxton, Alexander. *The Rise and Fall of the White Republic: Class Politics and Mass Culture in Nineteenth Century America.* New York: Verso, 1990.

Scarry, Elaine. "Consent and the Body: Injury, Departure, and Desire." *New Literary History* 21 (1990): 867–96.

Schlesinger, Arthur M., Jr. *The Disuniting of America: Reflections on a Multicultural Society.* New York: Norton, 1992.

Schmidgen, Wolfram. "The Principle of Negative Identity and the Crisis of Relationality in Contemporary Literary Criticism." *REAL* 11 (1995): 371–404.

Schultz, April R. *Ethnicity on Parade: Inventing the Norwegian American through Celebration*. Amherst: University of Massachusetts Press, 1994.

Schumacher, Joel, dir. *Falling Down*. Warner Bros., 1993.

Schwarz, Henry, and Richard Dienst, eds. *Reading the Shape of the World: Toward an International Cultural Studies*. Boulder, Colo.: Westview, 1996.

Scott, Jonathan. "Inside the White Corral." *Minnesota Review* 47 (1996): 93–103.

Segrest, Mab. *Memoir of a Race Traitor*. Boston: South End, 1994.

Shafir, Gershon, ed. *The Citizenship Debates: A Reader*. Minneapolis: University of Minnesota Press, 1998.

Shah, Nayan. *Contagious Divides: Epidemics and Race in San Francisco's Chinatown*. Berkeley: University of California Press, 2001.

Singh, Nikhil Pal. "Culture / Wars: Recoding Empire in an Age of Democracy." *American Quarterly* 50, no. 3 (1998): 471–522.

Sklar, Kathryn Kish. *Catharine Beecher: A Study in American Domesticity*. New Haven, Conn.: Yale University Press, 1973.

Slotkin, Richard. *The Fatal Environment: The Myth of the Frontier in the Age of Industrialization, 1800–1890*. New York: Atheneum, 1985.

——. *Gunfighter Nation: The Myth of the Frontier in Twentieth-Century America*. New York: Atheneum, 1992.

——. *Regeneration through Violence: The Mythology of the American Frontier, 1600–1860*. Middletown, Conn.: Wesleyan University Press, 1973.

Smith, Jeff. "Student Goals, Gatekeeping, and Some Questions of Ethics." *College English* 59, no. 3 (1997): 299–320.

Smith, John H. "The *Transcendance* of the Individual." *Diacritics* 19, no. 2 (1989): 80–98.

Smoot, Jeanne J. "Ambassador Unaware." In *The Fulbright Experience, 1946–1986: Encounters and Transformations*, ed. Arthur Power Dudden and Russell R. Dynes, 301–2. New Brunswick, N.J.: Transaction, 1987.

Sollors, Werner. "Ethnicity." In *Critical Terms for Literary Study*, ed. Frank Lentricchia and Thomas McLaughlin, 288–305. Chicago: University of Chicago Press, 1995.

——."For a Multilingual Turn in American Studies." *American Studies Association Newsletter* 20, no. 2 (1997): 13–15.

Southworth, E. D. E. N. *The Hidden Hand; Or, Capitola the Madcap*. 1859. Ed. Joanne Dobson. New Brunswick, N.J.: Rutgers University Press, 1988.

Spanos, William V. *America's Shadow: An Anatomy of Empire*. Minneapolis: University of Minnesota Press, 2000.

——. *Heidegger and Criticism: Retrieving the Cultural Politics of Destruction*. Minneapolis: University of Minnesota Press, 1993.

Spencer, Mary. *Salt Lake Fruit: A Latter-Day Romance*. Boston: Franklin, 1884.

Spiller, Robert. "American Studies, Past, Present, and Future." In *Studies in Ameri-*

can Culture: Dominant Ideas and Images, ed. Joseph J. Kwiat, 207–20. Minneapolis: University of Minnesota Press, 1960.

——. "Unity and Diversity in the Study of American Culture: The American Studies Perspective." *American Quarterly* 25, no. 5 (1973): 611–18.

Spillers, Hortense J., ed. *Comparative American Identities: Race, Sex, and Nationality in the Modern Text.* New York: Routledge, 1991.

Spivak, Gayatri Chakravorty. "Marginality in the Teaching Machine." In *Outside in the Teaching Machine*, 53–76. New York: Routledge, 1993.

Stanley, Amy Dru. *From Bondage to Contract: Wage Labor, Marriage, and the Market in the Age of Slave Emancipation.* New York: Cambridge University Press, 1998.

Stenhouse, Mrs. T. B. H. (Fanny). *Tell It All: The Story of a Life's Experience in Mormonism.* Hartford, Conn.: Worthington, 1890.

Stoller, Ann Laura. *Race and the Education of Desire: Foucault's History of Sexuality and the Colonial Order of Things.* Durham, N.C.: Duke University Press, 1995.

Stowe, David W. "Uncolored People: The Rise of Whiteness Studies." *Lingua Franca*, September–October 1996, 68–77.

Stowe, Harriet Beecher. *Uncle Tom's Cabin.* 1852. New York: Library of America, 1982.

Sullivan, Andrew. *Virtually Normal: An Argument about Homosexuality.* New York: Vintage, 1996.

Susman, Warren I. *Culture as History: The Transformation of American Society in the Twentieth Century.* New York: Pantheon, 1984.

Sweezy, Paul M., and Leo Huberman, eds. *F. O. Matthiessen, 1902–1950: A Collective Portrait.* New York: Schuman, 1950.

Switzer, Jennie Bartlett. *Elder Northfield's Home; Or, Sacrificed on the Mormon Altar.* New York: Brown, 1882.

Tchen, John Kuo Wei. "Modernizing White Patriarchy: Re-Viewing D. W. Griffith's *Broken Blossoms.*" In *Moving the Image: Independent Asian Pacific American Media Arts*, ed. Russell Leong, 133–43. Los Angeles: UCLA Asian American Studies Center and Visual Communications, 1991.

Telotte, J. P. "Definitely Falling Down." *Journal of Popular Film and Television* 24, no. 1 (1996): 19–25.

Thomä, Dieter. "Multikulturalismus, Demokratie, Nation: Zur Philosophe der deutschen Einheit." *Deutsche Zeitschrift für Philosophie* 43 (1995): 349–63.

Thomas, Kendall. " 'Ain't Nothing Like the Real Thing': Black Masculinity, Gay Sexuality, and the Jargon of Authenticity." In *Representing Black Men*, ed. Marcellus Blount and George P. Cunningham, 55–69. New York: Routledge, 1996.

Tocqueville, Alexis de. *Democracy in America.* Vol. 1. Trans. Henry Reeve, rev. Francis Bowen. Ed. Phillips Bradley. New York: Vintage, 1990.

Tomlinson, John. *Cultural Imperialism: A Critical Introduction.* Baltimore: Johns Hopkins University Press, 1991.

Tompkins, Jane. *Sensational Designs: The Cultural Work of American Fiction, 1790–1860.* Oxford: Oxford University Press, 1985.

Turner, Victor. "Social Dramas and Stories about Them." In *On Narrative*, ed. W. J. T. Mitchell, 137–64. Chicago: University of Chicago Press, 1981.

Tylor, E. B. *Primitive Culture*. London: Routledge, 1994.

Van Wagoner, Richard S. *Mormon Polygamy: A History*. Salt Lake City: Signature, 1989.

Veblen, Thorstein. *The Higher Learning in America: A Memorandum on the Conduct of Universities by Business Men*. 1918. New Brunswick, N.J.: Transaction, 1993.

Victor, Metta Victoria Fuller. *Mormon Wives: A Narrative of Facts Stranger than Fiction*. New York: Derby and Jackson, 1856.

Wagnleitner, Reinhold. *Coca-Colonization and the Cold War: The Cultural Mission of the United States in Austria after the Second World War*. Trans. Diana M. Wolf. Chapel Hill: University of North Carolina Press, 1994.

Wald, Alan. *Writing from the Left: New Essays on Radical Culture and Politics*. London: Verso, 1994.

Walker, Robert. "The Internationalization of American Studies." *American Studies International* 26, no. 1 (1988): 67–71.

Wall, Cheryl A., ed. *Changing Our Own Words: Essays on Criticism, Theory, and Writing by Black Women*. New Brunswick, N.J.: Rutgers University Press, 1989.

Wallerstein, Immanuel. *Geopolitics and Geoculture: Essays on the Changing World-System*. Cambridge: Cambridge University Press, 1991.

Ward, Maria [pseud.]. *The Mormon Wife: A Life Story of the Sacrifices, Sorrows and Sufferings of Women*. Hartford, Conn.: Hartford, 1872. Reprint of *Female Life among the Mormons*, 1855.

Ware, Vron. *Beyond the Pale: White Women, Racism, and History*. New York: Verso, 1992.

Warner, Michael. *The Trouble with Normal: Sex, Politics, and the Ethics of Queer Life*. New York: Free Press, 1999.

Warner, Susan. *The Wide, Wide World*. 1850. New York: Feminist Press, 1987.

Washington, Mary Helen. "Disturbing the Peace: What Happens to American Studies If You Put African American Studies at the Center?" *American Quarterly* 50, no. 1 (1998): 1–23.

Waswo, Richard. *The Founding Legend of Western Civilization: From Virgil to Vietnam*. Hanover, N.H.: University Press of New England, 1997.

Watkins, Evan. *Work Time: English Departments and the Circulation of Cultural Value*. Stanford, Calif.: Stanford University Press, 1989.

Weisbrod, Carol, and Pamela Sheingorn. "*Reynolds v. United States*: Nineteenth-Century Forms of Marriage and the Status of Women." *Connecticut Law Review* 10 (1978): 828–58.

Welsh, Alexander. *Strong Representations: Narrative and Circumstantial Evidence in England*. Baltimore: Johns Hopkins University Press, 1992.

Welter, Barbara. "The Cult of True Womanhood." *American Quarterly* 18, no. 2 (1966): 151–74.

West, Cornel. *The American Evasion of Philosophy: A Genealogy of Pragmatism*. Madison: University of Wisconsin Press, 1989.

——. "The Postmodern Crisis of the Black Intellectuals." In *Cultural Studies*, ed. Lawrence Grossberg, Cary Nelson, and Paula A. Treichler, 689–96. New York: Routledge, 1992.

Wexler, Laura. "Tender Violence: Literary Eavesdropping, Domestic Fiction, and Educational Reform." In *The Culture of Sentiment: Race, Gender, and Sentimentality in Nineteenth-Century America*, ed. Shirley Samuels, 9–38. New York: Oxford University Press, 1992.

Whitney, Helen Mar. *Why We Practice Plural Marriage*. Salt Lake City: Juvenile Instructor Office, 1884.

Wiegman, Robyn. *American Anatomies: Theorizing Race and Gender*. Durham, N.C.: Duke University Press, 1995.

Wilentz, Sean. "Integrating Ethnicity into American Studies." *Chronicle of Higher Education*, 29 November 1996, A56.

Willey, Basil. *The Seventeenth Century Background: Studies in the Thought of the Age in Relation to Poetry and Religion*. London: Chatto and Windus, 1949.

Williams, Raymond. *Culture and Society, 1780–1950*. New York: Columbia University Press, 1983.

——. *Politics and Letters: Interviews with New Left Review*. London: Verso, 1981.

——. *What I Came to Say*. London: Hutchinson Radius, 1989.

Williams, William Appleman. *The Tragedy of American Diplomacy*. Cleveland, Ohio: World Publishing, 1959.

Winant, Howard. *Racial Conditions: Politics, Theory, Comparisons*. Minneapolis: University of Minnesota Press, 1994.

Winnicott, D. W. *Playing and Reality*. London: Tavistock, 1971.

Winthrop, John. *The Journal of John Winthrop, 1630–1649*. 3 vols. Ed. Richard S. Dunn, James Savage, and Laetitia Yeandle. Cambridge, Mass.: Belknap, 1996.

Wise, Gene. " 'Paradigm Dramas' in American Studies: A Cultural and Institutional History of the Movement." *American Quarterly* 31, no. 3 (1979): 293–337.

Wixson, Douglas. *Worker-Writer in America: Jack Conroy and the Tradition of Midwestern Literary Radicalism, 1898–1990*. Urbana: University of Illinois Press, 1994.

Wolin, Sheldon S. *The Presence of the Past: Essays on the State and the Constitution*. Baltimore: Johns Hopkins University Press, 1989.

Wood, Gordon S. *The Creation of the American Republic, 1776–1787*. New York: Norton, 1972.

Worcester, Kent. *C. L. R. James: A Political Biography*. Albany: State University of New York Press, 1995.

Wray, Matt, and Annalee Newitz, eds. *White Trash: Race and Class in America*. New York: Routledge, 1997.

Wright, Lawrence. *Remembering Satan*. New York: Knopf, 1994.

Young, Ann Eliza. *Wife No. 19; Or, The Story of a Life in Bondage, Being a Complete Exposé of Mormonism, and Revealing Sorrows, Sacrifices and Sufferings of Women in Polygamy*. Hartford, Conn.: Dustin, Gilman, 1876.

Young, Elizabeth. *Disarming the Nation: Women's Writing and the American Civil War*. Chicago: University of Chicago Press, 1999.

Young, Kimball. *Isn't One Wife Enough?* New York: Holt, 1954.

Young, Marilyn. *The Vietnam Wars: 1945–1990.* New York: Harper, 1991.

Yung, Judy. *Unbound Feet: A Social History of Chinese Women in San Francisco.* Berkeley: University of California Press, 1995.

Zack, Naomi. *Race and Mixed Race.* Philadelphia: Temple University Press, 1993.

Zemeckis, Robert, dir. *Forrest Gump.* Paramount, 1994.

Žižek, Slavoj. "Eastern Europe's Republics of Gilead." *New Left Review* 183 (1990): 50–62.

Contributors

LINDON BARRETT is Associate Professor in the Department of English and Comparative Literature and the Program in African American Studies at the University of California, Irvine, and is author of *Blackness and Value: Seeing Double* (Cambridge University Press, 1999).

NANCY BENTLEY is Associate Professor of English at the University of Pennsylvania. She is the author of *The Ethnography of Manners: Hawthorne, James, Wharton* (Cambridge University Press, 1995), and is writing a book on nineteenth-century fiction and the politics of marriage in the United States.

GILLIAN BROWN is Professor of English at the University of Utah. She is the author of *Domestic Individualism: Imagining Self in Nineteenth-Century America* (University of California Press, 1990) and of the forthcoming *The Consent of the Governed: The Lockean Legacy in Early American Culture*.

RUSS CASTRONOVO is Associate Professor at the University of Miami, where he teaches English and American Studies. He is author of *Fathering the Nation: American Genealogies of Slavery and Freedom* (University of North Carolina Press, 1995), and is completing a book on depoliticization, citizenship, and the body politic.

ERIC CHEYFITZ is Professor of English and Comparative Literature at the University of Pennsylvania, where he is also a member of the graduate group in Urban Studies and an adjunct professor in the Law School. He has been awarded fellowships by the National Endowment for the Humanities, the Newberry Library, and the Society for the Humanities at Cornell and is the author of two books: *The Trans-Parent: Sexual Politics in the Language of Emerson* (Johns Hopkins University Press, 1981) and *The Poetics of Imperialism: Translation and Colonization from "The Tempest" to "Tarzan"* (University of Pennsylvania Press, 1991). He is currently at work for Columbia University Press on *The Columbia Guide to Native American Literature of the United States, 1945–2000*, of which he is the editor.

MICHAEL DENNING is Professor of American Studies at Yale University, and the author of *Cover Stories: Narrative and Ideology in the British Spy Thriller* (Routledge, 1987), *Mechanic Accents: Dime Novels and Working-Class Culture in America* (Verso, 1987; 1998), and, most recently, *The Cultural Front: The Laboring of American Culture in the Twentieth Century* (Verso, 1996). He has written widely on contemporary cultural studies and is a member of the National Steering Committee of Scholars, Artists, and Writers for Social Justice.

WINFRIED FLUCK is Professor of American Culture at the John F. Kennedy-Institute for North American Studies at the Freie Universität Berlin. His publications include books on the history of criticism of *Huckleberry Finn* (*Aesthetisches Vorverständnis und Methode* [Metzler, 1975]), theories and methods of Popular Culture Studies (*Populäre Kultur* [Metzler, 1980]), American Realism (*Inszenierte Wirklichkeit* [Fink, 1992]), theories of American literature (*Theorien Amerikanischer Literatur* [Universitätsverlag

Konstanz, 1987]), and the changing functions of fiction in the American novel (*Das kulturelle Imaginäre* [Suhrkamp, 1997]). He has published articles on the theory and method of American and cultural studies, on the American novel, on American popular culture, and on literary theory. In the United States, some of his essays have appeared in *New Literary History*.

CARL GUTIÉRREZ-JONES is Associate Professor of English at the University of California, Santa Barbara. He is the author of *Rethinking the Borderlands: Between Legal Discourse and Chicano Culture* (University of California Press, 1995). He is currently completing a book-length project treating the rhetoric of racial injury.

DANA HELLER is Associate Professor of English and Director of the Humanities Institute at Old Dominion University. Her publications include *Family Plots: The Deoedipalization of Popular Culture* (University of Pennsylvania Press, 1995) and *Cross-Purposes: Lesbians, Feminists, and the Limits of Alliance* (Indiana University Press, 1997). In the spring of 1997 she received a Fulbright grant to lecture on American literature and culture at Moscow State University in Russia. She returned to Moscow for the academic year 1998–99 in order to help establish an American Studies curriculum in the International College at Moscow State University.

AMY KAPLAN is Professor of English and American Studies at Mount Holyoke College. She is author of *The Social Construction of American Realism* (University of Chicago Press, 1988), and co-editor of *Cultures of U.S. Imperialism* (Duke University Press, 1993). Her essay in this volume, "Manifest Domesticity," is part of a forthcoming book, "The Limits of Empire in American Culture," and was awarded the Forster prize for the best article in *American Literature* in 1998.

PAUL LAUTER is A. K. & G. M. Smith Professor of Literature at Trinity College (Hartford). He is general editor of *The Heath Anthology of American Literature* and of the New Riverside Series (Houghton Mifflin). His latest book, in which a version of this essay appears, is called *From Walden Pond to Jurassic Park* (Duke University Press, 2001). With Ann Fitzgerald he has recently completed a collection titled *Literature, Class, and Culture* (Longman, 2001). For many years he worked in the SUNY faculty-staff union as well as in a variety of campus-based activist groups, like the MLA Radical Caucus and the magazine *Radical Teacher*. He was president of the American Studies Association in 1994–95.

GÜNTER H. LENZ is Professor of American Literary and Cultural Studies at Humboldt-Universität, Berlin (Germany). A member of the International Committee of the American Studies Association, his main areas of research, teaching, and publication are: the history and theory of American Studies, cultural theory and comparative Cultural Studies, multicultural American literature and culture of the twentieth century, African American Studies, documentary film and the fine arts, and dimensions of European American Studies. He is currently working on a book on American multicultural critique and international American culture studies.

GEORGE LIPSITZ is Professor of Ethnic Studies at the University of California, San Diego. His publications include *The Possessive Investment in Whiteness* (Temple University Press, 1998), *A Life in the Struggle: Ivory Perry and the Culture of Opposition* (Temple University Press, 1988; 1995), *Dangerous Crossroads* (Verso, 1994), *Rainbow at Midnight* (University of Illinois Press, 1994), *Sidewalks of St. Louis* (University of Missouri Press, 1991), and *Time Passages* (University of Minnesota Press, 1990).

LISA LOWE is Professor in the Department of Literature at the University of California, San Diego, and affiliated with the Ethnic Studies Department and Critical Gender Studies Program. She is the author of *Critical Terrains: French and British Orientalisms* (Cornell University Press, 1991) and *Immigrant Acts: On Asian American Cultural Politics* (Duke University Press, 1996), and co-editor with David Lloyd of *The Politics of Culture in the Shadow of Capital* (Duke University Press, 1997). Her current project considers race, sexuality, and modern epistemology.

WALTER BENN MICHAELS is Professor of English at the University of Illinois at Chicago. He is the author of *The Gold Standard and the Logic of Naturalism* (University of California Press, 1987) and *Our America: Nativism, Modernism, and Pluralism* (Duke University Press, 1995), and is currently at work on a project provisionally titled "History of Theory: 1966–1996."

JOSÉ ESTEBAN MUÑOZ is Assistant Professor of Performance Studies, Tisch School of the Arts, New York University. He serves on the board of directors for the Center for Lesbian and Gay Studies, City University of New York, and the New Festival, the New York Gay and Lesbian Film Festival. He is a member of the editorial collective for *Social Text* and series editor of Sexual Cultures: New Directions in Gay and Lesbian Studies from CLAGS. He co-edited *Pop Out: Queer Warhol* (Duke University Press, 1996) and *Everynight Life: Culture and Music in Latina/o America* (Duke University Press, 1997), as well as special issues of *Social Text* and *Women and Performance*. His latest book is *Disidentifications: Queers of Color and the Performance of Politics* (University of Minnesota Press, 1999).

DANA D. NELSON, Professor of English and Social Theory at the University of Kentucky, is most recently the author of *National Manhood: Capitalist Citizenship and the Imagined Fraternity of White Men* (Duke University Press, 1998). She has also co-edited two recent projects: first, a special issue of *American Literature* with Houston A. Baker on "Violence, the Body and 'The South' " (June 2001) and second, with Russ Castronovo, a collection of essays tentatively entitled "Materializing Democracy" (Duke University Press, 2002). She is currently at work on a new book-length project entitled *Representative/Democracy*.

RICARDO L. ORTÍZ is Assistant Professor of U.S. Latino/a Literature in the English Department at Georgetown University. He is currently finishing one book project on Cuban American Literature and developing another on the Chicano novelist John Rechy. He has published a number of articles on various queer Latino writers, including Rechy, Reinaldo Arenas, Arturo Islas, and Rafael Campo.

DONALD E. PEASE is the Avalon Foundation Chair of the Humanities at Dartmouth College. A graduate of the University of Chicago, Professor Pease received the Dartmouth Distinguished Teaching Award in 1981. Over the last fifteen years he has delivered close to one hundred lectures at professional conferences and in universities within the United States and abroad. The author or editor of seven books, Pease's *Visionary Compacts: American Renaissance Writing in Cultural Context* (University of Wisconsin Press, 1987) received the Mark Ingraham prize for the best book in the humanities in 1987. Pease has also been honored with Guggenheim and NEH Fellowships and has directed two NEH Seminars for College Teachers. He is the general editor for the book series New Americanists at Duke University Press.

JANICE RADWAY is Frances Hill Fox Professor in Humanities and Professor of literature at Duke University. She is the author of *Reading the Romance: Women, Patriarchy, and Popular Literature* (University of North Carolina Press, 1984) and *A Feeling for Books: The Book-of-the-Month Club, Literary Taste, and Middle-Class Desire* (University of North Carolina Press, 1997).

JOHN CARLOS ROWE teaches the literatures and cultures of the United States and critical theory at the University of California, Irvine. He is the author of *The Other Henry James* (Duke University Press, 1998), *At Emerson's Tomb: The Politics of Classic American Literature* (Columbia University Press, 1997), *The Theoretical Dimensions of Henry James* (University of Wisconsin Press, 1984), *Through the Custom-House: Nineteenth-Century American Fiction and Modern Theory* (Johns Hopkins University Press, 1982), and *Henry Adams and Henry James: The Emergence of a Modern Consciousness* (Cornell University Press, 1976), as well as the editor of *"Culture" and the Problem of the Disciplines* (Columbia University Press, 1998), *New Essays on The Education of Henry Adams* (Cambridge University Press, 1996), and, with Rick Berg, *The Vietnam War and American Culture* (Columbia University Press, 1991). His latest book is *Literary Culture and U.S. Imperialism: From the Revolution to World War II* (Oxford University Press, 2000).

WILLIAM V. SPANOS is the founding editor of *boundary 2*. He is the author of numerous essays and several books on postmodern literature and theory. His most recent books include *Repetitions: The Postmodern Occasion in Literature and Culture* (Louisiana State University Press, 1987), *The End of Education: Towards Posthumanism* (University of Minnesota Press, 1993), *Heidegger and Criticism: Retrieving the Cultural Politics of Destruction* (University of Minnesota Press, 1993), and *The Errant Art of Moby-Dick: The Canon, the Cold War, and the Struggle for American Literary Studies* (Duke University Press, 1995). His book *Empire's Shadow: An Anatomy of America* is forthcoming from the University of Minnesota Press.

ROBYN WIEGMAN is Margaret Taylor Smith Director of Women's Studies and a member of the literature program at Duke University. She has published *American Anatomies: Theorizing Race and Gender* (Duke University Press, 1995) and three edited collections: *Who Can Speak? Authority and Critical Identity* (University of Illinois Press, 1995), *Feminism Beside Itself* (Routledge, 1995), and *AIDS and the National Body: Writings by Thomas Yingling* (Duke University Press, 1997). She is currently completing a manuscript on feminist knowledge formations and the university called "Feminism after the Disciplines."

Index

616 / Index

Goldfarb, Jeffrey, 569–70
Gopinath, Gayatri, 88
Gordon, Avery, 546, 550
Gordon, Sarah Barringer, 344, 353–54
Gotanda, Neil, 78
Graduate Employees and Students Organizations (Yale University), 486, 520–25
Graff, Gerald, 401, 514–15, 517
Gramsci, Antonio, 34, 402, 429–30, 434, 445
Grossberg, Lawrence, 462–64, 468
Guillory, John, 222–25
Gulf War, 393
Gunn, Giles, 250–52, 458 n.1
Gupta, Akhil, 58

Hale, Sara Josepha: *Liberia,* 113, 115, 121–28, 133 n.18
Hall, Stuart, 49, 138, 250, 425, 429–30, 432
Harper, Frances: *Iola Leroy,* 357
Harper, Phillip Brian, 323, 330
Harris, Cheryl, 278–79
Hartz, Louis, 142
Harvey, David, 437
Hawthorne, Nathaniel: *The Blithedale Romance,* 540–41, 547–53
Heidegger, Martin, 390, 393, 399, 401, 403, 408–9, 411
Henderson, Mae, 321–22
Higher education, 84–86, 174, 176; and class, 487–92, 496–97, 501–5, 510–11, 519–26, 530; corporatization of, 513, 517, 519, 528, 531–33, 536–38; and professionalization, 211–16, 225, 226 n.1, 227 n.6; proletarianization of, 297, 526
Hirsch, E. D., 168, 173
Hofstadter, Richard, 456
Holocaust, 254–57
Hong, Grace, 87
Honig, Bonnie, 567–68, 572, 577 n.3
Horkheimer, Max, 421, 423, 426, 428
Horsman, Reginald, 125

Horwitz, Richard P., 208–9 n.18, 471–72
Hudson, Mary: *Esther the Gentile,* 347, 349, 353
Huntington, Samuel B., 203, 204

Ignatiev, Noel, 232, 245, 286, 288–90, 303 n.32
Immigration, 76, 152, 167, 168, 282–83, 288, 295, 442, 446; from Asia, 77–84, 87–90; restriction of, 76, 77–83, 88–89, 135, 140
Imperialism, 49–51, 53, 55–57, 60, 72 n.20, 76, 87–88, 89, 113, 167, 171–72, 177, 201, 389–90, 392–96, 399–400, 402–4, 409–10, 447, 450–51, 453, 456, 472–74, 481; internal, 54, 170. *See also* Domesticity: and imperialism

Jaluague, Eleanor, 87–88
James, C. L. R., 50, 93, 99–100, 423, 430, 449; and Immigration and Naturalization Service, 135–40, 143–44, 148–53; *Mariners, Renegades, and Castaways,* 137–40, 143–45, 146–59
Jameson, Fredric, 426–27, 435–36
Japanese Association for American Studies, 61
Jay, Gregory, 401, 512–14, 517
Johnson, James Weldon: *Autobiography of an Ex-Coloured Man,* 231–32, 233
Judy, Ronald, 396, 397–98
Jun, Helen, 87

Kaplan, Amy, 40–42 n.11, 452–53, 472–73
Kaprow, Allan, 94–96, 97
Kelley, Robin D. G., 86
Kelly, Gordon, 9
Kerr, Alva: *Trean; or The Mormon's Daughter,* 349–50, 352, 355
Kluckhohn, Clyde, 419–23
Kroeber, A. L., 419–23
Kroes, Rob, 479
Kuklick, Bruce, 9

LaCapra, Dominick, 257–58, 264 n.11
Lasch, Christopher, 40 n.8

Library of Congress Cataloging-in-Publication Data

The futures of American studies / edited by Donald E. Pease
and Robyn Wiegman.

p. cm.

Includes bibliographical references and index.

ISBN 0-8223-2957-3 (cloth : alk. paper)

ISBN 0-8223-2965-4 (pbk. : alk. paper)

1. United States—Study and teaching 2. United States—
American Studies. I. Pease, Donald E. II. Wiegman, Robyn.

E175.8 .F88 2002

973'.071—dc21   2002005424